BUILDING A JUST WORLD ORDER

Alfred de Zayas

Clarity Press, Inc.

© 2021 Alfred de Zayas

ISBN: 978-1-949762-42-6
EBOOK ISBN: 978-1-949762-43-3

In-house editor: Diana G. Collier
Cover design: A.B. Abrams

ALL RIGHTS RESERVED: Except for purposes of review, this book may not be copied, or stored in any information retrieval system, in whole or in part, without permission in writing from the publishers.

Library of Congress Control Number: 2021938315

Clarity Press, Inc.
2625 Piedmont Rd. NE, Ste. 56
Atlanta, GA 30324, USA
https://www.claritypress.com

*To my Socratic mentor, Justice Jakob Th. Möller,
former Chief of the Petitions Mechanisms at the UN Human Rights Office,
with whom I had the privilege of collaborating for 16 years in the service
of human dignity: A model of discretion, ethics, honour, integrity,
proportion, and professionalism.
A true friend.*

TABLE OF CONTENTS

UN REPORTS viii

GLOSSARY ix

TABLE OF ABBREVIATIONS xii

INTRODUCTION 1

CHAPTERS

  1. Mechanisms for the Democratic Pursuit
     of Human Rights 12

  2. Principles of International Order 46

  3. Peace as a Human Right 61

  4. Military Expenditures and Human Rights 88

  5. The Right of Self-determination of Peoples 117

  6. The Rule of Law and the Right to Truth:
     Information as a Key Element of Democracy. 173

  7. The Prohibition of Interference in the
     Internal Affairs of States 203

  8. Business and Human Rights 231

  9. Taxation and Human Rights 300

  10. World Bank Group 336

  11. The Adverse Impact of IMF Policies on Human Rights 371

  12. Mission to Venezuela 408

CONCLUSION: Reflections on the Way Forward 446

INDEX 455

UN REPORTS

Human Rights Council:

A/HRC/39/47/Add.1. Report of the Independent Expert on the promotion of a democratic and equitable international order on his mission to the Bolivarian Republic of Venezuela and Ecuador.
3 August 2018 • https://undocs.org/A/HRC/39/47/Add.1

A/HRC/37/63. Report of the Independent Expert on the promotion of a democratic and equitable international order on the achievements and the challenges of the mandate.
25 January 2018 • https://undocs.org/A/HRC/37/63

A/HRC/36/40. Report of the Independent Expert on the promotion of a democratic and equitable international order. The Word Bank Group and Human Rights.
20 July 2017 • https://undocs.org/A/HRC/36/40

A/HRC/33/40. Report of the Independent Expert on the promotion of a democratic and equitable international order. Business and Human Rights, World Trade Organization.
12 July 2016 • https://undocs.org/A/HRC/33/40

A/HRC/30/44. Report of the Independent Expert on the promotion of a democratic and equitable international order. Free Trade Agreements and Investor-State-Dispute-Settlement.
14 July 2015 • https://undocs.org/A/HRC/30/44

A/HRC/27/51. Report of the Independent Expert on the promotion of a democratic and equitable international order. Military expenditures. Disarmament for Development.
17 July 2014 • https://undocs.org/A/HRC/27/51

A/HRC/24/38. Report of the Independent Expert on the promotion of a democratic and equitable international order. Models of Democracy.
July 2013 • https://undocs.org/A/HRC/24/38

A/HRC/21/45. Report of the Independent Expert on the promotion of a democratic and equitable international order. Methodology of the mandate. Roadmap.
3 August 2012 •   https://undocs.org/A/HRC/21/45

General Assembly:

A/72/187. Promotion of a democratic and equitable international order. The Inernational Monetary Fund and human rights.
21 July 2017 • https://undocs.org/A/72/187

A/71/286. Promotion of a democratic and equitable international order. Tax havens and tax evasion.
4 August 2016 • https://undocs.org/A/71/286

A/70/285. Promotion of a democratic and equitable international order. The Ontology of States, the Ontology of Business. ISDS as contra bonos mores.
5 August 2015 • https://undocs.org/A/70/285

A/69/272. Promotion of a democratic and equitable international order. The right of self-determination of peoples.
7 August 2014 • https://undocs.org/A/69/272

A/68/284. Promotion of a democratic and equitable international order. Reforming the United Nations, reforming the Security Council.
7 August 2013 • https://undocs.org/A/68/284

A/67/277. Interim report of the Independent Expert on the promotion of a democratic and equitable international order. Human dignity as source of all human rights.
9 August 2012 • https://undocs.org/A/67/277

GLOSSARY

ab initio—from the beginning

ad fontes—to the sources

ad libitum—as one wishes

calumniare audacter, semper aliquid haeret (Plutarch, Francis Bacon)—defame with audacity, something always remains

Cassandara—Greek mythological figure who foresaw the future but no one paid attention to her warnings.

contra bonos mores—against good morals—a treaty, agreement or decision that contravenes fundamental principles of law and justice and shocks the conscience. A *contra bonos mores* treaty is invalid *ex tunc* (from the beginning) by virtue of article 53 of the Vienna Convention on the Law of Treaties. Investor protection chapters in free-trade agreements are *contra bonos mores* if they include investor-state-dispute-settlement arbitrations, because these create a "parallel" system of settlement of disputes that circumvents public courts and thereby undermine the rule of law.

contra legem—contrary to the law.

cui bono?—who benefits?

Demophobia—the fear of direct democracy, the fear of allowing the people to vote in referenda, the opposition to granting citizens the power of legislative initiative

erga omnes—obligations toward the entire international community

ex aequo et bono—based on what is equitable and right

ex nunc—from now, without retroactivity

ex tunc—from the outset

ex injuria non oritur jus—out of a violation of law, no new norm emerges

fetishism of law—a form of extreme or blind positivism in law, whereby the law must be obeyed, even it is unjust—thus legitimizing colonialism laws, slavery laws Apartheid, *dura lex sed lex* (the law is hard, but it is the law) approach, instead of Cicero's *summun jus, summa injuria* (the excess of law results in injustice).

fragmentation of international law—a scam to circumvent international law by creating "stand alone" legal regimes that function in parallel but are by nature incompatible

free, prior and informed consent—a requirement when dealing with indigenous peoples. See Declaration of the Rights of Indigenous Peoples, articles 10, 11, 19, 28, 29 32.

hard law—binding norms of domestic and international law.

holistic approach to international law—an effort to make international law internally coherent, an epistemology of law that does not accept the fragmentation of law.

Hostis humani generis—enemy of mankind.

humanitarian intervention—a noble concept that awaits appropriate application by the UN Security Council and by the international community but vulnerable to politicized adjudications. It could and should have been invoked during the Cambodian democide in the 1970s and during the Rwandan genocide in the 1990s, but it was not. It was wrongly invoked in the case of the bombardment of Serbia without any resolution from the UN Security Council. Similarly wrongly invoked in 2003 in the context of the invasion of Iraq and 2011 in the context of "regime change" and the assassination of Muhammar Gaddafi.

impunity—the absence of accountability or punishment. Article 2 of the Peace of Westphalia stipulated that all crimes committed during the war be consigned to "oblivion." The Evian accords that ended the Algerian war of independence similarly includes general amnesties.

indigenous peoples—the original native populations of many countries who were massacred and displaced by colonizers and settlers, rendering them minorities in their own countries. See the United Nations Declaration on the Rights of Indigenous Peoples.

international law *à la carte* —selectivity, double-standards, arbitrariness in the application of international law.

international solidarity—a concept underlying multilateralism and the UN Charter. The Declaration on the Right to international solidarity prepared by UN Special Rapporteur Virginia Dandan has not yet been adopted by the General Assembly.

iudex in causa sua—judge in one's own cause (subjective).

ius cogens—peremptory rules of international law, e.g. the prohibition of the use of force pursuant to Article 2(4) of the UN Charter, the prohibition of torture, the right of self-determination of peoples. Treaties incompatible with *ius cogens* are invalid pursuant to article 53 of the Vienna Convention on the Law of Treaties.

Lawfare—entails the instrumentalization of the administration of justice for purely political ends, particularly to prosecute former political leaders. It destroys the rule of law from within.

legibus solutus—exempt from the application of the law (enjoying impunity).

moral vertigo—what shocks the conscience, what is unethical in the extreme.

motu proprio—on one's own initiative.

nil nocere—do no harm.

nomen est omen—the name is an omen, a sign, it speaks for itself (Plautus).

non-interference, non-intervention—related principles of customary international law going back to the 18th century Swiss jurist Emmerich de Vattel, the League of Nations, the UN Charter, and General Assembly Resolutions 2131, 2625, 3314 and cited in numerous ICJ rulings, e.g. the 1986 ruling in the *Nicaragua v. U.S.* contentious judgment.

Non quia difficilia sunt non audemus, sed quia non audemus, difficilia sunt—"It is not because things are difficult that we do not dare; it is because we do not dare that they are difficult" (Seneca).

ontology of business, capitalism, investment—the taking of risks in order to generate a profit, while accepting that sometimes you win, sometimes you lose.

ontology of States—the responsibility to protect the public welfare, the duty to legislate and regulate economic activity to ward off harm from the population.

opinio juris—conviction that a law or practice is legally obligatory, as opposed to mere usage.

ordre public—the public interest.

Pax optima rerum—peace is the highest good (motto of the Peace of Westphalia 1648).

positivism—doctrine whereby only written law is valid, regardless of its injustice and in frequent contravention of general principles of law such as good faith, proportionality.

quis custodiet ipsos custodes—who will guard the gardians? (Juvenalis) A constitutional approach to the rule of law relying on the concept of checks and balances.

quod non est in actis non est in mundo—what is not recorded does not exist.

repetitio est mater studiorum—repetition is the mother of learning.

R2P—responsibility to protect, an Orwellian scam to circumvent the UN Charter, in particular to legitimize military intervention without Security Council approval, in contravention of article 2(4) of the Charter. It is contained in paragraphs 138 and 139 of UN General Assembly Resolution 60/1. It is advocated by States that have a geopolitical interest in interfering in the affairs of other States and want to place a mantel of "legitimacy" over it.

sanctions—only UN sanctions imposed by the Security Council under Chapter VII of the Charter are legal according to international law.

self-determination of peoples—a *jus cogens* right that goes beyond mere decolonization. Article 1 of the ICCPR provides in the first paragraph that "all peoples" have a right of self determination, without distinction. The third paragraph imposes on all States parties the obligation to pro-actively promote self-determination. Internal self-determination entails autonomy and/or federalism and should be anchored in the constitution. External self-determination entails secession.

sic utere tuo ut alienum non laedas—exercise rights without harming the rights of others.

si vis pacem, cole justitiam—if you want peace, cultivate justice (motto of the ILO).

Soft law—non-binding resolutions and declarations, e.g. the UN Declaration on the Rights of Indigenous Populations, the UN Declaration on the Right to Peace

Special procedures—the system of rapporteurs, independent experts and working groups created by the Commission on Human Rights and continued and expanded by the Human Rights Council.

supremacy clause—article 103 of the UN Charter. Any treaty or agreement by member States must be in conformity with the UN Charter or it must be revised.

territorial integrity principle—an international law principle to protect a State from foreign intervention, occupation or annexation. Paragraph 80 of the Advisory Opinion of the International Court of Justice in the Kosovo independence case clearly states that territorial integrity applies only in relations between states. It cannot be used internally to deny a "people" their right of self-determination.

ultra vires—beyond one's competence, without legal basis, illegitimate, invalid.

unilateral coercive measures—illegal sanctions imposed by States unilaterally, a form of State terrorism. UCMs are indiscriminate and impact the most vulnerable.

ubi jus, ibi remedium—where there is law, there must be a remedy.

uti possidetis—an outdated and dangerous principle of international order used first in the context of the wars of independence of Latin American settlers against the mother country Spain, according to which every "colony" was to retain its borders as they were before independence. This had nothing to do with self-determination, since the majority indigenous peoples were subjugated by the European settlers and had no voice in the matter. The principle was again used in the context of the decolonization of Africa with disastrous consequences for many ethnic, linguistic and religious groups, because the frontiers drawn by the European colonizers had no relationship to the identities of the populations they colonized. As a result, the artificial borders of African continent remain potentially a source of violent self-determination conflicts, e.g. in the Cameroons, Equatorial Guinea, Niger, Nigeria, Sudan, etc.

weaponization of human rights—the instrumentalization of some human rights to destroy other human rights, the politicization of human rights and their use to denounce targeted states, usually geopolitical or geoeconomics rivals.

World Parliamentary Assembly (United Nations Parliamentary Assembly)—an idea launched by Joseph Schwarzenberg and Andreas Bummel to democratize the United Nations by direct elections to a people's assembly with advisory powers, to work in tandem with the UN General Assembly, but not consisting of diplomats.

TABLE OF ABBREVIATIONS

AEDIDH—Asociación Española para el Derecho International de los Derechos Humanos
ASEAN—Association of South East Asian Nations
BITs—bilateral investment treaties
CAFTA—Central American Free Trade Agreement
CAT—UN Convention against Torture
CEDAW—UN Convention on the Elimination of Discrimination against Women
CEPR—Washington Center for Economic and Policy Research
CERD—UN Convention on the Elimination of all forms of Racial Discrimination
CERN—European Organization for Nuclear Research
CIA—Central Intelligence Agency
CRC—Convention on the Rights of the Child
DDA—Doha Development Agenda
DESA—UN Department of Economic Social Affairs
DRD—Declaration on the Right to Development
ECHR—European Convention on Human Rights
EU—European Union
FAO—Food and Agriculture Organization
FBHR—Forum on Business and Human Rights
FTA—Free Trade Agreement
GATT—General Agreement on Tariffs and Trade
GDP—gross domestic product
GIPRI—Geneva International Peace Research Institute
GMO—Genetically modified organisms
HRC—Human Rights Council
HRIA—human rights impact assessment
IBRD—International Bank for Reconstruction and Development
ICCPR—international Covenant on Civil and Political Rights
ICESCR—International Covenant on Economic, Social and Cultural Rights
ICJ—International Court of Justice
ICSID—World Bank's International Center for Settlement of Investment Disputes
IGWG—Inter-governmental working group
IHR—WHO's International Health Regulations
ILC—International Law Commission
ILO—International Labour Organisation
IMF—International Monetary Fund
IP—intellectual property

ISDS—investor-state-dispute settlement mechanisms, mostly by an arbitration tribunal of 3 arbitrators
ITO—International Trade Organization
ITU—Interparliamentary Union
MDGs—Millennium Development Goals
NAFTA—North American Free Trade Agreement
NATO—North Atlantic Treaty Organization
NGO—non-governmental organization
NSA—National Security Agency
PPP—public-private partnership
PWC—Price Waterhouse Coopers
SAIHRL—Spanish Association for International Human Rights Law
SIPRI—Stockholm International Peace Research Institute
SSG—Sustainable Development Goals
TRIMs—Agreement on Trade Related Aspects of Investment Measures
TTIP—Transatlantic Trade and Investment Partnership
UDHR—Universal Declaration of Human Rights
UNCITRAL—United Nations Commission on International Trade Law
UCM—Unilateral coercive measures
UNCTAD—United Nations Conference on Trade and Development
UNDP—United Nations Development Programme
UNDRIP—Declaration of the Rights of Indigenous Peoples
UNICEF—United Nations Emergency Children's Fund
UNODC—United Nations Office on Drugs and Crime
UNPFII—UN Permanent Forum on Indigenous Issues
VCLT—Vienna Convention on the Law of Treaties
WB—World Bank
WHO—World Health Organization
WIPO—World Intellectual Property Organization
WTO—World Trade Organization

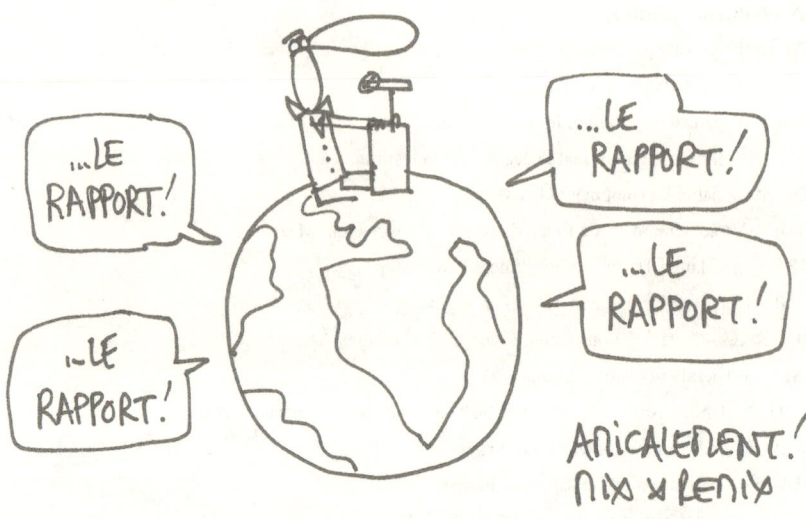

The famous Swiss cartoonist Philippe Becquelin, known as Mix & Remix, did several cartoons for me, including this one concerning my first report to the Human Rights Council. He sketched it before me, starting with my traditional bow-tie, and finished it in about one minute.

INTRODUCTION

"The central task of our time is to evolve a new system of world order based on principles of peace and justice."

RICHARD A. FALK[i]

Achieving a just world order has been the goal of philosophers and religious leaders for thousands of years. History is full of noble projects that have not been successful in establishing such an order. In recent times the League of Nations attempted to keep the peace and promote human rights, notably labour rights and minority rights. Yet, the League of Nations was incapable to prevent World War II. After the great catastrophe of 1939–1945, the Holocaust and the dawn of the atomic age with the nuclear annihilation of Hiroshima and Nagasaki, the world again attempted to establish a stable international order based on multilateralism and a commitment to peace and human dignity. [See my March 2018 report to the Human Rights Council, A/HRC/37/63, https://undocs.org/A/HRC/37/63.]

The United Nations Charter entered into force on 24 October 1945 and since then it has served as a kind of world constitution, a moral compass, a forum where international disputes can be settled peacefully through negotiation. Even if 76 years later, the United Nations still lacks the capacity to enforce its resolutions and decisions, it is certain that the world has benefited from its existence. It seems clear that without the United Nations the world would have stumbled into a new world war. There have been too many "close calls," moments of very high tension and uncertainty, which could easily have led to nuclear Apocalypse—the Cuban missile crisis of 1962 being only one example.

It is difficult to imagine the world without the United Nations, because its influence is ubiquitous. During its 76 years the United Nations has presided over the decolonization of peoples throughout the planet, and has established specialized agencies to advance public health, protect our environment, regulate telecommunications, intellectual property, patents, facilitate commerce, and provide for judicial adjudication of civil and criminal matters.

In the field of human rights, the United Nations was quick to establish a Commission on Human Rights, which drafted the Universal Declaration of Human Rights, adopted by the General Assembly on 10 December 1948. Since then major human

---

i Richard Falk, *The End of World Order: Essays on Normative International Relations* (New York: Holmes & Meier Publishers, 1983).

rights treaties and declarations have been adopted, including the International Convention on the Elimination of All Forms of Racial Discrimination, the International Covenant on Civil and Political Rights, the International Covenant on Economic, Social and Cultural Rights, the Convention against Torture, etc. The Commission and the General Assembly adopted resolutions on all fields of human activity, provided advisory services and technical assistance to countries requesting it, and established many monitoring mechanisms. In the 1980s human rights special rapporteurs and working groups were appointed with the mandate to study specific problems and formulate concrete, pragmatic and implementable recommendations. By virtue of General Assembly Resolution 48/141[1] the function of the United Nations High Commissioner for Human Rights[2] was created, with a vast mandate, including the provision of substantive and logistical support to the special rapporteurs and independent experts appointed by the Commission on Human Rights and its successor since 2006, the Human Rights Council.

This book describes the initiatives and reports of the United Nations Independent Expert on the Promotion of a Democratic and Equitable International Order, whose mandate was established pursuant to Human Rights Council Resolution 18/6 of 29 September 2011, which lays down the terms of reference of an inclusive rapporteurship.[3] The responsibilities of the mandate holder include the promotion of the principles and purposes of the United Nations Charter, in particular the building of a peaceful international order, a universal goal that had already found expression in numerous General Assembly resolutions following the historic Resolution 2131 (XX) of 21 December 1965 on the principle of sovereignty and the prohibition of intervention in the internal affairs of states,[4] Resolution 2625 of 24 October 1970 on the Principles of International Law concerning Friendly Relations and Co-operation among States,[5] Resolution 3201 of 1 May 1974 on the Establishment of a New International Economic Order,[6] Resolution 3314 of 14 December 1974 on the Declaration of the Illegality of Aggression, and Resolution 39/11 of 12 November 1984[7] on the Right of Peoples to Live in Peace.[8]

I was appointed the first UN Independent Expert on the Promotion of a Democratic and Equitable International Order on 23 March 2012 and assumed my functions on 1 May 2012. My six years' appointment ended on 30 April 2018, and I was followed by Dr. Livingstone Sewanyana from Uganda.

During my six years on the mandate, I issued thirteen thematic reports and one report concerning my official mission to Venezuela and Ecuador. I addressed cross-cutting human rights issues pertinent to the realization of a democratic and equitable international order, including:

- various models of democracy,
- the reform of the United Nations system, in particular the Security Council,
- the human right to peace; the right of self-determination of peoples,
- the social responsibility of business enterprises,
- bilateral investment treaties and free-trade agreements,
- investor-state dispute settlement (ISDS)
- military expenditures and the sustainable development goals,
- tax evasion, tax havens, and tax competition,
- enhanced coordination with international trade and financial institutions including the World Trade Organization, the World Bank and the International Monetary Fund, and
- domestic and international protection of human rights defenders including whistleblowers.

My report on my visit to Venezuela examines the concept of "humanitarian crisis" as a pretext to engage in a military "humanitarian intervention," the adverse impacts of unilateral coercive measures, and the relevance of article 7 of the Statute of Rome, which defines crimes against humanity under the jurisdiction of the International Criminal Court.

My fourteen reports evidence the added value of the mandate as a holistic directive to cast human rights in a concrete and coherent framework that invites cross-fertilization with other Special Procedures mandate holders. In my reports I took due account of the findings and recommendations of other rapporteurs and working groups, including those on international solidarity, extreme poverty, the right to health, the right to food, the right to housing, the right to water and sanitation, the right to truth, justice and reparation, the rapporteurs on foreign debt, illicit financial flows, unilateral coercive measures, indigenous peoples, the working groups on business and human rights, mercenaries, disappearances and arbitrary detention. I advocated new standard-setting initiatives such as:

- the declaration on the right to peace,[9]
- the declaration on the rights of peasants,[10]
- a binding legal instrument for transnational enterprises[11] setting out minimum social and environmental standards,
- the criminalization of environmental destruction,[12]
- a global bill of rights,[13]
- an international court on human rights,[14] and
- the creation of a world parliamentary assembly.[15]

My reports illustrated and commented on democratic deficits in many fields, and called for enhanced transparency and accountability by all governmental and non-state actors. Furthermore, the reports made evident that every exercise of power, particularly economic power, must be subjected to some kind of democratic controls, so that the protective functions of the State are not undermined. Similarly, the success of democracy as a system of government depends on transparency and accountability, access to reliable information, a pluralistic media and the assistance of "whistleblowers." Indeed, secrecy by government and the private sector may distort the democratic process and make it impossible for the citizenry to make judicious democratic decisions. Censorship by government or the private sector, including techno-giants and the new digital society, impact the reality of democracy, which means government by the people, not by a manipulated, deceived citizenry.

This is indeed a timely and necessary mandate, especially because it illustrates the inter-relatedness and inter-dependence of human rights, the natural convergence of civil, cultural, economic, political and social rights, and demonstrates that the so-called "fragmentation" of international law does not permit circumventing the holistic application of the Universal Declaration of Human Rights and of the ten core human rights treaties. There can be no "legal black hole" in the field of human rights, and in the twenty-first century the international human rights treaty regime permeates all fields of activity and imposes duties not only on States but also on non-state actors. By joining the dots, this hands-on mandate gives concrete expression to the Purposes and Principles of the United. It is in this spirit that I successfully campaigned with friends in the diplomatic community for the creation of the new mandates on the right to development and on the right to privacy. In 2018 I called for the establishment of new rapporteurships on the right of self-determination and on the right to peace, both aimed at addressing grievances in a timely fashion so as to promote local, regional and international peace and development. This book substantiates the wisdom of creating such mandates.

Besides my reports, I also issued more than a hundred press releases and media statements—and some fifty longer essays or "information notes"—that have sought to illustrate the variety of issues impacting the international order.

From 25 November to 9 December, I undertook the first official visit to Venezuela in 21 years by a UN rapporteur and one of the few UN missions to Ecuador.[16] Among the aims of the visit was to study how the alternative social and economic models of ALBA countries, in particular the *Revolución Bolivariana* in Venezuela and *the Revolución Ciudadana* in Ecuador, have impacted the international order, and vice versa. This two-country visit provided an opportunity to explore big picture challenges faced by all governments, in particular how economic, social and cultural rights can be given greater emphasis without restricting the enjoyment of civil and political rights.[17] Encouragingly, shortly following the visit, some of my specific recommendations were implemented, including the release by Venezuela of 80 political detainees and an enhanced cooperation with the United Nations, manifested by concrete agreements with UNDP, UNHCR, WHO and FAO.[18]

It is to be expected that in future years the potential of the international order mandate will continue to unfold. Admittedly, achieving a democratic and equitable international order requires overcoming formidable obstacles, including unilateralism, exceptionalism, economic wars, the misplaced priorities of some governments and international organizations, bias in favour of civil and political rights, the prevailing *demophobia* in many countries, where some States do not respond to the wishes of their citizens and ban or even criminalize referenda, the curses of positivism, selectivity and double standards and the propensity to go for short-term solutions instead of addressing the root causes of problems. Substantively, the continued existence of secrecy jurisdictions, tax havens, the impunity of States, inter-governmental organizations, transnational corporations, private security companies and other private sector actors are continuing impediments.

In addition to tackling these concerns, future mandate-holders will have to address the impact on a democratic and equitable international order of inter-governmental groupings such as the G7 and G20, private associations like the G 30, the United States Council on Foreign Relations, the World Economic Forum, the Bilderberg Group and the Trilateral Commission, and others, which are sometimes perceived as promoting world government outside the United Nations context,[19] and the World Social Forums since Porto Alegre 2001.

Major global challenges that should be studied from the international order perspective include achieving the sustainable development goals and the post-2030 development agenda, universal peace-keeping and the role of UN Peacekeeping missions, the growing impacts of globalization on the enjoyment of human rights, the consequences of climate change, natural disasters, pandemics, cultural imperialism, economic neo-colonialism, commodities speculation, vulture funds, and the unregulated activities of credit rating agencies and media conglomerates.

It would also be important to explore how the great world religions and non-denominational humanist and ethical unions could proactively advance a more peaceful, more democratic and more equitable international order. Moreover, the mandate might also explore the role of Peoples' Tribunals in ending impunity and helping to break the blackout on war crimes by powerful States and the complacent media conglomerates. The mandate would also benefit from additional country visits, although the mandate remains largely epistemological and primarily entails proposing the creation of norms and clarifying their concrete implications with a view to formulating pragmatic recommendations.

A democratic and equitable international order is one where the United Nations Charter is recognized as the world constitution, and the International Court of Justice operates as the World Constitutional Court, with due deference to the Charter's "supremacy clause."[20] Hitherto the advisory competence of the International Court of Justice has been under-utilized, and the acceptance and enforcement of ICJ advisory opinions has been particularly disappointing. It is imperative for the credibility of the ICJ and of the United Nations itself that States undertake to respect General Assembly resolutions as well as ICJ judgements and advisory opinions. Pursuant to the doctrine of "implied powers," the ICJ should also exercise the competence to issue advisory opinions *motu proprio*. Similarly, the UN Secretary General should be given the competence to ask the ICJ to issue advisory opinions on legal issues requiring an authoritative judicial resolution.

A democratic and equitable international order necessarily functions on the basis of multilateralism and international solidarity. It aims at promoting a culture of peace and dialogue among nations and peoples, fully respecting the sovereignty of States and ensuring that members of civil society in all countries have ample space to express themselves and to enjoy their individual and collective rights and to pursue their traditions, culture and identity. It bears repeating that a democratic and equitable international order is one where peoples and nations enjoy equitable representation not only in the UN General Assembly, but also in regional and international financial institutions, where they can exercise their right of self-determination, where the human right to peace is recognized in its individual and collective dimensions, where unilateral coercive measures are prohibited.

As the World Summit in September 2005 reaffirmed: "democracy is a universal value based on the freely expressed will of people to determine their political, economic, social and cultural systems and their full participation in all aspects of their lives." The Summit Outcome Document also stressed that "democracy, development and respect for human rights and fundamental freedoms are interdependent and mutually reinforcing," and pointed out that "while democracies share common features, there is no single model of democracy."[21]

Since the preamble of the Charter of the United Nations begins with the words "We the peoples," it is necessary to devise ways to give greater voice to civil society, to take the temperature of public opinion throughout the world so as to ensure that the will of peoples and nations is not supplanted by economic and geopolitical interests. At the same time, a proper balance must be found so that populism does not denature democracy and frustrate the nobler goal of serving the higher principle of human dignity.

What does it mean to be a United Nations Independent Expert or Rapporteur?

Independent Experts and Special Rapporteurs are part of what is known as the Special Procedures of the United Nations Human Rights Council, with headquarters in Geneva, established by General Assembly Resolution in 2006 and serviced by the Secretariat of the Office of the UN High Commissioner for Human Rights.

Special Procedures is the general name of the Council's independent fact-finding and monitoring mechanisms that address both thematic and country-specific problems in all parts of the world. This mechanism looks back on a 40-year history, having been originally established by the Commission on Human Rights in the 1980s to address the then acute problem of disappeared persons in Latin America. Over the course of the years some mandates have been terminated and new mandates have been created to respond to new challenges and formulate proposals to States, the General Assembly, inter-governmental organizations and civil society. These are concrete, pragmatic and implementable recommendations, which, however, are not always followed, partly because as of 2021, no follow-up mechanism has been created. As I told the General Assembly in October 2017, the Special Procedures mandate holders should be more than an "assembly of Cassandras." Mechanisms should be devised to facilitate the implementation of our recommendations.

Special Procedures' experts work on a voluntary basis; they are not UN staff and do not receive a salary for their work. They are independent from any government, inter-governmental organization or non-governmental organization, and serve in their individual capacity. They are bound to a strict code of conduct, formulated in Human Rights Council Resolution 5/2.

Before I summarize the substance of my 14 reports, I would like to elucidate my understanding of the function of a Rapporteur.

Every mandate requires that the expert be genuinely independent, keep an open mind, conduct his/her research objectively and without ideological prejudices, listen to all stakeholders and pro-actively seek the opinion of other experts, academics, diplomats, government officials and civil society.

Independence is the added value of any mandate—requiring not just bean-counting or compiling data and evaluations, but trying to understand the problems, identify their causes, the obstacles, the phoney explanations, and pushing back against intimidation, the psychological blackmail of "political correctness" and the consequent self-censorship. The essence of an independent expert is not merely his/her expertise—which must be considered a given—but the faculty of thinking both inside and outside the box, while rigorously respecting the terms of reference laid down in the resolution establishing the mandate and observing the code of conduct of rapporteurs.

A UN mandate is not intended to duplicate or rehash existing knowledge, to go along with mainstream views, to grandstand and condemn, but to offer new impulses, perspectives, emphases, and to formulate constructive proposals so as to advance the Purposes and Principles of the United Nations—with intellectual honesty and good faith.

As I understood it, my mandate entailed a generous symbiosis of civil, cultural, economic, political and social rights. The defining principle of my six years on the job was: *audiatur et altera pars*—listen to all sides. Another characteristic was going *ad fontes,* relying on primary sources rather than on mainstream media narratives, and putting facts and situations in their proper historical and social context, avoiding anachronisms and logical fallacies such as *post hoc ergo propter hoc*, always giving reason the priority over passion.

Methodologically a mandate holder should not rely on templates, but instead listen and remain open to correction, and avoid being identified with any ideology other than a commitment to human dignity. While an independent expert inevitably holds a certain cultural and educational predisposition, and must forego any preconceptions so as to get at the facts. Indeed, all mandate holders are human beings, children of their time, born into a particular culture, immersed in a specific *Zeitgeist.* They are not robots and have moods, preferences and prejudices. Hence, they must be aware of their own emotions and make a conscious effort to weigh the evidence dispassionately while remaining impervious to influences from governments, lobbies, non-governmental organizations, the OHCHR or even subtle "peer pressure" from other rapporteurs.

I have come to the conclusion that the overrated practice of "naming and shaming" rarely produces a solution to violations of human rights, nor does it facilitate the provision of adequate remedies to the victims. Experience shows that this practice is mostly counter-productive, because the party being named seldom recognizes the authority of the "namer," considers the accuser to be hypocritical and having ulterior purposes, and thus retrenches instead of opening up for dialogue. It's far more important that the rapporteur seek out the root causes of the violations, such as endemic inequalities, the persistence of privilege and the culture of violence, including structural violence. The anthropocentric approach is important too, and the commitment to devise measures to give recognition and reparation to the victims. The mandate holder must have the courage to formulate unpopular recommendations that entail more than a "band aid" and require changes of paradigm and mindset.

A rapporteur should have the courage to break the silence about taboo subjects, which are systematically avoided not only by States but, alas, also by what I would call the "human rights industry," the major non-governmental organizations, which have been increasingly influenced by donors from big business and special interests, who often succeed in dictating their agenda. However, my conscience required precisely that I tackle those taboo subjects that were being ignored. Accordingly, I had to endure uncomfortable pressures to self-censorship. Worse still, I endured mobbing, intimidation, insults and even anonymous threats. As I was warned when I became rapporteur, this comes with the job. But I already knew that from my career as Secretary of the Human Rights Committee and Chief of Petitions at the UN Office of the High Commissioner of Human Rights. One of my favorite Latin sayings has been that observation by plutarch, *"Calumniare audacter, semper aliquid haeret."* Indeed, something always sticks when one is slandered and libeled. And one is highly likely to be slandered when one is telling unwelcome truths.

I am convinced that the function of a rapporteur is to give impulses and concrete recommendations to governments and civil society, speak clear language, tear down pretences and double-standards. One thing the rapporteur must not be: a guardian of the *status quo*, a fig leaf for the international community, so that everybody can pretend to have a good conscience and continue "business as usual." Again and again, I see the OHCHR, the Human Rights Council, the Universal Periodic Review, the Special Rapporteurs, Independent Experts essentially copping out—instead of addressing the issues clearly and directly—taking a politicized, *Zeitgeist*-corrupted approach to universal problems. This always makes me think of one of Goethe's many clever maxims *"Wer das erste Knopfloch verfehlt, kommt mit dem Zuknöpfen nicht zu Rande."*[22] If you miss the first buttonhole, you will not finish well.... Ask the wrong questions—expect to get useless answers.

Mandate holders may draw some inspiration from Robert Frost's *The Road Not Taken*:

> *Two roads diverged in a yellow wood*
> *and sorry I could not travel both ...*
> *Two roads diverged in a wood, and I —*
> *I took the one less travelled by,*
> *And that has made all the difference*

They should also remember Horace's Epistles—*Dimidium facti, qui coepit, habet: sapere aude, / incipe* (I, 2, 40). Let's get started and then have the courage to use our judgment! Immanuel Kant also propagated this idea that became key to the Enlightenment—just two words: the imperative *sapere aude!*

The bottom line is that we need more than lip service to human rights, more than rhetoric, more than grandstanding. We need a new functional paradigm for human rights (see concluding chapter), a *mode d'emploi* to live in and for peace and human dignity, a renewed commitment to the spirituality of the Universal Declaration of Human Rights, to the ideals of Eleanor Roosevelt,[23] René Cassin, Charles Malik, P.C. Chang and John Humphrey.[24] Yes, a just world order is possible and it is our responsibility to build it.

Notes

1 General Assembly Resolution 48/141, High Commissioner for the promotion and protection of all human rights, A/RES/48/141 (7 January 1994), https://undocs.org/A/RES/48/141; "Brief History of UN Human Rights," United Nations Human Rights, *UNCHR*, https://www.ohchr.org/EN/AboutUs/Pages/BriefHistory.aspx.

2 Alfred de Zayas, "United Nations High Commissioner for Human Rights" in R. Bernhardt (ed.), *Encyclopaedia of Public International Law,* Vol. IV (Elsevier, Amsterdam 2000), pp. 1129–1132; de Zayas, "Human Rights, United Nations High Commissioner for" in Helmut Volger (ed.), *A Concise Encyclopedia of the United Nations,* 2nd Ed. (Leiden: Martinus Nijhoff, 2010), pp. 275–284.

3 "Mandate of the Independent Expert on the promotion of a democratic and equitable international order," United Nations Human Rights, *UNCHR,* https://www.ohchr.org/EN/Issues/IntOrder/Pages/mandate.aspx.

4 General Assembly Resolution 20/2131, Declaration on the Inadmissibility of Intervention in the Domestic Affairs of States and the Protection of Their Independence and Sovereignty, A/RES/20/2131 (21 December 1965), available at http://un-documents.net/a20r2131.htm;

Edward McWhinney, Q.C., "General Assembly Resolution 2131(XX) of 21 December 1965 Declaration on the Inadmissibility of Intervention in the Domestic Affairs of States and the Protection of their Independence and Sovereignty" (United Nations, 2010), https://legal.un.org/avl/pdf/ha/ga_2131-xx/ga_2131-xx_e.pdf.

5 General Assembly Resolution 25/2625, Declaration on Principles of International Law concerning Friendly Relations and Co-operation among States in accordance with the Charter of the United Nations, A/RES/25/2625 (24 October 1970), available at http://www.un-documents.net/a25r2625.htm.

6 General Assembly Resolution S-6/3201, Declaration on the Establishment of a New International Economic Order, A/RES/S-6/3201 (1 May 1974), available at http://un-documents.net/s6r3201.htm.

7 Definition of Aggression, United Nations General Assembly Resolution 3314 (XXIX) (14 December 1974), University of Minnesota Human Rights Library, http://hrlibrary.umn.edu/instree/GAres3314.html.

8 General Assembly Resolution 39/11, Right of peoples to peace, A/RES/39/11 (12 November 198), available at http://www.un-documents.net/a39r11.htm.

9 General Assembly Resolution 71/189, Declaration on the Right to Peace, A/RES/71/189 (19 December 2016), available at https://digitallibrary.un.org/record/858594?ln=en.

10 Fourth session of the open-ended intergovernmental working group on a United Nations declaration on the rights of peasants and other people working in rural areas, United Nations Human Rights Council, http://www.ohchr.org/EN/HRBodies/HRC/RuralAreas/Pages/4thSession.aspx.

11 Second session of the open-ended intergovernmental working group on transnational corporations and other business enterprises with respect to human rights, United Nations Human Rights Council, http://www.ohchr.org/EN/HRBodies/HRC/WGTransCorp/Session2/Pages/Session2.aspx.

12 "Transnational Corporations must be legally accountable for the negative human rights impacts of their activities," statement by Alfred de Zayas, Independent Expert on the Promotion of a Democratic and Equitable International Order, Workshop at the Human Rights Council 11-12 March 2014, http://www.ohchr.org/AR/NewsEvents/Pages/DisplayNews.aspx?NewsID=14340&LangID=E.

13 *Eleanor Lives! A Plan for Humanity,* https://www.eleanorlives.org.

14 https://www.workableworld.org/uploads/4/7/5/0/47500125/handout_-_multiple_page_program.pdf; "Creating a Workable World, October 15," *Alfred de Zayas Human Rights Corner,* 26 November 2015, https://dezayasalfred.wordpress.com/2015/11/26/creating-a-workable-world-october-2015/.

15 "UN's Independent Expert Alfred de Zayas: 'Time for a World Parliamentary Assembly,'" *UNPA Campaign,* 23 October 2013, http://en.unpacampaign.org/394/uns-independent-expert-alfred-de-zayas-time-for-a-world-parliamentary-assembly/.

16 "UN expert visits Venezuela and Ecuador to assess economic and social advancement," United Nations Human Rights, *UNCHR,* 27 November 2017, http://www.ohchr.org/en/NewsEvents/Pages/DisplayNews.aspx?NewsID=22457&LangID=E.

17 The report on these visits was presented at the 38th Session of the Human Rights Council in September 2018: Report of the Independent Expert on the promotion of a democratic and equitable international order on his mission to the Bolivarian Republic of Venezuela and Ecuador, A/HRC/39/47/Add.1 (3 August 2018), available at https://undocs.org/A/HRC/39/47/Add.1; "Ecuador and Venezuela: Rights expert urges greater cooperation with UN" (a press release following the mission), United Nations Human Rights, *OHCHR,* 12 December 2017, http://www.ohchr.org/EN/NewsEvents/Pages/DisplayNews.aspx?NewsID=22531&LangID=E.

18 "Venezuela: UN independent expert welcomes government action after his visit," United Nations Human Rights, *UNCHR,* 28 December 2017, http://www.ohchr.org/en/NewsEvents/Pages/DisplayNews.aspx?NewsID=22569&LangID=E.

19 See, e.g., Robert Eringer, *The Global Manipulators* (Bristol, England: Pentacle Books, 1980); Ian N. Richardson, Andrew P. Kakabadse and Nada K. Kakabadse, *Bilderberg People: Elite power and consensus in world affairs* (Hoboken, NJ: Routledge, 2011); and Holly Sklar (ed.), *Trilateralism: The Trilateral Commission and Elite Planning for World Management* (Boston: South End Press, 1980).

20 This provides that the Charter should prevail in the event of a conflict between the obligations of States as UN Members and their obligations under other international agreements. UN Charter, article 103.

21 General Assembly Resolution 60/1, 2005 World Summit Outcome, A/RES/60/1 (16 September 2005), available at http://un-documents.net/a60r1.htm.

22 Johann Wolfgang von Goethe, *Maximen und Reflexionen.* Aphorismen und Aufzeichnungen. Nach den Handschriften des Goethe-und Schiller-Archivs, edited by Max F. Hecker (1907).

23 *Eleanor Lives! A Plan for Humanity,* https://www.eleanorlives.org.

24 "John Humphrey (1905-1995)," *About McGill,* https://www.mcgill.ca/about/history/humphrey; A.J. Hobbins, A.J. "Humphrey and the High Commissioner: the Genesis of the Office of the UN High Commissioner for Human Rights," *Journal of the History of International Law,* Vol. III (2001), pp. 38–74.

Chapter 1

MECHANISMS FOR THE DEMOCRATIC PURSUIT OF HUMAN RIGHTS

"It isn't enough to talk about peace. One must believe in it. And it isn't enough to believe in it. One must work at it."

ELEANOR ROOSEVELT[i]

MANDATE AND METHODOLOGY

Professor Frank Cecil Newman[ii] *of Berkeley Law School used to come to the UN Commission of Human Rights and to the Sub-Commission on the Promotion and Protection of Human Rights every year. I used to meet with him in the 1980s and 90s when I was a staff member of the UN Division of Human Rights, later the Centre for Human Rights and Office of the UN High Commissioner for Human Rights. Frank was not only a distinguished law professor, he was also a judge in the Supreme Court of California and a very committed man, convinced that we could all make a difference, an optimistic believer in the possibility of a just world order based on ethics, equity and human dignity. Among the many wise things he used to say is that we had to look back in order to move forward. We were not the pioneers of human rights, but the disciples of philosophers, poets, religious leaders and politicians, who for thousands of years have been striving toward a better, kinder world. We were not reinventing the wheelbarrow, but building on the labour of giants—and of simpler folk like us.*

He liked to refer to Franklin Delano Roosevelt and his Four Freedoms.[iii] *He was also an admirer of Eleanor Roosevelt,*[iv] *whose courage and constancy made*

---

[i] *Voice of America,* 11 November 1951.

[ii] "Creative and Dynamic Strategies for Using United Nations Institutions and Procedures: The Frank Newman File," Chapter 7 (pp. 89–102) in *Human Rights from Exclusion to Inclusion; Principles and Practice: An Anthology from the Work of Theo Van Boven* (Leiden, Netherlands: Martinus Nijhoff Publishers, 2000).
Jennifer DeMarco, "The Newman Oral History: An Introduction," *HeinOnline,* https://heinonline.org/HOL/LandingPage?collection=journals&handle=hein.journals/calegh1&div=6&id=&page=.

[iii] "FDR and the Four Freedoms Speech," Franklin D. Roosevelt Presidential Library and Museum, https://www.fdrlibrary.org/four-freedoms.

[iv] Eleanor Roosevelt, "The Promise of Human Rights," *Foreign Affairs,* April 1948, in Allida Black, *Courage in a Dangerous World: The Political Writings of Eleanor Roosevelt* (New York: Columbia University Press, 1999), 156–68.
https://www.humanrights.com/voices-for-human-rights/eleanor-roosevelt.html

the adoption of the Universal Declaration of Human Rights[i] possible—together with René Cassin, Charles Malik, P.C. Chang, John Humphrey and many others. Frank believed that human rights were juridical, justiciable and enforceable. But human rights were not self-executing, and it was our responsibility to create the mechanisms so that governments would respect the human rights of all persons living under their jurisdictions, so that individuals would have effective recourse to public courts, so that victims would actually find just remedies. All regions of the world should expand their national human rights institutions and human rights tribunals and—one day—the United Nations should establish an international human rights court whose judgments would be binding and enforceable.

This was also the goal of the first Director of the UN Division on Human Rights, Professor John Humphrey (1905-1995), with whom I shared fruitful conversations during his frequent visits to Geneva. This towering figure was enormously inspiring to his students at McGill University, including my wife Carla Edelenbos. John was crucial to the drafting of the UDHR and navigated through difficult political storms, all in the name of human dignity. This too was the goal of Humphrey's successor as Director of the Division, Professor Theo van Boven, who recruited me in 1980 into UN service.[ii]

The San Francisco non-governmental organization Eleanor Lives (www.eleanorlives.org) and its founder Dr. Kirk Boyd are devoted to building on the work of Newman and Humphrey, reproducing and advancing Roosevelt's legacy. In 2010 Dr. Boyd published a prescient book, *2048, Humanity's Agreement to Live Together,* a reference to the adoption of the UDHR in 1948 and the hope that by 2048 the world will have an updated International Bill of Human Rights that every citizen and every lawyer can carry in his/her vest pocket, a bill of rights encompassing all the rights of the UDHR and the treaties that have followed, reformulated in user-friendly language, or incorporated by reference, a true restatement of the law of human rights. In November 2009 Berkeley Law School hosted a major conference, attended among others by Dr. Boyd, Professor David Caron, Professor Theodor Meron, Dr. José Ayala Lasso, the first UN High Commissioner for Human Rights,[iii] the Acting High Commissioner for Human Rights Dr. Bertrand Ramcharan, the UN Special Rapporteur on Torture Manfred Novak, Dr. Bruna Molina, Dr. Mishana Hosseinioun and myself.

Already back in the 1980s and 90s many of us were thinking about the need for an updated international bill of rights and the feasibility of creating the function

---

i "Universal Declaration of Human Rights," 10 December 1948, United Nations, https://www.un.org/en/about-us/universal-declaration-of-human-rights.

ii Bertrand Ramcharan, *The Advent of Universal Protection of Human Rights, Theo van Boven and the Transformation of the UN Role* (Cham, Switzerland: Springer Nature Switzerland AG, 2018).

iii Ayala Lasso, José. In: Encyclopedia of Human Rights, edited by David P. Forsythe. New York and Oxford: Oxford University Press, 2009), Volume 1, pp. 130–2.

of the UN High Commissioner for Human Rights and an incipient International Court of Human Rights. Back then I was a member of a small brainstorming group at the Centre for Human Rights under the direction of USG Jan Martenson. It was this little think tank that prepared the working papers and resolutions that eventually led to the decision to launch the 1993 World Conference on Human Rights in Vienna.[i]

At our little think tank we also debated the importance of coordinating United Nations Human Rights work and the timeliness of again floating the High Commissioner idea, which had been around for three decades but had not reached fruition because of the East/West divide and the Cold War.

I attended the extremely successful two-week World Conference in Vienna, preceded by a frantically busy preparatory week, and was pleased that part II, paragraphs 17 and 18, of the Vienna Declaration and Programme of Action incorporated our old dream—the creation of the function of the High Commissioner.[ii] We were confirmed in our hopes when we learned that the General Assembly on 20 December 1993 actually delivered on the Vienna recommendation and established the Office of the High Commissioner for Human Rights by Resolution 48/141, *"reaffirming the commitment made under Article 56 of the Charter to take joint and separate action in cooperation with the United Nations for the achievement of the purposes set forth in Article 55 of the Charter,"* and *"emphasizing the need for the promotion and protection of all human rights to be guided by the principles of impartiality, objectivity and non-selectivity, in the spirit of constructive international dialogue and cooperation."*[iii]

---

i Our member, Judge Jakob Th. Möller wrote on the Possible Reform of the Complaints Procedures, Dr. Markus Schmidt wrote about human rights in security matters and on the follow-up procedure of the UN Human Rights Committee, Dr. Eric Tistounet wrote about Reporting Procedures and I wrote seven short papers on The Relevance of Roosevelt's Four Freedoms Today, Migration and Human Rights, Human Rights and Refugees, Human Rights and Humanitarian Law, Strengthening the Secretariat Servicing the Treaty-Based Complaints Procedures, An International Court of Human Rights, and An International Criminal Court. In *Nordic Journal of International Law,* 1992–93, Volumes 61/62, pp. 193–271.

ii Vienna Declaration and Programme of Action, Adopted by the World Conference on Human Rights in Vienna on 25 June 1993, United Nations Human Rights, *OHCHR,* https://www.ohchr.org/EN/ProfessionalInterest/Pages/Vienna.aspx.

17. The World Conference on Human Rights recognizes the necessity for a continuing adaptation of the United Nations human rights machinery to the current and future needs in the promotion and protection of human rights, as reflected in the present Declaration and within the framework of a balanced and sustainable development for all people. In particular, the United Nations human rights organs should improve their coordination, efficiency and effectiveness.

18. The World Conference on Human Rights recommends to the General Assembly that when examining the report of the Conference at its forty-eighth session, it begin, as a matter of priority, consideration of the question of the establishment of a High Commissioner for Human Rights for the promotion and protection of all human rights.

iii General Assembly Resolution 48/141, High Commissioner for the promotion and protection of all human rights, A/RES/48/141 (7 January 1994), https://undocs.org/A/RES/48/141.

Pursuant to the resolution the High Commissioner shall *"be guided by the recognition that all human rights—civil, cultural, economic, political and social—are universal, indivisible, interdependent and interrelated and that, while the significance of national and regional particularities and various historical, cultural and religious backgrounds must be borne in mind, it is the duty of States, regardless of their political, economic and cultural systems, to promote and protect all human rights and fundamental freedoms."* Furthermore the High Commissioner shall *"recognize the importance of promoting a balanced and sustainable development for all people and of ensuring realization of the right to development, as established in the Declaration on the Right to Development,"* and to this end provide *"advisory services and technical and financial assistance, at the request of the State concerned."*

This resolution reminds us of Franklin Roosevelt's Four Freedoms, which embraced humanity's fundamental entitlements—two focussing on civil and political rights and two addressing economic and social rights. Indeed, freedom of speech and freedom of worship are crucial to the pursuit of happiness and essential to the consolidation of a free and democratic society. At the same time, freedom from want and freedom from fear are enabling rights that render it possible to enjoy all other rights, recognizing the human family's right to the fundamental conditions of existence—food, water, shelter, and the universal aspiration to be able to live in peace and dignity.

Full of enthusiasm and hope, I welcomed the challenge to help build a just world order and presented my initial report to the Human Rights Council on 12 September 2012. In it I formulated preliminary views on the conceptual and legal framework of the mandate and highlighted some of the epistemological challenges inherent in the notion of democracy at the national and international levels. I also endeavoured to identify obstacles to the equitable distribution of the world's natural resources, the implications of a culture of greed, the growing gulf between rich and poor countries and the sin of indifference to victims of assaults on human dignity. —AdeZ

* * *

A. Human Rights Council resolution 18/6

1. In its resolution 18/6 of 29 September 2011, the Human Rights Council established, for a period of three years, a new special procedure entitled "Independent Expert on the promotion of a democratic and equitable international order." The mandate holder is requested:

(b) To identify possible obstacles to the promotion and protection of a democratic and equitable international order, and to submit proposals and/or recommendations to the Human Rights Council on possible actions in that regard;

(c) To identify best practices in the promotion and protection of a democratic and equitable international order at the local, national, regional and international levels;

(d) To raise awareness concerning the importance of promoting and protecting a democratic and equitable international order;

(e) To work in cooperation with States in order to foster the adoption of measures at the local, national, regional and international levels aimed at the promotion and protection of a democratic and equitable international order through concrete proposals enhancing subregional, regional and international cooperation, including by holding subregional and regional consultations in that regard;

(f) To work in close coordination, while avoiding unnecessary duplication, with intergovernmental and non-governmental organizations, other special procedures of the Human Rights Council, international financial institutions, as well as with other relevant actors representing the broadest possible range of interests and experiences, within their respective mandates, including by attending and following up on relevant international conferences and events;

(g) To integrate a gender perspective and a disabilities perspective into his or her work;

(h) To report regularly to the Human Rights Council and the General Assembly.

2. Pursuant to paragraph 17 of the above-mentioned resolution, the Human Rights Council requests the Independent Expert to present his first report to the Council at its twenty-first session. Bearing in mind that the mandate holder assumed his functions on 1 May, this initial report should be understood as a *tour-d'horizon* of the multiple aspects of the mandate. While the mandate may appear overbroad or abstract, the intention of the Council is to give practical application to human rights norms in the international order, thus requiring the mandate holder to formulate pragmatic solutions. The individual and collective

dimensions of the resolution will be taken into account, recognizing the individual's entitlement to civil, political, economic, social and cultural rights, and the inter-State commitment to respect one another's sovereignty, ensuring the equitable participation of all States in the international order, including global decision-making and equitable commercial and financial relations.

1. The mandate calls for the identification of obstacles and best practices and for the formulation of proposals and recommendations on possible action. While norms and mechanisms exist, an important implementation gap prevails. The mandate holder is consulting stakeholders and will formulate recommendations on ways to make the international order more democratic and equitable. He is committed to cooperate with other mandate holders to avoid duplication, recognizing, however, that ""duplication" in the field of human rights may also open other perspectives and assist in the process of education, stocktaking and reflection. One task is to identify trends and desires for reform of the international order and to energize public opinion to demand and carry out such reforms at the local and regional levels, ultimately affecting the international order from the grass roots up. The Independent Expert will be guided by relevant General Assembly resolutions, including 61/160, 63/189 and 65/223.

B. The concepts of democracy and equity

A preliminary task of the mandate is a review of the various definitions of the notion of "democracy," which States use with varying content. The bottom line is that the people (*demos*) should meaningfully influence the policies and practices of government. Democracy is not merely a formal State structure or a pro forma holding of elections, but the correlation between the will of the people and the actions of its elected representatives. The will of the people must also be genuine and not the result of populism, demagoguery, manipulation by national or international lobbies, distortion through consumerism, intimidation or fear. It should also be kept in mind that although "democracy" is a better form of government than others, it is not a panacea for all the ills of mankind; thus it is necessary to come to grips with the paradoxes of democracy, freedom, the rule of law, and ethical values. Majority rule must not negate minority rights, the right to be different, the right to practice one's own culture, or the right to one's individuality and identity. Democracy without equity and without caritas can engender inhuman and degrading consequences, including extreme poverty and food insecurity. Democracy must always be tempered by a constant awareness of the inherent dignity of the human being, by the over-arching principle of social justice, bearing in mind that while competition is necessary and useful for material progress, in the absence of a sense of solidarity, competition may become predator behaviour. Indeed, democracy is more than just a political concept; it also has economic, social, anthropological, ethical and religious dimensions. The rule of law is not identical with positivism, but must be animated by Montesquieu's *Esprit des Lois* (1748), the existence of an independent judiciary, moderation, a culture of dialogue, negotiation and compromise, and a conviction that in human rights terms there cannot be any "legal black holes." Finally, it should be remembered that the ritual invocation of the word "democracy" does not make it happen. Societies must work in good faith to make it function, ensuring genuine participation by the population. At the same time, common sense also tells us to beware of the excesses of "militant democracy," a rather bizarre concept, which in some circumstances may take totalitarian overtones, and to abandon the fantasy that democracy can be exported or imposed by force. The respect for national sovereignty mandated in the Charter of the United Nations also means respect for the national identity of countries.

Democracy can be understood internally but also internationally, since the will of a majority of States in the General Assembly deserves respect. Whereas every member of the General Assembly has an equal right to vote, consideration must also be given to the fact that some States have very large populations and only a single vote, posing a problem of weighting. Moreover, the unequal economic and political power of States may lead to inequitable results, especially when a few powerful States frustrate the expressed will of democratically elected Governments representing hundreds of millions of human beings. This has led to the formation of informal voting blocks that do not always serve the cause of international equity. A problem of credibility arises when a large number of General Assembly resolutions remain unimplemented, although adopted by near unanimity.

The Independent Expert acknowledges earlier pronouncements of the General Assembly concerning democracy, e.g. in resolutions 55/96 on promoting and consolidating democracy, 57/221 on strengthening the rule of law, and 59/201 on enhancing the role of regional,[1] subregional and other organizations and arrangements in promoting and consolidating democracy, as well as resolution 50/172 on respect for the principles of national sovereignty and non-interference in the internal affairs of States in their electoral processes, in which the Assembly recognized that there is no single political system or single universal model for electoral processes equally suited to all nations and their peoples, and that political systems and electoral processes are subject to historical, political, cultural and religious factors. Similarly, the Human Rights Council, in its resolution 19/36 on human rights, democracy and the rule of law, reaffirms in a preambular paragraph that while democracies share common features, there is no single model of democracy and that democracy does not belong to any country or region, and stresses the necessity of due respect for sovereignty and the right to self-determination. Thus, it should be clear that the way toward democracy—both nationally and internationally—is arduous and that countries should devise their own democratic institutions and mechanisms consistent with their culture and traditions, but also grounded in universal human rights.

The mandate holder will also explore the practical scope of the concept of equity, going back to the Socratic notion of moderation and the Aristotelian approach to justice (*Ethics*) as equality of treatment, i.e. like cases being treated alike, unlike cases differently.

How can the existing international order evolve so that it will be more democratic and more equitable? Certain conditions appear necessary, foremost among them peace in the holistic sense, encompassing not only the absence of war but also positive harmony, the absence of structural violence, cultural hegemonism, neo-colonialism, exploitation, discrimination and the eradication of extreme poverty as envisaged in the Millennium Development Goals. At the request of the Human Rights Council, OHCHR organized an expert workshop on the right of peoples to peace, held in Geneva on 15 and 16 December 2009, in which experts and civil society participated. The report on the workshop (A/HRC/14/38) was presented to the Council in June 2010 and led to the adoption of resolution 14/3, in which the Council tasked the Advisory Committee with drafting a declaration on the right to peace, which also entails reducing the gap between rich and poor in all countries, whether developed or developing, through a process of gradual implementation of social justice. Pursuant to Council resolution 17/16 and Advisory Committee recommendation 8/4, the Advisory Committee submitted to the Council its draft declaration on the right to peace (A/HRC/20/31, annex). At its twentieth session, the Council considered the draft, and adopted resolution 20/15 establishing an open-ended working group to continue the codification process, taking duly into account all preparatory work.

Normative framework

A. Charter of the United Nations as a World Constitution

In a very real sense the Charter of the United Nations can be described as a World Constitution. All States are bound by it and should orient their policies and practices according to its purposes and principles. Paramount is the commitment "to save succeeding generations from the scourge of war" through meaningful disarmament and to fulfil the promise to turn swords into ploughshares, and end internal and international warfare.

The Universal Declaration of Human Rights is an emanation of the Charter and constitutes a minimum standard which must be respected not only by States but also by individuals.

The world financial crisis is a result not only of toxic loans by irresponsible bankers but also of the enormous waste caused by recurrent armed conflicts and by the inordinate proportion of national budgets devoted to the development of all kinds of armaments, including weapons of mass destruction, which threaten the survival of humanity[2] and violate article 6 of the International Covenant on Civil and Political Rights.[3] The Charter also stipulates the promotion of human rights, development and friendly relations based on respect for the principle of equal rights and self-determination of peoples. The application of the Charter is further governed by general principles of law, such as equity, good faith, victims' right to reparation, estoppel (*ex injuria non oritur jus*), and the overarching principles of equality, non-discrimination and the common heritage of mankind.

Relevant instruments

The Universal Declaration of Human Rights constitutes "a common standard of achievement for all peoples and all nations." Of particular relevance to the present mandate are the rights to freedom of opinion and expression (art. 19), freedom of peaceful assembly and association (art. 20), the right to take part in the conduct of public affairs (art. 21), the right to a social and international order in which the rights and freedoms set forth in the Declaration can be fully realized (art. 28), and everyone's "duties to the community in which alone the free and full development of his personality is possible" in the light of "the general welfare in a democratic society" (art. 29).[4]

For the realization of an international order that is more democratic, it is necessary that States observe the rights stipulated in both the International Covenant on Civil and Political Rights and the International Covenant on Economic, Social and Cultural Rights. With regard to civil and political rights, particularly crucial are the right to hold opinions without interference and the right to freedom of expression, including freedom to seek, receive and impart information, regardless of frontiers (art. 19), as well as the right to peacefully assemble (art. 21) and the right to freedom of association (art. 22). The right to due process in civil and criminal proceedings as well as the independence of the judiciary (art. 14) are central to every democracy, as is the right of every citizen to take part in the conduct of public affairs, directly or through freely chosen representatives, and to vote and be elected at genuine periodic elections (art. 25), and the autonomous right to equality (art. 26).

The International Covenant on Economic, Social and Cultural Rights stipulates conditions for the promotion of an equitable international order, in particular the rights to work (art. 6), to form and join trade unions (art. 8), to social security (art. 9), to an adequate standard of living and to be free from hunger (art. 11), to the enjoyment of physical and mental health (art. 12) and to education (art. 13).

The International Convention on the Elimination of All Forms of Racial Discrimination and the Convention on the Elimination of All Forms of Discrimination against Women contain many relevant provisions. With regard to gender discrimination and gender mainstreaming, the Independent Expert will explore the implications of the Committee on the Elimination of Discrimination against Women's general recommendation No. 23 (1997) on women in political and public life. The Convention on the Rights of Persons with Disabilities, the International Convention on the Protection of the Rights of All Migrant Workers and Members of Their Families and the 1951 Convention relating to the Status of Refugees provide additional perspectives relevant to the present mandate.

The Vienna Declaration and Programme of Action of 1993 commits States to "an international order based on the principles enshrined in the Charter of the United Nations, including promoting and encouraging respect for human rights and fundamental freedoms for all and respect for the principle of equal rights and self-determination of peoples, peace, democracy, justice, equality, rule of law, pluralism, development, better standards of living and solidarity." The United Nations Millennium Declaration of 2000 proclaimed: "We will spare no effort to promote democracy and strengthen the rule of law as well as respect for all internationally recognized human rights and fundamental freedoms, including the right to development" (para. 24)." The Millennium Development Goals reaffirm these commitments, in particular to end extreme poverty and promote universal education and gender equality.[5] The World Conference against Racism, Racial Discrimination, Xenophobia and Related Intolerance, held in Durban, South Africa, in August/September 2001, adopted the Durban Declaration and Programme of Action, reaffirmed in the outcome document of the Durban Review Conference, adopted on 24 April 2009, and in the declaration of the high-level meeting of the General Assembly to commemorate the tenth anniversary of the adoption of the Durban Declaration and Programme of Action, proclaimed by the Assembly in its resolution 66/3.

Particularly relevant to Human Rights Council resolution 18/6 are General Assembly Resolutions 3201 (S-VI) on the Declaration on the Establishment of a New International Economic Order, 2625 (XXV) on friendly relations and 3314 (XXIX) on the definition of aggression, and more immediately resolution 65/223, in which the General Assembly affirms that a democratic and equitable international order requires the realization of, inter alia, the right of peoples to self-determination, permanent sovereignty over natural resources, development and peace.

The mandate holder will build on the studies already conducted by the Commission on Human Rights, by the Human Rights Council and its Advisory Committee, including the Advisory Committee report on enhancement of international cooperation in the field of human rights (A/HRC/AC/8/3), as well as by the Sub-Commission on the Promotion and Protection of Human Rights, including those of the Special Rapporteur Awn Shawkat Al-Khasawneh, tasked with preparing a study on the human rights dimensions of population transfers, which identify numerous gross violations of democracy and equity that accompany every form of "ethnic cleansing,"[6] and the final report of Special Rapporteur Miguel Alfonso Martínez on treaties, agreements and other constructive arrangements between States and indigenous populations (E/CN.4/Sub.2/1999/20). He will also build on the work of the family of special rapporteurs of the Human Rights Council, the General Assembly and the Commission on Human Rights, in particular with respect to resolutions on the right of peoples to peace (Assembly resolution 39/11 and Commission resolution 2002/71). The pertinent conventions and directives of specialized agencies, such as the International Labour Organization (ILO), will be incorporated into the analysis of thematic issues in future reports.

Ethical and historical perspective

It is appropriate to recall that the objectives of the present mandate reflect aspirations expressed by the leaders of many countries, even before the creation of the United Nations. For instance, President Franklin Roosevelt of the United States of America articulated universal hopes in his "Four Freedoms" address of 6 January 1941, notably the freedom from want and the freedom from fear. These principles were confirmed in the eight-point peace plan known as the Atlantic Charter of August 1941, subsequently adhered to by 26 governments in the Declaration by United Nations of 1 January 1942. Article 2 of the Atlantic Charter stipulates that the anti-Hitler coalition "desire to see no territorial changes that do not accord with the freely expressed wishes of the peoples concerned"; its article 3 provides that "they respect the right of all peoples to choose the form of government under which they will live," its article 4 commits States to promote "the enjoyment by all States, great or small, victor or vanquished, of access, on equal terms, to the trade and to the raw materials of the world which are needed for their economic prosperity"; and its article 8 reaffirms the need for disarmament.

For centuries secular and religious thinkers have promoted peace and social justice. A central thesis of Immanuel Kant's philosophy was the imperative to recognize that humans are ends and should not be used as mere means to an end. Mahatma Gandhi propounded the philosophy of *satyagraha*[7] in his campaigns to reform Indian society and to awake Indian consciousness to the necessity of his social agenda. He condemned discrimination and immorality, inequality and exploitation. He struggled not merely for independence from England but for social justice within India: "Unless poverty and unemployment are wiped out from India . . . I would not agree that we have attained freedom."[8] In the same vein, on 28 August 1963, Martin Luther King expressed his hope that there can indeed be social progress: "I have a dream that one day this nation will rise up and live out the true meaning of its creed: 'We hold these truths to be self-evident that all men are created equal.'" Similarly, Nelson Mandela, upon receiving the Nobel Peace Prize on 10 December 1993, stated: "We speak here of the challenge of the dichotomies of war and peace, violence and non-violence, racism and human dignity, oppression and repression and liberty and human rights, poverty and freedom from want ... countless human beings, both inside and outside our country, had the nobility of spirit to stand in the path of tyranny and injustice, without seeking selfish gain. They recognised that an injury to one is an injury to all and therefore acted together in defence of justice and a common human decency."

As to freedom from fear, Aung San Suu Kyi expressed it well: " "Within a system which denies the existence of basic human rights, fear tends to be the order of the day. Fear of imprisonment, fear of torture, fear of death, fear of losing friends, family, property or means of livelihood, fear of poverty, fear of isolation, fear of failure. A most insidious form of fear is that which masquerades as common sense or even wisdom, condemning as foolish, reckless, insignificant or futile the small, daily acts of courage which help to preserve man's self-respect and inherent human dignity. It is not easy for a people conditioned by fear under the iron rule of the principle that might is right to free themselves from the enervating miasma of fear. Yet even under the most crushing state machinery courage rises up again and again, for fear is not the natural state of civilized man.[9]

In his book *Indignez-vous!* (Time for Outrage), Stéphane Hessel similarly calls for taking responsibility in our hands and demanding change. Such courage is being expressed in many countries by civil society, indignant at the failures and abuses by government. For centuries it has been the role of poets and novelists to use literature to promote a more ethical order, from Aristophanes to Ibn Rushd, Erasmus of Rotterdam, Jean-Jacques Rousseau, Friedrich von Schiller, Harriet Beecher Stowe, Wilfred Owen, Lu Xun, Anna Akhmatova, Gabriel García Márquez, Vaclav Havel, Arundhati Roy and Wole Soyinka.

Complementarity and coordination with other mechanisms

The Independent Expert will endeavour to liaise with charter-based and treaty-based mechanisms and build on United Nations initiatives such as the Global Compact.[10]

The United Nations treaty bodies are seized of situations and individual cases on matters relating to the present mandate and have adopted many pertinent decisions in this respect. Their jurisprudence in the form of case law,[11] concluding observations and general comments will enrich the reports of the Independent Expert; he will also rely on recommendations resulting from the universal periodic review and on the work of special procedures, in particular the reports of the Independent Expert on human rights and international solidarity; the Independent Expert on the effects of foreign debt and other related international financial obligations of States on the full enjoyment of all human rights, particularly economic, social and cultural rights; the Independent Expert on the issue of human rights obligations related to the enjoyment of a safe, clean, healthy and sustainable environment; the Special Rapporteurs on the promotion and protection of the right to freedom of opinion and expression, on the rights to freedom of peaceful assembly and of association, on the independence of judges and lawyers, on the promotion of truth, justice, reparation and guarantees of non-recurrence, on the right to education, in the field of cultural rights, on the rights of indigenous peoples, on extreme poverty and human rights, on contemporary forms of racism, racial discrimination, xenophobia and related intolerance, on the right to food, on the right of everyone to the enjoyment of the highest attainable standard of physical and mental health, on the human right to safe drinking water and sanitation, on adequate housing as a component of the right to an adequate standard of living, and on the human rights of internally displaced persons; the Working Group on the issue of human rights and transnational corporations and other business enterprises; and the Forum on Business and Human Rights.

The mandate holder will follow the work of the 26-member United Nations high-level panel on post-Millennium Development Goals, established in 2012, and seek synergies with the Special Adviser on Post-2015 Development Planning. Attention will be paid to the programmes established by several United Nations agencies with objectives relating to those of this mandate. In the field of labour law, the ILO promotes social justice through standard setting and monitoring; its motto *"si vis pacem, cole justitiam"* (if you desire peace, cultivate justice) could well be the motto of the present mandate and report. This motto is also written on a document buried at the foundation of the old ILO building in Geneva, today the headquarters of the World Trade Organization (WTO). WTO has the opportunity to promote a more equitable international order by mainstreaming human rights principles into its policies and programmes, including the Doha Development Agenda, pursuant to its commitment to achieve the agreed objective of rebalancing trade rules so that developing countries can benefit from enhanced equitable commerce. The Independent Expert will consider how WTO may promote equity in the global trade regime with fairness for all, especially for poor and vulnerable countries. He will study the relevant reports of the World Bank, International Monetary Fund and the United Nations Conference on Trade and Development (UNCTAD) and evaluate criticism by think tanks, academics and civil society.[12] The United Nations Educational, Scientific and Cultural Organization (UNESCO) advances international understanding through culture and is committed to the promotion of world peace, as expressed in the preamble of its Constitution: "Since wars begin in the minds of men, it is in the minds of men that the defences of peace must be constructed." In this spirit the Director-General of UNESCO proclaimed in 1997 the Declaration on the Human Right to Peace. Of continued relevance are the UNESCO programme on a Culture of Peace and the Declaration and Programme of Action on a Culture of Peace (General Assembly Resolution 53/243). On 12 November 1997 the General Conference of UNESCO adopted the Declaration on the Responsibilities of the Present Generations towards Future Generations (see www.unesco.org/cpp/uk/declarations/generations.pdf).

The Independent Expert will seek synergies with civil society and intergovernmental initiatives, including those of the Inter-Parliamentary Union, of the Alliance of Civilizations, United Nations Institute for Disarmament Research and of regional organizations, which may further contribute to the realization of a more democratic and equitable international order. He will study the future report Fostering cross-cultural understanding for building peaceful and inclusive societies.

In particular, the mandate holder recalls civil society initiatives that have borne fruit, for example the World Campaign on the Human Right to Peace conducted by the Spanish Society for the Advancement of International Human Rights Law, which concluded on 10 December 2010 with the adoption of the Santiago Declaration on the Human Right to Peace at the International Congress on the Human Right to Peace, held in Santiago de Compostela, Spain, in the context of the World Social Forum on Education for Peace.[13] This Declaration revised the earlier Luarca Declaration on the Human Right to Peace[14] in the light of inputs from different cultural sensibilities.[15] At the same Congress the Statutes of the International Observatory of the Human Right to Peace were adopted,[16] becoming operative on 10 March 2011, and which enjoy the endorsement of some 2,000 civil society organizations, as well as of numerous public institutions and the 22 member States of the Ibero-American Summit.[17]

Obstacles to the realization of a more democratic and equitable international order

The Independent Expert has already held consultations with stakeholders to learn what they perceive to be major obstacles and good practices for the realization of an international order that is more democratic and equitable. Focused questionnaires have been sent and further questionnaires will be addressed to all stakeholders over the next three years.

Through informal consultation with members of permanent missions, intergovernmental organizations and NGOs, in particular the academic communities of several countries, and subsequent study of relevant literature, the mandate holder has become aware of numerous concerns that require further study, including the postulate of a hierarchy of human rights as one of the remaining ideological debates between developed and developing countries. In his view, civil, political, economic, social and cultural rights are not only interdependent, but they also have equal value and importance.

With regard to a more democratic international order, some observers have signalled the need to reform the United Nations and, in particular, the composition of the Security Council so as to make it more responsive to the needs of the 193 States Members of the United Nations. A General Assembly task force on Security Council reform is committed to explore the modalities of Security Council reform. In his report entitled "In larger freedom: Towards development, security and human rights for all," submitted to the 2005 World Summit, the Secretary-General proposed an enlargement of the Security Council to 24 members (A/59/2005, paras. 168–170). Such enlargement could theoretically be achieved through amendment of the Charter of the United Nations (pursuant to Article 108), provided that the permanent members of the Security Council agree.

Other observers have pointed out that the theoretical equality of the Westphalian State system is put to question by the realities of power politics, economic imbalance and adverse trade relationships. Indeed, the overwhelming economic power of some countries renders illusionary the aspirations of sovereignty of many poorer countries. In the United Nations, votes are often influenced by economic carrot-and-stick practices, and some weaker economies must bend to diplomatic and other forms of pressure.

In the above-mentioned report (A/59/2005, para. 32), the Secretary-General observed:

> In 2005, the development of a global partnership between rich and poor countries . . . needs to become a reality. . . . Each developing country has primary responsibility for its own development—strengthening governance, combating corruption and putting in place the policies and investments to drive private-sector-led growth and maximize domestic resources available to fund national development strategies. Developed countries, on their side, undertake that developing countries which adopt transparent, credible and properly costed development strategies will receive the full support they need, in the form of increased development assistance, a more development-oriented trade system and wider and deeper debt relief. All of this has been promised but not

delivered. That failure is measured in the rolls of the dead— and on it are written millions of new names each year.

Some observers have expressed concern over "market fundamentalism," a philosophy that has much in common with social Darwinism and assumes that a laissez-faire policy is always the optimal solution.[18] "Corporatocracy," unfair taxation, uncontrolled markets, currency speculation and runaway finance impact negatively on both democracy and equity.

It has long been noted that certain transnational corporations are wealthier and more powerful than some States. Strategies and guidelines must be developed to ensure that international business and trade promote rather than hinder a democratic and equitable international order. The new Working Group on the issue of human rights and transnational corporations and other business enterprises, established by the Human Rights Council at its seventeenth session (resolution 17/4), is tasked with promoting human rights in this sensitive area. The Independent Expert will consult with the members of the Working Group in order to cross-fertilize and avoid duplication.

Globalization raises many human rights issues[19] and it is in the interest of governments, transnational corporations and civil society that the opportunities offered by globalization be used to advance and not to restrict the enjoyment of human rights. The Independent Expert will explore the impact of globalization on the realization of an international order that is more democratic and more equitable, and how to reconcile the tensions between, on the one side, the legitimate interest in profit and trade expansion[20] and, on the other side, the right of States, large and small, to sovereignty and control over their natural resources, and the right of peoples to self-determination,[21] to decide their domestic policies of full employment and equity.

Military expenditures, the power of the military-industrial complex, the overt and covert trade in weapons, international organized crime, in particular drug trafficking, money-laundering and corruption[22] of government officials and non-state actors continue to have a deleterious effect on the proper functioning of democracy in many countries. The impact of the "war on drugs" and of the "war on terror" on the rule of law also deserves close attention. The killing and harassment of journalists, reprisals against human rights defenders, censorship and deliberate disinformation by government and private sector media frustrate the democratic goal of empowering the population to develop responsible opinions upon which to act in the political arena. Frequently news reporting and commentary avoid the crucial issues and distract attention with red herrings of all kinds. Observers have noted that all too often the "elephant in the room" is ignored. Such practices undermine democracy.

The Independent Expert considers that the emergence of a democratic international order would be advanced by the participation of a growing number of States which implement democratic principles domestically.

Concern has been expressed about the role of religious institutions in the conduct of public affairs. The Independent Expert would like to explore how religious institutions can also contribute to a more democratic and equitable international order.

Greater efforts are needed to limit current attempts to shrink the space of civil society at the international and domestic levels. Arbitrary and undue restrictions on the effective enjoyment of fundamental freedoms, including the freedoms of association, peaceful assembly and expression, seriously obstruct the realization of a more democratic international order.

From the domestic perspective, obstacles to the promotion of a more democratic international order also include a lack of correlation between the will of the people and the policies and practices adopted by their governments, even democratically elected governments, and reflect an epistemological and perception gap between the governing elites and the population at large. This lack of correlation may be attributed in part to the psychology of power, but also to the deliberate distortion or manipulation of public opinion.[23]

It is generally recognized that a well-informed citizenry is a condition of democracy. A country where public opinion is manipulated by the government or private media cannot have a functioning democracy. Censorship, whether conducted by States or by press conglomerates, distorts reality and undermines democracy. Who is financing the media and what gets broadcasted or released are important issues in understanding the degree of press freedom, also to what extent big media smother out the independent press. Self-censorship as a result of intimidation or social pressures, sometimes referred to as " political correctness," constitutes a serious obstacle to the proper functioning of democracy. It is important to hear the views of all persons, including the "silent majority," and to give ear to the weaker voices. There is little hope for an international democratic order as long as democracy is lacking at the national level. Therefore, it is imperative to focus attention on education and access to information, including via the Internet, to enable persons to develop freely their own opinions. Direct or indirect censorship, whether through State or private sector agencies, undermines opinion-building and constitutes an obstacle for the individual and society at large to exercise civic responsibilities, including the right to participate in the conduct of public affairs.

The Human Rights Committee has stated: "Freedom of opinion and freedom of expression are indispensable conditions for the full development of the person. They are essential for any society. They constitute the foundation stone for every free and democratic society. The two freedoms are closely related, with freedom of expression providing the vehicle for the exchange and development of opinions. Freedom of expression is a necessary condition for the realization of the principles of transparency and accountability that are, in turn, essential for the promotion and protection of human rights."[24] Some pressure groups, lobbies and professional public relations companies may hijack political decision-making and leave large parts of the population effectively disenfranchised.

While the outward face of democracy may be a multiparty system and regular elections, some observers contend that there is a substantial difference between the right to vote and the right to choose policies. If the choice of candidates for election does not correspond to the desires of the people, then a pro forma election among candidates who have been put up by political machines does not further the credibility or legitimacy of such "democracies." This is not democracy but "partitocracy" (Sartori). Similarly, if the only choices possible are between candidate A and candidate B, whose programmes are often very similar, and the people do not have an opportunity to vote for a candidate C with a different programme, then the pro forma election of A or B does not satisfy the essence of what democratic government should be. In such cases, the two-party system avers itself to be only twice as democratic as the one-party system. Even in multiparty systems, it often occurs that the number of representatives in parliament does not correspond proportionally to the votes cast, and in some cases a party does not succeed in having a single representative in parliament, although proportionally it would have been entitled to some representation.

Another obstacle to the right to choose freely is the combination of policies that make up the cocktail of any party platform. Should the citizen be obliged to choose between two "package deals," one represented by party A and the other by party B? In many cases, the electorate may agree with as little as 30 per cent of the programme of party A, 30 per cent of the programme of party B, and find no candidate at all to espouse 40 per cent of his or her wishes. In such or similar cases confidence in the electoral process is undermined and results in high levels of electoral absenteeism in many countries. Indeed, democracy requires real choices as well as transparent and accountable governance and administration in all sectors of society. In other cases, party machines fail to advance a representative number of female candidates. Citizens have a right to be given greater opportunity to participate in the conduct of public affairs, particularly by general consultations through referenda on issues, not merely by voting for individuals whose loyalties are not always with their electorates but more often than not with the rich sponsors who financed their political campaigns. In this context many observers have noted that election campaigns in many countries entail enormous expenditures and that the choice of candidates is frequently dependent on their financial strength, resulting in a kind of elitist 'elective dictatorship.'

Obstacles of a more general nature are the historical inequities left by centuries of slavery, colonialism, imperialism and foreign occupation (that persist in some areas even today).[25] It is obvious that those persons and countries currently enjoying privileges may have an interest in maintaining the status quo and be reluctant to relinquish their advantages. In many countries, including developed countries, there is a growing gap between rich and poor. It is worth recalling the words of Justice Louis Brandeis, who said it simply: "You can have wealth concentrated in the hands of a few, or democracy, but you cannot have both."

Other generic obstacles include lack of ethics,[26] latent social Darwinism, endemic power asymmetry, racism, arbitrary embargoes, marginalization, taboos, "conspiracies of silence," political correctness, mobbing, self-censorship, lack of transparency (particularly in the financial sector), lack of accountability, false prioritizing, the instrumentalization of some human rights for purposes of power and exclusion, abuse of rights, the tendency to selectivity, lack of objectivity, double standards, international law *à la carte*, unilateral coercive measures, discrimination among victims, intellectual dishonesty, political hubris, bigotry, perpetuation of privilege and common greed.

Aware that the status quo itself hampers the realization of an international order that is more democratic and equitable, the mandate holder intends to explore ways and means to overcome these obstacles. The dynamics of economic power must change if progress and a more inclusive and balanced growth paradigm are to be achieved.

There is much room—as well as need—for improvement. States, the United Nations, intergovernmental organizations, NGOs and civil society all need to identify and overcome obstacles in their respective areas of competence and influence. This is required by the international order intended by the Charter of the United Nations, which entails a post-predator world consensus.

Good practices and promising trends

As a democratic international order demands well-functioning interaction between the democratic will of peoples and the concrete policies that affect them, an equitable international order requires a correlation between production and wealth, performance and reward, and rejects the excesses of the uncontrolled financial markets that have more than once adversely impacted on the world economy, causing hardship such as the unemployment and loss of savings and pensions of millions of people. In the light of the persistence of extreme poverty in the world, including in developed countries, exorbitant salaries and bonuses, as well as currency speculation, constitute unethical practices. Efforts in many countries to regulate the financial markets are commendable but risk remaining insufficient.

Any progress in the fields of codification, monitoring and enforcement of human rights is welcome, even if achieved by homeopathic doses. In her 2012 report on strengthening the United Nations human rights treaty body system (A/66/860), the High Commissioner for Human Rights welcomed greater ratification of the core human rights treaties. The goal is universal ratification, accompanied by education so that greater awareness of human rights permeates government and society in a sustainable manner. At this stage, the Independent Expert has not yet developed benchmarks to assess, measure and compare what qualitatively could be considered "best practices." He will further consult stakeholders in this respect.

With respect to a democratic international order, the mandate holder values the progress achieved in the empowerment of women in many countries, the greater transparency shown in elections, and the added value of election monitoring by many actors. As stated earlier, a democratic international order is best secured by a growing number of democratic States and by the constant improvement of democratic institutions. Democracy also requires an informed citizenry that can articulate its wishes and can choose among policies in periodic elections and by referenda. A democratic international order requires greater transparency and respect for the needs and aspirations of peoples in all regions of the world, regardless of economic power or geopolitical strategic importance, giving due regard to national sovereignty and the right of self-determination.

The mandate holder is studying the democratic traditions of many countries and practices of popular initiatives, referenda, recall and impeachment. He intends to explore the feasibility of using aspects of the "direct democracy"[27] model more broadly, which would give populations the opportunity to choose among policies and not only persons. It should be remembered that the right to vote is not identical with the right to choose. The manifold aspects involved in giving civil society the right to initiate legislation by petition, which could be put to a general vote if a certain number of signatures is reached, and the possibility of referenda on legislation already passed will be explored. Perhaps combining aspects of direct democracy and representative democracy could be appropriate for some countries.

Among practices to be studied are enhanced press freedom, access to the Internet worldwide, regular elections and election monitoring. Current developments in social media may contribute insights. In her statement at the fall session of the United Nations System Chief Executives Board for Coordination, held in New York in October 2011, the High Commissioner for Human Rights noted that "human rights, democracy and the rule of law are as much a part of the UN brand as peacekeeping and development assistance." In her opening statement for the nineteenth session of the Human Rights Council, she stated:

Much of this historic period has been marked by public demands of people to live a life of dignity and enjoyment of human rights. Although most striking in several countries of the Arab region where we have seen tens of thousands of women, men and young people take to the streets to voice their claims, popular movements denouncing exclusion, inequality, discrimination, absence of genuine political participation and lack of economic and social rights have emerged on all continents, as people have shown themselves unwilling to accept impunity and lack of accountability for the actions of Governments, international institutions and the transnational and national private sectors. People are demanding freedom: freedom from fear, and freedom from want. They are demanding respect of the rule of law—including in the economic sphere—and full participation in decisions that affect their lives.

With regard to an international order that shall be more equitable, the Independent Expert commends those countries that have met their commitments under the Millennium Declaration, in particular the Millennium Development Goals, as well as progress achieved in technology transfer and access to medical services and drugs. Foreign investment is necessary in developing countries, provided that the profits therefrom are equitably shared. Praiseworthy, too, is the growing consciousness that the products we buy at a grocery store or elsewhere should come from equitable production and trade, as illustrated by the growing popularity of fair trade coffee, flowers and other products. The mandate holder will endeavour to obtain more precise information on good practices through questionnaires and consultations.

Women's peace movements have raised major issues relating to war and conflict situations. Without doubt, these movements to wage peace have accomplished historical inroads in influencing public opinion and are reflected in Security Council resolutions 1325 (2000), 1820 (2008), 1888 (2009) and 1889 (2009), bringing a gender perspective into peace negotiations.

The Independent Expert is aware of State and private-sector programmes of cultural cooperation and mutual improvement of school textbooks and curricula. Textbooks should mainstream human rights and democratic values and eliminate stereotypes.

Among good practices in the United Nations system the Independent Expert will study the successes of OHCHR in providing advisory services and technical assistance to countries in transition to democracy, and the operation of the ILO tripartite system in achieving more equitable labour conditions worldwide. At Rio +20 (the United Nations Conference on Sustainable Development, held from 20 to 22 June 2012), the follow-up conference to the Earth Summit of 1992 and Agenda 21, the participating States committed themselves to a "green economy," adopting an outcome document entitled "The Future We Want," aiming at sustainable development.

The mandate holder will study the results of the Human Rights Council's universal periodic review, which is one step towards international democratic order through dialogue among stakeholders. The Governments–United Nations–civil society triangle should be further developed. Without a doubt, individuals and peoples have emerged as interlocutors with governments and agencies. As former Director of the United Nations Division on Human Rights Theo van Boven has emphasized: People Matter.

UNDERSTANDING AND DEFINING DEMOCRACY

My second report to the Human Rights Council continued the analysis of various aspects of democracy and attempted a definition. I drew inspiration from Theo van Boven's book, particularly his statements on "human rights and the new international order," the "broadening and deepening of the human rights programme," and "Victims of discrimination, in particular Indigenous Populations"[i] *—AdeZ*[ii]

* * *

---

[i] Theo van Boven, *People Matter* (Amsterdam: Meulenhoff, 1982).

[ii] General Assembly Human Rights Council, Twenty-fourth Session (Agenda item 3), Report of the Independent Expert on the promotion of a democratic and equitable international order, Alfred-Maurice de Zayas, A/HRC/24/38 (1 July 2013), available at http://daccess-ods.un.org/access.nsf/Get?Open&DS=A/HRC/24/38&Lang=E.

Democracy entails a correlation between the public interest as expressed by a majority of the population and the governmental policies that affect them. The term encompasses various manifestations, including direct, participatory and representative democracy, but Governments must be responsive to people and not to special interests such as the military-industrial complex, financial bankers and transnational corporations. Democracy is inclusive and does not privilege an anthropological aristocracy. It requires that the basic rules establishing and organizing the State and its relationship with society be put in place and accepted by the citizens. It requires consultation with the people and respect of the will of the voters. Although founded on majority rule, a democratic society must recognize and apply individual, minority and group rights. In other words, majority rule must be understood within the context of the rule of law and human dignity. As highlighted by the European Court of Human Rights, "Pluralism, tolerance and broadmindedness are hallmarks of a 'democratic society.' Although individual interests must on occasion be subordinated to those of a group, democracy does not simply mean that the views of a majority must always prevail: a balance must be achieved which ensures the fair and proper treatment of people from minorities and avoids any abuse of a dominant position."[28] This resolves the tension between populism and human rights, since democracy must not be abused to diminish human rights, e.g. by legitimizing torture or capital punishment, even if public opinion could be invoked or manipulated to demand it. Thus, it is necessary to strengthen the enforcement of national and regional bills of rights to provide a process and atmosphere for democracy to flourish, ensured by an independent judiciary that provides the necessary protection of both majority and minority interests.

Democracy has an old evolutionary history and has been adjusted to the needs of many different societies and cultures. There is no single "model" of democracy,[29] and no one should pretend that "one size fits all" and that one particular manifestation of democracy should be exported to countries that function differently, where the political process corresponds to other traditions. When approaching the concept of democracy, one should look beyond the label and ask the crucial question: What is the correlation between the needs and the will of the people and the political decision-making affecting them? A corollary to that question is: To what degree was truthful, reliable and pluralistic information available to facilitate genuine participation by the people in the development of law and practice? Democracy is not the end product, but the means to the end, which is the enjoyment of human rights by all.

In order to test the existence or otherwise of international democracy in recent times, one may ask whether States and peoples, including non-represented peoples, have had a democratic opportunity of participating in decisions concerning important issues, such as war and peace, global warming, the environment, trade relations, access to medicine and the common heritage of humankind. More concretely, would a majority of States approve the application of sanctions regimes selectively and not uniformly? Would they have approved the use of force against Serbia in 1999, against Iraq in 2003 and against Libya in 2011? Should the international community have had a voice in determining whether all avenues of peaceful negotiation had been exhausted? Should civil society be allowed a degree of participation on "technical" decisions on free trade and other agreements that result in widespread unemployment? And with regard to regional arrangements and regional constitutional law, should the citizens of the countries concerned be allowed to vote directly in favour or against treaties entailing a significant restriction of national sovereignty, e.g. should the citizens of the European Union have had an opportunity to vote by referendum on the adoption of the Treaty of Lisbon? Should they have had a say in decisions to impose or lift embargoes in situations of civil war? With regard to the reunification of the island of Cyprus, would a constitutional convention in which all Cypriot communities would have had an opportunity to negotiate a grass-roots constitution have resulted in a democratic instrument that could have bridged the impasse by involving all stakeholders?[30] This non-exhaustive list of international disorder illustrates that consultation has been flawed or entirely missing, precisely in cases where public participation would have been most necessary.

In order to test the existence or otherwise of domestic democracy in recent times, it may be instructive to explore how decisions such as those on the increasing electronic and video surveillance of individuals, arrest, indefinite detention, social security, health care, employment, marriage, abortion, etc. have been taken and are being taken, and the degree of genuine public participation in these decisions. More concretely, would a majority of the population accept the grave restrictions of human rights following the terrorist attacks of September 11, 2001? Would it accept the priorities imposed by Governments with regard to so-called "austerity measures"? Would it approve the bailout of the banks? Would it approve increasing militarization and the enormous slice of the budget allocated to the "defence" industry? Would it consent to the participation of their respective countries in military adventures not supported by resolutions of the Security Council and not allowed under Article 51 of the United Nations Charter? Would it consent to the sale of weapons to belligerents in foreign civil wars? Would it consent to the use of drones regardless of civilian casualties and collateral damage? Would the citizens of the 54 nations that cooperated with the system of rendition, secret prisons, "black holes," etc. have approved illegal acts committed in the name of the "war against terrorism"?[31] Would they consent to the use of military commissions to try civilians? What has been the role of some media in creating an atmosphere of imminent threat and fear through disinformation and skewed reporting, in contravention of the prohibition of war propaganda stipulated in article 20 ICCPR? Would a public referendum approve adoption of infants by same-sex couples? What does it mean when mass protests demanding democratic reforms and human rights are met with excessive use of force by police? Can laws be adopted top-down without public debate and in spite of widespread protest by the population? Are populations hostage of parliamentarians and incapable of influencing policy until the next elections, which may or may not allow a choice of policies but only of candidates whose decisions are sometimes a surprise to the electorate? Many of these issues demand public debate and consultation and should not be short-circuited and decided over the heads of the people.

UNITED NATIONS REFORM

In my 2013 report to the General Assembly I addressed possible ways of reforming the United Nations, in particular the Security Council. —AdeZ

* * *

An obvious obstacle to a democratic and equitable order is the use and abuse of the veto privilege in the Security Council. To any neutral observer, the record of veto practice over six decades demonstrates that it has often been used inconsistently with the purposes and principles of the Charter, notably against the right of self-determination, and to block sanctions against or mere condemnation of countries and situations that violate United Nations principles. The abuse of the veto power has become so predictable that frequently resolutions are not even tabled because of the certainty of a veto against their adoption. Necessary discussion is thereby suppressed. . . .

Scholars have produced numerous studies concerning the modalities of reforming the United Nations. While many believe that reform is necessary for the stability and credibility of the system, there is no consensus on the reforms that should be undertaken, nor a road map thereto.

In 2013, the United Nations University is publishing a book by Joseph Schwartzberg entitled *Transforming the United Nations System: Designs for a Workable World*. The book discusses the need for voting reform in the General Assembly, the possibility of a weighted voting system, proposals for a popularly elected World Parliamentary Assembly of civil society representatives, options on how best to reform the Security Council, increasing its membership and eliminating the veto, a transformation from the Economic and Social Council to a new structure of regional caucuses, a strengthened Human Rights Council, the coordination of specialized agencies, funds and commissions of the United Nations system, and enhanced participation of non-governmental organizations and other non-state actors.

In the opinion of the Independent Expert, this book, replete with statistics and tables, provides a credible architecture for global governance and explains how to go about reforms that will advance the goal of building a democratic and equitable order.

The unfair composition of the Security Council is largely acknowledged. The principal defects are the anachronistic privileges of the five permanent members of the Council and the Council's insufficient representativeness. Mr. Schwartzberg has proposed an increase in membership, divided into 12 regional seats, each with a weighted vote. He employs a simple mathematical formula that would allow a small, objectively determined number of leading States to hold Council seats in their own right, while the remaining seats would be allocated to multinational regions. Mr. Schwartzberg argues that a fairer voting system in both the General Assembly and the Security Council would enhance the legitimacy of United Nations decisions and contribute to promoting a democratic and equitable international order.

Any reform of the Security Council will require an amendment of the Charter of the United Nations under Article 108. Some observers feel that the veto power as practised since 1945 is the Achilles heel of the United Nations and of the contemporary international order. While a majority of United Nations Member States and observer States would agree to amend article 27 (3) of the Charter, this may be blocked by any of the members possessing the power of veto. Abandoning the veto, therefore, will have to envisage a substantial quid pro quo. Mr. Schwartzberg suggests workable trade-offs, for example, by providing for enhanced voting weights for the permanent five in the General Assembly in a reformed and more empowered Assembly.

It is not likely that a bargain could now be struck that would allow eliminating the veto privilege by simple Charter amendment. Thus, Mr. Schwartzberg proposes to phase it out in stages, over a transitional period of 15 years. This process could be advanced by gradually increasing the number of permanent five States whose dissenting votes could block resolutions from a single dissenting State to two dissenters and then three, and so forth. Thus, in the first five years of the reform period, two negative votes by permanent five States would constitute a veto, in the next five years three. Moreover, there should be a phased reduction of the range of subjects to which the veto may apply. The first step could be to prohibit a veto by any of the permanent five members in a case in which that member itself is a principal party. Subsequently, vetoes might be proscribed if they concern egregious violations of human rights, especially in respect to genocide and crimes against humanity.[32] Subsequently, vetoes could be precluded in respect to resolutions calling for the use of inspection teams or monitors in situations deemed to constitute a threat to the peace. Most importantly, any permanent five State exercising the veto power should be required to submit to the General Assembly a detailed legal explanation of its reasons for doing so.

While the use of the veto privilege has too often led to human rights violations, it is not the only problem with the operation of the Security Council (which because of its composition remains heavily under the influence of the permanent members), where majority votes have been secured for resolutions that have actually harmed thousands of victims.

It is thus important to recognize that the Security Council cannot be above the Charter or above *jus cogens,* and that its decisions and resolutions must become subject to scrutiny. Some of the grave problems that beset the international order today are attributable to the kind of decisions adopted and the resolutions not adopted by the Security Council. Some observers have pointed out that the Security Council can be, and has been, manipulated into adopting resolutions and decisions that are incompatible with the Council's mandate, defined in Article 24 (2) of the Charter: "In discharging these duties the Security Council shall act in accordance with the Purposes and Principles of the United Nations." In conformity with that provision, if a resolution or decision is contrary to human rights or has results that violate provisions of United Nations human rights treaties, such resolution or decision is *ultra vires.* This could be tested by the General Assembly through referral to the International Court of Justice for an advisory opinion pursuant to Article 96 of the Charter. A priori, there can be no conflict between the Charter and United Nations human rights treaties which could bring Article 103 of the Charter into play. Accordingly, if conflict appears to arise between a Council resolution and United Nations human rights treaties, the compatibility of the resolution with the purposes and principles of the United Nations could be tested.[33]

World Parliamentary Assembly

Among other civil society initiatives, the launching of a World Parliamentary Assembly or United Nations Parliamentary Assembly is worth exploring. As former Secretary-General Boutros Boutros-Ghali stated: "A United Nations Parliamentary Assembly—a global body of elected representatives—could invigorate our institutions of global governance with unprecedented democratic legitimacy, transparency and accountability."[34]

The idea is to remedy democracy deficits by giving voice to global public opinion, including citizens in global decision-making through elected officials. Such an Assembly could be set up by a vote of the General Assembly under Article 22 of the Charter or it could be created on the basis of a new international treaty between Governments, followed by an agreement linking it to the United Nations. Neither mechanism requires Charter amendment or reform. Global decisions would gain greater legitimacy through citizen input and involvement in an independent World Assembly with consultative functions, or in a United Nations Parliamentary Assembly representing people as well as States.

On 16 May 2013, the Independent Expert convened an expert consultation to discuss aspects of the mandate. In a statement delivered at the meeting, the representative of the Campaign for a United Nations Parliamentary Assembly, Andreas Bummel, stressed that democratization of the international order should aim at promoting the dignity and worth of every person and the equality of all world citizens. Bearing in mind that the United Nations is a State-based organization, Mr. Bummel noted that the challenge is to find ways to create a space within this setup that nonetheless allows connecting global decision-making more directly with the world's citizens as individuals. A parliamentary body will give the world's citizens a voice at the United Nations through more direct representation. The members of this new body could be designated by existing parliaments, or countries could choose to have them directly elected. Referring to the parliamentary organs of the European Union, the Council of Europe and the African Union, Mr. Bummel emphasized that such a new body in no way would contradict the intergovernmental nature of the United Nations. With reference to ongoing international discussions on post-2015 development goals, Mr. Bummel stated that steps towards citizen-based global democratic governance should be part of the new framework and that serious consideration should be given to the contribution that a parliamentary assembly at the United Nations could make to the mechanisms which can assure accountability, reporting, monitoring and continued dialogue regarding the fulfilment of the post-2015 goals.[35]

Recommendations

Whereas in his initial report to the General Assembly (A/67/277), the Independent Expert preferred not to formulate recommendations, he considers it appropriate at this stage to make a number of suggestions. Convinced that hackneyed prescriptions, platitudes or cosmetic proposals will not serve General Assembly Resolution 67/175, the Independent Expert offers these considerations in the spirit of the Roman Stoic philosopher Seneca: "It is not because things are difficult that we do not dare; it is because we do not dare that they are difficult" (*Non quia difficilia sunt non audemus, sed quia non audemus, difficilia sunt, Epistuale Morales* 104.26):

(a) States may consider taking a fresh look at the Charter of the United Nations and activate underutilized provisions, including Articles 33, 57, 63 and 73.

(b) Efforts at reforming the United Nations with a view to making it more democratic and equitable should continue, in particular Security Council reform, so that henceforth it better reflects the needs and priorities of present and future generations instead of the 1945 world order.

(c) States should practice multilateralism and abandon unilateral actions that adversely affect a democratic and equitable international order, refraining from the threat or use of force. They should apply international law uniformly, abandon overreliance on "positivism" and efforts to circumvent treaty obligations or invent loopholes. As "nature abhors a vacuum" (Spinoza, Ethics), human rights law abhors "legal black holes."

(d) The General Assembly may consider mandating the Human Rights Council to entrust one of the existing special procedures with monitoring the impact of unilateral coercive measures on the enjoyment of human rights and to ensure accountability.

(e) States should ratify the individual complaints procedures of the United Nations human rights treaties, adhere to and utilize the inter-State complaints procedures, and globalize the reach of the International Criminal Court.

(f) States should revise their budgetary priorities away from military expenditures and into the promotion and protection of human rights for all. In so doing, States should ensure fiscal and budget transparency and facilitate participation by civil society in decision-making processes.

(g) States should review their legislation and practice, identify endemic obstacles to democratic processes, and adopt corrective measures to ensure greater popular participation. In this context, the instruments of direct democracy should be increasingly utilized, namely opinion polling, independent inquiry, popular initiative, referendum, recall and impeachment.

(h) The General Assembly should promote the equitable participation of all States in the World Bank, the International Monetary Fund and the World Trade Organization, for instance, by placing these institutions under the authority of the United Nations and subordinating them to the purposes and principles of the Charter of the United Nations, pursuant to Articles 57 and 63 thereof.

(i) The General Assembly may consider expanding the mandate of the Human Rights Council to allow the examination of reports from financial institutions and transnational corporations under the universal periodic review procedure.

(j) States should repeal legislation that intimidates and criminalizes citizens in the exercise of their rights concerning the establishment of political parties, non-governmental organizations, freedom of peaceful assembly and association, the right to access information, the right to freely debate and express one's own opinions. States should implement paragraph 49 of general comment No. 34 of the Human Rights Committee by repealing so-called "memory laws."

(k) The General Assembly may consider reviewing the rules granting consultative status to non-governmental organizations so as to enhance the opportunity of independent civil society to interact with the Human Rights Council and other United Nations bodies.

(l) The budget priorities of the United Nations should promote the prevention of armed conflict, protection of the common heritage of humankind and the realization of human rights for all. This may require an overall budget increase.

(m) The General Assembly may consider referring specific legal questions to the International Court of Justice for advisory opinions, including issues of self-determination, unilateral coercive measures, threats and use of force, and debt cancellation.

(n) The General Assembly may consider revisiting the reality of self-determination in today's world and refer to the Special Committee on Decolonization and/or other United Nations instances communications by indigenous and unrepresented peoples wherever they reside, inter alia, in Alaska, Australia, Canada, Chile, China, the Dakotas, French Polynesia, Hawaii, Kashmir, the Middle East, Yemen, the Cameroons, the Bubis of Bioko Island, the Moluccas, Bougainville, Ryukyu, New Caledonia, Northern Africa, Sri Lanka and West Papua, with reference to Chapter XI of the Charter of the United Nations. The General Assembly may also consider amending its rules and procedures to allow for the participation of indigenous and non-represented peoples. Meanwhile, the Assembly should urge States to implement the Declaration on the Rights of Indigenous Peoples. It should ensure that indigenous, non-represented peoples, marginalized and disempowered peoples, and peoples under occupation have a genuine opportunity to participate in decision-making processes.

(o) The General Assembly may consider convening a conference to discuss promising initiatives such as the creation of a World Parliamentary Assembly and a World Court of Human Rights.

* * *

The Independent Expert finds hope in the words of Arundhati Roy. —*AdeZ*

Another world is not only possible; she is on her way... On a quiet day . . . I can hear her breathing.[36]

Notes

1 See the Inter-American Democratic Charter adopted by the Organization of American States on 11 September 2001.

2 Mikhail Gorbachev, "Resetting the nuclear disarmament agenda," *Geneva Lectures Series*, 5 October 2009.

3 Human Rights Committee general comment 14 (1984) on nuclear weapons and the right to life.

4 See also the report of the Special Rapporteur on Human Rights and Human Responsibilities (E/CN.4/2003/105); Declaration on the Right and Responsibility of Individuals, Groups and Organs of Society to Promote and Protect Universally Recognized Human Rights and Fundamental Freedoms (General Assembly Resolution 53/144, annex).

Jeffrey Sachs notes: "No class war is needed or intended. Yet as America's greatest businessmen, from Andrew Carnegie to Bill Gates, Warren Buffett, and George Soros, have known, those with great business skills have great responsibilities as well." In *The Price of Civilization: Economics and Ethics After the Fall* (New York: Random House, 2011), p. 263.

5 See also Bertrand Ramcharan, *Contemporary Human Rights Ideas*, Global Institutions Series (2008), especially chapters 5 to 7 ("Equality," "Democracy," and "Development"); and Jeffrey Sachs, *The End of Poverty: How We Can Make It Happen In Our Lifetime* (New York: Penguin Books, 2005). Harvard's Program on Human Rights in Development under the directorship of Stephen Marks has made outstanding contributions to an understanding of the correlation between development and human rights (see https://www.hsph.harvard.edu/phrd/).

6 See, in particular, the 1997 report, including a 13-point declaration (E/CN.4/Sub.2/1997/23 and Corr.1), endorsed by the Commission on Human Rights and the Economic and Social Commission but never elevated to the General Assembly for adoption. The first United Nations High Commissioner for Human Rights stated at the opening of an expert consultation convened by Mr. Al-Khasawneh in February 2007:

Sub-Commission resolutions 1994/24, 1995/13 and 1996/9 recognize " that practices of forcible exile, mass expulsions and deportations, population transfer, 'ethnic cleansing' and other forms of forcible displacement of populations within a country or across borders deprive the affected populations of their right to freedom of movement."

But I would go further, because the right to live in one's native land is a very precious and fundamental right. Compulsory population transfers, including the implantation of settlers and settlements are a serious matter, not only because they affect many people, but also because they violate the whole gamut of civil and political rights, economic, social and cultural rights.

See further A. de Zayas, "Forced population transfer," in Wolfrum, ed., *Max Planck Encyclopedia of Public International Law*, Vol. IV (2012), pp. 165–75; Felix Ermacora et al., *Grundrechte der europäischen Volksgruppen* (1993); Christian Tomuschat, "Das Recht auf die Heimat: Neue rechtliche Aspetke" in J. Jekewitz et al., eds., *Des Menschen Recht zwischen Freiheit und Verantwortung* (1989) pp. 183–212.

7 *Satyagraha* (Sanskrit), "insistence on truth," is a philosophy relating to non-violent resistance.

8 India, *Collected Works of Mahatma Gandhi* (Ministry of Information and Broadcasting), vol. 87, p. 452, as cited in Norman G. Finkelstein, *What Gandhi Says: About Nonviolence, Resistance, and . . .* (OR Books, 2012), p. 62.

9 Aung San Suu Kyi, "Freedom from Fear," acceptance message for the 1990 Sakharov Prize for Freedom of Thought, 1991.

10 See www.unglobalcompact.org/issues/human_rights/.

11 See, for example, Jakob Th. Möller and Alfred de Zayas, *United Nations Human Rights Committee Case Law 1977–2008: A Handbook* (Kehl am Rhein: Engel, 2009); Manfred Nowak, *U.N. Covenant on Civil and Political Rights*, 2nd revised ed. (Kehl am Rhein: Engel, 2005).

12 Naomi Klein, *The Shock Doctrine: The Rise of Disaster Capitalism* (London: Picador, 2007).

13 See AEDIDH (Asociación Española para el Derecho Internacional de los Derechos Humanos), http://www.aedidh.org/?q=node/1853.

14 Carmen Rosa Rueda Castañón and Carlos Villán Durán, eds., *La Declaración de Luarca sobre el Derecho Humano a la Paz*, 2nd ed. (2008); Carlos Villán Durán y Carmelo Faleh Pérez, *Contribuciones Regionales para una Declaración Universal del Derecho Humano a la Paz* (Luarca, España: AEDIDH, 2010).

15 Villán Durán and Faleh Pérez, *Contribuciones*.

16 See AEDIDH, http://www.aedidh.org/?q=node/www.aedidh.org/.

17 Carlos Villán Durán, "The human right to peace: A legislative initiative," *Spanish Yearbook of International law, Volume XV, 2009* (2011), pp. 143–71 and Carlos Villán Durán, "Civil society organizations contribution to the Universal Declaration on the Human Right to Peace," *International Journal on World Peace*, vol. 28 (2011), pp. 59–126. See also A. de Zayas, "Peace as a human right: the *jus cogens* prohibition of aggression" in A. Eide et al., eds., *Making Peoples Heard* (Leiden, Netherlands: Martinus Nijhoff, 2011), pp. 27–42.

18 See, *inter alia*, George Soros, *The New Paradigm for Financial Markets: The Credit Crisis of 2008 and What It Means* (Public Affairs, 2008); *Bill Moyers Journal*, interview with George Soros, 10 October 2008, available from www.pbs.org/moyers/journal/10102008/watch.html; Michael Sandel, *What Money Can't Buy: The Moral Limits of the Markets* (2012).

19 See, *inter alia*, Dani Rodrik, *The Globalization Paradox: Democracy and the Future of the World Economy* (New York: W. W. Norton & Co., 2011) and Jeffrey Sachs, *The Price of Civilization* (note 4 above).

20 Trade expansion, however, should not be achieved at the expense of local farmers and local industry, thus causing a destruction of local economies and increased unemployment. Nor is it ecologically sustainable to relocate production and thereby increase the consumption of fuel for transportation purposes.

21 See Cliff Durand and Steve Martinot, eds., *Recreating Democracy in a Globalized State* (Atlanta: Clarity Press, 2012); Noam Chomsky, *Profit over People: Neoliberalism and Global Order* (New York: Seven Stories Press, 1999).

22 See United Nations Convention against Corruption, in force 2005, 161 States parties; United Nations Convention against Transnational Organized Crime and the Protocols thereto.

23 See, *inter alia*, Tzvetan Todorov, *Les ennemis intimes de la démocratie* (Paris: Robert Laffont, 2012); Edward S. Herman and Noam Chomsky, *Manufacturing Consent* (New York: Pantheon Books, 2002).

24 General comment no. 34 (2011) on the freedoms of opinion and expression, paras. 2 and 3.

25 See, *inter alia*, Eduardo Galeano, *Open Veins of Latin America* (New York: Monthly Review Press, 1997); case law of the Human Rights Committee on indigenous matters, e.g. *Onimayak and the Lubicon Lake Band v. Canada*, "Historical inequities to which the State party refers, and

certain more recent developments threaten the way of life and culture of the Lubicon Lake Band, and constitute a violation of article 27 so long as they continue" (para. 33), as cited in Möller and de Zayas (note 11 above), p. 447. Nancy Fraser, "Egalité, identités et justice sociale," *Le Monde diplomatique*, June 2012, p. 3.

26 See the analysis of the concepts of legal and ethical norms in A. de Zayas "Normes morales et normes juridiques. Concurrence ou conciliation" in A. Millet-Devalle, *Religions et Droit International Humanitaire* (Paris, 2008), pp. 81–85; see also the analysis of "democracy" and "value" in China by Harro von Senger, "Wert in China,'' in Ivo de Gennaro, ed., *Value: Sources and Readings on a Key Concept of the Globalized World (Studies on the Interaction of Art, Thought and Power)* (Leiden: Brill, 2012), pp. 399–414; Hans Küng, *Anständig Wirtschaften. Warum Ökonomie Moral Braucht* (Piper, 2010).

27 See Johannes Reich, "An interactional model of direct democracy: Lessons from the Swiss experience" (University of Zurich, 2008). Available from http://papers.ssrn.com/sol3/papers.cfm?abstract_id=1154019; Jon Elster, ed., *Deliberative Democracy* (New York: Columbia University, 1998); Carne Ross, *The Leaderless Revolution: How Ordinary People Will Take Power and Change Politics in the 21st Century* (New York: Blue Rider Press/Penguin, 2011); Takis Fotopoulos, *Towards an Inclusive Democracy: The Crisis of the Growth Economy and the Need for a New Liberatory Project* (London: Cassell, 1997).

28 European Court of Human Rights, *Case of Leyla Sahin vs. Turkey,* Application no. 44774/98, para. 108.

29 Preamble, Human Rights Council Resolution 19/36, 23 March 2012.

30 Andreas Auer et al., *A principled basis for a just and lasting Cyprus settlement in Light of International and European Law* (Brussels, 2005). Andreas Auer/Vasiliki Triga, *A Constitutional Convention for Cyprus* (Berlin, 2009). Alfred de Zayas, "The Annan Plan," *The Cyprus Yearbook of International Relations* (2006), pp. 163–178.

31 See A/HRC/22/52.

32 See Ariela Blätter, "The Responsibility not to Veto: A Way Forward," *Minerva,* No. 37, pp. 47–53, www.globalsolutions.org.

33 See the Views of the Human Rights Committee in the *Sayadi and Vinck v. Belgium* case, Communication No. 1472/2006, holding that the application of Security Council sanctions by Belgium entailed the violation of articles 12 and 17 of the International Covenant on Civil and Political Rights. Jakob Möller and Alfred de Zayas, *United Nations Human Rights Committee Case Law 1977–2008: A Handbook,* chap. VII, pp. 526, 527, 530–3 (N.P. Engel, Publisher, 2009).

34 "Time for a global United Nations Parliamentary Assembly – UN Independent Expert," UN Human Rights, 29 October 2013, https://newsarchive.ohchr.org/EN/NewsEvents/Pages/DisplayNews.aspx?NewsID=13920. See also Boutros Boutros-Ghali, "The Missing Link of Democratization," *OpenDemocracy,* 9 June 2009; Joseph Schwartzberg, *Creating a World Parliamentary Assembly* (Berlin: Committee for a Democratic United Nations, 2012); Richard Falk and Andrew Strauss, "Toward Global Parliament," *Foreign Affairs* (Jan./Feb. 2001).

35 See https://www.unpacampaign.org/documents/en/201305statement.pdf. See also Andreas Bummel, *Developing International Democracy: For a Parliamentary Assembly at the United Nations* (Berlin, Committee for a Democratic U.N., 2010); Andreas Bummel, "The Composition of a Parliamentary Assembly at the United Nations," Background paper No. 3 (Berlin, Committee for a Democratic U.N., 2010); Dieter Heinrich, *The Case for a United Nations Parliamentary Assembly* (Berlin, Committee for a Democratic U.N., 2010).

36 Arundhati Roy, "Not Again," Stanford University, *Peer,* https://ccrma.stanford.edu/~peer/arundhatiRoy.html.

Chapter 2

PRINCIPLES OF INTERNATIONAL ORDER[i]

> "War may sometimes be a necessary evil. But no matter how necessary, it is always an evil, never a good. We will not learn to live together in peace by killing each other's children."
>
> — JIMMY CARTER
> The Nobel Peace Prize Lecture

My seventh thematic report to the Human Rights Council, presented in March 2018 (A/HRC/37/63), formulated 23 principles of International order, which summarized my theoretical and practical approach to the subject in the light of the empirical experience of administering the mandate. These norms of international law and practice derive their legal basis from the Principles and Purposes of the UN Charter, key General Assembly resolutions (notably resolutions 2131 (XX), 2625 (XXV), 3314 (XXIX), 39/11 and 55/2), core UN Conventions, inter alia the Convention on the Prevention and Punishment of the Crime of Genocide, Vienna Convention on the Law of Treaties, the Vienna Convention on Diplomatic and Consular Relations and other universal treaties such as the Geneva Red Cross Conventions and Additional Protocols. They reflect the progressive development of international law as created and applied by the United Nations and its specialized agencies, and propose a vision of a peaceful, democratic and equitable international order based on the cooperation of all stakeholders—both States and non-state actors, sovereign countries, inter-governmental organizations, transnational enterprises, peoples and minorities striving for self-determination, indigenous peoples, religious institutions and civil society. Grateful for criticism and input from friends and peers, I undertook a redrafting and regrouping of the list, incorporating two additional benchmarks.

These guiding principles should be understood in a holistic way, rejecting any kind of "fragmentation" of international law into "stand alone" legal regimes in competition with each other. The authority and credibility of the system of international law depends on its internal coherence and on rules of interpretation that recognize a logical hierarchy as well as a horizontal mutual reinforcement. Admittedly, these standards encompass not only hard law but also soft law and general notions of ethics and justice. They are offered in the hope

---

i These 25 principles are updated from my 2018 report to the Human Rights Council A/HRC/37/63, containing 23 principles.

that a concise restatement of principles will prove useful not only for specialists in international law but also for politicians, journalists, religious leaders and all who are concerned with strengthening coherence and stability in public affairs and international order. Like Virginia Dandan's Draft Declaration on the Right to International Solidarity,[ii] the Nijmegen Principles and Guidelines on Interim Measures for the Protection of Human Rights,[iii] the UN Declaration on the Right of Indigenous Peoples,[iv] the Commission on Human Right's Declaration on the illegality of forced population transfers,[v] and John Ruggie's Guiding Principles on Business and Human Rights,[vi] these principles on international order are not exhaustive and are intended to serve as useful criteria or standards to evaluate and better understand the complexities of the evolving international order. The reader must keep this caveat in mind: Principles and norms are not self-executing. Indeed, as the Bible has not resolved the problem of sin, and the UN Charter has not ended aggressive war and exploitation, these principles shall not eo ipso guarantee a democratic and equitable international order in the 21st century. Realistically speaking, even if all of these principles and declarations one day were to become UN treaties, they would still need political will, good faith, and an effective enforcement mechanism in order to make a difference. —AdeZ

* * *

1. **The paramount principle of international order is Peace**. *Pax optima rerum*.[1] Peace is not the peace of cemeteries. The United Nations Charter commits all States to promoting *Peace with Justice*. The Preamble and articles 1 and 2 of the Charter stipulate that the principal goal of the Organization is the promotion and maintenance of peace. This entails the prevention of local, regional and international conflict, and in case of armed conflict, the deployment of effective measures aimed at peace-making, reconstruction and reconciliation. The production and stockpiling of weapons of mass destruction constitutes a continuing threat against peace.[2] Hence, it is necessary that States negotiate in good faith for the early conclusion of a universal treaty on general and complete disarmament under effective international control[3]. Peace is much more than the absence of war, and necessitates an equitable world order, characterized by the gradual elimination of the root causes of conflict, including extreme poverty, endemic injustice, privilege and structural

---

ii https://undocs.org/A/72/171

iii https://www.ru.nl/law/ster/research/nijmegen-principles-and-guidelines-on-interim/

iv https://www.un.org/development/desa/indigenouspeoples/declaration-on-the-rights-of-indigenous-peoples.html

v Annex to document E/CN.4/Sub.2/1997/23.

vi https://www.ohchr.org/Documents/Publications/GuidingPrinciplesBusinessHR_EN.pdf

violence. Already in 1933 the League of Nations entrusted Albert Einstein and Sigmund Freud with the question "Why War?" Their answers are valid today.[4] In 2017 I held up the Einstein/Freud book to the assembled delegates at the Human Rights Council and again before the Third Committee of the General Assembly, and garnered applause at the conclusion of my presentations in both occasions.[5] In order to achieve universal peace, it is necessary to create and safeguard the conditions of peace, including economic development and progressive social legislation. The motto of the International Labour Organization deserves being recognized as the universal motto for our time: *si vis pacem, cole justitiam* (if you want peace, cultivate justice). Moreover, peace must be recognized an enabling right, a pre-condition to the enjoyment of civil, cultural, economic, political and social rights.[6]

2. **The UN Charter takes priority over all other treaties** (Article 103, known as the "supremacy clause"[7]). There is a hierarchy of international norms which places the United Nations Charter at the top of the system, as a kind of world constitution. States have a duty to ensure that all treaties and conventions are in conformity with the purposes and principles of the United Nations as laid down in Articles 1 and 2 of the Charter. Concretely, this imposes a responsibility on States to adopt effective domestic legislation and concrete measures to promote the Purposes and Principles of the United Nations, and an *erga omnes* obligation on all States to safeguard the coherence of the system of collective security, development and human rights.

3. **Resolutions and decisions of the UN Security Council are legally binding.** Pursuant to Article 25 of the Charter, "the members of the United Nations agree to accept and carry out the decisions of the Security Council in accordance with the present Charter." But the Security Council itself is not above international law, and in discharging its duties, it "shall act in accordance with the Purposes and Principles of the United Nations" (Article 24), i.e. the Security Council cannot adopt decisions or resolutions incompatible with the core principles of peace, human rights and development.[8] Such decisions would be *ultra vires* and would lack legitimacy. In a specific case, the International Court of Justice, the highest judicial instance of the United Nations, would have the competence to investigate and make pertinent findings in an Advisory Opinion pursuant to article 65 of the ICJ statute. Understanding that the Security Council is not omnipotent and must act in conformity with its terms of reference resolves the fundamental rule of law question *quis custodiet ipsos custodes?*[9]

4. **International law and human rights law must be applied uniformly and in good faith.** The arbitrary interpretation or selective application of international law, double-standards and selectivity undermine the authority

of the law and frustrate its function to ensure stability and predictability (*Rechtssicherheit*).

5. **International humanitarian law and international human rights law are mutually reinforcing legal regimes, grounded in the principles of respect for human dignity and justice.** According to paragraph 25 of the 1996 Advisory Opinion of the International Court of Justice on Nuclear Weapons: "The Court observes that the protection of the International Covenant on Civil and Political Rights does not cease in times of war, except by operation of Article 4 of the Covenant, whereby certain provisions may be derogated from in a time of national emergency. Respect for the right to life is not, however, such a provision. In principle, the right not arbitrarily to be deprived of one's life applies also in hostilities."[10] Similarly, the UN Human Rights Committee has repeatedly reaffirmed that international humanitarian law cannot be invoked to weaken the international human rights treaty regime.[11]

6. **States must respect not only the letter of the law, but also the spirit of the law** (Montesquieu, *De l'Esprit des lois, 1749*), which is the core and *raison d'être* of the rule of law, what enables the legislator to codify specific norms, which are not immutable, but always subject to progressive development. Blind positivism (*dura lex, sed lex*) frequently destroys the spirit of the law, *summum jus, summa injuria* (law taken to the extreme results in injustice, Cicero *De officiis* 1, 10, 33).

7. **General principles of law (Statute of the International Court of Justice, Article 38, para 1(c)) inform the interpretation and guide the application of international law.** Among general principles of law we recognize good faith, estoppel, reciprocity, proportionality, *ex injuria non oritur jus* (a breach of law does not give rise to new law), the prohibition of the abuse of rights, *sic utere tuo ut alienum non laedas* (use your rights but do not encroach on others), the prohibition of contracts or treaties that are *contra bonos mores* (against good morals), the impartiality of judges, non-selectivity, the principle of non-intervention in the internal affairs of States[12], *audiatur et altera pars (all sides must be heard), actori incumbit onus probandi (plaintiff carries the burden of proof)*, presumption of innocence, the customary rule that domestic law cannot be invoked to undermine international treaties,[13] and the "unwritten laws" of humanity.[14]

8. **International law is dynamic and progresses with the adoption of new treaties and conventions by the United Nations and its specialized agencies, with inter-State practice and the adoption of treaties within the framework of regional inter-governmental organizations, as well as with the binding resolutions of the Security Council, General Assembly, and**

the jurisprudence of the International Court of Justice, the International Criminal Court and the UN human rights treaty bodies. International law doctrine recognizes that certain principles may advance to the category of peremptory norms (*jus cogens*), as for instance the right of self-determination of peoples, the prohibition of the use of force, and the prohibition of torture. Article 53 of the Vienna Convention on the Law of Treaties establishes that a treaty that is contrary to peremptory norms is null and void. Article 64 stipulates that when a new norm of *jus cogens* emerges, treaties must be in conformity with it.

9. **The principles of humanity and human dignity are the source of all human rights**, which since their progressive codification beginning with the 1948 Genocide Convention and the 1948 Universal Declaration of Human Rights, have expanded into an international human rights treaty regime, many aspects of which have become customary international law. A just world order requires the eradication of extreme poverty,[15] the guarantee of food and water security, and a level playing field. The international human rights treaty regime necessarily has priority over military alliances, trade and other agreements (see my 2016 report to the Human Rights Council A/HRC/33/40, paras. 18–42), which must be interpreted and applied in conformity with the International Covenant on Civil and Political Rights (ICCPR), the International Covenant on Economic, Social and Cultural Rights (ICESCR), the International Convention on the Elimination of all Forms or Racial Discrimination (ICERD), the Convention against Torture (CAT) and other pertinent treaties. Commercial agreements cannot infringe on pre-existing human rights treaty obligations undertaken by States.

10. **The right of self-determination of peoples as stipulated in the Charter and in common article 1 of the ICCPR and ICESCR is a fundamental principle of international law (*jus cogens*) and international public policy (*ordre public*)**. All peoples without exception are rights-holders of self-determination. The duty bearers are all States members of the UN. The exercise of self-determination is an expression of democracy, as democracy is an expression of self determination. It attains enhanced legitimacy when a referendum is organized and monitored under the auspices of the United Nations. Although the enjoyment of self-determination in the form of autonomy, federalism, secession or union with another State entity is a human right, it is not self-executing. Timely dialogue for the realization of self-determination is an effective conflict-prevention strategy (see my 2014 report to the General Assembly, A/69/272, paras. 63–77). The United Nations has an essential mediating role between States and peoples, and should conduct self-determination referenda as a conflict-prevention measure, because self-

determination grievances often develop into a threat to the peace or a breach of the peace for purposes of Article 39 of the UN Charter. The right of self-determination has not only a collective but also an individual dimension. Moreover, the right to call for and conduct a referendum is protected by article 19 ICCPR.

11. **"The scope of the principle of territorial integrity is confined to the sphere of relations between States."** Thus rules the International Court of Justice in paragraph 80 of its Advisory Opinion on the Unilateral Declaration of Independence by Kosovo.[16] Admittedly, the principle of territorial integrity is a core principle of international law, aiming at promoting international stability and strengthening the mutual respect and sovereign equality of States. Nevertheless, this principle is not absolute, having primarily external application. In other words, State A may not invade or encroach upon the territorial integrity of State B. Yet, the principle cannot be invoked internally to deny or hollow out the right of self-determination of peoples, [17] which has emerged as a norm of *jus cogens*.

12. **Statehood depends on four criteria: population, territory, government (effective control) and the ability to enter into relations with other States.** While international recognition is desirable, it is not constitutive of statehood but only declaratory. A *de facto* or *de jure* new State is bound by the principles of international order, including respect for human rights. De facto States that emerge from the exercise of legitimate self-determination claims, like Nagorno Karabagh, deserve universal recognition. De facto States that arise as a consequence of naked aggression, like the so-called Turkish Republic of Northern Cyprus, must be brought to the negotiating table and made to conform with the UN Charter and the International Covenant on Civil and Political Rights.[18]

13. **Every State has an inalienable right to choose its political, economic, social and cultural systems, without interference in any form by another State,** as stipulated in numerous United Nations resolutions, the 1993 Vienna Declaration and Programme of Action,[19] the 2001 Durban Declaration,[20] the Outcome Document of the 2005 World Summit.[21] Already in 1530 the Spanish Dominican Francisco de Vitoria,[22] Professor of Law in Salamanca and advocate of the Roman law concept of *ius gentium* (the law of nations), stated that all peoples had the right to govern themselves and could adopt the political regime they wanted.[23]

14. **Peoples possess sovereignty over their natural resources.** A "people"[24] is not only the collective people of a given state but necessarily encompasses a people living under domination by another people. If a people's natural

resources were "sold" or "assigned" pursuant to colonial, neo-colonial or "unequal treaties" or contracts, these agreements must be revised in the light of the UN Charter to vindicate the sovereignty of peoples over their own resources; indigenous peoples are entitled to reparation for the lands and resources that were stolen from them. Any future agreements concerning indigenous lands and resources are conditioned on free, prior and informed consent.[25]

15. **All peoples have the right to their homeland, their culture and identity.**[26] Although closely related to the right of self-determination, the right to the homeland comprises deeper psychological elements, a metaphysics of the mind. Demographic manipulations, forced population transfers, "ethnic cleansing" and other racist measures constitute war crimes and crimes against humanity pursuant to articles 7 and 8 of the Statute of Rome of the International Criminal Court. If certain conditions under article 2 of the 1948 Genocide Convention prevail, forced population transfer and "ethnic cleansing" may constitute genocide under the provisions of the 1948 Genocide Convention and pursuant to article 6 of the Statute of Rome. Such measures are contrary to the ICCPR, ICESCR and the International Convention on the Elimination of all Forms of Racial Discrimination. Refugees and expellees have a right to return to their homelands.[27]

16. **States shall refrain in their international relations from the threat or use of force against the territorial integrity or political independence of any other State** or in any other manner inconsistent with the Purposes of the United Nations (Charter, Article 2 (4), OAS Charter articles 3, 19, 20). In the absence of a resolution adopted by the Security Council under Chapter VII of the Charter, the use of force is illegal[28] and may amount to the crime of aggression under article 5 of the Statute of Rome of the International Criminal Court pursuant to the Kampala definition.[29] States have the duty to refrain from propaganda for war (International Covenant on Civil and Political Rights, art. 20 (1)).[30] Propaganda for war was condemned by the UN General Assembly in numerous resolutions, including 110 (II) and 2625 (XXV).

17. **States have a positive duty to negotiate and settle their international disputes by peaceful means** in such a manner that international peace, security and justice are not endangered (Charter, Article 2 (3)). Chapter VI of the UN Charter, in particular Articles 33 and 34 stipulate that the Security Council may call upon States to seek solutions by negotiation, enquiry, mediation, conciliation, arbitration, judicial settlement or resort to regional agencies or arrangements. The Security Council may investigate any situation

which might lead to international friction and endanger the maintenance of international peace and security.

18. **The principle of non-intervention is part of customary international law.** States may not organize or encourage the organization of irregular forces or armed bands, including mercenaries, for incursion into the territory of another State. No State may organize, assist, foment, finance, incite or tolerate subversive, terrorist or armed activities directed towards the violent overthrow of the regime of another State, or interfere in civil strife in another State.[31] Whereas a State may be invited by the government of another State to assist in containing an internal armed conflict, it is not permitted for any State to support financially or otherwise the insurgency in another State.[32] The fact that such interventions occur with impunity when the perpetrators are permanent members of the Security Council does not give rise to new international law (*ex injuria non oritur jus*). Such interventions constitute continuing violations of international law, which justify investigation and prosecution by the International Criminal Court, ad hoc tribunals and Peoples' Tribunals.

19. **States must refrain from interfering in matters within the internal jurisdiction of another State.**[33] No State may use or encourage the use of economic, political or any other type of measures to coerce another State in order to obtain from it the subordination of the exercise of its sovereign rights and to secure from it advantages of any kind. Unilateral coercive measures are incompatible with the United Nations Charter. Only the Security Council can impose sanctions under Chapter VII of the Charter. Therefore, States shall refrain from imposing unilateral coercive measures, sanctions and financial blockades on other countries. When unilateral coercive measures cause widespread hunger and death, they may amount to crimes against humanity under article 7 of the Statute of the International Criminal Court[34]. While the promotion of human rights is of legitimate international concern, and there is an *erga omnes* obligation of States parties to the ICCPR and ICESCR to ensure their enforcement, the doctrines of "humanitarian intervention" and "responsibility to protect"[35] have been demonstrably counter-productive, and harbour grave dangers of selectivity and abuse, as evidenced in the General Assembly debate on R2P in July 2009,[36] and empirically shown in the chaos visited upon the people of Libya in the name of humanitarian intervention by great power instrumentalization of Security Council Resolution 1973 not for purposes of humanitarian assistance but for purposes of inducing "regime change."[37]

20. **States have a duty to protect and preserve the natural environment and the common heritage of humankind.** The crime of ecocide[38] entails the irreversible degradation or destruction of the human environment. It constitutes a crime against humanity that must be suppressed by the international community and prosecuted under article 7 of the Rome Statute of the International Criminal Court.

21. **State sovereignty is superior to commercial and other agreements.**[39] The principle *pacta sunt servanda* is not absolute and presupposes that the agreements are not contrary to *ordre public* and the general welfare of the population. The principle of non-retrogression[40] in human rights prevents a State from entering into commercial agreements that would prevent it from fulfilling its obligations under ICCPR and ICESCR. Non-state actors have not only rights but also duties under international law and States are obliged to ensure that enterprises registered and/or operating under their jurisdiction do not adversely impact human rights. The ontology of States is to legislate in the public interest. The ontology of capitalism, investment and business enterprises is to take risks to generate profit. It is axiomatic in the nature of business that enterprises sometimes win, but sometimes they lose; profit cannot be privatized while losses are socialized and born by the State. Any treaty that provides for one-way protection for investors and establishes arbitration commissions that circumvent the public courts system and encroach on the regulatory space of States is by nature *contra bonos mores*, as incompatible with the ontological functions of every State. Experience has shown that the investor-state dispute settlement mechanism (ISDS) lacks transparency and accountability and constitutes a frontal attack on fundamental concepts of the rule of law. ISDS cannot be reformed; it must be *abolished*.[41] Free-trade agreements and bilateral investment treaties that contain *contra bonos mores* provisions must be revised and such provisions must be eliminated pursuant to the principle of severability, otherwise known as the doctrine of separability.

22. **Everyone has the right to international solidarity as a human right.**[42] Pursuant thereto States have the duty to cooperate with one another, irrespective of the differences in their political, economic and social systems, in order to maintain international peace and security and to promote international economic stability and progress. To this end, States are obliged to conduct their international relations in the economic, political, social, cultural, technical and trade fields in accordance with the principles of sovereign equality and non-intervention. States should promote a culture of dialogue and mediation.

23. **The right to know and the right to access reliable information is an essential component of the national and international democratic order,** and finds its legal basis *inter alia* in article 19 ICCPR. Government and private sector secrecy rules and covers-up are enemies of the democratic order. Hence, whistleblowers are necessary human rights defenders, because they disclose information about crimes and omissions of governments, transnational corporations and other non-state actors. Transparency and accountability are crucial to every democratic society and the rule of law. A Charter of Rights of Whistleblowers is urgently needed, as I proposed in my reports to the Human Rights Council and General Assembly. The right of freedom of opinion and expression necessarily encompasses the right to publish research contrary to mainstream conceptions, and entails the right to be wrong. Penal laws that are enacted to suppress dissent and so-called "memory laws,"[43] which pretend to crystalize history into a politically correct narrative are totalitarian, offend academic freedom and endanger not only domestic but also international democracy (see my 2013 report to the Human Rights Council A/HRC/24/38, para. 37). The right to truth was recognized by the UN Commission for Human Rights Resolution 2005/66, which determined that there was an "inalienable and autonomous right" to truth,[44] in the United Nations Principles to Combat Impunity (2005), and in General Assembly Resolution 60/147. In 2011 the Human Rights Council created the function of a UN Special Rapporteur on the Promotion of Truth, Justice and Reparation.[45] While modern technology can advance the right to truth, it can also frustrate it. Access to information is already being manipulated in the digital world. Indeed, algorithms and artificial intelligence applications have become a critical part of the information environment. We encounter them throughout the internet, on digital devices and in technical systems, in search engines, social media platforms, messaging applications, and public information mechanisms. While algorithms are potentially useful to facilitate access to information, they are already being misused, particularly by search engines that give visibility primarily to mainstream narratives and frequently suppress non-conforming views.[46]

24. **Violations of international law and international human rights law by powerful States and/or permanent members of the Security Council do not create legal precedents, change the UN Charter, or result in a "new international law."** Such violations, however, weaken the integrity of the UN system and the cohesion of the international order. They constitute on-going violations until an international tribunal like the ICJ or ICC becomes seized of the matter and suppresses them. Impunity does not sanctify the crime, it only manifests the absence of effective UN enforcement mechanisms.

25. Wherever there is a violation of international law or human rights law, there is a State obligation to provide prompt, adequate and effective remedies (*ubi jus, ibi remedium*[47]). Enforcement of international judgments and other commitments frequently presupposes the existence of national enabling legislation that confer domestic legal status to international obligations. Enforcement depends on political will and international cooperation, entailing a balancing of vital interests, geopolitics and *opinio juris*. Enforcement must not be confused with punishment or with the imposition of sanctions. The UN Security Council can impose arms embargoes so as to facilitate dialogue and peace-making. On the other hand, economic sanctions and other coercive measures can result in greater injustice, as happened with the UN sanctions regime against Iraq 1991–2003, with an estimated one million deaths, affecting the most vulnerable.[48] Enforcement of international law commitments must build on international consensus, international solidarity and the good offices of the United Nations and its specialized agencies, which are always ready to furnish advisory services and technical assistance. Enforcement is the measure of international order. Such enforcement is furthered by a strengthening of the regional human rights courts system and by the establishment of an international court of human rights equipped with a monitoring and implementation mechanism[49]. The rule of *pacta sunt servanda* (treaties must be implemented),[50] is particularly relevant to the enforcement of the UN Charter.

Notes

1 Peace is the highest good (motto of the Peace of Westphalia, 1648). Alfred de Zayas, "Westphalia, Peace of" in Rudolf Bernhardt (ed.), *Encyclopaedia of Public International Law*, Vol. IV, (Amsterdam: Elsevier, 2000), pp. 1465–1469.

2 The UN Human Rights Committee regularly issues "general comments" to elucidate the scope of its provisions. See General Comments Nos. 6 and 14 on the right to life, which condemn the production and stockpiling of weapons of mass destruction that may destroy life on Earth:
CCPR General Comment No. 6: Article 6 (Right to Life) Adopted at the Sixteenth Session of the Human Rights Committee, 30 April 1982, https://www.refworld.org/docid/45388400a.html;
CCPR General Comment No. 14: Article 6 (Right to Life), Nuclear Weapons and the Right to Life, adopted at the Twenty-third Session of the Human Rights Committee, 9 November 1984, https://www.refworld.org/docid/453883f911.html.

3 See my 2014 report to the Human Rights Council A/HRC/27/51, paras. 6, 16, 18 and 44. The United Nations Treaty on the Prohibition of Nuclear Weapons entered into force on 22 January 2021: https://www.un.org/disarmament/wmd/nuclear/tpnw/.
"UN treaty banning nuclear weapons set to enter into force in January," *UN News*, 25 October 2020, https://news.un.org/en/story/2020/10/1076082.

4 Albert Einstein, Sigmund Freud, *Why War* (Geneva: International Institute of Intellectual Cooperation, League of Nations, 1933). "Why war? A letter from Albert Einstein to Sigmund Freud," *UNESCO Courier*, https://en.unesco.org/courier/may-1985/why-war-letter-albert-einstein-sigmund-freud.

5 There is a general practice according to which there can be no applause during debates in the Human Rights Council debate. This relates to the role of the Chairperson in maintaining order in the room. See rule 106 of the HRC's rules of procedure. Were applauses to be accepted, this would trigger a race towards those speakers attracting the most applauses and reciprocally those who attract booing. Hence, if delegations or NGOs were to applaud, which is extremely rare, the Chairperson is supposed to interrupt them. In my case the applause was not interrupted. It is the only instance I have experienced of a rapporteur being applauded.

6 Alfred de Zayas, "Peace," in William Schabas (ed.), *Cambridge Companion to International Criminal Law* (Cambridge: Cambridge University Press, 2016), pp. 97–116.

7 Prof. Robert Kolb gave a lecture at the Hague Academy of International Law in 2014 under the title "L'article 103 de la Charte des Nations Unies," *Collected Courses of the Academy*, Vol. 367, 2014.

8 See "Views" of the UN Human Rights Committee in a case concerning UN Security Council sanctions *Sayadi v. Belgium*, Case No. 1472/2006, U.N. Doc. CCPR/C/94/D/1472/2006 (HRC 2008), in particular the separate concurring opinions of Sir Nigel Rodley and Yuyi Iwasawa (new Japanese member of the International Court of Justice), Human Rights Committee Ninety-fourth session, 13–31 October 2008, http://www.worldcourts.com/hrc/eng/decisions/2008.10.22_Sayadi_v_Belgium.htm

9 Juvenalis, *Satires*, 6, 347.

10 "Legality of the Threat or Use of Nuclear Weapons," International Court of Justice Advisory opinion of 8 July 1996, https://www.icj-cij.org/public/files/case-related/95/095-19960708-ADV-01-00-EN.pdf, p. 240.

11 The Human Rights Committee's General comment No. 29 on derogations stipulates: "The Covenant requires that even during an armed conflict measures derogating from the Covenant are allowed only if and to the extent that the situation constitutes a threat to the life of the nation." CCPR General Comment No. 29: Article 4: Derogations during a State of Emergency, adopted at the Seventy-second session of the Human Rights Committee, 31 August 2001, para. 3, https://www.refworld.org/docid/453883fd1f.html. United Nations Human Rights, *International Legal Protection of Human Rights in Armed Conflict* (New York and Geneva: United Nations, 2011), https://www.ohchr.org/Documents/Publications/HR_in_armed_conflict.pdf.

12 General Assembly Resolutions 2131 (XX), 2625 (XXX), 3314 (XXXIV), 36/103

13 Article 27 of the Vienna Convention on the Law of Treaties

14 It is not only the written law that must be applied, but also the broader principles of natural justice as already recognized in Sophocles' *Antigone*, affirming the unwritten laws of humanity, and the concept of a higher moral order that prohibits taking advantage of a weaker party as happens with "unequal treaties," which may be considered as economic neo-colonialism or neo-imperialism.

15 In 2012 the Human Rights Council adopted Guiding Principles on Extreme Poverty and Human Rights, https://www.ohchr.org/EN/Issues/Poverty/Pages/DGPIntroduction.aspx. See Joseph Wronka, *Human Rights and Social Justice* (Sage Publications, 2017).

16 "Accordance with International Law of the Unilateral Declaration of Independence in Respect of Kosovo," International Court of Justice Advisory opinion of 22 July 2010, https://www.icj-cij.org/public/files/case-related/141/141-20100722-ADV-01-00-EN.pdf: "Several participants in the proceedings before the Court have contended that a prohibition of unilateral declarations of independence is implicit in the principle of territorial integrity. The Court recalls that the principle of territorial integrity is an important part of the international legal order and is enshrined in the Charter of the United Nations, in particular in Article 2, paragraph 4, which provides that: 'All Members shall refrain in their international relations from the threat or use of force against the territorial integrity or political independence of any State, or in any other manner inconsistent with the Purposes of the United Nations.' In General Assembly Resolution 2625 (XXV), entitled 'Declaration on Principles of International Law concerning Friendly Relations and Co-operation among States in Accordance with the Charter of the United Nations,' which reflects customary international law (*Military and Paramilitary Activities in and against Nicaragua (Nicaragua v. United States of America*), Merits, Judgment, I.C.J. Reports 1986, pp. 101–103, paras. 191–193), the General Assembly reiterated '[t]he principle that States shall refrain in their international relations from the threat or use of force

against the territorial integrity or political independence of any State.' This resolution then enumerated various obligations incumbent upon States to refrain from violating the territorial integrity of other sovereign States. In the same vein, the Final Act of the Helsinki Conference on Security and Co-operation in Europe of 1 August 1975 (the Helsinki Conference) stipulated that '[t]he participating States will respect the territorial integrity of each of the participating States' (Art. IV). Thus, the scope of the principle of territorial integrity is confined to the sphere of relations between States."

17 See my 2014 report to the General Assembly, A/69/272, paras. 21, 28, 69 and 70, https://undocs.org/A/69/272.

18 Security Council Resolutions 365, 367, 541, 544, 550.

19 Vienna Declaration and Programme of Action adopted by the World Conference on Human Rights in Vienna, 25 June 1993, https://www.ohchr.org/EN/ProfessionalInterest/Pages/Vienna.aspx

20 World Conference against Racism, Racial Discrimination, Xenophobia and Related Intolerance, Durban, South Africa, 31 August–8 September 2001, https://www.un.org/WCAR/durban.pdf.

21 "2005 World Summit Outcome," Resolution adopted by the General Assembly on 16 September 2005 [without reference to a Main Committee (A/60/L.1)] 60/1, https://www.un.org/en/development/desa/population/migration/generalassembly/docs/globalcompact/A_RES_60_1.pdf

22 See Ramón Hernández, O.P., "The Internationalization of Francisco deVitoria and Domingo de Soto," *Fordham International Law Journal,* Vol. 15, Issue 4, 1991, Article 4, http://ir.lawnet.fordham.edu/cgi/viewcontent.cgi?article=1325&context=ilj.

23 See Élaina Gauthier-Mamaril, "The Foundations of Human Rights : Human nature and jus gentium as articulated by Francisco de Vitoria" (Dominican University College, Ottawa, Canada), *Academia,* www.academia.edu/7222085/The_Foundations_of_Human_Rights_Human_nature_and_jus_gentium_as_articulated_by_Francisco_de_Vitoria. See also the Outcome Document of the 2005 Millennium plus 5 Summit, General Assembly Resolution 60/1, paragraphs 22 and 135: "We reaffirm that democracy is a universal value based on the freely expressed will of people to determine their own political, economic, social and cultural systems and their full participation in all aspects of their lives. We also reaffirm that while democracies share common features, there is no single model of democracy, that it does not belong to any country or region, and reaffirm the necessity of due respect for sovereignty and the right of self-determination. We stress that democracy, development and respect for all human rights and fundamental freedoms are interdependent and mutually reinforcing."

24 See the definition of "peoples" by Justice Michael Kirby in "People's Rights and Self-Determination," UNESCO International Meeting of Experts, Budapest, Hungary, 25-29 September 1991, https://www.michaelkirby.com.au/images/stories/speeches/1990s/vol24/906-Peoples%27_Rights_and_Self_Determination_-_UNESCO_Mtg_of_Experts.pdf.
See also my 2014 report to the General Assembly, para. 4, https://undocs.org/A/69/272.

25 Declaration on the Rights of Indigenous Peoples, articles 9, 10, 28, 29, 32.

26 Alfred de Zayas, *Heimatrecht ist Menschenrecht* (Munich: Universitas, 2002). de Zayas, "Ethnic Cleansing: Applicable Norms, Emerging Jurisprudence, Implementable Remedies" in John Carey (ed.), *International Humanitarian Law: Origins* (New York: Transnational Press, 2003), pp. 283–307.

27 Alfred de Zayas, "Forced Population Transfers," in Rüdiger Wolfrum (ed.), *Max Planck Encyclopaedia of Public International Law,* Vol. IV (Oxford, 2012), pp. 165–175. See also UN Declaration on the illegality of forced population transfers, Sub-Commission document E/CN.4/Sub.2/1997/23.

28 "Iraq war illegal, says Annan," *BBC News,* 16 September 2004, http://news.bbc.co.uk/2/hi/middle_east/3661134.stm.
Patrick E. Tyler, "Annan Says Iraq War Was 'Illegal'," *The New York Times,* 16 September 2004, https://www.nytimes.com/2004/09/16/international/annan-says-iraq-war-was-illegal.html.

29 Hans-Peter Kaul, "The Crime of Aggression after Kampala – Some Personal Thoughts on the Way Forward," remarks made at the international law symposium "Beyond Kampala: The ICC, the Crime of Aggression, and the Future of the Court," International Criminal Court, 13 May 2011, https://www.icc-cpi.int/NR/rdonlyres/2054CCC9-4FB7-4839-B847-292206BF6E16/283357/12052011_TheCrimeofAggressionafterKampala.pdf.

Claus Kreß and Stefan Barriga (eds.), *The Crime of Aggression: A Commentary* (Cambridge: Cambridge University Press, 2017), reviewed by Alexandre Skander Galand in *European Journal of International Law,* 30 December 2020, https://academic.oup.com/ejil/article/31/3/1176/6055180. Anouk T. Boas, "The Definition of the Crime of Aggression and Its Relevance for Contemporary Armed Conflict," *ICD Brief 1,* International Crimes Database, June 2013, http://www.internationalcrimesdatabase.org/upload/documents/20131030T045349-ICD%20Brief%201%20-%20Boas.pdf

30 Michael Kearney, *The Prohibition of Propaganda for War in International Law* (Oxford: Oxford University Press, 2007). See also Michael G. Kearney, "Propaganda for War, Prohibition," *Max Planck Encyclopedia of Public International Law,* https://socialglobalstudies.com/LAW%2012/maxplanckpropagandaforwar.pdf.

31 "Military and Paramilitary Activities in and against Nicaragua (Nicaragua v. United States of America)," *Merits, Judgment. I.C.J. Reports 1986,* p. 14. Available at www.icj-cij.org/files/case-related/70/070-19860627-JUD-01-00-EN.pdf.

32 Pietro Pustorino, "The principle of non-intervention in recent non-international armed conflicts," *Questions of International Law,* 30 September 2018, http://www.qil-qdi.org/principle-non-intervention-recent-non-international-armed-conflicts/. Louise Doswald-Beck, "The Legal Validity of Military Intervention by Invitation of the Government," *British Yearbook of International Law,* Vol. 56, Issue 1 (1985), pp. 242–244, https://academic.oup.com/bybil/article-abstract/56/1/189/276792?redirectedFrom=fulltext. Laura Visser, "Russia's Intervention in Syria," *EJIL: Talk!,* 25 November 2015, https://www.ejiltalk.org/russias-intervention-in-syria/.

33 Alfred de Zayas, "Report of the Independent Expert on the promotion of a democratic and equitable international order on his mission to the Bolivarian Republic of Venezuela and Ecuador," transmitted to the UN General Assembly Human Rights Council, Thirty-ninth session, 10-28 September 2018, https://undocs.org/A/HRC/39/47/Add.1, paras. 29–39.

34 See my 2018 report to the Human Rights Council on my mission to Venezuela: https://undocs.org/A/HRC/39/47/Add.1, paras. 34–39. See also the Preliminary Conclusions of the UN Special Rapporteur on unilateral coercive measures, Alena Douhan, https://www.ohchr.org/EN/NewsEvents/Pages/DisplayNews.aspx?NewsID=26747&LangID=E.

35 General Assembly Resolution 60/1, para. 138.

36 See my 2012 report to the General Assembly, https://undocs.org/A/67/277, paras. 14–15.

37 United Nations Security Council Resolution S/RES/1973 (2011), https://www.un.org/securitycouncil/s/res/1973-%282011%29. Also see "Russia accuses NATO of going beyond UN resolution on Libya," *RT,* 17 April 2011, https://www.rt.com/news/russia-nato-un-resolution-libya/; Micah Zenko, "The Big Lie About the Libyan War," *Foreign Policy,* 22 March 2016, https://foreignpolicy.com/2016/03/22/libya-and-the-myth-of-humanitarian-intervention/; Matthew Green, "To What Extent Was the NATO Intervention in Libya a Humanitarian Intervention?," *E-International Relations,* 6 February 2019, https://www.e-ir.info/2019/02/06/to-what-extent-was-the-nato-intervention-in-libya-a-humanitarian-intervention/.

38 "Polly Higgins," *Stop Ecocide,* https://www.stopecocide.earth/polly-higgins; Sophie Yeo, "Ecocide: Should killing nature be a crime?," *BBC Future Planet,* 5 November 2020; "European Parliament Urges Support for Making Ecocide an International Crime," *Stop Ecocide,* 21 January 2021, https://www.stopecocide.earth/press-releases-summary/european-parliament-urges-support-for-making-ecocide-an-international-crime.

39 See my 2016 report to the Human Rights Council, A/HRC/33/40, paras. 43–54.

40 Ben Warwick, *Unwinding Retrogression, Human Rights Law Review,* Volume 19, Issue 3, November 2019, pp. 467–490, https://www.escr-net.org/resources/progressive-realisation-and-non-regression. Limburg principles https://www.escr-net.org/resources/limburg-principles-implementation-international-covenant-economic-social-and-cultural. See also D. M. Johnson, *The Historical Foundations of World Order: The Tower and The Arena* (Leiden: Martinus Nijhoff, 2008).

41 See my 2015 report to the Human Rights Council, A/HRC/30/44, paras. 8, 12, 17 and 53, and my 2015 report to the General Assembly, A/70/285, paras. 54 and 65.

42 "About International Solidarity and human rights," *United Nations Human Rights,* https://

www.ohchr.org/EN/Issues/Solidarity/Pages/InternationalSolidarity.aspx.

43 Human Rights Committee, General Comment No. 34 (2011) on article 19 ICCPR, Freedom of opinion and expression: "Laws that penalize the expression of opinions about historical facts are incompatible with the obligations that the Covenant imposes on States parties in relation to the respect for freedom of opinion and expression. The Covenant does not permit general prohibition of expressions of an erroneous opinion or an incorrect interpretation of past events." https://www.refworld.org/docid/4ed34b562.html para. 49. See also Alfred de Zayas and Aurea Roldan, "Freedom of Opinion and Expression," in *Netherlands International Law Review,* 2012, pp. 425–454.

44 "Right to the truth," Human Rights Resolution 2005/66, UN Commission on Human Rights, 20 April 2005, https://www.refworld.org/docid/45377c7d0.html

45 "Special Rapporteur on the promotion of truth, justice, reparation and guarantees of non-recurrence," United Nations Human Rights, https://www.ohchr.org/EN/Issues/TruthJusticeReparation/Pages/Index.aspx. "International Day for the Right to the Truth Concerning Gross Human Rights Violations and for the Dignity of Victims (24 March)," *United Nations,* https://www.un.org/en/observances/right-to-truth-day.

46 "Report on Artificial Intelligence technologies and implications for freedom of expression and the information environment," *United Nations Human Rights,* https://www.ohchr.org/EN/Issues/FreedomOpinion/Pages/ReportGA73.aspx.

47 Jakob Th. Möller and Alfred de Zayas, *United Nations Human Rights Committee Case-Law* (Strasbourg: N.P.Engel, 2009), chaps. 6 and 7. See also the 1928 Judgement of the Permanent Court of International Justice in the *Chorzow Factory Case,* https://jusmundi.com/en/document/decision/en-factory-at-chorzow-merits-judgment-thursday-13th-september-1928. See also "Basic Principles and Guidelines on the Right to a Remedy and Reparation for Victims of Gross Violations of International Human Rights Law and Serious Violations of International Humanitarian Law," adopted and proclaimed by General Assembly Resolution 60/147 of 16 December 2005, https://www.ohchr.org/EN/ProfessionalInterest/Pages/RemedyAndReparation.aspx.

48 Hans-Christof Graf von Sponeck, *A Different Kind of War: The UN Sanctions Regime in Iraq* (New York: Oxford, 2006). Barbara Crossette, "Iraq Sanctions Kill Children, U.N. Reports," *New York Times,* 1995 December 1, https://www.nytimes.com/1995/12/01/world/iraq-sanctions-kill-children-un-reports.html.
"Sanctions have caused 1.6 million deaths, Iraq claims," *CBC News,* 28 December 2001, https://www.cbc.ca/news/world/sanctions-have-caused-1-6-million-deaths-iraq-claims-1.269576.

49 The non-governmental organization *Eleanor Lives* was established with the task of drafting a new international bill of rights together with the statute of an international court of human rights: www.eleanorlives.org. Alfred de Zayas, "An International Court of Human Rights" *Nordic Journal of International Law,* 1993, one of seven working papers I submitted to the Vienna World Conference on Human Rights, pp. 239–277. See also Kirk Boyd, *International Bill of Rights,* articles 27–34 (San Francisco, 2021) and Kirk Boyd, *2048: Humanity's Agreement to Live Together,* (San Francisco: Berrett-Koehler, 2010.

50 Vienna Convention on the Law of Treaties, article 26.

Chapter 3

PEACE AS A HUMAN RIGHT

"Peace cannot exist without justice, justice cannot exist without fairness, fairness cannot exist without development, development cannot exist without democracy, democracy cannot exist without respect for the identity and worth of cultures and peoples."

RIGOBERTA MENCHÚ
Nobel Peace Prize Laureate, 1992[i]

INTRODUCTION

Undoubtedly, there is nothing more crucial to building a just world order than to promote and protect local, regional and international peace. This goes beyond the prohibition of war and entails the elimination of structural violence and those root causes of conflict that have plagued the world over thousands of years.

In December 2009 the United Nations High Commissioner for Human Rights, Navi Pillay, convened a special workshop to discuss peace as a human right. I was one of the six experts who contributed in producing an important document, which was subsequently used in debates in the Human Rights Council and its Advisory Committee[ii] The concept of peace as a human right was championed by a group of civil society activists around Professor Carlos Villán Durán of the University of Alcalá de Henares in Spain. Profesor Villán Durán was and is still

---

i Rigoberta Menchú, *I, Rigoberta Menchú: An Indian Woman in Guatemala* (Second Edition), Verso Books, 2009, p. 22.

ii In its resolution 8/9, the Human Rights Council requested OHCHR to convene a workshop which took place on 15–16 December 2009 in Geneva. The outcome of the workshop is contained in document A/HRC/14/38 and was presented to the 14th session of the Human Rights Council. In its resolution 14/3 the Council noted with satisfaction the outcome of the workshop and further requested the Advisory Committee in consultation with Member States, civil society, academia and all relevant stakeholders, to prepare a draft declaration on the right of peoples to peace, and to report on progress to the Council at its 17th session. At its 5th session the Advisory Committee established a drafting group on the draft declaration on the right of peoples to peace. Several consultations were held during which primarily the United States and European delegations blocked the consensus driven by so-called third world countries, academia and civil society. https://www.ohchr.org/EN/HRBodies/HRC/RightPeace/Pages/WGDraftUNDeclarationontheRighttoPeace.aspx https://www.ohchr.org/EN/NewsEvents/Pages/RightToPeace.aspx https://www.ohchr.org/EN/ProfessionalInterest/Pages/RightOfPeoplesToPeace.aspx

the President of the Spanish Association for International Human Rights Law,[i] of which I have been a member since 2004 and was honoured to contribute to the drafting of the Declaración de Santiago de Compostela on the Human Right to Peace of 10 December 2010.[ii] It was on the basis of this Declaration, which was submitted to the Human Rights Council, that the Council on 5 July 2012 requested its Advisory Committee to prepare a draft, which was then the basis of discussions at an intergovernmental open ended working group.[iii]

Whereas feedback from the international civil society consultations conducted by the SAIHRL over a period of three years in all regions of the world was resolute and clear about what it wanted, it soon became apparent that the major powers had no interest in advancing the concept of peace as a human right. When we all sat down to drafting with government representatives, it turned out that precisely those countries that claim to be the leaders of the democratic and human rights movement—the United States and the members of the European Union—became the most hostile to the peace endeavour and the most procedurally inventive in undermining civil society's aspiration for peace. Not only would they not come on board; they actually did everything in their power to subvert the draft and ultimately to defeat the purpose of the exercise. Again and again these States claimed that the Human Rights Council was not the right venue to discuss matters of peace and security, that there was no legal basis for the right to peace and that, in any event, it would be a collective right, not an individual right that could ever be justiciable. The governmental opposition against the declaration was evidently coordinated, as none of the powerful states were willing to envisage a condemnation of the arms race, a meaningful reduction on nuclear stockpiles, a program to eliminate the root-causes of conflict, or any kind of monitoring mechanism.

---

i http://aedidh.org/es/
See Carlos Villán Duran y Carmelo Faleh Pérez (eds.), *Contribuciones Regionales para una Declaración Universal del Derecho Humano a la Paz*, Asociación Española para el Derecho Internacional de los Derechos Humanos, Luarca, Asturias, España, 2010; *Paz, Migraciones y libre determinación de los Pueblos*, Luarca 2012; *El Derecho Humano a la Paz y la Inseguridad Humana*, Luarca 2017. https://www.reei.org Villán Duran, C. and Faleh Perez (Directors), *The International Observatory of the Human Right to Peace*, Guipuzkoako Foru Aldundia, 2013.

Rueda Castañón, Carmen Rosa, y Villán Durán, Carlos (eds.): *La Declaración de Luarca sobre el derecho humano a la paz*, MADÚ Ediciones, Siero, Asturias, 2007. See also pertinent publications of the Geneva International Peace Research Institute, https://gipri.ch/, and of the Stockholm International Peace Research Institute, https://www.sipri.org/.

ii http://www.aedidh.org/sites/default/files/Santiago-Declaration-en.pdf
iii https://ohchr.org/EN/HRBodies/HRC/RightPeace/Pages/WGDraftUNDeclarationontheRighttoPeace.aspx
https://ohchr.org/EN/HRBodies/HRC/RightPeace/Pages/FirstSession.aspx

I exposed my arguments in favour of the Advisory Committee's draft declaration at an expert meeting held on 26–27 November 2012 in Caux, Switzerland, hosted by Professor Villán Durán.

What follows are excerpts from that meeting, the full text of which is on the OHCHR website.[i] *—AdeZ*

* * *

The question whether human rights are individual or collective, or more particularly, whether the human right to peace is individual or collective—is artificial and misleading, a kind of red herring. This phony discussion leads nowhere and actually delays progress in making all human rights more accessible and justiciable. What is needed is legislative action, clear drafting of laws that define the elements of the rights, the manner in which the rights can be claimed, the kind of remedies that are available, and the mechanisms of enforcement.

Of course, there are still some Governments and academics who question whether a right to peace exists at all. I have no hesitation in affirming its existence—not only in natural law, but also in positive international law. Nevertheless, this fundamental right has not been given the attention that it deserves, and positivists continue to deny its relevance. Perhaps the conceptual problem lies in the fact that peace is not a simple right like the right to property. It is more in the nature of an enabling right, prior and indispensable to other rights—an immanent or inherent right.

Much has been written concerning the legal principles underlying the right to peace. Surely the UN Charter, which can be seen as the world constitution, imposes *erga omnes* obligations on States, particularly the obligation to refrain from the threat or the use of force in international relations (UN Charter Article 2 (4)) and a positive obligation to negotiate in good faith so as to settle disputes peacefully (Article 2 (3)). This is a negative expression of the positive right to peace.

Bearing in mind that the Preamble of the UN Charter begins with the statement "We the Peoples" of the United Nations, it is also clear that in this respect not only States but also peoples and individuals are stakeholders, and as such they can and must articulate their demand that States observe their commitments under the Charter. Moreover, the General Assembly has repeatedly reaffirmed the Purposes and Principles of the Charter, particularly the mandate to preserve succeeding generations from the scourge of war, as reflected inter alia in Resolution 2625 on Friendly Relations and Resolution 3314 on the Definition of Aggression.[1]

---

i https://www.ohchr.org/EN/Issues/IntOrder/Pages/AlfredDeZayas.aspx

On the other hand, the scope of the human right to peace must not be limited to the issue of prevention of armed conflict. The right to peace is an all-encompassing individual and collective right that deserves outlining in its many facets. As the Outcome Document of the 2005 World Summit affirmed: "peace and security, development and human rights are the pillars of the United Nations system and the foundations for collective security and well-being. We recognize that development, peace and security and human rights are interlinked and mutually reinforcing."[2]

Article 1 of the **Advisory Committee's Draft Declaration on the Right to Peace** begins with the words "Individuals and peoples have a right to peace."

Article 2 of the Draft Declaration stipulates that everyone has the right to security of person, this being eminently an individual human right, reflected in article 9 of the International Covenant on Civil and Political Rights. Article 2 of the Draft Declaration also makes reference to the freedoms from fear and from want, which we know from President Franklin Roosevelt's "Four Freedoms" speech of 6 January 1941. Whereas at first sight such rights may appear to be collective in nature, they clearly have a very concrete meaning to each individual who is entitled to enjoy personal security and integrity.

It is difficult not to see the human right to peace as an individual human right. Indeed, the individual has the right to life, which is also stipulated in article 6 of the ICCPR. This right to life is undoubtedly an individual right, which in many ways depends on the realization of the right to peace, since the violation of the right to peace through structural, economic, cultural or other violence including armed conflict, significantly threatens the right to life. In this context it is worth mentioning the two General Comments issued by the UN Human Rights Committee on the Right to Life, both of which condemn the threat posed to the individual right to life and the larger threat to humanity posed by the production and stockpiling of nuclear and other weapons of mass destruction.

It bears repeating that the Human Rights Committee is the preeminent UN treaty body that deals with individual rights, and that the Committee's jurisprudence under the Optional Protocol focuses primarily on individual rights such as the rights to life, security and conscientious objection.

Article 2 of the Draft Declaration further clarifies what is meant by positive peace, which necessarily includes freedom of thought, conscience, opinion, expression, belief and religion.

To those doubters who contend that economic, social and cultural rights are not individual rights and therefore not justiciable, I should point out that the Optional Protocol to the International Covenant on Economic, Social and Cultural Rights, establishing an individual petitions procedure, has been adopted and opened for signature, and that it is likely to enter into force in the near future, since it is short of only two more ratifications. The Committee on Economic, Social and Cultural Rights is currently adopting its rules of procedure to deal with complaints under this new Optional Protocol.

Article 2, paragraph 3 of the Draft Declaration stipulates that everyone has the right to be protected from genocide, war crimes, the use of force in violation of international law, and crimes against humanity. In other words, every individual is entitled to protection—not only from violence perpetrated by governments but also violence emanating from non-state actors including paramilitary forces, mercenaries, private military or security companies, or terrorists. Here again, the individual and collective right to protection from violence becomes evident and justiciable. The doctrine of responsibility to protect (R2P), if applied objectively and non-selectively, may contribute to the realization of the right to peace. On the other hand, we all agree that this doctrine can be understood only in the context and consistently with the Purposes and Principles of the United Nations. Under no conditions can R2P be used as a pretext to erode the Charter's supreme commitment to peace, in particular the injunction formulated in Article 2 (4) of the Charter. The 2009 discussion of R2P in the General Assembly is worth recalling, especially the four conditions or benchmarks formulated by the then President of the General Assembly, Miguel d'Escoto Brockmann, on 23 July 2009.[3] Indeed, while the international community must be vigilant to prevent a repetition of the Rwanda genocide anywhere in the world, we all must be wary of trigger-happy countries who have their own agendas and would misuse R2P and the resuscitated "just war" doctrine, as a pretext to advance other economic or geopolitical interests, or to impose "regime change" such as occurred with regard to Libya in 2011, when Security Council Resolution 1973[4] was instrumentalized to bombard Libya.[5]

In this context **Article 2, paragraph 4**, stipulates that the United Nations shall include in mandates of peacekeeping operations the comprehensive and effective protection of civilians as a priority objective, while **paragraph 6** reaffirms the right of every human being to demand from his or her Government the effective observance of the norms of international law, including international human rights law and international humanitarian law.

Article 3 of the Draft Declaration deals with the issue of **disarmament**, which is crucial to the prevention of armed conflict. Not only is article 6 of the ICCPR in play, but also the right to individuals to meaningfully participate in the conduct of public affairs, as stipulated in article 25 of the ICCPR. There is a very obvious disconnect between governments and the people, and a worrisome lack of transparency. In many countries it is quite evident that the military-industrial complex exercises a thoroughly undemocratic influence over government policies and that the voice of the people that demands education and health care instead of more guns is not being heard. The whole contemporary discussion over "**austerity measures**" gains a particular relevance in connection with military expenditures which are not democratically decided by the people, and would certainly be rejected if there were the least attempt to carry out referenda thereon. In this context the establishment of a **United Nations Parliamentary Assembly** should be explored.[6] Such an Assembly would give greater voice to the real needs of peoples and could also facilitate, coordinate or conduct world referenda or opinion polling that would better reflect vox populi.

When it comes to determining the **priorities** of governmental expenditures, there must be much more transparency and the voice of those who want to see austerity with regard to military expenditures must be listened to. Each individual who is denied social services, ostensibly because there is no money to finance such services, has a right to demand them, because social services constitute an *aquis*, a hallmark of the social market economy. Governments that engage in military expenses, frequently consuming a high percentage of the national budget, and neglect their commitments under the International Covenant on Economic, Social and Cultural Rights, have violated the rights of their constituents under this Covenant, and arguably article 5 of the Covenant, which is intended to prohibit **retrogression**.[7]

Article 3, paragraph 2, of the Draft Declaration is particularly relevant in stipulating that all peoples and individuals have a right to live in a world free of weapons of mass destruction. Moreover, the use of weapons that damage the **environment**, in particular radioactive weapons, is contrary to international humanitarian law, the right to a healthy environment and the right to peace. Such weapons are prohibited and must be urgently eliminated, and States that have utilized them have the obligation to restore the environment by repairing the damage caused. This obviously also entails the necessary clean-up of those areas polluted by the use of depleted uranium weapons and cluster bombs, and the imperative need for accountability.

Article 3, paragraph 4, draws the logical conclusion from the above in affirming that all peoples and individuals have the right to have the resources freed by disarmament allocated to the economic, social and cultural development of peoples and to the fair redistribution of natural wealth, responding especially to the needs of the poorest countries and of groups in situations of vulnerability.

As everyone knows, one of the main obstacles to achieving the right to peace is **psychological**. Still many countries maintain a **culture of war**, where military honour is at the top of the scale of values. It is important to break away from this millennia-old indoctrination.

Many still pretend that there is some legitimacy to Horace's maxim *dulce et decorum est pro patria mori* (Odes III.2.13)—it is sweet and proper to die for one's country. There is urgent need to abandon this way of thinking. Indeed it should be *dulce et decorum est, pro patria vivere*. The British poet Wilfred Owen expressed it well in his poem, Dulce et Decorum, where in the last stanza he called it an **old lie**.

> *If you could hear, at every jolt, the blood*
> *Come gargling from the froth-corrupted lungs,*
> *Obscene as cancer, bitter as the cud*
> *Of vile, incurable sores on innocent tongues,*
> *— My friend, you would not tell with such high zest*
> *To children ardent for some desperate glory,*
> *The old Lie: Dulce et decorum est*
> *Pro patria mori.*

It is in this sense that **Article 4** of the Draft Declaration stipulates the right to education for peace. Indeed we must unlearn war, unlearn the predator in us, unlearn privilege and discrimination. And this right to education is very much an individual right, a right not to be indoctrinated into war, not to be manipulated as the hero in Erich Maria Remarque's *All Quiet in the Western Front* had been by his teachers in secondary school. Only too late did young Paul Bäumer recognize how he had been lied to, and so he died because of the old lie. The nineteen-year-old boy had finally understood.

> *How senseless is everything that can ever be written, done, or thought, when such things are possible. It must be all lies and of no account when the culture of a thousand years could not prevent this stream of blood being poured out, these torture chambers in their hundreds of thousands. A hospital alone shows what war is.*

This sense of disgust at war is also expressed by Albert Camus in *The Plague*: "When a war breaks out, people say: 'It's too stupid, it can't last long.' But though a war may be 'too stupid,' that doesn't prevent its lasting."

It is the responsibility of educators to help young persons understand and claim their rights, to move away from ingrained prejudices in favour of war, with the widespread confusion of honour and glory with military virtues. There is enough good literature that reveals the horrors of war. It is this literature that must be taught. Aristophanes' Lysistrata is a powerful anti-war satire, as valid today as during the Peloponnesian war 400 years before Christ. It is as valid as Tacitus Agricola, where he condemns the **euphemisms** of war and says it as it was and still is: the victors "plunder, they slaughter, and they steal: this they falsely name Empire, and where they make a wasteland, they call it peace" *ubi solitudinem faciunt, pacem appellant.*

Yet another concrete and pragmatic individual right stipulated in the Draft Declaration is to be found in **article 4, paragraph 4**:

> *Everyone has the right to denounce any event that threatens or violates the right to peace, and to participate freely in peaceful political, social and cultural activities or initiatives for the defence and promotion of the right to peace, without interference by Governments or the private sector.*

This means that anti-war activists must not be harassed or persecuted by government or non-state actors, must not be subjected to surveillance, breach of privacy, wire-tapping, mobbing and humiliation, must not be defamed or ostracised, must not be restricted in their freedom of movement. We know that anti-war activists have been subjected to house searches, arbitrary arrests and even disappearances, in violation of articles 9, 12, 17, 19, 21 and 25 ICCPR. This is a matter of considerable gravity, especially because there is legislation in some countries that imposes penalties for pacifist activities, when these are considered unpatriotic or even treasonable. Anti-war activists are entitled to protection by State authorities pursuant to article 9, paragraph 1, of the ICCPR.

Indeed, what is illegal is not waging peace, but engaging in aggressive war, which constitutes the **crime against peace** as defined in Point 6a of the Nuremberg indictment and in the compromise text of the meeting of States parties to the International Criminal Court at Kampala in 2010, which gave content to article 5 of the Rome Statute of the ICC. What is illegal is not manifesting for peace, but engaging in propaganda for war, which is specifically prohibited in **article 20 of the ICCPR**.

Part of the problem remains the old history of ethnic and religious rivalry in many countries. Such rivalry is continuously fed by cheap chauvinism, jingoism, yellow journalism, and even by negative stereotyping in **school textbooks**. This is why **Article 4, paragraph 5**, of the Draft Declaration imposes an obligation on States:

> *to remove hate messages, distortions, prejudice and negative bias from textbooks and other educational media, to prohibit the glorification of violence and its justification and to ensure the*

basic knowledge and understanding of the world's main cultures, civilizations and religions and to prevent xenophobia.

This is very much the vocation of UNESCO and of the Office of the High Commissioner for Human Rights through its manifold training courses.

In Germany the **Georg-Eckert Institut** in Braunschweig has done constant and solid work in organizing expert meetings between German and Polish, German and American historians, etc. aimed at mutually eliminating stereotypes from textbooks. I myself participated in the German-American schoolbook discussions back in 1979 and 1980. The goal is thus to establish a *culture of peace* based on historical truth of mutual respect.

Much progress has indeed been made, but prejudices die hard. In this sense we know that education can be employed for good and bad purposes. In the Rodgers and Hammerstein musical *South Pacific*, Lieutenant Cable sings a bitter song about it:

*You've got to be taught
to hate and fear
You've got to be taught
from year to year,*

*It's got to be drummed in your dear little ear
You've got to be carefully taught.*

*You've got to be taught to be afraid
Of peoples whose eyes are oddly made,*

*And people whose skin is a different shade,
You've got to be carefully taught.*

*You've got to be taught before it's too late
before you are six or seven or eight,*

*To hate all the people your relatives hate,
You've got to be carefully taught.*

Article 5 of the Draft Declaration stipulates the right of **conscientious objection** to military service. This is an eminently individual human right, and a right that has been recognized in the case-law of the Human Rights Committee under the Optional Protocol. In cases Nos. 1321-1322/2004 (*Myung-Jin Choi and Yeo-Blum Yoon v. The Republic of Korea*) the Committee noted that "to compel a person to use lethal force, although such use would seriously conflict with the requirements of his conscience or religious beliefs, falls within the ambit of article 18 ... the authors' conviction and sentence, accordingly amounts to a restriction of their ability to manifest their religion or belief. Such restriction must be justified by the permissible limits described in paragraph 3 of article 18 ... however, such restriction must not impair the very essence of the right in question."[8]

Not only is there an individual right to conscientious objection, based on the right to freedom of belief and conviction stipulated in article 18 ICCPR, individuals have also the right to be protected in the effective exercise of this right. Moreover, members of any military or other security institutions have the **right to disobey** orders that are manifestly contrary to international law and international human rights law. The duty to obey military superior orders does not exempt from the observance of these obligations, and disobedience of illegal orders shall in no case constitute a military offence.

Article 7 of the Draft Declaration lays down yet another individual right—the **right to resistance**. Pursuant to this article the individual has "the right to resist and oppose oppressive colonial, foreign occupation or dictatorial domination (domestic oppression). Moreover, everyone has the right to oppose aggression, genocide, war crimes and crimes against humanity, violations of other universally recognized human rights, and any propaganda in favour of war or incitement to violence and violations of the right to peace, as defined in the present declaration. This is both an individual and a collective right."

In this context it is important to recall the language of preambular paragraph 3 of the Universal Declaration of Human Rights: "Whereas it is essential, if man is not to be compelled to have recourse, as a last resort, to rebellion against tyranny and oppression, that human rights should be protected by the rule of law."

This provision has many implications and may have concrete manifestations that States would surely reject. One such expression of resistance would be the refusal to pay taxes to finance an aggressive war. This right has not been recognized by any human rights body such as the Human Rights Committee, but it deserves being discussed, because if citizens in a democratic society decide to organize and massively refuse to pay taxes for military budgets and aggressive war, there would surely be consequences.

Article 10 focuses on the right to a safe and healthy environment, which is part and parcel of the right to life and may be considered a condition to the enjoyment of first generation individual rights. This right encompasses the right to free and meaningful participation in the development and implementation of environmentally friendly policies.

Article 11 reaffirms the individual right to redress, as reflected in article 2 of the ICCPR. Accordingly, every victim of a human rights violation has the right to an appropriate remedy; to obtain the investigation of facts, as well as identification and punishment of those responsible; to obtain effective and full redress, including the right to rehabilitation and compensation; to measures of symbolic redress or reparation; and to guarantees that the violation will not be repeated. In its jurisprudence under the Optional Protocol, the Human Rights Committee has formulated a whole spectrum of concrete remedies to individual victims.[9] Moreover, the Human Rights Council appointed in 2012 a new Special Rapporteur on the Right to Truth, Justice and Reparation, Pablo de Greif from Colombia, who has presented preliminary reports to the Council (A/HRC/21/46) and the General Assembly (A/67/368)[10] in this respect.

Article 12 postulates the right to refugee status as falling within the scope of the right to peace. I confess that since the time of the adoption of the **Luarca Declaration** in 2006, I have been sceptical about this point. Whereas I do see the individual right to seek refuge abroad in situations of armed conflict, and the right of conscientious objectors to seek asylum from persecution, and I do recognize the non-refoulement obligation of States, i.e. the prohibition to return conscientious objectors to their countries of origin, I suggest that the current text of article 12 is overbroad. While the protection from refoulement of conscientious objectors to war and military service is undoubtedly germane to the human right to peace as an individual right, I remain to be persuaded that one can claim, as part of the human right to peace, that "all individuals have the right to seek and to enjoy refugee status if there is a well-founded fear of being persecuted for reasons of race, religion, nationality, membership of a particular social group or political opinion, is outside the country of one's nationality and is unable or, owing to such fear, is unwilling to avail oneself of the protection of that country; or who, not having a nationality and being outside the country of his former habitual residence as a result of such events, is unable or, owing to such fear, unwilling to return to it." This provision would expand the scope of article 14 of the Universal Declaration of Human Rights and of the 1951 Geneva Refugee Convention beyond what States may be willing to accept. It does not seem to me that this provision is essential to the Declaration on the right to peace.

I am more persuaded by the text of article 12, paragraph 2, which stipulates that refugee status should include "the right to voluntary return to one's country or place of origin or residence in dignity and with all due guarantees, once the causes of persecution have been removed and, in case of armed conflict, it has ended." This is related to the right to one's homeland,[11] which was vindicated in numerous Security Council resolutions during the ethnic cleansing phase of the Yugoslav conflict and made justiciable through the provisions of the Dayton

Accords and implemented by the Human Rights Chamber for Bosnia and Herzegovina,[12] which helped thousands of people in their return in safety and dignity to their places of origin.

Justiciability of the constitutive elements of the right to peace

When one talks about individual rights, one expects that these rights be justiciable before domestic and international instances. It is important to note that many of the constitutive elements of the right to peace are already justiciable. Violations of the right to life also constitute a violation of article 6 of the International Covenant on Civil and Political Rights. Pursuant to the Optional Protocol to the ICCPR, the UN Human Rights Committee possesses the competence to examine complaints concerning violations of article 6 submitted by individuals. Threats to the right to peace may be dealt with under article 9 ICCPR, which stipulates the State's obligation to ensure security of the person. Freedom to engage in anti-war activities, to manifest for peace and to create pacifist organizations is protected under articles 19, 21 and 22 ICCPR. Conscientious objection to military service is a right protected under article 18 ICCPR. Moreover, conscientious objectors and other persons have the right to leave any country including their own pursuant to article 12 ICCPR. Persons who have fled armed conflict and persecution, or who have left their countries of origin because of conscientious objection have a right seek asylum; as refugees, they have a right not to be subjected to refoulement, and this to right is protected under article 7 ICCPR and article 3 of the Convention against Torture. These categories of persons also have the right to return in safety and dignity to their countries of origin pursuant to article 12 ICCPR. Propaganda for war is prohibited under article 20 ICCPR, and such violation by Governments or the private sector can be justiciable if States adopt the appropriate legislation, as they should by virtue of having ratified the ICCPR. Moreover, in case of violation of these constitutive elements of the right to peace, victims have a right to a remedy under article 2 ICCPR.

The Human Rights Council by virtue of Resolutions 18/6 and 21/9 has affirmed its commitment to achieve an international order that is more democratic and more equitable. Both resolutions refer to the human right to peace as a condition to such an international order. And yet States are still caught in the logic of force, the logic of economic and military power, as we are all in a greater or lesser degree caught in a culture of violence.

States, even democratic States, have not listened to a majority of their constituents who do believe in the UN Charter, who want negotiated settlements and who genuinely oppose war. We cannot forget that in March 2003 a number of ostensibly democratic States formed a so-called "coalition of the willing" and dragged their peoples into an illegal war in Iraq, as Kofi Annan described it in more than one occasion.[13] Each individual victim of that illegal war, whether Iraqi civilians and soldiers or NATO personnel had their right to life under article 6 ICCPR violated, and that violation entailed also the breach of the individual right to peace.

This is one more reason why civil society has taken matters into its hands and launched a peoples' movement for peace. It is the great merit of the Spanish Society for International Human Rights Law to have adopted the Luarca Declaration on the Human Right to Peace in 2006 and to have conducted a four-year world-wide consultation leading to the adoption of the Declarations of Bilbao, Barcelona and Santiago de Compostela in 2010. Without this preparatory work, the Human Rights Council would not be seized of the matter, and we would not be here today discussing the Advisory Committee's Draft Declaration.

In conclusion let us recognize that although the Western conception of human rights is oriented toward individual rights, everyone knows that individuals make a collectivity and that the collectivity in turn has the right and the responsibility to promote and protect the rights of its individual members. When the collective right to peace has been achieved, each individual can best exercise his or her rights, not against others, but in harmony with the society in which he/she lives. Yet, as stated above, the discussion over collective and individual rights is sterile. What is important is to devise the mechanisms to make all rights justiciable.

Furthermore we have come to recognize that the holistic concept of peace goes well beyond the strict absence of armed conflict. Positive peace is linked to the eradication of structural violence resulting from the economic and social inequalities in the world, a situation that must be remedied if we are to realize an equitable international order. Let us accept that peace is not a band-aid, it is not just a cease fire, it is not just stopping war—it is creating sustainable structures that will ensure peace as proposed by Immanuel Kant in his essay Perpetual Peace—*Zur ewigen Frieden*:

> *Da es nun mit der unter den Völkern der Erde einmal durchgängig überhand genommenen Gemeinschaft so weit gekommen ist, dass die Rechtsverletzung an einem Platz der Erde an allen gefühlt wird: so ist die idee eines **Weltbürgerrechts** keine phantastische und überspannte Vorstellungsart des Rechts, sondern eine notwendige Ergänzung des ungeschriebenen Kodex sowohl des Staatsand Völkerrechts zum öffentlichen Menschenrechte überhaupt, und so zun ewigen Frieden...*

This Kantian concept of the ***Weltbürgerrecht* to peace** or the right of all human beings as citizens of the world to a peaceful order is of great relevance to the work of the inter-governmental working group of the Human Rights Council. Kant's principle of an international solidarity borrows from Montesquieu's *Esprit des Lois* and the non positivistic idea that the violation of the right of one person in one particular place constitutes a threat to all of us.

While some may demur that the human right to peace is only a duplication of what already exists in the core human rights treaties, there can never be enough emphasis on human rights, and a little duplication is salutary as a form of education through repetition. Indeed, *repetitio est mater studiorum*.

DEFINING THE MANDATE OF THE UN INDEPENDENT EXPERT[1]

In my 2013 report to the General Assembly (A/68/284) I was still in the process of defining the mandate and setting priorities. I addressed a number of issues which eventually became my 25 principles of international order (chapter 2). I was concerned with developing strategies to move the human rights agenda forward through the promotion of a social and economic environment conducive to respect for human dignity, a new social contract based on peace and justice. It is patent that individuals subjected to structural violence, coercion and war cannot fully exercise their human rights. It is thus important to reaffirm the credo of the Charter of the United Nations that peace is a condition for the enjoyment of all human rights. —AdeZ

* * *

In February 2013, the Independent Expert attended the first session of the Human Rights Council's Open-ended Intergovernmental Working Group on the Draft United Nations Declaration on the Right to Peace.[14] He was invited to take the floor and agreed with some speakers that the Working Group's mandate encompasses the progressive development of international law and mechanisms of implementation, for law is a living instrument. Here lies the added value of the Declaration as dynamic development, not mere reaffirmation of norms. It is indicative of the increased role played by civil society that this standard-setting exercise was spearheaded not by Governments but by scholars,[15] in response to the worldwide aspiration of individuals and peoples to live in peace. This confirms the spirit of the Charter of the United Nations, which begins with the words "We the Peoples."

i https://undocs.org/A/68/284

At the session, some delegates expressed skepticism about the legal basis of the right to peace. Some participants, however, pointed out that the legal basis rests on the Charter's preamble and Articles 1 and 2, as well as on General Assembly resolutions, including resolution 2625 (XXV) (friendly relations) and resolution 3314 (XXIX) (definition of aggression). Legal basis is also provided by article 28 of the Universal Declaration of Human Rights, which stipulates that everyone is entitled to a social and international order in which the rights and freedoms set forth in this Declaration can be fully realized, and by the United Nations human rights treaties. Many of the elements of the right to peace have been codified as articles of the International Covenant on Civil and Political Rights, the International Covenant on Economic, Social and Cultural Rights and other United Nations treaties. While some States still harbour doubts about the justiciability of the right to peace as a norm of international law, participants indicated that constitutive elements of the right to peace already exist and that a significant body of regional and international jurisprudence has emerged.

Seen from the perspective of individual rights, the Human Rights Committee is competent to examine individual complaints[16] concerning violations of the International Covenant on Civil and Political Rights. Thus, a breach of the right to life such as extrajudicial executions and potentially also illegal wars can be considered as a breach of article 6. Bearing in mind that two general comments on article 6 and general comment No. 29 on states of emergency postulate the State obligation to disarmament, a test case in this context may be justiciable. Threats to the right to peace may potentially be examined under article 9, which imposes on the State an obligation to ensure security of the person. Freedom to engage in anti-war activities, to demonstrate for peace and to create pacifist organizations is protected under articles 19, 21 and 22. The prohibition of the recruitment of children as soldiers in armed conflicts breaches article 24 and the Optional Protocol to the Convention on the Rights of the Child on the involvement of children in armed conflict, and will be justiciable under the third protocol to the Convention when it enters into force. The right of conscientious objection to military service has been repeatedly affirmed in the general comments of the Human Rights Committee and case law as inherent to article 18, which stipulates the right to freedom of conviction and belief. Conscientious objectors and other persons have the right to leave any country, including their own, pursuant to article 12. Persons who have fled armed conflict and persecution or who have left their countries of origin because of conscientious objection have a right to seek asylum; as refugees, they have a right not to be subjected to refoulement, a right protected under article 7 of the International Covenant on Civil and Political Rights, article 3 of the Convention against Torture and the 1951 Convention relating to the Status of Refugees. They also have the right to return in safety and dignity to their countries of origin pursuant to article 12 of the International Covenant on Civil and Political Rights. Propaganda for war is specifically prohibited under article 20 of the Covenant. The liability of State officials for warmongering and State responsibility for incitement by non-state actors may be considered by the Human Rights Committee under the State reporting and the Optional Protocol procedures. In case of violation of these constitutive elements of the right to peace, victims have a right to a remedy under article 2 of the Covenant.

The human right to peace also has important economic, social and cultural components. Following the entry into force of the Optional Protocol to the International Covenant on Economic, Social and Cultural Rights on 5 May 2013, individuals can invoke violations before the Committee on Economic, Social and Cultural Rights. Thus, the right to, *inter alia,* health, a safe environment, food, water and education has acquired even more resonance in the life of each individual.

Attention must be given to the penal consequences of violations of the right to peace, including the punishment by domestic courts or in due time by the International Criminal Court of those who have engaged in aggression and propaganda for war.

Developing a culture of peace requires education for peace. Everyone—not only children—should be educated in compromise, cooperation, empathy, solidarity, compassion, restoration, mediation and reconciliation.[17] Negotiation skills must be taught so as to prevent breaches of the peace and other forms of violence as well as to ensure a peaceful continuation of life after conflict. A philosophical paradigm change is necessary to break out of the prevailing culture of violence, the logic of power, practices of economic exploitation, cultural imperialism and impunity. A road map to this culture of peace entails a strategy to identify and remove obstacles, among which are the arms race, unilateralism and the tendency to apply international law à la carte.

It is encouraging that some countries have specific provisions on peace in their Constitutions,[18] and that pertinent national case law has emerged.[19]

The human right to peace as a collective and individual right logically derives from the Charter of the United Nations and other treaties. It is strengthened by the Nuremberg and Tokyo precedents condemning crimes against peace and by the definition of aggression adopted by the Assembly of States Parties to the Rome Statute of the International Criminal Court. The Independent Expert is persuaded that recognition of peace as a human right will promote a democratic and equitable international order and that national and international democratization will reduce conflict, since peoples want peace. It is governments that stumble into war.

Threat and Use of Force

Threats of the use of force and the use of force constitute obstacles to the building of a just world order. As Benjamin Ferencz, United States Prosecutor at Nuremberg, observed in his book *Enforcing International Law: A Way to World Peace:* "As an instrumentality for the maintenance of peace and human dignity, the promise of international law exceeds its performance. Law has not yet been able to bring order to the world. All nations pay lip service to prohibiting the use of force, yet very few are prepared unconditionally to abide by their professed restraints."[20] It is a tragedy that notwithstanding the Charter of the United Nations, States have not given up predator instincts, that the danse macabre of the weapons manufacturers and traders continues, and that international law is applied à la carte. The adoption by the General Assembly of the landmark Arms Trade Treaty on 2 April 2013 is a step in the right direction.[21]

World peace is continually threatened by the paranoia of power, as internal and international conflicts plague humanity. Confronted by the danger of weapons of mass destruction, humanity must take effective measures towards disarmament. Albert Einstein warned us: "I know not with what weapons World War III will be fought, but World War IV will be fought with sticks and stones."[22]

Human Rights Council resolution 18/6 establishing the mandate of the Independent Expert lays the foundations for the enhancement of international cooperation for the promotion and protection of human rights, which should be carried out with full respect for the "non-use of force or the threat of force in international relations and non-intervention in matters that are essentially within the domestic jurisdiction of any State."

Nevertheless, wars, structural and other forms of coercion persist—expressions of injustices, which should be addressed not only by the States immediately concerned but by the international community in solidarity with each other. The root causes of armed conflict, among them the race for natural resources, economic imbalances, and ethnic and religious tensions must be resolved, respecting the obligation to settle disputes by peaceful means under Article 2 (3) of the Charter. The obligation to negotiate is *jus cogens,* "negotiation" meaning dialogue and compromise, not the dictates of the stronger over the weaker.

THE SWORD OF DAMOCLES AND NUCLEAR ANNIHILATION

In my 2014 report to the Human Rights Council I addressed the enormous threat posed by the production and stockpiling of nuclear weapons. Here an excerpt from that report. —AdeZ

* * *

Since the invention of the atomic and hydrogen bombs, mankind has possessed the capacity to annihilate itself many times over.[23] Winston Churchill was one of many alerting us to the grave dangers inherent in weapons of mass destruction, noting that "the Stone Age may return on the gleaming wings of science, and what might now shower immeasurable material blessings upon mankind may even bring about its total destruction."[24] More recently, this has been echoed by senior statesmen, including Vaclav Havel, Ricardo Lagos, Fernando Cardoso, Yasuo Fukuda, Ruud Lubbers and Helmut Schmidt, who launched the Global Zero campaign[25] to advocate total nuclear disarmament.

Eminent figures like Mikhail Gorbachev[26] have pointed out the constant danger that nuclear weapons pose for humanity and the consequent necessity to eliminate this danger, because nuclear destruction may occur not only as a result of a deliberate first strike by an aggressor but also by human, electronic or technical error. In view of numerous "close calls" since 1945, it is a miracle of Providence that a technological glitch has not ushered in the end of humanity.[27]

The General Assembly has adopted many resolutions concerning the nuclear threat, most recently resolution 68/40 in 2013, in which it urged States to take the measures necessary to prevent the proliferation of nuclear weapons in all its aspects and to promote nuclear disarmament, with the objective of eliminating nuclear weapons, requested the Secretary-General to intensify efforts and support initiatives that would contribute towards the full implementation of the seven recommendations identified in the report of the Advisory Board on Disarmament Matters that would significantly reduce the risk of nuclear war and urged States to convene an international conference, as proposed in the United Nations Millennium Declaration, to identify ways of eliminating nuclear dangers.

Disarmament is not just an idle promise; it is also a commitment under Article 26 of the Charter of the United Nations, which stipulates: "In order to promote the establishment and maintenance of international peace and security with the least diversion for armaments of the world's human and economic resources, the Security Council shall be responsible for formulating plans to be submitted to the Members of the United Nations for the establishment of a system for the regulation of armaments." The world is waiting for an effective system of disarmament that will ensure human security without warfare.

In this context it is useful to recall the Nuremberg Judgment of 1946 holding that "To initiate a war of aggression... is not only an international crime; it is the supreme international crime differing only from other war crimes in that it contains within itself the accumulated evil of the whole."[28] In the post-nuclear world, a war of aggression would not only be a crime, but quite possibly would mean the destruction of any and all international order.[29] The existence of zero nuclear weapons may sound utopian, but the effort is required in the name of humanity. We must not forget the sword of Damocles still suspended over our heads.[30]

Considering that trillions of dollars will be required to address the consequences of climate change and the achievement of the Sustainable Development Goals, the Independent Expert has encouraged States to significantly reduce military budgets and transform military economies into peacetime economies equipped to finance climate change mitigation and the improvement and expansion of social services. To this end, in his 2014 report to the Council (A/HRC/27/51), the Independent Expert proposed that States develop conversion strategies to reorient resources formerly used for military expenditure towards social services, the creation of employment in peaceful industries and greater support to the post-2015 development agenda.[31]

ANNEX I

Statement on Nuclear Disarmament and the Right to Peace before the Vienna Conference on the Humanitarian Impact of Nuclear Weapons

Vienna, 9 December 2014

As the UN Independent Expert on the promotion of a democratic and equitable international order I join the many voices in this conference in reaffirming the human right to peace and the right to total nuclear disarmament. The right to peace, by the way, is on the agenda of the Human Rights Council and an intergovernmental working group is currently negotiating a draft declaration for eventual adoption by the General Assembly. This declaration, must, of course, go beyond GA Resolution 39/11 of November 1984. It must recognize the collective and individual dimensions of the right and provide for a monitoring mechanism.

I also endorse the proposal to draft and adopt a Convention on the Prohibition of Nuclear Weapons. The process of elaborating such a treaty would heighten awareness of the Damocles Sword suspended over all our heads and constitute eloquent recognition of the crimes against humanity perpetrated on the populations of Hiroshima and Nagasaki sixty-nine years ago, acts of pure terror.[32]

In the light of yesterday's film by Peter Anthony concerning the near Apocalypse of 1983, concerning the research of Eric Schlosser, Bruce Blair and others, including Chatham House's publication, *Too Close for Comfort*, we know that the only safe policy for humanity is the zero option—i.e., total nuclear disarmament.

From the purely international law aspect, it should be remembered that article 6 of the International Covenant on Civil and Political Rights stipulates the right to life, a right from which no State can derogate. The Human Rights Committee, Secretary of which I was for several years, issued two general comments on article 6, both of which specifically contain a prohibition of the threat or use of nuclear weapons. Beyond that, it is worth recalling that international humanitarian law rests on two fundamental principles—the principle of distinction and the principle of proportionality, both of which would be violated by the use of nuclear weapons, which by their very nature are indiscriminate. Moreover, it is worth recalling that the International Court of Justice in its 1996 Advisory Opinion on the Use of Nuclear Weapons noted in paragraph 25 that the regimes of human right law and international humanitarian law apply side by side in times of armed conflict.

So, do we really need a new Convention? I say yes, because we must give a name to the animal so that we can tame it. *Nomen est omen*. Accordingly, we must raise consciousness about the ever present threat and make sure that existing stockpiles are dismantled, that nuclear tests stop, that mining for uranium ends, that depleted uranium weapons are never used. Thus, the draft proposal of the Cuban Delegation has added value. Indeed, we need an explicit and very public rejection of nuclear weapons.

In my 2014 report to the Human Rights Council I focused on the dangers to democracy posed by the military-industrial complex and by lobbyists who exert undue pressure on

Parliaments. I welcome the excellent resolution adopted by the Inter-Parliamentary Union during its 130th Assembly this spring and I encourage all Parliamentarians to promote disarmament as a necessary step toward development and an enabler of human rights.

According to SIPRI statistics, the world spent 1.75 trillion U.S. dollars in the military in 2013. According to studies conducted by the World Bank, SIPRI and UNICEF, some countries have spent 20, 30 or even 40 percent of their discretionary budgets for the military. This is an insult to the millions of children who go to bed hungry, to the millions who die for lack of health care.

There is talk about a financial crisis, but the military is flourishing and NATO is pushing for increased military expenditures. At the same time, we hear about "austerity measures" which are being taken at the expense of education, health and social services and which have significantly aggravated unemployment. A downsizing of the military and a reorientation of resources toward achieving human security and the sustainable development goals must be undertaken.

For this we need coordinated efforts such as those of the International Peace Bureau and its Global Campaign on Military Spending. We need synergies with the media so that the public is informed about the unconscionable waste of resources—particularly in further nuclear research and research into horrendous new weapons such as the killer robots or lethal autonomous weapon systems.

Ladies and gentlemen, we are not facing a financial crisis, but a moral crisis and a crisis of priorities. We urgently need a change of mind-set and the realization that "national security" does not justify the risk of destroying the planet. What we need is conflict-prevention strategies and mutual respect.

As we learned from Colonel Petrov in yesterday's documentary film, we must learn to listen to each other, to practice international solidarity on a daily basis. The American people do not want to annihilate the Russian people, the Russian people do not want to annihilate the American people. But our politicians sometimes live in their own bubble, and it is imperative to tone down the rhetoric. That is why I have recommended that a "de-escalation committee" be established in the General Assembly, a neutral forum where politicians can withdraw from unreasonable positions without losing face. We should not allow politicians to gallop away with rhetoric that violates article 20 of the International Covenant on Civil and Political Rights. We cannot allow sabre-rattling and war-mongering that may indeed lead to a dynamic of war. All human beings have the right to live in peace. And governments have the responsibility to ensure this right.

Indeed, we must learn to live together as brothers so that we are not compelled to die together as dinosaurs.

ANNEX II

Draft Declaration on the Human Right to Peace[i]

A draft declaration on the right to peace prepared by the Advisory Committee of the Human Rights Council was followed by consultations and negotiations aimed at achieving a United Nations Declaration on the right to peace. States agreed only on the common goal of promoting peace, but the end result was much less than expected. Opponents of a human right to peace argued that there was no legal basis for such a declaration, notwithstanding the clear language of the UN Charter and of numerous General Assembly resolutions.

I participated in the consultations and proposed a draft declaration (below), which was not adopted. Perhaps a subsequent session of the Human Rights Council will again address the issue and adopt a stronger declaration than the empty shell of Resolution 71/189 adopted by the General Assembly on 19 December 2016,[ii] which gives less support to the idea of a human right to peace than that already formulated in GA resolution 39/11 of 12 November 1984.[iii]

Civil society remains resolute and will again push for the adoption of a new declaration with strong operative paragraphs. But, of course, the commitment to the human right to peace necessarily goes beyond the adoption of a GA resolution. It is an ethical imperative, a daily commitment. Civil society is ready, willing and able to launch another movement to oblige States to ensure world peace for our and future generations. —AdeZ

* * *

The General Assembly

Guided by the Purposes and Principles of the United Nations Charter and by the commitment of all Member States to promote peace, human rights and development,

Recognizing that the legal basis of the human right to peace is formulated in the UN Charter, UN Security Council, General Assembly, ECOSOC and Human Rights Council Resolutions, as well as in international treaties including the International Covenant on Civil and Political Rights, the International Covenant on Economic, Social and Cultural Rights,

Acknowledging that the legal basis of the human right to peace is strengthened by other universal instruments including the Vienna Declaration and Programme of Action, the Declaration on the Right to Development and the 2030 Sustainable Development Goals,

---

i De Zayas draft, discussed but not adopted.
ii https://www.refworld.org/docid/589c72134.html
iii https://www.ohchr.org/EN/ProfessionalInterest/Pages/RightOfPeoplesToPeace.aspx

Taking note that the constitutive components of the human right to peace are already contained in the Human Rights Covenants and are justiciable under the Optional Protocol Procedures of the Human Rights Committee and of the Committee on Economic, Social and Cultural Rights, among others the rights to life, liberty and security of person, the right to freedom of expression and peaceful assembly and association, the right to food, shelter, health and education,

Endorsing the General Assembly Declaration on the Preparation of Society for Life in Peace, the Declaration on the Right of Peoples to Peace and the Declaration and Programme of Action on a Culture of Peace,

Calling for the proactive implementation of General Assembly Resolution 2625 which contains the *Declaration on Principles of International Law concerning Friendly Relations and Cooperation among States in accordance with the UN Charter,*

Emphasizing the obligation of all Member States to negotiate and settle all disputes through peaceful means (UN Charter Art. 2 (3)) and to refrain in their international relations from the threat or use of force against the territorial integrity of political independence of any State (Art. 2(4)),

Recalling the commitments to nuclear disarmament contained in article 6 of the Non Proliferation Treaty, and endorsing the work of the Conference on Disarmament in the spirit of promoting development through disarmament and reallocation of resources,

Condemning propaganda for war as stipulated in article 20(1) of the International Covenant on Civil and Political Rights,

Taking note of the work of the Human Rights Council's Advisory Committee and its Draft Declaration on the Right to Peace as well as numerous civil society initiatives including the Declaration of Santiago de Compostela of 10 December 2010,

Aware that peace is not only the absence of war, but that it means the absence of economic and structural violence and requires a positive, dynamic, participatory process where root causes of conflict are addressed in a timely fashion and conflict-preventive measures are developed and applied uniformly and without discrimination,

Recalling that the recognition of the inherent dignity and the equal and inalienable rights of all members of the human family, women, men, children and elderly persons, is the foundation of freedom, justice and peace in the world,

Reaffirming that everyone is entitled to a social and international order in which the rights and freedoms set forth in the Universal Declaration of Human Rights and in the Human Rights Covenants can be fully realized, and that the rule of law demands the uniform application of norms and rejects selectivity, privilege and discrimination,

Recalling further that the commitment of the international community to eradicate poverty and to promote sustained economic growth, sustainable development and global prosperity for all and the need to address the growing inequalities among States and within them,

Recognizing that the asymmetries of trade, new forms of economic colonialism and exploitation, sanctions regimes and other forms of structural violence impede the enjoyment of the human right to peace and other human rights,

Recalling that a culture of peace and the education of humanity for peace, justice and liberty are indispensable to the dignity of human beings and constitute a duty that all nations must fulfill in international solidarity,

Welcoming the important contribution that civil society organizations have made and can continue to make in education for peace, building and preserving peace, as well as in strengthening a culture of peace,

Acknowledging that peace and human rights have a symbiotic relationship, that peace is a condition to the enjoyment of other human rights and that where human rights are fulfilled the outcome is peace,

Inviting regional courts and tribunals to examine appropriate cases concerning the human right to peace,

Inviting all stakeholders to embrace the philosophy of peace for development and the sacred commitment to preserve future generations from the scourge of war and continued oppression by endemic economic and structural violence,

And to that end, solemnly declares:

Article 1

The human right to peace in its individual and collective dimensions enables all persons and peoples to enjoy the spectrum of human rights.

Article 2

The constitutive elements of the human right to peace are already stipulated in the UN Charter and relevant provisions of the ICCPR and ICESCR. Individuals can assert the various components of the human right to peace by invoking the Optional Protocol procedures of the UN Human Rights Committee and Committee on Economic, Social and Cultural Rights, and by petitioning the regional human rights courts.

Article 3

All States shall address root causes of conflict and develop preventive strategies to ensure that grievances are addressed in a timely fashion and do not lead to violence.

Article 4

All States have an obligation to negotiate in good faith and settle disputes by non-violent means, shall refrain from the threat or use of force, from the imposition of unilateral sanctions, and shall suppress propaganda for war.

Article 5

All States have an obligation to gradually disarm and to eliminate stockpiles of weapons of mass destruction including nuclear weapons, chemical and biological weapons. Resources released through disarmament shall be devoted to the promotion and fulfillment of human rights treaty obligations.

Article 6

States, the United Nations and its specialized agencies shall take appropriate sustainable measures to implement the present Declaration. International, regional, national and local organizations and civil society should actively participate in the implementation of the Declaration.

Article 7

The Human Rights Council shall monitor progress in the implementation of this declaration as a permanent item in its agenda and as part of the UPR procedure.

Notes

1 William Schabas, "The Human Right to Peace," in Asbjorn Eide, J. Möller, I. Zeimele, *Making Peoples Heard* (Leiden: Martinus Nijhoff, 2011), pp. 43–58; A. de Zayas, "Peace as a Human Right" in Eide, op. cit., pp. 27-42; Theo van Boven, "The Right to Peace as an emerging Solidarity Right," in Eva Rieter and Henri de Waele, *Evolving Principles of International Law* (Leiden: Martinus Nijhoff, 2012), pp. 137–148.

2 UN General Assembly Resolution 60/1, para. 1 (16 September 2005).

3 Quoted in my report to the General Assembly A/67/277. See also http://www.globalresearch.ca/the-responsibility-to-protect/14537

4 https://www.un.org/securitycouncil/s/res/1973-%282011%29

5 In 1999 NATO countries invoked the earlier "humanitarian intervention" language to justify their illegal bombardment of Yugoslavia. See William Blum, *America's Deadliest Export: Democracy The Truth About US Foreign Policy and Everything Else* (Zed Books, 2013), p. 156. Russia brought the issue to the UN Security Council and tabled a resolution which, *inter alia*, would have affirmed "that such unilateral use of force constitutes a flagrant violation of the United Nations Charter." China, Namibia and Russia voted for the resolution, the United States, France and United Kingdom against, and the resolution failed to pass. Noam Chomsky quoted from the foreword to John Norris' 2005 book, *Collision Course: NATO, Russia, and Kosovo,* in which Strobe Talbott, then Deputy Secretary of State under President Clinton and the leading U.S. negotiator during the war, had written that "It was Yugoslavia's resistance to the broader trends of political and economic reform—not the plight of Kosovar Albanians—that best explains NATO's war."

6 Andreas Bummel, *Developing International Democracy for a Parliamentary Assembly at the United Nations* (Berlin 2010); *The Composition of a Parliamentary Assembly at the United Nations* (Berlin, 2010). See also http://www.bummel.org/texte/2012vnforum.pdf, and: http://www.opendemocracy.net/andreas-bummel/why-we-need-un-parliament

7 Statement before the General Assembly on 2 November 2012 http://www.ohchr.org/en/NewsEvents/Pages/DisplayNews.aspx?NewsID=12732&LangID=E
See also Press release concerning the Arms Trade Treaty
http://www.ohchr.org/en/NewsEvents/Pages/DisplayNews.aspx?NewsID=12397&LangID=E

8 Human Rights Committee, 2006 Report, particularly the concurring opinion of Committee member Hipólito Solari Yrigoyen. See also Human Rights Committee, General Comment No. 22, para. 11, and Jakob Möller/Alfred de Zayas, *United Nations Human Rights Committee Case Law* (Kehl, Strasbourg: N.P. Engel, 2009), pp. 349–353 and 536.

9 Jakob Möller, op. cit., chapter 5.

10 http://www.ohchr.org/Documents/HRBodies/HRCouncil/RegularSession/Session21/A-HRC-21-46_en.pdf

11 Alfred de Zayas, "The Right to One's Homeland, Ethnic Cleansing and the International Criminal Tribunal for the Former Yugoslavia," in *Criminal Law Forum*, Vol. 6 (1995), pp. 257–314. http://link.springer.com/article/10.1007%2FBF01097769?LI=true

12 Manfried Nowak, *Human Rights Chamber for Bosnia and Herzegovina, Digest of Decisions on Admissibility and Merits 1996-2002* (Kehl, Strasbourg: N.P. Engel Publisher, 2003). See also final report of the Rapporteur of the Sub-Commission on the Human Rights Dimensions of Population Transfers, E/CN.4/Sub.2/1997/23.

13 http://news.bbc.co.uk/2/hi/3661134.stm

14 See http://www.ohchr.org/EN/HRBodies/HRC/RightPeace/Pages/WGDraftUNDeclarationontheRighttoPeace.aspx.

15 See Carlos Villán Duran, International Observatory on the Human Right to Peace, *El derecho humano a la Paz: de la teoría a la práctica* (Oviedo, CIDEAL Foundation for Cooperation and Research, 2013). See http://www.aedidh.org.

16 See Jakob Möller and Alfred de Zayas, *United Nations Human Rights Committee Case Law, 1977-2008: A Handbook* (Kehl, Strasbourg: N.P. Engel Publisher, 2009).

17 In 1997, Costa Rica adopted the Law on the Alternative Resolution of Conflicts and Promotion of Social Peace, requiring peace education in every school and establishing the legal basis for alternative methods of conflict resolution.

18 Article 9 of the Constitution of Japan stipulates: "Aspiring sincerely to an international peace based on justice and order, the Japanese people forever renounce war as a sovereign right of the nation and the threat or use of force as means of settling international disputes."

Article 12 of the Costa Rican Constitution stipulates: "The Army as a permanent institution is abolished."

19 Costa Rican lawyer Luis Roberto Zamora filed a suit against the participation of Costa Rica in the "Coalition of the Willing." In 2004 the Supreme Court of Costa Rica held it to be against the Constitution, Costa Rica's neutrality declaration, international law and the United Nations system. See judgement No. 9992-04. See also Kofi Annan's interview on the illegality of the Iraq war, available from http://www.un.org/apps/news/story.asp?NewsID=11953&.

20 See http://www.benferencz.org/books/FerenczNewLegalFoundationsforGlobalSurvival.pdf.

21 See http://www.un.org/disarmament/ATT/.

22 See Alice Calaprice, *The New Quotable Einstein* (Princeton University Press, 2005), p. 173.

23 See www.nuclearsecurityproject.org/publications/next-steps-in-reducing-nuclear-risks-the-pace-of-nonproliferation-work-today-doesnt-match-the-urgency-of-the-threat.

24 See *The Sinews of Peace,* Fulton, Missouri, 5 March 1946, available from www.historyguide.org/europe/churchill.html.

25 See www.globalzero.org/ and www.globalzero.org/get-the-facts/cost-of-nukes.

26 Mikhail Gorbachev, "Resetting the Nuclear Disarmament Agenda," Geneva lecture, 5 October 2009, available from www.unitar.org/gls/third-edition. See also www.themoscowtimes.com/news/article/qa-25-years-on-gorbachev-recalls-nuclear-milestone/472644.html; and www.youtube.com/watch?v=9-Lk9m-Wqy0.

27 See Chatham House, *Too Close for Comfort: Cases of Near Nuclear Use and Options for Policy* (London, 2014), available from www.chathamhouse.org/publications/papers/view/199200. See also http://nsarchive.wordpress.com/2013/10/09/document-friday-narrative-summaries-of-accidents-involving-nuclear-weapons/;

www.theguardian.com/world/interactive/2013/sep/20/goldsboro-revisited-declassified-document; www.newyorker.com/arts/critics/books/2013/09/30/130930crbo_books_menand?currentPage=all; and Eric Schlosser, *Command and Control: Nuclear Weapons, the Damascus Accident, and the Illusion of Safety* (London: Penguin Press HC, 2013).

28 See www.roberthjackson.org/the-man/speeches-articles/speeches/speeches-related-to-robert-h-jackson/the-crime-of-waging-aggressive-war/.

29 A first strike would certainly be incompatible with the Advisory Opinion of the International Court of Justice on the Legality of the Threat or Use of Nuclear Weapons. See www.icj-cij.org/docket/files/95/7495.pdf. See also the United States deterrence fact sheet, available from www.whitehouse.gov/the-press-office/2013/06/19/fact-sheet-nuclear-weapons-employment-strategy-united-states; Francis Boyle, *The Criminality of Nuclear Deterrence* (Atlanta, Georgia, Clarity Press, 2002): see www.claritypress.com/files/BoyleI.html; and www.nytimes.com/2014/06/14/upshot/the-lack-of-major-wars-may-be-hurting-economic-growth.html?_r=1.

30 Cicero, *Tusculan Disputations*.

31 This concluding paragraph, returning to my central leitmotif, the *jus cogens* prohibition of the use of force and the necessity of codifying Peace as a human right, was submitted in my 2018 concluding report to the Human Rights Council, see https://undocs.org/A/HRC/37/63, para. 17.

32 The UN Treaty on the Prohibition of Nuclear Weapons entered into force on 22 January 2021. https://www.un.org/disarmament/wmd/nuclear/tpnw/

Chapter 4
MILITARY EXPENDITURES AND HUMAN RIGHTS

"The world is over-armed and development is underfunded."
SECRETARY GENERAL BAN KI-MOON

I wish to pay homage to the work done by the International Peace Bureau and in particular by its Secretary-General, Mr. Colin Archer, from whom I learned a great deal while preparing my 2014 report to the Human Rights Council, and who contributed significantly to the expert consultation I held in Brussels in May 2014.[i]

Human Rights Council resolution 25/15[ii] *reaffirms that a democratic and equitable international order requires the realization of the right of all peoples to peace and to this end urges all States to "do their utmost to achieve general and complete disarmament under effective international control, as well as to ensure that the resources released by effective disarmament measures are used for comprehensive development, in particular that of the developing countries."*

Disarmament for development constitutes a win-win proposition for both States and Peoples and a contribution to the implementation of Article 26 of the UN Charter which stipulates that "in order to promote the establishment and maintenance of international peace and security with the least diversion for armaments of the world's human and economic resources, the Security Council shall be responsible for formulating ... plans ... for the establishment of a system for the regulation of armaments." This is a noble task not only for the Security Council, but for the entire United Nations system including the Human Rights Council.

When we assert that disarmament is necessary for development, we mean that military expenditures must be reduced and that a strategy must be devised to gradually convert military-first economies into peaceful economies and thereby promote job creation. In light of the Covid-19 pandemic, global warming, increased frequency of natural disasters, and the many financial crises and growing

---

i https://www.ipb.org/yesterdays-news/sean-macbride-peace-prize-2016-to-be-awarded-to-secretary-general-colin-archer/attachment/colin-archer/
https://www.ohchr.org/EN/NewsEvents/Pages/DisplayNews.aspx?NewsID=14607
https://www.ohchr.org/EN/NewsEvents/Pages/DisplayNews.aspx?NewsID=14504
https://www.ohchr.org/EN/NewsEvents/Pages/DisplayNews.aspx?NewsID=15007
ii See also https://www.ohchr.org/en/NewsEvents/Pages/DisplayNews.aspx?NewsID=15111&LangID=E

budgetary deficits in most countries, we hear a call for "austerity" measures. But where should spending be decreased so as to reduce government deficits without violating the obligations of States under the Human Rights Covenants, notably their commitments to strengthen the rule of law, the administration of justice, the right to work, to education, health care and retirement benefits?

My 2014 report to the Human Rights Council surveys the level of military spending by States which, according to the Stockholm International Peace Research Institute, reached 1.75 trillion U.S. dollars in 2013, and according to the World Bank tables, consumed 20, 30 or even 40% of the national budgets of some countries. NATO Secretary-General Jens Stoltenberg does not cease to berate NATO members to increase their "defence" expenditures.[i] Meanwhile the real figures for the U.S. military budget exceeds one trillion dollars[ii] and corresponds to over 40% of the budget, according to some estimates 53%.[iii] It is here that spending cuts must be made. Yet, we see States cutting social services, reducing the number of teachers, civil servants and poverty-reduction programmes.

The "elephant in the room," about which the media consistently underreports, is the role of the military-industrial complex in all of its internal and international ramifications, including inciting "regime change" abroad and fueling armed conflict so as to sell even more weapons. We must come to grips with States' continued production and stockpiling of nuclear and other weapons of mass destruction, which constitute a sword of Damocles suspended over our heads. We must challenge the democratic legitimacy and the ethical justification of expenditures devoted to research into the development of new and frightful lethal autonomous weapon systems, killer robots, radiological weapons, unmanned combat aerial weapons, cluster munitions, as well as biological and chemical warfare.

Instead of focusing on real or imagined "national security" threats, States should endeavour to guarantee human security, a concept already found in Franklin Roosevelt's "Four Freedoms,"[iv] notably in the concepts of "freedom from fear" and "freedom from want." The 1994 UNDP Human Development Report defined human security as "[t]he security of people through development,

---

i Mr. Stoltenberg announced that in 2019 defence spending across European Allies and Canada increased in real terms by 4.6 %, making this the fifth consecutive year of growth. He also revealed that by the end of 2020, those Allies will have invested $130 billion more since 2016. Based on the latest estimates, the accumulated increase in defence spending by the end of 2024 will be $400 billion. Mr. Stoltenberg said: "This is unprecedented progress and it is making NATO stronger." https://www.nato.int/cps/en/natohq/news_171458.htm

ii https://www.nato.int/cps/en/natohq/news_171458.htm
https://www.pogo.org/analysis/2019/05/making-sense-of-the-1-25-trillion-national-security-state-budget/

iii https://www.nationalpriorities.org/analysis/2020/militarized-budget-2020/
https://www.thebalance.com/current-us-discretionary-federal-budget-and-spending-3306308

iv http://www.fdrlibrary.marist.edu/fourfreedoms

not arms; through cooperation, not confrontation; through peace not war." Expenditures for military nuclear research, production and stockpiling of nuclear weapons and weapons of mass destruction are staggering.

Since the invention of the atomic and hydrogen bombs, mankind has possessed the capacity to annihilate itself. Eminent figures like Mikhail Gorbachev[i] have pointed at the constant danger that nuclear weapons pose for humanity and the urgency to eliminate this danger, because nuclear destruction can occur not only as a result of a deliberate first strike by an aggressor but also by human, electronic or technical error. In view of numerous "close calls" since 1945, it is fortunate that a technology glitch has not already ushered in the end of humanity. The 2014 film documentary "The Man who saved the World," starring Kevin Costner, tells the story of Stanislav Petrov, a lieutenant colonel of the Soviet Air Defense Forces who could have unleashed World War III if he had believed what his computers mistakenly told him—that the U.S. had launched five intercontinental ballistic missiles against Russia.[ii]

In 1984 the Human Rights Committee adopted its General Comment Nr. 14 on article 6 of the International Covenant on Civil and Political Rights, the right to life,[iii] which reads in pertinent part:

> While remaining deeply concerned by the toll of human life taken by conventional weapons in armed conflicts, the Committee has noted that, during successive sessions of the General Assembly, representatives from all geographical regions have expressed their growing concern at the development and proliferation of increasingly awesome weapons of mass destruction, which not only threaten human life but also absorb resources that could otherwise be used for vital economic and social purposes, particularly for the benefit of developing countries, and thereby for promoting and securing the enjoyment of human rights for all.
>
> The Committee associates itself with this concern. It is evident that the designing, testing, manufacture, possession and deployment of nuclear weapons are among the greatest threats to the right to life which confront mankind today. This threat is compounded by the danger that the actual use of such weapons may be brought about,

---

i Mikhail Gorbachev "Resetting the Nuclear Disarmament Agenda," Geneva lecture 5 October 2009 http://www.unitar.org/gls/third-edition
http://www.themoscowtimes.com/news/article/qa-25-years-on-gorbachev-recalls-nuclear-milestone/472644.html
http://www.youtube.com/watch?v=9-Lk9m-Wqy0

ii https://www.bbc.com/news/world-europe-24280831; http://themanwhosavedtheworldmovie.com/#stanislav-petrov

iii https://www.refworld.org/docid/453883f911.html

not only in the event of war, but even through human or mechanical error or failure.

Furthermore, the very existence and gravity of this threat generates a climate of suspicion and fear between States, which is in itself antagonistic to the promotion of universal respect for and observance of human rights and fundamental freedoms in accordance with the Charter of the United Nations and the International Covenants on Human Rights.

The production, testing, possession, deployment and use of nuclear weapons should be prohibited and recognized as crimes against humanity. The Committee accordingly, in the interest of mankind, calls upon all States, whether Parties to the Covenant or not, to take urgent steps, unilaterally and by agreement, to rid the world of this menace.

With this in mind, senior statesmen launched the Global Zero[i] campaign advocating total nuclear disarmament. Many countries do want total nuclear disarmament, but the nine nuclear-weapon States do not and none of them ratified the UN Convention on the Prohibition of Nuclear Weapons, which entered into force on 22 January 2021.[ii] As of April 2021 only 54 States had adhered to the treaty.[iii]

Local military-employment concerns and a worrisome level of disinformation also hinder efforts to downsize the military. A frequently heard argument is that the military creates jobs. On the other hand, civilian investment actually generates more jobs than military investment.

On 29 January 2014 the Comunidad de Estados Latinoamericanos y Caribeños (CELAC)[iv] adopted a historic Declaration proclaiming the entire region a "zone of peace." This Declaration recalls the Treaty of Tlatelolco, which established a nuclear-free zone in Latin America and the Caribbean, 45 years ago. The establishment of zones of peace and cooperation in an increasing number of regions of the world is to be welcomed, as it carries the commitment of the governments towards a significant decrease in military budgets and spending.

In the spring of 2014 the International Peace Bureau in Geneva convened a panel attended among others by the Acting Secretary-General of the UN Disarmament Conference, a representative of the Stockholm International Peace

---

i https://www.globalzero.org/
ii https://www.un.org/disarmament/wmd/nuclear/tpnw/
iii https://cnduk.org/list-of-countries-that-have-signed-un-global-nuclear-weapons-ban-treaty/
iv https://caricom.org/institutions/the-community-of-latin-american-and-caribbean-states-celac/
https://www.nti.org/learn/treaties-and-regimes/community-latin-american-and-caribbean-states-celac/
http://celacinternational.org/celac-4/

Research Institute (SIPRI),[i] *and myself. There was consensus that budgetary decision-making should be open, with the reasons for spending clearly outlined so as to be understood by the electorate. Parliaments should monitor accountability in the budget decision process, with procurements controlled by rigorous procedures and subject to civilian control. Auditing of military spending should be regularly carried out, with improper practices investigated and prosecuted.*

The Universal Periodic Review procedure of the Human Rights Council provides an ideal opportunity to test the human rights commitments of States as reflected and implemented in their budgetary priorities. If a State is committed to the larger concept of human security, it will allocate the budget accordingly. Thus, a systematic examination of the level of military expenditures by States and a comparison with national expenditures in the social sector is necessary.

What follows are excerpts from the 2014 report to the Human Rights Council.[ii] —AdeZ

* * *

MILITARY BUDGETS vs. HUMAN SECURITY BUDGETS

"The global arms trade, and its accompanying glut of military spending, continues to represent the single most significant perversion of worldwide priorities known today. It buttresses wars, criminal activity and ethnic violence; destabilises emerging democracies; inflates military budgets to the detriment of health care, education and basic infrastructure; and exaggerates global relationships of inequality and underdevelopment. Without massive and coordinated action, militarism will continue to be a scourge on our hopes for a more peaceful and just 21st century."

—Oscar Arias, former President of Costa Rica and Nobel Peace Laureate[1]

INTRODUCTION

The present progress report should be read in conjunction with the Independent Expert's previous reports to the Human Rights Council and the General Assembly, which are cumulatively aimed at addressing the vast scope of Council resolutions 18/6, 21/9 and 25/15, taking due account of observations and proposals made by States, intergovernmental and non-governmental organizations, communications

---

i See Sipri's database on military expenditures, https://www.sipri.org/databases/milex
https://reliefweb.int/report/world/sipri-fact-sheet-april-2020-trends-world-military-expenditure-2019
ii https://undocs.org/A/HRC/27/51

addressed to the mandate holder, answers to a questionnaire and interactive dialogues. Inspired by the conviction that peace is an indispensable condition for achieving a democratic and equitable international order, the present preliminary report on disarmament for development corroborates the idea that disarmament must be a priority concern of the international community. Such disarmament must include cessation of the production and stockpiling of weapons, particularly weapons of mass destruction, accompanied by a significant reduction in the arms trade. Downsizing military budgets will enable sustainable development, the eradication of extreme poverty, the tackling of global challenges including pandemics and climate change, educating and socializing youth towards peace, cooperation and international solidarity. A concerted effort at the conversion of military-first economies into human security economies will also generate employment and stability.[2]

In this report the Independent Expert explores the adverse impacts of military expenditures on the enjoyment of human rights, and the possibilities of reducing military budgets and redirecting resources to the post-2015 development agenda. He is convinced that a democratic international order presupposes a commitment to a democratic domestic order, and that an international equitable order can best be achieved when the right to development is promoted. Such a world order cannot be achieved unless domestic and international priorities are changed. One way to change those priorities is to make economic and social rights enforceable in the courts of all countries, and to make decisions regarding those rights reviewable by regional courts as well as, perhaps, an international court of human rights. Budget and fiscal transparency are necessary tools to prevent the hijacking of the international order by the international military-industrial complex,[3] which seeks endless profits through the production and sale of weapons and thereby fuels conflict worldwide, hindering negotiation and peaceful solution of disputes.[4] However, transparency is not enough. Balanced spending for economic and social rights will only be achieved through the rule of law.

The United Nations has adopted countless resolutions reflecting that understanding shared by think tanks and civil society alike. Nevertheless, in spite of accurate diagnoses, there has been little progress in redirecting military expenditures toward peaceful industries. Indeed, one of the challenges faced by the present mandate is precisely how to transform the "ethically obvious" into the politically feasible. The present report on the links between disarmament and development and on the urgent need to reduce military expenditures worldwide can be seen as a preliminary report only, since the problem is endemic and strategies to solve it have hitherto failed. The Independent Expert intends to continue examining this vast issue as a component of the overall strategy to overcome obstacles to the establishment of a just international order.

Other crucial elements of all the Independent Expert's reports to date include a pertinent discussion of democracy and self-determination, which are closely related, both having individual and collective dimensions, as well as national and international implications. The ideal of direct democracy, including the power of legislative initiative of citizens and control of issues through genuine consultation and referenda has been partially achieved only in a few countries. The prevalent model of representative democracy is not perfect and needs improvement. Representative democracy deserves the predicate "democratic" only if and when parliamentarians genuinely represent their constituents. Elected members of parliament hold the trust of the electorate and must proactively inform the latter of relevant developments that impact on decision-making, including on the allocation of national budgets for the military, education and health care. They must be committed to inquiring into what the voters need and want. In other words, representatives are accountable to the citizens, must act transparently and regularly consult with their constituency, since they are not plenipotentiaries, but represent the people with a mandate limited in time and scope, which must be administered in good faith and not in usurpation of power.

Human security

Democracy and self-determination serve the overall goal of enabling human security and human rights. The concept of "human security" is not new. It is to be found, for example, in Franklin Roosevelt's "Four Freedoms," notably in the concepts of "freedom from fear" and "freedom from want."[5] The United Nations Development Programme Human Development Report (1994) defined human security as "the security of people through development, not arms; through cooperation, not confrontation; through peace not war."[6] It encompasses: "first, safety from such chronic threats as hunger, disease and repression. And second ...protection from sudden and hurtful disruptions in the patterns of daily life— whether in homes, in jobs or in communities. Such threats can exist at all levels of national income and development."[7] A major shift in priorities is necessary, because human security cannot be achieved for as long as governments, corporations, banks and universities continue to invest trillions in the technology of war rather than in the promotion and protection of human rights.[8] As the former Director-General of the United Nations Educational, Scientific and Cultural Organization (UNESCO), Federico Mayor, wrote in 1998, "Concepts of security must change. Until now we thought that investment in arms was the key to security. Now we know that our real enemies are poverty, ignorance, the destruction of the environment."[9]

One of the problems with addressing military spending is the lack of an all-encompassing definition. That absence allows governments to dissimulate certain expenditures by attributing them to budgets not immediately identified as military-related. Frequently, military expenditures are "secret" or concealed, thus frustrating the right of citizens to know how their taxes are being spent. Military expenditures may be allocated, not only to the Army, Navy and Air Force, but sometimes also to a department of energy,[10] to "research and development,"[11] "national security," "intelligence," "foreign relations," etc. A definition of military expenditures must include not only procurement of weapons of all kinds, nuclear arms, conventional arms, tanks, aeroplanes, submarines and drones, but also expenditures for military exercises, bases, weapons research, testing, environmental damage, removal of land mines and explosives, personnel costs, demobilization, rehabilitation, health care of veterans, national surveillance, global espionage, and—not to be forgotten—the interest paid on debts from ongoing and past wars.[12]

Military expenditures are staggering[13] and there is scant hope that disarmament negotiations will result in a significant reduction of military budgets and stop the trend to militarization in the foreseeable future. The Stockholm International Peace Research Institute (SIPRI) estimates that, in the year 2013, approximately 1,747 billion dollars were spent worldwide for the military.[14] The biggest spender devoted as much as 40 per cent of tax revenues to the military.[15] The Independent Expert joins the United Nations Secretary-General in deploring this situation; "the world is over-armed and development is underfunded."[16]

The Kennedy School of Government at Harvard University published a study on the cost of the Iraq and Afghanistan wars, estimating it at somewhere between four and six trillion United States dollars.[17] This study focused on the cost to the United States taxpayer, not to other members of the North Atlantic Treaty Organization (NATO), the "coalition of the willing," or to the populations of Iraq, Afghanistan and Pakistan. Much good could have been accomplished if a fraction of those military expenditures had been devoted to the promotion of the Millennium Development Goals.

The links between militarism and development as well as the connection between war and the environment must be taken into account. The environment requires protection from the testing of new weapons, their use in war and their continuing polluting effects, which cause long-term environmental and economic damage that should be factored in when the costs of militarism are computed. It is useful to recall principle 24 of the Rio Declaration of 1992: "warfare is inherently destructive of sustainable development. States shall therefore respect international law by providing protection for the environment in times of armed conflict and cooperate in its further development, as necessary."[18]

Many international statesmen have already pondered the issue of budgetary priorities. More than 60 years ago, the President of the United States of America, Dwight Eisenhower eloquently addressed the predicament: "Every gun that is made, every warship launched, every rocket fired signifies, in the final sense, a theft from those who hunger and are not fed, those who are cold and not clothed. This world in arms is not spending money alone. It is spending the sweat of its labourers, the genius of its scientists, the hopes of its children."[19] Expenditures for military nuclear research and the production and stockpiling of nuclear weapons and weapons of mass destruction have been astronomical, exceeding US$100 billion per year.[20]

Obstacles

In previous reports, the Independent Expert has identified multiple obstacles to the realization of a democratic and equitable international order. In the present report, he turns to the issue of spending imbalances prevalent in many countries, which privilege the military sector at the expense of peoples' basic needs.

Military spending is driven by a range of factors, including threat perceptions, which may be real or imagined, and which are exacerbated by warmongering and propaganda. During the Cold War the superpowers justified almost any level of spending by the "missile gap" numbers game. Today a new all-purpose enemy has been identified: national and international terrorism. This adversary gives military alliances and defence contractors a new lease on life. Yet, it would seem obvious to everyone, not only economists, that the law of diminishing returns applies, and that there is a level beyond which further militarization is futile. Focusing on the root causes of human insecurity is more important than trying to apply stopgap solutions here and there.[21]

Notwithstanding the *jus cogens* obligation to settle disputes by peaceful means as stipulated in Article 2, paragraph 3, of the Charter of the United Nations, the demonization of adversaries and sabre-rattling is practised by media and politicians alike, resulting in an atmosphere hardly conducive to fruitful negotiation. In fact, the prevalent culture of fear and paranoia adds oil to the fires of distrust and hostility among peoples and artificially creates a perceived need to buttress "security" by increasing military expenditures. This in turn provokes the designated "enemy" to reciprocate in kind, unleashing a spiral of armament and rearmament. The media could play a calming role in this cycle by encouraging solutions consistent with the Charter[22] and with article 20 of the

International Covenant on Civil and Political Rights, which specifically prohibits war propaganda, but the opposite is frequently the case. This culture of hostility appears to be nurtured by the military-industrial complex, which has an interest in greater profits through the production and use of weapons. It is not surprising that the value of the international arms trade reached $385 billion dollars in 2012.[23]

In recent years, international tensions were stirred up in a manner that gives reason to fear that some governments might manoeuvre themselves into positions that would not allow them to retreat without losing face. There is a dynamic to this kind of media- and government-sponsored "hype" regarding the use of force, whereby a supposed adversary is demonized in such a manner that it feels threatened and reacts nervously, thus giving ex post facto "justification" to those who claim that the adversary must be put down by force, and pulling the rug from under the feet of those who propose diplomatic solutions. As the Independent Expert illustrated in previous reports, the corporate media too often stand to gain from wars and emotive clickbait, which may explain the level of disinformation and profit-oriented propaganda disseminated. There is a need for a de-escalation committee with consultative competences in this regard.

Demonization of, and threatening gestures against, targeted States that are party to the Treaty on the Non-Proliferation of Nuclear Weapons (the Non-Proliferation Treaty) may induce them to withdraw from this treaty under its article 10.[24] That is exactly what the international community should avoid. In that context it would be more important to engage in serious disarmament as envisaged in article 6 of the Treaty. It is clear that if a State party to the Treaty genuinely feels threatened, it may want to join the club of nuclear weapon Powers—not as an aggressive measure, but in exercise of the fundamental right of self-preservation, in response to a legitimate concern over threats that contravene Article 2, paragraph 4, of the Charter of the United Nations.

In the light of continued warmongering by some States, it is apparent that resolutions of the General Assembly, including its resolution 68/28, have not succeeded in reducing tensions.[25]

The spiral of world military expenditures goes hand-in-hand with a false culture of "patriotism," "heroism" and chauvinism, which frequently equates love of country with promoting a large military force, while defaming sceptics and "pacifists" as unpatriotic or even as traitors. In many countries, the idea of being a good citizen is associated with military virtues and traditions, invoking a sense of awe towards the armed forces. Even in the twenty-first century young people in some countries are educated to believe that honour and glory are won on the battlefield, that "it is sweet and proper to die for one's country."[26] It would be preferable to teach that honour and glory can also be won through civil courage and working for social justice.

That militaristic trend is also facilitated by the lack of transparency in budgetary matters. Indeed, military expenditures are frequently treated as a matter of "national security" and shrouded in secrecy. A truly democratic country must proactively inform the public so that the public can decide on spending priorities.[27]

Following the end of the Cold War and the dissolution of the Soviet Union, the international community had a legitimate expectation that the world could be reoriented towards cooperation and solidarity and that the purposes and principles of the Charter of the United Nations would be vindicated. Billions of human beings were relieved to move away from needless distrust and confrontation. When, in 1991, the Warsaw Pact was dismantled, many considered that NATO had lost its raison d'être as a bastion against expansionist communism and that the expensive military alliance would be dissolved. Instead, NATO expanded eastward, and military expenditures continued. The hope of many that finally there would be long-term disarmament for sustainable development was dashed.

It is not unusual for regional military alliances to pressure their members to increase military expenditures,[28] even at the expense of education and social services. Would it not be better to leave peacemaking and peacekeeping in the hands of the United Nations as envisaged in its Charter? According to a 2014 report, the European Union is spending at least 315 million euros on drone-related projects.[29] Yet the use of armed drones against civilian targets having been found to be contrary to international humanitarian law, the research funds could certainly have been better spent elsewhere.[30] Drones are no substitute for foreign policy. On 25 February 2014, the European Parliament adopted a resolution condemning the use of drones.[31]

Those States that undergo domestic unrest frequently fail to extend the degree of protection which the population deserves. According to the doctrine of non-intervention, foreign interference in the domestic affairs of other States and the sale of weapons to the incumbent government or to insurgent groups are no solution. What is necessary is international solidarity in helping a State's authorities to better protect the human rights of its population. There is a distinct danger of politically-motivated recourse to the right to protect (R2P) doctrine (formerly the "humanitarian intervention" doctrine),[32] which would actually erode Article 2, paragraph 4 of the Charter of the United Nations and ultimately be counterproductive.

There are other obstacles to a democratic and equitable international order which cannot be examined in the present report, for instance the complications caused by the diversion of weapons to unauthorized groups or individuals.³³ While military expenditures for the procurement of nuclear weapons are not justified, expenditures for conventional weapons are also fraught with problems, including diversion, corruption, bribery, theft, etc. Organizations such as the Small Arms Survey serve an important function by monitoring small arms stockpiles held by States throughout the world, ferreting out corruption. The Government Defence Anti-Corruption Index published by Transparency International makes useful proposals on how to address corruption.³⁴

Another growing problem is the penetration of the military into universities and laboratories, creating a dangerous level of dependence, so that institutions of higher learning become reliant on government subsidies and research priorities are driven not by what science needs or what a population wants, but by what the military-industrial complex is willing to finance.³⁵ A regrettable misuse of brainpower contributes to the technological development of weapons of mass destruction and other weaponry. The military research sector has emerged as a powerful lobbyist for armaments budgets. Other competitors for research and development funds are at a disadvantage.

Local military-employment concerns and a worrisome level of disinformation also hinder efforts to downsize the military. A frequently heard argument, though fundamentally flawed, is that the military creates jobs. The truth is that civilian investment generates more jobs than military investment.³⁶

GOOD PRACTICES AND POSITIVE DEVELOPMENTS

The United Nations annual Reports on Military Spending, compiled from information submitted by States, are potentially a vital confidence-building tool for facilitating disarmament negotiations. Unfortunately, fewer than half of the States report in any one year. Here too, transparency is conducive to mutual reductions.³⁷ In view of this situation, the General Assembly, in its resolution 68/23, requested the Secretary-General "to establish a group of governmental experts, on the basis of equitable geographical representation, to review the operation and further development of the United Nations Report on Military Expenditures, including the establishment of a process for periodic reviews in order to ensure the continued relevance and operation of the Report, commencing in 2016, taking into account the views expressed by Member States on the subject and the reports of the Secretary-General on objective information on military matters, including transparency of military expenditures, and to transmit the report of the group of experts to the General Assembly for consideration at its seventy-second session.

United Nations Conference on Disarmament

The United Nations Conference on Disarmament, established in 1979 in Geneva, is the single multilateral disarmament negotiating forum for the entire world, and hence has a vital mandate which must translate into coordinated action worldwide.[38] Its mandate includes practically all multilateral arms control and disarmament issues, focusing on the need to stop the nuclear arms race and agree on the modalities of nuclear disarmament, the prevention of nuclear war, the prevention of an arms race in outer space, effective international arrangements to assure non-nuclear-weapon States against the use or threat of use of nuclear weapons, new types of weapons of mass destruction and new systems including radiological weapons. In general terms it promotes a comprehensive programme of disarmament and transparency in armaments. However, since 1996 the Conference has failed to agree on any programme of work. It is encouraging, however, that other initiatives are emerging. Michael Møller, the Acting Secretary-General of the Conference on Disarmament, made reference to the Second Conference on the Humanitarian Impact of Nuclear Weapons, held in Nayarit, Mexico, in March 2014,[39] which built on the 2013 Oslo Conference[40] and heightened the awareness of the catastrophic toll that any use, deliberate or accidental, of a nuclear bomb would have on every aspect of human life: "for humanity, real security and freedom from fear will never come about as long as nuclear weapons exist."[41]

Delegations at the Conference on Disarmament, held in Geneva in May 2014, again endorsed the commitments made in New York on 24 September 2010 at the high-level meeting on revitalizing the work of the Conference on Disarmament,[42] recalling the standard-setting of prior decades, including the Biological and Chemical Weapons Conventions, the Comprehensive Nuclear Test-Ban Treaty, and the Non-Proliferation Treaty.

General Assembly Resolutions and Secretary-General Pronouncements

The General Assembly adopts every year a resolution on disarmament and development with a focus on military spending. In resolution 68/37, it urged the international community to devote part of the resources made available by the implementation of disarmament and arms limitation agreements to economic and social development, with a view to reducing the ever-widening gap between developed and developing countries. The Assembly further expressed concern about nuclear weapons and the need to take measures to prevent any nuclear conflagration. In resolution 68/39, entitled "Towards a nuclear-weapon-free world: accelerating the implementation of nuclear disarmament commitments," the goal of complete nuclear disarmament is reaffirmed and the creation of nuclear-free zones endorsed. In paragraph 11, all States are urged to pursue the 2010 commitments to revitalize the Conference on Disarmament resolution.

Similarly, the United Nations Secretary-General, in his speech of 24 March 2014 at the Nuclear Security Summit in The Hague, called on all nations to honour security guarantees: "clearly the time has come to strengthen the rule of law in both disarmament and non-proliferation. Commitments to undertake disarmament negotiations in good faith must be honoured. So, too, must security assurances provided to non-nuclear-weapon States by nuclear-weapon States." He called on delegates to "address the legitimate interest of non-nuclear States in receiving unequivocal and legally-binding security assurances from nuclear-weapon States" and he concluded: "together we must ensure that nuclear weapons are seen by States as a liability, not an asset."[43] In December 2013, the United Nations High Representative on Disarmament observed: "any high-level meeting on nuclear disarmament advances nuclear disarmament, simply because it underlines the urgency of what needs to happen. The cornerstone of the whole architecture is clearly the Nuclear Non-Proliferation Treaty, which has three pillars. One of them is nuclear disarmament. But when you look at how much disarmament has actually taken place, it really isn't there. There's an increasing urgency on the part of those countries that do not have nuclear weapons to say to the nuclear weapons powers: you need to disarm, you need to fulfil your side of the bargain. Having a high-level meeting with many ministers underlined the fact that more needs to happen."[44]

Role of the International Court of Justice

Bearing in mind the dangers inherent in the mere existence of stockpiles of nuclear weapons, the Republic of the Marshall Islands filed applications before the International Court of Justice, on 24 April 2014, against nine nuclear-armed States for their alleged failure to negotiate in good faith for nuclear disarmament, as required under the Non-Proliferation Treaty.[45]

Many civil society organizations, including the Nuclear Age Peace Foundation, applauded the initiative of the Marshall Islands to engage the World Court in an overdue action against the nuclear-armed nations and the stagnation of negotiations. It should be remembered that the people of the Marshall Islands continue to suffer today from the effects of nuclear weapon tests that took place on their territory in the 1940s and 1950s, and they want to ensure that such devastation is never brought on anyone ever again.[46] Moreover, it is important to have a pronouncement of the International Court of Justice concerning the international legal obligations assumed by nuclear weapons States pursuant to article VI of the Non-Proliferation Treaty: "Each of the Parties to the Treaty undertakes to pursue negotiations in good faith on effective measures relating to cessation of the nuclear arms race at an early date and to nuclear disarmament, and on a treaty on general and complete disarmament under strict and effective international control."

While the current applications are of a contentious nature, the General Assembly could consider, pursuant to Article 96 of the Charter of the United Nations, referring a pertinent legal question to the International Court of Justice for an advisory opinion: What are the legal consequences of the non-respect of article VI of the Non-Proliferation Treaty?

Arms trade and zones of peace

On 2 April 2013, the General Assembly adopted the Arms Trade Treaty. As of July 2014, 118 States have signed the Treaty and 41 have ratified it.[47] Fifty ratifications are necessary for its entry into force. However, the mere existence of the Treaty provides an example of good international practice that slowly but surely can bear fruit.

On 28 and 29 January 2014 the Community of Latin American and Caribbean States (CELAC) held its second summit in Havana and adopted a declaration on 29 January 2014 proclaiming the entire region a "zone of peace."[48] The Declaration, which constitutes a strong and positive example for the entire world, is based on the desire of the inhabitants of the zone to preserve and consolidate peace through the promotion of friendly relations between States and the commitment of United Nations Member States to resolve differences through dialogue and peaceful means, in conformity with international law. It recalls the Treaty of Tlatelolco, which established a nuclear-free zone in Latin America and the Caribbean 45 years ago. The Declaration commits all members of the organization to strengthen regional integration with a vision to establish an international order based on the human right to peace.[49] That vision excludes the use of force and illegitimate means of defence, including weapons of mass destruction. This implies the need to negotiate in order to reach complete nuclear disarmament and arrive at a significant reduction in the production and stockpiling of conventional weapons and trade thereon. The establishment of zones of peace and cooperation in an increasing number of regions of the world is to be welcomed, as it would carry the commitment of the governments concerned towards a significant decrease in military budgets and spending.

Recent studies on the negative impact on economic growth of inequality in wealth distribution

In March 2013, the South Centre in Geneva issued a working paper illustrating that the fiscal contraction strategy in many countries, as well as specific austerity measures, are not conducive to socioeconomic recovery or the achievement of development and employment goals. Austerity with regard to social services is counterproductive. Austerity should instead begin by reducing military spending.[50]

In April 2014, the International Monetary Fund (IMF) published its *World Economic Outlook*,[51] followed by a paper concerning the negative consequences of wealth inequality for national and international economic growth.[52] The paper argues, inconsistently with the Fund's traditional position, that income inequality can actually lead to slower or less sustainable economic growth, while redistribution of income, when measured, does not hurt and may help the economy. This constitutes a welcome sign of a shift in IMF thinking about income disparity. "It would still be a mistake to focus on growth and let inequality take care of itself, not only because inequality may be ethically undesirable but also because the resulting growth may be low and unsustainable," according to the study.[53]

In June 2014, the International Labour Organization published the *World Social Protection Report 2014–15*,[54] providing a global overview of the organization of social protection systems, their coverage, benefits and public expenditures; analysing recent policy trends, including negative impacts of fiscal consolidation and adjustment measures; and calling on States to expand social protection for crisis recovery, inclusive development and social justice. The report notes that more than 70 per cent of the world population lacks proper social protection.

The United Nations Institute for Disarmament Research (UNIDIR) in Geneva conducts ongoing projects on a variety of subjects, including transparency and accountability in nuclear disarmament, concerning which it is endeavouring to develop a set of practical proposals based on the arms control experience of Russia and the United States to facilitate universal transparency and accountability in nuclear disarmament.[55]

The Human Rights Council and its Universal Periodic Review mechanism

The Human Rights Council is an appropriate forum in which to examine the human rights commitments of States as reflected in their budgetary priorities. If a State is truly committed to the larger concept of human security, which rests on the promotion and protection of human rights, it will allocate the budget accordingly, devoting not just a minimum of resources to education, health care, housing, infrastructure and the administration of justice,[56] but a progressively larger proportion thereof. If, however, a State practises a "military-first" policy and subordinates social services to a perceived "national security" need, then the Human Rights Council can make sensible recommendations on how to shift priorities so as to promote and protect human rights more effectively. Thus, a systematic examination of the level of military expenditures by States and a comparison with national expenditures in the social sector would be instructive. The two following examples from the nineteenth session of the universal periodic review illustrate contrasting approaches.

The draft report of the Working Group of the Universal Periodic Review on the Democratic People's Republic of Korea takes note of the Government's report and its explanation with regard to its "military-first" policy (*Songun*), namely that "safeguarding national sovereignty provided a guarantee for the enjoyment by people of their human rights.[57] The right to life was the foremost issue in guaranteeing human rights and of great importance to the people of the Democratic People's Republic of Korea, who had been exposed, for more than half a century, to persistent military threats by hostile forces. Military-first politics served to safeguard national sovereignty and had prevented the outbreak of war, making it possible to attain tangible achievements in the economic front."[58] By contrast, the universal periodic review compilation of United Nations information on the Democratic People's Republic of Korea quotes the Special Rapporteur on the Democratic People's Republic of Korea as expressing concern over the allocation of the country's resources for the elite and its "military-first" policy, to the detriment of the population.[59] In the summary of stakeholders' information, the Life Fund for North Korean Refugees claimed that the nuclear programme of the Democratic People's Republic of Korea was at the expense of basic needs of the population, and urged the Government not to divert precious resources to further military development.[60]

Many recommendations from the aforementioned report deserve exploring, including the recommendations that the Democratic People's Republic of Korea: "undertake profound legal reforms in accordance with international law, legalize and support free market activities that provide citizens with a livelihood, and release all prisoners detained for exercising private economic activities" (Germany); "consider further increase in State expenditures on the health sector with a view to meeting the demand for medical supplies, including essential drugs" (Belarus); "develop and implement more substantiated programmes and initiatives for the provision of enhanced level of the rights to education and health for all" (Cuba); "continue to promote economic, social and cultural development to provide better conditions for the enjoyment of all rights by its people" (China); and "strengthen measures to reinvigorate the national economy including allowing more people-to-people contact through engagement in economic, commercial activities, including tourism" (Malaysia).[61] Such constructive recommendations show how to convert from a military-first to a human security paradigm.

During the same universal periodic review session, the Council also examined the report of Bhutan. The compilation of United Nations information highlights the United Nations Children's Fund (UNICEF) assessment of the high share of public expenditure devoted by Bhutan to the social sectors. "The budget for 2011–2012 was confirmed as pro-poor, with about 25 per cent earmarked for the social sector, including 17 per cent for education and 7 per cent for health care. In the draft United Nations Development Assistance Framework, Bhutan ONE Programme 2014–2018, it was stated that the Bhutanese concept of gross national happiness (GNH) promoted a balanced approach to development, encompassing good governance, conservation and community vitality, in addition to traditional socioeconomic progress indicators, and that that development paradigm, prudent economic management and political stability had brought about a significant rise in living standards and an improvement in development indicators."[62] Besides praise, the draft report of the Working Group also gives practical recommendations. Among those are recommendations to: "attach more attention to job creation, especially addressing youth unemployment" (Turkey); "continue the programmes related to poverty reduction and continue the efforts to create a stronger system of social protection" (Kuwait); "continue the implementation of a more concrete system of social protection, through the initiatives listed in the national report and call on the international community to support those national efforts (Cuba)"; "remunerate the internship programmes and accompany them with technical education training processes with shared programmes with the country's economic sector (Mexico)"; "further consolidate successful health programmes that provide medical care that is universal, free and of quality for all Bhutanese" (Venezuela, Bolivarian Republic of).[63]

The above recommendations quoted prove that the universal periodic review procedure has the potential to become an excellent forum for promoting an international order that is more democratic and equitable, including in the context of fiscal and budget priorities, transparency, disarmament and peacemaking.

Human Rights Council workshop on unilateral State-imposed coercive measures

The Independent Expert participated in the one-day workshop convened in Geneva on 23 May 2014 pursuant to Human Rights Council resolution 24/14. He endorsed the pertinent study being conducted by the Advisory Committee, which was presented by Advisory Committee member Jean Ziegler. The consensus of the expert meeting was that economic sanctions can only be imposed by the Security Council and are contrary to international law when imposed unilaterally by States. Although this superficially "peaceful" form of coercion, it may result in structural violence whose effects are often incompatible with the purposes and principles of the United Nations.

Denis Halliday, a former Assistant-Secretary-General, stated that "in respect of unilateral coercive measures, this session needs to establish that all such measures are illegal, in violation of the Charter of the United Nations, and recommend complete cessation...[yet] recognizing unilateral measures will be hard to stop, we must find a means to demand close monitoring and accountability in respect of those States that illegally continue to impose such measures. Perhaps devices such as United Nations suspension, loss of General Assembly voting rights, payment of reparations, and payment of individual citizen compensation could be considered. Tight monitoring by the Human Rights Council would be required, with quarterly reporting to the General Assembly, or to a revitalized and operational International Court of Justice."[64]

The Independent Expert observed that unilateralism and exceptionalism are anachronisms under international law, incompatible with the spirit and letter of the Charter of the United Nations and with a democratic and equitable international order. Although sanctions, in particular unilateral sanctions, are sometimes imposed with spurious human rights justifications, they frequently have opposite effects to those intended. Considering that many victims of sanctions are not governments but innocent populations, it is important to test the legality of sanctions regimes on a case-by-case basis. This can be done through the individual complaints procedures established pursuant to several human rights treaties, including the Optional Protocol to the International Covenant on Civil and Political Rights. Sanctions regimes should also be reviewed in the context of State reporting procedures before the United Nations human rights treaty bodies and under the universal periodic review of the Human Rights Council.[65]

Experience confirms the futility of trying to coerce States to change their human rights performance simply by imposing sanctions, which more often than not are avoided by governments and result in injustices vis-à-vis innocent people. What is necessary is to persuade States that it is in their own interest to strengthen human rights in law and practice, for which the Office of the United Nations High Commissioner for Human Rights (OHCHR) can provide advisory services and technical assistance. The Independent Expert would also like to see the watchdog role of the media enhanced,[66] with more attention being devoted to the human rights consequences of sanctions regimes. It is the function of the media to alert the public about the suffering that sanctions bring to innocent human beings, not to sweep it under the rug. In totalitarian States citizen have no voice. In democratic countries, however, citizens bear responsibility for the decisions taken by their democratically elected officials. If crimes are committed in their name, it is their responsibility to demand accountability.

International Day of Peace and Global Day of Action on Military Spending

Since 1981, pursuant to General Assembly Resolution 36/67, the United Nations has celebrated the International Day of Peace on 21 September.[67] In 2011, civil society launched the Global Day of Action on Military Spending, which on 14 April 2014 was celebrated worldwide by the organization of conferences and other events.[68] Since part of the problem with regard to military spending has been lack of transparency and accountability, heightened awareness on the part of civil society will hopefully persuade governments that priorities must be shifted away from military spending and towards education and social services. In Geneva the International Peace Bureau convened a panel attended by, inter alia, the Acting Secretary-General of the United Nations Disarmament Conference, a representative of SIPRI and the Independent Expert. There was consensus that budgetary decision-making should be open, with the reasons for spending clearly outlined so as to be understood by the public. Parliaments should monitor accountability in the budget decision process[69] and implementation of expenditure, with procurements controlled by rigorous procedures and subject to civilian control. Auditing of military spending should be regularly carried out, with improper practices investigated and prosecuted.

From 6 to 10 June 2014, the Sarajevo Peace Event was attended by some 2,500 participants from 32 countries, who demanded an end to war and the threat of war. Probably the largest peace event in 2014, that civil society gathering included more than 190 workshops and cultural events as well as a youth camp in Sarajevo. As Nobel laureate Mairead Maguire said, "Let Sarajevo, where peace ended, be the starting point for the bold beginning of a universal call for peace through the wholesale abolition of militarism." Again the importance of the UNESCO Culture of Peace programme as an alternative to war and militarization was emphasized.[70] At the Peace Event it was announced that the Global Day of Action on Military Spending is now to become a year-round campaign.

Brussels Declaration

At the invitation of the European Parliament in Brussels, a fruitful two-day conference was held at the European Parliament on 18 and 19 October to discuss the enhanced participation of citizens in domestic and global decision-making, including on national priorities and military spending. The Independent Expert was invited in view of operative paragraph 6 of Human Rights Council resolution 18/6, which stipulates that a democratic and equitable international order requires: "(g) The promotion and consolidation of transparent, democratic, just and accountable international institutions in all areas of cooperation, in particular through the implementation of the principle of full and equal participation in their respective decision-making mechanisms; and (h) The right to equitable participation of all, without any discrimination, in domestic and global decision-making."

Human Rights Council resolution 24/8 on the right to equal political participation was also discussed, as well as working papers on the right to public participation prepared by the Danish Institute for Human Rights.[71] The Independent Expert argued that the right of public participation is not a vague promise, but actually has a solid legal basis in universal, regional and national legislation as well as in case law. Participation is a hallmark of democratic governance, entailing a measure of timely consultation so as to legitimize the exercise of governmental power.

Among the Independent Expert's recommendations was that a study be conducted by the Human Rights Council on how the establishment of a World Parliamentary Assembly could significantly advance the goal of making a democratic transition from military-first to human security budgets and helping to realize an international order that is more democratic and more equitable.[72] At the end of the conference, the Brussels Declaration was adopted.

CONCLUSIONS

Bearing in mind that peace is indispensable to achieving a democratic and equitable international order, every effort must be undertaken to settle disputes through peaceful means, to prevent armed conflict and to end ongoing wars. Disarmament and demilitarization are keys to development and human security. Both must be democratically decided and implemented. This requires an enduring consciousness of the threat of nuclear annihilation, and enhanced awareness of the waste of resources. Reduced military budgets will release funds for the promotion and protection of human rights and for addressing global problems such as pandemics, climate change, deforestation and acute water shortages.

For decades civil society has demanded the recognition of peace as a human right. The Human Rights Council has heard that call and its open-ended intergovernmental working group on a draft United Nations declaration on the right to peace has been carrying out important work on a draft declaration for adoption by the Council and the United Nations General Assembly. The draft is supported by civil society organizations, including PEN International, which adopted the Bled Manifesto of the Writers for Peace Committee in September 2013.

A democratic and equitable international order requires a comprehensive shift in priorities and a strategy for achieving human security through enhanced public participation in decision-making, in particular in the determination of domestic and international policy, including in budgetary matters. This entails more than a culture of transparency. States should proactively educate and inform their populations so that they can meaningfully exercise their democratic right of shaping policy and choosing among options. States should consult the electorate on budget priorities, including military expenditures, which must not be accepted as permanent features of government, nor shrouded in secrecy, nor justified on grounds of "national security." Civil society rejects fear-mongering and sabre-rattling. Only through resolute political will can the dynamics of the military-industrial complex be countered, the demands of which on the public purse lack democratic legitimacy and whose success relies on undemocratic lobbying activities.

Sustainable solutions to both the international financial crisis and the dislocated economies of many countries lie in part in the recognition that military budgets are woefully inflated and must be downsized, that large armies and nuclear arsenals are anachronisms. Civil society demands transparency, accountability and most importantly the right to effective participation in setting budgetary priorities, which must not be left in the hands of defence contractors and corporate lobbyists.[73] A significant downsizing of military budgets should result in the creation of jobs elsewhere—in social services, education, food security, clean water, health care, infrastructures, research into sustainable sources of energy and the control of pandemics. Austerity is necessary in the military—not in the progressive achievement of economic, social and cultural rights. Retrogression in the latter field entails violations of articles 2 and 5 of the International Covenant on Economic, Social and Cultural Rights.

RECOMMENDATIONS

As in his 2013 report, the Independent Expert is honoured to put forward a few pragmatic recommendations.

Recommendations to States

(a) States should be required to regularly report to the Human Rights Council on their military expenditures and contrast them with expenditures for education, health care, the administration of justice, etc. States should ensure that such expenditures are discussed within the framework of the Human Rights Council's universal periodic review mechanism and governments should be persuaded to devote a greater percentage of their budgets to the promotion of civil, cultural, economic, political and social rights, and required to make concrete proposals to convert from a military-first to a human security paradigm. Military expenditures incurred by States in conflict zones and internationally disputed territories that give rise to confiscation of territory and exploitation of the colonial and occupied peoples resources should also be examined under the universal periodic review.

(b) States should be required to report annually to the Secretary-General of the United Nations pursuant to General Assembly Resolution 66/20 on their military expenditures for the most recent fiscal year.[74]

(c) States should pro-actively inform their populations of military expenditures and encourage public participation in determining budgetary priorities. States should not conceal military expenditures by attributing them to other departments, such as "intelligence" or "research and development" or "energy." Secret funds, slush funds or "contingency funds" must be subject to regulation by parliament.

(d) States should significantly reduce military spending and develop conversion strategies[75] to redirect resources towards social services, the creation of employment in peaceful industries, and greater support to the post-2015 sustainable development agenda. States should individually and multilaterally devote savings released from reduced military spending to resourcing the economic and social transition required to respond to the global climate change challenge, as envisaged by the United Nations in establishing the Green Climate Fund established by the United Nations pursuant to the Framework Convention on Climate Change.[76] Furthermore, a portion of the financial resources released should be devoted to research and development of sustainable energy, including solar energy, and should be used to address the looming problem of water shortage, which has the potential to fuel future wars. An international effort to develop efficient desalination industries should be envisaged.

(e) States should increase funding for research into conflict-prevention, addressing the roots of conflict and promoting sustainable development, and significantly reduce funding for military projects at universities and other scientific institutes.

(f) States should ferret out waste, corruption and bribery in the arms trade and impose severe penalties on offenders. States should investigate the diversion of weapons, which sometimes fall into the hands of criminals and cause additional chaos and death.

Recommendations to parliaments

(a) Parliamentarians should regularly inform, and consult with, their constituents, particularly on matters of fiscal and budget priorities. They should resist the pressure of vested interests, and the lobbies of defence contractors and others belonging to the military-industrial complex.

(b) Parliamentarians should put in place specialized and well-resourced cross-party parliamentary defence committees with competence to oversee military spending and ferret out diversion, corruption and waste.

(c) Parliaments should organize training programmes for parliamentarians to assist them with the complexities of military budgets and with assessing the risks of diversion and corruption.

(d) Parliaments should develop interparliamentary capacity-building and cooperation programmes to strengthen oversight functions in young democracies at bilateral and multilateral levels.

(e) Parliaments should counter lobbyists who engage in undemocratic influence on behalf of the military-industrial complex.

Recommendations to civil society and national human rights institutions

(a) Civil society and national human rights institutions should demand public participation in defence policy and procurement and public participation in national budgeting, supporting the reallocation of military spending to meet urgent environmental and social needs, such as in the areas of climate change and income inequality, and call for conversion from military production to civilian production, including strategies to create employment in peaceful industries.

(b) Civil society and national human rights institutions should demand transparency and accountability from government officials in matters of fiscal and budgetary policy.

(c) Demand from government that it redirect its energy policies toward research into renewable energy, and transition to renewable energy in a manner consistent with the United Nations Decade of Sustainable Energy for All.

(d) Support the global campaign on military spending.[77]

(e) Launch petition campaigns for disarmament as a necessary condition for development.

(f) Build a wide alliance of groups that would benefit from a realignment of national budget priorities.

(g) Divest from funds and investments that are used for arms production, war and nuclear research.

Recommendations to the Human Rights Council

(a) The Council may consider tasking an existing mandate holder to focus on worldwide military expenditures and to report every year to the Council and to the General Assembly on trends and options.

(b) Under the universal periodic review procedure, the conduct of States should be reviewed with regard to unilateral and multilateral coercive measures that result in grave violations of the human rights of the affected populations.

(c) The Council may consider assigning to an existing mandate holder the task of monitoring war propaganda and fear-mongering worldwide, on the basis of the prohibition of war propaganda stipulated in article 20, paragraph 1, of the International Covenant on Civil and Political Rights.[78]

By way of conclusion, the Independent Expert would like to quote from a favourite poet, Walt Whitman:

> The greatest country, the richest country, is not that which has the most capitalists, monopolists, immense grabbings, vast fortunes, with its sad, sad foil of extreme, degrading, damning poverty, but the land in which there are the most homesteads, freeholds—where wealth does not show such contrasts high and low, where all men have enough—a modest living—and no man is made possessor beyond the sane and beautiful necessities of the simple body and the simple soul.

Notes

1 See "Fundación Arias para la Paz y el Progreso Humano," available from www.un-ngls.org/spip.php?page=amdg10&id_article=2592. See also http://arcwebsite.org/pages/vj_arc_oxfam_birm_jan06.htm.

2 Miriam Pemberton, "Demilitarizing the economy" (Institute for Policy Studies), available from www.ips-dc.org/blog/demilitarizing_the_economy_a_movement_is_underway; Replacing Defense Industry Jobs, available from http://newprioritiesnetwork.org/fact-sheet-replacing-defense-industry-jobs/http://www.ips-dc.org/staff/miriam; C. N. Makupula, "Disarmament and development: a South African perspective," in *Disarmament Forum* (United Nations Institute for Disarmament Research (UNIDIR), 2003). See UNCTAD, *World Investment Report 2014*, available from http://unctad.org/en/pages/PublicationWebflyer.aspx?publicationid=937, and commentary, available from www.rtcc.org/2014/06/24/sustainable-development-goals-face-2-5-trillion-funding-shortfall/. See also www.scidev.net/global/mdgs/feature/jeffrey-sachs-sdgs-big-science.html.

3 See http://jonathanturley.org/2014/01/12/perpetual-war-and-americas-military-industrial-complex-50-years-after-eisenhowers-farewell-address/.

4 See Rebecca U. Thorpe, *The American Warfare State: The Domestic Politics of Military Spending* (Chicago, University of Chicago Press, 2014).

5 See www.fdrlibrary.marist.edu/fourfreedoms.

6 See http://hdr.undp.org/sites/default/files/reports/255/hdr_1994_en_complete_nostats.pdf P.6.

7 See http://hdr.undp.org/sites/default/files/reports/255/hdr_1994_en_complete_nostats.pdf (p. 23).

8 See Colin Archer and Annette Willi, *Opportunity Costs: Military Spending and the UN's Development Agenda* (Geneva, International Peace Bureau, 2012). See also Colin Archer, *Warfare or Welfare: Disarmament for development in the 21st Century* (Geneva, International Peace Bureau, 2005), p. 9.

9 UNESCO International Conference of Experts, Barcelona, November 1998. See also Joseph Wronka, *Human Rights and Social Policy in the 21st Century* (New York, University Press of America, 1992).

10 See http://nnsa.energy.gov/aboutus/ourprograms/defenseprograms. See also https://www.osti.gov/opennet/forms.jsp?formurl=document/press/pc26.html.

11 See http://nnsa.energy.gov/aboutus/ourprograms/defenseprograms. See also https://www.osti.gov/opennet/forms.jsp?formurl=document/press/pc26.html

12 See International Peace Bureau, "Opportunity costs: military spending and the UN's development agenda" (Geneva, 2012), definition of military spending on p. 15. See also SIPRI definition, available from www.sipri.org/research/armaments/milex/milex_database/copy_of_sources_methods.

13 See http://data.worldbank.org/indicator/MS.MIL.XPND.GD.ZS.

14 SIPRI, Fact Sheet April 2014, "Trends in world military expenditure, 2013."

15 See Friends Committee on National Legislation, http://fcnl.org/action/alert/2014/0408/; https://www.warresisters.org/sites/default/files/FY2015piechart-BW.pdf; and https://www.nationalpriorities.org/budget-basics/federal-budget-101/spending/.

16 See www.un.org/disarmament/over-armed/. See also Melissa Gillis, *Disarmament: A Basic Guide* (New York, United Nations, 2012), available from www.un.org/disarmament/HomePage/ODAPublications/AdhocPublications/PDF/Basic_Guide-2011-web-Rev1.pdf#page=15. See also www.un.org/disarmament/HomePage/ODAPublications/AdhocPublications/PDF/guide.pdf.

17 See https://research.hks.harvard.edu/publications/workingpapers/citation.aspx?PubId=8956 Joseph Stiglitz and Linda Bilmes, "There will be no peace dividend after Afghanistan," *Financial Times*, 24 January 2013.

18 See www.un.org/documents/ga/confl51/aconfl5126-1annex1.htm.

19 Dwight D. Eisenhower, *The Chance for Peace*, 16 April 1953, available from www.edchange.org/multicultural/speeches/ike_chance_for_peace.html.

20 See www.icanw.org/the-facts/catastrophic-harm/a-diversion-of-public-resources/.

21 See Colin Archer, *Warfare or Welfare* (see endnote 8), p. 35.

22 See www.usip.org/publications/the-news-media-and-peace-processes-the-middle-east-and-northern-ireland www.globalresearch.ca/stop-the-disinformation-war-machine-support-independent-media/5311094.

23 See www.bloomberg.com/news/2014-01-31/lockheed-remains-top-in-weapon-sales-ranking-amid-russian-rise.html.

24 See www.un.org/disarmament/WMD/Nuclear/NPTtext.shtml.

25 Conclusion of effective international arrangements to assure non-nuclear-weapon States against the use or threat of use of nuclear weapons (General Assembly Resolution 50/68, 10th, 12th, 13th and 16th preambular paragraphs and paragraphs 2, 4 and 5).

26 *"Dulce et decorum est pro patria mori,"* Horace.

27 Colin Archer, *Whose Priorities?* (Geneva, International Peace Bureau, 2007).

28 Following the NATO meeting in Brussels on 24 and 25 March 2014, President Barack Obama stated that he was concerned that defence spending in Europe had fallen in several countries: "If we have collective defence it means everyone has to chip in." See www.globalsecurity.org/military/world/int/nato-spending.htm. See also www.whitehouse.gov/photos-and-video/video/2014/03/26/president-obama-holds-press-conference. Germany is accordingly increasing military spending: see ottawacitizen.com/news/national/defence-watch/germany-to-increase-defence-budget-but-rejects-gdp-percentage-method-for-mapping-levels-of-military-spending.

29 See www.tni.org/sites/www.tni.org/files/download/011453_tni_eurodrones_inc_br_3e.pdf.

30 Report of the Special Rapporteur on the promotion and protection of human rights and fundamental freedoms while countering terrorism, Ben Emmerson (A/HRC/25/59).

31 See www.europarl.europa.eu/sides/getDoc.do?pubRef=-//EP//TEXT+MOTION+P7-RC-2014-0201+0+DOC+XML+V0//EN.

32 See paragraphs 130–139 of the 2005 World Summit Outcome Document, available from www.unric.org/html/english/library/backgrounders/R2P.pdf.

33 Eric Berman, Small Arms Survey, various articles, available from www.smallarmssurvey.org/armed-actors/state-security-forces.html.

34 Transparency International, *Watchdogs? The quality of legislative oversight of defence in 82 countries* (London, September 2013).

35 See www.openmediaboston.org/content/subrata-ghoshroy-us-military-funding-academic-research.
36 Robert Pollin and Heidi Garrett: see www.peri.umass.edu/fileadmin/pdf/published_study/PERI_military_spending_2011.pdf.
37 United Nations Office for Disarmament Affairs, United Nations Report on Military Expenditures, available from www.un-arm.org/Milex/home.aspx.
United Nations Office for Disarmament Affairs, UNODA Occasional Papers, No. 20, November 2010 "Promoting further openness and transparency in military matters: An assessment of the United Nations standardized instrument for reporting military expenditures, available from www.un.org/disarmament/HomePage/ODAPublications/OccasionalPapers/PDF/OP20.pdf.
38 See www.un.org/News/Press/docs//2010/dcf457.doc.htm.
39 See www.reachingcriticalwill.org/disarmament-fora/others/hinw/nayarit-2014/report.
40 See John Borrie and Tim Caughley, After Oslo: Humanitarian Perspectives and the Changing Nuclear Weapons Discourse (Geneva, UNIDIR, 2013).
41 See www.unog.ch/80256EDD006B8954/%28httpAssets%29/CCB0AA6D778C809EC1257CDE0044CD66/$file/1316ASG+Moller%27s+address_AsDelivered.pdf.
42 See www.un.org/News/Press/docs//2010/dcf457.doc.htm.
43 See www.un.org/apps/news/story.asp?NewsID=47417.
44 See www.un.org/apps/news/newsmakers.asp?NewsID=100#sthash.T597InnU.dpuf.
45 See www.icj-cij.org/presscom/files/0/18300.pdf.
46 See www.wagingpeace.org/the-nuclear-zero-lawsuits-taking-nuclear-weapons-to-court/.
47 See www.un.org/disarmament/ATT/, www.un.org/sg/dsg/statements/index.asp?nid=514.
48 See www.ohchr.org/EN/NewsEvents/Pages/DisplayNews.aspx?NewsID=14215&.
49 Carlos Villán Durán, *The Emerging Right to Peace: Its Legal Foundations* (Cambridge, United Kingdom, Intersentia, 2014). David Cortright, *Peace: A History of Movements and Ideas* (Cambridge, United Kingdom, Cambridge University Press, 2008).
50 Isabel Ortiz and Matthew Commins, "The age of austerity: a review of public expenditures and adjustment measures in 181 countries" (Geneva, South Centre, March 2013).
51 See www.imf.org/external/pubs/ft/weo/2014/01/pdf/text.pdf.
52 "Redistribution, inequality, and growth," prepared by Jonathan D. Ostry, Andrew Berg, Charalambos G. Tsangarides (Washington D.C., IMF Research Department, April 2014). See Thomas Piketty, *Capital in the Twenty-First Century* (Cambridge, Massachusetts, Belknap Press, 2014). See also Pope Francis, *Evangelii Gaudium*.
53 See www.huffingtonpost.com/2014/02/26/income-inequality-economic-growth-economy_n_4860228.html.
54 See www.ilo.org/gimi/gess/ShowTheme.do?tid=3985.
55 The researcher in charge is Pavel Podvig. See www.unidir.org/programmes/weapons-of-mass-destruction/transparency-and-accountability-in-nuclear-disarmament.
56 Article 26 of the Draft International Bill of Rights provides for increased funding to strengthen the rule of law, recognizing that "the rule of law and rights herein benefit the citizens and businesses of all countries ... each country shall annually contribute one percent of its gross national product into an international fund for the use and support of educational, healthcare and judicial facilities and salaries internationally, including the Courts described in articles 27–34." See internationalbillofrights.org/wp-content/uploads/2013/10/IBORv9.pdf.
57 A/HRC/WG.6/19/PRK/1.
58 A/HRC/WG.6/19/L.8, para. 58.

59 A/HRC/WG.6/19/PRK/2, para. 68. See also A/HRC/13/47, para. 28.
60 A/HRC/WG.6/19/PRK/3, para. 63.
61 A/HRC/WG.6/19/L.8, para. 124.
62 A/HRC/WG.6/19/BTN/2, para. 9.
63 A/HRC/WG-6/19/L.6, para. 118.
64 www.ohchr.org/Documents/Events/Seminars/CoercitiveMeasures/DenisHalliday.pdf.
65 See www.ohchr.org/EN/NewsEvents/Pages/DisplayNews.aspx?NewsID=14639&LangID=E.
66 On 13 August 2013, the New York Times published an interview with Edward Snowden in which he deplored the failure of the media to inform the public. "After 9/11, many of the most important news outlets in America abdicated their role as a check to power—the journalistic responsibility to challenge the excesses of government—for fear of being seen as unpatriotic and punished in the market during a period of heightened nationalism." See www.nytimes.com/2013/08/18/magazine/snowden-maass-transcript.html?_r=0.
67 See www.un.org/en/events/peaceday/.
68 See www.cnduk.org/cnd-media/item/1899-monday-14-april-global-day-of-action-on-military-spending.
69 Willem van Eekelen, *The Parliamentary Dimension of Defence Procurement* (Geneva, DCAF, 2013).
70 See www.peaceeventsarajevo2014.eu/press-releases/articles/more-peace-action-are-needed.html.
71 See also DIHR, *The Right to Public Participation—A Human Rights Law Update* (Copenhagen, 2013).
72 Richard Falk, Andrew Strauss, *A Global Parliament: Essays and Articles*, with a foreword by Boutros Boutros-Ghali (Berlin, Committee for a Democratic U.N., 2011).
73 See James Carafano, *Private Sector, Public Wars: Contractors in Combat—Afghanistan, Iraq, and Future Conflicts* (Praeger, 2008). See also www.batr.org/corporatocracy/021914.html.
74 See the report of the Secretary-General on objective information on military matters, including transparency of military expenditures (A/68/131). See also www.un.org/disarmament/convarms/Milex/Publications/.
75 See www.ips-dc.org/blog/demilitarizing_the_economy_a_movement_is_underway
76 See www.gcfund.org, unfccc.int/cooperation_and_support/financial_mechanism/green_climate_fund/items/5869.php.
77 See www.ipb.org/web/.
78 This recommendation is similar to that on the creation of the mandate of the Special Rapporteur on contemporary forms of racism, racial discrimination, xenophobia and related intolerance (stemming from article 20, paragraph 2, of the International Covenant on Civil and Political Rights).

Chapter 5
THE RIGHT OF SELF-DETERMINATION OF PEOPLES

"In my view, it is very important to think of self-determination *as a process*. *The process of achieving self-determination is endless*. This is true of *all* peoples not only indigenous peoples. Social and economic conditions are ever-changing in our complex world, as are the cultures and aspirations of all peoples. For different peoples to be able to live together peacefully, without exploitation or domination— whether it is within the same state or in two neighboring states—they must continually renegotiate the terms of their relationships."

ERICA DAES
UN Special Rapporteur on Indigenous Peoples[i]

THE REALIZATION OF THE RIGHT OF SELF-DETERMINATION OF PEOPLES AS A CONFLICT-PREVENTION STRATEGY[II]

During my six years as independent expert, I repeatedly emphasized the importance of implementing the right of self-determination of peoples as an effective conflict-prevention strategy. Alas, since the Second World War and the Nuremberg Trials hundreds of wars have had their origin in the unjust denial of the right of self-determination of peoples.

The world witnessed the criminal efforts of colonial powers to hold on to their colonies, the continuing exploitation of indigenous peoples and the looting of their resources, the oppression by occupying powers over native populations, the implantation of settlers in order to change the demographics of a territory, the suppression of languages, cultural manipulations tantamount to cultural-destruction, the erasing of historical memory, and the adamant denial of autonomy or secession to peoples who had and have a legitimate right to determine their own future.

In the years 2012–18, I consistently demanded that the right of self-determination be included as a permanent agenda item of the Human Rights

---

i "Striving for Self-Determination for Indigenous Peoples," in *In Pursuit of the Right to Self-Determination*, Y. N. Kly and D. Kly, Clarity Press, 2001.

ii Updated version of the speech delivered at the European Parliament on 27 February 2018. https://www.ohchr.org/EN/Issues/IntOrder/Pages/AlfredDeZayas.aspx

Council, as it had been a permanent item in the agenda of the Commission on Human Rights. I advocated the creation of the mandate of a new special Rapporteur or a working group on the right of self-determination. Further, I proposed that the General Assembly create the function of a Senior Advisor of the Secretary-General on the issue of self-determination with an "early warning" mandate to investigate grievances that might develop into a threat to local, regional or international peace.

I argued that it is the function of the United Nations to facilitate the exercise of self-determination of peoples, to organize and monitor self-determination referenda at the earliest possible time, and not to wait until hundreds of thousands of persons have lost their lives and livelihoods in senseless struggles, reprisals and counter-reprisals. Indeed, the UN-organized referenda in Ethiopia/Eritrea, Timor Leste and Sudan could have been held much earlier. Today referenda are needed inter alia in Kurdistan, Kashmir, Western Sahara, Southern Yemen, Biafra, the Cameroons, Equatorial Guinea, Sri Lanka, West Papua, the Ryukyu islands (Okinawa, Liuqiu), Rapa Nui, the Mapuche territories in Chile, the Amerindian territories in the Amazon basin, but also in established European States, where the Catalans of Spain, the Scots of the United Kingdom, the Corsicans of France, the Armenians of Nagorny Karabagh and the Russians of Donetsk and Lugansk are pursuing legitimate aspirations.

Indeed, the right of self-determination of peoples did not expire with the end of colonialism, as we know from the emergence of new states including Estonia, Latvia, Lithuania, Georgia, Azerbaijan, Slovenia, Croatia, Bosnia and Herzegovina, etc. And even the decolonization of Africa and Asia did not deliver results valid in all eternity. In 1971 Bangladesh split from Pakistan after a bloody war. But other peoples were not successful, and their claims were no less valid. The Igbos and Ogonis of Biafra struggled to gain their independence from Nigeria, the Tamils from Sri Lanka, suffering enormous human losses.

In 2017 the General Assembly adopted resolution 71/292 requesting an advisory opinion from the International Court of Justice concerning the incomplete decolonization of Mauritius by the United Kingdom. On 25 February 2019 the Court ruled that the decolonization of Mauritius was improper and that the Chagos Islands should be returned to Mauritius.[i] The Bubi population of Bioko Island (Fernando Po), formerly a Spanish colony, have made submissions to the Commission on Human Rights[ii] and Human Rights Council demanding a

---

i https://www.icj-cij.org/en/case/169, https://www.icj-cij.org/public/files/case-related/169/169-20190225-ADV-01-00-EN.pdf

ii https://www.un.org/press/en/1998/19980324.HRCN824.html
https://infogalactic.com/info/Bubi_people

review of their *"decolonization,"* which merged them, without their consent, to another former Spanish colony, Equatorial Guinea.[i]

The Alaskan indigenous population and the Hawaiian natives have made strong submissions to the Human Rights Committee, arguing that the referenda organised by the United States in 1958 had been fraudulent and that the adoption of General Assembly Resolution 1469, releasing the United States from its obligations under Chapter XI of the UN Charter, was therefore fundamentally flawed and should be revisited.[ii] During my 6 years as UN independent expert I participated in numerous panels and side-events at the United Nations concerning the right of self-determination of the native peoples of Alaska and Hawaii. I also issued expert statements that were quoted in domestic United States jurisdictions.[iii]

In this connection it is important to clarify that the exercise of the right of self-determination is not identical with secession and should not be the cause of panic by countries that want to maintain their territorial integrity. On the other hand, it is immoral and contrary to the UN Charter and Article 1 of the International Covenant on Civil and Political Rights to pretend that the issue of self-determination is closed and that future aspirants are simply out of luck. Self-determination may also express itself in the form of autonomy, federalism or incorporation into another state entity, but first it is necessary to know what the peoples genuinely want. That is why UN-organized and monitored referenda would contribute significant *"added value"* in the common effort to ensure world peace while promoting social and cultural justice.

In my 2013 report to the General Assembly I made a number of recommendations, which were commented upon by several States. Paragraph 69(n) of the report contains this pragmatic proposal, which thus far the General Assembly has not implemented:

> The General Assembly may consider revisiting the reality of self-determination in today's world and refer to the Special Committee on Decolonization and/or other United Nations instances communications by indigenous and unrepresented peoples wherever

---

i https://www.amnesty.org/download/Documents/140000/afr240011999en.pdf
ii https://talesofhawaii.net/2020/10/17/5949/
https://www.transcend.org/tms/2020/04/a-call-for-review-of-the-historical-facts-surrounding-the-unga-resolution-of-1959-that-recognized-attainment-of-self-government-for-hawaii/
http://www.hawaiiankingdom.net/news
iii https://www.courthousenews.com/alaskan-native-tribes-face-health-and-government-challenges-with-fishing-season/
https://www.courthousenews.com/wp-content/uploads/2020/06/Alfred-de-Zayas-April-30-Memo-Alaska.pdf
https://nation.com.pk/06-Oct-2020/okc-hold-virtual-conference-on-sidelines-of-un-hrc
https://www.peaceforokinawa.org/news/un-official-dr-alfred-de-zayas-supports-hawaiis-independence

they reside, inter alia, in Alaska, Australia, Canada, Chile, China, the Dakotas, French Polynesia, Hawaii, Kashmir, the Middle East, the Moluccas, New Caledonia, Northern Africa, Sri Lanka and West Papua, with reference to Chapter XI of the Charter of the United Nations. The General Assembly may also consider amending its rules and procedures to allow for the participation of indigenous and non-represented peoples. Meanwhile, the Assembly should urge States to implement the Declaration on the Rights of Indigenous Peoples. It should ensure that indigenous, non-represented peoples, marginalized and disempowered peoples, and peoples under occupation have a genuine opportunity to participate in decision-making processes.[i]

In February 2018 I spoke on two occasions at the European Parliament in connection with the self-determination aspirations of the Catalans and of the Armenian population of Nagorno Karabagh (Artsakh).[ii] Of my 14 reports to the Human Rights Council and the General Assembly, it was my 2014 report to the GA that has had the most impact and has been invoked by numerous peoples in all five regions of the world. What follows is an updated version of my speeches before the European Parliament and excerpts from my 2014 report to the General Assembly, A/69/272. —AdeZ

* * *

International law is not static but dynamic. It is a work in progress, guided by the United Nations Charter and its Article 103, the supremacy clause. Some principles of international law, however, constitute peremptory rules, including the prohibition of the use of force, the prohibition of invading and occupying foreign territory, the prohibition of piracy, the prohibition of torture, and the principle of non-refoulement. The facts resulting from violation of *jus cogens* rules have no legitimacy and do not create new law, *ex injuria non oritur jus*.

The progressive development of international law responds to economic, social and political needs. New conventions and Security Council resolutions impact international law, as does the actual practice of States, which generates precedents. Sometimes the facts on the ground, even *faits accomplis* by peoples or by States that did not conform to international norms at the time of their occurrence, can evolve into law, if recognized by the international community

---

i https://undocs.org/A/68/284
ii https://www.ohchr.org/EN/Issues/IntOrder/Pages/AlfredDeZayas.aspx Presentation to the Brussels conference on self-determination, Centre for European and Policy Studies & European Parliament," 26-27/02/2018

and if they do not violate *jus cogens* rules. For instance, the unilateral declarations of independence and the subsequent secession of Estonia, Latvia, Lithuania, Ukraine, Slovenia, Croatia, Bosnia and Herzegovina, notwithstanding the fact that the constitutions of the Soviet Union and of Yugoslavia did not allow secession by unilateral declaration, resulted in the emergence of these States as United Nations members. Other States that separate from the mother country and function within the international community as State entities, even if they do not enjoy international recognition, are considered *de facto* States, among them Kosovo, Abkhazia, Taiwan.

While the UN Charter serves as a kind of world constitution, the political narrative does not always conform to this legality and there is a degree of "fragmentation" in international law, which States invoke self-servingly to apply international law selectively, violating general principles of law—not by accident, but deliberately and calculatingly, just to see whether they can get away with it. Any observer will confirm that the application of international law à la carte was common in the past, as it is in the present. In the absence of effective enforcement mechanisms, States will continue to breach international law with impunity, even in matters of *jus cogens* like flouting the prohibition of the use of force laid down in Article 2 (4) UN Charter.

In the international law of the 21st century, the right of self-determination of peoples plays and will continue to play an ever-increasing role. The international community should be ready to address self-determination grievances before they can grow into local, regional or international conflicts and thereby endanger the peace and security of humankind. Indeed, there are hundreds of peoples who have legitimate aspirations to exercise internal or external self-determination and the unjust denial of their right will lead to violence, as has happened in all continents. Indeed, the right of self-determination did not end with the partial achievement of decolonization in the 1960s and 1970s. Moreover, the sequels of colonialism, the irrational drawing of colonial frontiers, the perfunctory application of the obsolete rule of *uti possidetis* and the consequent emergence of artificial minorities will quite naturally lead to legitimate claims for adjustment in the name of ethnic, religious and historical considerations. It is time to recognize that self-determination is a *conditio sine qua non* for the establishment of a peaceful, sustainable, democratic and equitable international order.

My 2014 report to the General Assembly[1] was devoted entirely to the proposition that the realization of the right of self-determination is a vital conflict-prevention strategy. The report demonstrates that countless wars since 1945 found their origin in the unjust denial of self-determination, and argues that the United Nations should have exercised its responsibilities under Chapter VI of the UN Charter to facilitate mediation and negotiation in a timely basis and under Chapter VII to adopt preventive measures to avert the outbreak of hostilities. Pursuant to the UN's overarching objective of achieving sustainable peace, the UN could and should offer its good offices to facilitate dialogue and, where appropriate, organize self-determination referenda. It reflects badly on the United Nations, and on the international community in general, that self-determination referenda in Ethiopia/Eritrea, East Timor and Sudan were only organized after tens of thousands of human beings had lost their lives.

Rights holders of self-determination are all peoples. Common Article 1(1) of the International Covenant on Civil and Political Rights and of the International Covenant on Economic, Social and Cultural Rights, stipulates that "All peoples have the right of self-determination." Neither the text nor the *travaux preparatoires* limit the scope of "peoples" to those living under colonial rule or otherwise under occupation. Pursuant to article 31 of the Vienna Convention on the Law of Treaties, "All peoples" means just that—and cannot be arbitrarily restricted. Admittedly, the concept of "peoples" has never been conclusively defined, notwithstanding its frequent use in United Nations fora.

Pursuant to common article 1(3) of the Covenants, duty bearers of the right of self-determination are all States parties to the Covenants, who are not merely prohibited from interfering with the exercise of the right, but "shall promote" its realization proactively. In other words, States cannot pick and choose according to their whims and do not have the prerogative to grant or deny self-determination claims *ad libitum*. They must not only respect the right but implement it. Moreover, in modern international law, self-determination is an *erga omnes* commitment stipulated in numerous articles of the UN Charter and in countless Security Council and General Assembly resolutions. The empowerment of peoples to enjoy human rights without discrimination and to exercise a degree of self-government is crucial for national and international stability. Otherwise, a significant potential for conflict remains. A persistent obstacle to the realization of the right of self-determination of peoples has been the adamant insistence of some States not to negotiate with peoples living within their frontiers. We have witnessed this in the case of Sri Lanka, where as a sequel of an improper decolonization process, the Tamils and the Sinhalese were kept together in the island of Sri Lanka, instead of conducting a referendum to determine whether the Tamils and the Sinhalese were prepared to live together in one State or whether they preferred to emerge as two equal sovereign entitles. What has made the situation worse is the aggravating factor that the Sri Lanka government has wrongly labelled the Tamils as "terrorists" and contributed to the false narrative that the Tamils do not have a right of self -determination because they are "terrorists." This is a matter that the United Nations Rapporteur on Human Rights while countering terrorism must address resolutely, because it has become too easy for certain States to avoid their obligations under Article I ICCPR and Art. I ICESCR simply by branding peoples with a legitimate claim to self-determination as terrorists.[2] The narrative managers in the mainstream media bear considerable responsibility for the negative perception of national liberation movements as somehow "terroristic." It is worth recalling that the General Assembly adopted numerous resolutions recognizing the right of national liberation movements to engage in civil disobedience and in some cases in armed resistance against a central government that systematically ignores their right of self-determination.[3] Indeed, the right of liberation movements to have recourse to "all necessary means at their disposal"[4] including a *jus ad bellum*, and to invoke the *jus in bello*[5] has repeatedly been confirmed by the General Assembly.

In the case of the Catalan people of Spain, who have a thousand-year history, their own language, culture and identity, their elected leaders have always acted peacefully and in full compliance with their democratic mandates. In 2017 they kept their promise to the electorate by organising and conducting a self-determination referendum. However, in violation of various provisions of the ICCPR, and the European Convention on Human Rights and Fundamental Freedoms, the Spanish government prosecuted them for "sedition" and twelve of them are currently serving long prison sentences in Spain. Three ministers, including the 130th President of the Generalitat of Catalonia, Carles Puigdemont, have gone into exile. This means that there are political prisoners and political exiles in Europe, in breach of article 2 of the Treaty of Lisbon of the European Union. Such brazen suppression of the exercise of freedom of expression contravenes Spain's own Constitution, in particular Articles 10(2) and 96, which incorporate Spain's human rights treaty obligations into the Spanish legal order, including the right of self-determination of peoples, the right to freedom of expression and the right to peaceful assembly and association.[6]

Even though most professors of international law affirm that self-determination has emerged as a *jus cogens* right, superior to many other international law principles, including territorial integrity, it is not self-executing and never was. There have been many legitimate claimants to the right of self-determination who have seen their right denied with impunity by occupying powers, notably the Kurds, the Sahraouis, the Palestinians, the Kashmiris. Others possessing all the elements of entitlement, including the Igbos and Ogonis of Biafra, the Tamils of Sri Lanka, and the Bubis of Equatorial Guinea[7], have valiantly fought for their culture and identity and suffered exploitation, discrimination, disenfranchisement, disappearances, massacres and even genocide. Others, like the Bangladeshis, did succeed in obtaining their independence from Pakistan, but they had to fight a nearly genocidal war in 1971, with estimates of civilian deaths ranging from 300,000 to three million human beings.

Over the past decades, some peoples have achieved self-determination through effective separation from the State entities with which they had hitherto been associated, but their international status remains inchoate because of the political bickering among the great powers and consequent lack of international recognition, among them the Russian-Ukrainian entities of Lugansk and Donetsk, the Republic of Pridnestronia (Transnistria-Moldavia), the Republic of Artsakh (Nagorno Karabagh[8]), Abkhazia, and Southern Ossetia. Another case concerns the separation of the Crimea from the Ukraine by virtue of a referendum and a unilateral declaration of independence by the Crimean Parliament. Although this expression of self-determination with explicit reference to the Kosovo precedent did not receive international recognition, Crimean independence was followed by another act of self-determination—its formal application for reunification with Russia, which was granted by the Russian Duma on 20 March 2014 and held to be constitutional by the Russian Constitutional Court. With or without international recognition, the Crimean people are today Russian citizens. and it is not conceivable that Crimea will ever be separated from Russia, except through a major international war, a highly unlikely scenario.

Whether some political leaders in the world like it or not, *de facto* States can and do assert democratic legitimacy, since their populations have acted in pursuance of the right of self-determination, and are entitled to the full protection of the international human rights treaty regime. A solution to the impasse can only be through peaceful negotiation, since the use of armed force against self-determination would violate numerous international treaties, including the UN Charter, the human rights Covenants, and the Geneva Red Cross Conventions. In this context it is important to underline that there are no "legal black holes" when it comes to human rights, and that the human rights treaty regime prevails in conflict zones and the populations of all *de facto* States enjoy protection under the customary international law of human rights.

Different from the above is the situation in the Turkish Republic of Northern Cyprus, because this *de facto* State emerged out of an egregious violation of Article 2 (4) of the UN Charter by Turkey, an illegal aggression and invasion of the island of Cyprus in 1974, in violation of the UN Charter and UN Security Council resolutions, and accompanied by war crimes and crimes against humanity, including the expulsion and "ethnic cleansing" of some 200,000 Greek-Cypriots, whose ancestors had lived in Northern Cyprus for five thousand years. The criminal Turkish invasion was followed by the illegal settlement of Anatolia-Turks in Northern Cyprus, a deliberate attempt at demographic manipulation, which is specifically prohibited in article 49 of the 1949 Fourth Geneva Red Cross Convention.[9] Illegal settlers, of course, are not a "people" entitled to claim the right of self-determination in Cyprus.[10]

A very incomplete list of peoples who have the right of self-determination and who have expressed their aspirations of self-determination and international recognition include the Kurds, the Tamils, the Tibetans, the Catalans,[11] the Corsicans, the Austrians of the Southern Tyrol, the Veneto-Italians, the Trieste population,[12] the Kashmiris,[13] the people of Southern Yemen[14], the anglophone Cameroonians, many minority groups in post-colonial Africa, the Mapuches of Chile and Argentina, the peoples of Rapa Nui, West Papua, the Molukans, Aceh-Sumatrans, etc. The Palestinians are closer to achieving their goal since they already enjoy observer status at the United Nations and have been able to ratify numerous international treaties. On the other hand, looking at the checkered map of Palestine and as a direct consequence of Israel's illegal settlements policy and the on-going encroachment of Palestinian territory, even the Palestinian leadership is bending towards a one-State solution.[15]

The United Nations could make a considerable contribution to durable peace and conflict-prevention by convening an international conference to revisit the reality of self-determination today and consider referring the claims of many aspirant peoples to the General Assembly Committee of 24.[16] Moreover, the General Assembly should revisit the situation of *de facto* states, with a view to regularizing their status, so that their populations do not remain indefinitely in limbo. Indeed, we owe to these populations that they should be empowered to access the full benefits of being members of the UN family. We remember that for many decades the two Koreas were outside the UN system, because one power coalition would block one candidate, while the other coalition would block the other. The impasse was broken in 1991 when both countries were simultaneously welcomed into the UN pursuant to Security Council Resolution 702. Similarly, neither North Vietnam nor South Vietnam had ever achieved UN membership. This happened only after the reunification of North and South Vietnam and formal UN resolutions in 1977.[17]

THE PRINCIPLE OF TERRITORIAL INTEGRITY

My 2014 report to the General Assembly formulates a number of criteria that should be taken into account when addressing self-determination issues. Bearing in mind that the international community will have to address, rather sooner than later, the aspiration of so many peoples to self-determination, it is appropriate to review some of the norms that apply. —AdeZ

* * *

To address the multiple and complex issues involved in achieving self-determination, a number of factors have to be evaluated on a case-by-case basis. In this context, it would be useful if the General Assembly were to request the International Court of Justice to issue advisory opinions on the following questions: 1. What are the criteria that determine the legitimate exercise of self-determination by way of greater autonomy or independence? 2. What role should the United Nations play in facilitating the peaceful transition from one State entity to multiple State entities, or from multiple State entities to a single entity? 3. What are the consequences of the continued refusal of States to grant self-determination to peoples under their rule? 4. What can the international community do to further the realization of self-determination by all peoples?

All manifestations of self-determination are on the table: from a full guarantee of cultural, linguistic and religious rights, to various models of autonomy, to special status in a federal State, to secession and full independence, to unification of two State entities, to cross-border and regional cooperation.

The principle of territorial integrity must be understood as in Article 2 (4) of the UN Charter and as in countless UN Resolutions, including 2625 on Friendly Relations and 3314 on the definition of the crime of aggression. The principle of territorial integrity is an important element of international order, as it ensures continuity and stability. But it is a principle of *external* application, meaning that State A cannot encroach on the territorial integrity of State B. The principle is not intended for internal application, because this would automatically cancel out the *jus cogens* right of self-determination. Every single exercise of the right of self-determination that results in secession has entailed an adjustment to the territorial integrity of the previous State entity. There are too many precedents to count.

It is undisputable that international law is not a static concept and that it continues to evolve through practice and precedents. The independence of the former Soviet republics and the secession of the peoples of the former Yugoslavia created important precedents for the implementation of self-determination.

These precedents cannot be ignored when modern self-determination disputes arise. It is not possible to say yes to the self-determination of Estonia, Latvia, Lithuania, Slovenia, Croatia, Bosnia and Herzegovina, Kosovo, but then say no to the self-determination of the peoples of Abkhazia, Southern Ossetia or Nagorno Karabagh. All these peoples have the same human rights and must not be discriminated against. As in the case of the successful claimants, these peoples also unilaterally declared independence. There is no justification whatever to deny them recognition by applying self-determination selectively and making frivolous distinctions that have no basis in law or justice.

The primacy of the principle of territorial integrity was rejected when the international community accepted the destruction of the territorial integrity of the Soviet Union by recognizing the unilateral declaration of independence of its parts, ditto with regard to the unilateral declarations of independence by the Yugoslav republics. Most significantly, in 1999 NATO countries undertook a frontal attack on the territorial integrity of the Federal Republic of Yugoslavia, when it bombarded Yugoslavia without any decision of the Security Council under Articles 39-42 of the UN Charter or any pertinent resolution under Chapter VII. This massive violation of international law has remained unpunished to this day. But one clear consequence of that war was the tacit consent of the international community to abandoning the previously sacrosanct principle of territorial integrity.

This development was confirmed in the Advisory Opinion of the International Court of Justice in the case concerning the unilateral declaration of independence by Kosovo. Paragraph 80 of that advisory opinion states: "Several participants in the proceedings before the Court have contended that a prohibition of unilateral declarations of independence is implicit in the principle of territorial integrity. The Court recalls that the principle of territorial integrity is an important part of the international legal order and is enshrined in the Charter of the United Nations, in particular in Article 2, paragraph 4, which provides that: "All Members shall refrain in their international relations from the threat or use of force against the territorial integrity or political independence of any State, or in any other manner inconsistent with the Purposes of the United Nations." In General Assembly Resolution 2625 (XXV), entitled "Declaration on Principles of International Law concerning Friendly Relations and Co-operation among States in Accordance with the Charter of the United Nations," which reflects customary international law (*Military and Paramilitary Activities in and against Nicaragua (Nicaragua v. United States of America), Merits, Judgment, ICJ Reports 1986,* pp. 101–103, paras. 191–193), the General Assembly reiterated "[t]he principle that States shall refrain in their international relations from the threat or use of force against the territorial integrity or political independence of any State." This resolution then enumerated various obligations incumbent upon States to refrain from violating the territorial integrity of other sovereign States. In the same vein, the Final Act of the Helsinki Conference on Security and Co-operation in Europe of 1 August 1975 (the Helsinki Conference) stipulated that "[t]he participating States will respect the territorial integrity of each of the participating States" (Art. IV). Thus, the scope of the principle of territorial integrity is confined to the sphere of relations between States."[18]

CRITERIA FOR PEACEFULLY AND DEMOCRATICALLY INVOKING SELF-DETERMINATION

The concrete application of the above text is that the principle of territorial integrity cannot be used as a pretext to undermine the State's responsibility to protect the human rights of the peoples under its jurisdiction. The full enjoyment of human rights by all persons within a State's jurisdiction and the maintenance of peaceful coexistence among States are the principal goals that the United Nations and the international community must achieve.

Whereas guarantees of equality and non-discrimination are necessary for the internal stability of States, non-discrimination alone may not be enough to keep peoples together when they do not want to live together. The principle of territorial integrity is not sufficient justification to perpetuate situations of endemic ethnic or religious hostility leading to violence that may gradually fester and erupt into civil war, thus endangering regional and international peace and security.

Although the "remedial theory" of self-determination may have some appeal, especially if one considers the universal desire for justice and the general rejection of impunity for gross human rights violations, it is difficult to apply "remedial self-determination," because there is no objective measuring-stick and no one has defined where lies the threshold of violation under which self-determination would not be envisaged and above which it would require separation as punishment. It is far more practical to see self-determination as a fundamental human entitlement, not dependent on anyone's wrongdoing. It is a stand-alone right. All peoples have the right because they are peoples with their own culture, identity, traditions—not because someone committed a crime or otherwise violated international law. The right attaches to peoples by their very ontology. Similarly, the doctrine of "responsibility to protect" does not help our analysis, because R2P is highly subjective and can be easily abused, as the debate in the General Assembly on 23 July 1999 amply demonstrated.[19]

Pursuant to the UN Charter, the United Nations has a crucial role to play in the exercise of the right of self-determination by all peoples, and States should appeal to the Secretary General to take the initiative and assist in the preparation of models of autonomy, federalism and, eventually, referenda. A reliable method of determining public opinion and avoiding manufactured consent must be devised so as to ensure the authenticity of the expression of public will in the absence of threats of or the use of force. Longstanding historical links to a territory or region, religious links to sacred sites, the consciousness of the heritage of prior generations as well as a subjective identification with a territory must be given due weight. Agreements with persons who are not properly authorized to represent the populations concerned, and agreements with puppet representatives are a fortiori invalid and contrary to the fundamental principle of good faith. In the absence of a process of negotiation or plebiscites, there is a danger of armed revolt.

In order to ensure sustainable internal and external peace in the twenty-first century, the international community must react to early warning signs and establish conflict-prevention mechanisms. Facilitating dialogue between peoples and organizing referenda in a timely fashion are tools to ensure the peaceful evolution of national and international relations. Inclusion of all stakeholders must be the rule, not the exception.

Excerpts from my 2014 Report to the General Assembly follow. —AdeZ

* * *

INTRODUCTION

In its resolution 68/175, the General Assembly took note of the major changes taking place on the international scene and the aspirations of all peoples for an international order based on the principles enshrined in the Charter of the United Nations, including promoting and encouraging respect for human rights and fundamental freedoms for all and respect for the principle of equal rights and self-determination of peoples, peace, democracy, justice, equality, the rule of law, pluralism, development, better standards of living and solidarity. Bearing in mind that all States have a legal obligation to observe the purposes and principles of the United Nations and work to strengthen its three pillars—peace, development and human rights—the present report builds on paragraph 5 of resolution 68/175, in which the Assembly affirmed that a democratic and equitable international order required the realization of, among other things:

(a) The right of all peoples to self-determination, by virtue of which they can freely determine their political status and freely pursue their economic, social and cultural development;

(b) The right of peoples and nations to permanent sovereignty over their natural wealth and resources;

(c) The right of every human person and all peoples to development;

(d) The right of all peoples to peace.

In this connection, the Independent Expert has given attention to General Assembly Resolution 68/153 and to the report of the Secretary-General on self-determination (A/68/318), which recognize that universal realization of self-determination is a fundamental condition for the effective guarantee and observance of human rights. He further acknowledges the study on the impacts of the Doctrine of Discovery on indigenous peoples, including mechanisms, processes and instruments of redress, submitted to the Permanent Forum on Indigenous Issues, in which special rapporteurs are encouraged to play a role in establishing relevant standards (E/C.19/2014/3, para. 36). Since 2012, the Independent Expert has received an increasing number of appeals and communications from stakeholders concerning self-determination issues.[20]

In its essence, the right of self-determination means that individuals and peoples should be in control of their destinies and should be able to live out their identities, whether within the boundaries of existing States or through independence. More than an outcome, self-determination should be seen as a process subject to revision and adjustment, and its outcome must correspond to the free and voluntary choice of the peoples concerned,[21] within a framework of human rights protection and non-discrimination. Self-determination cannot be understood as a one-time choice, nor does it extinguish with lapse of time because. Like the rights to life, freedom and identity, it is too fundamental to be waived. As an ongoing democratic exercise, self-determination entails a people's equal participation[22] in decision-making, a continuous dialogue by virtue of which parties adjust and readjust their relationship for mutual benefit. It can be exercised at various levels, from enhanced empowerment, regional autonomy and federalism to secession. When populations are disenfranchised and cannot exercise their cultural identities, tensions may increase, culminating in armed conflict, the outcome of which might be their military success and consequent independence, or their defeat and decimation. The process did not end with decolonization, with the dissolution of the Soviet Union and Yugoslavia, or with the independence of South Sudan. It continues today as many minorities, indigenous peoples and peoples living under occupation strive to achieve higher degrees of self-administration and self-government. The international community should develop strategies to facilitate early warning and assist States in devising timely solutions.

At the outset, it is useful to clarify that the rights holders of self-determination are peoples, a concept that has never been conclusively defined, notwithstanding its frequent use in United Nations forums. Participants at a UNESCO expert meeting on self-determination endorsed what has been called the "Kirby definition,"[23] recognizing as a "people" a group of persons with a common historical tradition, racial or ethnic identity, cultural homogeneity, linguistic unity, religious or ideological affinity, territorial connection, or common economic life.[24] To this should be added a subjective element: the will to be identified as a people and the consciousness of being a people. A people must be numerically greater than just "a mere association of individuals within the State."[25] Their claim becomes more compelling if they have established institutions or other means of expressing their common characteristics and identity. In plain language, the concept of "peoples" embraces ethnic, linguistic and religious minorities, in addition to identifiable groups living under alien domination or under military occupation, and indigenous groups who are deprived of autonomy or sovereignty over their natural resources.

Duty bearers of the right of self-determination are all States Members of the United Nations, who must recognize and promote this right, individually and collectively, pursuant to *erga omnes* provisions of the Charter and human rights treaties. Empowerment of peoples to enjoy human rights without discrimination and to exercise a degree of self-government is crucial for national and international stability. Otherwise, a significant potential for conflict remains.

There are multiple ways of looking at self-determination. One understanding of the right focuses on the legitimacy of choice, so that every people may choose the form of government that it deems appropriate to its culture and traditions. Another perspective focuses on the right of two or more peoples to unify into one single State. An additional aspect emphasizes the possibility of exercising various degrees of cultural, economic and political autonomy within a State entity, and yet another expression of self-determination entails the aspiration to independent statehood. All these manifestations of self-determination should be interpreted in the context of the Charter and human rights treaties, which reject all forms of colonialism, neocolonialism and foreign occupation. As the Declaration on Principles of International Law concerning Friendly Relations and Cooperation among States in accordance with the Charter of the United Nations annexed to General Assembly Resolution 2625 (XXV) clarifies: "The establishment of a sovereign and independent State, the free association or integration with an independent State or the emergence into any other political status freely determined by a people constitute modes of implementing the right of self-determination by that people." In all the cases described, self-determination can be understood as a vector of peace and part of a democratic and equitable world order.

In this connection, the Independent Expert recalls that the post-Second World War international order has been frequently challenged and changed in response to the aspirations of non-self-governing peoples to achieve internal and external self-determination. In some States, federalism has guaranteed the self-determination right of parts of the population. In others, separation has been the result of armed conflict. It would have been preferable to see the implementation of the right of self-determination occur by virtue of the recognition of entitlement and good-faith negotiation instead of through the use of force. Considering that in the twenty-first century many peoples have not achieved self-determination, it is important for the international community to recognize their aspirations and devise a strategy to facilitate their realization without armed conflict.

For human rights, peace, security and stability to flourish, the relationships between peoples and governmental entities must be based on genuine and continuing consent, on the understanding of a *contrat social* and, if this *contrat* is violated by Government, the people as sovereign have the democratic right to redefine the relationship. As Michael van Walt has noted: "Peace cannot exist in States that lack legitimacy or whose governments threaten the lives or well -being of a section of the population. The international community, its members and institutions have an obligation to act where international law, including human rights and especially the right of self-determination, is violated."[26]

The present report builds on the Independent Expert's previous reports, which rest on the premise that the Charter of the United Nations is the world's constitution and that the best possibility for human advancement lies in the rule of law. A democratic and equitable international order requires that all States observe the Charter and apply international law uniformly. World peace and security are best served when States observe treaties in good faith (*pacta sunt servanda*) and do not hedge or invent loopholes in implementing treaties that defeat the object and purpose thereof. The credibility of law depends on its uniform application. Norms cannot be applied à la carte. Unilateralism and exceptionalism must be seen as anachronisms in the twenty-first century.[27]

In the report, the Independent Expert surveys applicable norms and practices and concludes that international peace and security are at risk as long as peoples have not achieved self-determination, and as long as they suffer occupation and exploitation by foreign Powers. Thus, to achieve a democratic and equitable international order, it is necessary to ensure the enjoyment of self-determination by all peoples, which necessarily includes the right to live in one's homeland without being threatened by ethnic cleansing or expulsion from one's roots, history, land and resources.

Although the present interim report focuses primarily on external self-determination, which is where most conflict potential exists, the Independent Expert stresses the advantages of the internal dimension of self-determination.

By internal self-determination, we understand participatory democracy, as laid down in article 25 of the International Covenant on Civil and Political Rights, and the right of a population group within the State to participate in decision-making at the State level, which may also entail the right to exercise cultural, linguistic, religious and political autonomy within the boundaries of an existing State. By external self-determination or full self-determination, we understand the right to decide on the political status of a people in the international order in relation to other States, including the right to secede from an existing State.[28]

When human rights are enjoyed by all peoples without discrimination and populations have the feeling that they are in control of their destinies, they will be less disposed to seek external self-determination. Arrogance, exclusion, arbitrariness and neglect by Governments can drive peaceful peoples to despair and violence. Instead, Governments owe it to all persons under their jurisdiction to protect their human rights and to deploy confidence-building measures so as to create peaceful societies under the rule of law.

The Independent Expert recalls the words of Federico Mayor, former Director-General of the United Nations Educational, Scientific and Cultural Organization (UNESCO), at a UNESCO conference on the right to self-determination:

> In today's global world, the official borders between States have been relativized.... Everything possible must be done to ensure that the immediate political interests of States do not compromise the aspirations of all peoples for freedom and other legitimate rights. There must be negotiation among all the parties involved so that conflict is prevented and peaceful solutions found ... The right to self-determination must include cultural, linguistic and communication rights alongside of social, economic and political rights. One depends on the other.[29]

NORMS AND PRACTICE

There is consensus among States, judges of international tribunals and professors of international law that self-determination is not only a principle but also a right that has achieved the status of *jus cogens*. Unfortunately, there is no authoritative definition of the right. As a political rather than a legal concept, self-determination can be traced back many centuries. It suffices to recall the Declaration of Independence of the United States of 4 July 1776, which proclaimed that Governments derive their powers from the consent of the governed and that, "whenever any Form of Government becomes destructive of these ends, it is the Right of the People to alter or abolish it." Similarly, the French revolution advanced the doctrine of popular sovereignty and considered that any annexation of territory should be by plebiscite.

When the President of the United States, Woodrow Wilson, championed the principle of self-determination during the First World War, it sounded utopian in an era of rampant imperialism, colonialism and unabashed exploitation of weaker peoples. The idea was applied very imperfectly at the Paris Peace Conference of 1919, which redrew European frontiers in a manner disadvantageous to the human rights of the defeated nations. Later, the Atlantic Charter of 14 August 1941 established in eight "common principles" a vision for a post-Second World War world order. The second principle enunciated the principle of self-determination as a commitment "to see no territorial changes that do not accord with the freely expressed wishes of the peoples concerned." The third principle affirmed "the right of all peoples to choose the form of government under which they will live."

The great step forward was the adoption of the Charter of the United Nations and its emphasis on the principle of self-determination as a cornerstone of peace. Implementing the right of self-determination, however, has posed enormous problems because it requires balancing with other competing interests, notably the principle of territorial integrity. It is with good reason that the Declaration on Principles of International Law concerning Friendly Relations and Cooperation among States refers to the norm that "the territorial integrity and political independence of the State are inviolable." This does not mean, however, that flexibility is not possible or that frontiers cannot be subject to adjustment by peaceful negotiation with a view to better serving the purposes and principles of the United Nations. Additional problems arise as a result of geopolitical considerations that frequently affect the consistency and logic of States that enthusiastically recognize the exercise of self-determination by some peoples and just as passionately oppose it in other cases.

A review of norms and practice appears appropriate, beginning with the commitments undertaken by all States Members of the United Nations pursuant to Article 1 (2) of the Charter, which lists among the purposes of the Organization to "develop friendly relations among nations based on respect for the principle of equal rights and self-determination of peoples, and to take other appropriate measures to strengthen universal peace." Pursuant to Article 14, the General Assembly may "recommend measures for the peaceful adjustment of any situation, regardless of origin, which it deems likely to impair the general welfare or friendly relations among nations." Pursuant to Article 24, the Security Council "shall act in accordance with the purposes and principles of the United Nations" in discharging its duties. Article 55 stipulates: "With a view to the creation of conditions of stability and well-being which are necessary for peaceful and friendly relations among nations based on respect for the principle of equal rights and self-determination of peoples, the United Nations shall promote...." Chapter XI is entitled "Declaration regarding Non-Self-Governing Territories,"[30] which imposes on the administrating Powers the "sacred trust" to advance the interests of the inhabitants, while Chapter XII established the international trusteeship system, the basic objectives of which were the promotion of "the political, economic, social and educational advancement of the inhabitants of the trust territories, and their progressive development towards self-government or independence" (Article 76).

In countless resolutions the General Assembly has affirmed the right of self-determination, notably resolution 2625 (XXV), by which the Assembly adopted the Declaration on Principles of International Law concerning Friendly Relations and Cooperation among States in accordance with the Charter of the United Nations, whose preamble states "that the principle of equal rights and self-determination of peoples constitutes a significant contribution to contemporary international law, and that its effective application is of paramount importance for the promotion of friendly relations among States." The Declaration recognizes that the foreign subjection, domination and exploitation of peoples violate their human rights and pose a threat to international peace and security. Among its principles the Declaration stipulates: "Every State has the duty to refrain from any forcible action which deprives peoples...of their right to self-determination and freedom and independence. In their actions against, and resistance to, such forcible action in pursuit of the exercise of their right to self-determination, such peoples are entitled to seek and to receive support in accordance with the purposes and principles of the Charter." Here, it is useful to recall that the international community can devise and employ innovative methods to support the bearers of the right of self-determination, to ensure the protection of their human rights while seeking to prevent or curtail violence and unrest.

The Vienna Declaration and Programme of Action, adopted in 1993, recognizes the right of self-determination in its preamble and stresses, in Part I, paragraph 2, that "all peoples have the right of self-determination.... Taking into account the particular situation of peoples under colonial or other forms of alien domination or foreign occupation, the World Conference on Human Rights recognizes the right of peoples to take any legitimate action, in accordance with the Charter of the United Nations, to realize their inalienable right of self-determination." The World Conference participants further fleshed out the links between the pursuance of self-determination and its interrelatedness with human rights by highlighting that the denial of self-determination is a violation of human rights.

While the above text recognizes self-determination as an inalienable right, it also points at the necessity of regulating its implementation in the light of other principles of international law, notably the maintenance of local, regional and international peace and security, as well as with principles of international human rights law, especially the right to be free from discrimination. The last part of paragraph 2 adds a caveat: "This shall not be construed as authorizing or encouraging any action which would dismember or impair, totally or in part, the territorial integrity or political unity of sovereign and independent States conducting themselves in compliance with the principle of equal rights and self-determination of peoples and thus possessed of a Government representing the whole people belonging to the territory without distinction of any kind." In other words, although territorial integrity is a reasonable principle of international stability, it is not an immutable norm of international relations and must be balanced against other principles, including human rights and self-determination, which are also conditions for international stability.

While General Assembly resolutions and the Vienna Declaration and Programme of Action constitute what may be termed "soft law," they have the virtue of reflecting a very large consensus on these central principles of the Organization. The "hard law" provisions on self-determination are best articulated in common article 1 of the International Covenant on Economic, Social and Cultural Rights and the International Covenant on Civil and Political Rights, which stipulates:

1. All peoples have the right of self-determination. By virtue of that right they freely determine their political status and freely pursue their economic, social and cultural development.

2. All peoples may, for their own ends, freely dispose of their natural wealth and resources without prejudice to any obligations arising out of international economic cooperation, based upon the principle of mutual benefit, and international law. In no case may a people be deprived of its own means of subsistence.

3. The States Parties to the present Covenant, including those having responsibility for the administration of Non-Self-Governing and Trust Territories, shall promote the realization of the right of self-determination, and shall respect that right, in conformity with the provisions of the Charter of the United Nations.

In its general comment No. 12, the Human Rights Committee stated: "The right of self-determination is of particular importance because its realization is an essential condition for the effective guarantee and observance of individual human rights and for the promotion and strengthening of those rights. It is for that reason that States set forth the right of self-determination in a provision of positive law in both Covenants and placed this provision as article 1 apart from and before all of the other rights in the two Covenants (para. 1)." The general comment underscores a particular aspect of the economic content of the right of self-determination, namely the right of peoples, for their own ends, freely to dispose of their natural wealth and resources. The general comment continues: "This right entails corresponding duties for all States and the international community. States should indicate any factors or difficulties which prevent the free disposal of their natural wealth and resources contrary to the provisions of this paragraph and to what extent that affects the enjoyment of other rights set forth in the Covenant (para. 5)."

Article 2 of the two International Covenants imposes legal obligations on States parties to implement all human rights, including the right of self-determination, and to provide redress for violations. The Basic Principles and Guidelines on the Right to a Remedy and Reparations for Victims of Gross Violations of International Human rights Law and Serious Violations of International Humanitarian Law (General Assembly Resolution 60/147, annex) further underline the obligation of States to respect, ensure respect for and implement international human rights law and international humanitarian law; to take appropriate measures to prevent violations from happening; to investigate violations; and to ensure victims equal and effective access to justice as well as effective remedies.

Accordingly, the right of self-determination must be implemented through specific measures, including legislation and adjudication. The bearers of the right of self-determination possess justiciable rights, not mere promises.

Lastly, the International Court of Justice has pronounced itself on the principle and application of self-determination, among others in its advisory opinions on Namibia (South West Africa), Western Sahara and the legal consequences of the construction of a wall in the Occupied Palestinian Territory, including commenting on the *erga omnes* character of self-determination.

Progressive development of international law

The world order before the Charter of the United Nations was neither democratic nor equitable. International law reflected the interests of the great Powers and was codified to strengthen colonial and imperial sustainability. Since 1945 international law has not ceased to evolve. Respect for human rights has become a paramount consideration of legality, and self-determination is now recognized as a principle of legitimacy underlying modern international law.

External self-determination can entail unification or secession, the latter being the most contentious aspect. Historically, the separation of one part of a country from another has not been accomplished simply by virtue of pre-existing law, but frequently by force. Whereas the friendly separation of Czechoslovakia into two independent States in 1993 took place without force, the implosion of Yugoslavia in the 1990s was accompanied by war and ethnic cleansing and entailed the destruction of the country's territorial integrity and its separation into new entities and six new States Members of the United Nations. Similarly, the dissolution of the Soviet Union resulted in 15 new States. These are not only historical events, but legal precedents that have expanded the meaning of self-determination beyond the context of decolonization and placed it in the context of the human right to freedom by the expressed will of the peoples concerned.

More recent history has shown that the former entities and new States are also subject to internal tensions reflecting ethnic and religious differences, and sometimes the feeling of parts of the population that they cannot fully exercise their human rights in the context of the new State entity. Ensuring all human rights for all parts of the population so that they may feel empowered and represented in the new State entity is in the interest of all parties concerned. Otherwise, existing grievances may develop into a desire for full independence. If the principle of self-determination is recognized with regard to the secession of parts of old State entities, it can equally be applied to parts of new State entities.

A violation of the right of self-determination gives rise to a legitimate human rights claim by individuals and groups and triggers State responsibility to make reparation. Any such violation of *jus cogens* also has third-party effects and imposes *erga omnes* obligations on other States, however. The Declaration on Principles of International Law concerning Friendly Relations and Cooperation among States reaffirms that "every State has the duty to promote, through joint and separate action, realization of the principle of equal rights and self-determination of peoples, in accordance with the provisions of the Charter, and to render assistance to the United Nations in carrying out the responsibilities entrusted to it by the Charter regarding the implementation of the principle."

In his final report, the Special Rapporteur of the Sub-commission on Prevention of Discrimination and Protection of Minorities on human rights and population transfer, Awn Shawkat Al-Khasawneh, addressed the *erga omnes* issue in article 10 of his proposed draft declaration on population transfer and the implantation of settlers (E/CN.4/Sub.2/1997/23 and Corr.1, annex II):

> Where acts or omissions prohibited in the present Declaration are committed, the international community as a whole and individual States, are under an obligation: (a) not to recognize as legal the situation created by such acts; (b) in ongoing situations, to ensure the immediate cessation of the act and the reversal of the harmful consequences; (c) not to render aid, assistance or support, financial or otherwise, to the State which has committed or is committing such act....

Self-determination and democracy

Self-determination is an expression of the individual and collective right to democracy, as democracy is an expression of the individual and collective right of self-determination. Both have national and international dimensions. The hallmark of self-determination must be public participation in decision-making and control over resources. In most cases this can be achieved within existing State entities, inter alia through federalism and other models of autonomy.

In the case of Non-Self-Governing Territories, self-determination referendums must be carefully organized so as to guarantee their democratic legitimacy and limit participation to those who really have a link to the Territory and not allow recent settlers and colonizers to participate therein on the same basis as natives;[31] nor can artificial barriers such as language tests be required, given that they sometimes exclude precisely those who are entitled to exercise self-determination. Articles 14, 18, 19, 21, 22 and 25 of the International Covenant on Civil and Political Rights should also inform every process of self-determination. The Vienna Declaration and Programme of Action added: "Democracy is based on the freely expressed will of the people to determine their own political, economic, social and cultural systems and their full participation in all aspects of their lives" (part I, para. 8). Support is also provided by the Forum on Minority Issues, the second session of which was devoted to minorities and effective political participation. It recommended:

> "Governments should take effective measures to end discrimination. They should consider, for instance, instituting independent monitoring and complaints mechanisms designed to prevent discrimination in voting, vote fraud, intimidation and similar acts that inhibit the effective participation of all, especially members of minorities, in electoral activities" (A/HRC/13/25, para. 10).

Unification in international law

The unification of States is a sovereign act and an expression of self-determination, consistent with the sovereign equality of States stipulated in the Charter. It cannot be frustrated by the geopolitical interests of third States. Thus, peoples who have been separated by the drawing of colonial or other arbitrary frontiers have a right to demand adjustment and reunification. Similarly, artificially separated States have a right to reunification, for example, when the two German States resulting from the surrender of Nazi Germany and the division of its territory into zones of occupation achieved reunification in 1990. Happily, this reunification occurred without the use of force and with the enthusiastic approval of the international community. In the twenty-first century there are other peoples who aspire to reunification. It is in the interest of peace and stability for the United Nations to address these concerns in a timely fashion and assist in coordinating negotiations in accordance with recognized international human rights standards.

RIGHT TO ONE'S HOMELAND

The right to one's homeland is the positive expression of the international prohibition of forced population transfers, recently referred to as ethnic cleansing. It is prior to and inseparable from self-determination. Several conventions specifically prohibit mass expulsions. Judgments and advisory opinions of the International Court of Justice and judgements of international human rights tribunals, including the European Court of Human Rights and the Inter-American Court of Human Rights, have held that forced transfers constitute massive violations of human rights and in particular of the right of self-determination.[32]

It would be too easy to frustrate the right of self-determination if it were legal to collectively uproot a population and bring in settlers so as to change the demographics of the territory concerned. In time of armed conflict this is specifically prohibited by article 49 of the Geneva Convention relative to the Protection of Civilian Persons in Time of War, of 12 August 1949 (Fourth Geneva Convention) ("Individual or mass forcible transfers, as well as deportations of protected persons from occupied territory to the territory of the Occupying Power or to that of any other country...are prohibited.") Article 17 (1) of Additional Protocol II of 1977 to the Geneva Conventions applies this prohibition to internal displacements ("The displacement of the civilian population shall not be ordered...."). The expulsion of civilian populations constitutes a "grave breach" under article 147 of the Fourth Geneva Convention and under article 85 of Additional Protocol I of 1977. Mass expulsions are prohibited in the Protocol No. 4 to the Convention for the Protection of Human Rights and Fundamental Freedoms (European Convention on Human Rights).

In the Rome Statute of the International Criminal Court, the States parties agreed that "deportation or forcible transfer of population" constitutes a crime against humanity under article 7 (d), and that "unlawful deportation or transfer" constitutes war crimes under article 8 (2) (a) (vii). Article 16 of International Labour Organization (ILO) Indigenous and Tribal Peoples Convention, 1989 (No. 169) affirms the prohibition of involuntary transfers with regard to indigenous peoples.

Self-determination is inextricably related to the right to live in one's homeland and not be subjected to forced assimilation or mass expulsion. This right was already recognized in academic circles and consecrated in a series of lectures by the French international law expert Robert Redslob, who emphasized that "the forcible transfer of a population cannot be allowed because it violates a fundamental right...and entails abandoning...a highest possession, which humankind demands on the basis of a sacred right which all men strive for: the Homeland.... There is a right to the homeland, and it is a human right."[33]

Awn Shawkat Al-Khasawneh affirmed the right to the homeland in his final report to the Subcommission, referred to above. Article 4 (2) of the draft declaration states: "No person shall be compelled to leave his place of residence." The then United Nations High Commissioner for Human Rights, José Ayala Lasso, expressed it thus in his introductory remarks to a United Nations expert meeting on population transfers[34] held in Geneva in March 1997: "Mass expulsions violate the gamut of civil, political, economic, social and cultural rights."[35]

On 28 May 1995, Mr. Ayala Lasso delivered a statement in Frankfurt, Germany, asserting that "the right not to be expelled from one's homeland is a fundamental human right," thus rejecting collective expulsions and "collective punishment on the basis of general discrimination."

An essential component of the right of self-determination and of the right to the homeland is the right to return in safety and dignity to one's home and possessions. This right has been affirmed in many resolutions of the Security Council and General Assembly concerning, among others, Afghanistan, Bosnia and Herzegovina, Croatia, Cyprus, Kosovo,[36] Palestine and Timor-Leste. Article 16 (3) of ILO Convention No. 169 affirms the right to return of indigenous peoples who have been displaced.

As the Human Rights Committee has stated in its general comment No. 17, "the right to return is of the utmost importance for refugees seeking voluntary repatriation. It also implies prohibition of enforced population transfers or mass expulsions to other countries" (para. 19).

The draft declaration on population transfer stipulates in its article 8:

> Every person has the right to return voluntarily, and in safety and dignity, to the country of origin and, within it, to the place of origin or choice. The exercise of the right to return does not preclude the victim's right to adequate remedies, including restoration of properties of which they were deprived in connection with or as a result of population transfers, compensation for any property that cannot be restored to them, and any other reparations provided for in international law.

The right to one's homeland is especially relevant to populations living under occupation, indigenous and non-self-governing peoples. Obstacles to the achievement of the implementation of the right to one's homeland, as an expression of the right of self-determination, are the conflicting geopolitical agendas of major powers and the economic interests of transnational corporations over the natural resources of weaker peoples. Frequently, advocates of self-determination are discredited as radicals or irredentists. It is clear that governmental paranoia about irredentism cannot trump a legitimate entitlement of self-determination. Labels aimed at incitement against minorities or indigenous peoples may entail violations of article 20 (2) of the International Covenant on Civil and Political Rights, which specifically prohibits incitement to discrimination, hostility or violence.

DECOLONIZATION

In the light of the Charter of the United Nations, it became clear that colonialism had to be dismantled, but it was not until the 1960s that the General Assembly adopted groundbreaking resolutions on the subject.

The preamble to resolution 1514 (XV) on the Declaration on the Granting of Independence to Colonial Countries and Peoples of 1960 establishes the symbiotic link between self-determination and friendly relations among nations.

However, decolonization alone would not have given the formerly colonized peoples a decent future and equal opportunity to participate in global decision-making. It was necessary to adopt resolution 1803 (XVII) on permanent sovereignty over natural resources in 1962, paragraph 1 of which declares: "The right of peoples and nations to permanent sovereignty over their natural wealth and resources must be exercised in the interest of their national development and of the well-being of the people of the State concerned."

Paragraph 7 stipulates: "Violation of the rights of peoples and nations to sovereignty over their natural wealth and resources is contrary to the spirit and principles of the Charter of the United Nations and hinders the development of international cooperation and the maintenance of peace."

The decolonization process had already begun on the Indian subcontinent in 1947, followed by the independence of Indonesia in 1949, continuing in Asia, the Pacific Islands, Africa and Latin America. Decolonization was frequently preceded and accomplished by violence, as was the case in numerous African and Asian territories including Algeria, Namibia, Timor-Leste and Zimbabwe.

Decolonization was not only just and consistent with the Charter; it was necessary to end violence. Initially, decolonization was conducted on the basis of the *uti possidetis* doctrine, which had characterized the liberation of

Latin American republics from Spanish and Portuguese rule, providing for the maintenance of the old colonial frontiers. In the African context, however, *uti possidetis* ushered in many potential conflicts.

From 1960 to 1962, the decolonized Belgian Congo experienced a war in which two of its ethnically different and mineral-rich provinces unsuccessfully attempted secession. From 1967 to 1970, the Igbos of Nigeria unsuccessfully attempted to separate and the Biafran war left 1 million casualties in its wake. In 1971, East Pakistan separated and emerged as the new State of Bangladesh. In 1975, Timor-Leste became independent from Portugal, was invaded and occupied by Indonesia and emerged as a new independent State in 2002. In 1991, after a 30-year war, Eritrea gained its independence from Ethiopia, following a referendum supervised by the United Nations. In 2011, after a 20-year war, South Sudan separated from the Sudan pursuant to a referendum also organized by the United Nations. Thus, it is clear that decolonization did not pronounce the last word on self-determination. To avert future armed conflict, timely adjustment of frontiers is a peace-promoting policy that should be applied with international solidarity. There is no reason to insist on the "sanctity" of national borders, which sometimes owe their existence to very unsaintly means.

Secession has also occurred outside the decolonization context in response to a people-centered perception that full independence is the only means to restore fundamental rights and freedoms. This aspect of self-determination draws its legitimacy from the fundamental right of rebelling against tyranny, a right of last resort specifically referred to in the preamble to the Universal Declaration of Human Rights.[37]

NON-SELF-GOVERNING AND INDIGENOUS PEOPLES

When the Charter was adopted, many peoples lived under foreign rule. Colonialism was widespread, peoples were subjected to military occupation and minorities and indigenous peoples had little or no international protection.

The process of self-determination did not end with decolonization and the independence of trust territories. Even today there are many unrepresented peoples and nations, peoples living under occupation and a majority of indigenous peoples in several continents who aspire to exercise self-determination, whether in the form of autonomy within existing States or independence. It is therefore necessary to devote attention to their situation, consult with the peoples concerned and ensure their right to participate in decision-making, in particular on all matters that directly concern them, their lands, their natural resources and their culture.

There is a list of 17 remaining Non-Self-Governing Territories for which the Special Committee on the Situation with regard to the Implementation of the Declaration on the Granting of Independence to Colonial Countries and Peoples carries out a degree of supervision.[38] This list is obviously incomplete, however, given that there are other non-self-governing peoples who aspire to have a voice before the Committee. The question thus arises whether other territories should be added to the list on the ground that the populations claim that they do not enjoy self-determination. Moreover, there are questions concerning the earlier delisting of some Territories for which the administrating Powers have ceased to report, but whose delisting has been described by observers as "irregular."

Even today, indigenous peoples and colonized and occupied peoples are not vested with their proper status at the national or international level. The United Nations could grant them such status as a corollary to the right of self-determination in a manner that allows for their equal participation and their free, prior and informed consent on all matters that affect them and at all levels within the United Nations system. Part of the problem with the delayed discussion on the self-determination of indigenous peoples was the fact that Governments essentially marginalized them. Moreover, the devastating impact of the policies applied by the colonizers, including massacres, spoliation, re-education and cultural dislocation paralyzed many indigenous peoples. Michael van Walt observed that "a number of first nations of the Americas...no longer exist as a result of genocide."[39] A partial recognition of the injustices is reflected in several apologies issued by Governments over the past two decades.[40] Such apologies are appropriate, but a proactive policy to reduce continuing effects and to heal the profound trauma inflicted on indigenous peoples is necessary.

As history has witnessed, indigenous peoples have been unable to achieve autonomy or self-government and obtain redress in the same ways as other rights bearers. This is attributable in part to the devastation of their numbers and the assault on their cultures, which rendered them too weak to assert their rights and frequently left them in extreme poverty, unable even to obtain adequate legal representation.[41] Greater access to the international forum and the permeation of human rights principles has allowed indigenous peoples to emerge from this past powerlessness.[42]

It is time to face "historical inequities"[43] and abandon the culture of silence. There are many open accounts worldwide that should be settled— peacefully—

through good-faith negotiation with indigenous peoples, whose inalienable rights have not been extinguished through lapse of time or through the racist and factually inapplicable doctrine of discovery (see E/C.19/2014/3). A breakthrough was achieved in 1992 in Australia when the High Court, in *Mabo and others v. Queensland*, overturned the *terra nullius* doctrine.[44] Similarly, the Supreme Court of Canada in a number of recent judgements has ruled in favour of the claims of First Nations to the return of their lands.[45] As the Permanent Forum study observes: "The Doctrine of Discovery is significant globally not only for abuses in the past, but also for its ongoing far-reaching consequences. Such colonial doctrines must not prevail in practice over human rights, democracy and the rule of law" (ibid., para. 32).

The adoption of ILO Convention No. 169 was of enormous importance, especially considering that indigenous populations are still subject to dispossessions and involuntary transfers.

The United Nations Declaration on the Rights of Indigenous Peoples constitutes a milestone in the struggle of indigenous peoples for self-determination and provides an important catalogue of rights and entitlements that should guide both Governments and the indigenous peoples themselves. Beginning in its preamble, the Declaration expresses concern "that indigenous peoples have suffered from historic injustices as a result of, inter alia, their colonization and dispossession of their lands, territories and resources, thus preventing them from exercising, in particular, their right to development in accordance with their own needs and interests." Article 3 stipulates: "Indigenous peoples have the right to self-determination. By virtue of that right they freely determine their political status and freely pursue their economic, social and cultural development." Article 8 (1) affirms that indigenous peoples and individuals have the "right not to be subjected to forced assimilation or destruction or their culture." Article 19 states: "States shall consult and cooperate in good faith with the indigenous peoples concerned through their own representative institutions in order to obtain their free, prior and informed consent before adopting and implementing legislative or administrative measures that may affect them." Article 28 (1) stipulates that indigenous peoples have the right to get back or be compensated when the lands, territories or resources have been wrongly taken away, occupied, used or damaged without their free, prior and informed consent. Article 32 further stipulates that indigenous peoples have the right to decide how they wish to develop their lands and resources. Governments must respect and protect these rights. Indigenous peoples' free, prior and informed consent must be obtained when any decisions are made that may affect the rights to their lands, resources or waters (see A/HRC/18/35). Justice and equity require that many of these articles be given some retroactive effect, so as to counter the continuing effects of earlier injustices and grant a measure of rehabilitation.

Unfortunately, some States reject the Declaration, considering it to be non-binding. In this regard, the Special Rapporteur on the rights of indigenous peoples, James Anaya, has observed:

> Debilitating to the Declaration are repeated assertions that the Declaration is non-binding, characterizations of the Declaration as granting privileges to indigenous peoples over others, and the position advanced by some States that the right to self-determination affirmed in the Declaration is different from self-determination in international law. These assertions and positions are each flawed... they only serve to weaken the force of the broad consensus underlying the Declaration and of its role as an instrument of human rights and restorative justice (A/68/317, para. 88).

With regard to sovereignty over natural resources, the Special Rapporteur has suggested that a new model more conducive to indigenous peoples' self-determination and their right to pursue their own priorities of development is needed, noting that direct negotiations between companies and indigenous peoples may be the most efficient and desirable way of arriving at agreed-upon arrangements for the extraction of natural resources (A/HRC/21/47, para. 70).

CRITERIA FOR THE EXERCISE OF SELF-DETERMINATION

Any process aimed at self-determination should be accompanied by participation and consent of the peoples concerned. It is possible to reach solutions that guarantee self-determination within an existing State entity, e.g. autonomy, federalism and self-government.[46] If there is a compelling demand for separation, however, it is most important to avoid the use of force, which would endanger local, regional and international stability and further erode the enjoyment of other human rights. Therefore, good-faith negotiations and the readiness to compromise are necessary; in some cases these could be coordinated through the good offices of the Secretary-General or under the auspices of the Security Council or the General Assembly.

To address the multiple and complex issues involved in achieving self-determination, a number of factors have to be evaluated on a case-by-case basis. In this context, it would be useful if the General Assembly were to request the International Court of Justice to issue advisory opinions on the following questions: What are the criteria that would determine the exercise of self-determination by way of greater autonomy or independence? What role should the United Nations play in facilitating the peaceful transition from one State entity to multiple State entities, or from multiple State entities to a single entity?

Some of the factors to be taken into consideration in the context of unification, autonomy or secession are described in the following paragraphs.

Self-determination has emerged as a *jus cogens* norm and is enshrined in Article 1 of the Charter as one of the purposes of the Organization. The right is not extinguished with lapse of time because, just as the rights to life, freedom and identity, it is too important to be waived. All manifestations of self-determination are on the table: from a full guarantee of cultural, linguistic and religious rights, to various models of autonomy, to special status in a federal State, to secession and full independence, to unification of two State entities, to cross-border and regional cooperation.

The implementation of self-determination is not exclusively within the domestic jurisdiction of the State concerned, but is a legitimate concern of the international community.

The rule of law entails more than positivism, which is seldom adequate to solve complex political situations that require flexibility and compromise. More important is the spirit of the law, those principles that underlie the codification of norms as an approximation of justice.

Neither the right of self-determination nor the principle of territorial integrity is absolute. Both must be applied in the context of the Charter and human rights treaties so as to serve the purposes and principles of the United Nations.

The principle of territorial integrity cannot be used as a pretext to undermine the State's responsibility to protect the human rights of the peoples under its jurisdiction. The full enjoyment of human rights by all persons within a State and peaceful coexistence among States are the principal goals to achieve. Guarantees of equality and non-discrimination are necessary for the internal stability of States, but non-discrimination alone may not be enough to keep peoples together when they do not want to live together. The principle of territorial integrity is not sufficient justification to perpetuate situations of internal conflict that may erupt in civil war and threaten regional and international peace and security.

International law evolves through practice and precedents. The independence of the former Soviet republics and the secession of the peoples of the former

Yugoslavia created precedents for the implementation of self-determination that must be considered whenever self-determination disputes arise.

The aspiration of peoples to fully exercise the right of self-determination did not end with decolonization. There are many indigenous peoples, non-self-governing peoples and populations living under occupation who still strive for self-determination. Their aspirations must be taken seriously for the sake of conflict prevention. The post-colonial world left a legacy of frontiers that do not correspond to ethnic, cultural, religious or linguistic criteria. This is a continuing source of tension that may require adjustment in keeping with Article 2 (3) of the Charter. The doctrine of *uti possidetis* is obsolete and its maintenance in the twenty-first century without possibility of peaceful adjustments may perpetuate human rights violations.

The United Nations could be called upon to assist in the preparation of models of autonomy, federalism and, eventually, referendums. A reliable method of determining public opinion and avoiding manufactured consent must be devised so as to ensure the authenticity of the expression of public will in the absence of threats of or the use of force. Longstanding historical links to a territory or region, religious links to sacred sites, the consciousness of the heritage of prior generations as well as a subjective identification with a territory must be given due weight.

Agreements with persons who are not properly authorized to represent the populations concerned and *a fortiori* agreements with puppet representatives are invalid. In the absence of a process of good-faith negotiation or plebiscites, there is a danger of armed revolt.

A consistent pattern of gross and reliably attested violations of human rights against a population negates the legitimacy of the exercise of governmental power. In case of unrest, dialogue must first be engaged in the hope of redressing grievances. States may not first provoke the population by committing grave human rights abuses and then invoke the right of self-defence in justification of the use of force against them. That would violate the principle of estoppel (*ex injuria non oritur jus*), a general principle of law recognized by the International Court of Justice. Although all States have the right of self-defence from armed attack under Article 51 of the Charter, they also have the responsibility to protect the life and security of all persons under their jurisdiction. No doctrine, not that of territorial integrity nor that of self-determination, justifies massacres; neither doctrine can derogate from the right to life. Norms are not mathematics and must be applied with flexibility and a sense for proportionality in order to reduce and prevent chaos and death.

Secession presupposes the capacity of a territory to emerge as a functioning member of the international community. In this context, the four statehood criteria of the Montevideo Convention on the Rights and Duties of States (1933) are relevant: a permanent population; a defined territory; government; and the capacity to enter into relations with other States.[47] The size of the population concerned and the economic viability of the territory are also relevant. A democratic form of government that respects human rights and the rule of law strengthens the entitlement. The recognition of a new State entity by other States is desirable but it has declaratory, not constitutive, effect.

When a multi-ethnic and/or multi-religious State entity is broken up, and the resulting new State entities are also multi-ethnic or multi-religious and continue to suffer from old animosities and violence, the same principle of secession can be applied. If a piece of the whole can be separated from the whole, then a piece of the piece can also be separated under the same rules of law and logic. The main goal is to arrive at a world order in which States observe human rights and the rule of law internally and live in peaceful relations with other States.

Sustainable internal and external peace requires the implementation of self-determination of peoples, which is an expression of democracy: government by consent of the governed. As Willy Brand said in his Nobel Peace Prize lecture, waging war is the *ultima irratio*. This is all the more so when a State uses force to suppress the legitimate rights and aspirations of its own population.

OUTLOOK AND RECOMMENDATIONS

Self-determination is a work in progress, a process of adapting and readapting to tensions between power and freedom. Rather than perceiving self-determination as a source of conflict, a better approach is to see armed conflict as a consequence of the violation of self-determination. There are many countries in which issues of enhanced democracy, autonomy and self-government require timely discussion.

A peaceful, democratic and equitable international order is best served by a symbiotic accommodation of the principle of territorial integrity, vindicated by States, and the right of self-determination held by peoples. Both are subject to adjustment and should not be treated as hyperboles of immutable law. While the extreme notion of sovereignty has a territorial fixation, sometimes the concept of self-determination is reduced to only one option: separation. There are multiple ways of exercising self-determination, the implementation of which constitutes an important strategy to promote national and international stability and prevent ethnic or religious tensions from developing into breaches of local, regional or international peace.

There is an emerging customary international law on self-determination that takes into account the emergence of new State entities following the dissolution of the Soviet Union and Yugoslavia and the friendly separation of Czechoslovakia. This customary international law is not self-executing, however.

International law being dynamic, it is no longer the same as it was at the beginning of the twentieth century, or at the end of the Second World War. There has been a progressive development towards the primacy of human rights over State rights. Many international lawyers, political scientists and sociologists recognize that, whereas States are pragmatic constructs that enable effective exercise of jurisdiction, and while many States have been shaped by imperial and colonial policies that disregard geographic, ethnic, religious, linguistic and historical realities, peoples constitute another kind of reality, an older and deeply felt force that binds generations and survives changes in boundaries and Governments. Whereas the principle of territorial integrity is a legal, political and pragmatic construct, the right of self-determination has a profound ethical basis.[48]

Meanwhile, the principle of territorial integrity no longer possesses a higher status in international law than the right of self-determination, which is anchored in the Charter of the United Nations and in the International Covenants on Human Rights. A balancing of rights and interests must be carried out, always with a view to achieving greater respect for human rights and widening the democratic space.

There remains insufficient consciousness in the international community of the enormity of the injustice that colonialism and settlement meant for the peoples of many continents. It is to be welcomed that gradually, politicians have found words to apologize. Apologies should, however, be followed by rehabilitation.

In recent decades, the international community has witnessed instances of the reunification of States and also the separation of States into independent State entities. Current and future conflicts concerning the implementation of self-determination should be solved by negotiation within the context of the Charter and the rule of law.

Bearing in mind that international law is universal, the criteria for exercising and recognizing the right of self-determination must be applied uniformly. Otherwise, the credibility and predictability of international law would be seriously compromised. The modern perspective on self-determination focuses on its function as a means to promote peace. In short: States have the sacred duty to ensure peace, while individuals and peoples have the right to peace.[49]

On the basis of the foregoing, and with the view to advancing the implementation of General Assembly Resolution 68/175, the Independent Expert recommends that States:

(a) Take measures to implement common article 1 of the International Covenant on Civil and Political Rights and the International Covenant on Economic, Social and Cultural Rights, which stipulates the right of all peoples to self-determination;

(b) Treat all populations under their jurisdiction in accordance with internationally accepted human rights norms, enable their participation in decision-making, consult them, provide legal remedies for violations of their rights and ensure enforcement of judicial decisions;

(c) Proactively report to the Human Rights Council on the enjoyment of self-determination by populations under their jurisdiction, pursuant to the universal periodic review procedure. They should similarly report on self-determination matters to the Human Rights Committee and to the Committee on Economic, Social and Cultural Rights;

(d) Demonstrate that they are prepared to work towards a peaceful change of status through democratic political means, especially in situations of protracted conflict;

(e) Assist post-secession States in establishing the rule of law and ensuring human rights;

(f) Surpass the minimum required by human rights treaties and implement soft law in the spirit of the Charter. They should not shun good-faith pledges and commitments merely because they do not constitute "hard law";

(g) Enforce treaties made with indigenous populations (see E/CN.4/Sub.2/1999/20) and negotiate only with their legitimate representatives. Decisions affecting indigenous peoples must be taken with their free, prior and informed consent. States should adopt appropriate national legislation to implement the provisions of the United Nations Declaration on the Rights of Indigenous Peoples and ILO Convention No. 169;

(h) Recognize and support indigenous peoples' legal systems and parliaments, which should have a special status so as to authentically represent their communities nationally and internationally.

He recommends that the General Assembly:

(a) Consider establishing a special mechanism to monitor the reality of self-determination today, in particular the situation of unrepresented peoples and non-self-governing peoples who are not currently being considered under

(b) Article 73 of the Charter, or assign more targeted functions to the Fourth Committee of the General Assembly, so as to supervise the proper application of Chapter XI procedures;

(c) Consider tasking the Human Rights Council with the examination of self-determination issues as a permanent item in its agenda or as part of the universal periodic review procedure, especially from the functional perspective of self-determination as a tool to promote international peace and security;

(d) Consider referring to the International Court of Justice for advisory opinions on specific legal questions concerning the scope of application of self-determination, its *erga omnes* implications, and issues of restitution and reparation to victims;

(e) Consider employing the good offices of the Secretary-General to advance the implementation of self-determination;

(f) Consider activating the special status of indigenous peoples and granting them, along with colonized and occupied populations, standing to participate in the General Assembly and its subsidiary bodies;

(g) Demonstrating the same realism shown in General Assembly Resolutions 1654 (XVI) and 1803 (XVII), proactively assist in the peaceful achievement of self-determination by non-self-governing peoples and peoples living under occupation in the twenty-first century, bearing in mind that the post-colonial world inherited ethnic, social and religious problems resulting from the arbitrary drawing of frontiers;

Consider developing programmes of assistance and transitional justice to support peoples who have recently attained self-determination, in cooperation with United Nations agencies including the United Nations Children's Fund, the United Nations Development Programme, ILO, the World Health Organization, UNESCO, the United Nations Environment Programme and the World Intellectual Property Organization.

ANNEX

THE APPLICATION OF THE RIGHT OF SELF-DETERMINATION IN THE CASE OF THE PEOPLE OF CATALONIA: CASE STUDY

While still Independent Expert, and in preparation of my presentation to the European Parliament, I drafted this opinion applying the criteria set out in my report A/69/272 to the Catalan people.

During the weeks preceding and following the self-determination referendum conducted in Catalonia on 1 October 2017, I issued several press releases and persuaded some of my rapporteur colleagues to join me in light of the violation of the right of self-determination, the right to freedom of opinion and expression, the right to peaceful assembly and association, the right to participate in the conduct of public affairs and the threat to the rule of law not only in Spain but in the European Union.[i]

I summarized the criteria for the exercise of the right of self-determination in a document (not included here) entitled *"Practical notes for the assessment of activities and allegations related to the peaceful and democratic exercise of the right of self-determination of peoples"* (hereinafter, the *"Notes"*[ii]), which contain the following legal conclusions about the right of self-determination of peoples (hereinafter, the *"right of self-determination"*):

1. The right of self-determination is jus cogens, a fundamental norm of superior hierarchical rank, recognized by the United Nations founding treaty, compulsory on national and international judicial and administrative

---

[i] https://www.ohchr.org/en/NewsEvents/Pages/DisplayNews.aspx?NewsID=22295&LangID=E
https://www.ohchr.org/en/NewsEvents/Pages/DisplayNews.aspx?NewsID=22197&LangID=E
https://www.ohchr.org/en/NewsEvents/Pages/DisplayNews.aspx?NewsID=22197&LangID=E
See also the 161-page Report by an International Expert Commission made up by Professors Nicolas Levrat, Sandrina Antunes, Guillaume Tusseau and Paul Williams, *Catalonia's Legitimate Right to Decide*, September, 2017.
See also https://www.change.org/p/jean-claude-juncker-solidarity-with-catalonia-for-the-right-to-peaceful-self-determination/u/22941620. On 23 June 2021 the Spanish Prime Minister Pedro Sanchez liberated the nine Catalonian self-determination activists, who had been imprisoned since 2017 and were serving sentences of up to 13 years. Political prisoners are entitled to rehabilitation and compensation. Hitherto the European Commission had tolerated the violation of the European Convention on Human Rights by the existence of prisoners of conscience in Europe. Clearly the Commission should have started an investigation against Spain under article 7 of the Treaty of Lisbon for an egregious violation of article 2. https://en.ara.cat/misc/its-outrageous-political-prisoners-spain_1_2800393.html

[ii] http://www.ohchr.org/EN/Issues/IntOrder/Pages/Articles.aspx (see under "Open Letter: Right to Free Determination , 12/22/2017").

instances, and superior to any national constitution or law that may conflict with it.*i*

2. The right of self-determination refers to the peoples' capacity to decide their political status. This includes the external exercise of the right of self-determination (secession or unification with another state) as well as its internal exercise (deciding on the degree of integration within a State). The exercise of the right of self-determination entails the equal participation of all peoples within the State in the decision-making in an ongoing dialogue in which the parties adjust and readjust their relationship for their mutual benefit. Self-determination is an expression of human dignity and an enabling human right necessary for the enjoyment of many other human rights in their holistic dimension—collective and individual.

3. The rights holders of the right of self-determination are "all peoples" without distinction. Although the definition of "people" does not yet exist internationally, in general it is recognized for a group of persons with a common historical tradition, an ethnic or racial identity, cultural homogeneity, linguistic unity, religious or ideological affinity, territorial connection or a common economic life, with the awareness of being a people and the willingness to be recognized as such. Any arbitrary limitation of the right of self-determination only to some peoples (for example, those subjected to military occupation or colonial domination) or only in certain historical moments in time (for example in situations of armed conflict) would be contrary to international law.

4. The duty bearer of the right of self-determination is "Every State," whose institutions should not only respect the exercise of that right (for instance refraining from external interference) but also proactively facilitate it, especially in relation to the peoples under its jurisdiction.

5. The principle of territorial integrity as laid down in the United Nations Charter (Article 2 (4)) and General Assembly Resolutions 2625 and 3314, is intended for external application. This means that a State cannot invade or encroach on the territorial integrity of other States. The principle of territorial integrity must not be invoked internally nor can it be used as a pretext to restrict the human rights of the peoples under a State's jurisdiction. The right

---

i In this respect, refer to the recent Judgment of the Court of Justice of the European Union of February 27, 2018, in Case C-266/16, which reaffirms once again the pre-eminence of the right of self-determination of peoples which is a "rule of general international law" fully applicable to the European Union, rejecting in the case in question the scope of application of an international agreement concluded by the European Union that did not take into account this fundamental right (full text of the Judgment at: http://curia.europa.eu/juris/document/document.jsf?text=&docid=199683&pageIndex=0&doclang=en&mode=lst&dir=&occ=first&part= 1 & cid = 446411)

of self-determination is a right recognized to peoples as right holders, and it is not the prerogative of the State to grant or deny, not even on the basis of the principle of territorial integrity, unless there is external interference. In case of conflict between the principle of territorial integrity and the human right of self-determination, it is the latter which prevails.

6. Peoples should exercise the right of self-determination in a peaceful and democratic manner. States should facilitate such an exercise effectively, under conditions of equality, securing a permanent dialogue in their mutual benefit. All the organs of the State are bound by it; creating obstacles to the exercise of the right of self-determination would amount to a serious violation of a fundamental human right and would result in the responsibility of the State (see Permanent Court of International Justice, Chorzow Factory Case).

7. The right of self-determination exists in the internal national order of all the Member States of the United Nations, since it is jus cogens, an imperative norm of superior hierarchical rank, of mandatory compliance in accordance with the Charter of the United Nations. Pursuant to Article 103 of the United Nations Charter (the supremacy clause), the Charter prevails over other treaties and agreements.

8. The denial of the right of self-determination (article 1 of the International Covenant on Civil and Political Rights) is frequently associated with the violation of other fundamental rights, including the right to personal integrity, the prohibition of torture and degrading treatment (article 7 ICCPR), the prohibition of arbitrary arrest or detention (art. 9 ICCPR), the right to a fair trial before a competent and impartial public court and the prohibition of trying civilians before military tribunals (art. 14 ICCPR), the right to access to information and freedom of expression (art. 19 ICCPR), the right to peaceful assembly (art. 21 ICCPR), the right to association (art. 22 ICCPR), the right to participate in the conduct of public affairs (art. 25 ICCPR), the right to equality and non-discrimination (art. 26 ICCPR) and the special rights of minorities (art. 27 ICCPR).

Given the interest and numerous inquiries received on the situation in Catalonia, this document examines the recommended application of the referred "Notes" to the specific case of the CATALAN PEOPLE, under the jurisdiction of the KINGDOM OF SPAIN. —AdeZ

* * *

A. On the ratification of the relevant international instruments, in this specific case

The first step in considering the application of the right of self-determination in a specific case is to establish whether the State in question has ratified one or more of the relevant international instruments and whether they are in force in relation to that State.

Regarding the most important instruments that recognize the right of self-determination, the situation in the case of Spain is as follows:

- **Charter of the United Nations** (CNU 1945).[50] In force in relation to Spain since 14 December 1955 through its Declaration of acceptance [51] of the obligations of the Charter and the entry of Spain into the United Nations. Reservations, interpretative declarations, objections or notifications: none.

- **International Covenant on Civil and Political Rights** (ICCPR 1966).[52] In force in relation to Spain since 27 July 1977 through the deposit of the corresponding Instrument of ratification.[53] Reservations, interpretative declarations, objections or notifications: none in relation to the right of self-determination.

- **International Covenant on Economic, Social and Cultural Rights** (ICESCR 1966).[54] In force in relation to Spain since 27 July 1977 through the deposit of the corresponding instrument of ratification.[55] Reservations, interpretative declarations, objections or notifications: none in relation to the right of self-determination.

In addition to its adherence to the most important international instruments on the right of self-determination, Spain has voted in favor of numerous resolutions of the United Nations to support it.

CONCLUSION: Spain has committed internationally to abide by the right of self-determination, without any reservation in that respect.

B. On the incorporation of those international obligations in the national legal order

The next step is to examine how these provisions, to which Spain is bound, are incorporated into the Spanish legal order.

Like many other States, Spain has incorporated them through its ordinary mechanism of reception of international law, which in the case of Spain is Article 96 (1) of the Spanish Constitution:

> 1. **Validly concluded international treaties, once officially published in Spain, shall form part of the internal legal order.** Their provisions may only be repealed, amended or suspended in the manner provided in the treaties themselves or in accordance with the general rules of international law.

As the Legal Advisor of the Spanish Parliament pointed out in his commentary on this article,[56]

> According to the constitutional drafting, the treaty is incorporated into the internal order through publication, provided it has been authentically

concluded. An internal normative act that transforms the content of the treaty is not required; nor can it be interpreted that the mere conclusion of the treaty without publication is sufficient for its internal applicability. The publication and valid conclusion are required.

Obviously, the three main instruments referred to in the previous section have been duly published in the Official State Gazette (*Boletín Oficial del Estado*, BOE) of Spain:

- **Charter of the United Nations**: BOE nr. 275, of November 16, 1990, pages 33862 to 33870;[57]

- **International Covenant on Civil and Political Rights**: BOE nr. 103, of 30 April 1977, pages 9337 to 9343;[58]

- **International Covenant on Economic, Social and Cultural Rights**: BOE nr. 103, of 30 April 1977, pages 9343 to 9347.[59]

Through these publications in the Official State Gazette, and in application of article 96 (1) of the Spanish Constitution, it is obvious that these international instruments are fully incorporated into the Spanish legal system. Given that such instruments include the recognition of the right of self-determination, it can be concluded that said right is in force in the Spanish legal system.

The fact that some States (though not Spain) may have decided to expressly mention the right of self-determination in their Constitutions is irrelevant. Article 96 (1) of the Spanish Constitution fully incorporates the right of self-determination in the Spanish legal system as if the Constitution had mentioned it explicitly (in the same way that any "treaty is incorporated into the internal order through publication," as noted by the Legal Advisor of the Parliament).

In fact, the right of self-determination exists in any case in the internal national order of all Member States of the United Nations, since it is a matter of *jus cogens*, a mandatory right of higher hierarchical order, whose implementation is compulsory according to the Charter of the United Nations. This was understood, for instance, by the United Kingdom and by Canada, which negotiated the holding of referenda in Scotland and Quebec respectively.

CONCLUSION: The right of self-determination is fully integrated and in force in the Spanish domestic legal system. It is not necessary to modify the Spanish Constitution in that respect.

C. On the application of the right of self-determination in the Spanish legal order

Once the validity of the right of self-determination in Spain has been confirmed, it is necessary to examine how it is regulated and how it is applied at the national level.

Spain has not yet explicitly developed rules regarding the exercise of this fundamental right. However, Article 10 (2) of the Spanish Constitution indicates how to interpret its exercise at the national level:

> 2. The principles relating to the fundamental rights and liberties recognized by the Constitution shall be interpreted in conformity with the Universal

Declaration of Human Rights and the international treaties and agreements thereon ratified by Spain.

Thus, in accordance with the Spanish Constitution, the right of self-determination is applicable in Spain in line with the provisions of international law, obviously including its normative and interpretative development. Indeed, the right of self-determination is a fundamental right recognized by the United Nations in its foundational Charter, as well as by the Spanish Constitution through its Article 96 (1) (see previous section), and its development is therefore automatically included by Article 10 (2) amongst those that will be interpreted in accordance with the international order ratified by Spain.

The generic description of the international order on the right of self-determination as explained in my Notes is valid for Spain because it has not made any reservation in relation to the application of that right.

- The principle of territorial integrity regulates the behavior of Member States amongst themselves, basically ensuring the safeguard of the territory against any external interference. The right of self-determination is a right recognized to peoples as rights holders, and it is not up to the State to grant it or deny it, not even based on the principle of territorial integrity, unless there is external interference. Otherwise, the exercise of this right would be completely emptied of content.

- It is entirely irrelevant to the specific case whether any other United Nations Member State may have violated the right of self-determination *vis-à-vis* any of its peoples, since it is obvious that the alleged violation of a fundamental right by another Member State (were that to be confirmed by a competent body) does not legitimize another Member to commit a similar violation.

The validity of the right of self-determination, thus defined, is consolidated by the Spanish Constitution at the highest level within the configuration of the Spanish legal system, and is therefore imposed on any norm or resolution of lower rank.

In that respect, any national rule must be interpreted in accordance with the right of self-determination, in the sense of facilitating it and not hindering it. Any internal rule in blatant contradiction (be it legislative, executive or judicial) must yield to this fundamental right and, ultimately, be considered as contrary to articles 96 (1) and 10 (2) of the Spanish Constitution, and therefore unconstitutional, null and void.

CONCLUSION: In accordance with the Spanish Constitution, the right of self-determination must be applied in Spain in line with the provisions of international law.

D. On the scope of the term "people"

Having thus established the validity of the right of self-determination in Spain within the parameters defined in international law, it remains to be determined whether there exists in Spain a "Catalan people" that can be considered as the holder of said right within the framework of the Charter of the United Nations, the International Covenants and the Spanish Constitution.

Although the definition of the term "people" has not been agreed to internationally, in general it is recognized as applying to all groups with a common historical tradition, an ethnic or racial identity, cultural homogeneity, linguistic unity, religious or ideological affinity, territorial connection or a common economic life, with an awareness of being a people and willingness to be recognized as such.

Notwithstanding the fact that there may be different opinions on the exact terms to be used to define what is a "people," it seems beyond doubt that, in any case, there is indeed a "Catalan people" in Spain, which is conscious of being a people and desirous of being recognized as such. For purposes of international law, it must be clear that the Catalan people, numbering more than seven million human beings, are not just a "minority" but a "people."

There are in fact more than enough historical, political, institutional, legal, linguistic, cultural, identity, customary and territorial evidences to consider that there is a group in Spain that considers itself as "Catalan people," and that is recognized by the State and by Spanish society as such, as well as by the international community.

From a political point of view, we can, for example, remember that the Generalitat of Catalonia as an institution of self-government has a medieval origin (from 1359 until this date there have been 132 presidents of the Generalitat of Catalonia). After its abolition following the War of the Spanish Succession and the Treaty of Utrecht (1713), and its subsequent restitution, the Spanish Constitution of 1978 declared the objective of "Protecting all Spaniards and *peoples of Spain* in the exercise of human rights, their cultures and traditions, languages and institutions," and recognized the "right to autonomy of the *nationalities* and regions that make it up."

The evidences of the existence of a Catalan people are so overwhelming and well-known that it seems superfluous to develop them in greater detail in this document. References to them are easily available in numerous official sources of the Kingdom of Spain and the Autonomous Community of Catalonia, among others.

The acknowledgment of the existence of a "people" (in this case the "Catalan people") is without prejudice to possible differences of opinion on the precise geographical area currently occupied by said people, as well as the criteria to define a personal belonging to it (for example, criteria of residence, filiation, self-designation or personal self-identification etc.). Indeed, it is not necessary to limit precisely these sociological questions, which are often fluid, to recognize whether a people exists as such or not.

Finally, it should be stressed that the existence of a Catalan people does not contradict that of a Spanish people. Both realities are not exclusive from a sociological point of view, but have been complementary for centuries.

For the legal purpose that concerns us, that is, the recognition or not of the validity in Spain of a right of self-determination for the Catalan people, it is the existence of the latter that is most relevant.

In this sense, the recognition of a "Spanish people" in Article 1 of the Spanish Constitution ("National sovereignty resides in the Spanish people, from which the powers of the State emanate") with the recognition of the right of citizenship is not legally contradictory with the self-determination of the "Catalan people," which logically flows from Articles 96 (1) and 10 (2) of the Spanish Constitution.

In effect, the Catalan people exercised their right of self-determination (internal) by voting in referendum in favor of the Spanish Constitution on 6 December 1978, in force in Spain's adherence to the Charter of the United Nations since 1955 and the International Covenants since 1977, incorporated by the previous regime. Voting in favor of article 1, but also of Articles 96 (1) and 10 (2) of the same Constitution, which form a whole and cannot be separated in the matter at hand, the Catalan people agreed to integrate their sovereignty into the framework of the Spanish people, thus establishing a framework of institutional relationship between the new Kingdom of Spain established by the 1978 Constitution, and the pre-existing Catalan people recognized in the Constitution.

In any case, even assuming *arguendo* that the Catalan people somehow had renounced their status as a political subject by voting in favor of Article 2 of the Spanish Constitution ("The Constitution is based on the indissoluble unity of the Spanish Nation, common and indivisible homeland of all Spaniards"), it should be remembered that, according to international human rights law, the right of self-determination is inalienable and not subject to statutes of limitations (like all fundamental rights), whereby the decision of the Catalans in 1978 cannot be seen as an immutable decision for all eternity and cannot deprive today's Catalan people (and future generations of Catalans) of their ongoing fundamental right of self-determination. Thus, today's Catalans are not in a straight-jacket of legalism and are free to assert their right of self-determination.

Finally, it should be recalled that, according to articles 26 and 27 of the Vienna Convention on the Law of Treaties (ratified[60] and integrated into the Spanish legal system), Spain cannot invoke any domestic regulation to escape its international obligations such as are derived from the adhesion of Spain to the right of self-determination:

> *Article 26. PACTA SUNT SERVANDA*
> Every treaty in force is binding upon the parties to it and must be performed by them in good faith.
>
> *Article 27. INTERNAL LAW AND OBSERVANCE OF TREATIES*
> A party may not invoke the provisions of its internal law as justification for its failure to perform a treaty.

Thus, articles 1 and 2 of the Spanish Constitution must be understood within the framework of the right of self-determination in force in Spain for the Catalan people according to articles 96 (1) and 10 (2) of the Constitution itself, as well as constitutional references to the "peoples of Spain" and to "the nationalities" of Spain, without there being any contradiction between these constitutional norms.

CONCLUSION: There is a "Catalan people" in Spain that holds the right of self-determination recognized by the United Nations and the Spanish Constitution. The guarantor of the peaceful and democratic exercise of this right is the Kingdom of Spain, which currently exercises jurisdiction over the Catalan people.

E. On the practical application of the right of self-determination

The conclusions of applying my Notes (sections 1 to 7) in relation to the Catalan people (paragraphs A to D above) are basically the following:

- The right of self-determination consists in the ability of peoples to decide their political destiny. The headlines are "all peoples," including the Catalan people (Article 1 of the Charter of the United Nations and the International Covenants, among others).

- The duty bearers of the right of self-determination are "all States," including the Kingdom of Spain in relation to the Catalan people (Article 1 of the International Covenants, among others).

- The principle of territorial integrity is only applicable in case of external interference by another State in Spanish territory, which is not at issue (Article 2 of the Charter of the United Nations, among others).

- The right of self-determination thus defined already exists in the Spanish legal system (Articles 96 (1) and 10 (2) of the Spanish Constitution), without it being necessary to reform the Constitution to integrate it.

- All the bodies and institutions of the Kingdom of Spain must facilitate the exercise by the Catalan people of the right of self-determination in a peaceful and democratic manner. To create obstacles to it would be to seriously attack a fundamental human right protected at the highest level by the United Nations and by the Spanish Constitution.

Having established these conclusions, it is appropriate to examine the practical consequences thereof, as well as to make recommendations in this regard within the framework of the mandate granted by the member states to the United Nations Independent Expert on the promotion of a democratic and equitable international order, in particular, the mandate "to support the strengthening and promotion of respect for human rights and fundamental freedoms throughout the world."

RECOMMENDATION 1: Refrain from OBSTRUCTING the peaceful and democratic exercise of the right of self-determination of the Catalan people.

It is recommended that all parties, as well as any organ, institution and public official, refrain from executing public actions or resolutions, whether administrative or judicial, whose objective or consequence is to hinder acts of peaceful and democratic pursuit of their exercise of the right of self-determination by the Catalan people. In effect, such actions or resolutions should be considered as serious violations of a fundamental human right protected by the Charter of the United Nations, by the International Covenants and by the Spanish Constitution, and normally null and void.

It is also recommended that public officials (state, regional or local) not be ordered to execute such actions or resolutions, and that conscientious objection be recognized if so alleged in view of the serious potential for violation of human rights.

Below are examples of public actions or resolutions that could be considered obstacles to the peaceful and democratic exercise of the right of self-determination (in addition to potentially violating other fundamental rights such as those of access to information, freedom of opinion and expression, of peaceful assembly and association, of public manifestation, and political participation). If so, such official's abstention would be recommended.

The list that follows is generic. For details on specific situations, there are hundreds of complaints from Catalan citizens, voters and demonstrators, as well as two criminal complaints with a list of specific cases forwarded by more than 600 jurists in December 2017 and February 2018 to the United Nations[61] and the Council of Europe,[62] and a report[63] about restrictions on freedom of information prepared by a group of journalists.

The Spanish Government and other authorities must refrain from adopting:

- Administrative or judicial actions or resolutions whose objective or consequence could be to hinder peaceful and democratic acts of information or demonstration about the right of self-determination of the Catalan people, for example:
  - hinder or prevent the peaceful holding of conferences and information events on the right of self-determination of the Catalan people, as well as the celebration of marches or peaceful demonstrations in support of it;
  - compel the identification for no apparent reason, and in an abusive and intimidating manner, of participants at said events;
  - withdraw or requisition documents of information or publicity about such events, or about the right of self-determination of the Catalan people in general; prohibit the use of separatist flags in events, and confiscating them;
  - block publications, as well as closing websites and web pages dealing with such events or the right of self-determination of the Catalan people in general;
- Administrative or judicial actions or resolutions whose objective or consequence could be to hinder peaceful and democratic acts of organization or support of a consultation or referendum to gather the opinion of the Catalan people on the exercise of their right of self-determination. Indeed, consultations or referendums conducted in a peaceful and democratic manner constitute a reliable method to poll public opinion and avoid artificial consent in order to guarantee the authenticity of the expression of public will in an environment free of threats and the use of force. There are standard instruments to facilitate the peaceful and democratic exercise of the right of self-determination, and actions or resolutions of hindrance could de facto prevent the exercise of such right, for example:
  - hinder or prevent the dissemination of information and publicity normally carried out in public and private media; make abusive entries and records in the media and identify journalists in an abusive manner; close websites, web pages and applications (even from a political party); withdraw and requisition information or advertising documents; remove posters, banners and advertisements from the public thoroughfare, even if they were in usual places to do so, and even remove them from private balconies; compel the identification of persons related to such acts in an abusive and intimidating manner;
  - hinder or prevent the peaceful holding of conferences, demonstrations and other events on the consultation or referendum; compel the identification for no apparent reason, and in an abusive and intimidating manner, of participants at said events;

- obstruct or prevent the logistical organization of the consultation or referendum; make abusive entries and registrations in official bodies and subcontracted companies; conduct wiretaps and stop, interrogate and / or imprison public officials and businessmen who could be facilitating the logistics of such consultation or referendum; hinder or prevent the normal use of public financing mechanisms; close logistic facilitation websites and web pages; requisition voting materials such as ballots; violate institutional and private correspondence and seize postal material related to such consultation or referendum.

RECOMMENDATION 2: Refrain from CRIMINALIZING the peaceful and democratic exercise of the right of self-determination of the Catalan people.

The criminalization of the peaceful and democratic exercise of as fundamental human right as the right of self-determination must not exist among the advanced democracies of the 21st century.

Therefore, it is recommended that all parties, as well as any organ, institution and public official, refrain from executing public actions or resolutions, whether administrative or judicial, whose objective or consequence is to criminalize acts of peaceful and democratic exercise of the pursuit of their right of self-determination by the Catalan people.

The following are examples of actions or public resolutions undertaken by the Spanish Government that could be considered as criminalization of the peaceful and democratic exercise of the right of self-determination, as well as serious impairment of the legitimate functioning of democratic institutions of the Catalan people, and serious impairment of electoral rights. and the representation of elected politicians by the Catalan people (in addition to violating other fundamental rights such as those of access to information, freedom of opinion and expression, of assembly and association, of manifestation, and of political participation):

- on the day of the consultation or referendum, violently assaulting crowds of citizens waiting to vote or peacefully demonstrating before polling stations, causing injuries of varying severity to 1066 persons (58% over 41 years old, 23 over 79 years old, 22 minors, two under 11 years old) who had to be treated according to official health sources[64] (including a myocardial infarct, loss of vision in one eye, 31 head injuries and 25 fractures); enter by force and cause material damage to schools and voting centers; confiscate ballot boxes and ballots, and close polling stations; use electronic measures to hinder the logistic management of the consultation or referendum. There are two reports of missions of independent international observers[65] that supervised the referendum as well as a great deal of audiovisual documentation.

- opening a criminal proceeding and condemning the 129th President of the Generalitat of Catalonia and members of his Government to political disqualification for promoting a non-binding popular consultation in 2014 to gather the opinion of the Catalan people on the exercise of their right of self-determination; opening and instructing a new and separate judicial proceeding for the same acts, preemptively seizing the private homes and other assets of the same persons for more than five million euros;

- ordering the opening of investigative proceedings by the Public Prosecutor's Office against 712 mayors (75% of Catalonia mayors) for giving peaceful support to a referendum or consultation by assigning voting premises, proposing their arrests in case of lack of cooperation;

- opening and instructing criminal proceedings, detaining and / or interrogating numerous persons such as school teachers, computer technicians, comedians or users of twitter, among others, for the treatment and dissemination of information related to the Catalan process and / or the referendum;

- opening and instructing criminal proceedings against high officials and officials of the Generalitat of Catalonia, particularly in the economic, police and technological fields, arresting and imprisoning some of them for several days, for supporting the Catalan process and / or the referendum;

- opening and instructing criminal proceedings against leaders of Catalan civil society, interrogating them and imprisoning them without prior trial for an indefinite period (from October 16, 2017) at the request of the Public Prosecutor, for an alleged offense of sedition;

- dismissing the 130th President of the Generalitat of Catalonia and the members of his Government, and intervening in the administration of Catalonia by placing it under the direct instruction of the Government of Spain, dismissing officials and removing charges, among others (note: these measures have been challenged, because Article 155 of the Spanish Constitution, on which they are based, does not attribute said powers to the Government of Spain);

- opening and instructing criminal proceedings against the newly dismissed President of the Generalitat, Vice President and members of the Government, at the request of the Public Prosecutor, for the alleged offense of rebellion, among others;

- interrogating and imprisoning without previous judgment the newly dismissed Vice-President of the Generalitat and several members of the Government, at the request of the Public Prosecutor; keeping the Vice President and a member of the Government in prison indefinitely (from 2 November 2017);

- issuing warrants of arrest against the newly dismissed President of the Generalitat and members of the Government residing in Brussels, at the request of the Public Prosecutor's Office (note: Spain requested Belgium to arrest and extradite the President and members of his Government residing in Brussels, but withdrew such a request just before the Belgian courts could decide, however, arrest warrants issued for the Spanish territory remain in force);

- dissolving the Parliament of Catalonia, calling for early elections, and supervising them directly by the Government of Spain on the basis of Article 155 of the Spanish Constitution (note: these measures have also been subject to several appeals for the reasons mentioned in a note previous);

- opening and instructing several criminal proceedings against the President of the Parliament of Catalonia and separatist members of the Parliament's Bureau, at the request of the Public Prosecutor's Office, for the alleged offense of rebellion, among others;

- interrogating, and imprisoning in a prison in Madrid for one night, after having transferred him in a police van while held with handcuffs, the President of the Parliament of Catalonia, the first authority of the country at that time, after the dismissal of the President of the Generalitat of Catalonia; requiring bail, withdrawing his passport and requiring weekly appearances to provisionally release him from prison;
- after the Government of Spain's calling early elections, preventing the participation in the electoral campaign of independent political candidates, including a head of the electoral list and a second head of the electoral list, keeping them in prison without trial; denying their departure at any time during the electoral campaign, thus imposing a situation of inequality of opportunity with respect to other candidates;
- after the holding of the elections, to continue keeping elected officials in pretrial detention and for an indefinite period, thus hindering their functions of political representation; denying them transfer to prisons in Catalonia, near their representatives and families (in contravention of article 10 ICCPR), keeping them away in prisons in Madrid; denying penitentiary permits so that they can attend plenary sessions of the Parliament of Catalonia, establishing a "prolonged legal incapacity," all without prior trial;
- after the holding of the elections, expanding the list of those investigated for rebellion to presidents and spokespersons of pro-independence parliamentary groups, as well as presidents and general secretaries of pro-independence political parties and the President of the Association of Independent Municipalities. According to the Spanish press,[66] the new resolutions "raise to 286 the total of those investigated by the Supreme Court in the case of rebellion. (...) The list could be extended, since the *Guardia Civil* attributes the criminal activities to other lower levels."
- after holding the elections, denying a prison permit enabling the candidate elected President of the Generalitat to leave prison for a few hours and be invested by Parliament as the 131st President of Catalonia, despite the elected candidate having all of his civil and political rights; denying such request without hearing the parties; denying also a non-face-to-face or delegated investiture, which does not need his physical presence in Parliament, thus ending by de facto denying his right to passive suffrage, all without prior trial.

In short, the actions by the Spanish Government listed above entail violations of articles 1, 7, 9, 10, 14, 19, 21, 22, 25, 26 and 27 of the International Covenant on Civil and Political Rights and should be brought before the United Nations Human Rights Committee for adjudication pursuant to the Optional Protocol to ICCPR, to which Spain is a State party.[67] Said actions by the Spanish Government also violate numerous provisions of the European Convention on Human Rights and Fundamental Freedoms and its Protocols, for which the European Court of Human Rights in Strasbourg is competent to adjudicate. Moreover, they are incompatible with the three pillars of the European Union—democracy, rule of law and human rights—contravening article 2 of the Treaty of Lisbon and requiring appropriate action under article 7 of the Treaty of Lisbon. The European Court of Justice in Luxembourg should adjudicate on the matter.

RECOMMENDATION 3: FACILITATE the peaceful and democratic exercise of the right of self-determination of the Catalan people.

My 2014 report to the General Assembly of the United Nations (A /69/272)[68] affirms and documents the proposition that the peaceful and democratic exercise of the right of self-determination contributes to greater enjoyment of human rights, peace and national and international stability. In effect, the modern perspective on the right of self-determination focuses on its function as a means to promote peace. Thus, respect for the right of self-determination on the part of the States allows maintaining harmonious relations with the peoples under their jurisdiction and constitutes an important strategy to promote national and international stability.

On the other hand, the violation of this right causes instability and can degenerate into situations of conflict that must be avoided through timely and good faith negotiations. In order for human rights, peace, security and stability to flourish, relations between peoples and governmental entities must be based on a genuine and permanent agreement, in turn based on a social contract. In case the government violates said contract, the people, as sovereign, must have the democratic right to redefine the relationship.

In this sense, it should be remembered that self-determination does not always mean secession. The right of self-determination entails the intrinsic capacity of the people to decide on their political future, being able to freely prioritize, at a specific historical moment, from a complete integration into a State even without differentiation with other regions (possibly guaranteeing specific cultural, linguistic and religious rights), all the way to secession and full independence, going through different models of regional empowerment, autonomy, or special status in a federal State (in all cases with varying degrees of cultural, economic and political autonomy).

In fact, when all peoples enjoy human rights without discrimination and populations feel that they hold the reins of their destiny, their interest in achieving external self-determination (secession) is lower. Arrogance, exclusion, arbitrariness and carelessness on the part of governments can lead a peaceful people to despair and violence. Governments have an obligation to protect the human rights of those under their jurisdiction and to adopt confidence-building measures to create peaceful societies governed by the rule of law. In most cases, this can be achieved within the framework of existing state bodies, among other ways, through federalism and other models of autonomy.

However, if there is an urgent demand for separation, the most important thing is to avoid responding by the use of force, which would endanger local, regional and international stability and further erode the enjoyment of other human rights. Negotiations in good faith and the willingness to compromise are therefore necessary.

In this regard the former Director General of UNESCO, Federico Mayor Zaragoza published the following reflection after the independence referendum on October 1, 2017:[69] "CATALUNYA: it's never too late for the meeting. It is never too late for the meeting and to approach with serenity the problems that, if they do not find a solution in time, can lead to undesirable situations for everyone. As I have repeatedly indicated in relation to the events that took place in Catalonia, I believe it is fundamental and urgent that a meeting of representatives of both parties takes place without conditions or a priori, addressing the different dimensions of the conflict with serenity and a high level of vision. to conclusions that allow to avoid the serious consequences that could derive. As former Director General of UNESCO, President of the Culture of Peace Foundation and co-President of the University Institute for Human Rights, Democracy and Culture of Peace and Non-Violence (DEMOSPAZ) I wish to join my voice to those who seek it, from different national and international instances, adequately resolve an issue that concerns and challenges us all."

Based on all of the above, **FIVE RECOMMENDATIONS** are proposed to facilitate a solution to a common problem, which is shared by the Spanish State and by the Catalan people:

(a) The immediate reconsideration of the measures adopted that may criminalize the peaceful and democratic exercise of the right of self-determination of the Catalan people, particularly those that affect the functioning of democratic institutions of the Catalan people and their fundamental human rights, especially those of elected representatives, without waiting for such measures to be formally questioned in international jurisdictional areas. In effect, measures to criminalize fundamental rights is contrary to international law, and from the outset they make a solution to the conflict difficult, with the potential to generate even more instability in the region. In this sense, it is understood, for example, that the Public Prosecutor has the power to modify his request for provisional measures so that elected deputies imprisoned without a trial can be released from prison and that they can begin to fully exercise their political rights in the Parliament of Catalonia.

(b) The recognition that the Catalan people have manifested over the last two decades, and persistently, an aspiration to peacefully and democratically modify their current framework of self-government, and that the representatives freely elected by the Catalan people are the legitimate interlocutors to negotiate with the Spanish State on their behalf (just as they were recognized as such by the State when the reform of the Statute of Catalonia was negotiated bilaterally in the last decade).

(c) The urgent start of a bilateral negotiation process in good faith between representatives of the Spanish State and the Catalan people, to jointly examine, without *a priori* impositions, the possibilities of reaching agreements satisfactory to both parties. In this regard, the international community (particularly at the European level and the United Nations) has extensive experience in the provision of mediation and good offices to assist the parties.

(d) The understanding of the parties that either of them should be able to submit proposals or results of said negotiating process to appropriate democratic validation mechanisms, whether representative (parliamentary) or direct democracy (consultation or referendum). In effect, any negotiating process must be accompanied by the participation and consent of the citizens concerned. The details of that can be included in the negotiation process (question, census, quorum and majorities etc.). European and United Nations bodies have extensive experience in the matter and can assist in the supervision of a consultation or referendum.

(e) The acceptance by the international community that a refusal of the Spanish State to participate, urgently, in good faith and with a willingness to compromise, in a bilateral dialogue process should, in the current situation, open the possibility to the Catalan people to prioritize alternative ways for the peaceful and democratic exercise of their legitimate right of self-determination, in particular the holding of a binding referendum of self-determination under the direct supervision of the international community. In this connection, one may refer to the UN-organized and monitored referendum held in 1999 in Timor Leste, against the wishes but ultimately with the consent of the occupying power, Indonesia, which realised that it could no longer stop it.[70]

Finally, as indicated in my report to the General Assembly, the application of the right of self-determination (like that of all fundamental rights) is not simply relegated to the exclusive competence of the national jurisdiction of the State in question, but is a legitimate concern of the international community, because of the consequences of its refusal for the peace and stability of the region. A democratic and equitable international order requires that all States observe the Charter and apply international law in a uniform manner. The best way to ensure world peace and security is for States to observe treaties in good faith and apply them in the light of the international human rights treaty regime.

The credibility of the common effort to realize human rights depends on its uniform monitoring, both in developing regions and in developed regions. The rules cannot be applied selectively or *à la carte,* as practiced by some states. In addition, the criminalization of the exercise of human rights, including the right to one's own identity and self-determination, is contrary to the obligation of states to observe treaties and conventions in force. The international community cannot accept repressive spirals anywhere. Exceptions are anachronisms in the 21st century.

For this reason, the United Nations and all its member states, the Council of Europe and all the Member States of the European Union are invited to ensure respect for human rights and fundamental freedoms also in Catalonia, and to ensure their proper application in relation to the Catalan people, with the aim of continuing to develop their potential to promote peace and stability in Europe.

Notes

1 https://undocs.org/A/69/272
2 https://www.ohchr.org/EN/Issues/Terrorism/Pages/SRTerrorismIndex.aspx
https://www.gopetition.com/petitions/tamils-fighting-for-freedom-are-not-terrorists.html
3 Konrad Ginter, "Liberation Movements" in R. Bernhardt (ed.), *Encyclopedia of Public International Law,* Vol. III, pp.211–215, Elsevier, Amsterdam, 1997.
4 GA Res. 2621 (XXV)
5 GA Res. 3103 (XXVIII)
6 https://www.ohchr.org/en/NewsEvents/Pages/DisplayNews.aspx?NewsID=22295&LangID=E
https://www.ohchr.org/en/NewsEvents/Pages/DisplayNews.aspx?NewsID=22197&LangID=E
https://www.ohchr.org/en/NewsEvents/Pages/DisplayNews.aspx?NewsID=22176&LangID=E
https://www.change.org/p/jean-claude-juncker-solidarity-with-catalonia-for-the-right-to-peaceful-self-determination/u/22941620

https://www.elnacional.cat/es/politica/zayas-onu-mediacion-catalunya-espana_251571_102.html
7 http://www.thebubis.com/index.html
8 http://asbarez.com/170928/international-legal-expert-affirms-artsakhs-right-of-self-determination/
9 Alfred de Zayas, "Forced Population Transfer" in Rüdiger Wolfrum (ed.), *Max Planck Encyclopedia of Public International Law,* Vol. IV, pp. 165-175, Oxford 2012. https://www.un.org/en/genocideprevention/documents/atrocity-crimes/Doc.33_GC-IV-EN.pdf
10 Alfred de Zayas, "The Annan Plan and the Implantation of Turkish Settlers in the Occupied Territory of Cyprus," *Cyprus Yearbook of International Relations,* 2006, pp. 163-179.
11 https://therift.eu/wp-content/uploads/2019/10/Alfred-de-Zayas-Urgent-Action-By-The-EU-Required-in-Catalonia.pdf
12 http://www.triest-ngo.org/un-expert-alfred-de-zayas-about-free-port-of-trieste/
13 https://kmsnews.org/news/2019/12/11/2020-commission-kashmir-launched-for-realising-kashmiris-birth-right/
https://nation.com.pk/21-Dec-2020/organisation-on-kashmir-coalition-issues-report-on-human-rights-day
http://www.radio.gov.pk/05-10-2020/speakers-call-for-settlement-of-kashmir-dispute-as-per-unsc-resolutions
14 https://en.stcaden.com/news/8793
https://www.thenationalnews.com/world/mena/yemen-southern-transitional-council-announces-self-determination-plan-1.1011145
15 Virginia Tilley, *The One State Solution,* University of Michigan Press, 2010.
16 https://www.un.org/dppa/decolonization/en/c24/about
17 https://www.un.org/en/member-states/index.html
18 https://www.icj-cij.org/public/files/case-related/141/141-20100722-ADV-01-00-EN.pdf
19 See my 2012 report to the General Assembly, https://documents-dds-ny.un.org/doc/UNDOC/GEN/N12/457/95/PDF/N1245795.pdf?OpenElement, para 14.
20 Including at the expert consultations convened by the Independent Expert in Geneva in May 2013 and in Brussels in May 2014, at which representatives of the Indigenous Peoples and Nations Coalition, the Indian Council of South America, representatives of Australian Aborigenes and the International Human Rights Association of American Minorities spoke.
21 International Court of Justice, *Western Sahara, Advisory Opinion, I.C.J. Reports 1975,* p. 12.
22 See Human Rights Council resolution 24/8.
23 Michael Kirby, speech delivered at the UNESCO International Meeting of Experts on Peoples' Rights and Self-Determination," Budapest, 25-29 September 1991. Available from www.michaelkirby.com.au/images/stories/speeches/1990s/vol24/906 -Peoples'_Rights_and_ Self_Determination_-_UNESCO_Mtg_of_Experts.pdf.
24 See M. van Walt and O. Seroo, eds., "The implementation of the right to self-determination as a contribution to conflict prevention: report of the International Conference of Experts held in Barcelona from 21 to 27 November 1998," UNESCO Centre of Catalonia, 1999. Available from www.unpo.org/downloads/THE%20IMPLEMENTATION%20OF%20THE%20RIGHT%20TO%20SELF.pdf).
25 UNESCO, "International meeting of experts on further study of the concept of the rights of peoples: final report and recommendations," 1989, UNESCO document SHS-89/CONF.602/7, p. 8. See also the definition of indigenous peoples proposed by José Martínez Cobo in the conclusions and recommendations of his *Study of the Problem of Discrimination against Indigenous Populations* (United Nations publication, Sales No. E.86.XIV.3), para. 379.
26 See endnote 24.
27 See, for example, Commission on Human Rights resolution 2004/64, para. 8.
28 See also Committee on the Elimination of Racial Discrimination, general recommendation No. 21.
29 See endnote 24.
30 See, in this regard, Makane Moïse Mbengue, "Non-Self-Governing Territories," in *Max*

Planck Encyclopedia of Public International Law (http://opil.ouplaw.com/home/EPIL). See also General Assembly Resolutions 9 (I), 66 (I), 146 (II), 1332 (XIII), 1466 (XIV), 1514 (XV) and 1803 (XVII). See further United Nations, "What the UN Can do to Assist Non-Self-Governing Territories," 2007, available from www.un.org/en/events/nonselfgoverning/pdf/What%20the%20UN%20can%20do.pdf.

31 Human Rights Committee, *Marie-Hélène Guillot et al. v. France,* communication No. 932/2000, views adopted on 15 July 2002. Cited in J. Möller and A. de Zayas, *United Nations Human Rights Committee Case Law* (Kehl/Strasbourg, N.P. Engel, 2009).

32 See Council of Europe, Parliamentary Assembly, "Enforced population transfer as a human rights violation," report of the Committee on Legal Affairs and Human Rights, document 12819, 9 January 2012. Available from http://assembly.coe.int/ ASP/Doc/XrefViewPDF.asp?FileID= 13204&Language=EN; A. de Zayas, "Forced population transfers," Max Planck Encyclopedia of Public International Law.

33 Robert Redslob, *Collected Courses of The Hague Academy of International Law,* vol. 37 (1931), p. 45; A. de Zayas, *Heimatrecht ist Menschenrecht* (Munich, Universitas, 2001), p. 39.

34 The expert group affirmed the right to live and remain in one's homeland, i.e. the right not to be subjected to forcible displacement, as a fundamental human right and a prerequisite to the enjoyment of other rights. Reference was made to the extensive discussion of this issue at the session of the Institute for International Law held at Siena, Italy, which had concluded that transfers of population entailed serious violations of human rights. See also A. de Zayas, "The right to one's homeland, ethnic cleansing and the International Criminal Tribunal for the Former Yugoslavia," *Criminal Law Forum,* vol. 6, No. 2 (1995), pp. 257–314.

35 See A. de Zayas, "Ethnic cleansing: applicable norms, emerging jurisprudence, implementable remedies," in J. Carey, W. Dunlap and R. J. Pritchard, eds., *International Humanitarian Law* (Martinus Nijhoff, 2003).

36 References to Kosovo shall be understood to be in the context of Security Council resolution 1244 (1999).

37 "[I]t is essential, if man is not to be compelled to have recourse, as a last resort, to rebellion against tyranny and oppression, that human rights should be protected by the rule of law."

38 In Africa: Western Sahara. In the Atlantic and Caribbean: Anguilla, Bermuda, British Virgin Islands, Cayman Islands, Falkland Islands (Malvinas), Montserrat, St. Helena, Turks and Caicos Islands, United States Virgin Islands. In Europe: Gibraltar. In Asia and the Pacific: American Samoa, French Polynesia, Guam, New Caledonia, Pitcairn and Tokelau.

39 See endnote 24.

40 Apology by the United States Government to the Hawaiian people, 1993; apology by the Government of Australia to Australia's indigenous peoples, 2008; apology by the United States Government to native peoples of the United States, 2010; apology by the Government of Canada for injustices to the native peoples, 1998; apology by the Government of Canada to former students of Indian Residential Schools, 2008; apology by the Government of Sweden to the Sami people, 1998; apology by King Harald V of Norway to the Sami people, 1997.

41 Bartolomé de las Casas, *Brevísima relación de la destrucción de las Indias (A Brief Account of the Devastation of the Indies)* (1542); Richard Drinnon, *Facing West* (University of Oklahoma Press, 1997); Frederick Hoxie, ed., *Encyclopedia of North American Indians* (Houghton Mifflin Harcourt, 1996), in particular the entry "Population: precontact to present"; David Stannard, *American Holocaust* (Oxford University Press, 1992); Eduardo Galeano, *Open Veins of Latin America* (Monthly Review Press, 1997).

42 See www.idlenomore.ca/.

43 *Chief Bernard Ominayak and the Lubicon Lake Band v. Canada,* communication No. 167/1984, views of the Human Rights Committee adopted on 26 March 1990, p. 33: "Historical inequities to which the State party refers, and certain more recent developments threaten the way of life and culture of the Lubicon Lake Band, and constitute a violation of article 27 [of the International Covenant on Civil and Political Rights] so long as they continue." Cited in Möller and de Zayas, p. 447.

44 www.aiatsis.gov.au/_files/ntru/resources/resourceissues/mabo.pdf.
45 See http://scc-csc.lexum.com/scc-csc/scc-csc/en/item/14246/index.do.
46 See the rationale for the judgement of the Supreme Court of Canada concerning Québec, available from www.scc-csc.gc.ca/case-dossier/info/dock-regi-eng.aspx?cas=25506.
47 See www.jus.uio.no/english/services/library/treaties/01/1-02/rights-duties-states.xml.
48 See endnote 24.
49 A. de Zayas, "Peace as a human right," in A. Eide, J. Möller and I. Ziemele, eds., *Making Peoples Heard* (Leiden, Martinus Nijhoff, 2011), pp. 27-43.
50 http://www.un.org/en/charter-united-nations/index.html
51 https://treaties.un.org/doc/source/docs/spain.pdf
52 http://www.ohchr.org/SP/ProfessionalInterest/Pages/CCPR.aspx
53 http://www.boe.es/buscar/doc.php?id=BOE-A-1977-10733
54 http://www.ohchr.org/SP/ProfessionalInterest/Pages/CESCR.aspx
55 https://www.boe.es/buscar/doc.php?id=BOE-A-1977-10734
56 http://www.congreso.es/consti/constitucion/indice/sinopsis/sinopsis.jsp?art=96&tipo=2
57 https://www.boe.es/buscar/doc.php?id=BOE-A-1990-27553
58 http://www.boe.es/buscar/doc.php?id=BOE-A-1977-10733
59 https://www.boe.es/buscar/doc.php?id=BOE-A-1977-10734
60 https://www.boe.es/buscar/doc.php?id=BOE-A-1980-11884
61 http://collectiupraga.cat/wp-content/uploads/2018/02/19-01-2018.-DENUNCIA-INTERNACIONAL-CAST..pdf
62 http://collectiupraga.cat/wp-content/uploads/2018/02/DENÚNCIA-CEDH-26-02-18.-Cast.-1.pdf
63 https://www.media.cat/2017/12/04/1o-llibertat-dinformacio-corda-fluixa/
64 http://premsa.gencat.cat/pres_fsvp/docs/2017/10/20/11/15/232799c8-755f-4810-ba56-0a5bbb78609c.pdf
65 http://www.cataloniavotes.eu/wp-content/uploads/2017/10/RESEARCH_GROUP_STATEMENT_ON_CATALONIA_REFERENDUM.pdf
http://www.cataloniavotes.eu/wp-content/uploads/2017/10/RESEARCH_GROUP_STATEMENT_ON_CATALONIA_REFERENDUM-1.pdf
66 http://www.elmundo.es/cataluna/2017/12/22/5a3cd8d3ca4741ee5d8b4590.html
67 Jakob Möller/Alfred de Zayas, *United Nations Human Rights Committee Case Law*, N.P. Engel, Strasbourg 2009.
68 http://www.un.org/ga/search/view_doc.asp?symbol=A/69/272&Submit=Search&Lang=S
69 http://federicomayor.blogspot.ch/2017/10/catalunya-nunca-es-tarde-para-el.html
70 John Taylor, *East Timor: The Price of Freedom* (Australia: Pluto Press, 1999).

Chapter 6

THE RULE OF LAW AND THE RIGHT TO TRUTH: INFORMATION AS A KEY ELEMENT OF DEMOCRACY

"The result of a consistent and total substitution of lies for factual truth is not that the lie will now be accepted as truth, and truth be defamed as lie, but that the sense by which we take our bearings in the real world—and the category of truth versus falsehood is among the mental means to this end—is being destroyed."

—HANNAH ARENDT[i]

EMPOWERING CIVIL SOCIETY

There are recurring themes in all of my reports to the Human Rights Council and General Assembly—among them the concept that the "rule of law" must evolve into the "rule of justice," that blind application of the law results in injustice, that in order to make democracy work, we must ensure the right to know, the right to truth, which requires governmental and private-sector transparency and accountability, access to pluralistic information and different perspectives without censorship or self-censorship. Again and again my reports identify obstacles to the establishment of a democratic and equitable international order, including the systematic manipulation of information by governments, the mainstream media, and also the alternative media. I have tried to warn about the ubiquitousness of "fake news," because phoney information eventually evolves into "fake history" in the sense of Orwell's dystopia.

My reports warn about the not-so-improbable emergence of a "Ministry of Truth" tasked with combatting "fake news" by special legislation, even penal legislation, aimed at suppressing dissenting views and imposing an official narrative. It is not only government that engages in this kind of manipulation, as we already see techno-giants like Google, Facebook, Twitter, and Youtube practicing so-called "fact-checking," closing users' accounts, filtering information and blocking access through algorithms, and censoring inconvenient voices. When an author is censored it is not only his/her right to freedom of expression that is being

---

i "Hannah Arendt Explains How Propaganda Uses Lies to Erode All Truth & Morality: Insights from The Origins of Totalitarianism," *Open Culture,* January 2017, https://www.openculture.com/2017/01/hannah-arendt-explains-how-propaganda-uses-lies-to-erode-all-truth-morality.html.

violated, but the rights of all potential listeners and readers who are denied the opportunity of hearing what that person has to say. An atmosphere of censorship is accompanied by a sense of intimidation and results in self-censorship. A modern "Ministry of Truth" wears the mask of the "rule of law," but it actually invents "facts," cements politically-useful narratives, "cancels" inconvenient dissent.

Worse still, we observe the corruption of language, the use of neologisms to confuse, not to elucidate, the deliberate misuse of legal terms, the re-interpretation of legal concepts, giving them a meaning significantly different than that originally intended by the drafters, the Machiavellism that accompanies globalization, with its focus on consumerism, the transformation of basic human necessities like water or shelter into mere "commodities" that can be bought or sold, the myths of the "invisible hand of the market" and the higher "efficiency" of privatization. The sum total of these aberrations leads to what I would call "fake law," "fake diplomacy," "fake democracy" and ultimately totalitarianism.

Access to information can be significantly manipulated and distorted in the digital world. Indeed, algorithms and artificial intelligence (AI) applications have become a critical part of the information environment. We encounter them throughout the internet, on digital devices and in technical systems, in search engines, social media platforms, messaging applications, and public information mechanisms. While algorithms are potentially useful to facilitate access to information, they are already being misused, particularly by search engines that give visibility primarily to mainstream narratives and frequently hide or suppress non-conforming views. David Kaye, the Rapporteur on freedom of opinion and expression, recommended in his 2018 report to the General Assembly: "When procuring or deploying artificial intelligence systems or applications, States should ensure that public sector bodies act consistently with human rights principles. This includes, inter alia, conducting public consultations and undertaking human rights impact assessments or public agency algorithmic impact assessments prior to the procurement or deployment of artificial intelligence systems. Particular attention should be given to the disparate impact of such technologies on racial and religious minorities, political opposition and activists. Government deployment of artificial intelligence systems should be subject to regular audits by external, independent experts."[i] As an independent researcher, historian and lawyer, I have observed how manipulative search engines are and have learned not to rely blindly on search results that offer zero guarantee of comprehensive coverage of the facts and analysis thereof.

It may appear unnecessary to repeat the truism that democracy depends on transparency and accountability, and yet, how often has the democratic order been betrayed by our democratically-elected leaders in the recent past? How

---

i https://www.ohchr.org/EN/Issues/FreedomOpinion/Pages/ReportGA73.aspx
https://www.undocs.org/A/73/348.

often has the media abandoned its essential watchdog function, how often has the "quality press" simply accepted the role of an echo-chamber for the powerful, whether government or transnational corporations? Among the many scandals and betrayals of democracy and the rule of law we recognize the persecution of inconvenient journalists by many governments and their helpers in the media. Perhaps the most scandalous and immoral example of the multinational corruption of the rule of law is the "lawfare" conducted against Julian Assange, the founder of Wikileaks, who in the year 2010 uncovered war crimes committed by the United States and its NATO allies in Afghanistan and Iraq.

In a world where the rule of law matters, these crimes would have been promptly investigated, indictments would have been issued and criminals would have been sentenced. This is an obligation of all States parties to the 1949 Geneva Conventions and the 1977 Additional Protocols. But no. The ire of the governments and the media focused on the journalist who had dared uncover these crimes. The persecution of this journalist was a coordinated assault on the rule of law by the United States, United Kingdom and Sweden, later joined by Ecuador. The instrumentalization of the administration of justice—not for purposes of doing justice, but to destroy a human being, gradually pulled more and more people into a cesspool, a joint-criminal scheme of defamation, trumped-up charges, deliberate delays, covers-up.

In April 2021 my colleague, Professor Nils Melzer, the UN Rapporteur on torture, published a meticulously researched and methodically unassailable documentation of this almost incredible saga. His book can well be called the "J'accuse" of our time, reminding us how our authorities have betrayed us, how four governments colluded in the corruption of the rule of law. Like Emile Zola, who in 1898 exposed the web of lies surrounding the frame-up of the French Colonel Alfred Dreyfuss in France, Nils Melzer shocks us 122 years later with proof of how countries that are ostensibly committed to the rule of law and human rights can betray the democratic ethos with the assistance and complicity of the mainstream media. Melzer writes about "concrete evidence of political persecution, gross arbitrariness on the part of the administration of justice and deliberate torture and abuse."[i]

This is an enormously important book because it requires us to abandon our "comfort zone" and demand transparency and accountability from our governments. Indeed, it is scandalous that none of the four governments involved in the frame-up cooperated with Professor Melzer's investigations and instead answered his precise questions with "political platitudes." As UN Independent Expert for 6 years, I too experienced a similar lack of cooperation from powerful countries to whom I had addressed notes verbales concerning allegations of serious

---

i Nils Melzer, *Der Fall Julian Assange*, Piper Verlag, Munchen 2021, p. 14.

violations of human rights. None of these countries responded professionally. Alas these are some of the same countries that demand adherence to "a rules-based international order" from Russia and China.

Melzer reminds us of Hans-Christian Andersen's fable "The Emperor's New Clothes." Indeed, everyone involved in the Assange frame-up has consistently maintained the illusion of legality, gone along with the scam, repeated a narrative full of demonstrable untruths, until an innocent child, who is not into the game of the adults, exclaims—but the Emperor has no clothes! That is the point. Melzer shows us that the administration of justice—at least in these four countries—has no clothes and instead of advancing justice, colludes in the persecution of a journalist, a true human rights defender. The reader is almost afraid to turn each page, because every new page of this remarkable book uncovers even more depravity on the part of precisely those authorities who are tasked with defending the rule of law. This has gravest implications for the survival of the democratic order. Melzer convinces us with facts—that we are living in a time of "post-truth," and that it is our responsibility to correct this situation now, lest we wake up tyranny.[i]

Aware of anti-democratic trends in my country of nationality, the United States of America, and witness to numerous instances of systemic incoherence and betrayal of "European values" by member states of the Council of Europe during my years as rapporteur, I had already started my second report to the Human Rights Council (2013)[ii] by recalling democratic and Voltairean fundamentals.
—AdeZ

* * *

The will of the people shall be the basis of the authority of government; this will shall be expressed in periodic and genuine elections which shall be by universal and equal suffrage and shall be held by secret vote or by equivalent free voting procedures.[1]

Democracy is based on the freely expressed will of the people to determine their own political, economic, social and cultural systems and their full participation in all aspects of their lives.[2]

A democratic and equitable international order is inherent in the fundamental human rights that humanity shares.[3] It is achievable, step-by-step, when every country and people act at the local, regional and international levels, aware that such an international order must be based on the United Nations Charter and

---

i Ibid., pp. 326–331.
ii https://undocs.org/A/HRC/24/38.

the human rights treaties, which together make up what effectively serves as the Constitution of the modern world, subject, of course, to necessary reforms. The Preamble and articles 1 and 2 of the Charter lay down the intention of the "peoples of the United Nations" to build an international order of peace, human rights and development.

With regard to an international democratic and equitable order, it is obvious that such international order depends on the sovereign equality of States, the right of peoples to self-determination and a commitment to sharing the riches of the planet in a spirit of international solidarity.[4] While self-determination is closely related to the idea of democracy, participation in international decision-making is still far from equal or even equitable. Indeed, the United Nations Security Council is not democratic, nor are the Bretton Woods institutions. There are other players which are not democratic in their structure or in their modus operandi, including certain elitist organizations such as the Trilateral Commission, the Atlantic Council and the Bilderberg Group, as well as better-known conferences of the G-7, G-20, the World Economic Forum, and military alliances such as the North Atlantic Treaty Organization (NATO). Meanwhile, transnational corporations exert increasing influence on global decision-making and impact on the options of sovereign States and on the enjoyment of human rights.[5] Corporations—whether national or multinational—do not operate on the basis of democratic principles but seek primarily profit, and their decisions affect the international order. Reforms are necessary so as to ensure the equitable participation of States, large and small, in global decision-making, especially concerning decisions on peacekeeping, the environment, trade relations and the common heritage of humankind.

In a democracy, it is the people who are sovereign. Therefore, with regard to the promotion of democracy at the local, country and regional levels, civil society must have a stronger voice in all political processes. The situation in some countries is grave, since freedom of expression, peaceful assembly and association, and free and fair elections, are not ensured; opposition leaders are arrested or killed; journalists, whistleblowers, vloggers and bloggers are harassed, intimidated and detained; public demonstrations are prohibited; peaceful demonstrators massacred, elections are reduced to masquerades, etc. Several Rapporteurs have documented these violations, the Human Rights Council has adopted pertinent resolutions, and the Human Rights Committee has adopted important jurisprudence thereon.[6] The Independent Expert is highly concerned about such situations where the rule of law and the respect for key principles such as free, fair and competitive elections are blatantly violated.

It is crucial that electoral systems be free and fair, ensure the free formation and operation of political parties, in accordance with best practices related to freedom of association, and respect the principle of non-discrimination so that all groups, including opposition groups or groups promoting dissenting views, can take part in the electoral process. These rules should apply not only for general or important elections, but also in local consultations. Participation is more than casting votes: it implies the ability for individuals and people to freely express their views, and for this voice to be heard "to shape the decisions that affect their community."[7]

But even in ostensibly democratic States, there is no reason for complacency. Although formally free elections are held, the electoral process in many countries is dysfunctional and election results and subsequent policies do not always correspond to the wishes of the electorate. In order to satisfy democratic requirements, there must be consultation of the public and the choice of candidates must be free and transparent. Methods to determine the will of the people, for instance, through frequent opinion polling and through referenda, should be put in place. As many observers note, representative democracy frequently manifests a disconnect between parliamentarians and the people, so that parliamentarians have agendas that do not correspond to the wishes of the electorate. This has led in many countries to apathy, cynicism and large-scale absenteeism in elections. What is needed is not only parliaments, but parliamentarians who genuinely represent the wishes of the electorate. In almost all countries, women are underrepresented and in many countries women are essentially disenfranchised.[8] Such disenfranchisement is undemocratic and demands corrective measures.

The Right to Know

A *conditio sine qua non* for democracy is the right to know. Indeed, a manipulated population cannot genuinely express what they really want and need. Many elections are bogus, in a sense "fake" elections, because the population only echoes the propaganda it has been fed, and contending parties offer no real choice, leading to a straight-jacket of pseudo-democratic, ritual elections.

Thus, the right to know has been a recurring *leitmotif* in all of my 14 reports. The right of access to truthful, reliable information as provided for in article 19 (2) of the International Covenant on Civil and Political Rights is indispensable both for domestic and international democracy, for transparency and accountability, and in a wider sense for the rule of law.

One premise of this 2013 report to the Human Rights Council is that democracy requires a free press that informs the public, enabling it to exercise conscientious judgment, free of government censorship and corporate-media manipulation. There is a legitimate democratic expectation that the media will have not only diversity of ideas but also diversity of ownership. Domestically, each government should take a close look at its telecommunications legislation, at the concentration of ownership in the media, and utilize anti-trust legislation to break up conglomerates that hinder open debate and diversity. What passes for journalism in many countries actually leaves the population indoctrinated, not informed. Too often journalism reflects a structural bias for the elites, the government and corporate interests.

Whereas freedoms of opinion, the media, peaceful assembly and association are absolutely essential to every democracy, these rights are lacking in some countries and hollowed out elsewhere. State censorship constitutes an obvious violation of article 19 of the ICCPR: a manipulated public. State interference with the media and Internet is a worldwide problem. Censorship is also practiced by the private sector, engendering the same undemocratic result: On 17 July 2011, the Human Rights Committee adopted General Comment 34, in which it addressed the threats to freedom of opinion and expression, including defamation laws, blasphemy laws, and memory laws, which interfere with the free flow of ideas and necessary debate thereon:

> Defamation laws must be crafted with care to ensure that they ... do not serve, in practice, to stifle freedom of expression. All such laws, in particular penal defamation laws, should include such defences as the defence of truth ... (paragraph 47);

> Prohibitions of displays of lack of respect for a religion or other belief system, including blasphemy laws, are incompatible with the Covenant.... (paragraph 48).

> Laws that penalize the expression of opinions about historical facts are incompatible with the obligations that the Covenant imposes on States parties in relation to the respect for freedom of opinion and expression. The Covenant does not permit general prohibition of expressions of an erroneous opinion or an incorrect interpretation of past events.... (paragraph 49).

Such laws have totalitarian implications and consequences, violate human dignity, the right to open debate, academic freedom, and ultimately lead to intellectual stagnation and self-censorship,[9] which have adverse consequences on the ability of people to participate in decision-making.

Access to truthful and reliable information from diverse sources is indispensable to a responsible citizenry and to the exercise of the vote. Freedoms of expression and peaceful assembly are not only rights but also civic duties that should be exercised freely and openly in every democracy. Freedom of expression is not just the right to echo politically correct ideas, but the right to express one's personal convictions, which necessarily includes the right to be wrong. In some countries, the right to demonstrate is significantly curtailed and plagued by red tape; in others, demonstrators are arrested or even killed.

Increasingly, it seems that some media carry primarily the views of the elites. Even on controversial issues, there is lack of balance and little competitive opportunity for views other than those of the advertisers. Relentless advertising and hyper-commercialization of the media also have the effect of misleading the public, distracting their attention from real issues and making the audience addicted to sensationalist, trivial or trash news. A corporate media that only seeks profit and neglects public interest fails the test of a democratic media.

Quite generally, it must be recognized that the profit system serves primarily the elites and all too frequently trumps the interests of society.

A democratic and equitable international order cannot be achieved as long as civil society lacks mechanisms to ensure change, e.g. by democratically enforcing a shift in priorities away from military expenditures and toward general disarmament, away from surveillance of citizens and toward the prosecution of corruption and criminality, away from "austerity measures" and toward social justice.

It would be good to report that States and civil society are advancing in the promotion of a culture of democratic thinking, democratic *feeling* and democratic acting. Unfortunately, most areas of human activity seem to be locked into their own logic and dynamic, where democracy is conjured to legitimize the *status quo,* while doing little to give life to the concepts of participation and consultation or to core values of the United Nations, including transparency and accountability. Yet, the spirit of democracy resides in the minds of women and men, and step by step each community, State, and region can claim and reclaim it. This culture of democracy must be home-grown and cannot be exported or imposed top-down. The conviction that the government should serve the people and that its powers must be circumscribed by a Constitution and the rule of law remains crucial. Juvenal's question *quis custodiet ipsos custodes* (who guards the guardians?) remains a central concern of democracy, since the people must always watch over the constitutional behaviour of the leaders and impeach them if they act in contravention of their duties. Constitutional courts must fulfil this need and civil society should show solidarity with human rights defenders and whistle blowers who, far from being unpatriotic, perform a public service to their countries and the world.

The "vital interests" of States must be made to conform to the Purposes and Principles of the United Nations, while respecting the sovereignty of States and the self-determination of peoples. The problem remains that, although there is talk on reforms, vested interests prevent their implementation; although there are *Indignados* and occupy movements, there is no effective mechanism to translate public protest into concrete reform. Soon everything returns to business as usual and the public remains irrelevant. Since public access to information, freedom of expression and the media are indispensable to carry out reforms, it is crucial to ensure the democratization of the media, so that it exercises its watchdog function. A media controlled by the State or held hostage by corporate interests undermines democracy. And whereas media hype can negatively impact decision-making, responsible media can advance a human rights agenda through information and education. The gap between institutionalized power and the people must be bridged. It bears repeating: Democracy means participation. "Formal democracy" is no democracy.

Recommendations

This 2013 report ends with some observations that remain valid today:

(a) States should strengthen the rule of law and implement the principle of separation of powers. In particular, States should take all necessary legislative and administrate measures to make civil society participation in decision-making more effective, in particular by allowing more direct democracy through the instruments of popular initiative, referenda, recall and impeachment. Moreover, not only the law but also actual practice must be assessed. Empowerment of the public requires education programmes on human rights, including the right to peace.

(b) States should adopt the necessary legislative, administrative and judicial measures to give effect to the Universal Declaration of Human Rights and States parties to the ICCPR should implement articles 2, 19, 21, 22 and 25 ICCPR, consistent with the principle expressed in the Advisory Opinion of the Permanent Court of International Justice, "according to which a State which has contracted valid international obligations is bound to make in its legislation such modifications as may be necessary to ensure the fulfilment of the obligations undertaken."[10]

(c) States are invited to go beyond the provisions of article 25 ICCPR to ensure pluralism in elections and enhanced consultation with stakeholders. In particular, States should implement the participation and consultation recommendations in the relevant General Comments of the United Nations treaty bodies.

(d) Multiparty electoral systems and the establishment of political parties representing a wide diversity of points of view should be facilitated. States should review their legislation on the establishment and prohibition of political parties. One-party systems suffer from an obvious democratic deficit, and if only one political party is allowed to operate, provision should be made to facilitate and encourage public participation in the formulation of policies and the possibility or articulating a diversity of views within the party.

(e) States should ensure access to public information[11] and repeal legislation that is incompatible with articles 18 and 19 of the ICCPR; in particular, blasphemy and memory laws and any laws that hinder open discussion of political and historical events. States should refrain from misusing anti-terror legislation to intimidate and suppress dissent and thus undermine participation in the democratic process.[12] States should ensure freedom of expression online and refrain from censorship except for reasons of health and morals.

(f) States should never impose reprisals against human rights defenders and repeal laws that hinder the right to peaceful assembly in public and private spheres, impose unreasonable fines or imprisonment on demonstrators, or restrict the right to association and collective bargaining.

INFORMATION DEFICITS

In my 2013 report to the General Assembly[i] I focused on certain obstacles to the rule of law, including the illusion of objectivity and the negative role of the corporate media in advancing or sabotaging democracy. Do the media contribute to the dissemination of truth, or do they manipulate the facts, transmit "fake news" and conspiracy theories, engage in political indoctrination? Do they fulfill their role as "watchdogs," ready to uncover abuse and corruption, or do they cover-up the crimes of government? Do they help the electorate understand what is being done in their name? What protection should be provided for whistleblowers? —AdeZ

* * *

According to Human Rights Council resolution 18/6, the promotion of a free, just, effective and balanced international information and communications order is necessary to achieve a democratic international order. Nevertheless,

---

i https://www.ohchr.org/EN/Issues/IntOrder/Pages/IEInternationalorderIndex.aspx

censorship and manipulation are practised in many parts of the world. Totalitarian Governments control news and education and prohibit any form of pluralism. In ostensibly democratic States, Governments interfere at various levels with access to information and academic freedom and freedom to question, including through "memory laws" that pretend to crystallize history and penalize the expression of non-conformist views. Such laws and the abuse in their application hinder freedom of research and have been found by the Human Rights Committee to be incompatible with article 19 of the International Covenant on Civil and Political Rights.[13]

Censorship and skewed reporting is also practised by the private-sector media, which often indoctrinate more effectively than Governments. Citizens and civil society should therefore assert their right to know and demand from their Governments that academic freedom as well as unencumbered access to information be guaranteed, which are essential to develop one's own opinions and exercise responsibly the right of democratic participation.

While in totalitarian regimes, government controls the media and criminalizes journalists, bloggers and human rights defenders who do not echo the State's propaganda, in numerous democratic countries, the media are largely in private hands—too few hands. Often media are controlled by conglomerates responsive to corporations and advertisers who determine the content of news and other programmes, frequently disseminating disinformation or suppressing crucial information necessary for democratic discourse. Indeed, the media blackout on important issues constitutes a grave obstacle to democracy, since absent sufficient information and without free and pluralistic media, democracy is dysfunctional and the political process, including elections, becomes a mere formality—not an expression of the will of the people. Some observers compare elections in some countries with sports events, where people are but spectators. Moreover, elections must not be mere interludes for pushing a lever and then retreating to passivity, for democracy demands committed participation in the daily workings of society.[14]

There is a growing feeling that some media have betrayed the public trust. Far from facilitating participation by the people in decision-making, they have contributed to the consolidation of decision-making by oligarchs. In many countries, observers criticize the apparent subservience of the press to the Government, noting the employment of a skewed moral compass and selectivity.[15] The gulf between public policy and public opinion can be bridged only by informed dialogue, not by slogans and caricatures.

Freedom of online and offline media is also linked to the right to privacy stipulated in article 17 of the International Covenant on Civil and Political Rights. The so-called "war on terrorism" since 2001 has eroded a spectrum of civil liberties essential to a democratic and equitable international order. Terrorism[16] poses a grave threat to a just order. As Secretary-General Ban Ki-moon has said, "Nothing can justify terrorism—ever. No grievance, no goal, no cause can excuse terrorist acts. At the same time, we must remove the conditions that feed the problem. Terrorism festers where conflicts are endemic... and where human rights, human dignity and human life are not protected and impunity prevails."[17] The Independent Expert considers that the answer to terrorism cannot be a huge surveillance system and policies that violate article 17 of the International Covenant on Civil and Political Rights,[18] or the criminalization of individuals voicing dissent or minority opinions. What must be researched and remedied are the causes of terrorism, which frequently originate in despair, hopelessness, social injustice and the growing gulf between the super-rich and the extremely poor—problems that will be corrected when there is political will. Fighting rogue terrorism by State terrorism[19] exacerbates matters and undermines the credibility of international law and ubiquitous commitment to the rule of law. Human rights and security are not in competition but complementary and interdependent.

Disclosures about the magnitude of covert State surveillance and well-known examples of intimidation of human rights defenders shock the conscience and require public discussion and corrective action in each country and by the international community. In a democratic society, it is crucial for citizens to know whether their Governments are acting constitutionally or are engaged in policies that violate international law and human rights. It is their civic duty to protest against Government secrecy and cover-ups, the chilling effect of disproportionate surveillance, acts of intimidation and harassment, arbitrary arrests and defamation of human rights defenders, including whistleblowers, as unpatriotic or even traitors, when in fact they may be the most effective defenders of the rule of law. These acts of surveillance and intimidation are hallmarks of totalitarianism, not of democratic governance.

The Independent Expert salutes the approach taken in 2009 by the Parliamentary Assembly of the Council of Europe in adopting the Convention on Access to Official Documents (CETS No. 205),[20] followed by resolution 1838 (2011) on Abuse of state secrecy and national security: obstacles to parliamentary and judicial scrutiny of human rights violations and by the adoption on 24 June 2013 of a report on National security and access to information, stating, inter alia:

> Most human rights abuses in the context of the "war on terror" were in fact brought to light through whistleblowers and investigative work by journalists and human rights organizations rather than through parliamentary or judicial oversight mechanisms.... Lack of

information on important issues of public interests prevents effective scrutiny and fosters a culture of secrecy and impunity which, in turn, threatens the democratic values upon which our societies rest.[21]

Equally incisive is the text adopted on 12 June 2013 by the Open Society Justice Initiative and 21 other international organizations entitled "Global Principles on National Security and the Right to Information."[22]

Civil society must take the space it needs to exercise democratic rights, while non-governmental organizations should have greater opportunity to participate in the conduct of domestic affairs and to contribute to the work of the Human Rights Council and other United Nations bodies. Economic and Social Council resolution 1996/31 has proved to be too restrictive, hindering legitimate non-governmental organizations from obtaining consultative status. By contrast, quasi-governmental non-governmental organizations ("GONGOS") have obtained consultative status through the existing scheme. Bearing in mind that the Human Rights Council reports to the General Assembly and not to the Economic and Social Council, as its predecessor did, it would be sensible for the Assembly to issue new rules for granting consultative status to non-governmental organizations.

Whereas in recent times there have been good developments and implementable proposals, a number of which are highlighted herein, the blockage by vested interests persists, obstructing change and confusing matters through obsolete dogmas about, inter alia, "efficient markets," "benign deregulation," "free-trade agreements" and accompanied by misleading arguments, weasel words, red herrings, cognitive dissonances and Orwellianisms.

Pursuant to article 29 of the Universal Declaration of Human Rights, emphasis should be placed on duties and obligations, not just on rights. It is a civic duty for peoples and individuals to act at both the domestic and international levels; to call for democratic elections and processes; not to keep silent when human rights are being violated and when propaganda for war is being disseminated. They should demand from Governments greater transparency and accountability, a shift of national budgets away from military expenditures and towards the promotion of human rights, an end to impunity for corruption. Civil society should also demonstrate solidarity with all victims, not only with "preferred victims," conscious of the fact that there is no monopoly on suffering, and that all victims, living and dead, share the same dignity. Competition among victims is deplorable and leads to discrimination and further injustice.

It may be permitted to propose a shift in thinking models that could advance the common agenda by discarding the obsolete division of rights into artificial categories of first, second and third generation rights—with their skewed value judgements. Human rights should henceforth be redefined in functional terms, recognizing human dignity as the source of all rights, whether individual or collective. This functional paradigm reveals the interrelatedness of human rights as the convergence of enabling rights (such as the rights to peace, food, health, homeland and environment), inherent rights (such as equality and non-discrimination), procedural rights (such as access to information, freedom of expression and due process) and what could be called outcome rights, that is, the practical realization of human dignity in the form of the right to our identity, to achieve our potential and to be just who we are, free to live our transcendence, practice our faith, enjoy our own culture, preferences and opinions, without intimidation, surveillance or pressures to behave in a prescribed "politically correct" mode or endure self-censorship. The absence of this outcome right to identity and self-respect is reflected in much of the strife we see in the world today.

STRENGTHENING THE RULE OF LAW[i]

In my final thematic report to the Human Rights Council I came back to issues of the rule of law, democratization of the media, self-determination and referenda. —AdeZ

* * *

Any process aimed at self-determination should be accompanied by the participation and consent of the peoples concerned. Thus, a reliable method of determining public opinion and avoiding manufactured consent must be devised to ensure the authenticity of the expression of public will in the absence of threats of or the use of force. In addition, while it is possible to reach solutions that guarantee self-determination within an existing State entity, e.g. autonomy, federalism and self-government, if there is a compelling demand for separation, it is extremely important to avoid the use of force, which would endanger local, regional and international stability and further erode the enjoyment of other human rights. Therefore, good-faith negotiations and a readiness to compromise are necessary; in some cases, these could be coordinated through the good offices of the Secretary-General and the High Commissioner for Human Rights or under the auspices of the Security Council or the General Assembly. The Independent Expert has also advocated for the United Nations to provide advice and technical

---

i https://undocs.org/A/HRC/37/63

assistance to States on viable models of autonomy, federalism and, eventually, referendums.

Lawyers have been called "pens for rent" and "intellectual mercenaries." Government lawyers have special responsibilities and should not act like "escape artists." They should endeavour to see their role as that of facilitators of enforcement of just laws both nationally and internationally. They should devote their efforts to translating international commitments into concrete action and crafting the necessary measures to comply with treaties and the rules of international judicial bodies. Alas, many government lawyers mistake their vocation for that of defence lawyers, paid to get their guilty clients off the hook. It is not their function to look for ways to dodge responsibility by concocting specious interpretations of the law, making bogus distinctions or inventing loopholes. Would it not be more sensible if lawyers endeavoured to make human rights law implementable—and not constantly try to drill holes into the vessel of human dignity?

Sterile legalisms, the fetishism of law—otherwise known as the doctrine of positivism—have emerged as a serious impediment to a world order based on the rule of law, which must also be the rule of justice. Alas, Governments and private sector actors, including transnational corporations, sometimes abuse the law to destroy justice.

To strengthen the international rule of law and multilateral law-making, the Independent Expert has recommended amendments to the Charter and the statute of the International Court of Justice, which would bolster the Court, giving the Court the necessary power to initiate the issuance of advisory opinions without being asked by the Security Council or General Assembly, and creating an enforcement mechanism for its judgments and advisory opinions. Furthermore, calls for a yet-to-be-established world parliamentary assembly or a United Nations parliamentary assembly seek to address international democratic deficits and give expression to global public opinion by including all citizens in global decision-making through the designation of representatives specifically elected for this purpose.

ANNEX I

EFFORTS TO TAKE THE MANDATE'S FINDINGS TO THE PUBLIC

During my six years as independent expert I issued some one hundred press releases and information notes, many of them devoted to the human right to peace, the right of self-determination of peoples, the need for a rules-based world order, the democratization of the media, the right to truth, the right of access to information, freedom of expression and a Charter of Rights of Whistleblowers.

It was not always easy to get these press releases issued by the Office, because some of them were considered as going against the mainstream narrative, and the OHCHR has traditionally tried to remain mainstream and not "rock the boat" too much, lest it lose voluntary donations from States, particularly from rich States that breach human rights as a matter of course and in total impunity.

Admittedly, the OHCHR does not have the right to censor a rapporteur, but censorship is indeed practiced, and the OHCHR can also sabotage a mandate it dislikes by simply withholding the substantive and logistical support that it is duty-bound to provide to all mandate-holders without discrimination. Alas, there are mandate-holders who receive enormous support, because their mandates are useful to powerful States, and other mandate-holders who get the short end of the stick and end up without assistants for prolonged periods of time, or whose assistants are changed every four to six months, thus depriving the mandate-holder of continuity of service.

Another practice that is hardly known outside OHCHR is that the UN secretariat writes a significant percentage of the reports and press releases of the mandate holders. It is actually not well seen, when a rapporteur "dares" to write his/her reports, press releases and info notes, or when the mandate-holder decides independently on his/her priorities, i.e. what reports to write. I welcomed input from the Secretariat, having been a Secretariat member myself for more than two decades and I acknowledged whatever assistance I was given, but again and again OHCHR tried to influence the choice of topics for my reports, dissuade me from writing certain reports or discourage me from conducting a particular country-visit. On one occasion an assistant failed to invite any of the experts I had placed on a list for an expert consultation, and other "experts" were invited instead, who, as it turned out, did not advance the research I was conducting and essentially only rehashed platitudes and generally created confusion. I do not know whether this happened deliberately, or whether it was just incompetence. On another occasion, following a disagreement about priorities, I was "punished" for my recalcitrance by being denied any assistance whatever when I travelled on official mission to the 2017 annual meeting of the IMF and World Bank. Actually, I do not know of any official mission by a UN rapporteur in which the mandate-holder did not have at least one OHCHR assistant with him/her to handle the logistics, reschedule interviews, contact potential experts, call taxis, take notes etc. Notwithstanding the handicap, the mission turned out a success and my report on the World Bank in September 2017 before the Human Rights Council garnered applause from NGOs and delegations, a very rare occurrence. My report to the General Assembly on the IMF in October 2017 was similarly received with applause. I was surprised when a delegate from a francophone African country came up to me at the Third Committee of the General Assembly and said "vous êtes le premier rapporteur qui parle la verité" (you are the first rapporteur who speaks the truth). For a fleeting moment I felt flattered and thought that—just maybe—I was making a difference with some delegations.

Nevertheless, what I internally flagged to OHCHR authorities and colleagues deserves being reflected in this book, because other rapporteurs have also shared with me their concern that OHCHR sometimes interferes with their independence and does not always provide the logistical and substantive support required by the Human Rights Council and General Assembly pursuant to the resolutions yearly adopted on each mandate. For instance, Council resolution 18/6 that created the international order mandate instructed "the United Nations High Commissioner for Human Rights to provide all the necessary human and financial resources for the effective fulfilment of the mandate by the independent expert."[i] My experience and the experience of several other rapporteurs is that OHCHR assistance is not always being provided equitably, and that some "popular" mandates enjoy enhanced support.

Looking back, I must recognize that alertness and resoluteness on my part was required to safeguard my independence from manifold influences by the Office and peer pressure from "politically correct" rapporteurs. In the course of my years as rapporteur, maybe a dozen of my draft press releases did not see the light of day, thus leaving me no alternative but to upload the texts onto my blog and indicate that they had originally been intended as OHCHR press releases, but that the Office had declined publication. Needless to say, my blog activity was not always appreciated, although it did amuse a certain number of colleagues in the Secretariat who congratulated me for my "candour." It flabbergasted me that some bureaucrats were not always prepared to accept the simple fact that the Council had appointed me "independent expert," that I took this independence

---

i Resolution 36/4 repeated this request so that I could "prepare a final report on his studies conducted during the last six years of his mandate, and to share it with the Human Rights Council at its thirty-seventh session." Similarly, GA resolution 71/149 requested "the Secretary-General and the United Nations High Commissioner for Human Rights to continue to provide all the human and financial resources necessary for the effective fulfilment of the mandate." https://www2.ohchr.org/english/bodies/hrcouncil/docs/18session/A.HRC.RES.18.6_English.pdf

seriously, and that for better or worse I was acting in good faith according to my conscience and using my professional judgment as professor of international law.

In December 2016, following the election of Donald Trump, there was considerable malaise at OHCHR, and I sensed a kind of anti-Trump agitation. The traditional Human Rights Day message, issued on 10 December, was drafted in a manner that did not accept nuances and dissenting views. It essentially sounded opportunistic and focused on populism and xenophobia—neglecting economic, social and cultural rights and other important concerns such as peace and human security. The Rapporteurs were invited to issue a press release on the occasion, but the text was not open to democratic drafting and did not reflect the spectrum of views of many Rapporteurs. True enough, I had been pro forma consulted, and I had made it very clear that I strongly disliked Trumpism, but I insisted that other urgent matters be addressed, including extreme poverty, the arms race and the adverse impact of unilateral coercive measures. None of my concerns were reflected in the final text, which I considered unbalanced and unduly confrontational.

Accordingly, and to the astonishment of some colleagues, I refused to be associated with it. A row followed and some rapporteurs were "uncomfortable" with me for not joining the "consensus," and even angrier when I reminded them that there was no consensus and that they were not acting independently as experts, but as members of a herd, engaging in "groupthink." My conscience told me that the independence of rapporteurs had to be vindicated and that the principle was much too important to abandon it. I felt that it was inappropriate to have statements issued in the name of all rapporteurs, when many of them did not agree with the text.

It became an uphill battle with the Office to insist that a "complementary" opinion be issued in my name and in the name of other rapporteurs who may be inclined to join me. Two others did join me, although I knew others who essentially agreed with me, but lacked the courage to go public.

My press release was issued as a "communiqué"[i] and, as expected, it caused consternation.[ii] Reportedly, the communiqué was quoted by the media more than the original joint press release of the other rapporteurs, and some press articles in France made quite a scandal of it, including "Mediapart,"[iii] which devoted a very long opinion piece to it. —AdeZ

* * *

---

[i] https://www.ohchr.org/en/NewsEvents/Pages/DisplayNews.aspx?NewsID=21057&LangID=E
[ii] https://www.ohchr.org/en/NewsEvents/Pages/DisplayNews.aspx?NewsID=21057&LangID=E
[iii] https://blogs.mediapart.fr/salim-koudil/blog/230117/le-conseil-des-droits-de-l-homme-de-lonu-ebranle

GENEVA (21 December 2016)—Three Special Procedures mandate holders[i] consider it appropriate to issue an opinion complementary to the communiqué which was published in the name of special procedures mandate holders on 9 December on the occasion of Human Rights Day.

"We call on the international community and specially on human rights mechanisms world-wide to engage in a constructive debate so as to identify objectively problems that affect the enjoyment of human rights by billions human beings—including the right to development, to food security, to clean water and sanitation, to education, to sovereign debt restructuring. Likewise odious debt, crushing "austerity measures," unilateral coercive measures, war or other violent action, whether by States or by non-state actors are issues of real concern as we stand on the threshold of the New Year.

Human Rights Day commemoration is also an occasion to endorse mechanisms to provide recourse and remedy to victims of human rights violations, to advance the idea of a human right to peace, to the proactive State protection of the family as the natural and fundamental group unit of society, to defend the right to privacy, culture and identity. We should not forget those who continue to suffer tragically from the denial of the right of self-determination, and those who endure war and occupation.

We must warn against war propaganda (prohibited in article 20(1) ICCPR), the persecution and prosecution of whistleblowers. Nor can we remain silent on the on-going discrimination and murder of persons suffering from albinism, the persecution of Christian and of other religious minorities in the Middle East and of Muslim minorities in South East Asia and elsewhere, on the impunity of non-state actors and transnational corporations for major human rights violations, including the destruction of the environment (ecocide).

The signatories consider that SPs should aspire to being the conscience of the Human Rights Council and observe a holistic approach to all human rights, aiming at the prevention of violations and not only at reacting *post hoc*. It is our function to identify the root causes of violations, so that we can better prevent them. It is not helpful to condemn "populism" if one is not willing to recognize that populists are merely filling the vacuum left by governments that for decades have been insensitive to the needs of the people, who have continued "business as usual," and not listened.

It is easy to condemn social phobias of which a fashionable few only are usually brought out, but there is need henceforth to cover the attacks on the broad range of internationally recognised minorities whose members are known to suffer shockingly across the world. Empathy for victims should not be selective. There is need also to reflect on the reasons for those multiple phobias, offering guidance as to how to defuse them in a manner consistent with human rights and human dignity.

Furthermore, care must be taken not to legitimize language that can be misused by those who want to destroy human rights by invoking other human rights. It is thus not desirable to denounce "hate speech" without pointing out normative dangers, since some national legislations are developing into major threats to democratic discourse and are

---

i This statement was signed by The Independent Expert on the promotion of a democratic and equitable international order, Alfred de Zayas; the Independent Expert on the enjoyment of human rights by persons with albinism, Ms. Ikponwosa Ero; and the Special Rapporteur on the negative impact of the unilateral coercive measures on the enjoyment of human rights, Mr. Idriss Jazairy.

being misused by numerous states to intimidate dissenters, threatening them with penal sanctions and engendering an anti-democratic chilling effect. The "hate speech" motive as well as the suppression of dissent under other motives is fostering the development of a new "franchise" for ostracism and sanctions. The claim that dissent jeopardizes an entity, whether it be a State, a social group or a professional community, is in essence totalitarian unless the dissenters' views have been previously discussed with them in search of a compromise expression of a common position.

Incitement to violence must, of course, be combated, but it is necessary for this purpose to clearly define what "hate speech" and what "incitement" mean, hence the necessity to scrupulously protect freedom of expression as laid down in articles 19(1) & (2) of ICCPR and respect the very narrow grounds for imposing limitations envisaged in article 19(3). Interpretation of "hate speech" cannot be left to the discretion of governments and prosecutors, as this would open the door to arbitrariness contrary to the rule of law and tantamount to censorship. Article 20(2) ICCPR, which prohibits certain types of advocacy leading to discrimination and violence, is an important provision, but it must be read in conjunction with article 19 ICCPR as a whole and with the Committee's general comment 34 on freedom of opinion and expression, and the relevant jurisprudence on the protection of privacy, religious convictions and the right to access to information.

We therefore appeal to the international community to recommit, on the occasion of the New Year 2017, to upholding all human rights enshrined in the Universal Declaration of Human Rights of 10 December 1948 and in all related Covenants and Treatises. Indeed all these rights are inter-related, inter-dependent and equally deserving of support. There is no priority to be established between them. As proclaimed in the Vienna Declaration of 25 June 1993 on Human Rights: "The international community must treat human rights globally, in a fair and equal manner, on the same footing and with the same emphasis."

ANNEX II

HUMAN RIGHTS WATCH DISAPPOINTS ON HUMAN RIGHTS[i]

Our concern about the weaponization of human rights and the double-standards manifested by many human rights NGOs was the subject of an essay that Idriss Jazairy and I published in the Interpress Service on 25 July 2019, three days after the publication of an article entitled "UN Chief Guterres has disappointed on Human Rights" by Kenneth Roth, Executive Director of Human Rights Watch. Sure enough, HRW issues many solid reports, e.g. its recent report

---

i http://www.ipsnews.net/2019/07/human-rights-watch-disappoints-human-rights/

concerning human rights violations in Palestine,[i] but sometimes its reports are disappointing, e.g. on Venezuela, which I fact-checked during my mission to Venezuela and found methodologically flawed. —AdeZ

* * *

GENEVA, July 25, 2019 (IPS)—On 22 July 2019, Kenneth Roth published an article in Publico, Lisbon, entitled: "UN Chief Guterres has disappointed on Human Rights."

This essay lampooning António Guterres is not a voice "against the tide" but very much mainstream—and demonstrably skewed. Major NGOs headquartered in rich advanced countries and enjoying generous funding from the Establishment may not always think "out of the box" and are as likely, as are the interest groups which support them, to politicize human rights and therefore to disappoint rights holders in smaller or weaker countries.

While they do contribute to exposing situations of human rights violations worldwide, they are not exempt from biases which reflect the structure of their central governing bodies or the cultural environment within which they operate. They cannot arrogate to themselves the sole legitimacy to speak in the name of the civil society of many countries, and when they claim to do so, they may disappoint rightsholders, particularly in the developing countries, whose priorities are frequently different from theirs.

Sober analysis and stocktaking are necessary to determine whether and to what extent the priorities and agendas of NGOs like HRW are set by the overall interests of the established power-structures and multiple elites in many countries. Kenneth Roth's article expressing disappointment at the human rights performance of Secretary General António Guterres fails to identify the root causes of human rights violations.

His admonitions have little or no preventative value, and do not formulate constructive recommendations such as, for instance, the provision of advisory services and technical assistance to many countries that need it and have asked for it.

HRW's "naming and shaming" strategy has been inconclusive at best because "naming and shaming" depends on the authority of the "namer" and the impartiality of the methodology. Kenneth Roth's bludgeoning of the UN Secretary General in this regard is yet another expression of grandstanding and even of a measure of arrogance. HRW's criticism of China, Russia, Cuba, Nicaragua, Venezuela, would be more persuasive if the organization addressed with the same intensity the egregious violations of human rights in many other countries.

For instance, Mr. Roth does not mention the denial of the right of self-determination to millions of people, the retrogression in the enjoyment of economic, social and cultural rights (prohibited by the Covenant on Economic, Social and Cultural Rights), the looting of natural resources and degradation of the environment by transnational corporations and their neocolonial schemes, the impunity enjoyed by politicians who engage in aggressive

---

i https://www.hrw.org/report/2021/04/27/threshold-crossed/israeli-authorities-and-crimes-apartheid-and-persecution
https://www.ijvcanada.org/ijv-commends-pivotal-human-right-watch-report-on-israeli-crimes-of-apartheid-persecution/

wars and by paramilitaries and private security companies, the devastating human rights impact of blockades by source countries and economic sanctions on the populations of Gaza, Syria, Iran and Venezuela, which have caused and continue to cause tens of thousands of deaths.

The politicization or as we now witness with concern, the "weaponization" of human rights is taking the world on a slippery slope. When the Universal Declaration of Human Rights (UDHR)was adopted in 1948, Eleanor Roosevelt, Charles Malik, René Cassin and others spoke of human dignity and the inalienable rights of human beings, but article 29 of UDHR also reminded us that "everyone has duties to the community."

Indeed, what is most necessary is global education in human rights, including the human right to peace, education in empathy and solidarity with others—compassion, not predatory competition in the "human rights industry" on a "holier than thou" ticket.

Meanwhile, Secretary-General António Guterres should not be expected to act as a Human Rights NGO. This high office is not that of an unaccountable activist. It is neither that of a general that can blast any state at will nor is it a secretary that has to be subservient to the prevailing powers that be.

That high official must recognize the reality of the power balance that he cannot fundamentally alter but must strive with obduracy and at times courage to stretch the international community towards more compliance with the purposes and principles of the United Nations. Most importantly this means the promotion of peace through conflict-prevention, good offices, impartial mediation, disarmament and yes, human rights. When all diplomacy fails and only then may "naming and shaming" become an option. But it is a default option and a sign of diplomatic failure.

In the experience of both of us as Special Rapporteurs of the Human Rights Council, we have delivered on our mandates, not by openly challenging the authority of states or claiming to teach them lessons in human rights but by giving quiet diplomacy a chance.

This is how one of us together with another Independent Expert facilitated a lifting of the sanctions on Sudan and this is how we are again currently engaging with protagonists of other conflicts. We have succeeded in confidence-building and contributed to the release of detainees. Persevering and discrete advocacy bears fruit.

We want an SG that puts values above politics in human rights matters and this is, in our opinion, what Guterres is doing. We have a Secretary General that can speak for truth and can at least listen to the narratives of the smaller and weaker states who have no access to the world media and whose action is distorted by biased reporting.

Of course the murder of Khashoggi is a tragedy because beyond the tragic loss of a human life, it is the freedom of expression that is targeted. But Kenneth Roth does not mention the thousands of migrants whose lives end in the liquid graves of the oceans because saving them at sea is becoming a criminal offence in some «enlightened» nations.

Are there different values attached to life according to the «exploitability» of its loss for political aims? We do not think that the Secretary General should go down along this road, even if this may cause disappointment in some quarters.

We would be really concerned if the Secretary general were to follow the path of selective indignation advocated implicitly by Mr Roth, because he would lose the moral leadership that we all, people of good will, can identify with across the world. THAT would be a major disappointment.

We welcome in António Guterres a Secretary General who does not hesitate to call a spade a spade, an SG who promotes peace and does not stoke conflict, who challenges unilateral economic sanctions, who supports the Right to Development1 and places the Secretariat of the United Nations in its service. We welcome an SG who, together with the new UN High Commissioner for Human Rights, Michelle Bachelet, are engaging all of humanity in the noble task—day by day—of implementing civil, cultural, economic, political and social rights in larger freedom—and in good faith.

Idriss Jazairy – *Special Rapporteur, UN Human Rights Council*
Alfred de Zayas – *Former Independent Expert, UN Human Rights Council*

ANNEX III

CALL FOR A CHARTER OF THE RIGHTS OF WHISTLEBLOWERS[i]

"It is time to recognize the contribution of whistleblowers."

—UN expert welcomes commutation of Manning's sentence

GENEVA (18 January 2017)—The United Nations Independent Expert on the promotion of a democratic and equitable international order, Alfred de Zayas, welcomes the commutation of Chelsea Manning's 35-year sentence for leaking classified military secrets. Mr. de Zayas calls on all Governments to protect whistleblowers instead of persecuting them.

"I welcome the commutation of sentence of Chelsea Manning and her forthcoming release in May. There are, however, many whistleblowers who have served the cause of human rights and who are still in prison in many countries throughout the world. It is time to recognize the contribution of whistleblowers to democracy and the rule of law and to stop persecuting them.

"I call on Governments worldwide to put an end to multiple campaigns of defamation, mobbing and even prosecution of whistleblowers like Julian Assange,[ii] Edward Snowden, the Luxleakers Antoine Deltour and Raphael Halet[iii] and the tax corruption leaker Rafi Rotem, who have acted in good faith and who have given meaning to article 19 of the International Covenant on Civil and Political Rights on freedom of expression. Whistleblowers who are serving prison sentence in many countries should be pardoned.

---

i https://news.un.org/en/story/2013/09/448712
ii https://www.ohchr.org/en/NewsEvents/Pages/DisplayNews.aspx?NewsID=17042&LangID=E
iii https://www.ohchr.org/en/NewsEvents/Pages/DisplayNews.aspx?NewsID=20212&LangID=E

"Whistleblowers are human rights defenders whose contribution to democracy and the rule of law cannot be overestimated. They serve democracy and human rights by revealing information that all persons are entitled to receive. A culture of secrecy is frequently also a culture of impunity. Because the right to know proclaimed in article 19 of the International Covenant on Civil and Political Rights is absolutely crucial to every democracy, whistleblowers should be protected, not persecuted.

"A democratic and equitable international order can best be achieved when States give prompt and effective consideration to the findings and recommendations of international human rights mechanisms, especially those of special procedures mandate holders and treaty bodies.

"Respect for human rights and human dignity must be vindicated by giving necessary protection to whistleblowers and adopting a Charter of Rights of Whistleblowers, as I proposed in my 2016 report to the United Nations General Assembly.[i] I urge the UK and Swedish Governments to strengthen the human rights system by giving effect to the recommendation of the UN Working Group on Arbitrary Detention.[ii] I am concerned that despite the opinion of the Working Group neither Government has taken steps toward implementation and Mr. Assange finds himself a refugee under the diplomatic protection of Ecuador.

"It is time for this abnormal and inhuman situation to end."

ANNEX IV

WORLD PRESS FREEDOM DAY
Information Note 3 May 2017

On the occasion of World Press Freedom Day the Independent Expert on the Promotion of a Democratic and Equitable International Order, Alfred de Zayas, reminds both private and public media that they hold an important trust for all of us, that they are obliged pursuant to article 19 of the International Covenant on Civil and Political Rights to ensure objective reporting and pluralistic dissemination of views so that civil society can arrive at their own opinion and thus exercise their right to public participation as envisaged in article 25 ICCPR.

George Orwell already warned us about "newspeak" and the tendency of both the public and the private sector to manipulate words, to disseminate false or incomplete information, what today we know as "fake news" and "disinformation." Indeed, it is not only governments that manipulate public opinion, but also private vested interest which aims to influence it. If articles 19 and 25 mean anything, they mean that in a democratic society, everyone must have access to reliable information so that a personal opinion can be formulated. It is this personal opinion that is protected by freedom of expression. It would be very sad if the only freedom of expression recognized by the law were the

---

i https://news.un.org/en/story/2013/09/448712
ii https://www.ohchr.org/Documents/Issues/Detention/A.HRC.WGAD.2015.docx

freedom to echo whatever nonsense we heard last night in the telejournal or read in the newspapers, in Facebook or Twitter.

The danger of neologisms, euphemisms and word-manipulations was recognized by Lewis Carroll in Alice in Wonderland:

> "When I use a word," Humpty Dumpty said, in rather a scornful tone, "it means just what I choose it to mean—neither more nor less."
> "The question is," said Alice, "whether you can make words mean so many different things."
> "The question is," said Humpty Dumpty, "which is to be master—that's all."
>
> —Lewis Carroll, *Through the Looking-Glass*[i]

Language indeed means something. The word can be more powerful than the sword. But language can also be emptied of content and used arbitrarily, today to mean something, tomorrow something else.

All journalists should always be mindful that what they write impacts society and may lead to reconciliation or more violence. Hence, they should keep in mind Article 20 ICCPR that prohibits propaganda for war and incitement to hate. Responsible journalists must report the truth without engaging in chauvinism or racism.

On World Press Freedom Day we must honour the work of journalists in many countries who labor daily to obtain information that we so urgently need. Many journalists give their lives in this effort. The number of journalists killed or jailed is appalling. I wish to salute the important work of whistleblowers, including the International Consortium of Investigative Journalists, who uncovered the scandals associated with tax evasion in tax havens including Panama and the Bahamas. I salute the work of whistleblowers like Edward Snowden who showed the world the degree to which our privacy is breached on a daily basis. I salute the work of Julian Assange, who was the recipient of many human rights awards, until he dared disclose crimes committed in Iraq, and who published the secret environmental, health, and investment protection chapters of international investment treaties, such as TPP, CETA and TTIP, thereby giving civil society the opportunity to discuss them and oppose them, even at a very late hour. In a very real sense, whisteleblowers are human rights defenders.

As I did in my report to the General Assembly 2016 (A/71/286), a Charter on the Rights of Whistleblowers should be adopted so that whistleblowers are no longer subjected to persecution and prosecution but do receive effective protection. The weight of the law should fall on the persons whose criminal acts are uncovered by the whistleblowers. But those who commit war crimes, those who engage in corruption, those who conspire to defraud States of their tax revenue, continue to enjoy impunity.

On World Press Freedom Day, let us salute the journalistic profession and encourage journalists, bloggers, whistleblowers to continue helping the world advance toward a more democratic and equitable international order, toward justice and peace based on truth.

---

i Lewis Carroll, *Through the Looking-Glass* (Hayes Barton Press, 1872), p.72.

Notes

1 Article 21(3), Universal Declaration of Human Rights.
2 Vienna Declaration and Programme of Action, paragraph 8.
3 See https://www.un.org/en/global-issues/democracy; *Democracy, Human Rights and the Emerging Global Order,* a Workshop hosted by the Brookings Institution's Managing Global Order project, 29–30 November 2012.
4 Report of the Independent Expert on human rights and international solidarity, A/HRC/23/45 and Add. 1.
5 Salvador Allende at the United Nations, 1972, *YouTube,* http://www.youtube.com/watch?v=knewNLlpkMw.
6 See, *inter alia,* reports from Independent Expert on minority issues: Special Rapporteur on the Independence of Judges and Lawyers; Special Rapporteur on the promotion and protection of the right to freedom of opinion and expression; Special Rapporteur on the promotion and protection of human rights while countering terrorism; Special Rapporteur on the promotion of truth, justice, reparation and guarantees of non-recurrence; Special Rapporteur on the situation of Human Rights Defenders; and Special Rapporteurs on Belarus, Cambodia, Côte d'Ivoire, Eritrea, Islamic Republic of Iran and Sudan.
7 See Report A/HRC/20/27 of the Special Rapporteur on the rights to freedom of peaceful assembly and of association.
8 Concluding observations of the Committee on the Elimination of Discrimination against Women (CEDAW), report A/HRC/23/50 of the Working Group on the issue of discrimination against women in law and in practice.
9 Human Rights Committee General Comment No. 25, para 4, Human Rights Committee General comment 34, para. 49. Alfred de Zayas and Aurea Roldan Martín, "Freedom of Opinion and Freedom of Expression: Some Reflections on General Comment No. 34 of the UN Human Rights Committee" in *Netherlands International Law Review,* 2012, pp. 425–454.
10 Advisory opinion concerning the Exchange of Greek and Turkish Populations Case, http://www.worldcourts.com/pcij/eng/decisions/1925.02.21_greek_turkish.htm.
11 2009 Council of Europe Convention on Access to Documents; Draft Model Law for African Union Member States on Access to Information; OAS model law on Access to Public Information.
12 Jim O. Madison, "How fusion centers spied on Occupy Wall Street," *United for Peace of Pierce County,* 25 May 2013, http://ufppc.org/us-a-world-news-mainmenu-35/11479/; see also Sheldon Wolin, *Democracy Incorporated: Managed Democracy and the Specter of Inverted Totalitarianism,* 2008.
13 See CCPR/C/GC/34 and Alfred de Zayas and Aurea Roldan, "Freedom of Opinion and Freedom of Expression," *Netherlands International Law Review* 2012 (vol. LIX, pp. 425–455).
14 See Noam Chomsky, *Hopes and Prospects* (Chicago: Haymarket Books, 2010), p. 101.
15 See David Cromwell, *Why are we the Good Guys? Reclaiming Your Mind from the Delusions of Propaganda* (London: Zero Press, 2012); Robert McChesney/John Nichols, *Our Media, Not Theirs: The Democratic Struggle against Corporate Media* (New York: Seven Stories Press, 2002).
16 See http://www.ohchr.org/EN/NewsEvents/Pages/DisplayNews.aspx?NewsID=13439&LangID=E.
17 See http://www.unmultimedia.org/radio/english/2013/01/nothing-can-justify-terrorism-ever-ban/.
18 See A/HRC/22/52 and A/HRC/23/40 and Corr.1. See also the press release of the High Commissioner for Human Rights of 12 July 2013 on mass surveillance, available from http://www.ohchr.org/EN/NewsEvents/Pages/Media.aspx?IsMediaPage=true&LangID=E.
19 See http://www.princeton.edu/~achaney/tmve/wiki100k/docs/State_terrorism.html.
20 See http://conventions.coe.int/Treaty/Commun/QueVoulezVous.asp?NT=205&CM=1&CL=ENG.
21 See http://www.assembly.coe.int/Communication/pressajdoc25_2013.pdf, paras. 9 and 11.
22 See http://www.freedominfo.org/2013/06/osi-issues-principles-on-national-security-rti/.

De Zayas with President Jimmy Carter

De Zayas with Noam Chomsky

De Zayas with Julian Assange

De Zayas with Ramsey Clark, former US Attorney General

De Zayas with Spanish Judge Baltasar Garzón

De Zayas being interviewed in his home by former Ecuadorian president Rafael Correa for RT-TV

De Zayas in his capacity as President of P.E.N. International Centre Suisse romand demonstrating for social justice before the Palais des Nations (UN Geneva Office) carrying the banner "misery kills" together with Dr. Fawzia Assaad, former P.E.N. president.

De Zayas with José Ayala Lasso, the first High Commissioner for Human Rights, at a Berkeley Law School Conference in 2009.

De Zayas with Virginia Dandan, the Independent Expert on International Solidarity, at the UN General Assembly (Third committee).

Chapter 7

THE PROHIBITION OF INTERFERENCE IN THE INTERNAL AFFAIRS OF STATES

"I just got this down from upstairs" [meaning the Secretary of Defense's office] ... This is a memo that describes how we're going to take out seven countries in five years, starting with Iraq, and then Syria, Lebanon, Libya, Somalia, Sudan and finishing off Iran."

GENERAL WESLEY CLARK[i]

NON-INTERFERENCE AND THE RIGHT TO DEMOCRACY

In my first report to the General Assembly I had already flagged the problem of the deliberate corruption of language in order to achieve results not foreseen or intended in the original texts. This practice entails among others what may be termed Orwellian "newspeak" or a kind of cognitive dissonance, when two mutually exclusive concepts are being simultaneously proposed by the narrative managers and accepted by the public as somehow legitimate, notwithstanding their incompatibility.

Orwell was prescient when in the beginning of his book 1984 he introduced the slogans for the nation of Oceania: War is Peace. Freedom is Slavery. Ignorance is Strength. These oxymorons are not taken from the realm of fiction, but actually reflect the practice of many governments and their state-of-the-art technological indoctrination. Indeed, we swim in an ocean of lies, and that is precisely why the right of access to information, the right to truth,[ii] the right to freedom of opinion and expression are absolutely crucial if we want democracy to survive.

Regrettably, we seem to have come to terms with the "fake news," "fake history," "fake law" that surrounds us. We allow governments to invoke "human rights," when we know that they are not interested in human rights, but in power. And when they visibly use human rights as a pretext to destroy human rights, we do not push back.

---

i General Wesley Clark in an interview with Amy Goodman, *Democracy Now!*, September 2001, https://www.youtube.com/watch?v=nUCwCgthp_E

ii On 30 September 2016 the Human Rights Council adopted a resolution on the Right to Truth. https://www.undocs.org/pdf?symbol=en/A/HRC/RES/33/19. This resolution reaffirms General Assembly Resolution 68/165 on the right to truth, https://undocs.org/en/A/RES/68/165

In the 1960s and 1970s there was renewed awareness of the concept of human dignity. The human rights language related to it became almost embedded in the public consciousness, especially after the UN General Assembly declaration on decolonization, Resolution 1514 of 14 December 1960.[i] At that time the concept of national liberation movements[ii] had become politically correct and the mainstream media applauded freedom fighters like Nelson Mandela. Today, regardless of the legitimacy of their claims to human rights and self-determination, those engaging in liberation movements are labelled terrorists. But peoples unquestionably are the right-holders of self-determination and governments are the duty-bearers, charged with the responsibility to implement their right. It is adding insult to injury to accuse the Sahraouis, the Kashmiris, the Tamils, the South Yemenites of being terrorists. On the contrary, it is governments that engage in State terrorism in suppressing their legitimate aspiration to achieve self-determination as stipulated in common article 1 of the ICCPR and ICESCR.

The corruption of language has made it possible to put forward concepts and policies that are clearly anti-democratic and which ultimately subvert human rights. In chapter 6 I discussed the overuse of the concept of democracy, which, judging by the way the U.S., UK and European Union use it, is a synonym for global capitalism, the neo-liberal economic system and has very little to do with concern for the welfare of the demos, for a genuinely democratic interest in consulting the public about their needs and priorities.

Neologisms have been created to allow intervention in the internal affairs of sovereign States. Surely there are strong arguments in favour of "humanitarian intervention" and "responsibility to protect," but these principles have never been applied justly or uniformly. There, where the principles could have been applied—to prevent democide in Cambodia in the 1970s and genocide in Rwanda in 1994, it was not invoked. Where it could have been applied in recent years—in the Palestine occupied territories, in Gaza, in Kahsmir, in Yemen, it was not. But where it had no application, e.g. in Libya and Syria, it was and is still being invoked. This reflects a high level of intellectual dishonesty on the part of governments, media and NGOs alike.

In my 2012 report to the General Assembly I wrote about the concept of democracy as it relates to the right to non-interference. —AdeZ

* * *

---

[i] https://www.un.org/dppa/decolonization/en/general-assembly
https://research.un.org/en/docs/decolonization/keydocs
[ii] Konrad Ginther, "Liberation Movements" in R. Bernhardt (ed.), *Encyclopedia of Public International Law,* Amsterdam, Elsevier, 1997, Vol. III, pp. 211–215.

Hitherto, democracy has been understood primarily in the domestic context. article 25 of the International Covenant on Civil and Political Rights stipulates that "every citizen shall have the right and the opportunity... to take part in the conduct of public affairs, directly or through freely chosen representatives." The Human Rights Committee, in its general comment No. 25 (1996) on article 25, confirmed that "[it] lies at the core of democratic government based on the consent of the people and in conformity with the principles of the Covenant," and that "[f]reedom of expression, assembly and association are essential conditions for the effective exercise of the right to vote and must be fully protected." Moreover, in addition to article 25, the case law of several States also refers to this principle. However, the implicit existence of a right of all peoples to democracy does not presuppose a prerogative of States to interfere in the domestic affairs of other States. Contrary to some trends and perceptions, the idea of the "responsibility to protect," contained in General Assembly Resolution 60/1, the World Summit Outcome, did not replace the Charter-mandated international law of non-interference in the internal affairs of sovereign States. The responsibility to protect is not a *lex specialis* that derogates from article 2, paragraphs 3, 4 and 7, or any other provision of the Charter. This is all the more true as in 2005 world leaders declared that "[e]ach individual State has the responsibility to protect its populations from genocide, war crimes, ethnic cleansing and crimes against humanity."[1] The principle of non-intervention remains very much valid and is confirmed in countless resolutions of the General Assembly and the Human Rights Council. Therefore, responsibility to protect must not be abused to circumvent the Charter or engage in sabre-rattling or propaganda for war, which is specifically prohibited by article 20 of the International Covenant on Civil and Political Rights. Any intervention in other States must satisfy strictly defined benchmarks and take place only as an *ultima ratio*. In July 2009, the General Assembly revisited the responsibility to protect doctrine, holding a plenary debate on the question. The President of the Assembly identified four benchmark questions that should determine whether and when the system of collective security could implement the responsibility to protect:

(a) Do the rules apply in principle, and is it likely that they will be applied in practice equally to all States, or, in the nature of things, is it more likely that the principle would be applied only by the strong against the weak?;

(b) Will the adoption of the responsibility to protect principle in the practice of collective security be more likely to enhance or undermine respect for international law?;

(c) Is the doctrine of responsibility to protect necessary and, conversely, does it guarantee that States will intervene to prevent another situation like the one that occurred in Rwanda?;

(d) Does the international community have the capacity to enforce accountability upon those who might abuse the right that the responsibility to protect principle would give States to resort to the use of force against other States?

In this context, it should be recalled that the Charter of the United Nations imposes certain *erga omnes* obligations on States. One of those obligations is to condemn the threat and the illegal use of force and to deny recognition of territorial changes arising from the illegal use of force. While there is an international responsibility to protect, there is, first and foremost, an international responsibility to protect humanity from the scourge of war and, most importantly, to protect humanity from weapons of mass destruction, including nuclear weapons.

Whereas international human rights law has traditionally been regarded in terms of States' relations with their inhabitants, the Independent Expert's mandate presupposes addressing the links between an international democratic order and domestic democracy. The Independent Expert is of the view that key elements of democracy—which include, inter alia, equity, participation, the rule of law and an independent judiciary backed up by accountability—are hardly present at the international level. International democracy is often questioned by the ability of some powerful States and non-state actors to subvert the clear will of the majority of the people and States. In this context, an example of what could constitute a form of international democracy is the application of international law as the basis for State conduct, and of the Charter as a world constitution. However, lack of enforcement of international norms, in particular human rights, refugee and humanitarian norms, is a reminder that the conduct of States is not always constrained by international law.

While international democracy is not a precondition for the existence of democracy at the national level, there is a need to recognize democracy "as an international principle, applicable to international organizations and to States in their international relations. The principle of international democracy does not only mean equal or fair representation of States; it also extends to the economic rights and duties of States."[2]

Moreover, the right of all peoples to participate in the conduct of public affairs at the national level must also be accompanied by their ability to do so in the international relations of States. In this context, meaningful participation of civil society in the conduct of public international affairs depends on the full realization of domestic democracy. This is particularly relevant as the legitimacy of the foreign actions of States must represent the actual wishes of the people, and facilitate the meaningful participation of independent civil society organizations in international decision-making bodies. We are in a unique period of history, when trends and aspirations are coming together. It is not only the social media and the new vistas of information and knowledge that the Internet has opened to civil society; it is a period of liberation from old taboos and empowerment of civil society. The concept of the *indignados,* the Occupy movements in various countries, shows that civil society wants to claim its democratic rights which external factors such as the markets have taken away.

International democracy should not be confined only to States Members of the United Nations. Due regard for the principle of self-determination as a peremptory norm of international law must be observed for non-self-governing territories and other unrepresented peoples. In its general comment No. 12 (1984) on self-determination, the Human Rights Committee called it "an essential condition for the effective guarantee and observance of individual human rights and for the promotion and strengthening of those rights."

FROM THE RESPONSIBILITY TO PROTECT TO THE RESPONSIBILITY TO ACT

In my 2016 report to the Human Rights Council I tackled the continued challenge posed to international law by the R2P concept and proposed developing it in a different direction.--AdeZ

* * *

The notion of the responsibility to protect[3] was formulated at the 2005 World Summit. Theoretically it has the potential, depending how it is interpreted and applied, to reaffirm the duty of each State to protect the population under its jurisdiction from internal and external dangers by the adoption of preventive and curative policies to counteract structural violence caused by State and non-state actors. On the other hand, a narrow interpretation of the responsibility to protect as a pretext to allow foreign intervention in the internal affairs of States poses dangers signaled at the General Assembly debate in July 2009, which revealed the potential geopolitical misuse of the responsibility to protect as a means to circumvent the jus cogens prohibition of the use of force stipulated in article 2 (4) of the Charter of the United Nations. While the responsibility to protect could advance human rights, its slogan-like mediatization and the dangers of arbitrary and selective application would erode the Charter.[4]

The Independent Expert proposes a reformulation of the doctrine to lift it out of the narrow focus on protecting populations from war crimes and genocide to a broader duty to protect populations from war, military interventions and structural violence. The international community has an interest in reaffirming a duty to protect and actively advance civil, cultural, economic, political and social rights. Governments, parliaments and courts have a responsibility to act in the public interest for economic stability, social development, environmental sustainability, food security, improvement of health and labour standards, through taxation, precautionary and preventive measures against the dangers of genetically modified organisms,[5] fracking,[6] open-pit mining, pesticides, air and water pollution, corruption, monopolies and asymmetrical trade. Those generic obligations of governance are the raison d'être of organized society. Rights holders of the responsibility to act are individuals and peoples, including indigenous peoples. Duty bearers are Governments, parliaments and courts.

Never must the courts become instruments of injustice. Never should they lend themselves to the execution of manifestly unjust investor-State dispute settlement awards. Courts should exercise their constitutional and implied powers to deny implementation in cases of abuse of rights, unjust enrichment or manifestly ill-founded awards, such as when arbitrators invent outrageously extensive interpretations.

The human rights and fundamental freedoms enshrined in the International Covenant on Civil and Political Rights, the International Covenant on Economic, Social and Cultural Rights, numerous regional human rights treaties like the Convention for the Protection of Human Rights and Fundamental Freedoms (European Convention on Human Rights), the European Social Charter, the American Convention on Human Rights and the African Charter on Human and Peoples' Rights, are binding treaty obligations, not mere pledges.

It appears that investors and transnational corporations understand human rights narrowly as the right to trade, the right to property and the right to profits. That perspective is supported by invoking the "laws of the market,"[7] a kind of ideological fundamentalism or groupthink reflected in a speech by the former WTO Director Pascal Lamy, who argued at a United Nations Institute for Training and Research conference on 26 September 2010 that "trade ensures concrete realization of human rights."[8] The "right to competition" is also a favourite neo-liberal "right." But trade, property and competition are not ends in themselves and must be seen in the context of other rights and subject to reasonable regulation. Competition presupposes a level playing field, which often necessitates affirmative action to correct imbalances. Competition without solidarity is predator behaviour, especially when competition is rigged in favour of mega-corporations and monopolies.[9]

HUMANITARIAN INTERVENTION

In my 2018 report to the Human Rights Council I returned to the issue of the prohibition of interference in the internal affairs of States. In paragraphs 32 and 33 of my report I reminded the Council of two epistemological challenges to the establishment of a democratic and equitable international order: the instrumentalization of "humanitarian assistance" for purposes of military intervention and forcing regime change under false pretences, and the problem of denial of the right of self-determination of peoples under the pretence of the sacrosanct principle of territorial integrity. —AdeZ

* * *

A democratic and equitable international order can only flourish in a peaceful environment. With conflict prevention being the overarching raison d'être of the United Nations, the hundreds of wars since 1945 indicate that the Organization must reform in order to live up to its purposes and principles. For that reason, war and war-mongering (prohibited by article 2 (4) of the Charter and article 20 (1) of the International Covenant on Civil and Political Rights) must be banned. Moreover, the so-called "responsibility to protect doctrine" should be discarded and replaced by the principle of the responsibility to act in the public interest (see A/HRC/33/40, paras. 13–17). The responsibility to protect cannot be seen as replacing the *jus cogens* prohibition of the use of force contained in article 2 (4) of the Charter, Under no condition can the international community tolerate that a State unilaterally invoke the R2P "doctrine" without Security Council approval. Instead, the Independent Expert has proposed that a standing group—administered by the United Nations and deployed by the Security Council, which receives its troops and support from current Security Council members—be ready for rapid deployment in the event of violations of article 2 (4) or future grave human rights abuses.[10]

The Independent Expert has also illustrated the relationship between aspirations for fulfilment of the right of self-determination and present-day challenges to peace and security (A/69/272). As a point of fact, the post-colonial world left a legacy of frontiers that do not correspond to ethnic, cultural, religious or linguistic criteria. This has been a continuing source of tension that may require adjustment in keeping with article 2 (3) of the Charter. The doctrine of *uti possidetis* is obsolete and its maintenance in the twenty-first century without the possibility of peaceful adjustments may perpetuate human rights violations. Thus, the implementation of the right of self-determination is not exclusively within the domestic jurisdiction of the State concerned, but is a legitimate concern of the international community.

UNILATERAL COERCIVE MEASURES: ECONOMIC SANCTIONS

During its 46th session in Geneva in March 2021, the UN Human Rights Council called upon states to stop imposing unilateral sanctions and condemned their use as a means of political and economic pressure. The resolution was adopted on 23 March by a vote of 30 countries. It is a disgrace that 15 nations, among them European Union members, the United Kingdom and Ukraine, voted against. Two nations—Armenia and Mexico—abstained. According to the resolution, the UN Human Rights Council "urges all States to stop adopting, maintaining or implementing unilateral coercive measures [...] in particular those of a coercive nature with extraterritorial effects." It further says that such measures must be lifted, because they are "not in accordance with the Charter of the United Nations and the norms and principles governing peaceful relations among States."

In my 2013 report A/68/284 to the General Assembly I flagged some obstacles to achieving a democratic and equitable international order, including brazen interference in the domestic affairs of States and the practice of imposing economic sanctions on States in the expectation to destabilize them, cause chaos and social unrest and eventually achieve "regime change." Although the Human Rights Council has frequently condemned UCMs, e.g. in Resolutions 27/21, 40/3 and 46/5, States that impose them do not lift them, as if they knew that they themselves would not be subject to counter-measures or United Nations sanctions. Thus, there is a situation of brazen violation of international norms in total impunity. —AdeZ

* * *

In April 2013, OHCHR, pursuant to Human Rights Council resolution 19/32, organized a workshop on the impact of the application of unilateral coercive measures on the enjoyment of human rights by the affected populations in the States targeted (see A/HRC/24/20). The workshop focused not only on unilateral measures, but also on coercive measures by regional groups without Security Council clearance, questioning their legality and legitimacy in the context of existing human rights obligations by the States imposing them. Participants noted the violation of sovereignty through threats or the imposition of economic sanctions in the name of human rights. They recalled general comment No. 8 of the Committee on Economic, Social and Cultural Rights, which states that economic sanctions are being imposed with increasing frequency, both internationally, regionally and unilaterally and that sanctions often cause significant disruption in the distribution of food, pharmaceuticals and sanitation supplies, jeopardize the quality of food and the availability of clean drinking water, severely interfere with the functioning of basic health and education systems, and undermine the right to work (see E/C.12/1997/8). Reference was made to the 1993 Vienna Declaration and Programme of Action, which calls upon States to refrain from any unilateral measure not in accordance with international law and the Charter of the United Nations that creates obstacles to trade relations among States and impedes the full realization of the rights of everyone to a standard of living adequate for their health and well-being, including food and medical care, housing and the necessary social services.[11]

A number of speakers argued that unilateral coercive measures constituted violations of the Charter, the International Covenant on Economic, Social and Cultural Rights and the multilateral trading system, adversely affecting the right to development. In particular, sanctions on the transfer of funds had prevented the importation of food and medicine. The 2012 thematic report by the High Commissioner for Human Rights was cited, stressing that coercive measures should be of limited duration, proportional and subject to human rights safeguards, including impact assessments and monitoring conducted by independent experts (see A/HRC/19/33, para. 38). Marc Bossuyt, President of the Constitutional Court of Belgium, observed that sanctions regimes must be periodically evaluated.

The then Chairperson of the Committee on Economic, Social and Cultural Rights, Ariranga Pillay, indicated that some coercive measures had extraterritorial effects that raised international law questions. Participants stressed that unilateral coercive measures created a regime of structural violence with disproportionate impacts on women and children, undermining the rule of law, constituting an obstacle to self-determination, infringing sovereign rights, jeopardizing peace, security and the human rights of ordinary people. The former President of the Human Rights Council, Ambassador Laura Dupuy Lasserre, noted that the Council had been seized of situations involving unlawful coercive measures, including the blockade of Gaza, the United States base at Guantánamo, targeted killings of non-state actors and the supply of weapons to parties in internal armed conflicts. Some participants proposed that the Council draw up guidelines to prevent, minimize and redress the adverse impacts of unilateral measures, establishing a special procedure to monitor them and ensure accountability.

In a 2012 paper for an earlier workshop on coercive sanctions, Mr. Bossuyt noted that the economic sanctions against Iraq had been imposed by the Security Council in its resolution 661 (1990) of 6 August 1990, followed by a comprehensive arms embargo imposed by its resolution 687 (1991). Over time, those sanctions had been criticized for inflicting huge suffering on the population (see S/2000/208). The Secretary-General himself had said that the population was not the intended targets of sanctions. Mr. Bossuyt concluded that it was not sufficient that the policy of the targeted country justify the imposition of economic sanctions. The impact of sanctions on the enjoyment of human rights by the population should be taken prominently into account. If the desired results could not be attained within a reasonable time period, the measures should be suspended. If not, the sanctions might not only lose their legitimacy, but might also become counterproductive.[12]

Already in 2000, Mr. Bossuyt had reported to the Sub-Commission on the Promotion and Protection of Human Rights on the adverse consequences of economic sanctions on the enjoyment of human rights (see E/CN.4/Sub.2/2000/33), expressing concern that such measures should always be limited in time, should not affect the innocent population, especially the most vulnerable, should not aggravate imbalances in income distribution, or generate illegal and unethical business practices.

Notwithstanding the Sub-Commission's concerns, the sanctions regime against Iraq continued until 2003, causing grave harm to the population, the situation being so serious that officials of the Food and Agriculture Organization of the United Nations (FAO)[13] in 1995 and the United Nations Children's Fund (UNICEF) estimated that at least 500,000 children had died as a consequence of the sanctions,[14] and two Assistant Secretary-Generals of the United Nations, Denis Halliday (1997–1998)[15] and Hans-Christof von Sponeck (1998–2000),[16] both of them Humanitarian Coordinators in Iraq, resigned in protest. While these resignations were treated as irrelevant and did not result in the lifting of the sanctions, the great suffering imposed on the Iraqi population eloquently illustrates systemic dysfunction, incompatible with the purposes and principles of the Charter.[17] Peeling the onion of Security Council sanctions on Iraq, one finds not even a thin layer of human rights, but instead power politics as insensitive as in centuries gone by.[18] In this context, the General Assembly may consider establishing an ad hoc committee on non-intervention, in the spirit of the Ad Hoc Committee on the Indian Ocean, which was established in 1971 in order to render the Indian Ocean a zone of peace and to persuade the great powers to abstain from further militarization.[19]

UNILATERALISM

At the expert workshop on the proposals of the Special Rapporteur on unilateral coercive measures held at the Palais des Nations in Geneva on 3 June 2017, I made the following statement. —AdeZ

* * *

In my 2013 report to the General Assembly (A/68/284), I identified unilateralism as a significant obstacle to a democratic and equitable international order and unilateral coercive measures as a threat to the realization of human rights, given the harm these measures cause to the world's most vulnerable populations.[20]

By restricting access to necessary medicines, food and essential goods and by degrading vital infrastructure, coercive measures—both multilateral and unilateral—have been shown to adversely impact the enjoyment of the rights to life, health, education, food, clean water and an adequate standard of living of individuals and groups.[21] In addition, particular harms suffered by historically marginalized persons, such as women, children and persons with disabilities, have raised the concerns of human rights and humanitarian actors.[22]

Unilateral coercive measures which flout States' international human rights obligations are a serious attack on the international order as they contravene international law and the purposes of the Charter.[23] By undermining the very norms which ground the multilateral system, including respect for state sovereignty, free trade and inter-state friendly relations, unilateral measures violate international treaties and United Nations resolutions and contribute to system incoherence.[24] Further, the embargo against Cuba can be taken as a specific example of the adverse impact of unilateral coercive measures on the enjoyment of human rights. Moreover, the contributory nature of unilateral coercive measures in ongoing human rights situations brought before the Human Rights Council—such as supplies of weapons to armed groups, the blockage of Gaza and targeted killings of non-state actors[25]—demonstrates the threats these measures pose to the maintenance of international peace and security.

I am concerned that, in practice, the imposition of unilateral coercive measures runs contrary to foundational human rights principles which are prerequisites to achieving a democratic and equitable international order, including fair representation, international cooperation and accountability. A culture of human rights also encompasses the necessity of international solidarity. Sanctions regimes constitute a flagrant example of absence of solidarity with the millions of human beings who have to endure the consequences of the sanctions. As outlined in a 2000 Report to the Sub-Commission on the Promotion and Protection of Human Rights, the underlying theory that coercive measures like sanctions bring about change by inspiring grassroots democratic pressure has not held true. Rather, at the expense of already disadvantaged communities, such measures are often instrumentalized by national elites to strengthen anti-democratic policies.[26] They are also employed by international power players to solidify already privileged positions on the world stage.[27]

Already in 2000, Professor Marc Bossuyt reported to the Sub-Commission on the Promotion and Protection of Human Rights on the adverse consequences of economic sanctions on the enjoyment of human rights (see E/CN.4/Sub.2/2000/33), suggesting that, to avoid adverse consequences, such measures should always be limited in time, should not affect the innocent population, especially the most vulnerable, should not aggravate imbalances in income distribution, nor generate illegal and unethical business practices. Moreover, all sanctions regimes should be periodically monitored and terminated when it becomes apparent that they do not serve any purpose other than to "punish" a given State without thereby enabling any political change that will enhance the enjoyment of human rights. Experience shows that such "punishment" has frequently led to targeted politicians digging in their heels even deeper and being even less inclined to dialogue and reform.

Several prominent stakeholders, including the Special Rapporteur on unilateral coercive measures, have also called for States to assess the human rights harms caused by unilateral coercive measures.[28] This can be done through the individual complaints procedures established pursuant to several human rights treaties, as well as through the communication procedures of the Human Rights Council's Special Procedures. The treaty bodies also have an under-utilized inter-State complaints procedure, which should be engaged and in some cases could facilitate negotiation and friendly settlement (e.g. Art. 41 ICCPR). Sanctions should also be tested in the context of the Universal Periodic Review of the Human Rights Council.[29]

As stated above, sanctions regimes constitute unlawful interference with free trade and are incompatible with numerous provisions of GATT and WTO agreements as well as free-trade agreements. States may consider challenging unilateral sanctions regimes pursuant to the contentious jurisdiction of the International Court of Justice. Individual investors, businesses and transnational corporations may consider invoking pertinent provisions of free-trade agreements before domestic courts and before international arbitral tribunals, the World Bank's International Center for Settlement of Investment Disputes, or before the WTO dispute settlement panels. It is indeed an anomaly that investors and transnational corporations that have suffered considerable losses as a result of sanctions regimes, have failed to challenge them, whereas they do challenge the exercise of legitimate regulatory measures by States in the fields of labour, environmental and health protection.[30]

Moreover, the General Assembly should consider formulating pertinent legal questions to be submitted to the International Court of Justice for advisory opinions under article 96 UN Charter, including the legality of sanctions in the light of the Purposes and Principles of the United Nations and article 103 of the UN Charter, the supremacy clause. Another legal question would concern the illegality of extra-territorial application of national legislation, its adverse impacts on the sovereign equality of States, and the level of reparation due for the unlawful imposition of sanctions regimes.

Further, beyond the condemnation of sanctions regimes by the Non-Aligned Movement[31] and CELAC[32] and multiplying calls for States to refrain from implementing such measures, such as that rightfully made by the General Assembly last year in response to the Cuba embargo,[33] it is essential that reparations be paid to those deprived of their rights as a consequence of such measures. There is clear evidence that the embargo against Cuba has directly led to the deaths of many persons as a result of lack of medicines and the impossibility to import medical equipment or replacement parts.[34]

I welcome the initiatives put forward by the Special Rapporteur on unilateral coercive measures to address human rights violations committed as a result of unilateral coercive measures. In this context, I would like to reiterate once again that sanctions should only be considered as an *ultima ratio*, which should be subject to periodic review and terminated as soon as possible, bearing in mind that thousands of innocent persons have suffered and are suffering because embargoes prevent goods, medical equipment or manufacturing supplies from reaching a particular country. Ending the impunity on the part of the States that impose sanctions will contribute to an environment consistent with article 28 of the Universal Declaration of Human Rights and advance humanity towards a more peaceful, democratic and equitable international order.

THE WEAPONIZATION OF HUMAN RIGHTS FOR PURPOSES OF REGIME CHANGE

In my report to the Human Rights Council on my mission to Venezuela I devoted a section to the customary international law principles of non-intervention and non-interference. Because of its general application to a democratic and equitable international order, I consider it best to introduce this discussion here rather than delaying it to chapter 12, which encompasses a more focused analysis of the Venezuelan crisis, its causes and possible solutions. —AdeZ

* * *

The Charter of the United Nations rests on the philosophy of multilateralism, a commitment to international cooperation, and the sovereign equality of States. Countries must not be isolated and boycotted, but helped in strengthening their democratic institutions. Over the past sixty years, non-conventional economic wars have been waged against Cuba,[35] Chile,[36] Nicaragua,[37] the Syrian Arab Republic[38] and the Bolivarian Republic of Venezuela in order to make their economies fail, facilitate regime change and impose a neo-liberal socioeconomic model. In order to discredit selected governments, failures in the field of human rights are maximized so as to make violent overthrow more palatable. Human rights are being "weaponized" against rivals. Yet, human rights are the heritage of every human being and should never be instrumentalized as weapons of demonization. Instead, measures of inclusion are necessary, as is reliance on the expertise of international organizations such as the United Nations Development Programme (UNDP),[39] the United Nations Children's Fund (UNICEF),[40] FAO,[41] WHO,[42] the Joint United Nations Programme on HIV/AIDS (UNAIDS),[43] the Office of the United Nations High Commissioner for Refugees (UNHCR),[44] UNODC,[45] ILO,[46] the United Nations Educational, Scientific and Cultural Organization (UNESCO)[47] and the Pan American Health Organization,[48] among others, to provide effective advisory services and technical assistance.

The principles of non-intervention[49] and non-interference[50] in the internal affairs of sovereign States belong to customary international law and have been reaffirmed in General Assembly resolutions, notably 2625 (XXV) and 3314 (XXIX). The 1993 Vienna Declaration and Programme of Action. article 32 of the Charter of Economic Rights and Duties of States, adopted by the General Assembly in 1974, stipulates that no State may use or encourage the use of economic, political or any other type of measures to coerce another State in order to obtain from it the subordination of the exercise of its sovereign rights.

In its judgment of 27 June 1986 concerning *Nicaragua v. United States*, the International Court of Justice quoted from resolution 2625 (XXV): "no State shall organize, assist, foment, finance, incite or tolerate subversive, terrorist or armed activities directed towards the violent overthrow of the regime of another State, or interfere in civil strife in another State." In the context of the inter-American system, the Court cited the Convention on the Duties and Rights of States in the Event of Civil Strife, which was confirmed by resolution 78 adopted by the General Assembly of the Organization of American States on 21 April 1972, in which it resolves "To reiterate solemnly the need for the member states of the Organization to observe strictly the principles of non-intervention and self-determination of peoples as a means of ensuring peaceful coexistence among them" and "To reaffirm the obligation of those states to refrain from applying economic, political, or any other type of measures to coerce another state and obtain from it advantages of any kind." Similarly, chapter 4, article 19, of the Charter of the OAS stipulates that "No State or group of States has the right to intervene, directly or indirectly, for any reason whatever, in the internal or external affairs of any other State. The foregoing principle prohibits not only armed force but also any other form of interference or attempted threat against the personality of the State or against its political, economic, and cultural elements."

While he was in the Bolivarian Republic of Venezuela, the Independent Expert had long personal conversations and email exchanges with Pasqualina Curcio, who published a well-documented book entitled *The Visible Hand of the Market*, analysing the economic war. She reminds readers that in 1970, when Salvador Allende was democratically elected President of Chile, Richard Nixon told Henry Kissinger that the United States would not tolerate an alternative economic model in Latin America and gave orders to "make the Chilean economy scream,"[51] and when all the boycotts and sanctions failed, Allende was removed by Pinochet's coup in September 1973.[52] The Spanish economist Alfredo Serrano, head of the Centro Estratégico Latinoamericano de Geopolítica, analyses the manipulation of the "country risk factor,"[53] the refusal of banks to process Venezuelan international transactions, the obstacles to obtaining insulin and other medicines,[54] the artificially induced inflation, and the arbitrary "dollar today" figures.[55] Furthermore, staff of the Banco Central de Venezuela explained to the Independent Expert that the pernicious exchange rate published on a website that was not grounded in factual purchase and sale transactions had been negatively impacting the economy, primarily, as a price marker, raising inflations levels, and constituting an instrument of war that had risen constantly, accumulating during the year an upward variation trend over 2,465 per cent.

According to Pasqualina Curcio, the manipulation of the exchange rate has been the most effective strategy to disrupt the Venezuelan economy. It has an impact not only on the foreign exchange market, but also price levels of the economy, leading to the loss of purchasing power, distortion of markets and production. She explains that:

> The variations of the parallel exchange rate published in websites since 2012 do not correspond to the historical behaviour of the ratio between international reserves and monetary liquidity. This leads us to uphold our theory that the levels of this type of parallel exchange rate do not respond to economic factors but rather to political ones in the framework of this manipulation of the economic warfare against the people in Venezuela.... The unconventional nonviolent warfare method that has been evidently used since 2012 to distort the Venezuelan economy and to provoke social unrest and political destabilization is known in economic terms as supply shock, generated by the inflation costs. The tool used is the manipulation of the exchange rate in the parallel black market.[56]

ANNEX I

UNILATERAL SANCTIONS AND INTERNATIONAL LAW

Excerpts of the lecture delivered at the Vienna Expert Meeting on Unilateral Coercive Measures on 27 June 2019[i]

The world order established by the UN Charter takes precedence over other international and regional treaties and imposes positive and negative obligations on member states, including the United States of America and the European Union. This is stipulated in article 103 of the Charter, **the supremacy clause.**

The question arises whether in the light of the UN Charter unilateral coercive measures could be considered compatible with modern international law? The orthodox answer is that only those sanctions that are imposed by the Security Council under Chapter VII can be considered legal. Article 41 of the Charter stipulates "The Security Council may decide what measures not involving the use of armed force are to be employed to give effect to its decisions." But even Security Council decisions and resolutions must be compatible with the purposes and principles enunciated in articles 1, 2, 55 and 56 of the UN Charter and not violate fundamental norms of international law, customary international law, or treaties such as the International Covenant on Civil and Political Rights and the International Covenant on Economic, Social and Cultural Rights, which stipulate *inter alia* the right to life, the right to health and the right to medical care. Allow me to quote from the 1993 Vienna Declaration and Programme of Action, which called upon States "to refrain from any unilateral measures ... that create obstacles to trade relations among states and impedes the full realization of the human rights set forth in the Universal Declaration of Human Rights."[57]

The Security Council is not above international law, as its mandate is circumscribed by Article 24 of the Charter.[58] Thus the imposition of sanctions regimes that are tantamount to "collective punishment" and cause widespread death and suffering[59] of innocent people are contrary to Article 24 of the Charter and therefore *ultra vires*. At some future date the International Court of Justice should demonstrate the courage to say exactly that, even as an *obiter dictum* in a pending contentious case or in an advisory opinion requested by the General Assembly under article 96 of the UN Charter.

In any event, nothing in the UN Charter can be read as authorizing in any way unilateral coercive measures, which are incompatible with general principles of international law, violate the prohibition of interference in the internal affairs of other states and violate their sovereignty. A problem arises when numerous powerful states become rogue States, deliberately ignore their *erga omnes* obligations and breach international law, and do it with impunity. The self-serving argument that a new State practice has thereby emerged is fallacious. This fundamentally flawed argument fails because it is incompatible with general principles of law (article 38 ICJ Statute) such as *ex injuria non oritur jus* (from

---

i Other speakers were Dr. Idriss Jazairy, Special Rapporteur on Unilateral Coercive Measures, Prof. William Schabas, Middlesex University, London, and Ignacio Ramonet, former Editor-in-Chief, *Le Monde Diplomatique*

a violation of law no new law can emerge). The very concept of the rule of law rejects the proposition that a violation of a norm invalidates the norm. The situation is different: A breach of international law occurs, which for the time being cannot be reversed in the absence of an effective enforcement mechanism. There are many historical precedents, e.g. Apartheid was incompatible with international law, human rights law, advisory opinions of the International Court of Justice, resolutions of the Security Council, and yet it persisted for decades.

On 1 November 2018, the UN General Assembly adopted its 27th resolution condemning the embargo (*bloqueo*) against Cuba (A/RES/73/8), nearly unanimously (189 votes in favour, 2 against (U.S. and Israel), and two non-voting.[60] This resolution, "Necessity of ending the economic, commercial and financial embargo imposed by the United States of America against Cuba," can be seen as a *restatement of the law* on unilateral sanctions. In its preambular paragraphs the resolution reaffirmed "the sovereign equality of States, non-intervention and non-interference in their internal affairs and freedom of international trade and navigation, which are also enshrined in many international legal instruments." It further expressed concern "about the continued promulgation and application by Member States of laws and regulations, such as that promulgated on 12 March 1996 known as 'the Helms-Burton Act,' the extraterritorial effects of which affect the sovereignty of other States, the legitimate interests of entities or persons under their jurisdiction and the freedom of trade and navigation."

In its operative paragraphs the resolution called upon all States "to refrain from promulgating and applying laws and measures of the kind referred to in the preamble to the present resolution, in conformity with their obligations under the Charter of the United Nations and international law, which, *inter alia*, reaffirm the freedom of trade and navigation." It further urged all States "that have and continue to apply such laws and measures to take the steps necessary to repeal or invalidate them as soon as possible in accordance with their legal regime."

This Resolution illustrates the fact that the primacy of the UN Charter entails a restriction of a State's prerogatives in international relations. An older view on unilateral sanctions had justified them as a form of "retorsion" or "countermeasure" against a State that had violated international law. The burden, however, was always on the sanctioning State to establish prior unlawful conduct by the targeted State. This requirement was rarely satisfied. That is why the better view (in unenforceable international law doctrine) is that States have relinquished unilateral coercive measures and recognized that economic sanctions can only be imposed by the Security Council. This, as we know from the reality of the unilateral sanctions against Cuba, Iran, North Korea, Syria, Venezuela, has not yet become operative. U.S. sanctions do not aim at persuading the targeted States to renounce previous "unlawful conduct" but are intended as economic war or regime-change strategy. Many UN rapporteurs have condemned unilateral coercive measures as incompatible with the UN Charter, but rapporteurs are little more than an assembly of Cassandras. What is needed is an advisory opinion by the International Court of Justice stating unequivocally that unilateral sanctions are incompatible with the UN Charter and in some cases constitute crimes against humanity. States that impose sanctions and claim that they are legal are not impartial but acting as *judex in causa sua*. . . .

The overthrow of Salvador Allende in Chile in September 1973 led to 17 years of dictatorship and torture under General Augusto Pinochet. So too did the overthrow of the governments in the Dominican Republic, Grenada, Haiti, Honduras, etc. But the U.S. client regimes and the oligarchic elites of those countries were happy to return to "the good old days" when the rich were rich and the poor were poor, and when the U.S. investors and transnationals could loot *ad libitum* the natural resources of these countries, all in the name of privatization and profit.

In order to discredit selected governments, failures in the field of human rights are maximized so as to make violent overthrow more palatable. Human rights are thus being "weaponized" against rivals. Yet, human rights are the heritage of every human being and should never be instrumentalized as weapons of demonization. Instead, measures of inclusion are necessary, as is reliance on the expertise of international organizations such as the United Nations Development Programme (UNDP), the United Nations Children's Fund (UNICEF), FAO, WHO, the Joint United Nations Programme on HIV/AIDS (UNAIDS), the Office of the United Nations High Commissioner for Refugees (UNHCR), UNODC, ILO, the United Nations Educational, Scientific and Cultural Organization (UNESCO) and the Pan American Health Organization, among others, to provide effective advisory services and technical assistance. The U.S.—and sometimes the EU—show little interest in such international solidarity and cooperation, since what is really intended is a forced return to uncontrolled capitalism and retrogression in economic, social and cultural rights. Thus, the first thing that the 2002 coup d'état in Venezuela attempted was the dismantlement of the social acquis of the Bolivarian Revolution. The Carmona decree[61] of the coup-presidency of Pedro Carmona[62] entailed the abrogation of 49 pieces of social legislation, the dismantlement of the Chávez National Assembly and even of the Supreme Court. The 48-hour coup ended with the restoration of Chávez, but the intent of the "model" had been shown, notwithstanding the legal principle of non-retrogression in human rights.[63]

The principles of non-intervention[64] and non-interference[65] in the internal affairs of sovereign States belong to customary international law and have been reaffirmed in countless General Assembly resolutions, including 2625 (XXV) and 3314 (XXIX), and in the 1993 Vienna Declaration and Programme of Action.

Article 32 of the Charter of Economic Rights and Duties of States, adopted by the General Assembly in 1974, stipulates that no State may use or encourage the use of economic, political or any other type of measures to coerce another State in order to obtain from it the subordination of the exercise of its sovereign rights.31.In its judgment of 27 June 1986 concerning *Nicaragua v. United States,* the International Court of Justice quoted from resolution 2625 (XXV): "no State shall organize, assist, foment, finance, incite or tolerate subversive, terrorist or armed activities directed towards the violent overthrow of the regime of another State, or interfere in civil strife in another State."

In the context of the inter-American system, the International Court of Justice cited the Convention on the Duties and Rights of States in the Event of Civil Strife, which was confirmed by resolution 78 adopted by the General Assembly of the Organization of American States on 21 April 1972, in which it resolves "To reiterate solemnly the need for the member states of the Organization to observe strictly the principles of non-intervention and self-determination of peoples as a means of ensuring peaceful coexistence among them" and "To reaffirm the obligation of those states to refrain from applying economic, political, or any other type of measures to coerce another state and obtain from it advantages of any kind."

Similarly, chapter 4, article 19, of the Charter of the OAS stipulates that "No State or group of States has the right to intervene, directly or indirectly, for any reason whatever, in the internal or external affairs of any other State. The foregoing principle prohibits not only armed force but also any other form of interference or attempted threat against the personality of the State or against its political, economic, and cultural elements."

Notwithstanding the above, it must be said that not every economic sanction is *ipso facto* illegal or contrary to the UN Charter. Indeed, arms sales embargoes may be justifiable against some countries like Saudi Arabia and Libya, in order to facilitate dialogue and peacemaking. Again and again, United Nations bodies have condemned unilateral coercive measures,[66] notably in the landmark 2000 study of the Sub-Commission on the Promotion and Protection of Human Rights,[67] documenting the adverse human rights impact of those measures.

As indicated above, multilateral sanctions, even those imposed by the Security Council under Chapter VII of the Charter, can also cause suffering and death. In the 1990s, two United Nations Assistant Secretary-Generals, Denis Halliday and Hans-Christof von Sponeck,[68] quit their Humanitarian Coordinator functions in Iraq to protest against UN sanctions, which had caused more than a million deaths among Iraqis, particularly children, and which they qualified as a form of genocide.[69]

On 23 March 2018, the Human Rights Council condemned unilateral coercive measures by a vote of 28 in favour, 15 against and 3 abstentions, recalling that economic sanctions demonstrably cause death, aggravate economic crises, disrupt the production and distribution of food and medicine, constitute a push factor generating emigration, and lead to violations of human rights. On 21 March 2019 the Council adopted a similar resolution.[70]

It is particularly shameful to note that in November 2017 Colombia refused to deliver antimalaria medicine to Venezuela that had been ordered to combat an outbreak in November 2017.[71] The absence of condemnation from the international community entails its joint responsibility for the aggravation of the crisis. In that case, the anti-malaria medicine had to be imported from India.

What is particularly pertinent and urgent today is to address the issue whether sanctions can amount to crimes against humanity under article 7 of the Rome Statute of the International Criminal Court. An investigation would be appropriate, but the geopolitical submissiveness of the Court may prevent this.

One thing that we must all realize is that today's economic sanctions and financial blockades[72] are comparable with medieval sieges of towns with the intention of forcing them to surrender. Twenty-first century sanctions attempt to bring not just a town, but sovereign countries to their knees. Contemporary blockades can also be compared with blockades during World War II. Thus, we recall that the Nazi siege of Leningrad, lasting for nearly 900 days, resulted in 670.000 deaths according to Russian sources, with a significant number attributable to starvation. Other estimates place the death toll as high as one million.

Another difference, perhaps, is that twenty-first century sanctions are accompanied by the manipulation of public opinion through "fake news," aggressive public relations and a pseudo-human rights rhetoric so as to give the impression that a human rights "end" justifies the criminal means. There is not only a horizontal juridical world order governed by the Charter of the United Nations and principles of sovereign equality, but also a vertical world order reflecting the hierarchy of a geopolitical system that links dominant States with the rest of the world according to military and economic power. It is the latter geopolitical system that generates geopolitical crimes in total impunity.

Economic asphyxiation policies as already practised against the people of Chile, the Democratic People's Republic of Korea, Nicaragua and the Syrian Arab Republic are criminal, but the mainstream media under-reports the level of suffering and death, and sometimes even argues that the sanctions are "targeted" and that they only affect government officials and not the populations of the countries concerned.

In January 2018, Middle East correspondent of the *Financial Times* and *The Independent*, Patrick Cockburn, wrote on the sanctions affecting Syria: There is usually a pretence that foodstuffs and medical equipment are being allowed through freely and no mention is made of the financial and other regulatory obstacles making it impossible to deliver them. An example of this is the draconian sanctions imposed on Syria by the U.S. and EU which were meant to target President Bashar al-Assad and help remove him from power. They have wholly failed to do this, but a UN internal report[73] leaked in 2016 shows all too convincingly the effect of the embargo in stopping the delivery of aid by international aid agencies. They cannot import the aid despite waivers because banks and commercial companies dare not risk being penalised for having anything to do with Syria. The report quotes a European doctor working in Syria as saying that "the indirect effect of sanctions makes the import of the medical instruments and other medical supplies immensely difficult, near impossible."[74]

In short: economic sanctions kill. Moreover, they violate the commitments undertaken by UN member States pursuant to articles 55 and 56 of the UN Charter and render the achievement of the Sustainable Development Goals impossible.

UN Workshops

The Office of the UN High Commissioner for Human Rights issued a thematic report in 2012 in which High Commissioner Navi Pillay condemned unilateral coercive measures because of their adverse human rights impacts. She recommended *inter alia,*

> States must refrain from adopting unilateral coercive measures that breach their human rights obligations... should avoid the application of any coercive measures having negative effects on human rights, particularly on the most vulnerable... adopt measures ensuring that essential supplies, such as medicines and food, are not used as tools of political pressure, and that under no circumstance should be deprived of their basic means of survival.[75]

Notwithstanding such clear statements by the Office of the High Commissioner, it is disconcerting that the murderous sanctions and financial blockade by the U.S. and EU against Cuba, Syria, Venezuela have not been clearly and unconditionally condemned by the major human rights NGOs.

The OHCHR has organized numerous workshops on unilateral coercive measures, in which Marc Bossuyt, Idriss Jazairy and myself—among many others—have participated. I duly reflected this in my 2013 report to the Human Rights Council[76] and General Assembly,[77] as well as in subsequent reports. The Advisory Committee to the Human Rights Council produced an indispensable report on this issue in 2015 (A/HRC/28/74).

For decades the United Nations Secretary General has been issuing reports on the adverse human rights impacts of sanctions regimes. In all of these reports, the violations of international law are documented. Year after year.

At a Workshop on sanctions held at the Office of the High Commissioner for Human Rights in April 2012, Professor Marc Bossuyt, then President of the Belgian Constitutional Court, presented a paper on the "Adverse Effects of Economic Sanctions on the Enjoyment of Human Rights." He referred to the earlier Sub-Commission report dating back to 2000 (E/CN.4/Sub.2/2000/33), submitted pursuant to decision 1999/111 of 26 August 1999, of the UN Sub-Commission on the Promotion and Protection of Minorities. This report was the follow-up to resolution 1997/35 of 28 August 1997, in which the Sub-Commission had stressed four specific points concerning economic sanctions, namely that:

(i) They should always be limited in time;

(ii) They must not affect the innocent population, especially the most vulnerable;

(iii) They must not aggravate imbalances in income distribution;

(iv) They must not generate illegal and unethical business practices.

Benchmark questions were proposed to evaluate sanctions, namely:

(i) Are the sanctions imposed for valid reasons?

> Sanctions under the United Nations system must be imposed only when there is a threat of or actual breach of international peace and security. Sanctions should not be imposed for invalid political reasons and should not arise from or produce an economic benefit for one State or group of States at the expense of the sanctioned State or other States.

(ii) Do the sanctions target the relevant parties?

> Sanctions should not target civilians who are not involved with the threat to peace or international security, nor should they target, or result in collateral damage to "third party" States or peoples.

(iii) Do the sanctions target the relevant goods or objects?

> Sanctions should not interfere with the free flow of humanitarian goods and they should not target goods required to ensure the basic subsistence of the civilian population, nor essential medical provisions or educational materials of any kind. The target must have a reasonable relationship to the threat of or actual breach of peace and international security.

(iv) Are the sanctions reasonably time-limited?

Legal sanctions may become illegal when they have been applied for too long without meaningful results. Sanctions that continue for too long can have a negative effect long after the wrongdoing ceases.

(v) Are the sanctions effective?

Sanctions must be reasonably capable of achieving the desired result in terms of threat or actual breach of international peace and security. Sanctions that are targeted in ways that would not affect the wrongdoing, may be viewed as ineffective.

(vi) Do the sanctions violate the "principles of humanity and the dictates of the public conscience?

Profressor Bossuyt noted:

that it is not sufficient that the policy of the targeted country justifies the imposition of economic sanctions. There should also be a reasonable expectation that the measures taken may lead to the desired result. Within regular intervals of not more than one year at the maximum, the effects of sanctions must be evaluated. The impact of sanctions on the enjoyment of human rights by the population should be taken prominently into account. If the desired results cannot be attained within a reasonable time period, the measures should be suspended. If not, the sanctions may not only lose their legitimacy, but may also become counter-productive.

It should also be borne in mind that the intent of the party imposing unilateral sanctions is less important than the foreseeable consequences thereof. It is no excuse that the death of civilians was (implausibly) "unintended" or was merely "collateral damage." Such collateral damage is legally *imputable* to the State imposing the sanctions, which has thereby committed an internationally wrongful act, for which there is State responsibility and the obligation to make reparations. Professor Bossuyt concluded that the whole theory behind economic sanctions is fallacious. It is assumed that pressure on civilians will in turn translate into pressure on the Governments for change. However, in regimes where political decision-making is not democratic, there is simply no pathway through which civilian pressure can bring about change in the Government. As sanctions are generally imposed on countries where the Governments are not periodically subjected to free and transparent elections, the population has no chance to penalize their leaders that pursue a policy resulting in sanctions being imposed upon them. It is also unlikely that those leaders, once they become aware of the suffering their policy entails for their population, will modify that policy.

In the light of the above, allow me to formulate the following Recommendations:

1. The General Assembly should refer the following legal questions to the International Court of Justice and request an advisory opinion pursuant to article 96 of the UN Charter:
    a. Under what conditions can unilateral coercive measures be deemed legal?

b. Assuming that a sanctions regime was legitimate at its outset, does it lose its legality when coercive measures cause large-scale suffering and death?
c. What is the legal responsibility to make reparation to victims of unilateral sanctions?

2. The Human Rights Council should reject the apologetics of powerful countries intent on imposing neo-imperialist sanctions and unanimously condemn sanctions regimes.

3. The Independent Expert on the adverse effects of unilateral coercive measures should be invited to draft guidelines on the strict limits of such measures and rules for reparation of the victims.

4. The Special Rapporteur on the promotion of truth, justice, reparation and assurances of non-recurrence should study the human rights impacts of sanctions against the populations of Cuba, Iran, Syria, Venezuela and other targeted countries, and make an estimate of the reparation due to the victim populations.

5. The International Criminal Court should start an investigation into the question whether certain sanctions can amount to "crimes against humanity" under article 7 of the ICC Statute.

6. the ICC should establish the international penal responsibility for the imposition of unilateral sanctions and make an estimate of the reparation due to the victims.

7. The ICC statute should be amended to add the categories of "geopolitical crimes" and "State terrorism."

8. Inter-State complaints before the Human Rights Committee under article 41 of the International Covenant on Civil and Political Rights should be submitted against those states that have imposed unilateral coercive measures and thereby violated provisions of the ICCPR.

9. World religions should unite in condemning economic sanctions. Pope Franciscus should remind Catholics that such sanctions are diametrically opposed to the letter and spirit of the Sermon on the Mount.[78]

ANNEX II

SUMMARY OF THE LAW AND PRACTICE ON UNILATERAL COERCIVE MEASURES

At the expert consultation convened by Professor Alena Douhan, Special Rapporteur on Unilateral Coercive Measures on 26 April 2021 in Geneva, I summarized the law and practice on unilateral coercive measures.

> Unilateral coercive measures (UCM) raise multiple issues of international law and ethics that should be defined in precise legal language, excluding loopholes and weasel words. The definition must take into account

empirical evidence drawn from decades of abuse by powerful countries and the human consequences endured by populations affected. The normative exercise must give due weight to the UN Charter as a kind of world constitution (supremacy clause, article 103), core principles of international law including sovereignty, sovereign equality, the prohibition of interference in the internal affairs of states, as reflected in GA resolutions 2131, 2625, 3314, 31/91, and the jurisprudence of the International Court of Justice in the *Corfu Channel* and *Nicaragua v. U.S.* cases. Since the entry into force of the UN Charter, the international legal order is multilateral and makes provision for economic sanctions only with regard to Security Council decisions under Chapter VII, which, pursuant to Article 24 of the Charter, must conform with the Purposes and Principles of the UN, namely the promotion of peace, development and human rights (see Human Rights Committee "Views" in *Sayadi v. Belgium*). By contrast, unilateral coercive measures have no legitimacy, and possible exceptions in cases of justified retorsion must be evidence-based, due process supported and subject to *ex ante/ex post* impact assessments.

Under no conditions can sanctions be used for purposes of "punishment" but only as an inducement to the targeted state to cease specific illegal conduct. UCMs have been examined by United Nations instances and found to be inconsistent with international human rights treaty obligations. See the 1997 General Comment 8 of the Committee on Economic, Social and Cultural Rights, the 2000 Sub-Commission report by Professor Marc Bossuyt, which established criteria and concluded that UCM must be reviewed every 6 months and lifted if ineffective in inducing change. High Commissioner Navi Pillay condemned them in her 2012 report (A/HRC/19/33), the Advisory Committee to the Human Rights Council in its 2015 report. The GA has adopted 28 resolutions demanding the lifting of the U.S. embargo against Cuba. Yet, these GA and HRC Resolutions have been ignored.

Thus, the ICJ should be requested to issue an Advisory Opinion declaring UCMs contrary to international law and fixing State responsibility for reparations to victims. Similarly, the ICC should examine whether UCMs constitute "crimes against humanity" under article 7 of the Rome Statute, when it is established that they have led to the untimely deaths of tens of thousands of persons due to lack of food, clean water, medicine and medical equipment, especially during times of pandemic.

Bottom line: economic sanctions kill and must be lifted NOW."

* * *

It appears appropriate to close this chapter with a quotation by Dr. Sashi Tharoor, the dashing Indian Under-Secretary General who was a serious contender for the post of Secretary-General in 2006. I think that under his leadership maybe the Libyan and Syrian calamities and the humanitarian scandal of unilateral coercive measures could have been averted as well as other military interventions initiated under the pretext of "humanitarian assistance," albeit what was always intended was to obtain "regime change" and geopolitical advantage. —AdeZ

The U.N. guards the vital principles entrenched in its charter, notably the sovereign equality of states and the inadmissibility of interference in their internal affairs. It is precisely because the U.N. is the chief guardian of both these sacrosanct principles that it alone is allowed to approve derogations from them.[79]

Notes

1 General Assembly Resolution 60/1, para. 138.
2 Universal Declaration on Democracy, adopted by the Governing Council (formerly the Inter-Parliamentary Council) of the Inter-Parliamentary Union at its 161st session (Cairo, 16 September 1997), art. 24.
3 www.un.org/en/preventgenocide/adviser/responsibility.shtml; A/63/677.
4 www.un.org/press/en/2009/ga10850.doc.htm.
5 www.globalresearch.ca/the-seeds-of-suicide-how-monsanto-destroys-farming/5329947.
6 www.alternet.org/environment/8-dangerous-side-effects-fracking-industry-doesnt-want-you-hear-about.
7 Words conceal more than they elucidate. "The market" is not a law of natural science, but a bundle of power relations. When a dogmatist invokes as a magic phrase "the laws of the market," he means what the mega-corporations want. "Investment" may or may not be beneficial. While the funding of long-term investment in socially useful activities must be promoted, the management of existing assets to milk them for rents, dividends and capital gains hurts society. Wealth extraction is different from wealth creation. Market fundamentalism and free-trade-populism constitute a utopian, millenarian faith in the "invisible hand" of the market, and in a non-existent "trickle down" effect.
8 www.wto.org/english/news_e/sppl_e/sppl172_e.htm.
9 Ha-Joon Chang, "Kicking away the ladder," Foreign Policy In Focus (Silver City, NM: Interhemispheric Resource Center, December 2003).
10 See the debate in the General Assembly on 23 July 2009, summarized in my 2012 report to the Assembly (A/67/277). Contrary to some trends and perceptions, the idea of the responsibility to protect, contained in General Assembly Resolution 60/1 (2005 World Summit Outcome), did not replace the Charter-mandated international law of non-interference in the internal affairs of sovereign States.
11 See http://www.unhchr.ch/huridocda/huridoca.nsf/%28symbol%29/a.conf.157.23.en, para. 31.
12 See http://www.ohchr.org/Documents/Events/WCM/MarcBossuyt_ WorkshopUnilateralCoercive Seminar.pdf.
13 See S. Zaidi and M. C. Smith-Fawzi, "Health of Baghdad's Children," *The Lancet*, vol. 346, No. 8988, 2 December 1995.
See http://www.thelancet.com/journals/lancet/article/PIIS0140-6736(95)92499-X/fulltext and http://ac.els-cdn.com/S014067369592499X/1-s2.0-S014067369592499X-main.pdf?_tid=96207b 30-f37f-11e2-9b60-00000aacb35f&acdnat=1374574188_ cd1dd38b2f89967c98330ac1462be4be.
14 See Ali MM, Shah IH, "Sanctions and childhood mortality in Iraq," *The Lancet*, vol. 355, No. 9218, pp. 1851-57, 27 May 2000, available from http://ac.els-cdn.com/S0140673600022893/1-s2.0-S0140673600022893-main.pdf?_tid=aacffdf6-f3b8-11e2-a825-00000aab0f02&acdnat=1374598704_cb7484ab864b941dd7a5edb154c32d86.

15 See Noam Chomsky, *Hopes and Prospects* (Chicago, Haymarket Books, 2010).

16 Hans-Christof von Sponeck, *A Different Kind of War: The UN Sanctions Regime in Iraq* (New York and Oxford, Berghahn Books, 2006).

17 See http://www.guardian.co.uk/world/2001/nov/29/iraq.comment.

18 For this aspect, see John Pilger, *The New Rulers of the World* (London 2003).

19 See http://www.slmission.com/news/17-other-news/746-ad-hoc-committee-on-the-indian-ocean.html.

20 http://www.un.org/Docs/journal/asp/ws.asp?m=A/68/284

21 See, e.g., General Comment No. 8 of the Committee on Economic, Social and Cultural Rights, E/C.12/1997/8; Sub-Commission on the Promotion and Protection of Human Rights, *The adverse consequences of economic sanctions on the enjoyment of human rights,* E/CN.4/Sub.2/2000/33, paras. 63-67, 79-82, 91-94.

22 See Office of the High Commissioner for Human Rights, *Thematic study on the impact of unilateral coercive measures on the enjoyment of human rights, including recommendations on actions aimed at ending such measures,* A/HRC/19/33, para. 36; E/CN.4/Sub.2/2000/33, para. 94; A/68/284 para. 45.

23 Notably, Charter of the United Nations, arts. 39, 41; Vienna Declaration and Programme of Action; International Covenant on Economic and Social Rights, arts. 11-13; International Covenant on Civil and Political Rights, art. 6.

24 General Assembly Resolution 2625, "Friendly Relations Resolution."

25 See A/68/284, para. 42

26 See E/CN.4/Sub.2/2000/33, paras. 48-51.

27 See John Pilger, The New Rulers of the World (London 2003).

28 See E/C.12/1997/8, paras. 12-14; A/HRC/19/33, para.. 38; A/68/284 report, para. 42.

29 A/68/284, para. 43.

30 See reports A/HRC/30/44, A/HRC/33/40 and A/70/285) where the lack of legitimacy of ISDS tribunals and their obstruction of the rule of law is discussed. It shocks the conscience that transnational corporations challenge the refusal of a permit to mine in an ecologically sensitive area, but fail to challenge the imposition of unilateral sanctions which interfere far more with existing contracts and established trade relations).

31 https://libya360.wordpress.com/2016/09/19/final-declaration-of-the-xvii-summit-of-the-non-aligned-movement-nam/

http://www.humanrightsvoices.org/site/developments/?d=13519

http://www.nam.gov.za/media/030227e.htm

32 https://peoplesdemocracy.in/2015/0517_pd/summit-americas-us-recognises-new-realities

33 Resolution adopted by the General Assembly on 26 October 2016: Necessity of ending the economic, commercial and financial embargo imposed by the United States of America against Cuba, A/RES/71/5.

34 https://www.amnestyusa.org/pdfs/amr250072009eng.pdf

https://www.ncbi.nlm.nih.gov/pmc/articles/PMC1380757/

http://medicc.org/ns/documents/The_impact_of_the_U.S._Embargo_on_Health_&_Nutrition_in_Cuba.pdf

35 www.amnestyusa.org/pdfs/amr250072009eng.pdf; www.cetim.ch/the-effects-of-the-us-embargo-against-cuba-and-the-reasons-of-the-urgent-need-to-lift-it/; www.cubavsbloqueo.cu/sites/default/files/InformeBloqueo2017/informe_de_cuba_sobre_bloqueo_20_17_ingles.pdf; www.sela.org/media/264635/t023600006305-0-cuba_ing.pdf.

36 United States of America, *Covert Action in Chile, 1963–1973: staff report of the Select Committee to Study Governmental Operations with Respect to Intelligence Activities* (94th Congress, Washington, 1975); National Security Council, "Options Paper on Chile" (NSSM 97), 3 No. 1970; "National Security Decision Memorandum 93, Policy Toward Chile," 9 November 1970; "Report on CIA Chilean Task Force Activities, 15 September to 3 November 1970."

37 www.washingtonpost.com/archive/opinions/1989/08/27/uncle-sams-money-war-against-the-sandinistas/f78e064a-1ca1-4e07-90d2-bebdeff1717d/?utm_term=.9dd20f649246.

38 https://theintercept.com/2016/09/28/u-s-sanctions-are-punishing-ordinary-syrians-and-crippling-aid-work-u-n-report-reveals/.
39 www.ve.undp.org/.
40 www.unicef.org/venezuela/spanish/unicef_venezuela_7741.htm.
41 www.fao.org/venezuela/programas-y-proyectos/en/.
42 www.paho.org/ven/index.php?option=com_content&view=article&id=416:rusia-entrego-a-venezuela-8-5-toneladas-de-medicamentos-con-el-apoyo-de-ops-oms&Itemid=0; www.paho.org/ven/index.php?option=com_content&view=article&id=418:venezuela-lanza-campana-de-vacunacion-para-interrumpir-la-circulacion-del-virus-del-sarampion&Itemid=0.
43 www.unaids.org/en/regionscountries/countries/venezuela.
44 www.unhcr.org/venezuela.html.
45 www.unodc.org/; www.unodc.org/unodc/treaties/CAC/country-profile/CountryProfile.html?code=VEN.
46 www.ilo.org/dyn/normlex/en/f?p=NORMLEXPUB:11110:0::NO::P11110_COUNTRY_ID:102880; www.ilo.org/gb/GBSessions/GB320/ins/WCMS_237898/lang--en/index.htm.
47 www.iesalc.unesco.org.ve/index.php?option=com_content&view=article&id=1202:venezuela-ingresa-al-consejo-ejecutivo-de-la-unesco&catid=11&Itemid=466&lang=es; https://en.unesco.org/countries/venezuela-bolivarian-republic?language=fr.
48 www.paho.org/ven/index.php?option=com_content&view=article&id=418:venezuela-lanza-campana-de-vacunacion-para-interrumpir-la-circulacion-del-virus-del-sarampion&Itemid=0. Between 2017 and 2018, thanks to the Pan American Health Organization revolving fund, nearly 7 million measles/mumps/rubella vaccines and more than 9 million vaccines against diphtheria and tetanus were distributed, as well as the syringes needed for vaccination.
49 Marcelo Kohen, "The principle of non-intervention 25 years after the *Nicaragua* judgment," *Leiden Journal of International Law*, vol. 25 (2012).
50 Naigen Zhang, "The principle of non-interference and its application in practices of contemporary international law, *Fudan Journal of the Humanities and Social Sciences*, vol. 9, No. 3 (September 2016).
51 https://nsarchive2.gwu.edu//NSAEBB/NSAEBB8/nsaebb8i.htm.
52 Peter Kornbluh, *The Pinochet File: A Declassified Dossier on Atrocity and Accountability* (New York, The New Press, 2003);
Gonzalo Martner, *Chile: Los mil días de una economía sitiada* (Caracas, Universidad Central de Venezuela, 1975);
www.usnews.com/opinion/world-report/articles/2018-03-03/new-evidence-the-trump-administration-is-meddling-in-venezuelas-elections.
53 www.coface.com/Economic-Studies-and-Country-Risks/Venezuela.
54 www.celag.org/las-pruebas-del-crimen-economico-venezuela/amp/; https://venezuelanalysis.com/analysis/13529.
55 https://dolartoday.com/.
56 Pasqualina Curcio Curcio, *The visible hand of the market: economic warfare in Venezuela* (2017), pp. 54 and 74.
https://lalenguatv.com.ve/wp-content/uploads/2017/03/ManoVisibleMercado.pdf. Pasqualina Curcio, *Hyperinflación*, Editorial Nosotros Mismos, Caracas 2018.
57 https://www.ohchr.org/EN/ProfessionalInterest/Pages/Vienna.aspx
58 "The Security Council shall act in accordance with the Purposes and Principles of the United Nations."
59 According to a study by Professor Jeffrey Sachs and Mark Weisbrot, sanctions on the Venezuelan people caused an estimated 40,000 deaths in 2018. http://cepr.net/publications/reports/economic-sanctions-as-collective-punishment-the-case-of-venezuela. http://cepr.net/press-center/press-releases/report-finds-us-sanctions-on-venezuela-are-responsible-for-tens-of-thousands-of-deaths
60 Resolutions adopted during the 73rd session https://undocs.org/en/A/RES/73/8 https://undocs.org/en/A/RES/72/4 Resolution 72/4, https://undocs.org/en/A/RES/72/4 https://www.un.org/press/

en/2018/ga12086.doc.htm
 61 https://www.aporrea.org/actualidad/n155077.html
 62 https://venezuelanalysis.com/news/2329
https://www.thenation.com/article/our-gang-venezuela/
 63 https://www.escr-net.org/resources/progressive-realisation-and-non-regression
 64 Marcelo Kohen, "The principle of non-intervention 25 years after the Nicaragua judgment," *Leiden Journal of International Law*, vol. 25 (2012).
 65 Naigen Zhang, "The principle of non-interference and its application in practices of contemporary international law, *Fudan Journal of the Humanities and Social Sciences*, vol. 9, No. 3 (September 2016).
 66 www.ohchr.org/EN/NewsEvents/Pages/DisplayNews.aspx?NewsID=22072&LangID=E. The Movement of Non-Aligned Countries has also repeatedly condemned sanctions. See https://venezuelanalysis.com/analysis/12896.
 67 www.ohchr.org/Documents/Events/WCM/MarcBossuyt_WorkshopUnilateralCoerciveSeminar.pdf;Sub-Commission on Human Rights resolution 2000/25
 68 Hans-C. von Sponeck, *A Different Kind of War: The UN Sanctions Regime in Iraq* (Berghahn Books, Oxford, 2006.
 69 http://news.cornell.edu/stories/1999/09/former-un-official-says-sanctions-against-iraq-amount-genocide. In a 1996 interview, when asked about reports that half a million children had died in Iraq owing to the sanctions, the United States Secretary of State, Madeleine Albright, replied "we think the price is worth it." See https://fair.org/extra/we-think-the-price-is-worth-it/.
 70 In favour (27): Angola, Bahamas, Bahrain, Bangladesh, Burkina Faso, Cameroon, Chile, China, Cuba, Democratic Republic of the Congo, Egypt, Eritrea, Fiji, India, Iraq, Nepal, Nigeria, Pakistan, Philippines, Qatar, Rwanda, Saudi Arabia, Somalia, South Africa, Togo, Tunisia and Uruguay.
Against (15): Australia, Austria, Brazil, Bulgaria, Croatia, Czech Republic, Denmark, Hungary, Iceland, Italy, Japan, Slovakia, Spain, Ukraine and United Kingdom of Great Britain and Northern Ireland.
Abstentions (5): Afghanistan, Argentina, Mexico, Peru and Senegal.
 71 www.colombiainforma.info/santos-bloquea-venta-de-medicamentos-a-venezuela/;https://venezuelanalysis.com/news/13782;http://m.avn.info.ve/contenido/venezuela-denuncia-que-euroclear-mantiene-secuestro-recursos-destinados-medicinas-y-alimen.
 72 Pasqualina Curcio, La Mano Visible del Mercado, Caracas 2016; Hiperinflación, Caracas 2018. https://www.aporrea.org/tiburon/a271967.html, http://www.15yultimo.com/2019/02/18/acelerar-el-colapso/
 73 https://assets.documentcloud.org/documents/3115191/Hum-Impact-of-Syria-Related-Res-Eco-Measures-26.pdf
 74 www.independent.co.uk/voices/economic-sanctions-north-korea-syria-hospital-supplies-a8168321.html.
 75 A/HRC/19/33. https://www2.ohchr.org/english/bodies/hrcouncil/docs/19session/a-hrc-19-33_en.pdf, paras 39-42.
 76 http://ap.ohchr.org/documents/dpage_e.aspx?si=A/HRC/24/38
 77 http://ap.ohchr.org/documents/dpage_e.aspx?si=A/68/284
 78 https://www.biblegateway.com/passage/?search=Matthew+5-7&version=NIV
 79 https://shashitharoor.in/

Chapter 8
BUSINESS AND HUMAN RIGHTS

"We want capitalism and market forces to be the slave of democracy rather than the opposite."

THOMAS PIKETTY[i]

ON FREE-TRADE AGREEMENTS, INVESTOR-STATE DISPUTE SETTLEMENT, AND THE WTO DISPUTE PANEL

My 2015 and 2016 reports to the Human Rights Council and my 2015 report to the General Assembly explore glaring rule-of-law problems arising from free-trade agreements and bi-lateral investment treaties. In particular, the report reviews the procedures and awards of ad hoc arbitration tribunals known as the investor-state dispute settlement mechanism. These ISDS tribunals are stipulated in the "investment protection" chapters of commercial treaties, creating a parallel system of dispute-settlement, which lacks transparency, accountability and appealability, and circumvents the domestic courts, often discarding domestic statutes, ignoring the judgments of the highest domestic tribunals, as well as the democratic decisions of local communities and sovereign States. On 20 March 2015 I visited Julian Assange at the Ecuadorian Embassy in London to learn about the Wikileaks publication of the super-secret investment protection chapters in free-trade agreements and learned about the deliberate effort of the corporate negotiators and their accomplices in government to keep outside experts, parliamentarians, potential critics, independent observers and the public out of the picture. The negotiation process of such agreements has been shown to be undemocratic and lacking a minimum of transparency to give them legality under the Vienna Convention on the Law of Treaties. Because of the secretive procedure of adopting such free-trade agreements and bearing in mind the experience made concerning the arbitrariness and incoherence of many ISDS awards, it has become clear to many observers that such tribunals are "toxic" to the common good of society and incompatible with the ontology of States as protectors of the population, particularly in the fields of environmental safety, health and morals. Because ISDS undermines the regulatory functions of States, ISDS must be abolished as contra bonos mores and contrary to article 53 VCLT. The ISDS cannot be reformed or replaced by any international investment court

---

i "Economist says U.S. inequality reaching 'spectacular' heights." Interview with Alain Sherter, *CBS News,* www.cbsnews.com, June 5, 2014.

scam providing only one-way jurisdiction. Below are excerpts from my 2015 report to the HR Council. —AdeZ

* * *

Pursuant to Human Rights Council resolutions 18/6, 21/9, 25/15 and 27/9, the Independent Expert has endeavoured to identify obstacles to the realization of a democratic and equitable international order, including lack of transparency and accountability (A/HRC/21/45 and A/67/277), lack of genuine democratic participation in domestic and global decision-making (A/HRC/24/38), asymmetric economic, financial and trade practices (A/68/284), military expenditures (A/HRC/27/51) and denial of self-determination (A/69/272).

In this report, the Independent Expert addresses the adverse impacts of free trade and investment agreements, whether bilateral or multilateral, on the international order. The report to the General Assembly will focus on the impacts of investor–State dispute settlement arbitrations. The Independent Expert has relied on the advice of economists and given attention to the reports of other Special Procedures mandate holders, including the Special Rapporteur on the right to food (A/HRC/19/59/Add.5 and A/HRC/10/5/Add.2); the Special Rapporteur on the right of everyone to the enjoyment of the highest attainable standard of physical and mental health;[1] the Special Rapporteur on the human right to safe drinking water and sanitation;[2] the Special Rapporteur on extreme poverty and human rights;[3] the Independent Expert on the effects of foreign debt and other related international financial obligations of States on the full enjoyment of all human rights, particularly economic, social and cultural rights;[4] the Special Rapporteur on the independence of judges and lawyers; the Special Rapporteur on the rights to freedom of peaceful assembly and of association (A/HRC/29/25); the former Special Representative of the Secretary-General on human rights and transnational corporations and other business enterprises;[5] and the Working Group on the issue of human rights and transnational corporations and other business enterprises (A/HRC/29/28, paras. 30–31). He strongly endorses articles 1 to 10 of the 2011 Guiding Principles on Business and Human Rights (A/HRC/17/31, annex) and the United Nations "Protect, Respect and Remedy" Framework.[6] He relies on pertinent general comments and concluding observations of treaty bodies including the Human Rights Committee, the Committee on Economic, Social and Cultural Rights, and the Committee on the Rights of the Child. He welcomes the perceptive diagnoses, recent conferences and pertinent reform initiatives by UNCTAD.[7] Advocates of free trade and investment agreements may question the analysis in this report because of a lack of hands-on experience. Critics, however, cannot delegitimize the human rights recommendations contained herein, which correspond to the Human Rights Council's resolutions pertaining to the mandate.

An international order of sovereign and equal States under the Charter of the United Nations, committed to the rule of law, transparency and accountability must not be undermined by private attempts to replace it with an international order ruled by transnational enterprises lacking democratic legitimacy.

This preliminary report on a complex and multifaceted subject does not question the axiom that, in principle, free trade is a good thing that has promoted development for centuries. A breakdown in trade can even usher economic contraction, as happened with the decline of the Roman Empire into the "dark ages." Although bilateral investment treaties and free-trade agreements may foster international exchanges, one should not be so optimistic as to equate trade with welfare or to pretend that "[o]ne could almost say that trade is human rights in practice."[8] Given that tariffs are already low, do they need to be reduced further at the expense of domestic regulation of social policy? The focus has shifted to non-trade barriers, which many countries—both developed and developing—maintain to protect their domestic markets. Some observers contend that bilateral investment treaties and free-trade agreements are geopolitical constructs having little to do with trade liberalization, while others like Professor Yash Tandon point to the history of trade as a form of imposing economic dominance.[9] In any case, a sensible compromise that allows foreign direct investment while ensuring the protection of human rights[10] is possible, as recognized by the Guiding Principles on Business and Human Rights. Such obligations are derived from customary law and treaty law, notably the International Covenant on Civil and Political Rights and the International Covenant on Economic, Social and Cultural Rights. By definition, every State's legitimacy depends on its ability to advance the welfare of the population under its jurisdiction. Every State under the rule of law must fulfil this responsibility and cannot divest itself of human rights obligations by outsourcing or privatizing activities that are fundamentally State functions. Before and after entering into international investment agreements, States should conduct human rights, health and environmental impact assessments.[11]

Many observers have expressed concern about certain investor–State dispute settlement arbitrations that have effectively overridden the State's fulfilment of its function to regulate domestic labour, health and environmental policies, and have had adverse human rights impacts, also on third parties, including a "chilling effect" with regard to the exercise of democratic governance. Arbitration tribunals are credible institutions only when they operate in a demonstrably independent, transparent and accountable manner, as required under article 14 (1) of the International Covenant on Civil and Political Rights concerning suits at law. Investor-State dispute settlement tribunals do not operate in a separate legal context, but are bound by the *erga omnes* obligations imposed by the international human rights regime,[12] which permeates all areas of human activity, including by non-state actors. Some observers consider certain arbitration awards frivolous and manifestly ill-founded, yet not appealable.

A fundamental problem arises concerning the tension between legally binding human rights treaties and the operation of international investment agreements. As Bohoslavsky has observed: "There is a need for coherence in order to avoid the fragmentation of an international legal order that aspires to legality and, consequently, consistency."[13]

Investment protection versus human rights protection

In a *New York Times* article entitled "On the wrong side of globalization," Joseph Stiglitz observed:

> Corporations everywhere may well agree that getting rid of regulations would be good for corporate profits. Trade negotiators might be persuaded that these trade agreements would be good for trade and corporate profits. But there would be some big losers— namely, the rest of us.[14]

International investment agreements are not new phenomena in the international arena. Bilateral investment treaties currently number over 3,200. After years of experience with investor–State dispute settlement, the International Centre for Settlement of Investment Disputes (ICSID) and other arbitrations, it has become apparent that the regulatory function of many States and their ability to legislate in the public interest have been compromised. The problem has been aggravated by the chilling effect of certain awards that have penalized States for adopting regulations to protect the environment, food safety, access to generic medicine and reduction of smoking, as required under the WHO Framework Convention on Tobacco Control. The legality of such awards is questionable as contrary to domestic and international *ordre public*, and may be considered, in some cases, *contra bonos mores*.

Observers have noted retrogression in the protection of rights including the rights to life,[15] food (A/HRC/25/57), water and sanitation,[16] health, housing, education, culture, improved labour standards, an independent judiciary, a clean environment and the right not to be subjected to forced resettlement. Moreover, there is a legitimate concern that international investment agreements might aggravate the problem of extreme poverty,[17] foreign debt renegotiation, financial regulation and the rights of indigenous peoples, minorities, persons with disabilities and older persons and other vulnerable groups.

The Working Group on business and human rights has stressed in its reports that the Guiding Principles on Business and Human Rights stipulate in principles 8 and 9 that "States should ensure that governmental departments, agencies and other State-based institutions that shape business practices are aware of and observe the State's human rights obligations" and that "States should maintain adequate domestic policy space to meet their human rights obligations when pursuing business-related policy objectives with other States or business enterprises, for instance through investment treaties or contracts." Accordingly, all international investment agreements under negotiation should include a clear provision stipulating that in case of conflict between the human rights obligations of a State and those under other treaties, human rights conventions prevail.

The 1994 North American Free Trade Agreement (NAFTA) is an example of an agreement that has led to relocation of manufacturing industries, resulting in loss of employment in the United States (estimated at 850,000 jobs) and the proliferation of assembly centres in Mexico, known as *maquiladoras*,[18] where labour costs are lower and social protection below ILO standards. NAFTA "provided investors with a unique set of guarantees designed to stimulate foreign direct investment and the movement of factories within the hemisphere.... Furthermore, no protections were contained in the core of the agreement to maintain labor or environmental standards. As a result, NAFTA tilted the economic playing field in favor of investors, and against workers and the environment."[19] Several international investment agreements are currently being negotiated, mostly in secret, including the Transatlantic Trade and Investment Partnership (TTIP), the Trade in Services Agreement, the Trans-Pacific Partnership and the Regional Comprehensive Economic Partnership.[20]

Numerous scholars and Nobel prize laureates in economics have already signalled the dangers to democratic governance and human rights. Stiglitz states: "These agreements go well beyond trade, governing investment and intellectual property as well, imposing fundamental changes to countries' legal, judicial, and regulatory frameworks, without input or accountability through democratic institutions. Perhaps the most invidious—and most dishonest—part of such agreements concerns investor protection. Of course, investors have to be protected against the risk that rogue governments will seize their property. But that is not what these provisions are about. There have been very few expropriations in recent decades, and investors who want to protect themselves can buy insurance from the Multilateral Investment Guarantee Agency, a World Bank affiliate (the U.S. and other governments provide similar insurance).... The real intent of these provisions is to impede health, environmental, safety, and, yes, even financial regulations."[21] With regard to developing countries, the 2014 report of the United Nations Conference on Trade and Development (UNCTAD) further notes:

"Foreign capital flows to developing and transition economies may support investment, economic diversification and growth, or generate macroeconomic instability, external imbalances and boom-and-bust-credit episodes.... For macroprudential and developmental reasons, governments need sufficient policy space to be able to manage foreign capital flows, influence their amount and composition, and channel them to productive uses."[22] This correctly points out that foreign direct investment and other capital flows can generate problems in areas beyond human rights.

Observers have noted grave democratic deficits with international investment agreements and investor–State dispute settlement tribunals and wondered why States continue to engage in negotiations, based on partisan studies and overly optimistic forecasts about gross domestic product (GDP) growth and employment. Not only is there a failure of States to proactively disclose information about the agreements, but key stakeholders are excluded from the negotiating table, where mostly corporate lawyers and lobbyists[23] participate. There is even an attempt to circumvent parliaments by "fast-tracking" the adoption of these agreements, manifesting a gross absence of due process and hence of democratic legitimacy.

There is no lack of good diagnoses about the challenge. The problem lies in part in an anachronistic and uncritical commitment to the philosophy of market fundamentalism. Joseph writes perceptively: "Free trade is not an end in itself. ...The fervour with which free trade advocates continue to promote their cause is astonishing."[24] Stiglitz notes the lack of empirical evidence that trade liberalization has significantly increased GDP and employment, notwithstanding dogmatic assertions to that effect and amazingly optimistic forecasts for agreements currently under consideration.[25] As Joseph observes, because trade law spills over into other areas of law, the desire for certainty cannot legitimately quarantine trade rules from allegedly non-trade considerations such as human rights and labour standards.[26] With regard to ongoing negotiations on the TTIP, Capaldo questions current assumptions and the projections: "Projections by different institutions have been shown to rely on the same Computable General Equilibrium Model that has proven inadequate as a tool for trade policy analysis. ...[W]e assess the effects of TTIP using the United Nations Global Policy Model, which incorporates more sensible assumptions on macroeconomic adjustment, employment dynamics, and global trade. We project that TTIP will lead to a contraction of GDP, personal incomes and employment. We also project an increase in financial instability and a continuing downward trend in the labor share of GDP."[27]

Investor–State dispute settlement: a challenge to democracy and the rule of law[28]

Among the major threats to a democratic and equitable international order is the operation of arbitral tribunals that act as if they were above the international human rights regime. Investor–State dispute settlement tribunals are made up of corporate arbitrators whose independence has been repeatedly questioned because of conflicts of interest.[29] Admittedly, corporate arbitrators are not natural guardians of the public interest, but of business interests and of a new "industry" that, as experience shows, has privileged investors over the public. The investor–State dispute settlement system entails a completely separate system of dispute settlement, not only outside the domestic court system, but above it, and without appeal. The mind reverts to Juvenal's question *quis custodiet ipsos custodes?* ("who guards the guardians?"). Can a democracy call itself democratic if it allows the creation of separate, non-transparent and non-accountable systems of dispute settlement?

Observers question the legitimacy of tribunals where the investor can sue the State but not vice versa.[30] Interpretations of terms such as "investment," "expropriation" and "fair and equal treatment" have been expansive and difficult to reconcile with the interpretation rules under articles 31 and 32 of the Vienna Convention on the Law of Treaties. Experience shows that arbitrators interpret international investment agreements without consideration of human rights or environmental constraints. Their procedures are not transparent, and it is not even known how many arbitrations have actually taken place, because most of them are not published. What becomes apparent is the strong business bias of the arbitrators and their feeling of being immune to general principles of law. In a 2012 report, UNCTAD noted that an "expansive interpretation of minimalist treaty language can give rise to a lack of predictability in the application of the standard. This, in turn, may lead to the undermining of legitimate State intervention for economic, social, environmental and other development ends."[31]

Spanish arbitrator Felipe Fernández-Armesto notes: "When I wake up at night and think about arbitration, it never ceases to amaze me that sovereign states have agreed to investment arbitration at all.... Three private individuals are entrusted with the power to review, without any restriction or appeal procedure, all actions of the government, all decisions of the courts, and all laws and regulations emanating from parliament."[32] Indeed, it is disturbing that arbitrators can disregard basic principles such as respect for the "margin of discretion" of States, State legislation and even the judicial pronouncements of the highest domestic courts. The one-way street of investor protection has not contributed to a culture of investor–State cooperation but fuelled an aggressive tendency to litigate and demonstrably generated a "regulatory chill." Arbitration may take place in Washington under the auspices of the World Bank's ICSID, but there is a worrisome degree of forum-shopping, and tribunals may meet before the London Court of International Arbitration, the International Chamber of Commerce, the Stockholm Chamber of Commerce, the Hong Kong International Arbitration Centre or the United Nations Commission on International Trade Law (UNCITRAL). There is a growing number of arbitrations that privilege profit over human rights.[33] According to UNCTAD, many investor–State dispute settlement arbitrations are completely confidential and information is available only regarding some 608 awards.[34] The Independent Expert refers to his forthcoming report to the General Assembly and flags a few cases in order to illustrate litigation practices and their human rights implications.

- In 2013, Lone Pine, a Calgary-based company registered in the United States sued Canada not under Canadian law, but under chapter 11 of NAFTA, challenged the moratorium by Quebec on fracking. The company did not give Canada time to weigh scientific studies showing that some fracking chemicals include carcinogens and hazardous air pollutants, justifying preventive measures.[35] Lone Pine contends that the moratorium is "arbitrary" and "capricious," and that it expropriates Lone Pine's profit.

- Ethyl Corporation, a Virginia corporation with a Canadian subsidiary, submitted a claim alleging that a Canadian statute banning imports of the gasoline additive MMT breached the obligations of Canada. Rather than fight, Canada withdrew the ban, notwithstanding health dangers.[36]

- *Metalclad v. Mexico* involved a corporation suing Mexico for refusing to allow it to build a waste disposal which would pollute the Mexican water supply. The arbitrators granted Metalclad $16.79 million in compensation for lost profits.[37]

- In 2013, the French transnational Veolia sued Egypt because of alleged loss of expected profits as a result of Egypt raising the minimum wage. The amount in controversy is $82 million.[38]

- *Aguas del Turani S.A. v. Republic of Bolivia* concerned a contract privatizing the water supply of Cochabamba, including 40-year concessions with a guaranteed annual cash flow. The deal was endorsed by the World Bank, which imposed privatization as a condition for credit. The majority shareholders of Aguas were the American company, Bechtel, and the Spanish multinational Abengoa. After the contract was implemented in 1999, water prices increased sharply. When people demonstrated for their right to an affordable water supply, the then-Government declared martial law and tried to quell protests by military force. After the death of a 17-year-old adolescent, the Plurinational State of Bolivia cancelled the privatization contract and Aguas sued for $50 million.[39]

- In 2009, the Swedish energy conglomerate Vattenfall sued Germany under the Energy Charter Treaty, demanding 1.4 billion euros in compensation for environmental measures restricting the use and discharge of cooling water into the River Elbe. Only after Germany agreed to lower its environmental standards was settlement reached, with adverse effects on the river and wildlife.[40] Following the Fukushima disaster, the German public demanded the closure of nuclear plants and the Government of Germany decided on a phase-out of nuclear energy. Vattenfall is currently seeking 4 billion in compensation.[41]

- One of the most egregious ICSID arbitrations concerned the case by United States–based Occidental Petroleum against Ecuador concerning the termination of an oil production site in the Amazon, and resulting in an award of $1.76 billion to Occidental ($2.4 billion with interest), which Ecuador accused of multiple human rights violations and environmental destruction.[42]

- In *Philip Morris (Switzerland) v. Uruguay* (2010), the multinational sued under the Switzerland–Uruguay bilateral investment treaty claiming that the Uruguayan anti-smoking legislation devalued its investments, blithely disregarding the WHO Framework Convention on Tobacco Control.[43] WHO submitted an *amicus curiae* brief.

- In 2009, an Ecuadorian court fined Chevron for environmental damage caused by its activities. Chevron refused to pay and turned to UNCITRAL to demand damages from Ecuador for lost profits.[44] Litigation is pending.

- When Philip Morris filed a claim against Australia[45] in 2011 challenging the Australian measures to reduce tobacco consumption, the Government stated that it rejected investor–State dispute settlement "provisions that would confer greater legal rights on foreign businesses than those available to domestic businesses.... The Government has not and will not accept provisions that limit its capacity to put health warnings or plain packaging requirements on tobacco products or its ability to continue the Pharmaceutical Benefits Scheme.... If Australian businesses are concerned about sovereign risk in Australian trading partner countries, they will need to make their own assessments about whether they want to commit to investing in those countries."[46]

Only gradually are governments and parliamentarians beginning to counter the corporate move against the fundamentals of State sovereignty. In the European Parliament, the issue of corporate blackmail has been raised in connection with the debate on the TTIP, arguing on the basis of *Vattenfall* and *Veolia* that multinational companies are using investor protection rules to achieve corporate aims, increasing the cost to the taxpayer of defending public policy and rules. A concept paper of the European Commission, "Investment in TTIP and beyond— the path for reform,"[47] outlines possible improvements in free trade agreement models so as to guarantee the State's policy space. Experience has shown that self-regulation has proven insufficient,[48] notwithstanding the Guiding Principles on Business and Human Rights, which should be made legally binding by treaty. In this context, it must be stressed that the possibility that arbitrations may find for the State and against the investor does not remove the danger nor legitimize the investor–State dispute settlement model, since the mere threat of such arbitration has dissuaded even developed States like Canada from adopting social legislation. Developing countries are even more vulnerable to the threat,[49] since they lack the resources to defend themselves against major transnational enterprises.

The manifest abuse of rights by investors is so brazen that one could imagine that one day the military-industrial complex might invoke investor–State dispute settlement when a country decides to reduce or terminate the production of anti-personnel landmines or cluster bombs because contrary to international humanitarian law, thus "expropriating" expected profits of the arms industry.

It is not just a question of reforming the investor-State dispute settlement system for the future, but imperative to review and revise existing bilateral investment treaties and free-trade agreements, which were never intended to become prisons for States. If investor–State dispute settlement and ICSID have since mutated into institutions of economic coercion, they must be dismantled and reinvented through the Vienna Convention on the Law of Treaties.

Normative framework

Although bilateral investment treaties and free-trade agreements have been on the international agenda for decades, their human rights impacts have been underreported. Apparently the siren call of potential profit and the over-optimistic forecasts promising GDP growth and significant creation of jobs have been so seductive to some governments that human rights considerations have been neglected and State functions compromised.

Among the sources of law recognized by the International Court of Justice are the general principles of law [art. 38 (1)(c) of the Statute of the International Court of Justice] which inform both national and international legal orders. Among those fundamental principles is good faith (*bona fide*), which has been incorporated into the civil codes and Constitutions of many States, and means that the law must be coherent and cannot be used antithetically to destroy rights. The Universal Declaration of Human Rights enshrines this principle in article 30, which is reflected in article 5 of the two Covenants. Other relevant general principles of law include the principles of proportionality, foreseeability, *rebus sic stantibus*, clean hands, estoppel (*ex injuria non oritur jus*), the prohibition of abuse of rights, entrapment and the prohibition of treaties or contracts that are *contra bonos mores*.

Most States have enshrined in their Constitution and legislation the concept of *ordre public*. A government that compromises its competence to defend and protect the interests of the persons living under its jurisdiction betrays its raison d'être and loses its democratic legitimacy.

The large body of existing human rights treaties, protocols and declarations create a constitutional framework that must be taken into account whenever a State enters into agreements with other States and/or private-sector actors, including financial institutions and transnational enterprises. The human rights regime, including international and regional human rights treaties and the relevant ILO and WHO Conventions, must be treated as superior to other agreements, including bilateral investment treaties and free-trade agreements. National courts and international tribunals and arbitration instances must be subordinated to this regime.

Among the rights that States must ensure are the rights to life, security of person, participation in the conduct of public affairs, homeland, movement, health, education, employment and social security. These commitments are enshrined, inter alia, in articles 1, 2, 6, 9, 12, 17, 25, 26, 27 of the International Covenant on Civil and Political Rights and articles 1, 2, 5, 6, 7, 9, 10, 11, 12 and 13 of the International Covenant on Economic, Social and Cultural Rights.

The process of elaboration, negotiation and adoption of bilateral investment treaties and free-trade agreements must conform with the requirement of article 25 (a) of the International Covenant on Civil and Political Rights to ensure participation by all stakeholders. This entails a proactive obligation on the part of Governments to disclose the necessary information and facilitate public participation. Access to information is an essential condition for the exercise of the right of freedom of opinion and expression under article 19 of the International Covenant on Civil and Political Rights. The added value of consultation and participation is building consensus which decreases the likelihood of onerous litigations. Parliaments have a high responsibility to carefully examine bilateral investment treaties and free-trade agreements and ensure that human rights and environmental impact assessments are carried out.

Trade negotiations conducted in secret (although not a matter of national security!) and excluding key stakeholders entail prima facie violations of articles 19 and 25 of the International Covenant on Civil and Political Rights.[50] As the Independent Expert explained in his 2013 report to the Council, democratically elected representatives do not have carte blanche from the electorate, but must consult with constituents and act according to their wishes.[51] Democracy is not exercised only once in a while, but entails a continuing dialogue between representatives and constituents. Had it not been for Wikileaks[52] publishing several chapters of the free-trade agreements under discussion, the necessary public debate could not even have gotten started.

The Committee on Economic, Social and Cultural Rights has issued pertinent general comments: No. 12 on the right to adequate food (art. 11), paragraphs 19 and 36 ("States parties should, in international agreements whenever relevant, ensure that the right to adequate food is given due attention"), No. 14 on the right to the highest attainable standard of health (art. 12), paragraph 39 ("In relation to the conclusion of other international agreements, States parties should take steps to ensure that these instruments do not adversely impact upon the right to health") and paragraph 41 prohibiting embargos or sanctions on medicines and medical equipment; No. 15, on the right to water (arts. 11 and 12), paragraphs 31 and 35–36 ("States parties should ensure that the right to water is given due attention in international agreements and, to that end, should consider the development of further legal instruments. With regard to the conclusion and implementation of other international and regional agreements, States parties should take steps to ensure that these instruments do not adversely impact upon the right to water"); No. 18 on the right to work (art. 6) and No. 19 on the right to social security (art. 9).[53]

These commitments are further strengthened by ILO Conventions 14, 29, 77, 78, 87, 95, 98, 102, 105, 138, 169 and 182. Also of relevance are WHO Conventions and other international treaties including the Convention for the Safeguarding of the Intangible Cultural Heritage, the Convention concerning the Protection of the World Cultural and Natural Heritage, and the United Nations Framework Convention on Climate Change.

Universal and regional human rights treaties, including the International Covenant on Civil and Political Rights and the International Covenant on Economic, Social and Cultural Rights, the European Convention on Human Rights, the American

Convention on Human Rights and the African Charter on Human and Peoples' Rights necessarily take precedence over other treaties. As the European Court of Human Rights decided in its 1989 judgment in *Case of Soering v. the United Kingdom*, the obligations under the European Convention on Human Rights prevail over those under extradition treaties, *mutatis mutandis* over bilateral investment treaties and free-trade agreements.

Systemic reform

Extraordinary problems require bold solutions. Anti-democratic investor–State dispute settlement paroxysms can be neutralized by revision or termination of such dispute settlement. If States can adopt extraordinary measures such as bailing out delinquent banks, *a fortiori* they can adopt measures to protect the welfare of the population. Protective actions by a State whose economy, agriculture or industry is in danger of failure because of the sometimes unpredictable effects of bilateral investment treaties and free-trade agreements may be justifiable under the *force majeure* principle.

The validity of bilateral investment treaties and free-trade agreements should be tested under the rules of the Vienna Convention on the Law of Treaties. For instance, a treaty may be void if it can be established that there was a manifest violation of the State's Constitution, errors relating to a fact or situation which was assumed to exist at the time the treaty was concluded and which formed an essential basis of its consent to be bound to the treaty (art. 48), fraudulent conduct by a negotiating party (art. 49), deliberately misleading or spurious claims, corruption (art. 50), coercion (arts. 51–52) or conflict with a peremptory norm of international law (art. 53). Treaties may also be terminated or their application suspended pursuant to the doctrine of material breach (art. 60), subsequent impossibility of performance (art. 61) or fundamental change of circumstances (art. 62). Normally, treaties contain provisions for denunciation or withdrawal. In the absence of such provisions, such a right may be implied by the nature of the treaty (art. 56). To the extent that bilateral investment treaties and free-trade agreements lead to violations of human rights, they should be modified or terminated. Articles 65 *et seq.* lay down the procedure.

In a famous article in the *American Journal of International Law*, Alfred Verdross elucidated which treaties can be considered *contra bonos mores*: "To this problem the decisions of the courts of civilized nations give an unequivocal answer. The analysis of these decisions shows that everywhere such treaties are regarded as being *contra bonos mores* which *restrict the liberty of one contracting party in an excessive or unworthy manner or which endanger its most important rights*. This and similar formulas prove that the law of civilized states starts with the idea which demands the establishment of a juridical order guaranteeing the rational and moral coexistence of the members. It follows that all those norms of treaties which are incompatible with this goal of all positive law—a goal which is implicitly presupposed—must be regarded as void."[54] Moreover, pursuant to the doctrine of severability, treaty provisions that are *contra bonos mores* can be severed without abandoning the entire treaty.

Any court ruling on the legality of a particular treaty or contract would have to look at its constitutionality. Hence the question whether, under any reasonable interpretation of a country's Constitution, a State can waive its ontological function to legislate in the public interest. In most jurisdictions, the courts would answer in the negative. Moreover, there is an ethical minimum threshold that underlies every contract or treaty. A treaty is *contra bonos mores* if it prevents the universally recognized tasks of the civilized State:

(a) maintenance of public order;

(b) defence of the State against external attacks;

(c) care of the bodily and spiritual welfare of persons under its jurisdiction at home; and

(d) protections of citizens abroad.[55]

Many States have in their Constitutions and legislation provisions concerning good faith and the illegality of unjust enrichment. Moreover, it is not only the written law that stands, but the broader principles of natural justice as already recognized in Sophocles' *Antigone*, affirming the unwritten laws of humanity (αγραφος νομος), and the concept of a higher moral law prohibiting unconscionably taking advantage of a weaker party, which could well be considered a form of economic neo-colonialism or neo-imperialism. Many Constitutions contain provisions concerning abuse of rights, which may find application when a transnational enterprise interferes in a government protecting employment, health, the environment and social order.

Investors might be tempted to invoke the principle *pacta sunt servanda* ("agreements must be kept," art. 26 of the Vienna Convention on the Law of Treaties), a kind of positivism akin to the "pound of flesh" mentality described in Shakespeare's *Merchant of Venice*, where the money-lender Shylock adamantly insists on specific performance of a contract stipulating the taking of a pound of flesh from the body of the borrower, the bankrupt merchant Antonio.[56] Undoubtedly Shylock had a right to reimbursement, but demanding a pound of flesh from Antonio's breast would have meant an attempt on his life. Shakespeare decides the competing rights in Antonio's favour. By analogy, it can be said that a petroleum company that is polluting the waters and causing major environmental damage cannot claim that its profits are guaranteed and that a State ordinance to prevent environmental damage should be repealed. Such legalistic nonsense borders on the criminal, and is invalidated by Article 103 of the Charter of the United Nations.

International criminal law and the Nuremberg precedents[57] might also be relevant in examining bilateral investment treaties and free-trade agreements, to the extent that transnational corporations and their lobbyists may have engaged in activities that contravene penal law. It would be appropriate to test whether the concept of "conspiracy" to commit acts that are *contra bonos mores* (or "joint criminal enterprise" as used by the International Criminal Tribunal for the Former Yugoslavia) can be applied to the method in which international investment agreements have been elaborated and negotiated in secrecy. Are States or some transnational corporations guilty of "conspiracy"? Actions in pursuance of such conspiracy could include deliberately giving false information; issuing false forecasts of GDP and employment growth; engaging think tanks, economists, universities or foundations in preparing "teleological reports"; and colluding with media conglomerates to ensure that only the "sunny" side of bilateral investment treaties and free-trade agreements is presented, and contentious issues are suppressed or minimized. The issue of corporate criminal responsibility for ecocide[58] and other offences deserves in-depth analysis in a future report.[59]

In reviewing the validity of the treaties, courts should also consider equitable arguments, both *intra legem* equity (within the rules of international law) and *praeter legem* equity (in the place of the rules of international law, applying the rules of justice or "substance over form"). Indeed, there is an inherent power for every court, including the International Court of Justice, to make decisions *ex aequo et bono* (based on what is fair and right), as in all agreements there is inherent equity. Each party who enters into an agreement tries to obtain the best possible deal, and when countries entered into bilateral investment treaties and free-trade agreements they were expecting GDP growth, job creation and development. None imagined that the agreements would include "Trojan horse" provisions such as unpredictable investor–State dispute settlement commitments and "survival clauses," nor dreamt that arbitrators would interpret concepts like "expropriation" as encompassing fiscal, budgetary, macroprudential, social, environmental or health measures that could potentially reduce investors' profits. Had this danger been clearly explained, probably no State would have consented. Thus, to the extent that there was inadequate disclosure of the risks, false representations and overly optimistic growth forecasts, there was no informed consent, and the Vienna Convention on the Law of Treaties provides grounds for modification or termination.

Substantively, investor–State dispute settlement tribunals cannot immunize investors from responsibility to make amends for damage caused, and the "polluter pays" principle cannot be trumped by a claim that paying fines is tantamount to an "expropriation." Such a claim would be rejected by any independent tribunal as blatantly frivolous and contrary to *ordre public*.

Pursuant to this analysis, the denunciation of international investment agreements is not only legitimate but also legal and their "survival clauses" must be seen as null and void when they are intended to perpetuate a system that violates human rights.

Outlook

"There is no fast or ready-paved road to sustainable and inclusive development; but the past three decades have demonstrated that delivery is unlikely with a one-size-fits-all approach to economic policy that cedes more and more space to the profitable ambitions of global firms and market forces. Countries should ultimately rely on their own efforts to mobilize productive resources and, especially, to raise their levels of domestic investment (both public and private), human capital and technological know-how. However, for this they need to have the widest possible room for manoeuvre to discover which policies work in their particular conditions, and not be subject to a constant shrinking of their policy space."[60]

Pursuant to article 28 of the Universal Declaration of Human Rights, States shall ensure "a social and international order in which the rights and freedoms set forth in this declaration can be fully realized." This is reinforced in article 2 of the International Covenant on Civil and Political Rights and article 2 of the International Covenant on Economic, Social and Cultural Rights.

The adoption of 10 core international human rights treaties and countless resolutions and declarations of the General Assembly, the Economic and Social Council and the Human Rights Council, pertinent ILO and WHO Conventions, the emergence of a system of regional human rights courts capable of adopting binding judgments, the 1993 Vienna Declaration and Programme of Action, the Millennium Development Goals—all these instruments over a period of many decades prove that a customary international law of human rights has emerged, manifesting *opinio juris* and international consensus on the primacy of human rights. Accordingly, globalization and targeted investment ought to foster an environment where human rights are fully realized through the State's regulatory functions. Alas, international investment agreements are usurping State functions as if the only rights were the rights to trade and to invest.

In the field of intellectual property, there is consensus that it deserves protection which must occur, however, in tandem with human rights considerations. Twenty-first century humanity functions on the basis of thousands of years of freedom of knowledge, or the free interchange of ideas and inventions. While there is justice in rewarding research and patenting new pharmaceuticals and inventions, monopolies must not contribute to greater inequality and Governments should regulate to ensure flexibility and prevent "evergreening" practices. Access to affordable medicine is essential to protect the right to life, and refusal to provide such affordable medicine is tantamount to the criminal offence of denial of humanitarian aid[61] or assistance to persons in danger. In other words, knowledge cannot be appropriated for profit, privatized or commoditized, but rather must be shared in international solidarity. Sharing knowledge without fee, as the European Organization for Nuclear Research shared the World Wide Web,[62] is in the best traditions of civilization.

Globalization cannot be allowed to become the grand global casino where investors rig the system to guarantee that they always win. A democratic and equitable international order is not possible if this "Hotel Brave New World" is allowed to ensnare States, letting them check in but never leave. Since the siren call of foreign direct investment has proven deceptive, Governments must move away from easy mythologies and demand empirical evidence of job creation and reject a "race to the bottom" in human rights terms. With good will, States can adjust international investment agreements for their benefit.

Transnational enterprises operate in the territory of States that are bound to the Charter of the United Nations, akin to a world constitution, whose Purposes and Principles are paramount for the achievement of a democratic and equitable international order. Transnationals cannot create a new legal order beyond the Charter of the United Nations, nor be *legibus solutus* or exempt from the rule of law, general principles of law and basic codes of conduct. Transnationals do not exist in a vacuum and are bound by the international human rights regime. Even their most cherished contribution to today's societies—creating jobs—is only possible thanks to laws that ensure the orderly functioning of market transactions, the clear assignment of property rights and reliance on effective courts. They operate in the context of accountability and checks and balances that took centuries to develop and cannot be waived. Wherever transnational corporations are registered or carry out operations, the home and host States have the responsibility to regulate them to prevent violations of human rights.

A State that fails to ensure the human rights of the population living under its jurisdiction is a failed State, even if it meets all its financial obligations. In order to prevent the emergence of a dystopian situation whereby a State cannot effectively protect human rights and transnational enterprises dictate public policy, States must reassert their sovereignty in a manner consistent with the Purposes and Principles of the United Nations, in particular with Articles 1 and 2 of the Charter of the United Nations. They must revise and, when necessary, terminate agreements that conflict with human rights.

Bearing in mind that the essence of capitalism and investment is risk taking, States must insist that investors accept the risk and subject themselves to national legislation in a manner similar to the Calvo doctrine,[63] which holds that jurisdiction in international investment disputes must lie with the country in which the investment is made. This doctrine has been adopted into the Constitutions of many Latin American States, and merits being used as a model for international investment agreements. Transnational enterprises cannot claim that State measures to protect the environment, health and hygiene standards entail unpredictable risks.

Modification or termination of international investment agreements may be a complex task, but much less problematic than, for example, dealing with armed conflict. The world economy has had to adjust time and again to advance the cause of human dignity. So it was with the prohibition of the lucrative slave trade, the abolition of slavery and decolonization, which were replaced by other economic models. For centuries slavery was the de facto economic model with implicit legality; colonialism was de facto the international order. Today these practices are seen as crimes against humanity. For decades, investor–State dispute settlement arbitrations have de facto upset the international order but they cannot trump the Charter of the United Nations. Just as other economic paradigms were abandoned, eventually investor–State dispute settlement will be recognized as an experiment gone wrong, an attempted hijacking of constitutionality resulting in the retrogression of human rights. The consequences of not modifying or terminating bilateral investment treaties and free-trade agreements are more serious than soberly accepting the necessity of revising them.

By way of conclusion, it would be appropriate to reaffirm that while free trade and investment agreements have their raison d'être, the primary role of the State is to act in the public interest. There are ample opportunities for corporations and investors to make legitimate profits and enter into genuine "partnerships" with States and not into asymmetrical relationships. The rule of thumb should be to:

(a) give to corporations what belongs to them—an environment in which to compete fairly;

(b) give back to States what is fundamentally and inalienably theirs—sovereignty and policy space;

(c) give parliaments what belongs to them—the faculty to consider all aspects of treaties without undemocratic secrecy and fast-tracking; and

(d) give to the people what is theirs: the rights to public participation, due process and democracy.

Plan of action

Seventy years after the entry into force of the Charter of the United Nations, it is appropriate to reaffirm its Purposes and Principles which, pursuant to Article 103, prevail over other treaties. Bearing in mind that a democratic and equitable international order can only be achieved gradually through the concerted action of States, national human rights institutions, intergovernmental organizations and civil society, the Independent Expert submits this preliminary plan of action with preventive and corrective recommendations.

Recommendations to States:

(a) States must ensure that all trade and investment agreements—existing and future—represent the democratic will of the populations concerned. Negotiations on current drafts must not be secret or "fast-tracked," but, on the contrary, must be subject to public participation on the basis of independent human rights, health and environmental impact assessments.

(b) States should ensure that parliaments, national human rights institutions and ombudspersons are involved in the process of elaboration, negotiation, adoption and application of trade and investment agreements.

(c) States must ensure that all trade and investment agreements recognize the primacy of human rights and specify that, in case of conflict, human rights obligations prevail. States must uphold their *erga omnes* obligation to implement human rights treaties and observe ILO and WHO Conventions.

(d) States must exercise due diligence to minimize the risk of violating human rights through the adoption and operation of bilateral investment treaties and free-trade agreements, and foreclose the danger of having to compensate foreign investors as a consequence of adopting necessary fiscal, financial and debt resolution measures or policies designed to respond to changing circumstances such as financial crises, new scientific findings or public demand for laws of general application.

(e) States that adhere to international investment agreements must ensure that a regulatory independent mechanism is also agreed upon, such as the office of an ombudsperson. Provision must be made for ex ante and ex post human rights and environmental impact assessments.

(f) States cannot compromise their obligation to ensure human rights by accepting investor–State dispute settlement agreements that allow investors to challenge the State's labour law, environmental legislation or health codes.

(g) States must ensure that international investment agreements do not undermine their ability to implement the industrial and macroeconomic policies needed for development, which is an essential objective of United Nations "constitutional" law, and take steps to revise promptly existing bilateral investment treaties and free-trade agreements with negative effects on human rights. States should test existing bilateral investment treaties and free-trade agreements for compliance under their respective Constitutions, and revise or terminate said agreements pursuant to the Vienna Convention on the Law of Treaties when they conflict with human rights obligations.

(h) States should keep essential services in governmental hands so as to ensure democratic transparency and accountability. Any privatization must be coupled with effective human rights safeguards.

(i) All future international investment agreements should provide for the settlement of disputes not by investor–State dispute settlement but by the national courts.

(j) States should take measures to ensure implementation of the guiding principles on human rights impact assessments of trade and investment agreements and make them legally binding in the domestic legal order.

(k) States should monitor respect for the Guidelines on Business and Human Rights by all transnational enterprises operating in their territory and make them legally binding in the domestic legal order.

(l) States should partner with civil society actors to counteract the negative impact of free-trade agreements on the enjoyment of human rights and provide for an enabling environment for civil society actors.

(m) States must deny effect to investor–State dispute settlement and ICSID awards that violate human rights; practice solidarity with States seeking to modify or terminate bilateral investment treaties, free-trade agreements or investor–State dispute settlement agreements or that deny effect to arbitral awards; and take measures vis-à-vis investors and transnational corporations violating international human rights law.

(n) States victims of *contra bonos mores* investor–State dispute settlement arbitrations should organize a concerted response, jointly refuse implementation and convene an assembly of States parties to modify or terminate investor–State dispute settlement agreements with immediate effect and to revise or terminate application of the Convention on the Recognition and Enforcement of Foreign Arbitral Awards when the awards entail human rights violations.

(o) States should include in bilateral investment treaties and free-trade agreements specific provisions on the legal responsibility of transnational corporations and investors to make reparation for environmental, health and other damages caused by their activities, and strengthen domestic criminal law provisions so as to address personal criminal liability of investors and corporation executives for environmental harm or gross human rights violations. To this end, States should establish a monitoring mechanism to assess investor compliance with human rights.

(p) States should invoke Article 96 of the Charter of the United Nations and request the General Assembly to refer pertinent legal questions to the International Court of Justice for advisory opinions.

Recommendations to parliaments:

(a) Bearing in mind that in representative democracies parliaments are the trustees of the will of the people, parliamentarians must consult with their constituents, proactively inform and seek the opinion of all sectors of the population, particularly those likely to be affected by international investment agreements. Fast-tracking treaties is incompatible with the democratic process and results in illegitimate treaties.

(b) Parliaments must ensure that international investment agreements contain general provisions on their periodic review and amendment, as well as provisions for termination, withdrawal or suspension without unreasonable "survival clauses."

(c) Parliaments must ensure that bilateral investment treaties and free-trade agreements advance food security, education, health, sanitation social and economic policies and decide on domestic budgetary and fiscal matters.

(d) Parliamentarians should resist the siren call of lobbies for transnational enterprises that make over-optimistic projections of growth and development. Parliamentarians must demand independent economic studies and independent human rights impact assessments.

(e) Parliamentarians should resist attempts to privatize essential governmental services, including the provision of safe water and sanitation.

(f) Regional parliaments and parliamentary assemblies should address the dangers to human rights of bilateral investment treaties and free-trade agreements, including ways to repeal and/or modify them according to the Vienna Convention on the Law of Treaties.

Recommendations to transnational enterprises and investors:

(a) Transnational enterprises must accept the adoption of State measures to implement progressively the rights contained in the International Covenant on Economic, Social and Cultural Rights and factor them in as a cost of doing business.

(b) They must refrain from interfering in a State's function to legislate in the public interest in implementation of human rights treaty obligations.

Recommendations to civil society, national human rights institutions, universities and religious institutions:

(a) Civil society organizations and universities should revisit the dogmas of market fundamentalism and test empirically the extent to which existing international investment agreements have fostered or hindered the enjoyment of human rights.

(b) Individuals and groups should reclaim their democratic right to participate in decision-making in the determination of governmental budgetary, fiscal, economic, trade and social policies. They should demand the primacy of human rights over investment privileges and vindicate the social contract, as reflected in an index of public satisfaction composed of both material and non-material indicators.

(c) Individuals and groups should demand periodic review of the success or otherwise of international investment agreements. When treaties conflict with human rights, they must be revised, amended or terminated.

(d) Individuals and groups should demand transparency and accountability from their elected officials, particularly with regard to the elaboration, negotiation, adoption and application of trade and investment agreements.

(e) Individuals and groups should engage national courts to determine the constitutionality of existing bilateral investment treaties and free-trade agreements and to define the parameters of possible future agreements.

(f) Individuals and groups should assert their rights by invoking the jurisdiction of regional human rights courts, and asking them to investigate and denounce violations of the civil, cultural, economic, political and social rights resulting from the application of international investment agreements or the implementation of investor–State dispute settlement awards.

(g) Law schools should include ethics in their curricula and teach prospective lawyers and arbitrators that they have a duty to serve society and uphold the letter and spirit of the law. They cannot aid and abet any system whose foreseeable consequences are the erosion of human rights and environmental standards. Students should see investment law as part of a legal framework that includes human rights. Law is not a game and the goal is not to "win" but to serve justice, aware that positivism in law must integrate human dignity. No one should seek to profit from injustice.

(h) Religious institutions should join forces to assess the compliance of bilateral investment treaties and free-trade agreements with human rights law and standards, and where relevant promote ways to modify or terminate those treaties that adversely impact on human rights.

(i) National human rights institutions should advise States against entering bilateral investment treaties or free-trade agreements that do not guarantee State sovereignty and regulatory space. National human rights institutions should advise States on how to modify or terminate treaties that hinder the implementation of human rights.

Recommendations to the Human Rights Council:

(a) The new Forum on Human Rights, Democracy and the Rule of Law should devote a session to the human rights impacts of bilateral investment treaties and free-trade agreements. This Forum may elaborate a plan of action to address existing problems and recommend implementable solutions, including the phasing out of investor–State dispute settlement.

(b) The Human Rights Council should systematically use its universal periodic review procedure to inquire into the impact of bilateral investment treaties and free-trade agreements on the enjoyment of human rights.

(c) The Council should consider tasking OHCHR with a global online consultation on the issue of adverse impacts of free trade and investment agreements on the enjoyment of human rights so as to provide input to the Accountability and Remedy Project, and allocate additional funds for this consultation.

(d) The Council should consider referring matters to the United Nations Security Council and to United Nations specialized agencies like the Food and Agriculture Organization of the United Nations, ILO, WHO and the United Nations Children's Fund and study the possibility of requesting injunctive relief to prevent the violation of civil, cultural, economic, political and social rights.

Recommendations to United Nations agencies and subsidiary organs:

(a) UNCTAD should consider convening a conference to explore the possibilities of revising or terminating existing bilateral investment treaties and free-trade agreements that contain provisions that have interfered with the State's duty to legislate human rights, implement economic policies and regulate in the public interest. Such a conference should advance the UNCTAD "action menu" and "road map" for reform.

(b) UNCTAD and OHCHR should provide advisory services and technical assistance how to reverse the negative human rights impacts of bilateral investment treaties and free-trade agreements and how to compensate victims.

(c) All United Nations agencies and subsidiary organs should put international investment agreements on their agenda and offer advisory services and technical assistance to States considering such agreements to ensure the protection of all human rights, including the rights to food, health, minimum wage, improved labour standards, gender equality and the rights of the child. In relevant ICSID and investor–State dispute settlement arbitrations they should submit amicus curiae briefs. They should use their competence under Article 96 (2) of the Charter of the United Nations to request pertinent advisory opinions from the International Court of Justice.

(d) WTO should integrate human rights into its mission statement and ensure that its dispute settlement mechanism fosters human rights.

(e) As the core legal body of the United Nations system in the field of international trade law, UNCITRAL[64] should mainstream human rights into its activities, in particular strengthen its transparency rules and ensuring that arbitrations systematically take obligations under the International Covenant on Civil and Political Rights and the International Covenant on Economic, Social and Cultural Rights into account and refrain from undermining human rights, national policy space and environmental protection measures. Arbitrations must migrate from the private law paradigm to a public law framework which promotes general interests.

THE CASE AGAINST THE INVESTOR-STATE SETTLEMENT REGIME

My 2015 report to the General Assembly continued the analysis started for the Human Rights Council, consciously avoiding duplication and providing additional examples of the kind of abuse that is being practised and the "revolving door" corruption associated with the "closed shop" of lawyers, arbitrators and transnational corporation managters. I had the opportunity of participating in panels organized by South Centre in Geneva, and in events hosted by the Transnational Institute and Corporate Europe Observatory[i] in Amsterdam, Brussels, Paris and Berlin, where I exchanged views with economists and other experts including Cecilia Olivet and Pia Eberhardt, whom I thank for their valuable reports. —AdeZ

* * *

According to the *World Investment Report 2015*, growing unease with the current functioning of the global international investment agreement regime, together with today's sustainable development imperative, the greater role of Governments in the economy and the evolution of the investment landscape, has triggered a move towards reforming international investment rules seeking to make them better suited for today's policy challenges. As a result, the regime is going through a period of reflection, review and revision. As is evident from the United Nations Conference on Trade and Development (UNCTAD) World Investment Forum, held in October 2014, from the heated public debate taking place in many countries, and from various parliamentary hearing processes, including at the regional level, a shared view is emerging on the need for reform of the international investment regime to ensure that it works for all stakeholders. The question is not about whether to reform or not, but about the "what," "how" and "extent" of such reform.[65]

The present report, the fourth by the Independent Expert to the General Assembly, should be read in conjunction with his report submitted to the upcoming thirtieth session of the Human Rights Council (A/HRC/30/44), in which he analyses the operation of international investment agreements. The present report focuses on the investor-State dispute settlements that accompanies many international investment agreements and their adverse impacts on a democratic and equitable international order. The Independent Expert integrates analyses of the UNCTAD *Trade and Development Report, 2014*[66] and the *World Investment Report 2015* as well as reports of the Working Group on the issue of human rights and transnational

---

[i] https://corporateeurope.org/en
https://corporateeurope.org/en/who-we-are
https://www.tni.org/en

corporations and other business enterprises of the Human Rights Council[67] and the special rapporteurs dealing with matters of foreign debt, food, water, health, the environment, extreme poverty, indigenous peoples, the independence of judges and lawyers and international solidarity. He acknowledges academic works in the field of the human rights obligations of non-state actors.[68]

The added value of the report lies in the identification of threats to the democratic and equitable international order posed by international investment agreements that are not anchored in human rights and by investor-State dispute settlement arbitration regimes because they reduce the State's regulatory space and do not oblige the arbitrators to give priority to human rights treaty norms. It underlines the urgency of crafting future agreements in a way that prevents the abuses of the past and calls for a revamping of the existing 3,200 international investment agreements, more than 1,500 of which are due to expire.[69] The Independent Expert provides a fresh look from an independent perspective that places human rights at its centre and highlights pertinent provisions of the Vienna Convention on the Law of Treaties with a view to the revision or termination of some of these agreements and to the abolishment of investor-State dispute settlement as *contra bonos mores* and incompatible with provisions of the International Covenant on Civil and Political Rights and the International Covenant on Economic, Social and Cultural Rights.

Pursuant to paragraph 6 of General Assembly Resolution 69/178, the Independent Expert acknowledges that a democratic and equitable international order requires, inter alia, the realization of the right of peoples and nations to permanent sovereignty over their natural wealth and resources; the right of every human person and all peoples to development; international solidarity; the promotion of equitable access to benefits from the international distribution of wealth through enhanced international cooperation, in particular in international economic, commercial and financial relations; and the shared responsibility of the nations of the world for managing worldwide economic and social development, as well as threats to international peace and security, which should be exercised multilaterally.

Pursuant to paragraph 11 of the resolution, he has endeavoured to identify obstacles and undertaken to continue working urgently for the establishment of a new international economic order based on equity, sovereign equality, interdependence, common interest and cooperation among all States. He is also conscious of the preventive aspect of the mandate and recalls the reaffirmation in paragraph 12 that the international community should devise ways and means to remove the current obstacles and meet the challenges to the full realization of all human rights and to prevent the continuation of human rights violations resulting therefrom.

In recent years there has been a growing awareness by States, intergovernmental organizations, non-governmental organizations and religious institutions,[70] that the international investment agreement regime poses grave dangers to the enjoyment of human rights, but no global solution has been devised, possibly because of the complexity of the issues and the power of transnational enterprises and investors, who consistently oppose reform. The unbiased observer will have no problem understanding the two basic ontologies at stake. First is the ontology of the State, which is to legislate in the public interest, adopting laws, regulations and practices for the welfare of the persons living under its jurisdiction, including improvement of labour standards, food security, clean water, medical care, a healthy environment, adequate shelter and the administration of justice by a transparent and accountable system of courts. This ontology is seen by some as a social contract.

The second ontology is that of investment, business, enterprise, banking and other free economic activity. By their very nature these activities entail risk-taking, which justifies an expectation of profit. But can there be a guarantee that an investor who speculates or a bank that gives loans without adequate equity will always draw a profit? No, because sometimes investors win, sometimes they lose. What is abnormal is for an investor to demand a guarantee of profit, to create a parallel system of extrajudicial dispute resolution, which often is not independent, transparent, accountable, or even appealable, and to seek to usurp the function of the State and encroach on government regulation of fiscal and budgetary matters in the public interest. The last 25 years have delivered numerous examples of abuse of rights by investors and unconscionable arbitral awards that have not only led to violations of human rights, but have engendered a "regulatory chill" or even a "regulatory freeze," stopping States from adopting regulations on waste disposal or tobacco control for fear of being sued before investor-State dispute settlement tribunals that protect speculators making risky investments and deny States their regulatory space, imposing instead "austerity measures" on social services. A parallel may be drawn between the bailout of delinquent banks during the financial crisis of 2007–2008, when billions of dollars were paid from the public treasury, and the current practice of rescuing speculative investors when they take risks without insurance. This is tantamount to the privatization of profits and the socialization of losses. The mandate-related question concerning obstacles to the realization of a democratic and equitable international order requires acknowledgement of the adverse impacts of international investor agreements and investor-State dispute settlement on human rights.

Paradoxes

Over the past 70 years, the United Nations has conducted a magnificent normative orchestra which has put on the world stage not only the Universal Declaration of Human Rights, but legally binding instruments including 10 core human rights treaties and countless declarations and resolutions such as the Declaration on the Establishment of a New International Economic Order, the Declaration on the Right to Development and the United Nations Declaration on the Rights of Indigenous Peoples. The noble task of codification and refining human rights norms continues. Moreover, the United Nations has established implementation mechanisms, including treaty-based bodies like the Human Rights Committee and the Committee on Economic, Social and Cultural Rights, which have advanced the work of standard-setting through the adoption of general comments on the provisions of the International Covenants and have engaged in monitoring activities, the examination of periodic State party reports and *in situ* visits. The Commission on Human Rights created the special procedures mechanism comprising working groups, special rapporteurs and independent experts, each of which is entrusted with a specific thematic or country mandate. Its successor, the Human Rights Council, has expanded on the issues covered by the special procedures and developed the universal periodic review. States have made pledges, for example, in connection with the Millennium Development Goals and the post-2015 development agenda. The Third International Conference on Financing for Development, held in Addis Ababa in July 2015, resulted in the Addis Ababa Action Agenda and agreement on a draft outcome document[71] for the United Nations summit to adopt the post-2015 development agenda to be held in New York in September 2015, which merits significant strengthening. While the Independent Expert welcomes greater attention to financing for development, he is concerned that the existence of 3,200 international investment agreements and, in particular, of investor-State dispute settlements may render the implementation of the Action Agenda illusory.

Regionally, we have seen the adoption of the Convention for the Protection of Human Rights and Fundamental Freedoms (European Convention on Human Rights) and its Protocols, the American Convention on Human Rights and the African Convention on Human and Peoples' Rights, all of them providing for human rights courts competent to adopt binding judgements. This enormous normative, monitoring and implementing activity manifests *opinio juris*, generating an international customary international law of human rights that no State or non-State actor can ignore. Much has been written about the *erga omnes* character of the international human rights regime. What is needed is an explanation of how best to implement it and a clear statement from the

International Court of Justice on the priority of human rights treaty obligations over other treaties.

Paradoxically, States enter into bilateral and multilateral free trade and investment treaties that hinder their compliance with human rights treaty obligations and result in the violation of civil, cultural, economic, political and social rights. Perhaps they follow the siren call of promised growth and employment, but seldom do they realize that investors are there for profit, will resist scrutiny by human rights bodies and reject legally binding obligations. Notwithstanding the foregoing, States are still bound by the International Covenants and must ensure that non-state actors operating in their territories do not violate human rights. States have a responsibility to protect, particularly with respect to the administration of justice. Article 14 of the International Covenant on Civil and Political Rights requires States to ensure that suits at law are examined by competent and independent tribunals in a regime of transparency and accountability.[72] Paradoxically, States have agreed to the creation of ad hoc investor-State dispute settlement tribunals that are frequently not independent, transparent or accountable. Studies have been published that manifest egregious abuses by specialized law firms in collusion with arbitrators and corporations using this system of "privatized justice" to escape adjudication before public courts under article 14. In the light of well-established and well-functioning domestic legal systems, investor-State dispute settlement offers no added value and yet, vested interests of powerful investors and transnational corporations have rendered it difficult to abolish it.[73]

Paradoxically, although States are bound to observe the public participation clause of article 25 of the International Covenant, they negotiate treaties in secret and exclude key stakeholders, including labour unions, consumer unions, health professionals and environmental protection groups. Sometimes, secret treaties are fast-tracked through parliaments so as to avoid public participation. This renders the agreements democratically illegitimate.

Are the legally binding obligations of States under human rights treaties then meaningless, just because there is no tribunal competent to impose sanctions on States that violate their responsibility to protect and no enforcement mechanism against investors? Are the legal obligations under human rights treaties inferior to treaty obligations under free trade and investment agreements? Are human rights treaties only a moral fig leaf for globalization?

Notwithstanding good diagnoses formulated, inter alia, by UNCTAD and the perceptive analysis of experts including Joseph Stiglitz, Paul Krugman and Jeronim Capaldo, pressures by transnational corporations continue to drive Governments to new international investment agreements with investor-State dispute settlement provisions that will aggravate matters and ultimately result in a breakdown of the system or even a crisis situation in which local, regional or international peace and security will be endangered.

A reason given for the establishment of investor-State dispute settlement tribunals is that investors did not trust national justice systems and preferred to create a separate jurisdiction for commercial disputes. It is difficult to understand why any State would accept the implicit disqualification of its national courts and consent to the creation of a privatized system of dispute settlement that has been widely recognized as lacking independence, transparency and accountability.

Core norms and principles

All States Members of the United Nations are bound by the Charter, which is akin to a world constitution. Article 103 of the Charter states: "In the event of a conflict between the obligations of the Members of the United Nations under the present Charter and their obligations under any other international agreement, their obligations under the present Charter shall prevail." This means that bilateral and multilateral free trade and investment agreements that contain provisions that conflict with the Charter must be revised or terminated, and incompatible provisions must be severed according to the doctrine of severability.[74]

Pursuant to the cardinal norm of international law *pacta sunt servanda*, enshrined in article 26 of the Vienna Convention on the Law of Treaties, existing treaties must be implemented "in good faith," and no subsequent treaty can be considered legitimate if it hinders the performance of commitments under existing treaties unless the parties explicitly agree to modify the previous treaties. Inadvertent incompatibilities can be resolved in good faith by interpreting the subsequent treaty in a manner consistent with the prior treaty, applying articles 31 and 32 of the Convention. Pursuant to Article 103 of the Charter, subsequent treaties must in any case conform to the Charter and are invalid if they impede the fulfilment of its purposes and principles, including its human rights provisions. The argument has merit that since most States parties to international investment agreements were already parties to United Nations human rights treaties, including the International Covenants, the principle of *pacta sunt servanda* requires the implementation of these United Nations treaties and the international investment agreements must be interpreted and applied in a manner that does not contravene the Charter or United Nations treaties, including the Indigenous and Tribal Peoples Convention, 1989 (No. 169) of the International Labour Organization (ILO), the Framework Convention on Tobacco Control of the World Health Organization (WHO), conventions of the Food and Agriculture Organization of the United Nations (FAO) and the United Nations Children's Fund (UNICEF) and the Convention on Access to Information, Public Participation in Decision-making and Access to Justice in Environmental Matters (Aarhus Convention) of the Economic Commission for Europe.

According to customary international law and article 53 of the Vienna Convention, treaties or treaty provisions that violate peremptory norms of international law (*jus cogens*) are *contra bonos mores* and therefore null and void.[75] This encompasses a category of contracts and treaties entailing unethical activities, or whose foreseeable consequences are contrary to the protective functions of the State. Thus, any treaty that hinders the ability of a State to fulfil its obligations under United Nations human rights treaties is incompatible with international *ordre public* and with the commitments undertaken by all States pursuant to the Charter. Similarly, so-called "leonine," or unequal, treaties, such as existed between some new States and former colonial Powers must be considered contrary to the Charter and incompatible with the principle of equality of States. The notion of *jus cogens* was further elucidated in the process of codification of article 41 of the draft articles on Responsibility of States for internationally wrongful acts (see A/56/10 and Corr.1), adopted by the International Law Commission in 2001.[76]

When addressing macroeconomic problems and human rights violations ensuing from the usurpation of State functions by transnational enterprises, the "general principles of law" referred to in article 38 (1) of the Statute of the International Court of Justice come into play, including estoppel, *ex injuria non oritur jus*, the prohibition of abuse of rights,[77] *ultra vires* conduct and the invalidity of *contra bonos mores* agreements. Indeed, all systems of justice recognize that there are certain unwritten laws of humanity, as in Sophocles' *Antigone*, the very spirit of the law (Montesquieu), which are immanent values that precede codification of norms. Experience with existing international investment agreements, in particular investor-State dispute settlement tribunals, raises multiple issues of abuse of rights. The essence of the doctrine of abuse of rights is found in the principle of Roman law, *sic utere jure tuo ut alienum non laedas*, which stipulates the exercise of individual rights in such a manner that does not harm others. Inherent to legal thinking is the notion that because all subjects of international law can abuse rights, controls on the exercise of such rights must be established as a matter of *ordre public*. Courts and arbitral tribunals must respect these general principles of law and the principle of equity recognized in the Statute of the International Court of Justice (art. 38 (2)).

Domestic and international criminal law as well as the Rome Statute of the International Criminal Court may be of relevance in the context of economic crimes, especially when economic and financial activities result in grave violations of human rights, including mass unemployment, dislocation of the agricultural sector, destruction of food security or even famine, food fraud, devastation of the environment, water pollution, radioactive contamination resulting in death from cancers and other health complications, genetic deformations and destruction of ecosystems (ecocide). Such activities are assaults on human dignity and crimes against humanity justiciable under article 7 (1) (k) of the Statute *juncto* the criminal law principle of reckless endangerment. Perpetrators can be the pharmaceutical industry; mining enterprises, in particular gold and uranium mining; and gas and petroleum extraction, fracking and ozone-destroying enterprises. Such crimes should be susceptible to universal jurisdiction.[78] The United Nations Convention against Corruption of 2003 may have relevance with regard to corporate activities, including bribing public officials. Hitherto, investor-State dispute settlement tribunals have not been required to take these treaties into account and have tended to privilege the economic interests of investors over the imperatives of protecting human rights and the environment.

Human rights treaties, general principles of law, customary international law, declarations and resolutions constitute a symbiosis of norms of hard law and soft law, an international *ordre public* essential to achieving a democratic and equitable international order. Together with domestic *ordre public* this legal regime overrides any attempt by investors to subvert the rule of law through international investment agreements that challenge the democratic safeguards of national legislative and judicial bodies.

It is consistent with the United Nations mandate to promote stability and cooperation by calling upon States to regulate the activities of investors and transnational enterprises registered or operating within their jurisdiction and to foreclose the threat or use of economic force in any manner inconsistent with the Charter.

Investor-State dispute settlement

Investor-State dispute settlement is a rather recent and arbitrary construction, a privatized form of dispute settlement that accompanies many international investment agreements. Rather than litigating before local courts or invoking diplomatic protection, investors rely on three arbitrators who in confidential proceedings decide whether their rights and investment have been violated by a State. Whereas investor-State dispute settlement tribunals can entertain suits by investors against States, they do not entertain suits by States against investors, for example, when investors violate national laws and regulations, pollute the environment and the water supplies, introduce potentially dangerous genetically modified organisms, etc. A birth defect of investor-State dispute settlement is its "Trojan horse" quality: it was introduced into international investment agreements without full disclosure as to its potentially intrusive application, without the participation of key stakeholders at the time of elaboration and without public referendum, hence lacking democratic legitimacy. Bearing in mind their impacts, Governments have a duty to proactively inform constituents. Not doing so amounts to violating articles 19 and 25 of the International Covenant on Civil and Political Rights. The texts of many international investment agreements have only been obtained through freedom of information suits and Wikileaks revelations.

The *World Investment Report 2015* surveys the situation and presents a menu of options. Among the reasons given for the establishment and maintenance of investor-State dispute settlement tribunals is that they provide an additional avenue of legal redress and a more effective system of enforcement. This argument does not address the question whether such an avenue is really necessary, and whether it contributes to a fragmentation of international law, inconsistency in *arbitral* jurisprudence and a general lack of predictability, introducing a "chilling effect" on legitimate State regulation in the public interest. Another argument sometimes made in favour of investor-State dispute settlement is avoidance of cumbersome diplomatic protection. But is this a valid argument in the light of the Charter and customary international law? Diplomatic protection does have a long history in international relations and has proven to be a useful and frequently effective way of settling disputes, wholly in the spirit of Articles 1 and 2 of the Charter.

There are multiple reasons to oppose investor-State dispute settlement, based on the necessities of democratic governance, the administration of justice through transparent and accountable courts, the doctrine of State sovereignty and human rights law. It is difficult to justify that investor-State dispute settlement grants foreign investors greater rights than domestic investors, thereby creating unequal competitive conditions. The lack of transparency of investor-State dispute settlement tribunals and concerns about the independence and impartiality of the arbitrators are fundamental problems that cannot be solved by "fixing" existing investor-State dispute settlement mechanisms, by using filters or limiting investors' access, for example by reducing the scope of the subject-matter. Investor-State dispute settlement creates artificial incentives to gain access to privatized arbitration, exposing host States to considerable legal and financial risks. Indeed, both the remuneration of arbitrators and lawyers' fees are unconscionably high. Investor-State dispute settlement awards have led States to abandon measures to protect public health and to lower environmental standards. The regulatory chill resulting from the mere existence of the investor-State dispute settlement system has dissuaded, and may in the future dissuade, States from taking measures to respect, protect and fulfil their human rights obligations and thus have a negative impact on the democratic and equitable international order.

Lori Wallach of the organization Public Citizen has shown how investment treaties "allow companies to challenge public interest regulations outside of domestic court systems before tribunals of three private-sector trade attorneys operating under minimal to no conflict of interest rules." Ska Keller, member of the European Parliament representing the European Greens, wrote that "[d]emocratic decision-making is forcefully going under the knife through international arbitration. The accused states have only two options: either they can be like others and take back the decisions they have made, or they can pay huge sums in compensation to the investor." Daniel J. Ikenson of the Cato Institute concludes that "investor-State dispute settlement turns national treatment on its head, giving privileges to foreign companies that are not available to domestic companies."[79] Indeed, investor-State dispute settlement poses a particular challenge to the democratic order, particularly when Governments that have been democratically elected to carry out specific social policies have been sued by investors precisely because of those democratically mandated policies.

Although international tribunals can and should declare frivolous cases inadmissible for abuse of the right of submission (see article 3 of the Optional Protocol to the International Covenant on Civil and Political Rights) or abuse of procedure, investor-State dispute settlement tribunals seldom do so and entertain frivolous and vexatious litigation at huge expense to the parties, which is particularly harmful to developing countries.

According to the *World Investment Report 2015* there are 608 known investor-State dispute settlement cases in which 99 Governments have been respondents to one or more known claims. In 2014 investors initiated 42 known cases, 35 of which were brought by investors from developed countries and 5 by investors from developing countries; in 2 cases the nationality of the claimants is unknown. Counting from the start, the most frequently cited home States were the United States of America (129), the Netherlands (67), the United Kingdom of Great Britain and Northern Ireland (51), Germany (42) and France (36). The respondent States most frequently concerned were Argentina (56), Venezuela (36), the Czech Republic (29) and Egypt (24). UNCTAD publishes a revealing chart showing the results of decisions on the merits indicating that 60 per cent were in favour of the investor and 40 per cent in favour of the State. It should be recalled that investor-State dispute settlement only takes cases of investors against States and does not accept suits by States against investors. Thus, the 60 per cent of cases lost by States do hurt and the billions of dollars awarded to investors are ultimately paid by the public, meaning that there is that much less money available for education, health care or infrastructure. Statistics show that about 64 per cent of the awards went to companies with over $10 billion in annual revenue and 29 per cent to companies with between $1 billion and $10 billion in annual revenue, or to individuals with a net wealth of over $100 million, indicating that the primary beneficiaries of financial transfers in investor-State dispute settlement awards have been ultra-large companies and super-wealthy tycoons. The largest award, in the *Yukos Universal Ltd. (Isle of Man) v. The Russian Federation* cases, amounted to over $50 billion and the legal fees exceeded $60 million. Other awards have affected countries like Ecuador which in 2012 was ordered to pay $2.3 billion to Occidental Petroleum (see para. 30 below).

A report to the General Assembly is too short to lay out the human rights incompatibilities of investor-State dispute settlement, but one may address a few symptomatic problems for which there is no "quick fix." The list of *contra bonos mores* investor-State dispute settlement awards is long. The present report cannot summarize them, not only because of space limitations, but out of moral vertigo.

Metalclad v. Mexico. A case under the North American Free Trade Agreement (NAFTA) concerned a waste management business, Metalclad, which sued Mexico, claiming indirect expropriation (E/CN.4/Sub.2/2003/9, paras. 33 ff). In 1993, Metalclad had purchased a local waste management company with a view to building and operating a waste landfill facility. The project was subject to permits from the municipal, state and federal levels of government. Although the municipality had previously denied the permit, Metalclad went ahead. Because of environmental concerns and the opposition of local inhabitants, municipal authorities never issued the permits. Finally, state authorities issued an ecological decree declaring the area a natural reserve, forcing the waste management project to close. The investor-State dispute settlement tribunal found that the Government had taken a measure tantamount to expropriation and ordered Mexico to pay $16.7 million in compensation. Mexico sought statutory review of the decision and the Government of Canada intervened in the proceedings. A justice of the Supreme Court of British Columbia found that:

> The Tribunal gave an extremely broad definition of expropriation for the purposes of Article 1110 [of the Agreement]. In addition to the more conventional notion of expropriation involving a taking of property, the Tribunal held that expropriation under the NAFTA includes covert or incidental interference with the use of property which has the effect of depriving the owner, in whole or in significant part, of the use or reasonably-to-be expected economic benefit of property. This definition is sufficiently broad to include a legitimate zoning of property by a municipality or other zoning authority.[80]

A study of the Subcommission on Promotion and Protection of Human Rights in 2003 noted:

> Such broad interpretations of expropriation provisions could have direct consequences for regulations intended to promote and protect human rights ... government action in relation to chemicals and toxic wastes has flow-on effects in relation to the enjoyment of human rights such as the right to health or the right to water. ... One commentator has suggested that broad interpretations of expropriation provisions could reverse the established tenet of environmental policy that the polluters should bear the cost of their pollution rather than be paid not to pollute (E/CN.4/Sub.2/2003/9, para. 35).[81]

Occidental Petroleum v. Ecuador. On 5 October 2012, a split tribunal of the International Centre for Settlement of Investment Disputes determined that Ecuador had breached a bilateral investment treaty between the United States and Ecuador and awarded damages of $2.3 billion, then the largest award ever issued by such a tribunal. The award demonstrates the vast power that tribunals wield and raises important normative questions about the International Centre.[82] Although the tribunal found that Occidental had illegally sold 40 per cent of its production rights to another firm without government approval, despite a specific provision in the concession contract stating that the sale of production rights without government pre-approval would constitute a material breach of the contract, and notwithstanding the fact that the contract explicitly enforced Ecuador's hydrocarbons law, which protects the Government's prerogative to vet companies seeking to produce oil in the environmentally sensitive Amazon region, two out of the three arbitrators decided to put aside Ecuador's concerns about the breach of contract by Occidental and found in favour of the transnational, applying an abstruse proportionality argument. The dissenting arbitrator expressed complete disagreement with the award.[83] Ecuador subsequently filed a request for annulment of the award; decision is pending.

Renco v. Peru. The Renco Group is currently using the investor-State dispute settlement mechanism to evade justice for causing massive pollution in La Oroya, Peru, where its subsidiary, Doe Run, has failed to fulfil its commitments to limit emissions and clean up grievous pollution. Peru gave Doe Run two extensions to halt the pollution. When the Government refused to grant a third extension on the company's unfulfilled 1997 commitment to install pollution mitigation devices and assume its liability for the health damage already caused, Renco used the investor-State dispute settlement tactic to pressure the Government to allow it to reopen its smelter without installing pollution-capturing devices. Investor-State dispute settlement has thus been used to evade justice in Peru. Meanwhile, in the United States, beginning in October 1997, 11 personal injury lawsuits against Renco and Doe Run were filed in Missouri state courts on behalf of 162 sick Oroyan children. Proceedings in the cases have stopped pending the outcome of the investor-State dispute settlement arbitration.[84]

Chevron v. Ecuador. This is one of the most problematic cases from the aspect of conduct *contra bonos mores* and abuse of rights on the part of the investor-State dispute settlement claimants. The case started with a series of judicial proceedings under Ecuadorian law against Texaco (previous corporate name) because of environmental damage caused by Texaco's operations in the Amazon. In a pristine rainforest environment, Texaco dug 350 oil wells and, upon leaving Ecuador, left behind some one thousand open-air, unlined waste pits filled with crude and toxic sludge. The pits subsequently leaked into the water table, polluting rivers and streams that tens of thousands of people depend on for drinking, cooking, bathing and fishing. Chevron is also accused of responsibility for dumping more than 18 billion gallons of toxic wastewater—a by-product of the drilling process—into the rivers. At the height of its operations, the company was dumping 4 million gallons per day, a practice outlawed in major United States oil-producing states decades before the company began operations in Ecuador in 1967. By handling its toxic waste in Ecuador in ways that were illegal in its home country, Texaco saved an estimated $3 per barrel of oil produced. A public health crisis of immense proportions occurred in the Ecuadorian Amazon, the root cause of which was massive contamination from 40 years of oil-drilling operations. The contamination contributed to cancers, miscarriages, birth defects and other ailments. In 2011 the Supreme Court of Ecuador sentenced Chevron to pay $ 9.5 billion in damages. Chevron refused to pay and instead sued Ecuador under the United States-Ecuador bilateral investment treaty for loss of profits (see A/HRC/21/47 and A/HRC/24/41). The case has been going on for several years and attorneys' fees are already in the millions of dollars.

Meanwhile, the Permanent Court of Arbitration at The Hague found in favour of Ecuador, which sought to pursue its claims for environmental damage against Chevron despite settlement of the case;[85] however, no one knows how the case will eventually play out.

Vattenfall v. Germany. The Swedish energy provider Vattenfall filed an investor-State dispute settlement suit against Germany in May 2012, pursuant to the Energy Charter Treaty, demanding a reported $5 billion for Germany's decision to phase out nuclear power, a decision adopted in response to widespread German public opposition to nuclear power generation in the wake of the 2011 Fukushima nuclear power disaster in Japan. The German Parliament amended the Atomic Energy Act to roll back a 2010 extension of the lifespan of nuclear plants and to abandon the use of nuclear energy by 2022. Vattenfall argues that Germany's policy change violates its obligations to foreign investors under the Energy Charter Treaty.

Whereas Germany objected to Vattenfall's claim as "manifestly without merit," the investor-State dispute settlement decided in 2013 to allow the claim to proceed.[86]

Philip Morris v. Uruguay. WHO has repeatedly warned about the global health dangers posed by tobacco and 180 States have adhered to the Framework Convention on Tobacco Control. It is estimated that 70 per cent of the 8.4 million deaths attributable to tobacco in 2020 will occur in developing countries. One country that has taken the Framework Convention seriously is Uruguay. In a "David v. Goliath" confrontation, tobacco giant Philip Morris is suing Uruguay for its anti-tobacco regulations. Uruguay's gross domestic product in 2013 was about $55.7 billion, while Philip Morris's revenues the same year reached $80.2 billion. Philip Morris wants $25 million in compensation from Uruguay. If Philip Morris wins, it is likely to seriously compromise the WHO anti-tobacco campaign.[87] A decision from the International Centre for Settlement of Investment Disputes is expected later in 2015.

Philip Morris v. Australia.[88] This case is similar on the merits, but procedurally it demonstrates the abuse of rights prevalent in the investor-State dispute settlement system. In order to sue Australia, Philip Morris established a "shell" or "mailbox" company in Hong Kong, to take advantage of the Hong Kong-Australia bilateral investment treaty.[89]

Vodaphone v. India.[90] Using its Dutch subsidiary, Vodafone is suing India for $2.2 billion in connection with India's taxation of Vodafone activities deriving from a transaction conducted in a tax haven (Cayman Islands), although all the assets are in India. At issue is whether a State can adopt legislation to end tax avoidance, for example, through the General Anti-Avoidance Rule of the Finance Act 2012.

Conflict with regional legislation, decisions of human rights tribunals and the constitutional separation of powers

Conflict between investor-State dispute settlement rulings and European Union law has led to legal uncertainty and conflicting obligations for member States. The *Micula v. Romania* case concerned a Swedish company which had invested in Romania before the country's accession to the European Union. The company had taken up business incentives offered by the Government of Romania.

However, when it acceded to the European Union, in order to comply with rules on State aid Romania discontinued its incentives programme. Micula sued Romania pursuant to the Romania-Sweden bilateral investment treaty. Investor-State dispute settlement awarded $250 million to Micula for violation of the investment agreement. In 2014, the European Union served an injunction on Romania provisionally ordering it not to pay the compensation because doing so would be contrary to European legislation. This situation illustrates the risk incurred by member States when bringing legislation into line with European Union standards.[91]

In the case involving the Marlin mine run by the Goldcorp company in Guatemala, the Inter-American Commission on Human Rights had found that the mine should be closed because of the dangers to health posed by its operation. Under considerable pressure, however, the recommendation of the Inter-American Court of Human Rights was withdrawn, although the case continues before the Court on the basis of failure to secure lack of free, prior and informed consent.[92] In the case of the Mayoc mine in Peru, the Court declared the case admissible but did not order the suspension of operations, notwithstanding the dangers to the health of the indigenous communities in the region.[93] In other mining cases, military forces have been used to suppress public protest, mostly against local indigenous populations.

In the ongoing *Chevron v. Ecuador* litigation, investor-State dispute settlement arbitrators have repeatedly ordered the executive branch in Ecuador to prohibit the enforcement of the highest judicial instances of the country. This is tantamount to dismantlement of checks and balances and a violation of article 14 of the International Covenant on Civil and Political Rights. If anything is *contra bonos mores* it is this attack on the rule of law and on the constitutional separation of powers.

Chilling effect of possible adverse judgments

In his 2014 report to the General Assembly (A/69/299), the Special Rapporteur on the right of everyone to the enjoyment of the highest attainable standard of physical and mental health noted that States are vulnerable to dispute settlement procedures when they give priority to their obligations under human rights treaties and thereby breach an obligation under an international investment agreement. This was the case when Ethyl Corporation submitted a claim against a public health decision by the Government of Canada to impose a trade ban on a gasoline additive produced by the corporation.[94] Canada chose to bend because of the high cost of arbitration and the danger of an adverse judgement. This illustrates how the mere existence of investor-State dispute settlement can create a chilling effect on States, dissuading them from fulfilling their right to health obligations.[95] Such disputes may also deplete the States' resources and affect their ability to progressively realize the resource-dependent aspects of the right to health. The fact that international investment agreements are treated as a "stand-alone legal code" and often do not contain references to the right to health contravenes *ordre public*. Hence, international investment agreements must be interpreted in a manner that does not conflict with human rights law because "the purpose of both development-stimulating investment treaties and human rights laws is to benefit individuals" (A/69/299, paras. 45 and 55).

The 2003 study of the Subcommission on Promotion and Protection of Human Rights referred to above had flagged the abuse of rights being perpetrated by investor-State dispute settlement tribunals (E/CN.4/Sub.2/2003/9, para. 32). That report gives many examples of the chilling effect, including the unconscionable suit brought by the Ethyl Corporation against Canada,[96] illustrating how government resources are wasted in litigation and how legitimate measures by States have been frustrated by investor-State dispute settlement.

The *Philip Morris v. Uruguay* case would probably have ended in surrender by Uruguay. Daunted by the prospect of paying contract lawyers $1,500 an hour for several years, President José Mujica almost settled the claim and only decided to defend Uruguay's laws after former President Vázquez voiced a protest and Michael Bloomberg, the former Mayor of New York City, decided to help finance Uruguay's defence team.[97] This justifies the establishment of an international fund for the defence of investor-State dispute settlement cases, modelled on the World Trade Organization (WTO) Technical Expertise Trust Fund for dispute settlement.[98] It is reported that the mere threat of an investor-State dispute settlement case stopped Canada from banning the words "light" and "mild" in its tobacco control laws.[99]

Environmental regulation has also been under attack in Canada, as a former government official reported: "I've seen the letters from the New York and [Washington] DC law firms coming up to the Canadian government on virtually every new environmental regulation [...]. Virtually all of the new initiatives were targeted and most of them never saw the light of day."[100]

Threats of expensive lawsuits against Governments are becoming more frequent than actual claims. Thus, investor-State dispute settlement has mutated from a corporate shield against allegedly unfair behaviour by States into a tactical weapon to delay, weaken and kill regulation. Specialized law firms actually encourage their multinational clients to scare Governments into submission: "It's a lobbying tool in the sense that you can go in and say, 'Ok, if you do this, we will be suing you for compensation.' It does change behaviour in certain cases."[101]

Dubious impartiality of investor-State dispute settlement tribunals

Critics of investor-State dispute settlement have pointed out that many arbitrators and corporations are "too close for comfort." A glaring example of the dysfunction of the annulment procedure for conflict of interests is provided by *Vivendi v. Argentina*.[102]

Argentina stated that one of the arbitrators, Gabrielle Kaufmann-Kohler, was acting as a member of the Board of Directors and a member of the Corporate Responsibility Committee of the Swiss bank UBS, which was the single largest shareholder in Vivendi. Argentina further argued that Ms. Kaufmann-Kohler was partially remunerated with UBS shares. While Argentina acknowledged that any issues regarding the ability of an arbitrator should be raised without delay during the arbitration proceeding, in this case it was not possible to do so because Argentina only learned about the facts and circumstances affecting her ability to serve as arbitrator in November 2007, after the award judgement of 20 August 2007 had been rendered. While the review committee was critical of the arbitrator's judgement and agreed with Argentina that the tribunal was not properly constituted and that annulment under article 52 (1) (a) of the Convention on the Settlement of Investment Disputes Between States and Nations of Other States could be supported, it declined to annul the award, holding that (a) the arbitrator's exercise of independent judgement was not actually impaired; (b) it would be unjust to deny the claimants the benefit of the award owing to the arbitrator's failures; and (c) the lengthy proceedings should "come to an end." This case, adjudicated by the International Centre for Settlement of Investment Disputes, illustrates that the International Centre's rules are insufficient to deal with conflicts of interest.

Under the current annulment procedure of the International Centre for Settlement of Investment Disputes, even ill-founded arbitral awards cannot be reversed. A review of the merits is not allowed; review is limited to grounds, such as irregular constitution or corruption of the arbitral tribunal, serious departure from a fundamental rule of procedure, failure to state reasons for the award or a manifest abuse of power. Hence, the International Centre annulment committee may find itself unable to annul or correct an award even after having identified "manifest errors of law."[103]

To counter investor-State dispute settlement abuse, domestic courts should deny enforcement of awards when such enforcement would be contrary to the public policy of their countries. This "public policy exception" to the enforcement of arbitral awards is found in article V (2) of the Convention on the Recognition and Enforcement of Foreign Arbitral Awards, 1958 (New York Convention) and the Model Law on International Commercial Arbitration, 1985 of the United

Nations Commission on International Trade Law (UNCITRAL).[104] Regulations and ethical codes of conduct should be activated against investor-State dispute settlement abuses[105] to remove the impunity hitherto enjoyed by investor-State dispute settlement. Lawyers who are found to have benefited directly or indirectly from the awards rendered, for example, when they are subsequently hired by the very investors they represented, should be investigated and, if necessary, disbarred. Investigations for breaches of ethical conduct should be systematically conducted into the activities of law firms and arbitrators under established rules on conflict of interest and conspiracy.

International investment agreements must undoubtedly be revisited to ensure that they are compatible with modern international law, in particular that they acknowledge the pre-eminence of the Charter of the United Nations pursuant to Article 103. The conclusion is inescapable that while international investment agreements can be reformed in a way that will further human rights and sustainable development, investor-State dispute settlement arbitral tribunals are ontologically and conceptually flawed and fail the test of compatibility with the Charter and human rights norms. Lessons learned over the past decades indicate that "good practices" in investor-State dispute settlement experience are few and far between and that the harm caused by the investor-State dispute settlement system justifies its abolition. A further question arises concerning the criminal responsibility of investors and transnational corporations when their activities cause serious harm to the environment, pollute water supplies, endanger public health, destroy food security or result in mass transfer of populations, for example, in connection with "mega-development" projects, sometimes accompanied by violence and death. International criminal law in this field is gradually emerging.[106] Until now, investor-State dispute settlement has seemed blithely immune to such considerations.

The most fundamental argument against investor-State dispute settlement is that it subverts the rule of law so laboriously constructed over the past two hundred years by attempting to privatize justice. The establishment of a parallel system of dispute settlement, which is not transparent, accountable or even independent, cannot be tolerated. Moreover, no injustice is done to investors, because they have valid recourse options and can always rely on a functioning domestic administration of justice and/or on diplomatic protection.

Outlook

"Investment arbitration as currently constituted is not a fair, independent, and balanced method for the resolution of disputes between sovereign nations and private investors."[107]

The UNCTAD "action menu" laid out in the *World Investment Report 2015* presents several reform options, but stops short of recommending abolition of investor-State dispute settlement. The Independent Expert strongly believes that maintaining investor-State dispute settlement is not an option and concludes that it should be abolished as a fundamentally flawed system having adverse human rights impacts and because its operation has upset the international order by debilitating States, encroaching on their regulatory space and aggravating inequality and inequity in the world. A history of abuse by arbitrators and interpretative practices well beyond articles 31 and 32 of the Vienna Convention on the Law of Treaties vitiates the system. Repeated findings by United Nations bodies notwithstanding, including the 2003 report of the Subcommission and the reports of several special procedures mandate holders,[108] have remained without effect, since the arbitrators have continued their practice of extensive interpretations and disregard of the human rights impacts. On the basis of the doctrine of abuse of rights and the prohibition of *contra bonos mores* agreements, investor-State dispute settlement should be abolished together with the "survival clauses," which provide for the continued application of treaties after their termination. This can be done pursuant to the doctrine of severability without abandoning the entire international investment agreements.

Investor-State dispute settlement could be replaced by any of the following options, or a combination thereof:

(a) A State-State dispute settlement mechanism similar to that of WTO. Under this procedure the home State would have discretion over whether to bring a claim and States would decide on the court that should hear the case, for example, the International Court of Justice or ad hoc tribunals with appeal chambers.

(b) Exclusive reliance on domestic dispute resolution. This option would abolish the right of investors to bring claims against host States in international tribunals and direct them to the jurisdiction of the States where they are operating and making a profit. This is the essence of the Calvo doctrine.[109]

The Independent Expert endorses the conclusions of the Special Rapporteur on the right to health contained in his previous report to the General Assembly, in particular his finding that although international investment agreements may contribute to the economic development of a country, States must ensure that protection of human rights, including the right to health, is incorporated into those agreements:

> Human rights must be respected, protected and fulfilled at all times, and should be the primary concern of all action by States.

International investment agreements should therefore expressly provide for States' human rights obligations, which should be able to override investors' rights in specific cases.

The ability of individuals to enjoy their right to health cannot be subject to contractual rights of investors, given that the right to health is fundamental to the dignity of individuals (A/69/299, paras. 57–58). The Independent Expert endorses the Special Rapporteur's finding that:

> The magnitude of violations by transnational corporations and the ease with which they can evade responsibility for such violations call for an international mechanism to hold them liable for human rights abuses. Such a mechanism should supplement domestic laws rather than diminish the importance of domestic law. The mechanism should therefore enable States and individuals to hold transnational corporations to account for their human rights violation (ibid., para. 38).

The Independent Expert concludes that the abolition of investor-State dispute settlement does no injustice to investors, who can still avail themselves of the domestic courts and/or the well-tried mechanism of diplomatic protection. In addition, the World Bank offers risk insurance, and this should be factored in as a normal cost of doing business. Notwithstanding the imposition of some necessary limits on the hybrid dogmas of market fundamentalism and the doxology of free trade, investors will continue making handsome profits and, precisely by accepting the principles of transparency, accountability and other reasonable public-oriented regulations, they ensure the continuation of a healthy system of free markets accompanied by sustainable development.

Recommendations

In the light of the obstacles to a democratic and equitable international order outlined above, the Independent Expert refers to the Plan of Action he formulated in his report to the Human Rights Council (A/HRC/30/44, sect. VII) and offers further recommendations.

A. To States

(a) States should abolish the investor-State dispute settlement system and replace it with State-to-State settlement before the International Court of Justice or by domestic courts bound by article 14 of the International Covenant on Civil and Political Rights.

(b) States should endeavour to modify or terminate existing international investment agreements and refrain from entering international investment agreements with investor-State dispute settlement provisions. Before entering any new international investment agreements, States should ensure that independent ex ante human rights, health and environmental impact assessments are conducted. Provision for ex post assessments should be made.

(c) States should use domestic and international law, including penal law, to suppress economic crimes and financial and banking speculation, apply and strengthen the precautionary principle in the protection of public health and the environment and rigorously enforce environmental and health standards.

(d) States should impose penal sanctions on white-collar crimes and corruption. They should ratify the United Nations Convention against Corruption.

(e) States should finish the elaboration of and adopt a legally binding convention that covers corporate social responsibilities and strengthens the implementation of the Guiding Principles on Business and Human Rights and the United Nations Declaration on the Rights of Indigenous Peoples.

(f) Until investor-State dispute settlement is abolished, States should establish a fund for the defence of investor-State dispute settlement cases modelled on the WTO Advisory Centre on WTO Law.

B. To the General Assembly

(a) The General Assembly may consider inviting UNCTAD to convene a conference to revise or terminate international investment agreements that have resulted in human rights violations.

(b) The General Assembly may consider tasking the Human Rights Council with a specific mandate on periodic monitoring of the adverse impacts of the international investment regime on the enjoyment of civil, cultural, economic, political and social rights, for example by expanding the scope of examination under the universal periodic review.

(c) The General Assembly may consider ways to put into effect the ILO and World Bank initiative for universal social protection[110] and provide for adequate financing thereof.

(d) The General Assembly may consider establishing a commission to monitor the impact of arbitral awards on the paramount obligation of States to promote and protect human rights.

(e) Bearing in mind that the International Court of Justice, as the highest judicial body of the United Nations can render an authoritative legal statement on international investment agreements, including investor-State dispute settlement, the General Assembly may, pursuant to article 96 of the Charter, request an advisory opinion on:

  i. The legal consequences of the priority of the Charter over all other treaties, pursuant to its Article 103, in particular with regard to international investment agreements and investor-State dispute settlement awards;

  ii. The priority of the international human rights regime, including the International Covenants as well as FAO, ILO, UNICEF and WHO conventions, over conflicting obligations under trade and investment agreements;

  iii. The application of norms of customary international law to non-state actors, in particular the respect for the sovereignty and independence of States and the prohibition of interference in matters that are essentially within the domestic jurisdiction of States;

  iv. The responsibility of a home or host State for the actions of a transnational corporation registered or operating in its territory;

  v. The scope of State sovereignty and the ontological obligation of every State to legislate and regulate for the welfare of the population, in particular the obligation of States pursuant to the international human rights treaties not to regress in human rights protection and not to allow external actors to dictate their fiscal, budgetary, social, labour, health, educational or environmental policies;

  vi. The application of article 53 of the Vienna Convention on the Law of Treaties to investment agreements that contain provisions that are *contra bonos mores* or violate *jus cogens*;

  vii. The legal status of privatized systems of justice that are not transparent or accountable nor subject to appeal, especially in the light of article 14 (1) of the International Covenant on Civil and Political Rights; the compatibility of investor-State dispute settlement tribunals with the principle of the rule of law; the obligation of investor-State dispute settlement arbitrators to take international human rights treaties into account;

  viii. The validity of investor-State dispute settlement awards, the necessity of appealability and the consequences of ex tunc invalidity;

ix. The primacy of State sovereignty over arbitral tribunals and the right of sovereign States to refuse to execute arbitral awards that entail violations of human rights;

x. The right of third States to refuse execution of arbitral awards that are *contra bonos mores,* notwithstanding the Convention on the Recognition and Enforcement of Foreign Arbitral Awards;

xi. The obligation of States to modify or terminate international investment agreements that have led to or are likely to lead to violations of human rights;

xii. The modalities of modification or termination of bilateral and multilateral free trade and investment agreements, pursuant to the Vienna Convention on the Law of Treaties, and the application of the principle of severability;

xiii. The responsibility of State courts to investigate corruption and collusion in connection with the operation of investor-State dispute settlement and to impose punitive damages on investors who engage in frivolous and vexatious litigation against the State's regulatory competences.

C. To transnational enterprises

(a) In the interrelated and interdependent world of the twenty-first century, plagued as it is by extreme poverty and where population growth announces threats to food security and the environment, energy scarcity, etc., international solidarity should engender concrete action. Enterprises should spend more of their profits for the promotion of human rights in the countries where they operate. They should take all necessary measures to ensure that their activities do not damage the environment, pollute, limit access to generic medicine, etc. They should comply with national and international regulations whereby the public must be informed of the dangers of tobacco consumption, genetically modified organisms, waste disposal, water pollution, etc.

(b) Transnational enterprises that are adversely affected by unilateral sanctions condemned by the General Assembly and the Human Rights Council should test their validity before the WTO dispute settlement mechanism, UNCITRAL or the International Centre for Settlement of Investment Disputes and/or invoke pertinent clauses in existing friendship, commerce and navigation treaties to refer disputes to the International Court of Justice.

D. To civil society

(a) Considering the grave democratic deficits of international investment agreements, in particular the secrecy of their elaboration and negotiation, the exclusion of key stakeholders and the adverse human rights impacts of international investment agreements and investor-State dispute settlement, civil society should demand that public referendums be held on all future international investment agreements, including bilateral investment treaties, the Trans-Pacific Partnership, the Trans-Atlantic Trade and Investment Partnership and the Trade in Services Agreement, and that referendums be organized concerning the urgent revision or termination of existing international investment agreements, including NAFTA and the Central America Free Trade Agreement (CAFTA).

(b) Individuals and groups should submit cases of human rights violations caused by the application of international investment agreements to regional human rights courts and denounce them in the social media.

(c) Civil society should demand the expansion of the concept of crimes against humanity to encompass economic crimes that entail the destruction of ecosystems or grave financial dislocations through manipulation of commodity markets or currency speculation resulting in the gravest consequences for millions of people.

WORLD TRADE ORGANIZATION RULES AND PRACTICE

Following my two reports on free-trade agreements and ISDS, the Human Rights Council requested me to continue research into this facet of international order.[i] It bears repeating that the World Trade Organization is the successor of the General Agreement on Tariffs and Trade,[ii] that neither the WTO itself nor the GATT have a mandate to promote human rights and that their focus must be on the facilitation of international commerce. However, there is no doubt that the WTO can contribute significantly to advancing human rights and, in particular,

---

[i] Paragraph 16 of Council Resolution 30/29 "Invites the Independent Expert to continue to develop studies on the adverse human rights impact of international investment agreements, bilateral investment treaties and multilateral free-trade agreements on the international order." https://undocs.org/en/A/HRC/RES/30/29. Accordingly, my 2016 report updates the prior reports, revisiting problems related to trade agreements and dispute settlement. These informative sections are omitted in this chapter—not because they overlap with what was already scrutinized, but because further elaboration of the subject lengthens this book and some readers may find it "redundant" in the light of the preceding, detailed analysis. Yet, the sections on the World Trade Organization and the WTO dispute settlement tribunal have added value.

[ii] https://www.wto.org/english/docs_e/legal_e/gatt47_e.pdf

the achievement of the sustainable development goals. On 1 March 2021 Ngozi Okonio-Iweala[i] became the seventh WTO Director-General, the first woman and first African to serve in this function. There are great hopes that Okonio-Iweala will revisit the commitments of member states to assist developing countries, in particular, deliver on their promise of technology transfer as part of the bargain struck with developing countries in exchange with their agreement to protect intellectual property rights. The WTO TRIPS Agreement aims precisely at facilitating the transfer and dissemination of technology as established in article 62.2, and specifically requires developed country members to provide incentives for their companies to promote the transfer of technology to least-developed countries.[ii] —AdeZ

* * *

The Independent Expert recognizes manifold human rights problems arising from commercial activity, but places trust in the existence of multilateral organizations like WTO. They have the opportunity and mechanisms to make trade work for human rights and development, as exemplified, for instance, by the adoption of the Doha Declaration, which is at the origin of an extended transition period for least developed countries exempting them from the obligation to enforce patents for pharmaceutical products.[111] The good will of States parties and a change of mindset toward more international solidarity offers a starting point.

Since the third Ministerial Conference, held in Seattle in 1999, and the civil society outcry against the adverse human rights impacts of commerce, WTO has become increasingly aware of the human rights dimensions of trade. In the wake of the global food crisis in 2008, the United Nations Secretary-General established the High-level Task Force on the Global Food Security Crisis, involving more than 20 international organizations, including WTO and the Office of the United Nations High Commissioner for Human Rights (OHCHR), towards a coordinated response to the crisis. A trilateral initiative with the World Health Organization (WHO) and the World Intellectual Property Organization (WIPO) also allows for policy dialogue and experience sharing. Since 2001, WTO has conducted a yearly Public Forum,[112] in which as many as 1,500 representatives from civil society, academia, business, media, Governments, parliamentarians and inter-governmental organizations share their knowledge and make recommendations on how to tap the potential for multilateral cooperation and growth and how best to implement the commitments of the Doha Development Agenda.

---

i https://www.wto.org/english/thewto_e/dg_e/dg_e.htm..
ii https://www.wto.org/english/tratop_e/trips_e/techtransfer_e.htm

While the Agreement on Trade-Related Aspects of Intellectual Property Rights (TRIPS Agreement) may allow some policy space to member States, allowing them to exclude from patentability those inventions that, if commercially exploited, might adversely impact human, animal, plant life or the environment, and could potentially be invoked to exclude genetically modified crops,[113] the State's policy space is far from being ensured, and the regulatory chill may still prevent States from adopting precautionary measures. The priority of human rights, health and environmental protection must be spelled out.

WTO held its tenth Ministerial Conference from 15 to 19 December 2015 in Nairobi. In a joint press release issued before it, the Special Rapporteurs on the right to food and on the right of everyone to the enjoyment of the highest attainable standard of physical and mental health joined the Independent Expert in urging Governments to deliver on the Doha Development Agenda (DDA) and not to betray commitments to address the needs of developing economies. "If trade is to work for human rights and development, it should contribute to the realization of the rights to adequate food, to the highest attainable standard of physical and mental health, and to live in a clean environment." There is no justification for defaulting on the Agenda: "Human rights obligations must be reaffirmed in the context of global trade rules to ensure that WTO negotiations and rules support development efforts to eliminate the root causes of hunger, ill-health and poverty, strengthen human rights protection and promotion and ultimately ensure that the newly adopted Sustainable Development Goals are achieved."[114]

A majority of States meeting in Nairobi favoured reaffirmation of the Doha framework, yet the opposition of some developed countries blocked consensus. Pressure on developing countries aimed at the introduction of new issues that would undermine the promotion of the right to development were reported. In response to the questionnaire sent by the Independent Expert, Saudi Arabia indicated that: "The WTO top priority should be concluding the DDA issues. The majority of WTO members are developing countries. A successful conclusion of the Doha Round would address developing country needs and contribute significantly to their economic growth and their integration into the global economy. Furthermore, concluding the Doha Development Round would address the trade distortions and imbalances in the WTO various agreements, and preserve the Special [and] Differential Treatment flexibilities granted to the developing countries.... The preamble of [the] Marrakesh agreement[115] establishing the WTO explicitly sets the objective to 'raise standards of living, ensuring full employment and a large and steadily growing volume of real income and effective demand.'"

While promoting trade, WTO should place people before profits, and development before the expansion of monopolies. As the Director at the Washington Centre for Economic and Policy Research, Deborah James, observed in 2015: "Despite the global consensus, the rules in the WTO remain unchanged from decades past. WTO rules do not allow developing countries that were not subsidizing in 1994 to subsidize beyond the *de minimis*... amount allowed to all WTO members. Meanwhile, the United States and Europe are allowed tens of billions a year in overtly trade-distorting subsidies for exported products, and have yet to implement the abolition of those subsidies to which they agreed nearly 10 years ago."

Implementation of those commitments would be facilitated if WTO were incorporated into the United Nations system and subordinated to the purposes and principles of the United Nations. Incorporation pursuant to articles 57 and 63 of the Charter would ensure that WTO not only actively contributes to the work of the Economic and Social Council, as it can proudly claim, but also gives proper weight to human rights as part of its own constitutional law.

The Nairobi Ministerial Conference reached some agreements on agricultural export subsidies, food aid and other issues. However, the Information Technology Agreement, covering products like Global Positioning System navigation systems and medical products such as magnetic resonance imaging machines, was primarily drafted by high income countries. None of the countries from the Group of Least Developed Countries were represented and only one of the lower-middle-income countries was represented.

It would have been desirable and in keeping with commitments to reduce poverty to adopt a clear statement on the legitimacy of public stockholding for food security that would allow countries to hold food stocks and enable them to deal with food shortages and fluctuations in global market prices.

While some developing countries were successful in securing concessions on cotton, an important issue for West African States, the rich countries won the deal on agricultural export subsidies, which did not abolish general subsidy schemes like the European Union Common Agricultural Policy. Observers noted that "the uneven WTO playing field, whereby rich countries' subsidy schemes are categorized as being 'allowable' while poorer countries are prevented from subsidizing their farmers, will continue."[116]

Barely three months after agreement on the Sustainable Development Goals, the Nairobi Ministerial Conference failed to implement target 17.10, pursuant to which States would "promote a universal, rules-based, open, non-discriminatory and equitable multilateral trading system under the World Trade Organization, including through the conclusion of negotiations under its Doha Development Agenda." That paradox highlights the need to rethink the global trading system and the skewed ideological approach taken by some negotiators. One problem with WTO, beyond Doha and Nairobi, is the prevalent vision that equates "progress" with the growth of trade volumes and exports or with a higher gross domestic product. The Charter of the United Nations advocates another vision of progress as development, solidarity and human rights in a progressively more democratic and equitable international order.

Notwithstanding press comments in the United States and the European Union declaring the Doha Development Agenda "dead," paragraphs 30, 31 and 34 of the Nairobi Declaration give reason for hope.[117] While acknowledging the stalemate, they indicate that the Doha Work Programme is a single undertaking, meaning that Western countries cannot cherry-pick which parts to prioritize. It appears relevant for the developing countries to continue the struggle on the negotiating agenda of the single undertaking of that Programme. Under no conditions can any conditional plurilateral agreements, as envisaged by the United States and the European Union, be incorporated into the WTO treaty framework, except when there is a consensus on them at a ministerial conference.[118] Yet, at the Bali Ministerial Conference, held in 2013, the developing countries surrendered their most powerful leverage when they conceded the Trade Facilitation Agreement as a separate accord. Bearing in mind that that Agreement has not entered into force, one may suggest the developing countries withhold deposit of their instruments of ratification until they secure their own demands, including Nairobi decisions on "deliverables," in a single protocol incorporating the results of the Doha Work Programme.

The outcome document of the eleventh session of the Parliamentary Conference on WTO, held on 13 and 14 June 2016, states: "We appreciate the decision on public stockholding for food security purposes and call for the conclusion of negotiations on finding a permanent solution to the issue.... We believe that the issue of food security is vital for developing countries and that WTO rules must support efforts to combat hunger. In line with the same decision, we also want to stress the importance of a speedy adoption of a proposal for a special safeguard mechanism.... Flexibility, openness, inclusiveness and political engagement will be key to advancing on all the remaining issues of the Doha Development Agenda."

World Trade Organization dispute settlement

On 24 February 2016, a WTO dispute panel adopted a decision against the efforts of India to create renewable energy through the extended use of solar panels.[119] One would think that, after the Conference of the Parties to the United Nations Framework Convention on Climate Change, everyone would support such initiatives, but WTO dispute panels seem to be caught in their own mantras and incapable of showing flexibility in accommodating the new priorities imposed by climate change. Despite some interesting initiatives in that field, such as the WTO Committee on Trade and Environment, there is still unwillingness to interpret broadly the general exceptions provided under the General Agreement on Tariffs and Trade 1994.[120]

The National Solar Mission of India, which aims at increasing the country's renewable energy in line with Sustainable Development Goal 7 on ensuring access to affordable, reliable, sustainable and modern energy for all, is a reasonable plan. It would create local jobs and bring clean energy to millions by generating 100 gigawatts of solar power annually, consistent with the goals of the Framework Convention on Climate Change. The WTO case was brought by the United States, which challenged the domestic content clause of India, which would require part of the solar cells to be produced nationally. India unsuccessfully tried to reach a settlement with the United States and now may have to adjust its solar programme to avoid WTO sanctions. The panel concluded that the measures of India were inconsistent with article 2.1 of the Agreement on Trade-Related Investment Measures and article III:4 of the General Agreement on Tariffs and Trade 1994, and were not covered by the derogation in article III:8 (a) of that General Agreement, or justified under the general exceptions in articles XX (j) and XX (d) of that General Agreement. The panel concluded that benefits accruing to the United States had been impaired. India appealed the decision on 30 April 2016,[121] and on 13 May announced that it would bring as many as 16 claims against the United States.[122]

Friends of the Earth has commented: "The WTO ruling against India's National Solar Mission shows how arcane trade rules can be used to undermine governments that support clean energy and local jobs. The ink is barely dry on the Paris Climate agreement, but clearly trade still trumps real action on climate change."[123] That is paradigmatic of what is wrong with the pro-business approach to the regulatory space of States and with the so-called "Washington consensus" that consistently opposes industrial policy-making by States.[124] A United Nations campaign is needed to mainstream human rights into the work of WTO and to establish clear guidelines for dispute settlement panels giving due weight to human rights, health and environmental concerns.

Preventive and corrective action

While endorsing the analyses of economists, sociologists and jurists, including Jeronim Capaldo,[125] Noam Chomsky,[126] Michael Hudson,[127] Deborah James,[128] George Kahale,[129] Richard Kozul-Wright,[130] Isabel Ortiz,[131] Max Otte,[132] Lauge Poulsen,[133] Jeffrey Sachs,[134] Joseph Stiglitz,[135] Gus van Harten[136] and Robert Wade,[137] and relying on the studies of other rapporteurs and working groups, the Independent Expert deems it urgent to demand that the Human Rights Council take action so that their good proposals are not rendered irrelevant by the corporate "so what?" Transnational corporations have become a kind of Leviathan that must be tamed. Indeed, every exercise of power, political or economic, that affects people's lives must be subject to democratic controls and compatible with the purposes and principles of the Charter of the United Nations. It is that spirit that has prompted the following recommendations.

Recommendations to States

(a) States should impose a moratorium on the execution of investor-State dispute settlement awards until the entire system is tested by the International Court of Justice. A new multilateral treaty should be elaborated stipulating that courts may not execute such awards without verifying their compatibility with human rights treaty obligations and *ordre public*.

(b) States should refrain from entering into new bilateral investment treaties and free-trade agreements, including the Trans-Pacific Partnership Agreement, the Transatlantic Trade and Investment Partnership, the Comprehensive Economic and Trade Agreement and the Trade in Services Agreement, unless human rights, health and environmental impact assessments have been conducted, and unless there is full disclosure, consultation with stakeholders and public participation. Where possible, referendums should be conducted.

(c) States should test the legality of provisions of bilateral investment treaties and free-trade agreements, investor-State dispute settlement and investment court system mechanisms, as well as WTO rules and practice, for compatibility with their own Constitutions and with their human rights treaty obligations.

(d) States may consider invoking the inter-State procedures of the Human Rights Committee (International Covenant on Civil and Political Rights, art. 41) and of regional human rights courts. European States should test the compatibility of the Comprehensive Economic and Trade Agreement and the Transatlantic Trade and Investment Partnership with their human rights obligations before the European Court of Human Rights. American

States should test the compatibility of trade agreements with the American Convention on Human Rights. African States should test compatibility with the African Charter on Human and Peoples' Rights. States members of the European Union should test the constitutionality of trade agreements before the European Court of Justice.[138]

(e) States should conduct ex post human rights, health and environmental impact assessments in connection with existing trade agreements and modify them where necessary.

(f) States should cooperate with the inter-governmental working group on the drafting of a binding treaty on corporate social responsibility and adopt it expeditiously. The treaty should put teeth on the Guiding Principles on Business and Human Rights and provide for monitoring and enforcement mechanisms. The treaty should give recourse and remedy to victims of abusive activities by transnational corporations.

(g) States should implement the Doha Development Agenda as envisaged in Sustainable Development Goal 17.10. The Trade Facilitation Agreement must not become operative until the Doha Development Agenda commitments have been met.

Recommendations to parliaments

(a) No parliament should approve trade agreements without exercising oversight functions and examining the compatibility of the agreements with human rights treaty obligations in the light of impact assessments.

(b) Parliaments should make it illegal for treaty negotiators to agree to anti-democratic lock-in periods in investment treaties.[139] The adding of riders to existing bills without democratic debate is unacceptable.

(c) Parliaments should invoke the pertinent revision and termination procedures laid out in the Vienna Convention on the Law of Treaties to modify commercial treaties and abolish investor-State dispute settlement.

(d) Parliaments and IPU should intensify their cooperation with WTO in the field of human rights, health and the environment.

Recommendations to domestic courts

(a) National courts and tribunals should execute foreign arbitral awards only after examining their legitimacy in the light of human rights treaty obligations. Arbitral awards that encroach on the regulatory space of States should be rejected as contrary to domestic and international ordre public.

(b) The public policy exception contained in article 5 of the New York Convention on the Recognition and Enforcement of Foreign Arbitral Awards should be used systematically to prevent interference in fundamental State functions.

Recommendations to the International Court of Justice

The International Court of Justice should pronounce in appropriate contentious cases or in an advisory opinion on the *erga omnes* obligations of States to comply with the human rights treaty regime. No trade agreement, investor-State dispute settlement or investment court system may obstruct the fulfilment of human rights treaty obligations. The supremacy clause of the Charter of the United Nations (Article 103) and general principles of law, including good faith, the prohibition of treaties that are *contra bonos mores* and the prohibition of abuse of rights, override conflicting trade agreements and arbitral awards.

Recommendations to the World Trade Organization

(a) WTO should mainstream human rights into all of its activities and issue directives to the dispute settlement panels so that human rights treaty violations are not adversely affected.

(b) WTO dispute panels should interpret the exceptions in the General Agreement on Tariffs and Trade 1994 to support initiatives on food security, health and the environment and facilitate solutions to climate change. WTO should harmonize policies with the Food and Agriculture Organization of the United Nations (FAO) and OHCHR.

Recommendations to the United Nations Conference on Trade and Development

UNCTAD should convene a world conference to revise existing bilateral investment treaties and free-trade agreements, abolish investor-State dispute settlement and declare the investment court system incompatible with United Nations constitutional law.

Recommendations to national human rights institutions and civil society organizations

National human rights institutions and civil society organizations should assist in conducting human rights, health and environmental impact assessments. They should disseminate information on commercial treaties and their human rights impacts and demand that referendums be held.

DRAFTING A BINDING TREATY ON CORPORATE SOCIAL RESPONSIBILITY

The OHCHR has been hosting a Forum on Business and Human Rights (FBHR) since 2012.[i] While I have attended for several years, I have never been invited to participate in any of their many panels, side-events, and other activities.[ii] notwithstanding my pertinent reports and concrete recommendations to the Human Rights Council and General Assembly on core issues concerning business and human rights. Indeed, most of the crucial issues related to business and human rights have been marginalized by this forum. This is why I have publicly termed this lavish self-congratulatory event the "forum on the business of human rights."

The forum is enormously well funded and invites all sorts of compliant non-governmental organizations devoted, not to advancing human rights or proposing genuine changes, but to creating the impression that someone is aware of the problems and is taking care of them. These corporate "operatives" publicize their "contributions" to "wokeness" in business, promote some cosmetic adjustments, cater to the lobbies for the extracting industries, for oil and gas, for gender and LGBT, and bottom line aim at preserving the status quo, because so many people are profiting from it, and, after all, because there is the beneficial "trickle down" effect.

Sadly, this spectacle is a Potemkin event—although few want to admit it. It resembles Hans Christian Andersen's fable of the King with no clothes. No one wants to say that the Forum has no clothes and no credibility. This is why numerous genuine NGOs like the Centre Europe Troisième Monde (CETIM)[iii]— and even some inter-governmental organizations like South Centre[iv]—boycott the FBHR. Some of these criticisms also apply to the UN Working Group on the issue

---

i https://www.ohchr.org/EN/Issues/Business/Forum/Pages/ForumonBusinessandHumanRights.aspx
https://www.ohchr.org/EN/Issues/Business/Forum/Pages/2020ForumBHR.aspx
  ii https://www.ohchr.org/EN/Issues/Business/Forum/Pages/2019ForumBHR.aspx
  iii https://www.cetim.ch/human-rights/
  iv https://www.southcentre.int/tag/business-and-human-rights/

of human rights and transnational corporations and other business enterprises, which was established by the Human Rights Council in 2011. Thus far the Working Group has been rather cautious—not to say timid—in tackling international investment agreements[i] and their adverse human rights impacts.

It bears repeating that so-called free-trade agreements have little to do with free-trade and much to do with increasing the stranglehold of transnational corporations on the policy space of sovereign countries, most negatively on the right to development of developing countries.[ii]

In my 2016 report to the Human Rights Council[iii] I addressed the urgent need to make the Guiding Principles on Business and Human Rights binding by drafting and adopting an appropriate treaty. —AdeZ

* * *

A democratic and equitable international order, as prescribed in the Charter of the United Nations, cannot be achieved through deregulation of trade, markets and financial services. While enterprises deserve protection from corrupt governments and arbitrary expropriations, governments also need protection from business scams, bribery and corruption by investors, speculators and transnational corporations. If responsibility to protect means anything, it means that governments have an obligation to protect individuals and peoples from abuse and to provide remedies against land-grabbing and exploitation.

Observers have long decried the anomaly that while businesses have secured privileged protection for their investments and have created privatized arbitral tribunals to enforce their view of the "law," there is no tribunal to protect governments from business abuse and no protection of individual victims from the negative consequences of business activities, business relocations, violations of labour laws, destruction of jobs, etc. This normative asymmetry must be corrected.

Fifty-five years after the adoption of the International Covenant on Civil and Political Rights and the International Covenant on Economic, Social and Cultural Rights, there is still no enforcement mechanism for these instruments of hard law. This absence of effective protection reduces the credibility of United Nations institutions that continue adopting "Views," "Opinions," declarations and resolutions, which many States and non-state actors ignore in total impunity.

---

i https://www.ohchr.org/EN/Issues/Business/Pages/IIAs.aspx
ii https://www.ohchr.org/EN/Issues/Business/Pages/WGHRandtransnationalcorporationsandotherbusiness.aspx
iii https://undocs.org/A/HRC/33/40. paras 77-84

Whereas there are enforcement mechanisms for trade and other agreements in WTO and investor-State dispute settlement, it is imperative to create them globally for human rights treaties as well. The promise of the United Nations Global Compact and the Guiding Principles on Business and Human Rights has not been realized, simply because self-regulation never works.

Binding obligations on investors and corporations must be incorporated into trade and investment agreements, and public courts must have jurisdiction to examine violations and impose sanctions on violators. Although the Guiding Principles are based on hard law, they are violated with impunity, as illustrated by bilateral investment treaties and free-trade agreements that encroach upon the regulatory space of States. The treaty should provide for its own monitoring and enforcement body or be incorporated into the International Covenant on Civil and Political Rights and the International Covenant on Economic, Social and Cultural Rights as optional protocols, stipulating that decisions are legally binding, as are those of the Inter-American Court of Human Rights and the European Court of Human Rights.

States must enact civil and penal legislation concerning the human rights impacts of business activity; the doctrine of State responsibility should be invoked to make abuses justiciable wherever the enterprises operate or are registered.

In June 2014, the Human Rights Council adopted resolution 26/9 creating an intergovernmental working group with the mandate to draft such an instrument.[140] In July 2015, the first session of the working group was held in Geneva;[141] its second session was held in October 2015. In 2017 the chairperson of the intergovernmental working group issued "Elements for the draft legally binding instrument." In July 2018, the IGWG presented the Zero Draft, followed by its draft Optional Protocol.[142] In October 2018 stakeholders provided input on the Zero Draft. In July 2019 a Revised Draft was published.[143] In August 2020, the Second Revised Draft was published.[144] The 6th session of the IGWG was held from 26 to 30 October 2020.

Beyond the treaty, there is an urgent need to strengthen national and international penal law, including anti-trust legislation, to address cases of corruption, fraud, bribery,[145] money-laundering, conspiracy, collusion, tax evasion, insider-trading, looting of pension funds, vulture fund transactions and reckless endangerment of life and the environment. In that context, the United Nations Convention against Corruption and the United Nations Office at Vienna could advance the process. Also pertinent is the United Nations Convention against Transnational Organized Crime, as certain activities of mining enterprises, including gold, diamond, lithium and coltan mining,[146] as well as the ivory trade,[147] entail criminal acts and gross human rights violations.

A treaty on corporate legal responsibility should not stop at defining the civil liability of transnational corporations. There must also be penal responsibility when corporate actions cause death or grievous harm, and when they destroy landscapes and the common heritage of mankind. Indeed, some activities of petroleum, gas and mining enterprises constitute a major attack on the environment, accompanied by reckless endangerment of millions of peoples' lives.

Such attacks, perpetrated not only by legal persons, but by individuals sitting in corporate boardrooms, may well be justiciable as crimes against humanity pursuant to article 7 (1) (k) of the Rome Statute of the International Criminal Court. In cases where business activity causes the involuntary displacement of populations, article 7 (1) (d) applies. The Nuremberg Trials showed the way in prosecuting and convicting business executives of the I.G. Farben, Flick and Krupp companies because of their complicity in Nazi crimes. In 1946 Bruno Tesch, a business executive responsible for the production of Zyklon B, was tried and convicted. Today the penal responsibility of enterprises producing indiscriminate weapons such as landmines, cluster bombs, depleted uranium ammunition and white phosphorus can and must come before the International Criminal Court. There is no justification for business executives enjoying impunity just because they are private-sector actors. Universal jurisdiction should also be tested in appropriate cases.

Hitherto, victims of corporate abuses have been left without adequate recourse or remedy. This poses a serious challenge to the Human Rights Council and calls not only for diagnoses but for concrete recommendations and implementable solutions. The strengthening of the human rights enforcement system is necessary to counter the prevalent architecture of corporate impunity.

Notes

1 A/69/299, A/HRC/11/12 and A/HRC/20/15/Add.2. See also E/CN.4/2005/51/Add.3 and www.ohchr.org/Documents/Issues/SForum/SForum2015/DainiusPuras.pdf.
2 "Extraterritorial violations may occur, for example, when ... (d) States fail to respect human rights or restrict the ability of others to comply with their human rights obligations in the process of elaborating, applying and interpreting international trade and investment agreements" (A/HRC/27/55, para. 71).
3 "States should take into account their international human rights obligations when designing and implementing all policies, including international trade, taxation, fiscal, monetary, environmental and investment policies" (A/HRC/21/39, para. 61).
4 Juan Pablo Bohoslavsky and Juan Bautista Justo, "The conventionality control of investment arbitrations: enhancing coherence through dialogue," *Transnational Dispute Management*, vol. 10, No. 1 (2013), pp. 1–12.

5 John Ruggie. See www.ohchr.org/EN/Issues/Business/Pages/SRSGTransCorpIndex.aspx.
6 business-humanrights.org/en/un-secretary-generals-special-representative-on-business-human-rights/un-protect-respect-and-remedy-framework-and-guiding-principles.
7 UNCTAD, World Investment Report 2015, Trade and Development Report 2014.
8 Pascal Lamy (former Director-General of the World Trade Organization (WTO)), "Towards shared responsibility and greater coherence: human rights, trade and macroeconomic policy," speech at the Colloquium on Human Rights in the Global Economy, Geneva, 13 January 2010. Available from www.wto.org/english/news_e/sppl_e/sppl146_e.htm.
9 Yash Tandon, *Trade is War: the West's War against the World* (OR Books, 2015). See also the history of the Opium Wars to force the opening of China to European trade in Jack Beeching, *The Chinese Opium Wars* (Orlando, Florida, Harcourt Brace Jovanovich, 1975); and Susanna Hoe and Derek Roebuck, *The Taking of Hong Kong: Charles and Clara Elliot in China Waters* (Richmond, Surrey, Curzon Press, 1999).
10 See Stephan W. Schill (ed.), *International Investment Law and Comparative Public Law* (Oxford University Press, 2010); Joseph François *et al.*, "Reducing transatlantic barriers to trade and investment: an economic assessment," IIDE Discussion Paper No. 20130401(Institute for International and Development Economics, 2013); V. S. Seshadri, "Trans-Atlantic trade and investment partnership," RIS Discussion Paper No. 185 (New Delhi, Research and Information Systems for Developing Countries, 2013); Jeffrey J. Schott and Cathleen Cimino, "Crafting a transatlantic trade and investment partnership: what can be done," Policy Brief No. PB13-8 (Washington, D.C., Peterson Institute for International Economics, 2013); and U.S. Business Coalition for TPP, "VOICES: Asia-Pacific Policy Experts Support TPP," 28 April 2015, available from tppcoalition.org/voices-asia-pacific-policy-experts-support-tpp-and-tpa.
11 See A/HRC/19/59/Add.5; www2.ohchr.org/english/issues/food/docs/report_hria-seminar_2010.pdf and www.humanrights.dk/business/impact-assessment.
12 Bruno Simma and Theodore Kill, "Harmonizing investment protection and human rights: first steps towards a methodology," in Christina Binder *et al.* (eds.), *International Investment Law for the 21st Century: Essays in Honour of Christoph Schreuer* (Oxford University Press, 2009).
13 Bohoslavsky (see endnote 4 above), p. 10. See also the report of the Study Group of the International Law Commission on fragmentation of international law: difficulties arising from the diversification and expansion of international law, *Yearbook of the International Law Commission 2006*, vol. II (Part Two), para. 251.
14 Joseph Stiglitz, "On the wrong side of globalization," *New York Times*, 15 March 2014. See also Pope Francis' statement http://www.pagina12.com.ar/diario/elpais/1-276806-2015-07-10.html.
15 The right to life is impacted when a person dies because of lack of access to medicine because pharmaceutical monopolies have "privatized knowledge" and, through "evergreening" of patents, delay or make the introduction of significantly cheaper generic medicine impossible. The right to life is also violated when farmers and other labourers have their livelihoods destroyed by "free trade" without protective governmental action. For instance, bilateral investment treaties and free-trade agreements impacted millions of farmers in India and caused a significant rise in suicides, see Devinder Sharma, "'Free' trade killing farmers in India," November 2007, available from www.bilaterals.org/?free-trade-killing-farmers-in.
16 www.cepal.org/es/publicaciones/3839-proteccion-del-derecho-humano-al-agua-y-arbitrajes-de-inversionhttp://cap-net-esp.org/document/document/181/agua_y_saneamiento_tratados_de_protecci%C3%B3n_a_las_inversiones.pdf.
17 www.globalresearch.ca/the-free-trade-agreements-the-asia-europe-peoples-forum-call-to-action/5416888?print=1.
18 See www.hrw.org/news/1996/08/17/mexicos-maquiladoras-abuses-against-women-workers; sdmaquila.blogspot.ch/2010/02/maquiladoras-101-english.html; and www.researchgate.net. publication/266820089_Human_rights_violations_in_the_Maquiladora_Industry.
19 Robert E. Scott, "The high price of 'free' trade: NAFTA's failure has cost the United States jobs across the nation," Briefing paper No. 147, Economic Policy Institute, 17 November 2003, available from www.epi.org/publication/briefingpapers_bp147.

20 See www.mfat.govt.nz/Trade-and-Economic-Relations/2-Trade-Relationships-and-Agreements/RCEP/; donttradeourlivesaway.wordpress.com/2015/06/11/press-statement-civil-society-raises-major-concerns-on-indias-engagement-with-the-massive-rcep-trade-deal/; and trade.ec.europa.eu/doclib/docs/2006/december/tradoc_118238.pdf. The European Free Trade Association is also negotiating free-trade agreements: see www.asean.org/images/2012/documents/Guiding%20Principles%20 and%20Objectives%20for%20Negotiating%20the%20Regional%20 Comprehensive%20Economic%2 0Partnership.pdf.

21 www.project-syndicate.org/commentary/us-secret-corporate-takeover-by-joseph-e--stiglitz-2015-05.

22 *Trade and Development Report, 2014* p. 145. Available from http://unctad.org/en/PublicationsLibrary/tdr2014_en.pdf. See also *UNCTAD World Investment Report 2015: Reforming the International Investment Regime*.

23 See www.washingtonpost.com/wp-srv/special/business/trade-advisory-committees/index.html.; big.assets.huffingtonpost.com/WarrenBrownTPPLetter.pdf; corporateeurope.org/pressreleases/2014/07/agribusiness-biggest-lobbyist-eu-us-trade-deal-new-research-reveals; www.publicintegrity.org/2005/07/07/5786/drug-lobby-second-none; www.citizen.org/documents/egregious-investor-state-attacks-case-studies.pdf; and www.opensecrets.org/lobby/methodology.php.

24 Sarah Joseph, *Blame it on the WTO? A Human Rights Critique* (Oxford University Press, 2011), p. 288.

25 Joseph Stiglitz and Andrew Charlton, *Fair Trade for All: How Trade can Promote Development* (Oxford University Press, 2005), p. 34.

26 Sarah Joseph (see endnote 24 above), citing Frank Garcia, "The global market and human rights: trading away the human rights principle," *Brooklyn Journal of International Law*, vol. 7 (1999), p. 51, at p. 65. See also Jeronim Capaldo, "The Trans-Atlantic Trade and Investment Partnership: European disintegration, unemployment and instability," GDAE Working Paper No. 14-03, Global Development and Environment Institute at Tufts University, available from http://ase.tufts.edu/gdae/policy_research/ttip_simulations.html.

27 Capaldo (see endnote above).

28 For investor–State dispute settlement cases in the database of publicly available investment cases under investment chapters of free-trade agreements and bilateral investment treaties, searchable by type of policy challenged by investor (for example, environment), but not updated after May 2010, see www.iiapp.org/. For texts of awards in investor–State dispute settlement cases, see www.italaw.com and unctad.org/en/Pages/DIAE/investor–State dispute settlement.aspx. See also www.baerbel-hoehn.de/fileadmin/media/MdB/baerbelhoehn_de/www_baerbelhoehn_de/investor– State dispute settlement_TAFTA_Bundestag.pdf; and www.iisd.org/pdf/2011/int_investment_law_and_sd_key_cases_2010.pdf.

29 See Pia Eberhardt and Cecilia Olivet, *Profiting from Injustice: How Law Firms, Arbitrators and Financiers are Fuelling an Investment Arbitration Boom* (Corporate Europe Observatory, Brussels, 2012), available from www.tni.org/sites/www.tni.org/files/download/profitingfrominjustice.pdf; acta.ffii.org/?p=2118; corporateeurope.org/sites/default/files/annex-2-still-not-loving-isds.pdf; corporateeurope.org/international-trade/2014/07/commission-isds-reform-plan-echo-chamber-business-views; www.bilaterals.org/?investor-to-state-dispute; and www.italaw.com/sites/default/files/case-documents/ita0221.pdf.

30 See John Hendy, "A threat to the sovereignty of courts and parliaments," *Graya*, No. 128 (2015), pp. 52–56.

31 *Fair and Equitable Treatment* (United Nations publication, Sales No. E.11.II.D.15), p. 2.

32 www.theguardian.com/commentisfree/2013/nov/04/us-trade-deal-full-frontal-assault-on-democracy.

33 European Center for Constitutional and Human Rights, "Human rights inapplicable in international investment arbitration?," available from www.ecchr.de/worldbank/articles/human-rights-inapplicable-in-international-investment-arbitration.html.

34 UNCTAD, *IIA Issues Note*, No. 1 (February 2015), available from unctad.org/en/PublicationsLibrary/webdiaepcb2015d1_en.pdf.
35 commonsensecanadian.ca/quebec-fracking-nafta-challenge-right-water-right-profit/.
36 www.international.gc.ca/trade-agreements-accords-commerciaux/topics-domaines/disp-diff/ethyl.aspx?lang=eng and www.citizen.org/documents/egregious-investor-state-attacks-case-studies.pdf.
37 www.citizen.org/documents/NAFTAReport_Final.pdf and solidarity-us.org/node/977. See also www.baerbel-hoehn.de/fileadmin/media/MdB/baerbelhoehn_de/www_baerbelhoehn_de/ISDS_TAFTA_Bundestag.pdf and www.oecd.org/daf/inv/internationalinvestmentagreements/40077817.pdf.
38 www.elstel.org/ISDS.html.en; infojustice.org/archives/34113.
39 www.citizen.org/cmep/article_redirect.cfm?ID=9208, documents.foodandwaterwatch.org/doc/ICSID_web.pdf and www.elstel.org/ISDS.html.en.
40 www.italaw.com/cases/documents/1655. Nathalie Bernasconi, "Background paper on *Vattenfall v. Germany*," IISD; Rechtsanwälte Günther (2012) Briefing Note. The Coal-fired Power Plant Hamburg-Moorburg.
41 www.fr-online.de/energie/atomausstieg-vattenfall-fordert-milliarden,1473634,21169258.html Power Shift (2012) Der deutsche Atomausstieg auf dem Prüfstand eines internationalen Investionsschiedsgerichts? Hintergründe zum neuen Streitfall Vattenfall gegen Deutschland. www.iisd.org/pdf/2012/powershift_forum_briefing_vattenfall.pdf.
42 One of the worst aspects of this case is that Ecuador was justified in terminating Occidental's permit under Ecuadorian law and the contract and still the investor–State dispute settlement tribunal penalised Ecuador, www.citizen.org/documents/oxy-v-ecuador-memo.pdf.
43 www.iisd.org/itn/2011/07/12/philip-morris-v-uruguay-will-investor-state-arbitration-send-restrictions-on-tobacco-marketing-up-in-smoke/.
44 www.italaw.com/cases/257. See also truth-out.org/news/item/23788, fpif.org/nafta-20-model-corporate-rule/, and content.time.com/time/world/article/0,8599,2053075,00.html.
45 www.italaw.com/cases/851 and /www.iisd.org/itn/2011/07/12/philip-morris-v-uruguay-will-investor-state-arbitration-send-restrictions-on-tobacco-marketing-up-in-smoke/.
46 www.acci.asn.au/getattachment/b9d3cfae-fc0c-4c2a-a3df-3f58228daf6d/Gillard-Government-Trade-Policy-Statement.aspx. The current Government of Australia may consider investor–State dispute settlement on a treaty-by-treaty basis.
47 trade.ec.europa.eu/doclib/docs/2015/may/tradoc_153408.PDF. See also the *UNCTAD World Investment Report 2015: Reforming International Investment Governance*, which presents an action menu for investment regime reform. UNCTAD, *IIA Issues Note*, May 2015.
48 ccsi.columbia.edu/files/2012/11/FDI-Perspectives-eBook-v2-Nov-2012.pdf.
49 Guatemala, www.theguardian.com/business/2015/jun/10/obscure-legal-system-lets-corportations-sue-states-ttip-icsid.
50 Article 1 of Wilson's 14 Points already warned against secret treaties. Article 102 of the Charter of the United Nations requires treaties to be published. Even if bilateral investment treaties and free-trade agreements have been partly published, they possess no democratic legitimacy unless the public can participate in negotiation and adoption. Some observers have articulated the fear that one reason for the worldwide surveillance of private citizens may be to predict when and where democratic movements are likely to arise so as to nip them in the bud. Hence the protection of the right to privacy and the prohibition of surveillance without warrant are mandated by articles 14 and 17 of the International Covenant on Civil and Political Rights.
51 A/HRC/24/38, paras. 15–24. See also Vienna Declaration and Programme of Action, para. 8.
52 Personal interview with Julian Assange at the Mission of Ecuador in London on 20 March 2015 wikileaks.org/tpp/pressrelease.html, wikileaks.org/tpp-investment/press.html, wikileaks.org/tisa/press.html and www.theguardian.com/media/2015/jun/03/wikileaks-documents-trade-in-services-agreement.
53 tbinternet.ohchr.org/_layouts/treatybodyexternal/TBSearch.aspx?Lang=en&TreatyID=9&DocTypeID=11.

54 Alfred Verdross, "Forbidden Treaties in International Law," *American Journal of International Law,* Vol. 31, No. 4 (1937), pp. 571 *et seq.* Verdross, "Les principes du droit et la jurisprudence internationale,» *Recueil des Cours de l'Académie de Droit International,* La Haye, (1935), pp. 195–249. Robert Kolb, *The International Court of Justice,* Oxford, 2013, p. 81. Irmgard Marboe and August Reinisch, "Contracts between States and foreign private law persons" in *Max Planck Encyclopedia of Public International Law*, vol. II, pp. 758–766. Oxford, 2012. felj.org/sites/default/files/elj/Energy%20Journals/Vol17_No1_1996_article_international.pdf.

55 law.wustl.edu/SBA/upperlevel/International%20Law/IntLaw-Mutharika2.pdf.

56 The contract between Shylock and the Merchant of Venice, Antonio, was contra bonos mores, because failure to reimburse a debt cannot have death as its consequence. By analogy, when a State cannot repay an investor, the consequence cannot be interventionism as practised in the nineteenth and twentieth centuries, when overt imperialism ruled, or more recently by IMF and central banks when imposing "austerity measures" and "privatizations"; A/65/260 and A/69/273.

57 Nazi entrepreneurs were held criminally responsible for the consequences of some of their business activities. www.roberthjackson.org/the-man/speeches-articles/speeches/speeches-related-to-robert-h-jackson/the-influence-of-the-nuremberg-trial-on-international-criminal-law/. Telford Taylor, *The Anatomy of the Nuremberg Trials: A Personal Memoir,* New York,1992. The principle applies also in the context of more recent human rights violations. Horacio Verbitsky, Juan Pablo Bohoslavsky (eds.), *Cuentas Pendientes. Los cómplices de la dictadura,* Siglo veintiuno, 2013.

58 Polly Higgins, *Eradicating Ecocide: Laws and Governance to Prevent the Destruction of our Planet,* London, 2010.

59 Harmen van der Wilt, "Corporate criminal responsibility for international crimes," *Chinese Journal of International law,* vol. 12 (Issue 1), pp. 43–77.

60 *UNCTAD Trade and Development Report, 2014.*

61 www.icrc.org/eng/resources/documents/misc/57jq32.htm.

62 https://home.cern/science/computing/birth-web https://home.cern/resources/video/computing/brief-history-world-wide-web

63 Patrick Juillard, "Calvo Doctrine/Calvo Clause," *Max Planck Encyclopaedia of Public International Law*, vol. I, pp. 1086–1093, Oxford, 2012. D. R. Shea, *The Calvo Clause: A Problem of inter-American and International Law and Diplomacy*, Minneapolis, 1955. C. K. Darymple, "Politics and foreign direct investment: the multilateral investment guarantee agency and the Calvo Clause," *Cornell International Law Review*, vol. 29, pp. 161–189.

64 www.uncitral.org/, www.uncitral.org/pdf/english/texts/arbitration/rules-on-transparency/Rules-on-Transparency-E.pdf, www.uncitral.org/pdf/english/texts/arbitration/ rules-on-transparency/Rules-on-Transparency-E.pdf.

65 UNCTAD, *World Investment Report 2015: Reforming International Investment Governance*, United Nations publication, Sales No. E.15.II.D.5, chap. IV, introduction.

66 United Nations publication, Sales No. E.14.II.D.4.

67 Available from www.ohchr.org/EN/Issues/Business/Pages/WGHRandtransnationalcorporations andotherbusiness.aspx.

68 A. Clapham, *Human Rights Obligations of Non-State Actors* (Oxford University Press, 2006); A. Clapham, ed., *Human Rights and Non-State Actors* (Elgar, 2013); O. De Schutter, "The accountability of multinationals for human rights violations in European law," New York University School of Law, 2004; O. De Schutter, "Human rights and transnational corporations: paving the way for a legally binding instrument," workshop convened by Ecuador on 11 and 12 March 2014 during the twenty-fifth session of the Human Rights Council; H. Verbitsky and J. Bohoslavsky, *Cuentas Pendientes: Los Cómplices Económicos de la Dictadura* (Buenos Aires, Siglo XXI, 2013); International Commission of Jurists, *Needs and Options for a New International Instrument in the Field of Business and Human Rights*; Amnesty International, "India: Court decision requires Dow Chemical to respond to Bhopal gas tragedy," 3 July 2013; J. Wronka, *Human Rights and Social Justice: Social Action and Service for the Helping and Health Professions* (Sage, 2008); V. Nerlich, "Core crimes and transnational business corporations," *Journal of International Criminal Justice*, vol. 8, No. 3 (July 2010), pp. 895–908.

69 UNCTAD, *World Investment Report*, chap. IV, p. 162.

70 See, inter alia, the speech by Pope Francis in Santa Cruz, Bolivia, on 10 July 2015: "The new colonialism takes on different faces. At times it appears as the anonymous influence of Mammon: corporations, loan agencies, certain 'free trade' treaties, and the imposition of measures of 'austerity' which always tighten the belt of workers and the poor." This is perhaps an echo of Saint Jerome: "*Homo mercator vix aut nunquam potest Deo placere*" ("A man who is a merchant can scarcely or never please God"). http://en.radiovaticana.va/news/ 2015/07/10/pope_francis_ speech_at_world_meeting_of_popular_movements/1157291; www.latribunadejulian romero.blogspot.com.es/2014/10/couple-of-couplespar-de-pares.html?m=1.

71 "Transforming our world: the 2030 agenda for sustainable development." Available from https://sustainabledevelopment.un.org/content/documents/7891TRANSFORMING%20OUR%20 WORLD.pdf.

72 Human Rights Committee, general comment No. 33 (2009).

73 P. Eberhardt and C. Olivet, *Profiting from Injustice: How Law Firms, Arbitrators and Financiers Are Fuelling an Investment Arbitration Boom* (Brussels/Amsterdam, Corporate Europe Observatory, 2012); Corporate Europe Observatory, "Profiting from crisis. How corporations and lawyers are scavenging profits from Europe's crisis countries," 2014.

74 See the summary records of the International Law Commission; Human Rights Committee, general comment No. 24 (1994); Roslyn Moloney, "Incompatible reservations to human rights treaties: severability and the problem of State consent," *Melbourne Journal of International Law*, vol. 5, No. 1 (May 2004).

75 Hersch Lauterpacht, in the first Report on the Law of Treaties to the International Law Commission, suggested that "rules of international morality so cogent" could constitute principles of international public policy that void treaties. See *Yearbook of the International Law Commission 1953*, vol. II. See also Michael Akehurst, who argues that morality underpins the process through which conventional or customary rules acquire a peremptory character. M. Akehurst, "The hierarchy of sources in international law," *British Yearbook of International Law*, vol. 47, No. 1 (1975), pp. 273, 283. See further International Law Commission, summary records of the 683rd meeting (A/CN.4/SR.683) (1963), para. 45, available from http://legal.un.org/ docs/ ?path=../ilc/documentation/english/summary_records/a_cn4_sr683.pdf&lang=EFS. Alfred Verdross advanced the position that the "higher interests of the whole international community" were capable of voiding "immoral treaties" in violation of a compulsory norm of general international law. A. Verdross, *Die Verfassung der Völkerrechtsgemeinschaft* (Vienna, Springer, 1926), pp. 21 ff. See further A. Verdross, "Jus dispositivum and jus cogens," in *International Law in the Twentieth Century*, L. Gross, ed. (New York, Appleton-Century-Crofts, 1969), pp. 222–223; Hermann Mosler, *The International Society as a Legal Community* (Springer, 1980), p. 142; R. Y. Jennings, "Nullity and effectiveness in international law" in *Cambridge Essays in International Law: Essays in Honour of Lord McNair* (London, 1965), pp. 64, 74; G. Hernandez, "A reluctant guardian: the International Court of Justice and the concept of 'international community'," *British Yearbook of International Law*, vol. 83, No. 1 (2012), pp. 13–60.

76 C. Tams and others, eds., *Research Handbook on the Law of Treaties* (Elgar, 2014). S. Talmon, "The duty not to recognize as lawful a situation created by the illegal use of force or other serious breaches of a *jus cogens* obligation" in C. Tomuschat and J.-M. Thouvenin, eds., *The Fundamental Rules of the International Legal Order* (Nijhoff, 2006).

77 A. Kiss, "Abuse of rights" in R. Wolfrum, *Max Planck Encyclopaedia of Public International Law*, vol. I (2006), pp. 20–26. M. Byers, "Abuse of rights: an old principle, a new age," *McGill Law Journal*, vol. 47 (2002), pp. 389–431. See for instance the reference to abuse of rights in *Trail smelter case (United States, Canada), Reports of International Arbitral Awards*, vol. III,p. 1905 and in article 300 of the United Nations Convention on the Law of the Sea: "States Parties shall fulfil in good faith the obligations ... in a manner which would not constitute an abuse of right." See also V. Paul, "Abuse of rights and bona fides in international

law" in Österreichische Zeitschrift *für* öffentliches *Recht und Völkerrecht* , vol. 28 (1977), pp. 107–130; B. O. Iluyomade, "The scope and content of a complaint of abuse of right in international law," *Harvard International Law Journal*, vol. 16 (1975), pp. 47–92.

78 H. Pontell and G. Geis, eds., *White Collar and Corporate Crime* (Springer, 2007). Cf. Cesare Lombroso, "Delitti vecchi e deliti nuove," 1902, anticipating Edwin Sutherland's *White Collar Crime*, 1949.

79 http://csis.org/files/publication/141029_investor_state_dispute_settlement.pdf. See also http://ttip2015.eu/blog-detail/blog/isds%20risks.html.

80 *The United Mexican States v. Metalclad Corporation* , Supreme Court of British Columbia, Reasons for judgement of the Honourable Mr. Justice Tyson, 22 May 2001, para. (99).

81 Citing *Private Rights, Public Problems: A Guide to NAFTA's Controversial Chapter on Investor Rights* (Winnipeg, Canada, International Institute for Sustainable Development and World Wildlife Fund, 2001), p. 33. See also https://gusvanharten.files.wordpress.com/ 2015/05/ appendix-c-opinion-articles-of-g-van-harten.pdf.

82 http://kluwerarbitrationblog.com/blog/2012/12/19/icsids-largest-award-in-history-an-overview-of-occidental-petroleum-corporation-v-the-republic-of-ecuador/.

83 International Centre for Settlement of Investment Disputes, *Occidental Petroleum Corporation v. Ecuador* (case No. ARB/06/11), award, 5 October 2012, para. 527.

84 www.italaw.com/cases/906. https://systemicdisorder.wordpress.com/tag/ trans-pacific-partnership/.

85 http://business-humanrights.org/en/hague-tribunal-rules-for-ecuador-in-investment-arbitration-with-chevron-govt%E2%80%99s-settlement-with-firm-did-not-preclude-oil-pollution-case-by-ecuadorian-plaintiffs.

86 www.isdscorporateattacks.org/#!energy/cqoo.

87 www.who.int/fctc/signatories_parties/en/. www.triplepundit.com/2015/04/philip-morris-vs-uruguay-lawsuit-a-threat-to-smoking-restrictions-worldwide/. www.italaw.com/cases/460.

88 *Philip Morris Asia Limited v. The Commonwealth of Australia* , Order of the High Court of Australia (Tobacco Plain Packaging Act). www.italaw.com/sites/default/files/case-documents/italaw1103.pdf. www.ag.gov.au/tobaccoplainpackaging.

89 www.iisd.org/pdf/2012/iisd_itn_january_2012_en.pdf.

90 www.southcentre.int/wp-content/uploads/2015/07/IPB3_India's-Experience-with-BITs_ENdf.

91 www.beuc.eu/blog/the-micula-case-when-isds-messes-with-eu-law/.

92 https://intercontinentalcry.org/inter-american-commission-on-human-rights-gives-in-to-pressure-from-guetamala/; www.oas.org/en/iachr/indigenous/protection/precautionary.asp; http://en.centralamericadata.com/en/article/home/Temporary_Closure_of_Marlin_Mine_Ordered_in_Guatemala. http://en.centralamericadata.com/en/search?q1=content_en_le:%22Inter-American+Commission+on+Human+Rights+%28IACHR%29%22.

93 www1.umn.edu/humanrts/cases/69-04.html.

94 *Ethyl Corporation v. Canada*, award on jurisdiction, judgement of 24 June 1998.

95 D. Gantz, "The evolution of FTA investment provisions: from NAFTA to the United States-Chile Free Trade Agreement," *American University International Law Review*, vol. 19, No. 4 (2003), p. 684.

96 The Ethyl Corporation case (1996–1998) is discussed in *Private Rights, Public Problems*, pp. 71–72.

97 R. Stumberg, "Safeguards for tobacco control: options for the TPPA," *American Journal of Law and Medicine*, vol. 39, Nos. 2 and 3 (2013), pp. 382–441. TPPA stands for Trans-Pacific Partnership Agreement.

98 www.acwl.ch/e/disputes/tech_exp_fund.html.

99 www.citizen.org/documents/NAFTAReport_Final.pdf.

100 http://corporateeurope.org/international-trade/2014/04/still-not-loving-isds-10-reasons-oppose-investors-super-rights-eu-trade.

101 Ibid.

102   www.italaw.com/documents/VivendiSecondAnnulmentDecision.pdf.
103   UNCTAD, *World Investment Report 2015*, p. 180.
104   Winnie Ma, "Public policy in the judicial enforcement of arbitral awards," thesis submitted for the degree of Doctor of Juridical Science, Bond University, Australia, 2005.
105   C. Olivet and P. Eberhardt, *Profiting from Crisis: How Corporations and Lawyers are Scavenging Profits from Europe's Crisis Countries* (Amsterdam/Brussels, Transnational Institute and Corporate Europe Observatory, 2014). See also www.theguardian.com/commentisfree/2013/nov/04/us-trade-deal-full-frontal-assault-on-democracy.
106   www.chathamhouse.org/event/corporate-responsibility-international-crimes. www.chathamhouse.org/sites/files/chathamhouse/field/field_publication_docs/INTA91_1_03_Ainleypdf. At an important conference held at the International Law Department of the University of Jaén, Spain, from 20 to 24 July 2015 on issues of economic crimes and universal jurisdiction, including a panel entitled "Crimenes económicos y financieros" moderated by Judge Baltasar Garzón and Professor Carmen Márquez, participants agreed that some economic crimes have consequences such that subjecting them to universal jurisdiction is justified. See also C. Wells, *Corporations and Criminal Responsibility*, 2nd ed. (Oxford University Press, 2002).
  L. Kaplan, "Some reflections on corporate criminal responsibility," address before the New York State Bar Association, 24 January 2007. Madrid Principles on Universal Jurisdiction, available from https://ujprinciples.wordpress.com/principles/.
107   Quoted in http://works.bepress.com/matthew_rimmer/178/ and reflected in an open letter signed by 100 leading professors, judges and lawyers from Trans-Pacific Partnership countries, including Justice Elizabeth Evatt, former member of the Human Rights Committee, urging the rejection of investor-State dispute settlement. Available from https://tpplegal.wordpress.com/open-letter/.
108   A/69/299, A/HRC/19/59/Add.5, A/HRC/25/57 and the forthcoming reports of the Independent Expert on the effects of foreign debt and other related international financial obligations of States on the full enjoyment of all human rights, particularly economic, social and cultural rights, and the Special Rapporteur on the rights of indigenous peoples to the General Assembly at its present session.
109   P. Juillard, "Calvo Doctrine/Calvo Clause," in Wolfrum, pp. 1086–1093 (2012). See also International Law Commission, "Third report on diplomatic protection by John Dugard, Special Rapporteur" (2002) (A/CN.4/523/Add.1); C. Dalrymple, "Politics and foreign direct investment: the Multilateral Investment Guarantee Agency and the Calvo Clause," *Cornell International Law Journal*, vol. 29, No. 1 (1996), pp. 1161–1189.
110   www.ilo.org/global/about-the-ilo/who-we-are/ilo-director-general/statements-and-speeches/WCMS_378984/lang--en/index.htm.
111   see the 2001 Doha Declaration https://www.who.int/medicines/areas/policy/doha_declaration/en/
  https://www.wto.org/english/tratop_e/dda_e/dohaexplained_e.htm .
112   Formerly known as "public symposium," www.wto.org/english/forums_e/public_forum_e/public_forum_e.htm.
113   See above endnote 111.
114   www.ohchr.org/en/NewsEvents/Pages/DisplayNews.aspx?NewsID=16870&LangID=E.
115   www.wto.org/english/docs_e/legal_e/04-wto_e.htm.
116   www.globaljustice.org.uk/blog/2015/dec/23/what-really-happened-wto-summit.
117   www.wto.org/english/thewto_e/minist_e/mc10_e/mindecision_e.htm.
118   http://thewire.in/17950/news-of-dohas-death-may-be-premature-but-india-china-must-fight-to-save-the-day/; Chakravarthi Raghavan, *The Third World in the Third Millennium CE* (Penang, Third World Network, 2014).
119   www.wto.org/english/news_e/news13_e/ds456rfc_06feb13_e.htm;
  www.ictsd.org/bridges-news/biores/news/us-launches-new-wto-challenge-against-india-solar-incentives; and www.wto.org/english/tratop_e/dispu_e/cases_e/ds456_e.htm.

120 www.wto.org/english/docs_e/legal_e/06-gatt_e.htm.
121 www.wto.org/english/news_e/news16_e/ds456apl_20apr16_e.htm.
122 www.pv-magazine.com/news/details/beitrag/india-confirms-it-will-file-16-solar-cases-against-us-under-wto-dispute_100024597/#axzz49OIWaEFn
123 www.bbc.com/news/world-asia-india-35668342.
124 Robert Wade, "The role of industrial policy in developing countries," in UNCTAD, Rethinking Development Strategies after the Global Financial Crisis, vol. I, pp. 67–80; José Salazar-Xirinachs, Irmgard Nübler and Richard Kozul-Wright (eds.), Transforming Economies: Making industrial policy work for growth, jobs and development (Geneva, ILO, 2014).
125 https://stopttipitalia.files.wordpress.com/2014/02/capaldottip_rejoinder.pdf.
126 Noam Chomsky, *Who Rules the World?* (London, Penguin, 2016); www.youtube.com/watch?v=P2lsEVlqts0.
127 www.counterpunch.org/2016/05/11/the-dangers-of-free-trade-agreements-ttips-threat-to-europes-elderly; Michael Hudson, *Killing the Host* (Petrolia, Counterpunch Books, 2015).
128 www.globalexchange.org/events/speaker/deborah-james.
129 Douglas Thomson, "Kahale calls for overhaul of BIT system," *Global Arbitration Review*, Vol. 9, No. 3 (11 April 2014); www.chambersandpartners.com/global/person/50001/george-kahale-iii.
130 www.euractiv.com/section/trade-society/news/un-blasts-eu-for-backing-global-deal-for-isds-but-not-for-country-bailouts/.
131 www.ilo.org/newyork/events-and-meetings/WCMS_237980/lang--en/index.htm; www.ilo.org/global/docs/WCMS_214366/lang--en/index.htm.
132 www.youtube.com/watch?v=P_FBjYZBWH0. Max Otte calls investor-State dispute settlement "a complete disempowerment of politics."
133 www.gov.uk/government/uploads/system/uploads/attachment_data/file/260380/bis-13-1284-costs-and-benefits-of-an-eu-usa-investment-protection-treaty.pdf; www.rowmaninternational.com/books/rule-makers-or-rule-takers
134 www.theguardian.com/global-development-professionals-network/2015/mar/24/could-the-ttip-trade-deal-undo-development-gains;
www.huffingtonpost.com/roger-hickey/economist-jeffrey-sachs-s_b_5823918.html.
135 Joseph Stiglitz, *Rewriting the Rules of the American Economy* (New York, W.W. Norton, 2015); *The Great Divide: Unequal Societies and what we can do about them* (New York, W.W. Norton, 2015).
136 http://thetyee.ca/Opinion/2016/01/18/TPP-Foreign-Investors/; http://thetyee.ca/Opinion/2013/11/12/Harper-Gives-Up-Sovereignty/.
137 Robert Wade "Growth, inequality, and poverty: arguments, evidence, and economists," in *Global political economy*, John Ravenhill, ed. (Oxford, Oxford University Press, 2014); "Current thinking about global trade policy," *Economic and Political Weekly*, vol. 49, No. 6. (8 Feb. 2014); "'Market versus State' or 'market with State': how to impart directional thrust," *Development and Change*, vol. 45, No. 4 (July 2014).
138 On 4 May 2016, the European Court of Justice upheld the 2014 Tobacco Products Directive against challenges from British-American Tobacco (BAT) and Philip Morris, http://curia.europa.eu/jcms/upload/docs/application/pdf/2016-05/cp160048en.pdf?version=meter+at+null&module=meter-Links&pgtype=article&contentId=&mediaId=&referrer=https%3A%2F%2Fwww.google.ch%2F&pri ority=true&action=click&contentCollection=meter-links-click.
139 Typically they range from 10 to 30 years in investment treaties, when one accounts for the minimum terms plus survival clauses. The Independent Expert is not aware of other treaties that have such long lock-in periods that hinder future elected Governments from revisiting treaties. Democratic Governments must never be bound by such treaties generation after generation.
140 http://business-humanrights.org/en/binding-treaty/un-human-rights-council-sessions. https://www.business-humanrights.org/en/big-issues/binding-treaty. . 20
141 Kinda Mohamadieh and Daniel Uribe, "Business and Human Rights," *South Bulletin*, vols. 87-88, 23 November 2015. On 25 September 2015, Pope Francis said before the General Assembly:

"We must avoid every temptation to fall into a declarationist nominalism which would assuage our consciences. We need to ensure that our institutions are truly effective in the struggle against all these scourges," http://w2.vatican.va/content/francesco/en/speeches/2015/september/documents/papa-francesco_20150925_onu-visita.html.

142 https://www.business-humanrights.org/en/big-issues/binding-treaty/zero-draft-unofficial-summary/

143 https://www.business-humanrights.org/en/big-issues/binding-treaty/revised-draft-unofficial-summary/

144 https://www.ohchr.org/Documents/HRBodies/HRCouncil/WGTransCorp/Session6/OEIGWG_Chair-Rapporteur_second_revised_draft_LBI_on_TNCs_and_OBEs_with_respect_to_Human_Rights.pdf

145 www.theage.com.au/interactive/2016/the-bribe-factory/day-1/the-company-that-bribed-the-world.html.

146 www.congoweek.org/en/coltan-facts.html.

147 http://iworry.org/crisis/?gclid=COnuwKXxks0CFVIaGwod6hMH2g.

Chapter 9

TAXATION AND HUMAN RIGHTS

> "Our international banking system allows banks to accept funds gained from tax evasion and other crimes and thereby facilitates and encourages embezzlement by public officials, especially in developing countries, as well as tax evasion and tax avoidance by multinational corporations."
>
> THOMAS POGGE
> Director of the Global Justice Program and
> Leitner Professor of Philosophy and International Affairs at Yale University[i]

Trillions of dollars are necessary to deliver on the Sustainable Development Goals and on COP21 commitments. More trillions will be necessary to tackle pandemics, natural and man-made disasters, desertification, volcanic eruptions, asteroid threats. Yet it is estimated that as much as thirty-two trillion dollars are held offshore in secrecy jurisdictions, escaping just taxation. Every year governments worldwide—developed and developing economies alike—lose huge sums of tax revenue through various schemes of tax avoidance and evasion, and hitherto most perpetrators have enjoyed impunity.

A human-rights-based-approach to taxation and stricter measures against tax fraud, tax evasion and tax havens are urgently needed, bearing in mind that a short-fall in tax revenues handicaps countries in the fulfillment of their ontological function to promote the well-being of all persons living under their jurisdiction and meeting their human rights treaty obligations, in particular under the International Covenant on Economic, Social and Cultural Rights.

As I outlined in my 2014 report to the Human Rights Council (A/HRC/27/51), one way of liberating funds for development lies in drastically reducing extravagantly high military expenditures, and stopping the obscene arms race and R&D into weapons of mass destruction, including chemical and biological weapons.

Another way of generating funds for public use consists in adopting legislative and administrative measures to ensure transparent and accountable fiscal and budgetary policies, so that individuals and corporations pay their fair share of taxes. Tax fraud by individuals and transnational corporations is not a gentleman's peccadillo, but a crime that should be systematically investigated, prosecuted and punished. Taxes collected from tax evaders and funds confiscated

---

i Source: https://truthout.org/articles/thomas-pogge-on-the-past-present-and-future-of-global-poverty/

from organized crime activities, drug trafficking, human trafficking, prostitution, bribery, currency speculation, embezzlement, illicit arms trade, trade in endangered species, etc. should be redirected to human rights programmes. Illicit deposits by kleptocrats[i] must be returned to the countries of origin.

As elucidated in my 2016 report to the General Assembly, a third source of revenue would be through the imposition of a financial transactions tax, which offers the additional advantage of curbing speculation and reducing the volatility of financial markets.[ii]

For decades the General Assembly has been concerned with these issues, adopting since the early 1970's pertinent resolutions on a new international economic order.[iii] After the millennium summit in 2000, the Assembly began addressing the promotion of a democratic and equitable international order, e.g. in its Resolution 70/149 of 17 December 2015 affirming that "the responsibility for managing worldwide economic and social issues ... must be shared among the nations of the world and should be exercised multilaterally." The resolution underlines "the importance of a global and inclusive post-2015 development agenda for the promotion of a democratic and equitable international order. ... [and for] the establishment of a new international economic order based on equity, sovereign equality, interdependence, common interest and cooperation among all States." My mandate is concerned because the achievement of a just world order requires significant changes in the current economic and financial regime, including just taxation worldwide.

Others experts are similarly concerned, including Jean Ziegler, former member of the Advisory Committee of the Human Rights Council, who prepared an in-depth report on vulture funds.[iv] Magdalena Sepúlveda, the former Special Rapporteur on extreme poverty, also focused on taxation issues, and the Independent Expert on foreign debt, Juan Pablo Bohoslavsky, has elucidated the impact of illicit financial flows and the necessity of sovereign debt restructuring.[v]

In the wake of the Bahamas leaks[vi] scandal, Bohoslavsky, Ziegler and another member of the Advisory Committee, Obiora Okafor, since 2018 Independent Expert on International Solidarity, issued a press release with recommendations similar to those I made in my 2016 report to the General Assembly, stressing

---

i https://www.unodc.org/documents/corruption/AddisEGM2017/Accelerated-International-Momentum-to-Return-Stolen-Assets_UNODC_IATF-Issue-Brief.pdf
https://www.thoughtco.com/kleptocracy-definition-and-examples-5092538

ii http://www.un.org/en/development/desa/news/policy/wess2012.html

iii A/RES/S-6/3201; A/RES/63/224; amongst others

iv https://www.thoughtco.com/kleptocracy-definition-and-examples-5092538
https://digitallibrary.un.org/record/847976

v https://www.ohchr.org/EN/Issues/Development/IEDebt/Pages/Debtrestructuringvulturefundsandhumanrights.aspx

vi https://www.icij.org/tags/bahamas-leaks/

that governments must eliminate tax haven secrecy and offshore tax evasion, and coordinate action to establish a United Nations body with a mandate to eliminate tax haven secrecy and offshore tax avoidance and evasion. They wrote: "When individuals and corporations hide unreported assets abroad to escape taxes or launder money, they are effectively stealing from the public. The proceeds from these illicit activities could and should be devoted to funding public services, such as health care, housing, schools, transportation infrastructure, social security, law enforcement and courts."[i] In this context it should be recalled that illicit financial flows include funds that, through legal loopholes and other artificial arrangements, circumvent the spirit of the law, including, for example, tax avoidance schemes facilitated by the use of offshore corporations. Hence, the United Nations should take efficient measures to prevent illegal activities of offshore companies located in tax havens. Worldwide tax justice and the successful fight against money-laundering will not be possible unless states cooperate to regulate the fiscal activities of offshore companies and ensure transparency and accountability, including through appropriate penal legislation. Moreover, States must set uniform minimum taxation floors, to prevent individuals and business entities from shopping for the lowest possible tax rates.

In my 2016 report to the General Assembly I urged the GA and Secretary-General António Guterres to take concerted action against abuses by individuals, speculators, hedge funds, vulture funds and transnational enterprises who skirt taxes and loot governments. Indeed, corruption, bribery, tax fraud and tax evasion have grave effects on human dignity, human rights, and human welfare and must be prosecuted nationally and internationally, including by virtue of universal jurisdiction. I urged the General Assembly to consider convening a World Conference to establish a United Nations Tax body and draft a convention that would facilitate the phasing-out of tax-havens, reduce tax competition among States and declare so-called "sweetheart deals" to be a form of illegitimate subsidy contrary to international ordre public.

While the end of tax havenry is not in sight, governments are gradually coming to realize that it is in their own interest to phase-out secrecy jurisdictions. An international tax convention is necessary to make country by country reporting meaningful and ultimately to stop competition among tax jurisdictions and abolish secrecy. Transparency and a prohibition of harmful aggressive tax avoidance should be the two main components of the treaty.

Since 2012 the G77 and China have proposed that the UN's Committee of Experts on International Cooperation in Tax Matters be transformed into a global, inclusive norm-setting body for international tax cooperation at the intergovernmental level. This Committee of 27 experts has a consultative

---

i https://www.ohchr.org/EN/NewsEvents/Pages/DisplayNews.aspx?NewsID=20644

function, but it is not a rule-making body. The idea of a UN Tax body has been gaining momentum with lawyers, economists, civil society and numerous non-governmental organizations. In preparation for the Third UN Conference on Financing for Development held in Addis Ababa in July 2015, several civil society organizations called for the establishment of a UN global tax body[i], as the most effective way to achieve an equitable global tax system, increase domestic resource mobilization and reduce intra-State and inter-State inequality.[ii] While the new Platform on Tax Collaboration of the UN, IMF, World Bank, and OECD aims for greater cooperation, only a broad representation will allow decisions on global tax rules. The UN is the only organization that can provide a space for a global political discussion on tax competition and tax cooperation.

There are three serious challenges to be faced. One is the collusion of banks, accounting firms and lawfirms in establishing phoney entities whose purpose is to hide wealth and avoid taxation. A second is the need to promote transparency and accountability and provide protection to whistleblowers. The third is the need to adopt a binding treaty on corporate social responsibility.

Euphemisms constitute an obstacle to reform, because sub-consciously many politicians, legislators, businessmen, investors, transnational corporations, the press and even the public do not "feel" that certain business activities are toxic for the human rights of billions of human beings. Tax-manipulators are euphemistically referred to as "legal providers." The very concept of a tax "haven" is a sympathetically sounding weasel word, implying the legitimacy of sheltering funds (however accrued) from predatory governments (irrespective of however such revenues might be spent).

"Tax havens" or "shelters" are really corruption ports. In the absence of specific criminal legislation, so-called "tax optimization" may be "legal," but some forms are borderline with what otherwise would constitute tax fraud, racketeering, or conspiracy to defraud. How else can one judge the collusion of business lobbies, politicians, tax lawyers, banks, accounting and consulting firms in the creation of a thoroughly artificial system with special tax laws, "incentives" and loopholes that serve no economic or job-creating purpose but allow companies to cheat governments of tax revenue?

The present Guiding Principles on Business and Human Rights do not contain any provision concerning the obligation of businesses to pay their fair share of taxes. There is no mention of tax evasion, tax fraud or tax havens. Maybe this obligation to pay taxes could be interpreted into the Guiding Principles under the rubric "due diligence," but, of course, it would not be binding unless incorporated into a treaty.

---

i http://www.globaltaxjustice.org/wp-content/uploads/2015/02/FINAL_GATJ_FFD_position-paper_20March2015.pdf

ii http://www.globaltaxjustice.org/the-world-needs-a-un-global-tax-body-now/

Exploitation of loopholes directed by an organised tax avoidance industry dominated by four accounting firms and avidly copied by others is having disastrous impacts on human rights. *"Accounting firms have set the standards to suit themselves... working in collusion with company executives to boost their rewards by hyping shareholder value at the expense of investment, social interests and long term survival."*[i] Not only does this behaviour illustrate a selfish approach to business driven by short-term profit, but most importantly it severely undermines democracy and the welfare of the people.

Whistleblowing is one of the most effective methods of shining light on corruption.[ii] Thanks to their revelations a public debate on tax havens has started that is providing momentum for legislative changes to abolish secrecy jurisdictions. But whistleblowers often pay a heavy price. It is in the spirit of a democratic and equitable international order to adopt legislation to protect whistleblowers and witnesses from reprisals and to provide them with easy-to-access avenues to make disclosures. As civil society has found, there are important shortcomings especially concerning the absence of anonymous channels for employees to discreetly report sensitive information.[iii] Hence, a charter on the rights of whistleblowers and a "protected disclosure defence" should be adopted by the United Nations, pursuant to which criminal or civil liability for protected disclosures is waved and an "authorized channel" is provided for such disclosures.

Because the tax activities of domestic and transnational corporations have significant direct and indirect socioeconomic impacts, a binding legal instrument on corporate social responsibility should be adopted, stipulating the obligation to pay taxes where the profits are generated and a prohibiting corporations from shifting profits to secrecy jurisdictions. This would encourage responsible tax behaviour that does not harm global financial stability, development, and human rights.

There is an urgent need for a paradigm shift. While it is generally assumed that companies bring in foreign direct investments and create employment, this should not become a pretext to let them operate outside or even against any framework. It is not acceptable that companies invest faceless, make immense profit while forcing population displacement and do not subscribe to the most basic environment and human rights standards. This must cease.

---

i Austin Mitchell, Prem Sikka, *The Pin-Stripe Mafia: How Accountancy Firms Destroy Societies*, 2011. Jim Cousins, Austin Mitchell, Prem Sikka, Race to the Bottom: The case of the accountancy firms, 2004.

ii see the 2015 report of the Advisory Committee of the Human Rights Council on the negative impact of corruption on the enjoyment of human rights https://undocs.org/A/HRC/28/73

iii https://www.transparency.de/fileadmin/pdfs/Themen/Hinweisgebersysteme/Whistleblower-Protection-Laws-in-G20-Countries-Priorities-for-Action.pdf

A democratic and equitable international order as envisaged in the United Nations Charter requires international solidarity to achieve sustainable development and human rights for all.

It is time for the General Assembly to convene a World Conference under the auspices of the United Nations Conference on Trade and Development with a mandate to outlaw tax havens and establish a global, inclusive norm-setting body for international tax cooperation at the intergovernmental level.

What follows are excerpts from my 2016 report to the General Assembly.[i]
—AdeZ

* * *

INTRODUCTION

Since the early 1970s the General Assembly has adopted resolutions on a new international economic order.[1] After the turn of the millennium, the Assembly began to address the promotion of a democratic and equitable international order.[2] In its resolution 70/149, the Assembly affirmed that the responsibility for managing worldwide economic and social issues, as well as threats to international peace and security, must be shared among the nations of the world and should be exercised multilaterally, and that efforts to make globalization fully inclusive and equitable must include policies and measures at the global level that corresponded to the needs of developing countries and countries with economies in transition and were formulated and implemented with their effective participation. The Assembly underlined the importance of a global and inclusive post-2015 development agenda for the promotion of a democratic and equitable international order and of the establishment of a new international economic order based on equity, sovereign equality, interdependence, common interest and cooperation among all States, irrespective of their economic and social systems, which would correct inequalities, redress existing injustices and make it possible to eliminate the widening gap between the developed and the developing countries.

A peaceful and just world order has long been a concern of the international community, and in particular of the Commission on Human Rights,[3] the Subcommission on Promotion and Protection of Human Rights,[4] the Human Rights Council[5] and its special procedures and Advisory Committee,[6] the United Nations Conference on Trade and Development (UNCTAD),[7] as well as intergovernmental organizations, including the Organisation for

---

i Excerpts of my remarks to the General Assembly on 20 October 2016, https://www.ohchr.org/en/NewsEvents/Pages/DisplayNews.aspx?NewsID=20805&LangID=E

Economic Co-operation and Development (OECD), all of which have provided invaluable reports. Alas, seldom do their recommendations result in thoroughgoing reform of international financial rules or investment regimes. Cosmetic changes are not enough. What is needed is bold and concerted action by Governments, not more diagnoses.

Notwithstanding the hard-law quality of the international human rights treaty regime, there are no adequate enforcement mechanisms. The reality is that "the economy" seldom takes into account the needs of destitute people but reflects the interests of elites, who mostly oppose reforms. Pursuant to the Charter of the United Nations, the Organization has the mandate to change the rules so that human rights, including the right to development, take priority over economic mantras. At various United Nations summits, in the United Nations Millennium Declaration, in the Sustainable Development Goals, at the twenty-first session of the Conference of the Parties to the United Nations Framework Convention on Climate Change, held in Paris in December 2015, and at the United Nations conferences on human settlements,[8] States rhetorically recognized the need to reorient the economy; but pledges and soft law rarely achieve results, and even legally binding treaties do not deliver unless there is transparency, accountability and enforcement. The announcement by the Group of Twenty (G-20) in 2009 that the "era of bank secrecy was over" has been followed by some good initiatives, notably the OECD Global Forum on Transparency and Exchange of Information for Tax Purposes[9] and the development of the Standard for Automatic Exchange of Financial Account Information (the Common Reporting Standard); but these have only made a dent on tax havens.[10]

The current international economic order manifests growing inequalities among States and within States. How should these inequalities be corrected and by whom? Whereas the United Nations is not a world government, but only a coordinator of global activities, the real powers that set the economic order are the major economic powers, transnational corporations and three international organizations—the World Trade Organization, the World Bank and the International Monetary Fund (IMF)—none of which is subject to direct supervision by the United Nations and only have loose association agreements with the United Nations system.[11] It is time to harmonize the policies of these three organizations with the purposes and principles of the Organization and to ensure that their actions do not conflict with or even frustrate the implementation of United Nations programmes.

There are systemic obstacles to changing this situation, among them asymmetrical power relationships; unfair taxation; lack of transparency and accountability; unjust enrichment; widespread corruption;[12] bribery;

embezzlement; secrecy; collusion among lobbies, accounting and consulting firms and law firms; and vested interests of domestic and transnational corporations. These should be met by stricter implementation of domestic and international penal law.[13] Current practice has a detrimental impact on human rights as it deprives States of resources needed to fulfil their human rights treaty obligations concerning the administration of justice, maintenance of infrastructures, health care, education and housing, and prevents them from implementing pledges for the Sustainable Development Goals and for environmental protection pursuant to the Paris Agreement.

The Independent Expert recognizes that a democratic and equitable international order cannot be achieved without adequate funding. A human rights-based approach to taxation and stricter measures against tax fraud, tax evasion and tax havens are urgently needed because a shortfall in tax revenues handicaps Governments in meeting human rights treaty obligations. Trillions of dollars are needed. As the Independent Expert outlined in his 2014 report to the Human Rights Council (A/HRC/27/51), one way of liberating funds is by drastically reducing military expenditures. Another way is by ensuring transparent and accountable fiscal and budgetary policies, so that individuals and corporations pay their fair share of taxes. Tax fraud should be systematically prosecuted and punished, and funds confiscated from organized crime activities, drug trafficking, illicit arms trade, trade in endangered species, etc. should be redirected to human rights programmes. Illicit deposits by kleptocrats must be returned to the countries of origin.[14] A further source of revenue would be through the imposition of a financial transactions tax, which would have the additional advantage of curbing speculation and reducing the volatility of financial markets.[15]

In a report submitted to the Human Rights Council at its twenty-sixth session, the Special Rapporteur on extreme poverty and human rights, Magdalena Sepúlveda, focused on fiscal and budgetary policy as a major component of human rights implementation, especially when tackling inequality and generating revenue for sustainable development, poverty reduction, education and job-and infrastructure-creation. Taxation must foster stronger governance, accountability and participation in public affairs. Principles of non-discrimination and equality and the duty of international cooperation and assistance should inform taxation policies at the global and national levels.[16]

At the twenty-eighth session of the Human Rights Council, the Independent Expert on the effects of foreign debt and other related international financial obligations of States on the full enjoyment of human rights, particularly economic, social and cultural rights, Juan Pablo Bohoslavsky, submitted an interim report on illicit financial flows and the post-2015 development agenda (A/HRC/28/60 and Corr.1). In his final report he observed, rather diplomatically:

> Financial institutions that facilitate tax evasion and transnational corporations that employ aggressive tax planning strategies must recognize that their actions may have negative human rights impacts. They can demonstrate respect for human rights through appropriate policies and due diligence procedures, through country-by-country reporting, including publishing information about the taxes they pay to each country in which they operate. Similarly, the professionals that make up the tax planning industry, such as lawyers, accountants, bankers and wealth managers, must take responsibility for their contributions to the harms caused by tax abuse. (A/HRC/3161, para. 56).

The author of the present report would speak, more pointedly, of white-collar criminality that has enjoyed a high level of anonymity and impunity. Indeed, it is the infrastructure of intermediaries, including tax advisers, law firms, accountants and trust service providers, that facilitates tax evasion and avoidance as well as cross-border illicit financial flows. Every strategy to tackle the intermediaries, euphemistically called "enablers" or "service providers," must be part of the effort to tackle tax evasion.

The present report is an interim report on the adverse impacts of unfair fiscal and budgetary policies on the international order, in which the Independent Expert gives due attention to the professional analysis of intergovernmental organizations such as the Geneva-based South Centre and the OECD and its Tax Inspectors Without Borders initiative,[17] as well as research conducted by civil society organizations including the International Bar Association,[18] Global Policy Forum,[19] Global Justice Now,[20] Global Alliance for Tax Justice,[21] Oxfam,[22] Centre Europe-tiers monde,[23] Business and Human Rights Resource Centre,[24] Tax Justice Network,[25] Center for Economic Policy Research,[26] Centre for Economic and Social Rights,[27] Shift,[28] Citizens for Tax Justice,[29] Transparency International,[30] Independent Commission for the Reform of International Corporate Taxation,[31] Global Reporting Initiative,[32] Organized Crime and Corruption Reporting Project,[33] Friedrich Ebert Stiftung,[34] AllianceSud,[35] Comité catholique contre la faim et pour le développement-terre solidaire,[36] Secours Catholique-Caritas France,[37] Plateforme paradis fiscaux et judiciaires[38] and others. The Independent Expert adds his voice to those of the various groups and organizations which have undertaken initiatives in this area and calls on Governments to take urgent action to correct the glaring injustices perpetuated by the systematic avoidance of taxes through tax havens that siphon off trillions of dollars from the economies of many countries, including developing countries.

In May 2016 more than 300 leading economists and lawyers appealed to Governments to work for fiscal transparency. Olivier Blanchard, Angus Deaton, Nora Lustig and Thomas Piketty expressed the view that tax havens served no economic purpose, and that they should end. In particular, they called on Governments to adopt global rules requiring companies to publicly report taxable activities in every country in which they operated and to ensure that all territories publicly disclosed information about the real owners of companies and trusts. "As the Panama Papers and other recent exposés have revealed, the secrecy provided by tax havens fuels corruption and undermines countries' ability to collect their fair share of taxes."[39]

The Special Adviser to the Secretary-General on the 2030 Agenda for Sustainable Development, Jeffrey Sachs, stated: "Tax havens do not just happen. The British Virgin Islands did not become a tax and secrecy haven through its own efforts. These havens are the deliberate choice of major governments, especially the United Kingdom and the United States, in partnership with major financial, accounting, and legal institutions that move the money."[40]

Part of the problem lies in the mantras of market fundamentalism and the belief that financial markets should be deregulated because this ultimately benefits everyone, including the poor. Although no empirical evidence exists to back this up, transnational corporations and the super-rich have succeeded in creating an enabling environment for systematic looting of society. Collusion between the world's biggest banks, specialized law firms, and consulting and accounting firms has led to a global system designed to hide money and avoid taxes by virtue of secretive offshore structures. This is unethical, and should be perceived as such by professional associations, law schools and business schools. Yet, instead of prohibiting activities that are clearly *contra bonos mores*[41] and may amount to conspiracy, or even a form of racketeering, States have entered into a kind of self-destructive competition among themselves to see which jurisdiction offers greater secrecy facilities. The situation has been a bonanza for lawyers and accounting firms and become toxic to the fiscal health of many countries, particularly since financial globalization expanded in the 1980s and 1990s. The offshore world corrupts and distorts markets and investments, shaping them in ways that have nothing to do with efficiency.[42]

Whistle-blowing is one of the most effective methods of shining a light on corruption. Thanks to the revelations of whistleblowers a public debate on tax havens has started that is providing momentum for legislative changes to abolish secrecy jurisdictions. But whistleblowers often pay a heavy price. It is in the spirit of a democratic and equitable international order to adopt legislation to protect whistleblowers and witnesses from reprisals and to provide them with easy-to-access avenues to make disclosures. Transparency International has published a report on whistleblower protection laws,[43] and a recent study by several institutions entitled "Whistleblower protection laws in G20 countries: priorities for action" analyses the state of whistleblower protection rules and finds important shortcomings, especially concerning the absence of anonymous channels for employees to discreetly report sensitive information.[44] Luxembourg Leaks ("LuxLeaks"), "SwissLeaks" and the Panama Papers lay bare the way that financial secrecy facilitates corruption when individuals and corporations can hide behind layers of anonymous companies, trusts and foundations.

In the period following his 2015 report to the General Assembly, the Independent Expert sent communications to States and questionnaires to Governments and intergovernmental organizations, and participated in international conferences, academic symposia and United Nations side events as outlined in his report to the Human Rights Council (A/HRC/33/40).

FACTS AND IMPLICATIONS

OECD had defined a tax haven as "a country which imposes a low or no tax, and is used by corporations to avoid tax which otherwise would be payable in a high-tax country [T]ax havens have the following key characteristics: No or only nominal taxes; Lack of effective exchange of information; Lack of transparency in the operation of the legislative, legal or administrative provisions."[45] OECD subsequently set up the Global Forum on Transparency and Exchange of Information for Tax Purposes and implemented a rigorous peer review process with ratings to determine compliance with international standards in tax transparency.[46]

The Whistleblower Justice Network suggests the following definition: "a country (or territory) whose laws make the country attractive as a tax shelter for foreign money."[47]

According to Tax Justice Network, there are over 100 "secrecy jurisdictions," a term preferred over tax havens for which there is no definition based on objectively verifiable criteria. The Network's global analysis reveals that there is a spectrum of financial secrecy in most jurisdictions assessed and that what is needed is a reform of the system, rather than looking for "unproblematic" jurisdictions.

Also according to Tax Justice Network, an estimated $21 -$32 trillion of private financial wealth is located offshore, untaxed or lightly taxed, in secrecy jurisdictions around the world. Estimated revenue losses are on the order of $190 billion annually.[48] According to UNCTAD, this costs developing countries more than $100 billion annually.[49]

The Tax Justice Network Financial Secrecy Index ranks jurisdictions according to their secrecy and the scale of their offshore financial activities (see annex). The top three jurisdictions listed in the 2015 index were Switzerland, Hong Kong, China,[50] and the United States.[51] Other high-profile jurisdictions include the United Kingdom of Great Britain and Northern Ireland and its Overseas Territories and Crown Dependencies, Luxembourg, the Netherlands, Belgium, Malta,[52] Cyprus, Singapore, Liberia[53] and Panama.

According to Tax Justice Network, illicit cross-border financial flows have been estimated at $1.6 trillion per year, dwarfing the $135 billion devoted globally to "foreign aid." It is estimated that since the 1970s African countries alone have lost over $1 trillion in capital flight, while combined external debts are less than $200 billion. Viewed from this perspective, Africa is a major creditor to the world, but its assets are in the hands of a wealthy elite, protected by offshore secrecy, while the debts are shouldered by populations already suffering from extreme poverty. European countries such as Greece, Italy and Portugal have also endured decades of tax evasion via offshore secrecy.

According to University of California, Berkeley economist Gabriel Zucman, tax evasion costs Governments approximately $200 billion annually.[54]

According to OECD, the artificial schemes of base erosion and profit shifting (BEPS) result in global corporate income tax revenue losses of $100–$240 billion annually.[55]

According to Oxfam, United States corporations hide at least $1.3 trillion in tax havens.[56] Profit shifting by United States multinationals suggests that about 25-30 per cent of global profits are shifted into jurisdictions with no corresponding real economic activity.

Tax havens host a substantial portion of the world's foreign direct investment.[57]

Fifty-one of the 68 companies that borrowed money from the World Bank's private lending arm in 2015 to finance investments in sub-Saharan Africa use tax havens.[58]

OBSTACLES AND BAD PRACTICES

Euphemisms constitute an obstacle to reform, because subconsciously, many politicians, legislators, business people, investors, transnational corporations, journalists and even the public do not "feel" that business activity and trade can be toxic for the human rights of billions of human beings. They perceive business as always beneficial, and tax manipulators are euphemistically referred to as "legal providers." Many do not immediately see "tax havens" or "shelters" as corruption ports, and endorse dubious forms of "tax optimization" as perfectly "legal," although some forms are borderline activities that would otherwise constitute tax fraud, racketeering or conspiracy. How else can one characterize the collusion of business lobbies, politicians, tax lawyers, banks and accounting and consulting firms in the creation of a thoroughly artificial system with special tax laws, "incentives" and loopholes that serve no economic or job-creating purpose, but allow companies to cheat Governments of tax revenue? The Guiding Principles on Business and Human Rights do not contain any provision concerning the obligation of businesses to pay their fair share of taxes. There is no mention of tax evasion, tax fraud or tax havens. Nor is there even in the commentary of the International Bar Association.[59] It's as if businesses were exempt from human rights obligations in the field of taxation. Perhaps this obligation could be interpreted in the Guiding Principles under the rubric "due diligence," but it should have merited at least one separate article.

Exploitation of loopholes directed by an organized tax avoidance industry dominated by four accounting firms (Deloitte, PricewaterhouseCoopers, KPMG and Ernst and Young), and avidly copied by others, is having a disastrous impact on human rights. As reports have documented, "they are setting the standards to suit themselves ... working in collusion with company executives to boost their rewards by hyping shareholder value at the expense of investment, social interests and long-term survival." Not only does this behaviour illustrate an unsophisticated and selfish approach to business driven by short-term profit only, but, most importantly, it severely undermines democracy and the welfare of the people. Depriving them of essential resources for health care, education, security and other basic needs, it has led numerous Governments "to shift taxes away from giant corporations and wealthy elites to labour, consumption and savings, depressing ordinary people's purchasing power and causing economic crises."[60]

Another obstacle is a sense of false security that "someone is working to solve the problems," emanating from the fact that organizations like the OECD exist. At a meeting in New York in April 2016, a representative of Financing for Development Group, stated: "Rich countries [get] together in a closed room and decide on what they call global tax rules."[61] She noted that the current OECD-coordinated process is "extremely undemocratic" and that the rules disadvantage developing countries. For example, according to OECD rules, when a company operates in more than one country, taxes should generally be paid in the country where the company has its headquarters. This favours OECD member countries, where headquarters are often located, and disadvantages developing countries, where companies perform substantial parts of their operations. To counter this situation, the Group of 77 (G-77) and China, representing 134 Member States, have urged the United Nations to take a greater role in global tax coordination for development, arguing that that this would strengthen international cooperation in this field and allow countries, including developing countries, to have an equal say on issues related to tax matters. Unfortunately, this proposal was rejected in the Addis Ababa Action Agenda of the Third International Conference on Financing for Development, which confirmed OECD control over global tax matters. Observers feel that the exclusion of more than 100 developing countries from the opaque rule-making processes is a reason why the global tax system has become so "fragmented, dysfunctional and unfit to meet the needs of the developing world."[62] The recently launched BEPS framework aims at addressing this point.

Meanwhile intra-company royalty payments are becoming a preferred vehicle for aggressive tax avoidance. Legislation should be adopted to prohibit this kind of artificial intra-company arrangement, which serves no purpose other than to deprive the State of legitimate tax revenue.[63] The World Economic Forum would be a good place to discuss these issues, but it may be that some of the big players still cherish fiscal paradises and will delay doing away with them.[64]

Panama Papers

In April 2016, the International Consortium of Investigative Journalists (ICIJ)[65] released the Panama Papers, nearly 12 million leaked documents that detail financial information on shell companies and tax havens by a single law firm in Panama, revealing the tip of an iceberg of tax avoidance, tax evasion and kleptocracy. One may ask how many other law firms in how many other secrecy jurisdictions are doing the same thing. The publication by ICIJ in May 2016 of a searchable database of over 214,488 offshore entities created in 21 jurisdictions, stretching from Nevada to Hong Kong, China to the British Virgin Islands,[66] may provide answers.

There has been a convergence of powerful interests working hand in hand to take advantage of any loophole in tax laws and to create dubious entities and shell companies that serve no economic or entrepreneurial purpose; their principal purpose is to hide great fortunes, including those of developing world kleptocrats who have looted their countries.[67] In some cases these entities have served to launder money that has been generated through questionable activities. These practices have contributed to the worsening of economic inequality. The Panama Papers are not about Panama, or about the law firm Mossack Fonseca,[68] but about the worldwide network of secrecy jurisdictions.

In an answer to the questionnaire on the impact of tax evasion and tax havens on human rights sent by the Independent Expert,[69] the OECD stated the following:

> While it's easy to focus on the bad news from the Panama Papers and other leaks, it is important to recognize the good news as well. It is clear from the information that has become available that the steps that the global community has been taking to address transparency of ownership information are starting to work. The figures presented by the ICIJ, for example, show that the number of bearer share companies formed by Mossack and Fonseca has been in decline for some time and had fallen to almost zero in 2015. All of the jurisdictions which were used to create these companies have now either immobilized bearer shares, including Panama itself, which immobilized them in 2015, or, as in the case of Seychelles, eliminated bearer shares entirely. What all this shows is that we are on the right track and that financial centres around the world are responding to the new environment with continued improvements in the area of tax transparency. What remains to be done is to ensure the implementation of the global tax transparency and exchange of information standards in full.

Thus far, the consequences of the Panama Papers scandal have been remarkably mitigated. Only one Head of Government resigned, the Prime Minister of Iceland.[70] It appears, as in other situations involving white-collar abuses, that impunity continues. The Special Rapporteur on the rights to freedom of peaceful assembly and of association, Maina Kiai, observed at the end of an official visit to the United States in July 2016 that Wall Street bankers had looted billions of dollars through crooked schemes, devastating the finances of millions of Americans and saddling taxpayers with a massive bailout bill. He noted that as yet, he had not heard any suggestions for a "war on Wall Street theft" (similar to the "war on drugs").[71]

Tax havens and corruption

In March 2016, the *Huffington Post* published the results of a months-long investigation into Unaoil, a Monaco-based firm registered in a tax haven, the British Virgin Islands. Unaoil and its subcontractors are reported to have bribed foreign officials to help major multinational corporations win contracts, as tens of thousands of the company's internal documents allegedly show. "The investigation illustrates just how complicit big Western companies are in corruption overseas. It also shows that by enabling corruption, these companies fuel the kind of political instability that allows insurgencies like the self-described Islamic State to grow."[72]

The Unaoil bribery scandal reveals systematic bribery by numerous transnational enterprises. Besides issues of corruption, this raises issues of tax evasion, since bribes were presumably not reported or taxed. Where are these moneys harboured? According to the leaked information, government contracts worth billions of dollars were allegedly awarded to the British enterprise Rolls-Royce, the United States multinational Halliburton, the Australian company Leighton Holdings and Republic of Korea corporations Samsung and Hyundai, thanks to bribes paid on behalf of the firms. The Federal Bureau of Investigation, the United States Department of Justice and anticorruption authorities in Australia and the United Kingdom have launched a joint investigation into the "bribes-for-contracts" scandal.

The art of creating "unreality": Innovative schemes by major accounting firms

In November 2014 ICIJ obtained from a source thousands of leaked documents revealing an intricate web of tax avoidance based in Luxembourg.

Global auditing firms are the architects of offshore banking. The ICIJ website offers the following account: For more than a decade, PricewaterhouseCoopers helped Caterpillar move profits produced in the United States to a tiny subsidiary in Switzerland. Although parts were shipped from suppliers to the United States and then shipped from the warehouse to independent dealers, the profits were booked by the Swiss subsidiary, which paid corporate taxes of less than 6 per cent a year, far lower than Caterpillar's 29 percent rate in the United States. By 2008, partners at the accounting firm worried that the strategy might be threatened by Caterpillar's decision to move some managers to the United States, a shift that would underline the parts business' small footprint in Switzerland. A PricewaterhouseCoopers partner who had helped design the tax-savings plan wrote to a colleague that they needed to "create a story" that "put some distance" between the managers and the spare-parts business. The colleague noted that, in any case, both would be retired before the strategy came up for audit. At a hearing before the United States Congress in 2015, Senator Carl Levin criticized the profit-shifting strategy as an exercise in the art of "creating unreality." An investigation revealed that the accounting firm had exploited legal loopholes to help Caterpillar shift $8 billion in paper profits from the United States to Switzerland, reducing the equipment maker's United States tax bill by $2.4 billion.[73]

ICIJ goes on to explain how internal company documents in Luxembourg revealed that PwC helped PepsiCo, Ikea and other corporate giants implement abstruse profit-shifting strategies allowing them to slash their tax bills by billions of dollars. Meanwhile, in the United States, authorities were investigating another major accounting firm, KPMG, for promoting offshore tax shelters that created billions of dollars in fake losses and allegedly misled the Internal Revenue Service about the shelters. In New York, another accounting firm, Deloitte, was being investigated for helping a British bank violate sanctions against the Islamic Republic of Iran, submitting a "watered-down" report to regulators.

In Dubai, Ernst and Young allegedly helped the largest gold refiner in the Middle East with obscure practices that may violate international standards aimed at combating trafficking in "conflict gold" from regions where competition for the mineral has led to bloodshed.

Although KPMG and PwC contend that they have strict codes of conduct for everyone working under their banners worldwide,[74] there seems still to be a very long way to go for accounting firms to understand what ethics, accountability and social justice mean.

The issue arises whether Governments see the major accounting firms as they viewed the big banks, "too big to fail." This attitude discourages reform, because partners know that Governments will only go so far in punishing bad behaviour. Most worrisome are revolving door practices and the infiltration of Government by the major auditing firms, which have gained influence and inside knowledge by helping Governments write the laws that establish the offshore system's rules of engagement, and by lobbying heavily to keep the rules to their liking. Austin Mitchell, a former Member of Parliament in the United Kingdom, has gone so far as to call the auditing firms "more powerful than government."[75] Critics contend that executives of the major accounting firms shuttle between the accounting industry and government so often in Europe and other regions that it undermines authorities ' efforts to police the industry and enforce tax laws.

LuxLeaks and the protection of whistleblowers

The Luxembourg Leaks investigation is based on a confidential cache of secret tax agreements approved by Luxembourg authorities that provide "tax relief" for more than 350 companies around the world. Although against national and international *ordre public*, the private deals are technically legal in Luxembourg.[76] The fact that the then President of Luxembourg became President of the European Commission in 2014 raises questions as to his commitment to end tax avoidance.[77] Unfortunately, the European Parliament failed to establish a committee of inquiry into the LuxLeaks scandal, as demanded by numerous parliamentarians.[78]

The whistleblowers who revealed the tax abuse were tried in the first half of 2016.[79] On 29 June, two former PricewaterhouseCoopers employees received suspended sentences of 12 and 9 months[80] respectively for leaking documents revealing how Luxembourg granted lucrative tax breaks that saved firms including Apple, Ikea and PepsiCo billions of dollars in taxes.[81] We seem to live in an upside-down world, in which whistleblowers are convicted and those who loot society are not. Whistleblowers are heroes of our time, serving society and human rights. It is urgent for parliaments to adopt robust legislation not only to protect whistleblowers, but also to reward them for contributing to ethics and integrity, especially in a sector where professional secrecy is at a peak.[82]

Instead of thoroughly investigating and, where necessary, taking penal measures against those involved in the LuxLeaks scandal, in May 2016 the European Union approved the Directive on the protection of undisclosed know-how and business information (trade secrets) against their unlawful acquisition, use and disclosure,[83] which civil society fears may enable lawsuits against journalists, trade unionists or whistleblowers who publish internal information from a company.[84]

Other whistleblowers involved in litigation are:

- Daniel Schlicksup, whose whistleblower retaliation suit against Caterpillar in 2012 led to the hearing of the United States Senate Permanent Subcommittee on Investigations on "Caterpillar's Offshore Tax Strategy."
- Bradley Charles Birkenfeld, whose disclosures led to a massive fraud investigation against the Swiss bank UBS and other banks by the United States Government; Mr. Birkenfeld was sentenced to prison in 2009.
- Swiss auditor Rudolf Elmer, who has been pursued by Swiss courts, allegedly for breaking Swiss banking secrecy while he was working in the Cayman Islands.
- Stéphanie Gibaud, who worked for UBS in Paris, was harassed and eventually fired after she made allegations about the company. In March 2015 a French labour tribunal ruled that she had been bullied by the bank.
- Rafi Rotem, who exposed a serious case of corruption in the Israeli Tax Authority and was fired.

Tax competition and "incentives"

Competition among States to see which will tax less can only lead to further impoverishment of States and aggravation of domestic and international inequality.[85] In her report on taxation and human rights (A/HRC/26/28 and Corr.1), the Special Rapporteur on extreme poverty and human rights, Magdalena Sepúlveda, deplored the difficulties in reaching an international agreement on tax cooperation, observing that low-income States and States with high debt levels or loans from international financial institutions had lost sovereignty over their tax policy and that their actions were frequently constrained by powerful countries, international financial institutions and business interests. She noted that tax sovereignty was also undermined by competition for foreign investment between developing countries, creating a "race to the bottom" in terms of both corporate tax rates and incentives, and that many States granted tax incentives to corporations as they competed to attract foreign investment, in particular in the agriculture and mining sectors. She concluded that such incentives warranted a heightened level of scrutiny in human rights terms because they restricted the State's revenue and therefore the resources it was able to devote to the realization of human rights. Losses to developing countries could reach $138 billion per year. The author of the present report concurs, and asserts that such harmful competition must be banned.

In 1997 the European Union Economic and Financial Affairs Council (Ecofin) adopted a non-binding Code of Conduct on business taxation,[86] under which States undertake to avoid harmful tax practices. The criteria for what constitutes "potentially harmful tax measures" include tax benefits reserved for non-residents and lack of transparency. However, the Code of Conduct Group refrained from discouraging the use of "sweetheart" deals, and latest data suggest that the use of such arrangements has been increasing. Meanwhile, article 87 of the Treaty establishing the European Community prohibits State aid that threatens to distort the European single market. The application of article 87 was laid out in the "Commission notice on the application of the State aid rules to measures relating to direct business taxation" (1998), according to which actions taken by the member State may be considered State aid if they are specific or selective, rather than general in nature. Moreover, the measure is not required to be a direct subsidy. Paragraph 22 of the notice stipulates: "Every decision of the administration that departs from the general tax rules to the benefit of individual undertakings in principle leads to a presumption of State aid and must be analysed in detail." Accordingly, the European Commission has opened investigations into alleged "sweetheart" deals for multinational companies including Apple[87] in Ireland, Starbucks[88] in the Netherlands, Fiat,[89] Amazon.com[90] and McDonald's[91] in Luxembourg.

On 11 January 2016, the Commission found that selective tax advantages granted by Belgium under its "excess profit" tax scheme violated European Union State aid rules. The scheme, benefiting at least 35 multinationals, must end and the multinationals must now return unpaid taxes to Belgium. The "excess profit" tax scheme, applicable since 2005, allowed certain multinational group companies to pay substantially less tax in Belgium on the basis of tax rulings which reduced the corporate tax base of the companies by 50–90 per cent, to discount so-called "excess profits" allegedly resulting from being part of a multinational group. The Commission's in-depth investigation, opened in February 2015, concluded that the scheme had derogated from normal practice under Belgian company tax rules and the so-called "arm's length principle."[92]

The above illustrates the widespread nature of the abuse and the necessity of insisting on public country-by-country reporting to display the massive misalignment between business activities elsewhere and profits declared in Belgium, Ireland, Luxembourg, the Netherlands and other countries at advantageous tax rates. The European Parliament has called for the key elements of "sweetheart" deals to be made public, but this proposal has not been endorsed by the European Commission nor by the Council of the European Union.

Organisation for Economic Co-operation and Development and Directive of the Council of the European Union

On 21 June 2016, the Council of the European Union agreed on a draft directive addressing tax avoidance practices commonly used by large companies. The directive is part of a January 2016 package of Commission proposals and builds on 2015 OECD recommendations to address BEPS.[93] The directive has been heavily criticized by civil society: Oxfam has said that Governments have been unable to agree on an effective approach against parking profits in tax havens at a time when repeated tax scandals are calling for immediate and efficient action; what is needed to end tax dodging are rules that require big companies to disclose where they make their profits and where they pay their taxes.[94] In 2015, the Independent Commission for the Reform of International Corporate Taxation issued a declaration in which it expressed reservations concerning the "targeted reforms" of the BEPS system.[95]

United Nations Conference on Trade and Development

The fourteenth session of the United Nations Conference on Trade and Development (UNCTAD XIV) took place in July 2016. In spite of constructive proposals made by many delegations, the outcome documents failed to give UNCTAD a clear mandate to expand its work on the impacts of taxation and tax avoidance on development. In order to facilitate the achievement of the Sustainable Development Goals and promote a democratic and equitable international order, the mandate of UNCTAD requires strengthening with respect to specific competences concerning international cooperation on taxation, abolishing tax havens, controlling financial flows and providing technical assistance, while ensuring that all States participate on an equal footing in international tax forums. Unfortunately, developed countries blocked relevant proposals.

GOOD INITIATIVES AND PRACTICES

The Convention on Mutual Administrative Assistance in Tax Matters, the most comprehensive multilateral instrument for tax cooperation, was elaborated by the OECD and the Council of Europe in 1988 and amended by Protocol in 2010. The G-20 has consistently encouraged countries to sign the Convention, including most recently at the meeting of the G-20 finance ministers and central bank governors in February 2016.[96] Ninety-eight jurisdictions currently participate in the Convention, representing a wide range of countries including all G-20 countries, the BRICS countries (Brazil, the Russian Federation, India, China and

South Africa), all OECD countries, major financial centres and an increasing number of developing countries.

A United Nations tax cooperation body

Within the United Nations, since 2012 the G-77 and China have proposed that the Committee of Experts on International Cooperation in Tax Matters be transformed into a global, inclusive norm-setting body for international tax cooperation at the intergovernmental level. This idea has been gaining momentum with numerous non-governmental organizations,[97] including Global Alliance for Tax Justice. In preparation for the Third United Nations Conference on Financing for Development, held in Addis Ababa in September 2015, Global Alliance submitted a position paper calling for a global tax body.[98] Following up on the conference, Global Alliance again called for the creation of a global tax body as the most effective way to achieve an equitable global tax system, increase domestic resource mobilization and reduce intra-State and inter-State inequality.[99]

On 9 June 2016, the President of Ecuador, Rafael Correa, endorsed the proposal to create a world institution to eliminate tax havens, and pledged to make a request to include this important issue in the agenda of the General Assembly agenda and to coordinate with G-77 countries to ban offshore secrecy.[100]

Another positive development was the announcement at the United Nations Conference of the Addis Tax Initiative,[101] pursuant to which developing countries will be assisted to build their domestic revenue systems. In the declaration issued by the partners to the Initiative, the participating countries and international organizations affirm that domestic resource mobilization and effective use is the crux of the common pursuit of sustainable development and achieving the Sustainable Development Goals. The partners commit to support countries that need assistance, including by substantially increasing official development assistance and technical assistance to build tax and fiscal management capacity, particularly in least developed countries; moreover, they agree to cooperate to combat tax evasion as well as tax avoidance.

Common Reporting Standard

Pursuant to the Common Reporting Standard devised by the OECD in 2014, automatic exchange of financial account information will take place as of 2017 without the need for the recipient jurisdiction to make a request. In response to the Independent Expert's questionnaire, the OECD stated that the impact of the Common Reporting Standard and improved transparency was already apparent, with at least €50 billion in additional revenues identified in countries that had put in place voluntary disclosure programmes and similar initiatives to allow taxpayers to come forward to correct their past tax transgressions. Observers, however, have identified loopholes concerning the high thresholds of ownership that prevent beneficial owners—the true owners of shell corporations—from being identified and facilitate the possibility of avoiding the identification of owners who hide behind an "active non-financial entity." Moreover, the Standard explicitly restricts the use of the information received to tax purposes and explicitly prohibits sharing the information with law enforcement authorities. Although the OECD clarified that information might be exchanged with other law enforcement agencies if the sending party explicitly agreed, these restrictions might prevent cost-free synergies for fighting corruption and money-laundering.

BEPS refers to tax planning strategies that exploit gaps and mismatches in tax rules to artificially shift profits to low or no-tax locations where there is little or no economic activity. Although some of the schemes used are illegal, most are technically legal. BEPS has the potential to solve some aspects of multinational tax avoidance, but hitherto has failed to address key issues that face developing countries. The OECD has also developed an inclusive framework on BEPS. In October 2015, the OECD unveiled a campaign to end tax havens and loopholes.[102] It has also developed a model tax convention.[103]

In September 2013, G-20 leaders endorsed the comprehensive Action Plan on Base Erosion and Profit Shifting.[104] Two years later, the G-20 proposed reinforced international standards and measures to help countries tackle BEPS. The package provides tools to ensure that profits are taxed where economic activities are performed and where value is created.

Speaking in Abu Dhabi on 22 February 2016, IMF Managing Director Christine Lagarde expressed the view that the BEPS project did not go far enough in creating an effective international tax system. She said that while the project had made significant progress, more work needed to be done in terms of both substance and scope. The BEPS rules had been designed to work within the traditional architecture for international taxation, developed nearly a century ago in a world where cross-border trade was less important and consisted almost entirely in physical goods. Today's challenges included the taxation of traded services and the shifting of intellectual property across borders, which was why an international tax system truly fit for the twenty-first century that would work for all economies was needed.[105]

On 14 April 2016, Ms. Lagarde advocated the strengthening of international efforts to curtail aggressive tax avoidance, so that the international tax system would no longer have loopholes available for rich people and companies to exploit. A perception that the rules are skewed towards some or do not apply to everyone constitutes a threat to the global economy. She warned that the world could no longer tolerate taxation being treated "as a local matter associated with sovereignty."[106]

The European Parliament has launched several initiatives to combat tax evasion,[107] while the European Commission has developed useful indicators to measure aggressive tax planning, including tax exemptions for royalties, advances and similar income derived from patents in respect of inventions, copyright and trademarks.

On 21 June 2016, the Special Committee on Tax Rulings II of the European Parliament adopted recommendations including the creation of a European Union public register of beneficial owners of companies, a tax-havens blacklist, sanctions against non-cooperative tax jurisdictions, action against abuse of patent box regimes for intellectual property revenues, a code of conduct for banks and tax advisers, tax good governance rules in all European Union trade agreements and a withholding tax on profits leaving the Union.[108] The European Parliament approved the recommendations on 6 July 2016.[109]

In order for Governments to be able to fund Sustainable Development Goals and deliver on their human rights obligations to provide public health care, education, water and sanitation, affordable housing and transportation, all countries must have an equal seat at the table to determine equitable international tax practices.

A financial transactions tax

In the *World Economic and Social Survey 2012*, titled *In Search of New Development Finance*, the United Nations proposed an international tax, combined with other innovative financing mechanisms, to raise more than $400 billion annually for development and global challenges such as fighting climate change.[110]

In October 2012, Christine Lagarde said that a financial transactions tax was a step in the right direction.[111] According to the Centre for Economic and Policy Research,[112] a set of scaled transactions taxes, imposed on transfers of stock and other financial assets, could raise more than $100 billion a year. This revenue could be used for environmental protection and sustainable development worldwide. Although there is growing momentum,[113] such a "Tobin tax" is far from being adopted.[114]

Development agenda of the United Nations Conference on Trade and Development

The *World Investment Report 2015: Reforming International Investment Governance* devotes an entire chapter to international tax and investment policy coherence. Awareness of the problems, however, is only a first step towards solving them. UNCTAD observes:

> Tax avoidance and the lack of transparency in international financial transactions are global issues that require a multilateral approach, with adequate developing-country participation.... International cooperation is fundamental to prevent harmful tax competition; competition to attract investment should not lead to a race to the bottom. International cooperation is also important for the success of transparency initiatives, such as the Extractive Industries Transparency Initiative.... Such initiatives should ideally not focus only on governments, but also on companies.

The report further states that "tax avoidance practices are responsible for a significant leakage of development finance resources. An estimated $100 billion of annual tax revenue losses for developing countries is related to inward investment stocks directly linked to offshore hubs." Oxfam has adopted this figure as the estimated loss for developing countries as a result of corporate tax dodging. For the purpose of its research, UNCTAD identifies offshore investment hubs with reference to the OECD 2000 list of tax havens, plus jurisdictions that shelter special purpose entities IMF defines special purpose entities as "autonomous legal entities, directly or indirectly wholly foreign owned, that are part of a group of companies, without substantial real economic links with the host economy, engaged in a variety of cross-border financial activities, which are aimed at the passing through of all types of financial and non-financial assets, liabilities and related income to third countries." They include Austria, Hungary, Luxembourg and the Netherlands, with the latter two accounting for the bulk of transit foreign direct investment. UNCTAD recognizes that the list of jurisdictions publishing special purpose entity investment data is increasing rapidly.[115]

At UNCTAD XIV, delegations prevented a neoliberal takeover of the future UNCTAD agenda and succeeded in including useful language in the outcome document:[116]

Given growing concerns about external debt sustainability, public debt management to prevent and pre-empt financial and debt crises is important. The need for a central data registry, including information on debt restructuring, has also been recognized. In this regard, the longstanding work of UNCTAD on debt issues within the United Nations, including through promotion of its Principles on Promoting Responsible Sovereign Lending and Borrowing, is recognized. The work of the United Nations, the International Monetary Fund and the World Bank remains important.

...

Effective taxation will be critical in the mobilization of resources for implementation of the Sustainable Development Goals and overall economic advancement of developing countries. This includes reducing opportunities for tax avoidance, as well as addressing illicit financial flows and the activities that underlie their occurrence, such as tax evasion, illegal exploitation of natural resources, corruption, embezzlement and fraud. This is a global issue that requires further multilateral cooperation. Current initiatives should also be more inclusive with regards to the participation of developing countries.

International Monetary Fund: Change of mindset?

A recent paper by IMF economists Jonathan Ostry, Prakash Lougani and Davide Furceri[117] and statements by Christine Lagarde[118] give reason for hope that international organizations like IMF can gradually abandon neoliberal mantras and start applying a human rights-based approach to their short-, medium- and long-term programmes. It is obvious that capital inflows in the form of portfolio investment and banking and speculative debt influxes do not boost growth and put populations at risk. Capital account liberalization has given way to the recognition that capital controls are needed to deal with the volatility of capital flows.

Taxes and military expenditures

As the Independent Expert substantiated in his 2014 report to the Human Rights Council (A/HRC/27/51), lobbies for the military-industrial complex exercise an undemocratic influence on parliaments and many countries devote an unconscionably high percentage of their discretionary budget to military-related activities. Bearing in mind that article 18 of the International Covenant on Civil and Political Rights recognizes the right to conscientious objection to war, the question arises whether individuals have a right to withhold taxes that are used for war or military research, e.g., for lethal autonomous weapons systems.[119] A parliamentary bill in the United Kingdom aims at recognizing the right of individuals to opt out of war for moral reasons and to opt out of paying taxes for war, since through taxes they would be financing what they deem immoral. If Governments were to recognize this right and devote the taxes of conscientious objectors to conflict-prevention measures, this would be a significant step for civilization.[120]

CONCLUSIONS

Tax avoidance, tax evasion and tax havens deprive countries of revenue needed to fulfil human rights treaty obligations, alleviate poverty, improve the administration of justice, ensure that remedies are available to victims of human rights violations, build infrastructures, create jobs and provide social security, quality health services and free education.

Because the tax activities of domestic and transnational corporations have significant direct and indirect socioeconomic impacts, a binding legal instrument on corporate social responsibility[121] stipulating the obligation to pay taxes where the profits are generated and a prohibition on shifting profits should be adopted. This would encourage responsible tax behaviour that does not harm global financial stability, development and human rights.

While the end of tax havens is not in sight, Governments are gradually coming to realize that it is in their own interest to phase out secrecy jurisdictions. An international tax convention is necessary to stop competition among tax jurisdictions and abolish secrecy.

Taxation should be used to advance human rights. Fiscal and budgetary policy should be reformed with a view to achieving fair taxation by abolishing tax havens and "sweetheart" deals, closing loopholes and rejecting *contra bonos mores* schemes and abuse of rights.[122] Progressive redistributive taxation polices will produce funding for vital public services that will reduce inequality and poverty and lead to sustainable development.

RECOMMENDATIONS

Bearing in mind that taxation has an impact on human rights and on the international order, the Independent Expert suggests the following action plan:

States should:

(a) Establish an intergovernmental tax body under the auspices of the United Nations with the mandate to elaborate a United Nations convention on taxation and international cooperation in tax matters;

(b) Adopt a common United Nations standard for multilateral and automatic exchange of tax information;

(c) Implement corporate tax and financial transparency, including public registries of ultimate beneficial ownership;

(d) Ensure that multinational corporations are treated as single entities conducting business across international borders;

(e) Enact legislation requiring country-by-country reporting and automatic and multilateral exchange of financial information, so as to reveal the misalignment between where business activity takes place and where profits are declared and taxes paid. Data should be made fully public so that citizens can hold multinationals and tax authorities to account;

(f) Abolish "sweetheart" tax deals; States members of the European Union should revise the Code of Conduct on business taxation to specifically prohibit "sweetheart" deals;

(g) Conduct systematic human rights impact assessments to monitor the spillover effects of their tax policies and agreements domestically and overseas. These should be periodic and independently verified;

(h) Impose criminal penalties for abusive tax practices and abolish tax amnesties;

(i) Enact legislation to protect whistleblowers and witnesses, and ensure that individuals who want to share information about corporate tax practices which harm human rights are not prosecuted or subjected to reprisals; States should cease punishing individuals for disclosing information that the public has a right to receive pursuant to article 19 of the International Covenant on Civil and Political Rights. A charter on the rights of whistleblowers and a "protected disclosure defence" should be adopted, pursuant to which criminal or civil liability for protected disclosures is waved and an "authorized channel" is provided for such disclosures;

(j) Introduce a financial transactions tax and enforce it;

(k) Pursue efforts to collect taxes, imposing fines on tax evaders, and use the revenue to fulfil human rights treaty obligations, in particular the administration of justice, health and education. States should cease imposing "austerity measures" in the social sector and exercise austerity with regard to military expenditures;

(l) Agree on a minimum corporate tax rate and curb tax competition among countries, acknowledging that this policy facilitates corruption, bribery and money-laundering;

(m) Audit banks, law firms and accounting and consulting firms that specialize in establishing anonymous, shell or mailbox companies that serve no purpose other than to avoid taxes;

(n) Test the inter-State complaints procedure under article 41 of the International Covenant on Civil and Political Rights and article 10 (1) of the Optional Protocol to the International Covenant on Economic, Social and Cultural Rights, e.g., concerning the extraterritorial liability of States for the activities of transnational corporations and banks, in particular concerning the loss of tax revenues through the operation of tax havens. These matters should be systematically reviewed when State party reports are examined.

Parliaments should:

(a) Exercise their oversight functions concerning the human rights impacts of fiscal policies and the domestic and extraterritorial effects of tax havens;

(b) Proactively inform their constituents of the aims and consequences of fiscal policies and endeavour to achieve tax justice domestically and internationally;

(c) Adopt robust legislation to protect whistleblowers and witnesses from harassment and/or prosecution.

The General Assembly should:

(a) Revise the Guiding Principles on Business and Human Rights and support the adoption of a legally binding instrument on corporate social responsibility prohibiting "aggressive tax avoidance," tax fraud, tax evasion and tax havens;

(b) Refer relevant legal questions to the International Court of Justice for advisory opinions.

UNCTAD should develop a strategy to protect the policy space of States in controlling capital flows, in particular to curb and criminalize illicit financial flows and the flight of moneys to tax havens, in cooperation with the Office of the United Nations High Commissioner for Human Rights and the United Nations Office on Drugs and Crime (UNODC).

OECD should facilitate the sharing of information collected under CRS by the recipient jurisdiction with other relevant government authorities to tackle corruption and money-laundering.

The International Monetary Fund, the World Bank and central banks should refuse loans to countries that harbour tax havens. No project should be subsidized if the enterprises involved use secrecy jurisdictions.

Domestic banks should investigate the origin of the deposits and investments they administer and return illicit funds held by corporations and kleptocrats to the countries of origin.

The International Court of Justice should issue an advisory opinion holding that tax havens are *contra bonos mores* and against international *ordre public*.

Members of civil society should:

(a) Demand more direct democracy in matters such as taxation. They should demand participatory democracy and expose so-called "representative democracy" when it ceases to represent the voice of the people and becomes subservient to corporate lobbies;

(b) Demand referendums on important issues, including a financial transactions tax, the outlawing of tax havens and runaway military expenditures;

(c) Demand a reduction of military expenditures. Bearing in mind that article 18 of the International Covenant on Civil and Political Rights protects the right of conscientious objection, this right should also shield citizens from prosecution if they engage in peaceful civil disobedience and refuse to contribute to the arms race and to governmental activities that threaten article 6 of the International Covenant on the right to life, and violate article 20 (1) of the International Covenant, which prohibits propaganda for war. Conscientious objectors should insist that their taxes be used for conflict-prevention policies;

International non-governmental organizations such as Amnesty International, Human Rights Watch, International Service for Human Rights and International Federation for Human Rights should add tax fairness and the abolition of tax havens to their urgent goals.

Law schools and business schools should:

(a) Include ethics and corporate social responsibility as obligatory disciplines in their curricula. Bar associations should test candidates thereon. The legal profession must not be silent when members of the bar seriously undermine social policies by creating fraudulent companies and other schemes for tax avoidance purposes;

(b) Instil a sense of responsibility in students as prospective lawyers and business executives. They must be taught that they have a duty to serve society and to promote human rights. Teaching "aggressive tax avoidance" is unethical. Students must understand the difference between legitimate profit and looting of society.

* * *

It is precisely in this spirit that I wish to end the chapter with a quote by Professor Jeffrey Sachs who for years has argued that tax havens have no economic justification and must be abolished. —AdeZ

> This is a system that has been created over time for the convenience of very rich and powerful people. There is no more direct example of how the rich and the powerful really control the levers of finance than these tax havens.... We see from the Panama Papers these are simply conduits for massive illegality, corruption, tax evasion and many other nefarious deeds. They just need to end.[123]

Notes

1 Most notably resolution 3201 (S-6), containing the Declaration on the Establishment of a New International Economic Order, and resolution 3281 (XXIX) containing the Charter of Economic Rights and Duties of States.

2 See, for example, resolutions 55/107, 56/151, 57/213, 61/160 and 63/189.

3 See Commission resolutions 2004/64 and 2005/57.
4 Report on the realization of economic, social and cultural rights by the Special Rapporteur, Danilo Türk (E/CN.4/Sub.2/1992/16).
5 See, for example, resolution 28/5.
6 Report on the issue of the negative impact of corruption on the enjoyment of human rights (A/HRC/23/9).
7 Annual world investment reports and trade and development reports. See in particular http://unctad.org/en/PublicationChapters/tdr2014ch7_en.pdf; and http://unctad.org/en/PublicationChapters/wir2015ch5_en.pdf.
8 See http://unhabitat.org/un-habitat-presents-world-cities-report-to-european-audience/.
9 See www.oecd.org/tax/forum-on-tax-administration/ftajitsicnetwork.htm; www.oecd.org/ctp/bribery-and-corruption-awareness-handbook-for-tax-examiners-and-tax-auditors-978926420 5376-en.htm; www.oecd.org/ctp/crime/effective-inter-%20agency-cooperation-report.pdf; www.oecd.org/tax/crime/Oslo-Dialogue-flyer.pd; and http://www.ipsnews.net/2016/08/ developing-nations-seek-tax-body-to-curb-illicit-financial-flows/.
10 See www.theguardian.com/world/2009/apr/02/g20 -summit-tax-havens.
11 Pursuant to Articles 57 and 63 of the Charter. See A/HRC/33/40, para. 63.
12 The United Nations Convention against Corruption states that "the illicit acquisition of personal wealth can be particularly damaging to democratic institutions."
13 Ndiva Kofele-Kale, The International Responsibility for Economic Crimes: Holding State Officials Individually Liable for Acts of Fraudulent Enrichment (Routledge, 2006) and Sol Picciotto, Regulating Global Capitalism (Cambridge, 2011).
14 See www.thedailybeast.com/articles/2016/05/03/how-the-kleptocrats-12-trillion-heist-helps-keep-most-of-the-world-impoverished.html. See also Human Rights Council resolution 31/22.
15 See www.un.org/en/development/desa/news/policy/wess2012.html; and www.bbc.com/news/business-15552412.
16 "Tax abuse includes tax evasion, fraud and other illegal practices, including the tax losses resulting from other illicit financial flows, such as bribery and money laundering .[G]lobally, approximately $3 trillion of government revenue is lost to tax evasion every yearIn 2011, developing countries lost $946.7 billion owing to illicit financial flows, according to OECD more than seven times official development assistance for that year. Tax abuse is thus nota victimless practice; it limits resources that could be spent on reducing poverty and realizing human rights, and perpetuates vast income inequality" (A/HRC/26/28 and Corr.1, paras. 58-59).
17 See www.oecd.org/tax/taxinspectors.htm.
18 See www.ibanet.org/LPD/Taxation_Section/Taxes/Publications.aspx.
19 See www.globalpolicy.org/home/272-general/52850-panama-papers-when-tax-abuse-is-human-rights-abuse.html.
20 See www.imf.org/en/News/Articles/2015/09/28/04/53/sp011216.
21 See www.globaltaxjustice.org/, http://www.globaltaxjustice.org/the-world-needs-a-un-global-tax-body-now/; and www.globaltaxjustice.org/wp-content/uploads/2015/02/UN-Tax-Body-Briefing-for-Government-Delegations-with-Logos.pdf.
22 See www.oxfam.org/en/tags/tax-havens, https://www.oxfam.org.au/wp-content/uploads/2016/06/OXF003-Tax-Havens-Report-FA-WEB.pdf; and www.theguardian.com/world/2016/apr/14/ us-corporations-14-trillion-hidden-tax-havens-oxfam.
23 See www.cetim.ch/wp-content/uploads/Right-t http://cepr.org/o-development.pdf; and www.cetim.ch/wp-content/uploads/report_10.pdf.
24 See https://business-humanrights.org/en/tax-avoidance-0.
25 See www.taxjustice.net/topics/inequality-democracy/human-rights/.
26 See http://cepr.org/, http://cepr.org/active/publications/discussion_papers/dp.php?dpno=8570.
27 See www.cesr.org/section.php?id=229, http://cesr.org/downloads/Tax_Evasion_ETOs_2014.pdf.
28 See www.shiftproject.org/article/tax-abuse-business-and-human-rights-issue.
29 See http://ctj.org/ctjreports/2015/10/offshore_shell_games 2015.php#.V4OtIfl97IU.

30 See www.transparency.org/glossary/term/tax_haven.
31 See www.icrict.org/declaration/.
32 See www.globalreporting.org/Pages/default.aspx.
33 See www.occrp.org/en/daily/5133-unaoil-leaks-investigation-spotlights-global-oil-industry-bribes-for-contracts-scandal.
34 See library.fes.de/pdf-files/iez/global/04669.pdf.
35 See www.alliancesud.ch/en/publications/downloads/5769_alliancesud_news_nr%2079_GzD.pdf.
36 See http://ccfd-terresolidaire.org/infos/partage-des-richesses/paradisfiscaux/.
37 See www.secours-catholique.org/actualites/sur-la-piste-des-banques-francaises-dans-les-paradis-fiscaux.
38 See www.stopparadisfiscaux.fr/.
39 See www.oxfam.org/en/pressroom/pressreleases/2016-05-09/tax-havens-serve-no-useful-economic-purpose-300-economists-tell. See also https://panamapapers.icij.org/. In defence of tax havens, see www.internationalman.com/articles/the-moral-case-for-tax-havens.
40 See www.theguardian.com/world/2016/may/09/tax-havens-have-no-economic-justification-say-top-economists.
41 Alfred Verdross, "Forbidden treaties in international law," *American Journal of International Law,* vol. 31, No. 4 (Oct. 1937), pp. 571 ff; A. Verdross, "Les principes généraux du droit et la jurisprudence internationale," *Collected Courses of the Hague Academy of International Law,* vol. 52 (1935), pp. 195-249; Olivier Corten and Pierre Klein, eds., *The Vienna Convention on the Law of Treaties: A Commentary,* Volume I (Oxford University Press, 2011), p. 146; and Robert Kolb, *The International Court of Justice* (Oxford University Press, 2013), p. 81. There is an ethical minimum standard for treaties, and a treaty which subverts *ordre public* or is otherwise *contra bonos mores* is void, e.g., if it prevents the universally recognized tasks of a civilized State such as maintenance of public order, care of the bodily and spiritual welfare of citizens and protection of nationals abroad. Bruno Simma, "The contribution of Alfred Verdross to the theory of international law," *European Journal of International Law,* vol. 6 (1995), pp. 33–54; and Gleider Hernandez, "A reluctant guardian: the International Court of Justice and the concept of 'international community'," *British Yearbook of International Law,* vol. 83, No. 1 (2012). See also Sir Hersch Lauterpact on "overriding principles of international law" in *Yearbook of the International Law Commission 1953,* vol. II (United Nations publication, Sales No. 59.V.4, Vol. II), p. 155; Alexander Orakhelashvili, ed., *Research Handbook on the Theory and History of International Law* (Elgar, 2011); and https://law.wustl.edu/SBA/upperlevel/International%20Law/IntLaw-Mutharika2.pdf.
42 See http://hack.tion.free.fr/mvtsoc/Attac/www.attac.org/fra/toil/doc/oxfam2.htm.
43 See www.transparency.org/topic/detail/whistleblowing/.
44 See www.transparency.de/fileadmin/pdfs/Themen/Hinweisgebersysteme/Whistleblower-Protection-Laws-in-G20-Countries-Priorities-for-Action.pdf.
45 See www.oecd.org/ctp/glossaryoftaxterms.htm. See also www.taxjustice.net/cms/upload/pdf/oxfam_paper_-_final_version_06_00.pdf.
46 For lists of secrecy jurisdictions, including a list of "uncooperative tax havens," see www.oecd.org/countries/monaco/listofunco-operativetaxhavens.htm. For other lists, see www.imf.org/external/NP/ofca/OFCA.aspx; www.bis.org/statistics/dsd_cbs.pdf; and www.gao.gov/assets/290/284522.pdf.
47 See https://whistleblowerjustice.net/what-is-a-tax-haven/.
48 See www.taxjustice.net/cms/upload/pdf/Price_of_Offshore_Revisited_120722.pdf.
49 See www.taxjustice.net/2015/03/26/unctad-multinational-tax-avoidance-costs-developing-countries-100-billion/.
50 See www.scmp.com/business/markets/article/1880426/crackdown-caribbean-tax-havens-surprise-boon-hong-kong.

51 See www.bloomberg.com/news/articles/2016-01-27/the-world-s-favorite-new-tax-haven-is-the-united-states.

52 See www.independent.com.mt/articles/2016-06-12/local-news/Malta-is-the-EU-s-number-four-corporate-tax-haven-Oxfam-International-6736159237; and www.oxfam.org/en/pressroom/pressreleases/2013-05-22/tax-private-billions-now-stashed-away-havens-enough-end-extreme.

53 See www.financeuncovered.org/investigations/liberia-americas-outpost-financial-secrecy/.

54 *The Hidden Wealth of Nations, the Scourge of Tax Havens* (University of Chicago, 2015).

55 See www.theguardian.com/global-development-professionals-network/2016/may/10/were-losing-240bn-a-year-to-tax-avoidance-who-really-ends-up-paying.

56 See www.theguardian.com/world/2016/apr/14/us-corporations-14-trillion-hidden-tax-havens-oxfam; www.oxfamamerica.org/static/media/files/Broken_at_the_Top_4.14.2016.pdf; and www.taxjustice.net/cms/upload/pdf/oxfam_paper_-_final_version__06_00.pdf. Reportedly, Apple has $181 billion offshore, General Electric $119 billion and Microsoft $108 billion.

57 See https://tax.network/ddharmapala/what-problems-and-opportunities-are-created-by-tax-havens/.

58 See www.oxfam.org/en/pressroom/pressreleases/2016-04-11/majority-world-banks-private-investments-go-companies-have.

59 See https://business-humanrights.org/sites/default/files/documents/IBA_Practical_Guide.pdf; and www.ibanet.org/Article/Detail.aspx?ArticleUid=c9bd50c6-c2b3-455b-b086-a7efbfe1f6a5.

60 Austin Mitchell and Prem Sikka, *The Pin-Stripe Mafia: How Accountancy Firms Destroy Societies* (Association for Accountancy and Business Affairs, 2011). Auditing firms advise transnational corporation and super-rich individuals how to structure their accounts in order to minimize tax and lobby Governments and supranational organizations to keep loopholes open for transnationals and to block transparency, devise new tax avoidance scams, advise Governments on new tax rules to ensure that the privileges of transnationals are preserved or expanded, undemocratically influence the development of tax law, engage in revolving door practices, act as a quasi-legitimate face for tax havens and fund think tanks to frame tax debates in a race to the bottom. See also Jim Cousins, Austin Mitchell and Prem Sikka, *Race to the Bottom: The Case of the Accountancy Firms* (Association for Accountancy and Business Affairs, 2004).

61 See www.ipsnews.net/2016/04/developing-countries-left-out-of-global-tax-decisions/.

62 See www.globaltaxjustice.org/the-world-needs-a-un-global-tax-body-now/.

63 See www.alliancesud.ch/en/publications/downloads/5769_alliancesud_news_nr%2079_GzD.pdf.

64 See www.ipsnews.net/2005/01/world-economic-forum-corporations-in-search-of-paradise-fiscal-that-is/.

65 See https://panamapapers.icij.org/; and www.cesr.org/article.php?id=1834 Center for Economic and Social Rights, when Tax abuse is Human Rights Abuse.

66 See https://panamapapers.icij.org/blog/20160509-offshore-database-release.html; https://offshoreleaks.icij.org/nodes/61034; and https://www.icij.org/offshore#_ga=1.183963814.1052794772.1467974903.

67 See the series of articles by ICIJ on secret deals in Africa, available from https://panamapapers.icij.org/.

68 On 16 June 2016, The *New York Times* reported that a Mossack employee had been arrested in Geneva as a suspected whistle-blower. See www.counterpunch.org/2016/04/18/panama-and-the-criminalization-of-the-global-finance-system/.

69 Available from www.ohchr.org/EN/Issues/IntOrder/Pages/IEInternationalorderIndex.aspx.

70 See www.theguardian.com/world/2016/apr/05/iceland-prime-minister-resigns-over-panama-papers-revelations.

71 See www.ohchr.org/EN/NewsEvents/Pages/DisplayNews.aspx?NewsID=20317&Lang ID=E.

72 See www.huffingtonpost.com/entry/unaoil-scandal-explained_us_56fbd2f0e4b0daf53aee0cff; and www.theguardian.com/business/2016/jul/19/serious-office-opens-criminal-investigation-into-unaoil.

73 See www.icij.org/project/luxembourg-leaks/big-4-audit-firms-play-big-role-offshore-murk.
74 Ibid.
75 See www.theaccountant-online.com/features/political-donations-are-a-way-of-influencing-policy-and-buying-influence-austin-mitchell-former-mp-4583932/.
76 See www.icij.org/project/luxembourg-leaks/explore-documents-luxembourg-leaks-database.
77 See www.theguardian.com/world/2014/dec/14/jean-claude-juncker-luxembourg-tax-deals-controversy.
78 See www.euractiv.com/section/euro-finance/news/parliament-despondent-after-failure-of-luxleaks-committee/.
79 See www.transparency.org/news/feature/whats_it_like_to_be_a_whistleblower.
80 See www.bbc.com/news/world-europe-36662636.
81 See criticism of the decision by civil society at www.transparency.org/news/pressreleas e/transparency_international_condemns_prosecution_and_sentencing_of_luxleaks.
82 See www.ohchr.org/EN/NewsEvents/Pages/DisplayNews.aspx?NewsID=20212&LangID=E#sthash.vCPcNjq5.dpuf.
83 See http://eur-lex.europa.eu/legal-content/EN/TXT/PDF/?uri=CONSIL:PE_76_2015_INIT&from=EN.
84 See http://corporateeurope.org/power-lobbies/2016/05/trade-secrets-protection-directive-still-dangerous-freedoms-and-rights.
85 OECD, *Harmful Tax Competition: An Emerging Global Issue* (Paris, 1998), pp. 13-14; and Africa Progress Panel, *Equity in Extractives: Stewarding Africa's Natural Resources for All: Africa Progress Report 2013*, p. 65.
86 See http://ec.europa.eu/taxation_customs/taxation/company_tax/harmful_tax_practices/index_en.htm.
87 See www.theguardian.com/technology/2016/jan/15/apple-european-commission-ruling-back-taxes-ireland.
88 See www.theguardian.com/business/2015/oct/21/starbucks-and-fiat-tax-deals-with-eu-nations-ruled-unlawful.
89 See http://ec.europa.eu/competition/elojade/isef/case_details.cfm?proc_code=3_SA_38375.
90 See http://europa.eu/rapid/press-release_IP-14-1105_en.htm.
91 See http://europa.eu/rapid/press-release_IP-15-6221_en.htm.
92 See http://europa.eu/rapid/press-release_IP-16-42_en.htm.
93 See http://www.consilium.europa.eu/en/press/press-releases/2016/06/21-corporate-tax-avoidance/.
94 See www.oxfam.org/en/pressroom/reactions/eu-finance-ministers-unwilling-address-tax-avoidance.
95 See www.icrict.org/wp-content/uploads/2015/06/ICRICT_Com-Rec-Report_ENG_v1.4.pdf.
96 See www.oecd.org/tax/exchange-of-tax-information/conventiononmutualadministrativeassistanceintaxmatters.htm.
97 See https://business-humanrights.org/en/ngos-call-for-greater-representation-of-developing-countries-in-global-tax-talks-emphasise-need-for-un-global-tax-body.
98 See www.globaltaxjustice.org/sites/default/files/FINAL_GATJ_FFD_position-paper_20March2015.pdf.
99 See www.taxjustice.net/wp-content/uploads/2013/04/GATJ-statement-GlobalTaxBodyPanamaPapers_18Apr2016.pdf.
100 See www.andes.info.ec/en/news/president-rafael-correa-commits-end-offshore-secrecy.html; and
http://www.telesurtv.net/news/Correa-propone-consulta-popular-sobre-paraisos-fiscales-en-Ecuador-20160715-0003.html.
101 See www.taxcompact.net/documents/Addis-Tax-Initiative_Declaration.pdf.
102 See www.telegraph.co.uk/finance/economics/11912495/OECD-unveils-global-push-to-end-tax-havens-and-loopholes.html.
103 See www.oecd.org/ctp/treaties/2014-model-tax-convention-articles.pdf.

104   See www.oecd.org/ctp/BEPSActionPlan.pdf.
105   See www.publicfinanceinternational.org/news/2016/02/international-tax-reforms-do-not-go-far-enough-says-lagarde.
106   https://next.ft.com/content/9ce6c362-0262-11e6-af1d-c47326021344 (subscription required).
107   See www.europarl.europa.eu/sides/getDoc.do?pubRef=-//EP//TEXT%20REPORT%20A7-2013-0162%200%20DOC%20XML%20V0//EN.
108   See www.europarl.europa.eu/news/en/news-room/20160621IPR33011/MEPs-call-for-tax-haven-black-list-patent-box-rules-CCCTB-and-more.
109   See http://www.europarl.europa.eu/sides/getDoc.do?pubRef=-//EP//TEXT+TA+P8-TA-2016-0310+0+DOC+XML+V0//EN&language=EN#BKMD-14.
110   See www.un.org/en/development/desa/news/policy/wess2012.html; and www.un.org/esa/ffd/wp-content/uploads/2012/03/2011esm_NGO1.pdf.
111   See http://robinhoodtax.org.uk/content/response-imf-chief-christine-lagarde-supporting-financial-transaction-tax.
112   See http://cepr.net/documents/publications/financial-transactions-tax-2008-12.pdf.
113   See http://cepr.net/documents/Support_for_FTT_09 -14.pdf.
114   See http://mondediplo.com/2016/05/08tobin.
115   See http://unctad.org/en/PublicationsLibrary/wir2015_en.pdf; .https://www.iosco.org/library/pubdocs/pdf/IOSCOPD243.pdf https://www.iosco.org/library/pubdocs/pdf/IOSCOPD308.pdf.
116   The text quoted is from the final agreed negotiated text of the consensus document (Nairobi Maafikiano), chap. I, sect. A, sub-theme 1, Challenges and opportunities in multilateralism for trade and development. As of the date of submission of the present document, the final report of the conference had not been issued.
117   See www.imf.org/external/pubs/ft/fandd/2016/06/ostry.htm.
118   See www.imf.org/en/News/Articles/2015/09/28/04/53/sp041116; www.imf.org/en/News/Articles/ 2015/09/28/04/53/sp040516; and www.imf.org/en/News/Articles/2015/09/28/04/53/sp011216.
119   See www.unog.ch/80256EE600585943/(httpPages)/37D51189AC4FB6E1C1257F4D004CAFB2.
120   See www.conscienceonline.org.uk/wp-content/uploads/2016/06/Taxes-for-Peace-Bill-2016.pdf: "Every gun that is made, every warship launched, every rocket fired signifies, in the f inal sense a theft from those who hunger and are not fed, those who are cold and are not clothed. This world in arms is not spending money alone. It is spending the sweat of its labourers, the genius of its scientists, the hopes of its children. Dwight D. Eisenhower."
121   See Human Rights Council resolution 26/9; and www.globalreporting.org/Pages/FR -CSX-2016.aspx.
122   "The doctrine of abuse of rights (or *abus de droit*) is one of the many outgrowths of the legal principle of good faith." Sir Robert Jennings, ed., *Oppenheim's International Law*, 9th ed., p 407. "The doctrine prevents a Party to an agreement from exercising its rights in a way that is unreasonable in the light of the spirit of the agreement. Used frequently in international courts, the idea behind the abuse of rights doctrine is being increasingly recognized as a norm of international law." According to Sir Hersch Lauterpacht, the concept of abuse of rights is present in most developed legal systems and "it is only at a rudimentary stage of legal development that society permits the unchecked use of rights without regard to its social consequences." *The Development of International Law by the International Court* (1958), p. 162. See also Lauterpacht, *The Function of Law in the International Community* (1933), chap. 14 and a review of the 2011 republication of this work by Isabel Feichtner in *European Journal of International Law*, vol. 22, No. 4 (2011), pp. 1177–1179; G.D.S. Taylor, "The content of the rule against abuse of rights in international law," *British Yearbook of International Law*, vol. 46 (1972–1973), also citing Lauterpacht; and Alexandre Kiss, "Abuse of rights" in R. Wolfrum (ed.), *Max Planck Encyclopedia of Public International Law*, vol. I (2012), pp. 20–26.
123   https://www.bbc.com/news/av/business-36247017

Chapter 10
WORLD BANK GROUP

"During my three years as chief economist of the World Bank, labor market issues were looked at through the lens of neoclassical economics. 'Wage rigidities'—often the fruits of hard-fought bargaining—were thought part of the problem facing many countries. A standard message was to increase labor market flexibility. The not-so-subtle subtext was to lower wages and lay off unneeded workers. They had a strategy for job destruction. They had no strategy for job creation."

JOSEPH STIGLITZ[i]

Introduction[ii]

Back in 2015 the UN Special Rapporteur on Extreme Poverty, Philip Alston, described the World Bank as a "human rights–free zone."[iii] While this criticism still has validity, my impressions from attending the 2017 spring meeting of the World Bank and IMF and assessing the recent work of the World Bank Group give me reason to harbour moderate optimism. Certainly an awareness of the human rights impacts of the lending policies of the Bretton Woods institutions has been growing in and outside the World Bank institutions and numerous internal papers and new inspection mechanisms indicate that some reforms are on the way.

The Bretton Woods institutions were founded in 1944, even before the San Francisco Conference that adopted the United Nations Charter. While the International Bank for Reconstruction and Development, otherwise known as the World Bank, and the IMF both have association agreements with the United Nations, they operate independently from—and not always in tandem with—the General Assembly, Security Council, ECOSOC, UNCTAD, the Human Rights Council and other UN organs.

In my reports, I call on both the World Bank and the IMF to amend their Articles of Agreement so as to participate more fully in the achievement of the Purposes and Principles of the United Nations. Indeed, sometimes the activities of the international financial institutions do enter into conflict with the human rights and development goals of the United Nations, an anomaly that must be

---

i "Interview with Joseph Stiglitz." Lucy Komisar, *The Progressive*, June 2011.
ii This introduction is adapted from my introductory statement to the Human Rights Council on 13 September 2017, https://www.ohchr.org/en/NewsEvents/Pages/DisplayNews.aspx?NewsID=22075&LangID=E
iii https://www.ohchr.org/en/NewsEvents/Pages/DisplayNews.aspx?NewsID=16517&LangID=E

changed sooner rather than later. In particular, article IV, section 10, of the World Bank's Articles of Agreement, the so-called prohibition of "political activity" is often cited as preventing the Bank from integrating human rights considerations into its work.

There is no reason to consider the promotion of human rights as falling under this prohibition. But since some officials at the World Bank still refer to it, the Articles of Agreement should now be updated and brought into the 21st century, so that human rights considerations are no longer perceived as conflicting with the economic priorities of the institutions.

Neither the World Bank nor the IMF can escape the international human rights treaty regime, much of which, by 2017, has surely emerged as customary international law. Indeed, all States members of the World Bank and IMF are bound by provisions of numerous human rights treaties, including the International Covenant on Civil and Political Rights and the International Covenant on Economic, Social and Cultural Rights. As UN Member States, all Bank Members are also individually bound by the UN Charter, and required to uphold the Purposes and Principles of the United Nations. Member States and Observer States of the Human Rights Council should prevail upon the international financial institutions to live up to the human rights expectations that flow from these instruments. Indeed, there are no longer any human rights–free zones.

Whereas the World Bank has the word "Development" in its name, what does this mean in law and practice? Hitherto the Bank has understood development as growth in terms of gross domestic product (GDP), *increased trade and greater consumption. In my report I endorse an understanding of "development" as an improved standard of living, food security, clean water, sanitation, healthcare, housing, education, a level playing field, equal pay for equal work, and a more equitable distribution of wealth in larger freedom. Alas, we observe instead that the inequalities among States and within States have been growing.*

For many years, civil society has signalled human rights abuses committed by companies benefitting from World Bank financing. Non-governmental organizations including Human Rights Watch, Inclusive Development International, the Oakland Institute, Oxfam, the International Consortium of Investigative Journalists, Action for Solidarity Environment Equality and Diversity-Europe, the NGO Forum on the Asian Development Bank, Social Justice Connection, Amnesty International, the Bretton Woods Project, Earth Rights International and many others have issued expert publications that document these abuses. Among the most egregious violations are land-grabbing, brutal evictions, involuntary resettlement, forced labour, child labour, sexual abuse, massive pollution, destruction of the environment, reliance on tax havens, corruption and money-laundering. My report summarizes a few salient cases which are representative of widespread violations.

I also highlight concerns about the Bank's promotion of public-private partnerships, notwithstanding evidence showing that these partnerships often do not benefit the public. Although seen as a solution to constrained State budgets, such partnerships can result in encroachments by the private sector into the policy space of governments. When services delivered are of low quality, correspond to the interests of private partners instead of to the needs of the public, or when the projects fall through at great cost to governments, it is communities that suffer because their rights to water and sanitation, health care and education go unfulfilled.

Beyond the direct harm caused by some World Bank projects, I also take note of reports that the Bank has been funding harmful projects indirectly, through intermediary banks. Some of these projects would not ordinarily meet the Bank's own operational standards, either because the projects at issue result in serious environmental degradation or because the contracted companies have a history of complicity in grave human rights violations.

Finally, the Bank must concern itself with cases of reprisals against those who have opposed Bank projects. This is an issue that has been raised by the High Commissioner for Human Rights, by other Special Procedures mandate holders, and also by civil society. It bears repeating that communities must not be prevented from raising concerns about ineffective and harmful projects, especially when such projects threaten their environment and livelihoods, or otherwise violate their rights.

All this said, I acknowledge a number of positive features in the World Bank's practice that should be enhanced to build a human rights-based approach to inclusive development. For example, I applaud the World Bank for its recent report_highlighting the unequal access of populations to water, sanitation and adequate hygiene and for tying this inequality to the realization of the sustainable development goals.

In addition, in April 2017 I had the opportunity to attend several events held during the spring meetings of the World Bank and IMF in Washington, where I also met with lawyers and economists of both institutions as well as with representatives of civil society. I was pleased to observe a heightened awareness of human rights issues and a positive attitude toward preventing the negative impacts of the Bank's current lending practices, mega-projects, public-private partnerships and austerity conditionalities. In particular, I see promise in the World Bank's new Environmental and Social Framework, which sets out social standards against which projects are to be evaluated, including those related to labour conditions, environmental impacts, preservation of natural resources and the protection of indigenous peoples and cultural heritage. The chapter devoted to indigenous populations is particularly necessary—and should be further strengthened—given that indigenous communities have been despoiled of their natural resources for centuries and have had their livelihoods devastated by the destruction of their environment, land-grabbing and involuntary resettlement in violation of their right to free, prior and informed consent, as laid down in the Declaration on the Rights of Indigenous Peoples.

During the 2017 World Bank Spring meeting, I also had the opportunity to discuss monitoring and redress mechanisms with senior staff of the Bank's Inspection Panel and Compliance Advisor Ombudsman, two mechanisms whose excellent work should be given greater visibility and whose findings deserve expeditious implementation. The Inspection Panel receives complaints from individuals who believe they have been, or are likely to be, harmed by a Bank-financed project. It has also begun producing an "Emerging Lessons" series, which is a series of reports that highlight historically problematic issues drawn from the Panel's past cases. In my report, I also welcome the work of the Ombudsman, which is an internal accountability mechanism conducting independent investigations of the Bank's private sector activities. These mechanisms should be further strengthened, since they don't, in themselves, have enforcement power. To that end, I recommend that the World Bank take prompt and effective action consistent with the findings of these monitoring bodies, and that it widely disseminate their recommendations inside and outside the Bank. It is also imperative that victims are made aware of how to utilize these redress mechanisms.

Beyond amending its Articles of Agreement, I recommend in my report that the World Bank take full responsibility for the outcomes of its investments and implement preventive measures, including by conducting systematic human rights, health and environmental impact assessments before projects are approved. The Bank should ensure corrective measures with the effective participation by all stakeholders and protection of human rights defenders on the ground. Financing should be suspended when serious human rights violations occur, and no project affecting the lives and culture of indigenous peoples should be approved without the free, prior and informed consent of the peoples concerned. Further, when Bank-financed projects result in violations, victims must be ensured both recourse and effective remedy.

Procedurally, one of the challenges that must be addressed is the World Bank's undemocratic decision-making structure, which creates inequitable and sometimes counterproductive priority setting. Thus, the gentleman's agreement that World Bank leadership will be held by citizens of certain States should be gradually phased out. Further, as other rapporteurs have noted, the underrepresented voices of the developing world must be upgraded.

I further propose that the World Bank embark on an inclusive process for drafting a new and separate human rights policy, which should embody a commitment to integrate human rights into its work by analysing human rights issues relevant to development in the context of country strategies, advise *governments how to advance compliance with their human rights commitments, and identify human rights risks linked to its investments or advice. The Bank's Board of Directors should issue directives that mainstream human rights into the Bank's manifold activities. I also recommend that the Bank enhance cooperation with UN agencies and other international organizations, including ECOSOC, UNCTAD, ILO, WHO, UNESCO, UNICEF, UNHCR, and, of course, the Office of the High Commissioner of Human Rights, all of which have plans of action to advance development and human rights.*

In particular, the Bank should adopt and implement the Universal Social Protection Initiative and the ILO's Social Protection Floors Recommendation No. 202. It should support the inclusion of enforceable labour provisions based on ILO standards, and repeal investor-state-dispute settlement mechanisms that undermine governments' ontological right and responsibility to regulate for the wellbeing of all persons living under their jurisdiction.

The challenges to a democratic and equitable international order, as envisaged by this Council in September 2011, are numerous and require the cooperation and solidarity of all international institutions, including the international financial institutions. To meet these challenges—and to achieve the Sustainable Development Goals—I call on the World Bank to make the protection of human rights a core characteristic of its policy and practice.

The following are excerpts from my 2017 reports to the Human Rights Council in Geneva. —AdeZ

* * *

The present report is submitted pursuant to Human Rights Council resolution 33/3, in which the Council invited the Independent Expert to continue his research into the impact of the financial and economic policies pursued by international organizations and other institutions, in particular the World Bank and the International Monetary Fund, on a democratic and equitable international order.

Following an expert consultation hosted by the Office of the United Nations High Commissioner for Human Rights (OHCHR) in Geneva in October 2016, the Independent Expert decided to focus his report to the Council on the World Bank, and to devote his report to the General Assembly to International Monetary Fund (IMF) issues. The two reports should be read together, conscious that in the twenty-first century there are no "human rights–free zones,"[1] that all States, international organizations and non-state actors must respect the customary international law of human rights, and that the so-called "fragmentation" of international law cannot create "stand-alone regimes" or "legal black holes."

While international financial institutions can advance human rights and development, some of their policies have resulted in the erosion of the enabling of the human rights environment in some countries, especially through the promotion of neoliberal policies that weaken the public sector and hinder States in the fulfilment of their human rights treaty obligations in the fields of education, health care, labour standards and an adequate standard of living. Moreover, by financing enterprises that evade taxes, the World Bank abets the diversion of public resources away from public services. Increased Bank support for public-private partnerships enhances the private sector at the expense of communities, especially when investments go awry and result in greater costs to governments. Henceforth, international financial institutions should take a human rights-based approach to lending, consult stakeholders, conduct impact assessments, take action to counter reprisals, combat corruption and accept legal responsibilities by waiving "absolute immunity."

The Independent Expert believes that, since the World Bank and IMF have association agreements with the United Nations, they must support the General Assembly, the Economic and Social Council and the United Nations Conference on Trade and Development (UNCTAD) in advancing the purposes and principles of the United Nations, as set out in the Charter of the United Nations, and in advancing human rights and sustainable development, while respecting the sovereign equality of States and the principle of non-intervention in the domestic affairs of States. It bears repeating that the member States of the World Bank and IMF are also States parties to numerous United Nations human rights treaties, notably the International Covenant on Civil and Political Rights and the International Covenant on Economic, Social and Cultural Rights, and that they must ensure that the policies of financial institutions and the projects they support do not have adverse effects on human rights.[2]

Bearing in mind that States have an obligation to ensure that investors and transnational corporations do not violate human rights,[3] States should use their leverage to strengthen the human rights regime whenever they negotiate deals with governments to finance specific projects.[4] In that regard, the Independent Expert recalls the commitments made in 2015 by States at the United Nations summit for the adoption of the post-2015 development agenda and the adoption by the General Assembly of the Sustainable Development Goals (see General Assembly Resolution 70/1). The Addis Ababa Action Agenda of the Third International Conference on Financing for Development, adopted in 2015, also calls upon all development banks to establish or maintain social and environmental safeguards systems (see General Assembly Resolution 69/313).

In January 2016, the Independent Expert sent questionnaires to the World Bank, IMF, States, intergovernmental organizations and non-governmental organizations (NGOs). He expresses deep appreciation for their cooperation and the many statistics and clarifications received.

In April 2017, he attended several events at the spring meeting of the World Bank and IMF, conducted bilateral exchanges with lawyers and economists in both institutions, and liaised with civil society organizations. He endorses the pertinent studies and reports of OHCHR and special procedure mandate holders who have focused on manifold aspects of the work of international financial institutions . He draws insight from substantive studies prepared by NGOs[5] and academics.

The World Bank Group is composed of the International Bank for Reconstruction and Development (IBRD), the International Finance Corporation (IFC), the International Development Association (IDA), the Multilateral Investment Guarantee Agency and the International Centre for Settlement of Investment Disputes. Since 2012, Jim Yong Kim has been President of the World Bank Group. The present report focuses on the work of IBRD and IFC.

The publications of the World Bank Group document their awareness of impacts on human rights. The evolution of the Bank's own social assessment framework acknowledges the Bank's human rights responsibilities. The present report does not aspire to tell the Bank what it already knows or what its experts are busy trying to address. It hopes to formulate realistic recommendations, applying a human rights-based approach. In that regard, the Bank's Articles of Agreement should be amended to integrate the promotion of human rights, and directives should be issued by the Board of Governors to mainstream human rights. A revised mission statement that reconciles the economic and financial priorities with human rights is desirable.[6] Even the words written on the great wall at the entrance of the Bank ("Our dream is a world free of poverty") serve as a call for action.

Over the past 60 years, the activities of IFC, which was established in 1956, have given rise to more criticism than that usually directed at the World Bank. As the Bank's private lending arm, IFC also has idealistic language on its website, where it boasts that the Bank's mission "is to fight poverty with passion and professionalism, for lasting results."[7] The Independent Expert agrees that that mission is achievable.

POSITIVE FEATURES

The World Bank acknowledges that "sustainable development recognizes that growth must be both inclusive and environmentally sound to reduce poverty and build shared prosperity for today's population and to continue to meet the needs of future generations. It is efficient with resources and carefully planned to deliver both immediate and long-term benefits for people, planet, and prosperity."[8]

To that end, in 2006 the Bank adopted the Environmental and Social Framework, comprising:

- A vision for sustainable development, which sets out the Bank's aspirations regarding environmental and social sustainability;
- An environmental and social policy for project financing, setting out mandatory requirements for projects it supports;
- Ten environmental and social standards, setting out mandatory requirements for borrowers and projects.

The vision statement of the new Environmental and Social Framework formulates a strategy that "sets out the corporate goals of ending extreme poverty and promoting shared prosperity in all its partner countries," including goals relevant to human rights, such as environmental sustainability, social inclusion and the preservation of resources. Within the Framework, 10 environmental and social standards, which are designed to support borrowers' projects, focus on: (a) social risks and impacts; (b) labour and working conditions; (c) pollution prevention; (d) health and safety; (e) land acquisition, land use and involuntary resettlement; (f) sustainable management of living natural resources; (g) indigenous peoples; (h) cultural heritage; (i) financial intermediaries; and (j) stakeholder engagement and information disclosure.

The vision goes beyond "do no harm" and aims at maximizing development gains. Thus, where the borrower's environmental and social assessment has identified potential development opportunities associated with a project, the Bank will discuss with the borrower the feasibility of incorporating those opportunities into the project. Moreover, the Bank is committed to work with borrowers to identify strategic initiatives and goals to address national development priorities and maintain dialogue on environmental and social issues with donor governments, international organizations, countries of operation and civil society.

There is no shortage of opinions about the impact of the World Bank on the international order. Some observers contend that the Bank and IMF have a greater impact on world affairs than all the resolutions of the United Nations General Assembly and the Economic and Social Council combined. While the supremacy clause in Article 103 of the Charter of the United Nations stipulates that the Charter shall prevail over all other international agreements, the fact is that the Bretton Woods institutions are not subordinated to the General Assembly and the Security Council and that they will continue to have a determining effect on world affairs, including the enjoyment of civil, cultural, economic, political and social rights.

Many in academia have been studying the impact of World Bank policies on human rights and the international order. Already in 2003 the Tilburg Guiding Principles on World Bank, IMF and Human Rights were adopted.[9] A follow-up conference at the University of Tilburg in the Netherlands entitled "Globalization and Transnational Human Rights Obligations," led to the adoption of the Tilburg-Glothro Guiding Principles in 2015. Similarly, in 2009, the Indian Law Resource Centre issued the "Principles of International Law for Multinational Development Banks,"[10] in which scholars refuted the argument that the international financial institutions are somehow above the law and that they only have to honour their charters and constitutions.

Whereas the Bank has the word "development" in its name, the question must be answered what development means for the purposes of the Articles of Agreement. Hitherto, both in doctrine and in practice, the Bank has understood development to mean growth in terms of gross domestic product (GDP), increased trade and greater consumption. Observers have been proposing a different understanding of "development," as a more equitable distribution of wealth, food security, clean water, sanitation, health care, housing, education and employment. The inequalities among States and within States, however, have been growing in many countries, where unemployment has increased, particularly affecting young people, and the actual standard of living has dropped.

CHALLENGES

Notwithstanding the positive developments described above, both the Bank and IMF continue pressing for increased reliance on purely market-based solutions, following the perspective of "market fundamentalism" that Joseph Stiglitz often decried.[11] In 2016, there was increased cooperation among multilateral development banks, with a focus on mega-infrastructure projects, a reliance on public-private partnerships[12] as a way to circumvent constrained fiscal space, and a continued effort to impose so-called labour flexibilization and other obsolete conditionalities on States.

As Naomi Klein recalls in her seminal work, *The Shock Doctrine,* the main problem remains the commitment of international financial institutions to the philosophy of laissez-faire economics, reflecting Milton Friedman's Chicago school and characterized by the almost religious belief that privatization and deregulation will advance GDP, notwithstanding its endemic boom and bust cycles and its minimization of social costs.[13]

For many years, civil society has signalled human rights abuses committed by companies benefiting from World Bank financing, with numerous publications documenting those abuses. Among the most egregious violations are land-grabbing, brutal evictions, involuntary resettlement, forced labour,[14] child labour, sexual abuse, massive pollution, destruction of the environment, reprisals against human rights defenders, corruption and money-laundering. The present report summarizes a few salient cases that are representative of widespread violations.

Ahead of the Bank spring meeting in April 2016, Oxfam released a report entitled "The IFC and tax havens," in which it revealed that 51 of the 68 companies in which IFC had invested in sub-Saharan Africa in 2015 used tax havens.[15] As described in the Independent Expert's 2016 report to the General Assembly (A/71/286), that deprives countries in the region of essential tax revenue which could be used to meet their human rights obligations, fulfil the Sustainable Development Goals and repay foreign debts. In fact, UNCTAD estimates that developing countries lose $100 billion annually in tax revenue, from which lost revenues and uninvested earnings yield a total development finance loss in the range of $250-300 billion.[16] It is time for the Bank to blacklist projects with companies that fail to pay their taxes.

There is ample evidence that projects financed by the Bank cause harm to millions of people. A 2015 report by the International Consortium of Investigative Journalists states that from 2009 to 2013, the Bank pumped $50 billion into projects graded the highest risk for "irreversible or unprecedented" social or environmental impacts.[17] The report also indicates that the Bank and IFC have financed governments and companies accused of human rights violations, including murder and torture. In some cases, they continue to finance those borrowers, notwithstanding the evidence.[18]

Environmental degradation, evictions and forced resettlement[19]

Among the vulnerable groups that have suffered as a consequence of major prospecting, mining, logging and hydroelectric enterprises are indigenous peoples whose lands have been taken away or devastated though industrial activity, without consultation and without their free, prior and informed consent.[20]

In 2015, the International Consortium of Investigative Journalists determined that 3.4 million persons had been physically or economically displaced by projects funded by the Bank, including the Ethiopian Anuak, who faced a violent campaign of mass evictions funded through the diversion of funds from a Bank-supported project.[21]

In 2016, the Consortium reported on the Bank's support to an agribusiness project that violated safeguards for indigenous people in Tanzania. Following massive protests by NGOs, the Bank initially retreated, but in March 2016 the Bank's

Board granted a full waiver of its safeguard policy (Operational Policy 4.10), creating an unfortunate precedent. At issue was a $70 million loan to the Southern Agricultural Growth Corridor of Tanzania (SAGCOT), a government initiative that evicted indigenous herders in the Barabaig region in order to transfer fertile agricultural lands to investors.[22] The Consortium has also reported on abuses in the mining sector,[23] including those connected with gold mining in Peru.[24]

The waiver of the Bank's Operational Policy on Indigenous Peoples was the subject of a communication addressed in February 2017 to the Bank by the Special Rapporteur on the rights of indigenous peoples and the Independent Expert on the effects of foreign debt and other related international financial obligations of States on the full enjoyment of all human rights, particularly economic, social and cultural rights. The communication noted that:

> The SAGCOT project may have a significant impact on nomadic and semi-nomadic pastoralist groups that self-identify as indigenous peoples, including the Barbaig, the Datoga, the Hadzabe and the Maasai, who depend on lands in the project areas for their daily livelihood and survival . . . we think that it is essential that projects aimed at improving the social safety net in Tanzania are designed in such a manner that Indigenous People can benefit from them . . . and that Indigenous People are fully consulted.[25]

The Special Rapporteur and the Independent Expert concluded that "the granting by the Board of waivers to OP 4.10 . . . is problematic both from a normative and an operational point of view. By taking for granted the unilateral contention that OP 4.10 contradicts the provisions of the national constitution . . . this generates evident protection gaps with relation to the rights of indigenous groups."[26]

In its response of March 2017, the Bank argued that "the project preparation team drew upon the advice of local and international experts and Indigenous Peoples' representatives. In particular, the government agreed to prepare a safeguards instrument aligned with the requirements of OP 4.10, known as the Vulnerable Groups Planning Framework (VGPF)."[27]

It further clarified that:

> The World Bank's Board of Executive Directors took account of the project design, the legal documents including the legal covenants related to the VGPF, and approved the SAGCOT Investment Project . . . the sub-project eligibility criteria has been designed to limit the potential impact of sub-projects on the land rights of host communities — the Project will not support investments that involve the reallocation of land from smallholders to agribusinesses.[28]

Human Rights Watch has also highlighted instances in which the Bank failed to observe its own policy of protecting indigenous peoples' rights. For example, it documented the forcible transfer of the semi-nomadic Nuer people in the Gambella region of Ethiopia, noting an operational link between World Bank projects and a government relocation programme known as "villagization." The matter came before the Bank Inspection Panel, which indeed found that the Bank "did not carry out the required full risk analysis, nor were its mitigation measures adequate."[29]

In 2014, the Bank approved a $73 million grant for the Inga hydropower project in the Democratic Republic of Congo, despite the Board noting "significant implementation risks." In July 2016, the Bank suspended funding. The NGO International Rivers commented that the Bank should not have been involved in the project in the first place, because "Inga represents a failed development model which bypasses the poor for the benefit of extractive industry and export markets."[30]

Labour rights violations

Civil society has also drawn attention to labour rights violations in connection with World Bank projects. Human Rights Watch's "Toxic Toil" report, for example, documents the flagrant violation of children's rights and the exposure of child labourers to mercury poisoning in Tanzania. In it, Human Rights Watch calls upon the gold mining industry to establish a thorough due diligence process, including regular monitoring, to eliminate child labour in supply chains.[31]

Further, in commenting on the Bank's compliance investigation into an IFC investment in Indian tea plantations, Human Rights Watch notes:

> The IFC invested millions ... without taking into account serious labor and other human rights abuses in the sector. ... The IFC failed to identify and address basic risks, including the grossly inadequate living conditions for workers and child labor. ... IFC deficiencies have been in part due to its culture and incentives that measure results in financial terms, encouraging staff to "overlook, fail to articulate, or even conceal potential environmental, social, and conflict related risks.[32]

Moreover, in the past, the IFC has failed to properly measure the risks of oil and mining projects, such as in the case of the Chad-Cameroon pipeline. In that case, a law intended to earmark oil revenues for education, health care and other social needs was gutted in Chad and the Bank ultimately had to suspend its loan to the country.[33]

Although Cameroon has ratified most of the International Labour Organization (ILO) Conventions regulating labour and workers' living conditions, and World Bank clients are obliged to enforce Bank directives on occupational health and safety, violations of workers' rights continue unabated. One example concerns China International Water and Electric Corporation, which participates in the Bank-financed Lorn Pangor Hydro Power Project, which has witnessed repeated complaints made to the Bank concerning environmental and social management problems. In January 2014, a report by the Cameroon Network of Human Rights Organizations called the human rights situation on the project site deplorable. The Electricity Development Corporation of Cameroon and the labour inspector have failed to compel the Corporation to respect labour legislation.[34]

Circumventing rules by outsourcing lending

Beyond the direct harm caused by some World Bank projects, civil society advocates have pointed out that the Bank has been funding human rights-insensitive corporations indirectly, through intermediary banks. A discrete or "invisible" way of doing that occurred when IFC financed six Indian commercial banks that in turn financed abusive companies. As reported by Inclusive Development International:

> Recipients of indirect IFC funds include Vedanta Resources, NHPC Limited and Jindal Steel & Power, which have well-documented records of complicity in grave human rights violations and environmental destruction. These companies would have little chance of receiving direct assistance from the IFC. Yet by outsourcing its development funds to for-profit commercial banks, the IFC is ... concealing its support from public scrutiny. In doing so, the IFC is providing little oversight in how its funds are used.[35]

Inclusive Development International has identified 68 Indian companies or projects implicated in serious harmful environmental impacts or abusive human rights practices that received funding from IFC intermediaries. As noted in the report, "we're seeing a worrying trend—not just at the World Bank but other development banks too—of hands-off lending through third parties to projects they would never usually touch. At the same time, the Bank is washing its hands of the mounting human and environmental costs—to forests, rivers and communities."[36]

Similarly, an October 2016 briefing note by Oxfam states:

> Over the past six years, the International Finance Corporation has channelled over $50bn to the financial sector, and its long-term

investments in financial intermediaries such as commercial banks and private equity funds have dramatically risen by 45 per cent. . . . However, the evidence continues to grow that . . . the World Bank Group has little control over how a great deal of this money is spent. This lack of accountability is having devastating impacts on many poor communities.[37]

While some progress is being achieved, as Oxfam commented at the end of the 2017 World Bank and IMF meeting, still more could be done, "we're encouraged by the IFC's commitments to improve oversight and be more selective of its high-risk financial intermediary investments. . . . What we're still waiting for, and which is key, is transparency from the IFC to show where their money is really ending up."[38]

Public-private partnerships

Many civil society organizations have protested the Bank's apparent commitment to the promotion of public-private partnerships, notwithstanding the challenges they pose to the regulatory space of governments, especially in the fields of clean water and sanitation, health services and education. In fact, the year 2016 was characterized by an intensified push for megaprojects and public-private partnerships.[39]

However, experience shows that public-private partnerships have not served developing countries well. For example, it appears that the flagship health public-private partnership of IFC threatens to disrupt health-care programmes in Lesotho. In 1999, the Queen Mamohato Memorial Hospital, a new hospital run by the private sector and financed through an IFC loan, was built to replace the old main public hospital in Lesotho. Lesotho finds itself locked into an 18-year contract that is already consuming more than half of the country's health budget, while producing high returns to the private partner.[40] That constitutes a dangerous diversion of scarce public funds from primary health-care services in rural areas, where three quarters of the population live. Not only are health public-private partnerships high risk and costly, they fail to advance the goal of universal and equitable health coverage.

In another case, in August 2016, the Minister of Education of Uganda announced the closure of 63 nursery and primary schools operated by Bridge International Academies, a private education services provider partly financed by IFC. The Minister stated that the decision was based on "danger from poor hygiene and sanitation on the life and safety of the innocent children."[41]

Similarly, in its response to the questionnaire sent by the Independent Expert, Open Society, Armenia, observed that, despite spending more than $100 million to support the Armenian education system, almost no systemic impact or improvement was recorded from an education public-private partnership supported by the Bank. On the contrary, the loans served to increase unequal access to quality education. Elsewhere in Europe, after examining the use of public-private partnerships in Portugal, the Organisation for Economic Co-operation and Development (OECD) warned that public-private partnerships "should be chosen only when they represent good value for money, not because they allow the government to escape budget restrictions by building up off-balance sheet liabilities."[42]

Worryingly, however, OECD has continued to endorse public-private partnerships, stating that "the government should consider expanding its remit to local public-private partnerships and water, sewage and waste sectors."[43]

Reprisals

Although development banks increasingly acknowledge the importance of public participation for effective development, a growing number of governments have embarked upon broad and sometimes brutal campaigns to shut down the space for civil society activity, in some cases going so far as to criminalize independent human rights work.[44] Those abusive measures exclude people from participating in decision-making, from publicly opposing development projects that may harm their livelihoods, and from complaining about initiatives that are ineffective.

In its response to the questionnaire sent by the Independent Expert,[45] Human Rights Watch noted that international financial institutions have done little to prevent reprisals against critics of projects that they finance. A 2015 Human Rights Watch report on reprisals against critics of World Bank Group projects describes how people in Cambodia, India, Uganda, Uzbekistan and elsewhere have faced reprisals from governments and powerful companies in connection with their critique of Bank projects.[46]

An Uzbek human rights defender, in exile after raising the issue of forced labour in projects benefiting his Government's cotton sector, stated, "the World Bank has not taken any meaningful measures to ensure that independent human rights defenders like me can monitor for abuses linked to the projects they fund. Nor have Bank staff spoken out against the government's attacks on my colleagues and me."[47] The defender, whose case was raised with the Government of Uzbekistan by special procedure mandate holders, was allegedly detained and ill-treated in connection with his monitoring of the sector,[48] although the Government denies that.[49]

Human Rights Watch further documents the fact that in Azerbaijan, although the Extractive Industries Transparency Initiative[50] prevailed upon the Government to stop its crackdown on independent civil society, and despite the fact that the Bank endorsed that recommendation, project funding continued unabated.[51]

In addition, reprisals are routinely inflicted by enterprises on indigenous and other persons who oppose land-grabbing and pollution. One of the most notorious cases, which has been regularly raised by the special procedure mandate holders, is that of Berta Cáceres, who was killed in March 2016.[52] Two of those facing charges for her murder were employees of a company involved in the construction of the Agua Zarca dam, a project financed not by the Bank but by Dutch, Finnish and Central American banks. Although the Bank was not responsible for financing that project, it was hit by so much collateral outrage that it became necessary to issue a press release, in which Bank President Jim Yong Kim stated:

> We deplore the high level of fear and violence in Honduras. Berta Cáceres was one of dozens of environmental activists who have been killed during the last six years. We urge the Government to address the deep-rooted land conflict in the region and bring this violence to an end. We know that strong environmental and social policies are key to achieving our goals of ending extreme poverty and boosting shared prosperity. This makes it all the more important that voices of people like Berta are not silenced.[53]

The United Nations High Commissioner for Human Rights also observed:

> Over the past year, at least six more campaigners have been killed in Honduras, including . . . José de los Santos Sevilla, the leader of the indigenous Tolupán people. Seven were killed in Colombia, Guatemala and Mexico during a single week in January, in connection with hydroelectric dams, mining and agribusiness projects. . . . In addition to murder, the tools of repression include curbs on peaceful assembly, clampdowns on non-governmental organizations, attacks on independent media, state censorship, draconian antiterror laws, state-sponsored vilification, surveillance, arbitrary detention, torture and disappearances. In some countries, punitive laws and special law-enforcement agencies have been created specifically to protect investors' interests.[54]

Business bias

In 2002, the Bank started the Doing Business project,[55] with the mandate to rank countries on how their national regulations operate in favour of the "ease of doing business." From its inception, the project was criticized for promoting deregulation and the lowering of social and environmental standards. The Bank responded by removing the project's "employing workers" indicator from its scoring methodology, because it undermined labour standards and internationally recognized workers' rights.[56] The Oakland Institute has decried that and other flawed benchmarks, including the "paying taxes" indicator, which rewards the reduction of all types of corporate taxes, including environmental and social taxes levied to protect citizens and the planet.[57] The most recent Doing Business report actually notes as "good reforms" the abolition of environmental protection fees for corporations in Spain[58] and Viet Nam,[59] and praises the reduction of private sector taxes in a total of 28 countries.[60] Another example of incomprehensible interference in the necessary regulatory space of States is the bad score given to Tanzania as "punishment" for introducing a workers' compensation tariff to be paid by employers,[61] and the bad grade accorded to Malta for increasing employers' maximum social security contribution.[62]

Based on the Doing Business model, the Bank initiated the Enabling the Business of Agriculture project in 2013. It scores countries on a range of agriculture-related "good regulatory practices," including how governments facilitate the importation and distribution of chemical fertilizers, implement intellectual property rights in agriculture,[63] enable private seed companies to increase profits, or facilitate the marketing of industrial seeds as opposed to seeds produced and exchanged by farmers, which are cheaper, more diverse and readily available in developing countries.

Those indexes are followed by investors and used by the Bank and bilateral donors to guide their funding. The Bank's Investment Climate department[64] provides advisory services to countries relying on the Doing Business scores. According to the Oakland Institute, "in many countries such interventions have assisted with the creation of 'one-stop shop' agencies to attract foreign direct investments, notably through offering cheap land leases, water access and tax breaks to corporations."[65] Whereas no scientific evidence[66] supports the selection of benchmarking topics by the Doing Business and Enabling the Business of Agriculture projects, or proves their effectiveness in fighting poverty, the Bank leverages such indexes to influence policy reforms around the world.

It is not without significance that over 280 civil society organizations, farmers' groups, unions and think tanks have endorsed the Oakland Institute's "Our Land

Our Business" campaign, which denounces the Bank's imposition of normative, standardized sets of reforms.[67]

Ahead of the Bank's release of the 2017 "Enabling the Business of Agriculture" report,[68] 157 organizations and academics from around the world criticized "the Bank's scheme to hijack farmers' right to seeds, attack on food sovereignty and the environment."[69] The statement decries the fact that "the EBA dictates so-called 'good practices' to regulate agriculture and scores countries on how well they implement its prescriptions." In reality, however, as the Oakland Institute adds, "the EBA has become the latest tool to push pro-corporate agricultural policies, notably in the seed sector."

Immunity of the World Bank from litigation in domestic courts?

Hitherto the World Bank has been shielded from liability for human rights abuses by virtue of the Convention on the Privileges and Immunities of the Specialized Agencies.[70] However, as international law evolves, and in a similar way as Head of State immunity was loosened since the Pinochet arrest warrant in 1998,[71] the time has come for international financial institutions to be made accountable for harm resulting from loan practices and lack of due diligence.

Earth Rights International, a non-governmental advocacy group focused on the environment, has filed two claims against IFC in United States federal courts,[72] in which it argues that absolute immunity is an anachronism.[73] The first, *Jam v. International Finance Corporation,* came before Washington D.C. district and circuit courts regarding the negative impacts of the Tata Mundra coal power plant in India.[74] In that case, IFC had provided $450 million for a power plant that the plaintiffs showed had degraded the environment and destroyed their livelihoods. While the courts have to date held that IFC enjoys absolute immunity,[75] the plaintiffs continue to challenge the decision and, at the time of writing of the present report, are requesting permission to present their arguments *en banc,* or before a full seating of all D.C. circuit court judges.[76]

In a second lawsuit, *Juana Doe v. IFC,* Earth Rights charges the Bank with responsibility for systematic human rights abuses committed by Dinant, a sprawling palm-oil plantation accused of engaging in bloody land-grabbing, intimidation and murder of indigenous persons in the Bajo Aguán region of Honduras.[77] The lawsuit alleges that since the mid-1990s, IFC, together with a financial intermediary, the IFC Asset Management Corporation, has invested millions of dollars in Honduran palm-oil companies. For nearly two decades, farmer cooperatives have challenged Dinant's claims to 16 palm-oil plantations, alleging that land was taken from the farmer cooperatives through fraud, cocrcion and actual or threatened violence. For its part, Earth Rights contends that IFC has "repeatedly and consistently provided critical funding to Dinant, knowing that Dinant was waging a campaign of violence, terror, and dispossession against farmers, and that their money would be used to aid the commission of gross human rights abuses." The claimants cite United States government sources to substantiate allegations that more than 100 farmers have been killed since 2009.[78] Furthermore, the suit relies in part on reports of the IFC internal watchdog, the Compliance Advisor Ombudsman, who determined that the Bank had failed to spot or deliberately ignored the serious social, political and human rights context when implementing the project.

Credit-rating agencies

Every exercise of power, including economic power, must be subject to democratic controls, transparency and accountability. Many countries believe that inadequate or even deliberately false credit ratings and questionable rating processes were key contributors to the Asian financial crisis,[79] and more recently to the global financial crisis of 2007/08.[80] It is obvious that reforms are necessary, but it appears that the Bank is not yet tackling the impact of those institutions, whose ratings influence the Bank's decisions to grant or deny loans. It is the view of the Independent Expert that the Bank has a responsibility to test the reliability of the ratings by private sector agencies, or develop its own rating mechanisms and institutions[81] that can perform more objectively and effectively.[82]

Ongoing research

Without a doubt, the World Bank has enormous potential for good and its staff of brilliant lawyers and economists is capable of devising policies and mechanisms to advance an agenda of economic growth cum human rights. Many of their studies recognize the key importance of human rights for development and formulate pertinent recommendations. However, those recommendations are not always put into effect.

Yet some products of World Bank researchers are not above criticism. The environmental and social justice organization Action for Solidarity Environment Equality and Diversity Europe[83] notes:

> The World Bank is the institution with one of the largest research budgets globally and has no rival in the field of development economics.... A number of researchers and scholars have questioned the reliability of the World Bank-commissioned research.... Regarding the World Development Report (WDR)

series, for example, Nicholas Stern, an Oxford professor in economics and former World Bank chief economist says that many of the numbers used by the Bank come from highly dubious sources, or have been constructed in ways which leaves one skeptical as to whether they can be helpfully applied.[84]

Since the Bank is aware of that criticism, there is hope that sooner rather than later the paradigm will change.

GOOD PRACTICES

For several decades now, human rights have emerged as global priorities that the World Bank no longer ignores. In 2000, universal primary education became a Millennium Development Goal. In 2011, the Guiding Principles on Business and Human Rights were adopted.[85] In 2013, the Bank and the World Health Organization (WHO) committed to universal health coverage. In 2015, the Bank and ILO agreed on an integrated set of policies designed to ensure income security and support to all people across the life cycle, known as the Universal Social Protection Initiative.[86] At the same time, there is keen awareness about environmental issues at the Bank, and efforts are under way to address them, such as the adoption of the Climate Change Action Plan, aimed at helping States implement their obligations under the Paris Agreement reached at the twenty-first session of the Conference of the Parties to the United Nations Framework Convention on Climate Change.[87]

Environmental and Social Framework

In April 2016, after a four-year process, the World Bank Board approved a new Environmental and Social Framework to replace the existing safeguards.[88] The Independent Expert welcomes it as a basis upon which further developments can be advanced. For instance, the new policy on free, prior and informed consent sets a standard for companies and financial institutions, including the 72 export credit agencies and private banks that commit to the Equator Principles—a voluntary set of standards for identifying and managing social and environmental risk in project financing.[89] However, while the free, prior and informed consent policy in the new Environmental and Social Framework requires collective consent, it is also important to ensure that minority viewpoints are not overlooked.

Even strong critics of the World Bank have identified the potential of the new framework, particularly the requirement that IFC clients secure the free, prior and informed consent of indigenous communities prior to launching development activities. The President of Oxfam America observed that "IFC has been widely criticized for funding socially and environmentally risky projects that, in some cases, have had negative impacts on local communities, but IFC's efforts to improve its lending policies are a step in the right direction." The executive director of Oxfam Australia noted that "the revised IFC Sustainability Framework has the potential to help indigenous people get their fair share of natural resource wealth, particularly in emerging economies and conflict-prone countries."[90]

While much in the Environmental and Social Framework is welcome and imaginative lawyers will press for more transparency and accountability, civil society organizations have signalled some regrettable lacunae,[91] including the failure to make a binding commitment to the protection of human rights, especially when it comes to balancing competing rights and interests,[92] and the failure to commit to implementing the core ILO Conventions.

Amnesty International pointed out, after contributing to the elaboration of the Environmental and Social Framework through several submissions, that "the Bank's refusal to address its own responsibility to respect human rights . . . means that it is lagging behind other International Financial Institutions and risks creating major reputational risks for the institution."[93] Amnesty urged the Bank "to ensure that the ESF allows for adequate human rights due diligence in order to identify, prevent and/or mitigate all potential negative impacts on human rights."[94]

Similarly, the NGO Forum on the Asian Development Bank (ADB) and Social Justice Connection cautioned that "gains have been largely undermined by the replacement of clear time-bound requirements with vague language, loopholes, flexible principles and reliance upon 'borrower system'."[95] The International Trade Union Confederation raised additional concerns over the absence of any reference to the ILO core conventions, which prohibit discrimination, child and forced labour, and require respect for freedom of association and the right to collective bargaining. The director of the Confederation's Washington office commented that "it should be an imperative for the Bank to ensure full consistency with the norms of the recognised international standard-setting bodies, including the ILO for labour."[96]

The Independent Expert considers that the Environmental and Social Framework should have explicitly required that all decisions on financing of projects be preceded by ex ante human rights, health and environmental impact assessments and that review mechanisms be devised to continue monitoring impacts for the duration of every project.

Inspection Panel

In 1993, the World Bank Executive Board established an Inspection Panel[97] as an independent complaints mechanism for persons who believe they have been, or are likely to be, harmed by a Bank-funded project. Over the past 24 years, the Panel has taken steps to maintain and improve accountability in the Bank and assist management to implement transformational projects. Composed of three members who respond directly to the Bank's Executive Board and remain independent of the Bank's management, the Panel's mission is to ensure accountability for the Bank's human rights and environmental obligations. All reports that are prepared by the Panel, including the initial complaint, are made public, but the identities of the complainants remain confidential, if they so wish.

The Inspection Panel has jurisdiction over projects financed by IBRD and IDA. Complaints about IFC and Multilateral Investment Guarantee Agency-supported projects are dealt with by the Office of the Compliance Advisor Ombudsman.[98]

Owing to its ability to conduct compliance investigations, the Inspection Panel has growing potential to redress injustices associated with the Bank's loans. The kind of dispute resolution provided can address core concerns of affected communities through negotiation and provide an opportunity to remedy abuses. In that regard, the Panel has investigated the alleged harm to people's livelihoods or environmental degradation resulting from infrastructure projects. The Panel has also considered projects affecting the rights of indigenous peoples, including land rights and sacred sites, projects affecting natural habitats, stress on water sources, adverse impacts on wetlands, deforestation, loss of biodiversity, and projects involving forced relocation, owing, for example, to the building of a dam, road, pipeline, landfill or power plant. The Panel's mandate, however, does not extend to issues relating to the procurement of goods or services, suspected fraud or corruption. The latter can be reported to the World Bank's Integrity Vice Presidency.[99]

In 2013, 20 years after the creation of the Inspection Panel, the Panel introduced its Pilot for Early Solutions programme as a second chance deferral process that entails putting an investigation on hold while allowing World Bank management time to resolve community complaints. Whereas the Pilot's second implementation in Paraguay seems to have worked well, experience elsewhere has shown that removal of a complaint from the Panel's transparent process may perpetuate the power imbalance, leaving the communities to negotiate directly with the same Bank staff and government officials responsible for the problems.[100] Thus, the Pilot programme should be reformed or terminated.

In response to the Human Rights Watch report on reprisals, several international financial institution accountability mechanisms are developing guidelines to prevent, monitor and respond to reprisals. For example, on 30 March 2016, the Inspection Panel published guidelines to reduce retaliation risks and respond to retaliation during the Panel process.[101] The Panel also collaborates with other complaints mechanisms, such as the European Investment Bank, with whom it completed a joint investigation in Kenya in 2015, adopting a mediation process. According to the Panel's 2015/2016 Annual Report,[102] the Panel carried out investigations in cases concerning Kenya and Uganda, and Kosovo,[103] and is engaged in pending cases in Armenia, Colombia, Mongolia and Uganda.In addition to the guidelines, the Inspection Panel launched its Emerging Lessons Series in 2016, in which errors are acknowledged and solutions proposed.[104] The first in the series, published in April 2016, concerns involuntary resettlement,[105] the second concerns indigenous peoples (October 2016),[106] while a third focuses on environmental assessment (April 2017). Those are important tools for the Bank, governments, businesses and civil society.

In the opinion of the Independent Expert, who is a former Chief of Petitions at OHCHR, the Inspection Panel holds enormous promise for petitioners and should ensure continuous monitoring of World Bank projects. The downside of the procedure is that the Panel does not have the authority to enforce its recommendations. Nevertheless, that is a challenge also shared by United Nations treaty bodies like the Human Rights Committee and the Committee on Economic, Social and Cultural Rights, both of which have complaints procedures.[107]

Taking preventive and corrective action

While *ex ante* impact assessments are necessary, a system of monitoring ongoing projects and the mechanism to suspend financing when human rights, health or environmental problems arise should be strengthened. For instance, in 2016, the Bank learned of widespread sexual abuse of workers in a $250 million bank-financed road construction project in Uganda. After unsuccessful attempts to correct the situation, financing was terminated. Yet *ex post* termination is insufficient. As World Bank President Jim Yong Kim stated:

> The multiple failures we've seen in this project—on the part of the World Bank, the government of Uganda and a government contractor—are unacceptable.... It is our obligation to properly supervise all investment projects to ensure that the poor and vulnerable are protected in our work.... I am committed to making sure we do everything in our power ... first to fully review

the circumstances of this project and then to quickly learn from our and others' failures so they do not happen again.[108]

An Inspection Panel report led to further action by the Bank and a 2017 Bank management response containing concrete proposals for reparation and lessons learned. It stated:

> Management has undertaken steps on two fronts—both project-level and system-wide, to address these issues. At the project level this has included steps to provide support for the victims of child abuse; to complete the compensation process; to address construction issues; to support capacity-building of the implementing agency; and support for response to gender-based violence.[109]

In 2014, the Bank had to reconsider a cotton industry project in Uzbekistan, when it learned of widespread forced labour, including child labour. As a senior international financial institutions researcher at Human Rights Watch noted, "the World Bank's proposals fall short in Uzbekistan, where forced labor in the cotton sector is uniquely government-orchestrated and supported by repressing independent groups.... The World Bank needs to ensure that independent groups and journalists can monitor World Bank projects and report forced labor without fear of reprisal."[110]

Compliance Advisor Ombudsman

As mentioned above, the Office of the Compliance Advisor Ombudsman, created in 1991, is the independent accountability mechanism for IFC and the Multilateral Investment Guarantee Agency (MIGA). The Office of the Compliance Advisor Ombudsman is mandated "to serve as a fair, trusted, and effective independent accountability mechanism and to improve the environmental and social performance of IFC and MIGA." The Office of the Compliance Advisor Ombudsman chooses its investigations independently and reports directly to the President of the World Bank Group.

Among its recent investigations, the Office of the Compliance Advisor Ombudsman has made useful recommendations concerning the failure of the IFC to monitor the environmental and social performance of the Amalgamated Plantations Private Limited project in India. It concluded:

> CAO has made a number of noncompliance findings.... These cover IFC's pre-investment E&S (environmental and social) review as well as its supervision of the project ... IFC underestimated the E&S challenges associated with the project. Addressing these

in accordance with IFC requirements will require the dedication of resources and relevant sectoral expertise beyond that which IFC has made available to the client to date.... In light of the noncompliance findings ... CAO will keep this investigation for monitoring ... until actions taken by IFC assure CAO that IFC is addressing its noncompliance findings.[111]

In another case, the Office of the Compliance Advisor Ombudsman audited IFC investment in a coal-fired power plant near the port town of Mundra in Gujarat, India. Complainants were fisher people living in the vicinity of the project who suffered environmental impacts of the plant operation. The audit concluded that:

IFC's E&S review ... did not support the formation of a robust view as to whether the project could be expected to meet requirements of the Performance Standards over a reasonable period of time. ... Weaknesses in IFC's E&S review process also meant that required opportunities to consider alternative project designs to avoid or minimize E&S impact were missed.... CAO has concerns that a framework for managing E&S impact that can be audited and monitored has yet to be established: the lacking elements being a consolidated statement of the requirements against which performance is monitored, using verifiable data.... Confidence among the IFC team in the client's E&S capacity and commitment, combined with a view that the project is performing well from an E&S perspective, have meant that IFC has not treated the Complainants' concerns as compliance issues. In accordance with the CAO Operational Guidelines, this audit will remain open and subject to CAO monitoring until CAO is assured that IFC has moved back into compliance with its E&S commitments.[112]

It must be stated that, as with the Inspection Panel, the Ombudsman does not have the authority to remedy abuses himself. As Human Rights Watch has observed, the Office of the Compliance Advisor Ombudsman investigates, but "it is the IFC that determines how to address the investigator's findings and often it chooses not to."[113]

A WAY FORWARD

The Independent Expert welcomes the many positive measures already taken by the World Bank to address systemic and extrinsic problems and encourages the Board of Governors to strengthen World Bank governance and accountability through enhanced and facilitated access to justice when abuses occur. The Bank is in a position to give effect to its commitment to end poverty and help achieve the Sustainable Development Goals ahead of 2030. There is reason for optimism, since the Bank is conscious of the problems, has a formidable staff and benefits from the input of civil society organizations that do not cease producing excellent studies, diagnoses and pragmatic recommendations.

Bearing in mind that multilateral development banks, including the World Bank, receive large injections of public money, their biased approach in support of the private sector in developed and developing countries must be transformed into a human rights-based approach that carefully weighs the needs of the populations concerned.

The Independent Expert believes that a fundamental rethink is necessary and should result in an explicit definition of new priorities that puts the interests of billions of human beings who are deprived of the necessities of life ahead of those of foreign investors. The rules of the game must be changed so that loans are not granted on purely economic considerations and that the loan "conditionalities" henceforth aim at advancing the well-being of the populations concerned. The Independent Expert admires the impressive rhetoric and the beautiful publications of the World Bank and suggests that fewer resources should be devoted to public relations and the packaging of the product, and much more to risk-assessment, monitoring and implementation.

To that end, the Independent Expert proposes a change of paradigm that would require not only amending the Articles of Agreement of 1944 (adopted at Bretton Woods, New Hampshire, and last amended on 16 February 1989), but also clear directives from the Board of Governors. Pursuant to article V, section 8 (a) of the Articles of Agreement, the Bank should cooperate with international organizations having specialized responsibilities in related fields, including the Economic and Social Council and UNCTAD, which have proposed plans of action to advance development and human rights.[114]

At present, article IV, section 10, of the Articles of Agreement could be interpreted as an obstacle to that paradigm change. That obsolete provision stipulates that "the Bank and its officers shall not interfere in the political affairs of any member; nor shall they be influenced in their decisions by the political character of the member or members concerned." However, there is no reason to consider the promotion of human rights and environmental protection to fall under the scope of the prohibited "political activity" of the Bank. Indeed, all States parties to the World Bank Agreement are also United Nations members and all are bound by the Charter of the United Nations and numerous human rights treaties.

Of relevance is the Agreement between the United Nations and the International Bank for Reconstruction and Development, which came into force on 15 November 1947, and its Protocol, signed at New York on 15 April 1948, which came into force on 1 July 1948. Pursuant to article IV of the agreement, the United Nations and the Bank shall consult and exchange views on matters of mutual interest. Formal recommendations may be made after such consultation. Moreover, "the Bank recognizes that the United Nations and its organs may appropriately make recommendations with respect to the technical aspects of reconstruction or development plans, programmes or projects." Article VIII specifically authorizes the Bank "to request advisory opinions of the International Court of Justice on any legal questions arising within the scope of the Bank's activities." Hence, it would be appropriate to make better use of the Articles of Agreement so as to effectively coordinate the work of the United Nations and the Bank in a manner that will advance implementation of United Nations human rights, development and environmental commitments. In particular, the Bank should request an advisory opinion on the overall priority of human rights treaties over commercial and other arrangements and how best to integrate customary human rights norms into the Bank's loan conditionalities.

Bearing in mind that the Bank's Articles of Agreement and the Agreement between the United Nations and the Bank were adopted prior to the adoption by the General Assembly of the Universal Declaration of Human Rights, and before the entry into force of the International Covenant on Civil and Political Rights, the International Covenant on Economic, Social and Cultural Rights and many other human rights treaties, it is not unreasonable to expect that the human rights obligations of States members of the Bank should be advanced and not hindered by Bank policies. Article XIII of the Agreement between the United Nations and the Bank stipulates that the agreement is subject to revision and both parties are authorized to make supplementary agreements. That is a window of opportunity for the Bank to commit itself to certain key principles of the United Nations, including respect for the sovereignty of all States and non-interference in the domestic affairs of States. That requires acceptance of the fact that States, particularly developing countries, need flexibility and policy space to implement social policies aimed at ensuring food security, raising the standard of living, strengthening labour laws and ensuring access to water and education, which some privatization projects financed by the Bank have been known to undermine. Any amendment to the association agreement should strengthen the cooperation between the Bank and the United Nations, particularly with UNCTAD.

In addition to amending its Articles of Agreement, the World Bank must take full responsibility for the outcomes of its investments and implement preventive and corrective measures to ensure effective participation by all stakeholders and protection of human rights defenders on the ground. Procedurally, one of the challenges that must be addressed is the World Bank's undemocratic decision-making structure, which creates inequitable and sometimes counterproductive priority setting. Thus, the gentleman's agreement that Bank leadership will be held by citizens of certain States should be gradually phased out. Further, as other rapporteurs have noted, the underrepresented voices of the developing must be upgraded.

The Independent Expert agrees with the Director of Global Programs at the World Bank Institute, who said in 2006, that "it would be tantamount to a virtual 'fig leaf' for any institution to claim that much is being contributed to enhancing human rights in a country simply because development projects—such as on water or rural roads—are being funded."[115] If the Bank really has development at heart, it will change the conditionalities away from privatization, deregulation and lower corporate taxation and put the emphasis on reducing military expenditures, ensuring that progressive tax legislation is enacted and enforced, that tax havens are outlawed, and that a financial transactions tax is adopted and the revenues used to build "A World Free of Poverty" through international solidarity.

CONCLUSIONS AND RECOMMENDATIONS

The World Bank should:

(a) Embark on an inclusive process for drafting a new and separate human rights policy, which should embody a commitment to integrate human rights into its work by analysing human rights issues relevant to development in the context of country strategies, advise governments how to advance compliance with their human rights commitments, and identify human rights risks linked to its investments or advice;

(b) Adopt and implement the Universal Social Protection Initiative and the ILO Social Protection Floors Recommendation, 2012 (No. 202).[116] It should support the inclusion of enforceable labour provisions based on ILO standards, as well as the repeal of investor-State dispute settlement mechanisms that undermine governments' right to regulate (see A/HRC/30/44 and A/HRC/33/40);

(c) Cease promoting labour market deregulation, including through its funding conditionalities, and instead help to reverse the rise in income inequality by supporting social dialogue and collective bargaining;

(d) Formulate tax policies and implement due diligence tools that go beyond asking simply for legal compliance from the companies to which it lends money;

(e) Hold IFC accountable for the development and implementation of a tax-responsible investment policy, which should be developed in consultation with civil society and include, at a minimum, due diligence beyond legal compliance to ensure that IFC cannot invest in companies with aggressive or abusive tax practices;

(f) Support initiatives to upgrade the Committee of Experts on International Cooperation in Tax Matters to an intergovernmental body that will prevent harmful international tax competition, negative spillovers from shifts of tax policies and illicit financial flows;

(g) Inform affected and prospectively affected communities about the Inspection Panel and the Compliance Advisor Ombudsman and how to approach them;

(h) Incorporate human rights chapters in its borrower country agreements, give policy advice to States on how best to promote fiscal responsibility and transparency in all sectors, including States' military expenditures;

(i) Address, as a matter of urgency, reprisals against critics of World Bank projects. Accountability mechanisms should systematically analyse the risk of reprisals and other security risks linked to every complaint received and discuss them with complainants; take all necessary measures to ensure confidentiality for complainants who ask that their identities be kept confidential; actively monitor for reprisals including by asking each of the complainants whether they or people closely associated with them have faced any problems, particularly following community visits; develop an early warning system to identify threats or other security issues particularly for those who have filed or are considering filing a complaint or are otherwise critical of a project; and work with World Bank management to respond to any reprisals linked to their cases to ensure that the security of complainants and others is restored;

(j) Issue operational procedures that involve Bank management in preparing and making public biannual reports tracking progress in implementing management action plans approved by the Board in response to Inspection Panel investigations;

(k) Create mechanisms to ensure that the reports and recommendations of the Inspection Panel and the Compliance Observance Advisor are publicized and implemented. Empower the Inspection Panel and the Compliance Advisor

Ombudsman to reference human rights in their reports and recommendations, including by expressly referencing the recommendations of human rights treaty bodies and special procedure mandate holders;

(l) Be alert to any information about misuse of funds and ensure that human rights violations that occur in connection with the granting or use of loans are referred to the appropriate civil and penal tribunals and that cases of corruption do not enjoy impunity but are prosecuted in domestic courts;

(m) Advise governments about their responsibility to regulate the practices of businesses to ensure that they do not violate human rights and that they pay taxes in the jurisdictions where the projects operate;

(n) Intensify its cooperation with OHCHR, UNCTAD, ILO and WHO;

(o) Waive institutional immunity when gross violations of human rights have occurred.

IFC should immediately terminate all links with corporations and projects engaged in dodging taxes, and stop lending money to borrowers that directly or indirectly operate with tax havens and thereby deprive countries of their legitimate tax revenues, crucial to implement human rights obligations.

The World Bank Board of Governors should issue a clear directive that the International Centre for Settlement of Investment Disputes must refrain from interfering with the ontological functions of the State, which are to regulate in the public interest, including through environmental, health, social and labour legislation. The International Centre for Settlement of Investment Disputes should not lend its services to litigation that puts those functions of the State into question. Rather the International Centre for Settlement of Investment Disputes should discover its vocation to serve in an advisory capacity.[117] To the extent that there is risk involved, the investor should take advantage of the Bank's Multilateral Investment Guarantee Agency and obtain risk insurance there (see A/HRC/30/44, A/HRC/33/40 and A/70/285).

Countries that benefit from World Bank financing should ensure that all loans they request and all foreign direct investment they receive are used in a manner that advances the enjoyment of human rights and does not result in the enrichment of a few at the expense of the many. In particular, monitoring mechanisms must be in place to ensure transparency and accountability, regular monitoring of business activity and easy recourse and remedy to persons adversely affected by World Bank-funded projects and IMF-funded government loans and "bail outs."

Donor countries should:

(a) Demand that their money be used only in ways that promote the common good;

(b) Deny funds unless and until there is an effective procedure for providing redress and reparation to victims of possible violations;

(c) Terminate financing of ongoing projects whenever it is clear that human rights violations are being committed, and rule out a return to direct budget support until there is significant improvement in the human rights situation;

(d) Recognize their responsibility by insisting on independent investigations, without the participation of governments suspected of corruption or other violations.

The media should objectively inform about abuses associated with loan agreements when they occur, particularly instances of evictions, destruction of the environment, child labour and corruption.

The International Consortium of Investigative Journalists should focus on early warning so as to help prevent abuses accompanying World Bank–financed projects and should ferret out cases of corruption, money-laundering and collusion with tax havens.

Civil society organizations should alert the public to the dangers of megaprojects and assist affected communities in presenting complaints to the World Bank Inspection Panel[118] and to the Compliance Advisor Ombudsman.[119]

Notes

1 See www.ohchr.org/EN/NewsEvents/Pages/DisplayNews.aspx?NewsID=16517&LangID=E and www.nytimes.com/2016/06/27/opinion/the-world-bank-should-champion-human-rights.html.

2 See the text of the draft articles on the responsibility of international organizations prepared by the International Law Commission and published in the report on its sixty-third session (A/66/10), para. 87.

3 See the Guiding Principles on Business and Human Rights: Implementing the United Nations "Protect, Respect and Remedy" Framework.

4 See the International Covenant on Economic, Social and Cultural Rights, art. 2 (1).

5 See www.oxfam.org/en/tags/world-bank and www.oxfam.org/en/pressroom/pressreleases/2016-10-03/new-links-expose-world-bank-group-investments-and-human-rights.

6 See www.youtube.com/watch?v=TyOUputeq2Y.

7 See www.ifc.org/wps/wcm/connect/corp_ext_content/ifc_external_corporate_site/about+ifc_new/ IFC+Governance.

8 See www.worldbank.org/en/topic/sustainabledevelopment/overview.

9 See Willem van Genugten, *The World Bank Group, the IMF and Human Rights: A Contextualized Way Forward* (Cambridge, Intersentia, 2015).

10 See http://scholar.law.colorado.edu/cgi/viewcontent.cgi?article=1001&context=free-prior-and-informed-consent. See also Günther Handl, "Multilateral Development Banking," available from www.meraki-autoworks.com/multilateral-development-banking-environmental-principles-and-concepts-reflecting-general-international.pdf.

11 See Joseph Stiglitz, "Moving beyond market fundamentalism to a more balanced economy," *Annals of Public and Cooperative Economics*, vol. 80, No. 3 (2009). See also www.globalpolicy.org/social-and-economic-policy/the-three-sisters-and-other-institutions/internal-critics-of-the-world-bank-and-the-imf/42796-joseph-stiglitz.html.

12 See www.worldbank.org/en/topic/publicprivatepartnerships, https://ppp.worldbank.org/public-private-partnership/overview/world-bank-group and https://ieg.worldbankgroup.org/Data/reports/lp_Health_PPP_1116.pdf.

13 See www.ipsnews.net/2017/06/east-asian-miracle-myth-making/.

14 See www.theguardian.com/global-development/2017/jun/27/world-bank-funds-linked-to-forced-labour-in-uzbekistan.

15 See www.oxfamsol.be/sites/default/files/documents/bn-ifc-tax-havens-110416-embargo-en.pdf. See also www.oxfam.org/en/pressroom/pressreleases/2016-04-11/majority-world-banks-private-investments-go-companies-have and
www.oxfam.org/en/pressroom/pressreleases/2016-12-12/worlds-worst-corporate-tax-havens-exposed-oxfam-report-reveals.
www.oxfam.org/sites/www.oxfam.org/files/bp-race-to-bottom-corporate-tax-121216-en.pdf.

16 See UNCTAD, *World Investment Report 2015*, chap. V, available from unctad.org/en/PublicationsLibrary/wir2015_en.pdf. See also
www.taxjustice.net/2015/03/26/unctad-multinational-tax-avoidance-costs-developing-countries-100-billion/.

17 See www.counterpunch.org/2017/03/24/world-bank-declares-itself-above-the-law/.

18 See www.icij.org/blog/2015/04/icijs-world-bank-probe-draws-global-attention.

19 Alfred de Zayas, "Forced Population Transfer," in *The Max Planck Encyclopaedia of Public International Law, Vol. IV*, Rüdiger Wolfrum, ed. (Oxford, Oxford University Press, 2012), pp. 165–175.

20 See the United Nations Declaration on the Rights of Indigenous Peoples, arts. 10–11, 19, 28, 30 and 32.

21 See www.icij.org/blog/2015/04/new-investigation-reveals-34m-displaced-world-bank and http://projects.huffingtonpost.com/worldbank-evicted-abandoned/new-evidence-ties-worldbank-to-human-rights-abuses-ethiopia.

22 *Bretton Woods Observer*, Autumn 2016, p. 7. Available from www.brettonwoodsproject.org/wp-content/uploads/2016/09/Observer_Sept_16_online.pdf. See also http://documents.worldbank.org/curated/en/215191467995074230/pdf/103990-SU-P125728-IDA-SU2016-0001-OUO-9.pdf and www.huffingtonpost.com/entry/world-bank-allows-tanzania-to-sidestep-rule-protecting-indigenous-groups_us_57607769e4b09c926cfd6b1c.

23 See www.brettonwoodsproject.org/2014/06/world-bank-mines-threatening-livelihoods/.

24 See http://projects.huffingtonpost.com/worldbank-evicted-abandoned/how-worldbank-finances-environmental-destruction-peru.

25 See https://spcommreports.ohchr.org/TMResultsBase/DownLoadPublicCommunicationFile?gId=22932.

26 Ibid.

27 See https://spcommreports.ohchr.org/TMResultsBase/DownLoadFile?gId=49127.

28 Ibid.

29 See www.hrw.org/news/2015/02/23/world-bank-address-ethiopia-findings.

30 *Bretton Woods Observer*, Autumn 2016, p. 2. Available from www.brettonwoodsproject.org/wp-content/uploads/2016/09/Observer_Sept_16_online.pdf.

31 See www.hrw.org/report/2013/08/28/toxic-toil/child-labor-and-mercury-exposure-tanzanias-small-scale-gold-mines.

32 See www.hrw.org/news/2016/11/08/world-bank-group-india-tea-investment-tramples-rights.

33 See www.oxfamamerica.org/press/aid-group-lauds-new-world-bank-policies-on-indigenous-rights-and-oil-and-mining-transparency/.
34 *Bretton Woods Observer,* Autumn 2016, p. 3. Available from www.brettonwoodsproject.org/wp-content/uploads/2016/09/Observer_Sept_16_online.pdf.
35 See www.inclusivedevelopment.net/new-report-reveals-the-world-banks-murky-financial-entanglements-with-indias-most-irresponsible-corporations/ and www.inclusivedevelopment.net/wp-content/uploads/2017/04/Outsourcing-Development-India.pdf.
36 See www.inclusivedevelopment.net/new-report-reveals-the-world-banks-murky-financial-entanglements-with-indias-most-irresponsible-corporations/.
37 See www.oxfam.org/sites/www.oxfam.org/files/file_attachments/bn-ifc-owning-outcomes-031016-en_0.pdf.
38 See www.oxfam.org/en/pressroom/reactions/no-breakthrough-big-issues-spring-meetings.
39 See www.brettonwoodsproject.org/2017/02/bank-imf-2016-year-review/ and www.brettonwoodsproject.org/2017/04/world-bank-undermines-right-universal-healthcare/.
40 See www.oxfam.org/en/research/dangerous-diversion.
41 *Bretton Woods Observer,* Autumn 2016, p. 2. Available from brettonwoodsproject.org/wp-content/uploads/2016/09/Observer_Sept_16_online.pdf.
42 See www.oecd-ilibrary.org/economics/oecd-economic-surveys-portugal-2012_eco_surveys-prt-2012-en, p. 26.
43 www.oecd.org/eco/surveys/Portugal-2017-OECD-economic-survey-overview.pdf, p. 25.
44 See www.hrw.org/news/2016/07/14/defending-human-rights-development.
45 See www.hrw.org/news/2017/04/25/human-rights-watch-submission-re-international-financial-institutions-and-human.
46 Human Rights Watch, *At Your Own Risk: Reprisals against Critics of World Bank Group Projects* (2015). Available from www.hrw.org/sites/default/files/report_pdf/worldbank0615_4up.pdf.
47 See www.hrw.org/news/2016/07/14/defending-human-rights-development.
48 See https://spcommreports.ohchr.org/TMResultsBase/DownLoadPublicCommunicationFile?gId=19586.
49 See https://spcommreports.ohchr.org/TMResultsBase/DownLoadFile?gId=48790.
50 See https://eiti.org/.
51 Human Rights Watch, *Harassed, Imprisoned, Exiled: Azerbaijan's Continuing Crackdown on Government Critics, Lawyers, and Civil Society* (2016). Available from www.hrw.org/sites/default/files/report_pdf/azerbaijan1016_web.pdf.
52 See www.ohchr.org/EN/NewsEvents/Pages/DisplayNews.aspx?NewsID=19805. See also public communications on the case, and government responses to them, available on the special procedures online communication database: https://spcommreports.ohchr.org/Tmsearch/TMDocuments.
53 See www.worldbank.org/en/topic/indigenouspeoples/brief/honduras-and-indigenous-people.
54 See www.miamiherald.com/opinion/op-ed/article136884218.html.
55 See www.doingbusiness.org/reports/global-reports/doing-business-2017.
56 See www.doingbusiness.org/Methodology/Changes-to-the-Methodology, www.ituc-csi.org/ituc-calls-on-world-bank-to?lang=en, www.law.cornell.edu/uscode/text/22/262p%E2%80%939 and old.brettonwoodsproject.org/update/70/bwupdt70_ai.pdf.
57 See www.oaklandinstitute.org/blog/world-bank%E2%80%99s-doing-business-rankings-relinquishing-sovereignty-good-grade.
58 See www.doingbusiness.org/Reforms/Overview/Economy/spain.
59 See www.doingbusiness.org/reforms/overview/economy/vietnam.
60 See www.doingbusiness.org/reports/thematic-reports/paying-taxes.
61 See www.doingbusiness.org/Reforms/Overview/Economy/tanzania.
62 See www.doingbusiness.org/Reforms/Overview/Economy/malta.
63 Alice Martin-Prével, "Down on the seed: the World Bank enables corporate takeover of seeds" (Oakland, California, Oakland Institute, 2017). Available from www.oaklandinstitute.org/sites/oaklandinstitute.org/files/down-on-the-seed.pdf.

64 See www.worldbank.org/en/topic/competitiveness/brief/investment-climate.
65 Letter to the Independent Expert dated 6 March 2017.
66 See T. Manuel et al., "Independent panel review of the Doing Business report" (2013). Available from http://hendrikwolff.com/web/Doing%20business%20review%20panel%20report%20with%20signatu res%20and%20Bibliography.pdf and www.socialwatch.org/sites/default/files/Joint-statement-Our-Land-Our-Business.pdf.
67 See www.oaklandinstitute.org/our-land-our-business, www.oaklandinstitute.org/world-bank-fuels-land-grabs-africa-through-shadowy-financial-sector-investments and www.oaklandinstitute.org/world-bank-sides-agribusinesses-against-farmers-indigenous-communities.
68 See http://eba.worldbank.org/.
69 See www.oaklandinstitute.org/civil-society-denounces-world-banks-scheme-hijack-farmers-rights-seeds.
70 See August Reinisch, ed., *The Privileges and Immunities of International Organizations in Domestic Courts* (Oxford, Oxford University Press, 2013).
71 See www.globalpolicy.org/component/content/article/163/29411.html.
72 See www.earthrights.org/sites/default/files/documents/jam_v_ifc_-_appellant_reply_brief.pdf.
73 See www.brettonwoodsproject.org/2016/04/ifc-claims-absolute-immunity-to-avoid-justice-but-will-it-hold-up-in-court/. See also European Court of Human Rights, *McElhinney v. Ireland* (application No. 31253/96) judgment of 21 November 2001 (dissenting opinion of Judge Loucaides).
74 See http://d2zyt4oqqla0dw.cloudfront.net/sites/default/files/documents/ifc_tata_mundra_complaint.pdf.
75 See http://www.allgov.com/india/news/top-stories/world-bank-cant-be-sued-rules-us-judge-in-denying-gujarati-villagers-lawsuit-160408?news=858610j; http://law.justia.com/cases/federal/appellate-courts/cadc/16-7051/16-7051-2017-06-23.html.
76 See www.earthrights.org/media/federal-appeals-court-rules-world-bank-group-cannot-be-sued-harming-communities-0.
77 See www.earthrights.org/media/honduran-farmers-sue-world-bank-group-human-rights-violations.
78 See https://systemicdisorder.wordpress.com/2017/03/22/world-bank-beyond-law/.
79 Naomi Klein, *The Shock Doctrine* (London, Penguin Books, 2008), pp. 267–276 and 426.
80 See http://unctad.org/en/Docs/osgdp20081_en.pdf.
81 See http://blogs.worldbank.org/developmenttalk/health/should-world-bank-issue-credit-ratings.
82 Jonathan Katz, Emanuel Salinas and Constantinos Stephanou, "Credit rating agencies," *Crisis Response*, Note No. 8 (Oct. 2009). Available from http://siteresources.worldbank.org/EXTFINANCIALSECTOR/Resources/282884-1303327122200/Note8.pdf. See also www.counterpunch.org/2017/06/07/muslims-are-very-strange-people/.
83 See www.aseed.net/pdfs/ASEED_Report_on_Worldbank_Conditionalities.pdf.
84 See www.counterpunch.org/2017/03/24/world-bank-declares-itself-above-the-law/.
85 See www.ohchr.org/Documents/Publications/GuidingPrinciplesBusinessHR_EN.pdf.
86 See www.ilo.org/global/topics/social-security/WCMS_378991/lang--en/index.htm and http://journals.sagepub.com/doi/pdf/10.1177/0020872815604814.
87 See www.worldbank.org/en/news/feature/2016/04/07/world-bank-group-sets-new-course-to-help-countries-meet-urgent-climate-challenges.
88 See www.brettonwoodsproject.org/2016/09/world-bank-approves-new-diluted-safeguards/.
89 See www.equator-principles.com/index.php/about-ep.
90 See www.oxfamamerica.org/press/aid-group-lauds-new-world-bank-policies-on-indigenous-rights-and-oil-and-mining-transparency/.
91 See https://medium.com/@OxfamIFIs/four-quick-ways-to-fix-the-world-banks-social-and-environmental-protection-policies-9e63721fe414.
92 See www.hrw.org/news/2017/04/25/human-rights-watch-submission-re-international-

financial-institutions-and-human.

93 See https://consultations.worldbank.org/content/submission-amnesty-international. See also the environmental and social safeguard policies of the African Development Bank, the United Nations Development Programme, the European Bank for Reconstruction and Development and the European Investment Bank, which all contain to differing extents a policy commitment to respect human rights in all their activities.

94 See https://consultations.worldbank.org/content/submission-amnesty-international.

95 *Bretton Woods Observer,* Autumn 2016, p. 8. Available from www.brettonwoodsproject.org/wp-content/uploads/2016/09/Observer_Sept_16_online.pdf.

96 Ibid., p. 8. See also www.ciel.org/news/safeguard-policy-endangers-rights/ and www.ituc-csi.org/IMG/pdf/ess2-wb_ituc-critique_0914.pdf.

97 See www.inspectionpanel.org and the Panel's 2015/2016 Annual Report, available from http://ewebapps.worldbank.org/apps/ip/Pages/Annual-Reports-2016.aspx.

98 See www.cao-ombudsman.org.

99 See www.worldbank.org/en/about/unit/integrity-vice-presidency/report-an-allegation.

100 *Bretton Woods Observer,* Autumn 2016, p. 5. Available from www.brettonwoodsproject.org/wp-content/uploads/2016/09/Observer_Sept_16_online.pdf.

101 See http://ewebapps.worldbank.org/apps/ip/PanelMandateDocuments/2016%20Retaliation%20Guidelines.pdf.

102 See http://ewebapps.worldbank.org/apps/ip/Pages/Annual-Reports-2016.aspx.

103 All references to Kosovo in the present document should be understood to be in compliance with Security Council resolution 1244 (1999).

104 See http://ewebapps.worldbank.org/apps/ip/Pages/Emerging-Lessons.aspx.

105 See www.youtube.com/watch?v=D4Ewnz4JcVE.

106 See www.youtube.com/watch?v=-0cuHodwjEA.

107 Jakob Th. Möller and Alfred de Zayas, *United Nations Human Rights Committee Case Law 1977–2008: A Handbook* (Kehl/Strasbourg, N.P. Engel Verlag, 2009).

108 See www.theguardian.com/global-development/2016/jan/12/world-bank-cancels-uganda-road-sexual-assault-claims.

109 http://documents.worldbank.org/curated/en/256791492009515078/pdf/Uganda-TSDP-1st-Progress-Report-REV-for-SVPOP-April-4-final-fdg-CLEARED-04062017.pdf, p. iv.

110 See www.hrw.org/news/2014/12/17/world-bank-investigate-uzbekistans-forced-labor.

111 www.cao-ombudsman.org/cases/document-links/documents/CAOInvestigationReportofIFCinvestmentinAPPL_EN.PDF, p. 11.

112 See www.cao-ombudsman.org/cases/document-links/documents/CAOAuditReportC-I-R6-Y12-F160.pdf, p. 5.

113 See www.hrw.org/news/2017/02/21/world-banks-view-through-looking-glass.

114 See World Bank, "Coherence, coordination and cooperation among multilateral organizations: 2009 progress report" (2009). Available from http://documents.worldbank.org/curated/en/589571468339611391/pdf/484000BR0SecM2101Official 0Use0Only1.pdf.

115 Daniel Kaufmann, "Human rights, governance, and development: an empirical perspective," in *Development Outreach,* World Bank Institute, October 2006, p. 19. Available from http://siteresources.worldbank.org/EXTSITETOOLS/Resources/KaufmannDevtOutreach.pdf.

116 See www.ilo.org/dyn/normlex/en/f?p=NORMLEXPUB:12100:0::NO::P12100_ILO_CODE:R202.

117 See Kinda Mohamadieh, Lean Ka-Min and Anna Bernando, *Investment Treaties: Views and Experiences from Developing Countries* (Geneva, South Centre, 2015). See also www.iisd.org/itn/2008/08/06/south-american-alternative-to-icsid-in-the-works-as-governments-create-an-energy-treaty/, http://old.brettonwoodsproject.org/art-561061, http://hsfnotes.com/publicinternationallaw/2012/01/19/venezuela-follows-bolivia-and-ecuador-with-plans-to-denounce-icsid-convention/, and Rafael Ramírez, *Nuestra Industria Petrolera es un Baluarte de Soberanía* (Caracas, Petroleros de Venezuela, 2014).

118 See http://ewebapps.worldbank.org/apps/ip/Pages/FileaRequest.aspx.

119 See www.cao-ombudsman.org/howwework/filecomplaint/ and https://www.cao-grm.org/.

Chapter 11
THE ADVERSE IMPACT OF IMF POLICIES ON HUMAN RIGHTS

"For decades, whenever the IMF "visited" a struggling country, it promoted "reforms" that led to the demolition of small businesses and the proletarisation of middle-class professionals. Abandoning the template in Greece would be to confess to the possibility that decades of anti-social programs imposed globally might have been inhuman and unnecessary."

YANIS VAROUFAKIS
former Finance Minister, Greece[i]

Philip Alston once called the World Bank a "human rights free-zone."[ii] *I agree with his assessment. But during my April 2017 participation in the annual meeting of the World Bank and IMF I had the opportunity of speaking with senior staff of both organizations and realized that at least at the World Bank there is an incipient awareness of the negative impact of its policies and concrete measures have been taken to control and monitor loan conditionalities.*

I delivered my sixth and final report to the General Assembly on 17 October 2017. This report responded to the invitation contained in General Assembly Resolution 71/190 "to continue [my] research into the impact of financial and economic policies pursued by international organizations and other institutions on a democratic and equitable international order, in particular by the World Bank and the International Monetary Fund." While my report to the Human Rights Council, presented on 13 September 2017 in Geneva, focused on the policies of the World Bank Group, the report to the General Assembly was devoted to the IMF loan conditionalities.

These two institutions established in 1944 in Bretton Woods were intended to help post World War II reconstruction. They preceded the San Francisco Conference, and the adoption of the United Nations Charter and the Universal Declaration of Human Rights. Both the World Bank and the IMF have association agreements with the United Nations, but in practice they operate independently

---

i Yanis Varoufakis, "Endgame for the IMF-EU Feud over Greece's Debt," *Der Spiegel*, https://www.spiegel.de/international/europe/op-ed-yanis-varoufakis-imf-eu-quarrel-over-greece-s-debt-a-1085203.html.

ii "'The World Bank is a Human Rights-Free Zone' – UN expert on extreme poverty expresses deep concern," *United Nations Human Rights*, 29 September 2015, https://www.ohchr.org/en/NewsEvents/Pages/DisplayNews.aspx?NewsID=16517&LangID=E

from—and not always in tandem with—the General Assembly, ECOSOC, UNCTAD and other UN organs. The time is overdue to call on both institutions to amend their Articles of Agreement so as to better serve the Purposes and Principles of the United Nations, precisely because, as I document in my reports, some of their activities have become conflictual with the human rights and development goals of the United Nations and impede the achievement of the Sustainable Development Goals.[i]

Article 103 of the UN Charter stipulates that its provisions should prevail over all other treaties and international agreements of Member States. However, both in structure and in practice, the international financial institutions are not subordinated to the provisions of the United Nations. This has generated tension between the commitment of States, as UN members, to respect and promote human rights and their agreements and activities as IMF members, which frequently generate adverse human rights impacts. Given this incoherence and the consequences it has had on the international order, I recommend that the General Assembly request an Advisory Opinion from the International Court of Justice on the primacy of the Purposes and Principles of the United Nations over the actions of all international financial institutions.

In my report, I also call on the IMF to abandon its misguided prioritization of economic growth above all other considerations, including human rights and the environment. Indeed, there is evidence that, within the institution, broader considerations, including income and gender inequalities, are already being discussed. In June 2016, the research department of IMF produced a paper entitled "Neoliberalism oversold?," in which it questioned the efficacy of the current guiding ideology of IMF. The paper begins with the ominous finding that: *"Instead of delivering growth, some neoliberal policies have increased inequality, in turn jeopardizing durable expansion,"* and concluding that the current policies did not deliver as expected. Tardy as they are, these 'wake-up calls' may yet bear fruit, although many in the IMF suffer from groupthink and still breathe the philosophy that any 'growth,' including such which only benefits the rich, will eventually benefit everyone, through the elusive—actually imaginary—'trickle-down' effect, reminiscent of the objectivist ethos of Ayn Rand.

Notwithstanding enlightened papers and seminars by experts at the World Bank and IMF, both institutions continue pushing the "market fundamentalism" which Joseph Stiglitz has so often decried. As Naomi Klein recalls in her seminal work, *The Shock Doctrine*, the main problem remains the institutions' commitment to Milton Friedman's Chicago school economics, characterized by the almost religious belief that privatization and deregulation will advance GDP, notwithstanding endemic boom and bust cycles and the consequent negative

---

[i] "The 17 Goals," United Nations Department of Economic and Social Affairs, Sustainable Development, https://sdgs.un.org/goals.

impacts on the rights of individuals and peoples. Correct diagnoses, good recommendations and fourteen years after *The Shock Doctrine*, there is still no implementation. On the contrary, in 2016 a renewed focus on mega-infrastructure projects, a greater reliance on public-private partnerships, and a continued effort to impose so-called labour flexibilization and other obsolete conditionalities on borrowing States illustrate the well-known inertia that characterizes the institution.

Moreover, rebranding exercises such as calling toxic structural adjustment programmes "Poverty Reduction and Growth" does not help, unless accompanied by macro-economic policies that allow an increase in social spending. Much more is needed than the IMF's recently touted "Inequality agenda." Oxfam has just released a 38-page study on IMF's Article IV inequality pilots and concluded that they are not promoting the policies needed to reduce inequality. I endorse Oxfam's ten-point policy recommendations.

The strict and selective loan conditions imposed by the IMF, such as the requirement that States demonstrate rapid economic growth, discourages States from making long-term investments in health, education and public infrastructure. Further, the lack of a global consensus on sovereign debt restructuring means that States which are not in a position to pay back loans may fall into vicious debt crises. Together, these factors can increase unemployment, worsen working conditions, reduce access to free quality education and weaken environmental protection. In a systematic sense, they also diminish States' capacity to guarantee rights and can lead to under-resourced public sectors which are vulnerable to breakdowns and emergencies.

At the 2017 Spring meeting of the World Bank and IMF, I had the opportunity to discuss a variety of issues with lawyers and economists at both institutions. I am persuaded that the IMF must change its priorities, give up the outdated loan conditions of privatization, deregulation of markets, and "austerity" in social services, which in the past have resulted in human rights violations, including in Greece, Argentina and Tunisia, to name but a few.

Bearing in mind that power dynamics are changing, it is time for the World Bank and IMF to discover a new vocation to promote development and human rights through "smart" lending practices that benefit not only banks and speculators, but billions of human beings.

Henceforth, IMF should make loans subject to a new set of conditions, including:

(a) A moratorium on military expenditure for the duration of the loan;
(b) Adoption of national legislation that ensures that national and transnational corporations pay their taxes, while profit-shifting and tax havens are outlawed;

(c) Adoption of legislation imposing fines on persons and corporations which evade taxes and obliging citizens who have moneys hidden offshore to repatriate their wealth within a defined period of time, or face penal sanctions;
(d) Adoption of legislation to prevent corruption and bribes, accompanied by effective monitoring mechanisms;
(e) Enactment of financial transactions tax legislation; and
(f) Assurances by borrower States that no part of any loan is used to satisfy claims by vulture funds.

These proposals would enable States to generate revenue to pay back IMF loans and satisfy the legitimate concerns of creditors. At the same time, it would ensure that States can continue to meet their human rights obligations and fulfil the Sustainable Development Goals. The human rights dimension in lending can no longer be ignored. No international financial institution, no transnational corporation and no trade agreement is above international law. All must respect the overarching international human rights treaty regime. Implementing these recommendations will benefit the entire human family. Only through the concerted efforts of IMF and the World Bank—together with the United Nations—will a more democratic and equitable international order emerge.

What follows are excerpts from my 2017 report to the General Assembly.
—AdeZ

* * *

INTRODUCTION

The present report examines the impact of financial and economic policies pursued by international organizations and other institutions on a democratic and equitable international order, in particular by the World Bank and the International Monetary Fund.

In the same spirit, in its resolution 71/236, entitled "Towards a New International Economic Order," the General Assembly reaffirmed that national development efforts need to be supported by an enabling international economic environment, including coherent and mutually supporting world trade, monetary and financial systems and strengthened and enhanced global economic governance, as well as by respect for each country's policy space, which set the stage for the present report.

The Independent Expert devoted his most recent report to the Human Rights Council (A/HRC/36/40) to an analysis of the human rights impacts of World Bank policies, as well as to redress mechanisms, including the Inspection Panel and the Compliance Advisor/Ombudsman. The present report focuses on the International Monetary Fund (IMF) and, in particular, on the "conditionality" of IMF loans. The reader will recognize the pertinence of the Independent Expert's report on the World Bank, but should bear in mind the differences between the two institutions, which each have their own Articles of Agreement[1] and specific mandates, in particular that while the World Bank finances projects, IMF lends to Governments.

The present report is focused on the impacts of IMF policies on the international order and human rights. It does not contain macroeconomic analyses or forecasts, but explorations of possible solutions to endemic problems that impede the enjoyment of human rights by the millions of human beings affected by the economic and financial decisions of Governments, international organizations, transnational corporations and banks.

There is no doubt that the World Bank and IMF have played major roles in today's international order. Both institutions have the potential to significantly contribute to the realization of the Sustainable Development Goals and should draw inspiration from Goal 16, which aims at promoting peaceful and inclusive societies for sustainable development, providing access to justice for all, and building effective, accountable and inclusive institutions at all levels (see General Assembly Resolution 70/1; and A/69/700). The draft declaration on the right of peoples and individuals to international solidarity, a promising *de lege ferenda* instrument, should also be a source of encouragement for IMF to ensure that no one is left behind (see A/HRC/35/35).

In response to the questionnaire sent by the Independent Expert, the IMF clarified that it had "a limited, technical mandate to promote freer international economic exchange and facilitate balance of payments adjustment by member countries."[2] However, even if the IMF is not a "development institution" as such, nothing would prevent it from advancing inclusive economic development and human rights. In that regard, in its response, the IMF acknowledged the following: IMF staff recognize the importance of respect for human rights and, in the discharge of its mandate under its Articles of Agreement, IMF contributes to the preconditions for the achievement of human rights. IMF activities indirectly promote human rights (in particular, social and economic rights) by helping to create an economic and institutional environment in which human rights can flourish.

According to its response, the IMF exercises its monitoring and financing competences to promote a stable economic and financial environment, which in turn facilitates the exercise of human rights in member States. As early as 2000, *World Economic and Social Survey 2000* called that optimistic projection into question. In a retrospective contained in the *World Economic and Social Survey 2017*, the conventional thinking called into question in *Survey 2000* was summarized as follows: "According to the logic of the [Washington] Consensus, stabilization, liberalization and privatization would automatically stimulate economic growth whose trickle-down effects should improve living standards."[3] In contrast, as noted in the *Survey*, factors that fostered the persistence of poverty traps, including weak aggregate demand and institutional constraints, such as the prevalence of highly unequal asset holdings (especially landholdings) were identified. The profession of faith in the "trickle-down" effect dies hard and reminds us of the work of Ayn Rand in *The Virtue of Selfishness*.[4]

The Independent Expert is of the view that, in the discharge of its functions, the IMF should ensure that its lending practices, and in particular the "conditionality"[5] thereof, do no harm to developed or developing economies and do not conflict with established human rights norms, such as by imposing privatization of government services, deregulation of markets or "austerity" measures that, as empirical evidence has shown in many cases, have led to widespread unemployment and misery. The Independent Expert does not suggest that the IMF staff is indifferent to human rights, rather he sees a need for the IMF to anticipate the consequences of the "conditionality" of its lending practices and to integrate *ex ante* human rights assessments so that its activities do not lead to violations of human rights. Moreover, there must be an effective mechanism in place to monitor the impacts of IMF activities and to apply prompt corrective measures as needed.

In its *Spotlight on Sustainable Development 2017* report submitted to the 2017 session of the high-level political forum on sustainable development, the Civil Society Reflection Group on the 2030 Agenda for Sustainable Development assessed how privatization and corporate capture were hijacking the 2030 Agenda for Sustainable Development. It observed that, while Governments committed in 2015 to a revitalized global partnership and declared that public finance had to play a vital role in achieving the Sustainable Development Goals, "the combination of neoliberal ideology, corporate lobbying, business-friendly fiscal policies, tax avoidance and tax evasion ha[d] led to the massive weakening of the public sector and its ability to provide essential goods and services."[6]

In the report, the shared responsibility of the international financial institutions in the weakening of the State through the imposition of structural adjustment programmes, in particular in highly indebted countries of the global South, is noted.[7]

Several special rapporteurs, independent experts and working groups have already addressed the issues referred to in resolutions 71/190 and 71/236 (see A/67/302, A/69/297, A/71/302, A/HRC/7/11/Add.2, A/HRC/26/28, A/HRC/29/31 and A/HRC/34/51),[8] and the Independent Expert endorses their findings and recommendations. The impact of IMF on the international order, and in particular on the enjoyment of civil, cultural, economic, political and social rights, has also been the subject of studies by lawyers, economists and civil society organizations. The object of the present report is not to pretend to do better than Naomi Klein in her seminal book *The Shock Doctrine*,[9] or surpass professors Joseph Stiglitz,[10] Thomas Piketty,[11] Jeffrey Sachs,[12] Paul Krugman,[13] Dani Rodrik,[14] William van Genugten,[15] Graham Bird and Dane Rowlands.[16] The present report contains a consideration of the current situation, with a view to formulating pragmatic recommendations and aligning the Bretton Woods institutions with the international human rights treaty regime, which applies not only to States, but to intergovernmental organizations and transnational corporations (see E/C.12/2016/1).[17] In the modern, globalized world, no one can opt out of what may be referred to as the customary international law of human rights.

There is no shortage of opinions about the impact of the World Bank and IMF on the international order. Some observers think that the Bretton Woods institutions have greater impact on world affairs than all the resolutions of the General Assembly, the Economic and Social Council and the United Nations Conference on Trade and Development (UNCTAD) combined. Whereas, in principle, the Charter of the United Nations should prevail over all other treaties and international agreements (Article 103), the fact is that those institutions are not formally subordinated to the United Nations.[18]

Although IMF is a "specialized agency" under the terms of the Charter of the United Nations, the Agreement Between the United Nations and the International Monetary Fund, adopted in 1947, stipulates that "the Fund is, and is required to function as, an independent international organization." In its responses, the IMF noted that "decisions by, inter alia, the General Assembly are not binding on IMF." Moreover, IMF indicated that: "As an institution concerned with economic issues, IMF is precluded from using its powers to support particular political systems or to directly engage in the promotion of human rights." That, however, cannot mean that there is no accountability or that IMF is absolved of responsibility for the adverse human rights impacts of its lending practices.

CHALLENGES

Ideological obstacles

Notwithstanding the existence of excellent empirical studies, accurate diagnoses and innovative reform proposals, a regrettable level of inertia prevails in IMF management. In *The Shock Doctrine,* Naomi Klein focuses on a fundamental problem: economic shock therapy and crisis opportunism. She describes how the doctrine "privatize or die" has been imposed on crisis-racked countries, noting that in the 1990s "the [United States] Treasury and the IMF became much tougher in their demands for instant privatizations."[19] She describes the "Tequila Crisis" in Mexico and the "Wild West" privatizations in the Argentina of Menem and the Bolivia of Goni and the Russian Federation of Yeltsin, which had devastating human rights consequences.

Some IMF insiders resisted this trend. For example, senior IMF economist Davison Budhoo memorably resigned, after accusing the Fund of using "statistical malpractice" in order to exaggerate the level of economic crisis in countries, following which IMF would propose its own solutions.[20] In Trinidad and Tobago, for example, the oil-rich country was made to look far less stable than it actually was. In another instance, Davison Budhoo contended that the Fund "invented, literally out of the blue," huge unpaid government debts. These "gross irregularities," which he claimed were deliberate and not mere "sloppy calculations," were taken as fact by the financial markets, which promptly classified Trinidad and Tobago as a bad risk and cut off financing.

This mismanagement in the Caribbean had its counterpart in Asia during the 1990s Asian financial crisis. Naomi Klein comments: "As far as the IMF was concerned, the crisis was going extremely well. In less than a year, it had negotiated the economic equivalent of extreme makeovers for Thailand, Indonesia, South Korea and the Philippines.... The IMF 'help' had turned crisis into catastrophe."[21] Even the IMF Independent Evaluation Office concluded that the structural adjustment demands imposed on Asian countries were "ill-advised," warning that the "crisis should not be used as an opportunity to seek a long agenda of reforms just because leverage is high."[22] In their book on the subject, Graham Bird and Dane Rowlands noted that "critics also argued that the design of programs in East Asia was inappropriate, involving excessive conditionality and much more emphasis on compressing domestic demand through fiscal austerity."[23] Sakib Sherani, a Pakistani economist, explained in an article entitled "A better multilateralism" that both the World Bank and IMF had often acted:

in concert with [United States] foreign policy—in effect, as a veritable instrument or extension of [United States] policy objectives. Evidence for this charge comes from two eminent sources: the Meltzer Commission report of 2000, commissioned by the [United States] Congress, and the IMF Independent Evaluation Office's first report released in 2001 (which found Pakistan's programmes to be "geopolitical" in nature).[24]

Prioritizing "growth" above all other considerations, including human rights and the environment, *The Managing Director's Global Policy Agenda: a more inclusive and resilient global economy,* a policy paper issued for the World Bank/IMF meeting in April 2017, manifests their continued commitment to neoliberal economic approaches. It does acknowledge, however, that inequality poses a problem:

> Staff will study how fiscal policies—including the progressivity of taxation, the design of social safety nets, and a basic income grant—could help address inequality and other side effects of economic integration and technology. Staff will also further explore the impact of structural reforms and financial sector policies on growth, income, jobs, and inequality.[25]

In fact, IMF advocacy of structural adjustment has privileged powerful corporate interests and created a vicious cycle of dependence for borrower countries. As noted by Peter Dolack:

> Ideology plays a critical role here. International lending organizations... consistently impose austerity. The IMF's loans, earmarked... to pay debts or stabilize currencies, always come with the same requirements to privatize public assets (which can be sold far below market value to multi-national corporations waiting to pounce); cut social safety nets; drastically reduce the scope of government services; eliminate regulations; and open economies wide to multi-national capital, even if that means the destruction of local industry and agriculture. This results in more debt, which then gives multi-national corporations and the IMF, which enforces those corporate interests, still more leverage to impose more control, including heightened ability to weaken environmental and labour laws.[26]

In his book *Capital in the Twenty-First Century,* Thomas Piketty observes that economic research is not designed to produce ready-made certainties, because there is no universal law of economics. Thus, while the ongoing debate among economists remains important, more crucial for the world is the effects that those theories and ideologies have on the ground, on the lives of real people.

Improving people's lives would require the IMF to abandon obsolete economic models and take a human rights-based approach. Indeed, the Independent Expert is of the view that a change, away from the Washington consensus of privatization, deregulation and "austerity measures" to a more "progressive" philosophy of inclusive development, is essential.

In response to the Independent Expert's questionnaire, Human Rights Watch noted that international financial institutions continued to argue that they had a "non-political" mandate, implying that "human rights" was a "political" issue they need not address. That mindset must be changed and the self-serving argument that international financial institutions are bound only by their own internal standards must go.

In that regard, Rutgers professor Radhika Balakrishnan and James Heintz set out the following explanation:

> In setting the conditions attached to loans to the poorest countries, the IMF has ignored the implications its policies have for governments' ability to meet their human rights obligations. Instead, the IMF narrows its focus to stable growth and lower inflation. Adding human rights into the mix involves more than an additional chapter tacked onto a Poverty Reduction Strategy. It requires a fundamental change in how the IMF supports development. Human rights obligations represent the constraints under which macroeconomic policies must operate, not the other way around.[27]

Rhetoric and reality

Recently, IMF has made a considerable effort at improving its image through the issuance of factsheets, discussion notes and public statements in order to demonstrate that it has taken on board the many criticisms of its practices. Yet one must still question whether the organization has really reformed itself and whether it is now protecting social spending and prioritizing health and education. In practice, as Alexander Kentikelenis, Thomas Stubbs and Lawrence King noted, "IMF has not lived up to its own hype on social protection."[28] Whereas a growing number of IMF loans do include social spending targets, experience shows that such targets have not been met—and cannot be met. The scholars elaborated as follows:

Stringent IMF-mandated austerity measures explain part of this trend. As countries engaged in excessive fiscal belt-tightening to meet the IMF's macroeconomic targets, few funds were left for maintaining social spending.... Under direct IMF tutelage, some of the poorest countries underfunded their social protection systems.... The organization still promotes targeted social assistance policies, at a time when global debates around the [Sustainable Development Goals] are overwhelmingly focused on the universal provision of key services...the IMF can help by aiding low-income countries in setting solid fiscal foundations for the development of social policies. This will entail abandoning pretences of reform in IMF-supported programmes, and overcoming institutional inertia.[29]

Selective conditionality

The IMF factsheet on conditionality indicates the following:

When a country borrows from the IMF, its Government agrees to adjust its economic policies to overcome the problems that led it to seek financial aid from the international community. These loan conditions also serve to ensure that the country will be able to repay the Fund so that the resources can be made available to other members in need. Lending reforms approved in 2009 streamlined IMF conditionality in order to promote national ownership of strong and effective policies.[30]

Guidelines on conditionality were revised in 2002 and 2009.[31] In addition, revised operational guidance was given to staff, in 2014, and issued as a policy paper, with the changes thereto primarily focused on conditionality in relation to "macrosocial" (or jobs and growth) issues, the better leveraging of surveillance, technical assistance in programme design, and improving partnerships with other institutions, in particular regional financing arrangements.[32]

Notwithstanding those reforms, the most obvious and common-sense loan condition should be a moratorium on military expenditure[33] for the duration of the loan. IMF has so far resisted that proposal, maintaining the following anachronistic position:

Fund policy prohibits the establishment of conditions that would require members to reduce the level of military spending. While the amount which the authorities of a member spend on the military may be very important for the country's macroeconomic position, the Fund has taken the position that the question of military spending is so inherently political in nature that it could not be appropriately made the subject of conditionality.[34]

That policy is not mandated by its Articles of Agreement, however, and even if it were, the articles are subject to amendment.

In addition to the selective exclusion of loan conditions relating to military expenditure, the European Network on Debt and Development (Eurodad),[35] a non-governmental organization working on issues relating to debt, development finance and poverty reduction, presents the argument that IMF conditionality constitutes an impediment to development policies and democratically defined sustainable development strategies. In the view of Eurodad, appropriate financing would empower peoples to chart their own paths towards development and ending poverty.

Scholars Radhika Balakrishnan and James Heintz have pointed out that the Group of 20, a group of States with hard-law human rights obligations, has bailed out the IMF using taxpayer money without applying a condition that IMF policies support human rights enhancement.[36] In the context of conditions these human rights obligations must now be brought on board as quid pro quo. "In exchange for the G-20's financial support, the IMF must be held accountable for advancing human rights for all."[37]

To the extent that IMF maintains its focus on imposing strict limits on government spending, it must be clearly defined what kind of government spending is toxic and what is not. Under no conditions should government spending for health and education be reduced. However, military procurement, research and development spending should be paused for the duration of IMF loans. Where security concerns exist, the United Nations and regional arrangements should provide what is known as "collective security."

COUNTRIES IN CRISIS

Greece

As the financial crisis in Greece demonstrates, IMF surveillance capacities are unequally applied, depending on the status of a member State's economy. Once an economic crisis hits, IMF may doggedly impose austerity measures as conditions, with variable consequences for rights realization in member States. Triggered by the Wall Street meltdown in 2008, the crisis in Greece dragged many weaker economies under, with disastrous consequences for economic, social and cultural rights. The IMF watchdog, its Independent Evaluation Office, determined that the IMF operated in a "culture of complacency" prone to "superficial and mechanistic" analysis.[38] A series of calamitous misjudgements were made, and the warning signs of impending crisis were ignored. In the report of the Office, it was noted that its own investigators were unable to obtain key records or penetrate the activities of secretive ad hoc task forces.

The results of an evaluation by the Independent Evaluation Office of the performance of the IMF in the run-up to the financial crisis pointed to inadequate surveillance in the euro area, which echoed a larger problem of IMF surveillance in advanced economies. Several factors were at play, including "a high degree of groupthink, intellectual capture, a general mindset that a major financial crisis in large advanced economies was unlikely, and incomplete analytical approaches."[39]

According to the Independent Evaluation Office, the IMF violated its own cardinal rule by signing off on a bailout in 2010, even though it could offer no assurance that the package would bring the country's debts under control or clear the way for recovery. An exception was made because of the risk of "systemic contagion." Indeed, the concern being addressed was saving the EU monetary union, not helping Greece out of its predicament. In the report, it was also noted that:

> Some officials in Europe stated to the [Independent Evaluation Office] that, in their view, the troika-supported programs, including in Greece, were a success because they averted a breakdown of the euro area and a widely-feared exit of Greece from the single currency. Consistent with these views, the European Court of Auditors...noted that the programs "addressed the need to safeguard the stability of the euro area or the [European Union] as a whole."[40]

Another critic, Stephen Lendman, described the series of disasters associated with the mismanagement of the Greek debt thus: "Even the Bretton Woods established/[United States] controlled loan shark of last resort IMF astonishingly called for Greek debt relief. It doesn't care about force-fed austerity harming ordinary people. It's concerned about contagion. If Greece implodes, expect continental fallout."[41]

The Independent Evaluation Office, however, only acknowledged the failure of the bailout, without addressing the adverse human rights impacts of the conditions imposed.

At the end of his country visit to Greece in December 2015, Juan Pablo Bohoslavsky, the Independent Expert on foreign debt and other related international financial obligations of States on the full enjoyment of all human rights, particularly economic, social and cultural rights, issued a statement voicing concern about those very impacts, including the fact that an estimated 2.5 million people were without health insurance as a result of the crisis. He went on to detail that the rights to work and social security were in a state of disarray, that youth unemployment remained at 47.9 per cent and only 1 out of 10 registered unemployed persons received unemployment benefits, while millions were left without basic social security. "After five years of adjustment policies, indicators tracking economic, social and cultural rights in Greece have not improved."[42]

Part of the problem had been the loan "conditionality imposed by the troika consisting of IMF, the European Commission and the European Central Bank. Juan Pablo Bohoslavsky regretted that "such far-reaching reforms...appear to be imposed by lenders with the sole goal of repayment, and the views of the Greek people are not seriously taken into consideration."[43] In the section of his report to the General Assembly on the mission (A/71/305, sect. II.B), he called for the IMF to significantly broaden its definition of "sustainability" under its Debt Sustainability Framework and respect the need to provide fiscal space to guarantee and ensure core human rights obligations.

In the same report, Juan Pablo Bohoslavsky also focused on integrating human rights into debt policies to counter new debt vulnerabilities and endorsed a statement of the Committee on Economic, Social and Cultural Rights on "Public debt, austerity measures and the International Covenant on Economic, Social and Cultural Rights" (E/C.12/2016/1). He recalled that "both borrowing States and lenders were required to carry out human rights impact assessments prior to the provision of loans concerned, in order to ensure that the conditionalities did not disproportionately affect economic, social and cultural rights, and did not lead to discrimination" (A/71/305).

In that connection, in its response to the questionnaire sent in the preparation of the present report, IMF indicated the following:

> [I]n IMF programme design, attention is focused on enhancing social spending, and this then informs the Debt Sustainability Framework assessment.... IMF separately performs extensive work with its members to boost fiscal space through technical assistance and capacity-building in revenue administration, tax policy and international tax issues.

With respect to the specific recommendations made by Juan Pablo Bohoslavsky in his report to the Human Rights Council (A/HRC/31/60/Add. 2), the IMF responded as follows:

> IMF has been at the forefront of efforts to secure debt relief for Greece and to avoid excessive fiscal adjustment.... The Fund has

called for additional fiscal measures ... because the Fund views the current Greek budget structure as unsustainable. There is a pressing need to reorient the budget to better support growth and social protection. IMF has called for reforms to ensure better coverage of the poorest populations, including the full implementation of the newly introduced guaranteed minimum income. IMF has also called for preserving labour market reforms introduced in 2011–12 to safeguard employment.... Further debt relief is now being discussed between the Greek authorities and their Eurozone partners in the context of the ongoing [European Stability Mechanism] adjustment programme.

Notwithstanding the above responses, the Independent Expert agrees with many who consider that the troika is continuing to fail in the ongoing crisis in Greece, which can only be resolved by debt relief and international solidarity. Additional "austerity measures" will only lead to continuing human rights violations.[44] He agrees with the findings contained in the preliminary report of the Truth Committee on Public Debt, led by Eric Toussaint and including contributions from the former Independent Expert on the effects of foreign debt and other related international financial obligations of States on the full enjoyment of all human rights, particularly economic, social and cultural rights, Cephas Lumina, which concluded that the Greek debt is an "odious debt" that should be repudiated.[45]

In that regard, in its statement to the thirtieth session of the Human Rights Council (A/HRC/30/NGO/18), Centre Europe-tiers monde criticized the IMF for facilitating the looting of Greece through privatization and anti-social austerity measures and endorsed the preliminary report of the Truth Committee on Public Debt, also referred to as the Greek Debt Truth Commission, the Truth Commission or the Greek Public Debt Audit,[46] and noted:

> IMF, as an international organization is bound by any obligations incumbent on it under general rules of international law.... The IMF is required to refrain from steps that would undermine the possibility of a borrowing State complying with its own national and international human rights obligations, as stated in the United Nations Guiding principles on foreign debt and human rights: 'International financial organizations and private corporations have an obligation to respect international human rights. This implies a duty to refrain from formulating, adopting, funding and implementing policies and programmes which directly or indirectly contravene the enjoyment of human rights.' In addition, the IMF, as

a specialized agency of the United Nations, is bound by the general aims and principles of the United Nations Charter, including respect for human rights and fundamental freedoms.[47]

The submission of Centre Europe-tiers monde continued as follows:

> Greece could legally take a unilateral act of repudiation. Such a decision is justified by peremptory considerations of justice and equity, but is also founded on sovereignty and self-determination. This is the case where there is an absence of good faith, based on article 26 of the Vienna Convention on the Law of Treaties.... The bad faith of the creditors consisted in rendering Greece financially subservient and imposing measures affecting the fundamental rights of the Greek people, in violation of national, European and international law. Bad faith was also evident in the ultimate goal of the creditors, which was not to help the Greek people but rather ... to transform private debt into public debt and thus save the big private banks.[48]

The Independent Expert endorses the conclusions of the audit that the Greek debt is odious and illegitimate and that:

> the increase in debt was not due to excessive public spending, which in fact remained lower than the public spending of other Eurozone countries, but rather due to the payment of extremely high rates of interest to creditors, excessive and unjustified military spending, loss of tax revenues due to illicit capital outflows, state recapitalization of private banks, and the international imbalances created via the flaws in the design of the Monetary Union itself.[49]

In a leaked IMF memo to the European Commission, it was estimated that Greece's debt would reach 200 per cent of GDP in two years without relief. In 1980, it was 22.6 per cent. In 2008, 127 per cent. In 2014, 177.1 per cent. Since the beginning of the financial crisis, the economy of Greece plunged by over 25 per cent. The IMF memo continues as follows: "Greece's debt can now only be made sustainable through debt relief measures that go far beyond what Europe has been willing to consider so far."

However, even these dire predictions have not stopped the imposition of system-shaking loan conditions, nor the devastating human rights consequences which result from them. In February 2017, the European Union and IMF decided to impose further "austerity measures" on Greece,[50] namely, to make a further

€7 billion payment to its creditors by July or risk defaulting on its entire debt, which remains at a staggering €330 billion. Whatever tactical differences may exist regarding the means to impose austerity on Greece, there are no conflicts over carrying it out. Regarding the substance of the "deal," it was noted in a Reuters report that: "Officials said the lenders would ask Greece to take 1.8 billion euros worth of new measures until 2018 and another 1.8 billion after 2018, focused on broadening the tax base and on pension cutbacks."[51] The new cuts represent 2 per cent of GDP—in human terms, a further €3.6 billion in austerity or taking another €327 from every man, woman and child in the country.

Sadly, the most succinct common-sense summation of the crisis in Greece was given by former Minister of Finance of Greece Yanis Varoufakis in an interview with Al-Jazeera, in which he stated that Greece was and is being subjected to "fiscal water-boarding."[52]

As a safeguard to prevent the further erosion of human rights in the country, the Independent Expert encourages all creditor States and financial institutions to revisit the "conditionality" of their past and future loans to Greece. Instead of demanding privatization, deregulation and reduction of social services, the IMF should consider applying a different set of conditions; no loan should be awarded to any country that continues spending for military procurement. In line with the recommendations made by the Independent Expert in his report to the Human Rights Council in 2014 (A/HRC/27/51), for the duration of a crisis and until the loans are paid back, a moratorium should be called on all military expenditure, save that for pensions and personnel. This means that Greece, a bankrupt country, must not be required by NATO to devote scarce resources to military expenditure.[53] Such a recommendation is desperately needed, given the results of the IMF survey on Greece conducted in 2010, in which "a significant reduction in military expenditure during the period" was envisaged.[54]

Argentina

In 1977, in an open letter to the Argentine military junta,[55] Roberto Walsh, an Argentinian journalist, denounced the crimes of the regime, the disappearances, systematic torture and other gross violations of human rights. "These events, which stir the conscience of the civilized world, are not, however, the greatest suffering inflicted on the Argentinean people.... It is in the economic policy of this government where one discovers not only the explanation for the crimes, but a greater atrocity which punishes millions of human beings through planned misery."⁵⁶ He placed the responsibility squarely with the "austerity" measures dictated by the IMF. Roberto Walsh was killed by police the following day.

The mismanagement of Argentine debt is not new. And, even if the blame is shared, the IMF has earned no laurels. As early as 2004, the wrong options were chosen.⁵⁷ The then Minister of Finance of Argentina, Roberto Lavagna, characterized Fund surveillance efforts as "ideological assessments," which blurred the capacity of the Fund to conduct objective assessments of policy reform.⁵⁸

Even the Independent Evaluation Office acknowledged that "IMF surveillance failed to highlight the growing vulnerabilities in the authorities' choice of policies and the IMF erred by supporting inadequate policies too long."⁵⁹ Roberto Lavagna agreed with the report's authors that a more participative decision-making process was needed: "the practice by certain prominent shareholders of bypassing the board raises serious transparency concerns."⁶⁰ Its correct diagnoses aside, interestingly enough, the words "human rights" do not appear in the report of the Office, which is only concerned with economic and financial matters.

Tunisia

Observers have similarly warned that the extreme conditions imposed on Tunisia by the IMF would reverse progress made in the country following the Jasmine Revolution. In March 2017, the International Trade Union Confederation warned that "IMF is pushing Tunisia to the brink of economic and political disaster with its refusal to release urgently needed funds at a time when the country most needs international support."⁶¹ According to the Government of Tunisia, the IMF suspended payments on its four-year, $2.8 billion loan "to pressure the Government into mass dismissals in the public sector, along with sales of government assets and possible cuts to pensions."⁶² Among other conditions, IMF demanded that Tunisia sell stakes in three State-owned banks, in addition to abolishing 10,000 public sector jobs.⁶³

The General Secretary of the International Trade Union Confederation contested those conditions, indicating that: "Ideological diktats like this from the IMF will throw thousands into poverty and destroy the progress that has been made and that Tunisians are determined to extend. A deepening economic crisis would lead to a resurgence of fundamentalism and increase the risk of terrorist attacks both in Tunisia and in nearby countries."

On 12 June 2017, the IMF Executive Board completed its first review of the economic programme of Tunisia, thereby enabling Tunisian authorities to draw an additional $314.4 million of IMF funds.⁶⁴ While Tunisia sought a waiver of some conditions, the Government did agree to privatizations, an increased value added tax and a scale-back of its public sector.[65] Participants at the meeting of the Group of 20 in Hamburg in July 2017 deplored the additional austerity measures forced on Tunisia by the IMF. As early as 2015, the Bretton Woods Project had noted: "The more things change, the more they stay the same.... Despite the IMF's promising rhetoric, IMF policies prescribed since 2011 bear an uncanny resemblance to the familiar pre-2011 policies."[66]

ROLE OF THE INTERNATIONAL MONETARY FUND IN THE INTERNATIONAL ORDER

Health emergencies

In addition to their potential to weaken public sector infrastructure, IMF conditionality has been shown to threaten the right to health. Researchers have noted that, with Governments required to demonstrate rapid economic growth and fiscal constraint, long-term investments, such as those required to improve health care, are discouraged, which leaves countries with under-resourced health sectors vulnerable to breakdowns and public health emergencies.

In a study entitled "The impact of IMF conditionality on government health expenditure: a cross-national analysis of 16 West African nations," scholars in the fields of sociology and public health linked IMF conditionality with reduced expenditure on health by Governments and consequently with setbacks in efforts to achieve universal health coverage. The academics indicate the following:

> We identify three pathways linking IMF-mandated policies to decreases in government health spending in the region: macroeconomic targets that reduce fiscal space for investment in health, limits to wage bills and civil service employment ceilings that inhibit hiring and retention of health staff; and decentralisation measures that amplify budget execution challenges in the health sector.[67]

The authors of the study concluded that the IMF should facilitate the process of achieving universal health coverage by allowing policy space for borrowing countries to invest in health and determine their health policies free from the influence of unduly restrictive conditions. "In doing so," they stated, "IMF can learn from and collaborate with its sister institution, the World Bank, that recently supported the goal of [universal health coverage]."[68]

Commentators have further drawn a connection between IMF conditionality, reduced health sector spending and the Ebola outbreak in West Africa.[69] As

Professor Alexander Kentikelenis explained in his article in *The Lancet Global Health*:

> Economic reform programmes by the IMF have required reductions in government spending, prioritisation of debt service, and bolstering of foreign exchange reserves. Such policies have often been extremely strict, absorbing funds that could be directed to meeting pressing health challenges. Although the IMF has responded to concerns about its programmes by incorporating "poverty-reduction expenditures" to boost health spending, these conditions were often not met. Thus, in 2013, just before the outbreak, whereas all three [of the most affected] countries achieved the IMF's macroeconomic policy prescriptions, they failed to meet targets for social spending.[70]

Writing in the *Washington Post*, professors Adia Benton and Kim Yi Dionne concluded the following:

> IMF and organizations like it have played an important role in creating a political environment in which the [Ebola] epidemic could emerge and become the deadliest on record... we argue that to ignore the effects of foreign aid and financial policies on local politics and social conditions is to miss an important part of the story.[71]

Scholars have likewise drawn attention to the impact of IMF conditionality on efforts to combat AIDS in developing countries.[72]

In another study, entitled "Impact of International Monetary Fund programs on child health," researchers found that IMF austerity policies may reduce parents' ability to look after their children's health in poor and middle-income countries. Involving some 2.8 billion people residing in 67 poor and middle-income countries from 2000 to 2005, the study examined five factors having an impact on children's health, including water, malnutrition, shelter, sanitation, and access to health care.[73]

Bearing in mind that the denial of adequate health care can lead to much suffering and death, the issue of accountability is inescapable. Admittedly, international organizations enjoy immunity from domestic legal action,[74] but that immunity is already being challenged in the United States of America, for example, by civil society groups like Earth Rights International.[75]

Corruption, tax evasion and fiscal transparency

In principle, IMF loans should ensure that the risk of corruption and tax fraud is avoided and that appropriate monitoring and follow-up is available. Although the IMF, in its publications, has recognized the importance of fiscal transparency and combating corruption, in practice, those standards are not uniformly raised.

As detailed by Human Rights Watch in its response to the Independent Expert's questionnaire:

> [International financial institutions] generally recognize the importance of avoiding corruption and of fiscal transparency and accountability. In practice, however, [International financial institutions] are selective when they raise these standards.... The IMF's Manual on Fiscal Transparency, which provides guidance on the implementation of its Fiscal Transparency Code, recognizes that these standards should apply to military revenue and expenditure, but in practice the institution has not used its leverage to support progress in this area.[76]

As an example, IMF chose not to raise with the Government of Egypt the matter of a lack of transparency and accountability over its military budget, when agreeing to a $12 billion loan. In the IMF Manual on Fiscal Transparency, which provides guidance on the implementation of its fiscal transparency code, it is recognized that those standards should apply to military revenue and expenditure, but in practice the institution has not used its leverage to support progress in that area. Other international financial institutions similarly fall short in that regard.[77]

On the other hand, the IMF has taken action in the past to stop disbursements of approved loans when it discovered corruption. Thus, in 2012, when a $32 billion dollar gap in the finances of Angola was discovered, Human Rights Watch[78] urged the IMF managing director and Executive Board to continue advocacy that had already begun for transparency and accountability in the use of public funds. Human Rights Watch further urged the IMF not to provide additional funds to Angola until the Fund and the public were able to verify both that the money was spent in the public interest and that there were reasons why financial oversight processes had been bypassed.

Special procedures mandate holders have also raised concerns about State-owned entities in Mozambique receiving loans for military purchases outside public knowledge.[79] While the IMF suspended its standby funding upon discovery of such "secret lending," the Working Group on the issue of human rights and transnational corporations and other business enterprises and human rights and the Independent Expert on the effects of foreign debt on human rights further encouraged the Fund to support an established commission of inquiry investigating the misconduct and the protection of human rights defenders facing reprisals for having demanded transparency. Moreover, they cautioned that disproportionate conditions and further cuts in funds could jeopardize public spending in the fulfilment of economic, social and cultural rights obligations.[80]

In addition to advocacy for increased transparency among borrower Governments, Oxfam and others have highlighted that IMF could play a role in the fight against tax evasion, in particular given growing inequalities between and within States. At the end of the World Bank–IMF meeting in 2017, Oxfam released a statement indicating the following:

> We're not seeing the leadership we need from these institutions. This is a tricky time—some countries are taking steps that put the hard-fought progress we've made at risk. If the IMF and the Bank want to fight inequality and make trade work for everyone, then cooperating and tackling tax competition will be indispensable.[81]

In response to the Independent Expert's questionnaire, IMF implied that its influence in that area was primarily through technical assistance. Relying on a staff policy paper of 2014, entitled "Spillovers in international corporate taxation,"[82] IMF concluded that limiting the adverse effects of tax avoidance and evasion on developing countries required capacity-building, addressing weaknesses in domestic law, and international arrangements. In that context, IMF promotes fiscal transparency.

However, in follow-up to the previous report of the Independent Expert to the General Assembly on the subject (A/71/286), the Independent Expert considers that IMF could be more proactive in making tax transparency a condition, by refusing to grant loans to those countries that are tax havens. Moreover, in order to ensure that Governments can pay back their debts, it is necessary for IMF borrower countries to adopt appropriate tax legislation and enforce it, including legislation establishing a financial transactions tax.

Sovereign debt restructuring

In 2001, Anne Krueger, then Deputy Managing Director of IMF, proposed a new approach to sovereign debt restructuring. Whereas in domestic law individuals and corporations have recourse to bankruptcy codes that give them protection from their creditors, sovereign States do not. She elaborated as follows:

> We lack incentives to help countries with unsustainable debts resolve them promptly and in an orderly way. At present the only

available mechanism requires the international community to bail out the private creditors.... Our aim would be to create a catalyst that will encourage debtors and creditors to come together to restructure unsustainable debts in a timely and efficient manner. This catalyst would take the form of a framework offering a debtor country legal protection from creditors that stand in the way of a necessary restructuring, in exchange for an obligation for the debtor to negotiate with its creditors in good faith and to put in place policies that would prevent a similar problem from arising in the future. The mere knowledge that such a framework was in place should encourage debtors and creditors to reach agreement of their own accord. Our model is one of a domestic bankruptcy court.[83]

Alas, her proposal was not endorsed by the ideology-bound IMF and the idea was essentially killed by Wall Street.[84] It is, however, still valid today.

The continuing work of IMF on sovereign debt restructuring[85] deserves expansion and implementation. Its report of 26 April 2013 on recent developments contained the following observation:

While creditor participation has been adequate in recent restructurings, the current contractual, market-based approach to debt restructuring is becoming less potent in overcoming collective action problems, especially in pre-default cases. In response, consideration could be given to making the contractual framework more effective, including through the introduction of more robust aggregation clauses into international sovereign bonds bearing in mind the inter-creditor equity issues that such an approach may raise.[86]

The Independent Expert encourages IMF to mainstream the Basic Principles on Sovereign Debt Restructuring Processes, as contained in General Assembly Resolution 69/319 of 10 September 2015.[87] Indeed, leaders in academia, the public sector and civil society—including Pope Francis[88] and economists Joseph Stiglitz and Thomas Piketty—have raised awareness of the need for a global bankruptcy process. The Basic Principles provide a road map for a future debt restructuring framework. Principles 1 and 8 deserve particular attention.

Bearing in mind that, in paragraph 2 of the resolution, the General Assembly invited all competent international organizations to support and promote the Ba sic Principles, IMF should join forces with other international financial institutions in facilitating debt relief programmes and removing aggressive vulture funds and hold-outs from the international financial landscape.

As the Independent Expert on the effects of foreign debt on human rights state, in his remarks to the Human Rights Council Advisory Committee in 2015:

> The Guiding Principles on Business and Human Rights oblige States to ensure adequate regulation of business enterprises operating within their jurisdiction to ensure respect for human rights. In my view, this also implies the need for adequate regulation of private commercial entities in the financial sector, such as vulture funds, that may through their behaviour or activities cause negative human rights impacts, irrespectively of where such impacts take place. If vulture fund litigation in one country may impede another country to repay its restructured bond holders or trigger a debt crisis in another country, there are certainly exterritorial effects on the enjoyment of economic, social and cultural rights that need to be considered.[89]

In response to the Independent Expert's questionnaire, IMF responded as follows:

> Regarding an international debt restructuring mechanism, no consensus exists in the international community towards such an outcome, something also recognized by UNCTAD. In this environment, IMF reforms have focused on strengthening the existing system incrementally, by: improving debt sustainability analysis, further improving its ability to predict debt distress while ensuring it does not stand in the way of needed borrowing; reducing the risk of holdout commercial creditors through enhanced bond contract clauses; reducing the risk of official hold-out creditors through reform of the lending into official arrears policy; and providing the right framework to encourage early debtor-creditor engagement and efficient and timely restructuring of debt when needed.

Interaction with the United Nations Conference on Trade and Development

UNCTAD *World Investment Reports* and *Trade and Development Reports* provide ample evidence that development requires the respect of the policy space of Governments, in particular in developing countries. In its response to the Independent Expert's questionnaire, IMF noted that it "interact[ed] regularly with UNCTAD on debt issues. We discuss challenges in debtor-creditor engagement, we collaborate in drafting the debt chapter in the reports of the Inter-Agency Task Force on Financing for Development—which provide an overview of debt developments and developments with the international architecture—and we both help to train country officials in dealing with debt issues." That current cooperation notwithstanding, the Independent Expert considers that there is not enough coordination between IMF and UNCTAD and would encourage an intensification of cooperation.

NEW FRONTIERS FOR THE INTERNATIONAL MONETARY FUND?

An International Monetary Fund "mea culpa"?

In June 2016, the research department of IMF produced a paper, entitled "Neoliberalism oversold?,"[90] in which it questioned the efficacy of the current guiding ideology of IMF. The paper begins with the ominous finding that: "Instead of delivering growth, some neoliberal policies have increased inequality, in turn jeopardizing durable expansion." It concludes with the following assessment:

> There are aspects of the neoliberal agenda that have not delivered as expected. Our assessment of the agenda is confined to the effects of two policies: removing restrictions on the movement of capital across a country's borders (so-called capital account liberalization); and fiscal consolidation, sometimes called "austerity," which is shorthand for policies to reduce fiscal deficits and debt levels. An assessment of these specific policies (rather than the broad neoliberal agenda) reaches three disquieting conclusions:
>
> (a) The benefits in terms of increased growth seem fairly difficult to establish when looking at a broad group of countries;
>
> (b) The costs in terms of increased inequality are prominent. Such costs epitomize the trade-off between the growth and equity effects of some aspects of the neoliberal agenda;
>
> (c) Increased inequality in turn hurts the level and sustainability of growth. Even if growth is the sole or main purpose of the neoliberal agenda, advocates of that agenda still need to pay attention to the distributional effects.[91]

Although, in the Independent Expert's view, it does not go far enough, the analysis in the paper is praiseworthy. It reasonably suggests that economic neoliberalism has not delivered the desired results in terms of both equity and sustainability, given that, as Oxfam reported in 2017, "the wealthiest 1 per cent in the world now has as much wealth as the rest of the planet's population combined."[92]

Moreover, IMF recently produced a video,[93] a staff paper[94] and a promising recent study on social protection,[95] illustrating an awareness of the harms of inequality. Contrary to prior thinking, the researchers note that: "Increasing the income share of the poor and the middle class actually increases growth while a rising income share of the top 20 per cent results in lower growth— that is, when the rich get richer, benefits do not trickle down."[96]

These tardy "wake-up calls" should be listened to. Unfortunately, however, as the Independent Expert observed during the World Bank–IMF meeting in 2017, many in the institution still breathe the philosophy that any "growth," including that which only benefits the rich, will eventually benefit everyone, through the imaginary "trickle-down" effect, reminiscent of the objectivist ethos of Ayn Rand.[97]

Gross national happiness

Beyond re-examining the paradigm and ideology that have so far guided IMF practice, IMF should consider re-evaluating what it evaluates in terms of countries' well-being. Since 2012, the Sustainable Development Solutions Network, a United Nations innovation initiative under the auspices of the Secretary-General, has been issuing *World Happiness Reports*,[98] in which it is illustrated that human happiness is not coterminous with GDP growth, expansion of trade and material consumption. Well-being entails food security, employment, shelter, satisfaction with social services, a healthy environment, justice, equity, peace, harmony with values, traditions, culture, empathy and solidarity. In establishing the world happiness index, the Network used, inter alia, data from the World Bank on four benchmarks, namely[99] government effectiveness, regulatory quality, rule of law, and absence of corruption, indicators which would further enable the fulfilment of States' human rights obligations.

The *World Happiness Reports* also align with General Assembly Resolution 65/309 of 19 July 2011, in inviting States to measure the happiness of their peoples and to use this in determining public policies. On 2 April 2012, the concept was further developed at the first high-level meeting on happiness.[100] Chaired by Prime Minister of Bhutan Jigme Thinley—Bhutan being the first country worldwide to have adopted gross national happiness as its main development indicator—the meeting referred to happiness as "a new economic paradigm."[101] Shortly thereafter, on 28 June 2012, the General Assembly, by its resolution 66/281, proclaimed March 20 the International Day of Happiness.[102] IMF could promote that goal through socially oriented conditions, advancing from the Hippocratic "do no harm" mode to the proactive development mode so as to achieve a democratic and equitable international order.

CONCLUSIONS AND RECOMMENDATIONS

Unlike the World Bank, which is increasingly aware of the risks and the consequences of its activities and which undertakes to investigate and take action, IMF still appears more committed to the obsolete neoliberal economic model. While the World Bank acknowledges problems and has established redress mechanisms like its Inspection Panel and its Compliance Advisor/Ombudsman, IMF is lagging behind and has been unable to correct unsustainable situations, such as the prevailing situation in Greece.

Despite its official function to safeguard global financial stability, IMF actions appear to lay bare a priority to safeguard the interests of creditors at the expense of debtors. Karin Lissakers, who served as United States representative to the IMF Executive Board for most of the 1990s, wrote in 1983 that the Fund was acting as an "enforcer of the banks' loan contracts" in Latin America, imposing harsh austerity on the debtors with the narrow objective of "free[ing] foreign exchange in order to service debts."[103]

Bearing in mind that power dynamics are changing the international order,[104] it is time for the World Bank and IMF to revisit their Articles of Agreement and discover their new vocation to promote development and human rights through "smart" lending practices that benefit not only banks and speculators, but billions of human beings. The challenge for the World Bank and IMF is to address the concerns formulated by civil society during the meeting of the institutions in 2017, including the fundamental issue of conditionality. Implementing the pertinent recommendations made by numerous special procedures mandate holders would be an initial step in the right direction.[105] The human rights dimension in lending can no longer be ignored.

International law will continue evolving for the good of mankind. At the same time, no international financial institution or commercial agreement is above international law. All must respect the overarching international human rights treaty regime.[106] In order to further elucidate the concrete application of human rights norms to international financial institutions, those institutions should request an advisory opinion from the International Court of Justice. In fact, article VIII of the Agreement between the United Nations and the International Monetary Fund explicitly authorizes IMF to request advisory opinions on any legal questions arising within the scope of its activities.

Civil society activism has significantly contributed to sensitizing both the World Bank and IMF about their responsibilities in the field of human rights. The many international conferences held concerning the Sustainable Development Goals and financing for development are reason for optimism. Perhaps a change of mindset is under way, one more in tune with a world populated by more than 7 billion human beings who demand food security, access to clean water and sanitation, health care and education. The shift should also be reflected in an amendment to the IMF Articles of Agreement.[107] In the *World Economic and Social Survey 2017*, the following is emphasized: "The implementation of an ambitious agenda for sustainable development requires both greater policy space for countries so that they can determine the policies that best reflect their own national context and sufficient flexibility in order to ensure an orderly recovery from situations of economic stress, as aimed for in target 17.15 under Sustainable Development Goal 17."[108]

As a complement to civil society activism, at the meeting of the Group of 20 held in Hamburg in July 2017, participants also demonstrated an increased awareness that inequality was no longer politically sustainable. Systematic tax avoidance by corporations and the super-rich cost poor countries an estimated $200 billion a year. Gradually, business leaders are coming to an understanding that the future of the world economy, and their own companies, depends on solving the poverty crisis, as recognized in the Sustainable Development Goals. Tackling that challenge requires that the World Bank, IMF and the business community come on board.[109]

Bearing in mind the legitimate interest of IMF in loan repayment, a legal and administrative environment which enables States to significantly increase their tax revenue, prevent waste and corruption and, if they occur, subject malfeasances to civil and penal sanctions, must be put into place. Domestic resource mobilization, mainly tax income, is essential to sustainable development. It is also necessary to make maximum resources available for the realization of rights (see A/71/304, para. 30). Thus far, however, international financial institutions and States have failed to enact the institutional reforms needed to make it happen. The Group of 77, which represents developing countries and thus the majority of Member States, has repeatedly asked for an intergovernmental tax body to be established under the auspices of the United Nations,[110] a proposal that the Independent Expert echoed in his previous report to the General Assembly, submitted in 2016 (A/71/286).

As in all human endeavours, there are priorities to be set and choices to be made. The Independent Expert is of the opinion that IMF should change its priorities and finally let go of the outdated conditions of privatization, deregulation of markets, and "austerity" in social services, which in the past have engendered human rights violations.

Henceforth, IMF should make loans subject to a new set of conditions, including:

(a) A moratorium on military expenditure (except for salaries and pensions) for the duration of the loan;

(b) Adoption of national legislation that ensures that national and transnational corporations pay their taxes, prohibits profit-shifting, and outlaws tax havens;

(c) Adoption of General Anti-Avoidance Rule legislation to address specific base erosion and profit shifting concerns;[111]

(d) Adoption of legislation imposing fines on persons and corporations which evade taxes and obliging citizens who have moneys hidden offshore to repatriate their wealth within a defined period of time, or otherwise face the risk of penal sanctions;

(e) Adoption of legislation to prevent corruption and bribes, accompanied by effective monitoring mechanisms;

(f) Enactment of financial transactions tax laws;

(g) Assurances by the borrower that no part of any loan is used to satisfy claims by vulture funds or hold-outs.

Furthermore, IMF should:

(h) Engage with and strengthen ongoing initiatives on international tax cooperation such as the automatic exchange of information and the base erosion and profit shifting initiatives and the Platform for Collaboration on Tax, as indicated in the *Global Policy Agenda* of April 2017;

(i) Assist jurisdictions in developing capacities to tackle illicit financial flows;

(j) Strengthen the global financial safety net with an adequately resourced, quota-based IMF at its centre;

(k) Increase coordination and cooperation with regional financial arrangements;

(l) Support public investments in energy-efficient infrastructure and climate change mitigation projects;

(m) Contribute to public investments in education, the care economy, water and sanitation, as well as other quality public services;

(n) Support sustainable pension systems as promised in the *Global Policy Agenda* of April 2017;

(o) Provide advisory services and technical assistance to States, including in drafting tax legislation and general anti-avoidance rules;

(p) Guarantee that, in cases of negative human rights impacts, victims have effective recourse and receive compensation, livelihood assistance and/or resettlement.

(q) Implementing these recommendations will benefit the entire human family. Indeed, as in the motto of Centre Europe-tiers monde: "There is not a developed world and an underdeveloped world but a single world badly developed." Only through the concerted efforts of IMF and the World Bank, together with the United Nations, will a more democratic and equitable international order emerge.

* * *

I would like to close this chapter with the words of Pope Francis. —AdeZ

The measure of the greatness of a society is found in the way it treats those most in need, those who have nothing apart from their poverty![i]

Notes

1 Available from www.imf.org/external/pubs/ft/aa/; and http://go.worldbank.org/Q53G3UP520.

2 See also International Monetary Fund, *Articles of Agreement* (Washington, D.C., 2016), article 1.

3 *World Economic and Social Survey 2017: Reflecting on Seventy Years of Development Policy Analysis* (United Nations publication, Sales No. E.17.II.C.1). Available from www.un.org/development/desa/dpad/wp-content/uploads/sites/45/publication/WESS_2017 -FullReport.pdf.

4 Ayn Rand, *The Virtue of Selfishness: A New Concept of Egoism* (New American Library, 1961); See also Naomi Klein, "Thanks a million, Ayn Rand, for setting the greedy free," *The Guardian* (28 September 2007). The author describes how Alan Greenspan discovered Ayn Rand in 1974, "What she did ... was to make me think why capitalism is not only efficient and practical, but also moral." Klein comments "Rand's ideas about the 'utopia of greed' ... infused [Greenspan] with a powerful new sense of mission: making money wasn't just good for him, it was good for society as a whole." Available from www.theguardian.com/commentisfree/2007/sep/29/ comment.comment.

5 International Monetary Fund, IMF Conditionality, 17 April 2017. Available from www.imf.org/en/About/Factsheets/Sheets/2016/08/02/21/28/IMF-Conditionality; Anna Yukhananov, "IMF loan conditions grow despite vows to limit them: study," Reuters, 2 April 2017. Available from www.reuters.com/article/us-imf-conditions-idUSBREA311SZ20140402; ActionAid Ghana, "Implications of IMF loans and conditionalities on the poor and vulnerable in Ghana," November 2010. Available from www.actionaid.org/sites/files/actionaid/implications_of_imf_loans_ and_conditionalities_on_the_poor_and_vulnerable_in_ ghana.pdf; Eurodad, "World Bank and IMF conditionaltiy: a development injustice," June 2006. www.eurodad.org/uploadedfiles/ whats_new/reports/eurodad_world_bank_and_imf_conditionality_report.pdf.

---

i Pope Francis, *The Spirit of St Francis: Inspiring Words on Faith, Love and Creation*, SPCK Publishing, 2015, p. 128.

6 Civil Society Reflection Group on the 2030 Agenda for Sustainable Development, *Spotlight on Sustainable Development 2017: Reclaiming Policies for the Public* (2017). Available from www.2030spotlight.org/en.

7 Ibid., p. 12.

8 See also the Reports of the Independent Expert on the effects of foreign debt and other related international financial obligations of States on the full enjoyment of all human rights, particularly economic, social and cultural rights, available www.ohchr.org/EN/Issues/Development/IEDebt/Pages/AnnualReports.aspx.

9 Naomi Klein, *The Shock Doctrine: The Rise of Disaster Capitalism* (London, Penguin, 2008).

10 See www.globalpolicy.org/social-and-economic-policy/the-three-sisters-and-other-institutions/internal-critics-of-the-world-bank-and-the-imf/42796-joseph-stiglitz.html.

11 Thomas Piketty, *Capital in the Twenty-First Century* (Cambridge, Massachusetts and London, England, Belknap Press of Harvard University Press, 2014); see also Thomas Piketty, "The IMF, the inequality debate, and economic research," 21 September 2016. Available from http://piketty.blog.lemonde.fr/2016/09/21/the-imf-the-inequality-debate-and-economic-research/; and Carlos Góes, "IMF working paper: testing Piketty's hypothesis on the drivers of income inequality: evidence from panel VARs with heterogeneous dynamics," working paper No. WP/16/160 (International Monetary Fund, 2016). Available from www.imf.org/external/ pubs/ft/wp/2016/wp16160.pdf.

12 Jeffrey Sachs, "Fixing the IMF and the World Bank," 4 October 1999. Available from www.project-syndicate.org/commentary/fixing-the-imf-and-the-world-bank?barrier=accessreg; Jeffrey Sachs, "A project in every port," *Finance and Development,* vol. 49, No. 4 (December 2012). Available from www.imf.org/external/pubs/ft/fandd/2012/12/people.htm; Jeffrey Sachs, "A warning on the eve of the G-20 summit," *Boston Globe,* 5 July 2017. Available from www.bostonglobe.com/opinion/2017/07/05/warning-eve-summit/TL2az8LWtbMYkNGklqjhPP/ story.html.

13 Paul Krugman, "Leave zombies be," *Finance and Development,* vol. 53, No. 4 (December 2016). Available from www.imf.org/external/pubs/ft/fandd/2016/12/krugman.htm; Paul Krugman, "The conscience of a liberal: opinion pages," *New York Times.* Available from https://krugman.blogs.nytimes.com/page/2/; Paul Krugman, "The case for cuts was a lie. Why does Britain still believe it?: The austerity delusion," *The Guardian,* 29 April 2015. Available from www.theguardian.com/business/ng-interactive/2015/apr/29/the-austerity-delusion.

14 Dani Rodrik, "The G20's misguided globalism," 6 July 2017. Available from www.project-syndicate.org/print/g20-misguided-globalism-by-dani-rodrik-2017-07; Dani Rodrik, *The Globalization Paradox: Democracy and the Future of the World Economy* (New York and London, W.W. Norton and Company, 2011), and Dani Rodrik, *Economics Rules: The Rights and Wrongs of the Dismal Science* (W.W. Norton and Company, New York and London, 2015).

15 Willem van Genugten, *The World Bank Group, the IMF and Human Rights: A Contextualised Way Forward* (Cambridge, United Kingdom, Intersentia, 2015).

16 Graham Bird and Dane Rowlands, *The International Monetary Fund: Distinguishing Reality from Rhetoric* (Cheltenham, United Kingdom and Northampton, Massachusetts, Edward Elgar Publishing, 2016).

17 See also Committee on Economic, Social and Cultural Rights, general comment No. 12 on the right to adequate food; and Committee on Economic, Social and Cultural Rights general comment No. 14 on the right to the highest attainable standard of health.

18 See William Holder, "The relationship between the International Monetary Fund and the United Nations," in *Current Legal Issues Affecting Central Banks,* vol. 4, Robert Effros, ed. (Washington, D.C., International Monetary Fund, 1997).

19 Naomi Klein, *The Shock Doctrine: The Rise of* (London, Penguin, 2008); see also John Perkins, *Confessions of an Economic Hitman* (New York, Plume, 2006).

20 Davison Budhoo, *Enough is Enough: Dear Mr. Camdessus...Open Letter of Resignation to the Managing Director of the International Monetary Fund* (New York, New Horizons Press, 1990), p. 102; and Naomi Klein, *The Shock Doctrine: The Rise of Disaster Capitalism* (London, Penguin, 2008), p. 10.

21 Naomi Klein, *The Shock Doctrine: The Rise of Disaster Capitalism* (London, Penguin, 2008).

22 Independent Evaluation Office of the International Monetary Fund, *The IMF and Recent Capital Account Crises: Indonesia, Korea, Brazil—Evaluation Report* (Washington, D.C., International Monetary Fund, 2003), p. 43. See also Allan Meltzer, "The report of the International Financial Institution Advisory Commission: comments on the critics," report prepared for Carnegie Mellon University Research Showcase, 2000. Available from https://pdfs.semanticscholar.org/6ac0/b262dd0bac92b27acf3aa3dd88ee1e5c6b35.pdf.

23 Bird and Rowlands, *The International Monetary Fund*, p. 3.

24 Sakib Sherani, "A better multilateralism," *Dawn,* 14 October 2016. Available from www.dawn.com/news/1289815.

25 International Monetary Fund, "The managing director's global policy agenda: a more inclusive and resilient global economy," 2017, p. 5. Available from www.imf.org/en/Publications/Policy-Papers/Issues/2017/04/18/md-spring-global-policy-agenda-a-more-inclusive-and-resilient-global-economy.

26 Pete Dolack, "World Bank declares itself above the law," 24 March 2017. Available from www.counterpunch.org/2017/03/24/world-bank-declares-itself-above-the-law.

27 Radhika Balakrishnan and James Heintz, "Making the International Monetary Fund accountable to human rights." Available from www.huffingtonpost.com/radhika-balakrishnan/making-the-international_b_549976.html (accessed 27 July 2017).

28 Alexander Kentikelenis, Thomas Stubbs and Lawrence King, "The IMF has not lived up to its own hype on social protection," *The Guardian,* 25 May 2016. Available from www.theguardian.com/global-development/2016/may/25/the-imf-international-monetary-fund-has-not-lived-up-to-hype-on-social-protection.

29 Alexander Kentikelenis, Thomas Stubbs and Lawrence King, "IMF conditionality and development policy space, 1985-2014," *Review of International Political Economy,* vol. 23, No. 4 (24 May 2016). Available from www.kentikelenis.net/uploads/3/1/8/9/31894609/ kentikelenis2016_imf_conditionality_and_development_policy_space.pdf.

30 www.imf.org/About/Factsheets/Sheets/2016/08/02/21/28/IMF-Conditionality?pdf=1.

31 International Monetary Fund, "Guidelines on conditionality," paper prepared by the Legal and Policy Development and Review Departments, 25 September 2002. Available from www.imf.org/External/np/pdr/cond/2002/eng/guid/092302.htm.

32 International Monetary Fund, "Revised operational guidance to IMF staff on the 2002 conditionality guidelines," 2014. Available from www.imf.org/en/Publications/Policy-Papers/Issues/2016/12/31/Revised-Operational-Guidance-to-IMF-Staff-on-the-2002-Conditionality-Guidelines-PP4889.

33 Stockholm International Peace Research Institute, SIPRI military expenditure database. Available from https://sipri.org/databases/milex.

34 Ross Leckow, "Conditionality in the International Monetary Fund," 7 May 2002. Available from www.imf.org/external/np/leg/sem/2002/cdmfl/eng/leckow.pdf;and Susan Jackson, "Military spending and the Washington consensus: the unrecognized link between militarization and the global political economy," PhD dissertation, University of Arizona, 2008. Available from http://arizona.openrepository.com/arizona/bitstream/10150/193513/1/azu_etd_2867_sip1_m.pdf.

35 See www.eurodad.org/; and www.eurodad.org/ Countdown-2017-UN-FfD-Forum.

36 Radhika Balakrishnan and James Heintz, "Making the International Monetary Fund accountable to human rights." Available from www.huffingtonpost.com/radhika-balakrishnan/making-the-international_b_549976.html (accessed 27 July 2017).

37 Ibid.

38 Ambrose Evans-Pritchard, "IMF admits disastrous love affair with the euro and apologises for the immolation of Greece," *The Telegraph,* 29 July 2016. Available from http://europeanpost.co/ imf-admits-disastrous-love-affair-with-euro-apologises-for-immolation-of-greece/.

39 Independent Evaluation Office of the International Monetary Fund, *The IMF and the Crises in Greece, Ireland, and Portugal* (Washington, D.C., International Monetary Fund, 2016), p. 37. Available from www.ieo-imf.org/ieo/files/completedevaluations/EAC%20%20Full%20Report.pdf.

40 Ibid., para. 80.

41 Stephen Lendman, "IMF: Greek debt untenable," 15 July 2015. Available from www.globalresearch.ca/imf-greek-debt-untenable/5462570.

42 Office of the United Nations High Commissioner for Human Rights (OHCHR), "UN human rights expert calls for debt relief to boost inclusive growth in Greece," 8 December 2015. Available from www.ohchr.org/EN/NewsEvents/Pages/DisplayNews.aspx?NewsID=16844 &LangID=E.

43 Ibid.

44 OHCHR, "UN human rights experts welcome Greek referendum and call for international solidarity," 30 June 2015. Available from www.ohchr.org/EN/NewsEvents/Pages/ DisplayNews.aspx?NewsID=16170&.

45 Truth Committee on Public Debt, preliminary report. Available from http://cadtm.org/IMG/pdf/Report.pdf.

46 See www.auditamosgrecia.org/en/executive-summary-greek-debt-audit/; see also http://greekdebttruthcommission.org/.

47 See www.cetim.ch/debt-and-austerity-measures-imposed-on-greece-violate-the-human-rights-of-the-greek-people-and-international-law/.

48 http://www.cetim.ch/debt-and-austerity-measures-imposed-on-greece-violate-the-human-rights-of-the-greek-people-and-international-law/.

49 Truth Committee on Public Debt, "Executive summary: Greek public debt audit report," 17 June 2015. Available from www.auditamosgrecia.org/en/executive-summary-greek-debt-audit/.

50 Robert Stevens, "EU and IMF demand more austerity measures from Greece," 13 February 2017. Available from www.globalresearch.ca/eu-and-imf-demand-more-austerity-measures-from-greece/ 5574554?utm_campaign=magnet&utm_source=article_page&utm_medium=related_articles.

51 Jan Strupczewski, "Euro zone, IMF agree on a common stance on Greece: official," Reuters (10 February 2017). Available from www.reuters.com/article/us-eurozone-greece-stance-idUSKBN15P11L.

52 Available from www.yanisvaroufakis.eu/2017/02/20/greeces-fiscal-waterboarding-continues-on-al-jazeera/.

53 Jon Stone, "NATO countries are not spending enough on defence, the alliance's chief says," Independent, 28 October 2016. Available from www.independent.co.uk/news/uk/politics/nato-jens-stoltenberg-military-spending-gdp-target-countries-not-enough-a7384236.html; and BBC News, "NATO defence spending target met, government insists," 14 February 2017. Available from www.bbc.com/news/uk-politics-38969697.

54 International Monetary Fund, "IMF survey: Europe and IMF agree €110 billion financing plan with Greece," 2 May 2010. Available from www.imf.org/en/News/Articles/2015/09/28/04/53/socar050210a.

55 Rodolfo Walsh, "Carta abierta de Rodolfo Walsh a la junta militar" (24 March 1977), Veredas do Direito, vol. 4, No. 8 (2007). Available from www.domhelder.edu.br/veredas_direito/pdf/ 26_160.pdf.

56 Benjamin Dangl, "After empowering the 1 per cent and impoverishing millions, IMF admits neoliberalism a failure," 31 May 2016. Available from https://towardfreedom.com/archives/globalism/after-empowering-the-1-and-impoverishing-millions-imf-admits-neoliberalism-a-failure/.

57 Edmund Conway, "IMF admits mistakes in Argentina crisis," The Telegraph, 30 July 2004. Available from www.telegraph.co.uk/finance/2891368/IMF-admits-mistakes-in-Argentina-crisis.html; and Paul Blustein, "IMF says its policies crippled Argentina: Internal audit finds warnings were ignored," 30 July 2004. Available from www.globalpolicy.org/component/ content/article/209/43078.html.

58 "IMF's 'role put into question': Argentina crisis evaluation," Bretton Woods Project, 21 September 2004. Available from www.brettonwoodsproject.org/2004/09/art-65659/.

59 Independent Evaluation Office of the International Monetary Fund, "IMF's Independent Evaluation Office announces release of report on the role of the IMF in Argentina," press release No. 04/02, 29 July 2004. Available from www.imf.org/External/NP/ieo/2004/pr/eng/pr0402.htm; and Independent Evaluation Office of the International Monetary Fund, The IMF and Argentina (Washington, D.C., International Monetary Fund, 2004). Available from www.imf.org/ External/NP/ieo/2004/arg/eng/index.htm.

60 "IMF's 'role put into question': Argentina crisis evaluation," *Bretton Woods Project*, 21 September 2004. Available from www.brettonwoodsproject.org/2004/09/art-65659/.
61 International Trade Union Confederation, "IMF stranglehold pushing Tunisia to the brink," 1 March 2017. Available from www.ituc-csi.org/imf-stranglehold-pushing-tunisia.
62 Ibid.
63 Tarek Amara, "Tunisia to accelerate reforms as IMF freezes loan: minister," Reuters, 26 February 2017. Available from www.reuters.com/article/us-tunisia-economy-idUSKBN16508T.
64 International Monetary Fund, "IMF executive board completes first review under the extended fund facility (EFF) arrangement with Tunisia," press release No. 17/217, 12 June 2017. Available from www.imf.org/en/News/Articles/2017/06/12/pr17217 -imf-executive-board-completes-first-review-under-eff-arrangement-with-tunisia.
65 International Monetary Fund, "Tunisia: first review under the extended fund facility, request for waivers of non-observance of performance criteria and rephasing of access," country report No. 17/203, July 2017. Available from www.imf.org/~/media/Files/Publications/CR/2017/ cr17203.ashx.
66 "Infographic: IMF policy in the MENA region," *Bretton Woods Project*, 18 December 2015. Available from www.brettonwoodsproject.org/2015/12/infographic-imf-policy-in-the-mena-region/.
67 Thomas Stubbs and others, "The impact of IMF conditionality on government health expenditure: a cross-national analysis of 16 West African nations," *Social Science and Medicine*, vol. 174 (February 2017). Available from www.sciencedirect.com/science/article/pii/ S0277953616306876.
68 Ibid., pp. 225-226; and Sanjeev Gupta, "Can a causal link be drawn? A commentary on 'the impact of IMF conditionality on government health expenditure: a cross-national analysis of 16 West African nations,'" *Social Science and Medicine*, vol. 181 (May 2017). Available from www.sciencedirect.com/science/article/pii/S0277953617301685, pp. 199–201.
69 Adia Benton and Kim Yi Dionne, "5 things you should read before saying the IMF is blameless in the 2014 Ebola outbreak," *Washington Post*, 5 January 2015. Available from www.washingtonpost.com/news/monkey-cage/wp/2015/01/05/5-things-you-should-read-before-saying-the-imf-is-blameless-in-the-2014-ebola-outbreak/.
70 Alexander Kentikelenis and others, "The International Monetary Fund and the Ebola outbreak," *The Lancet Global Health*, vol. 3, No. 2 (February 2015). Available from www.thelancet. com/ journals/langlo/article/PIIS2214-109X(14)70377-8/fulltext.
71 Adia Benton and Kim Yi Dionne, "5 things you should read before saying the IMF is blameless in the 2014 Ebola outbreak," *Washington Post*, 5 January 2015.
72 Adia Benton, *HIV Exceptionalism: Development through Disease in Sierra Leone* (University of Minnesota Press, 2015); and Rick Rowden, *The Deadly Ideas of Neoliberalism: How the IMF has Undermined Public Health and the Fight Against AIDS* (London, UK, and New York, NY, Zed Books, 2009). Rowden worked for development non-governmental organizations for nearly a decade and examines published research, official reports, conference declarations and parliamentary statements to document the failures of neoliberal reforms to improve health outcomes. In Part Three of the book Rowden "explains the ways in which ... support for strengthening public health systems and health workforces is being blocked by the IMF's fiscal and monetary policies and their associated budget restrictions and wage bill ceilings."
73 Adel Daoud and others, "Impact of International Monetary Fund programs on child health," *Proceedings of the National Academy of Sciences of the United States of America*, vol. 114,No. 25 (20 June 2017). Available from www.pnas.org/content/early/2017/05/09/1617353114, abstract; see also Alexander Kentikelenis, "Structural adjustment and health: a conceptual framework and evidence on pathways," *Social Science and Medicine*, vol. 187 (August 2017). Available from www.sciencedirect.com/science/article/pii/S0277953617301107.
74 Kristen Boon, "Privileges and immunities of international organizations," 11 June 2013. Available from http://opiniojuris.org/2013/06/11/privileges-and-immunities-of-international-organizations/; Niels Blokker and Nico Schrijver, eds., *Immunity of International Organizations* (Brill, 2015); *Convention on the Privileges and Immunities of the Specialized Agencies of the United Nations* (General Assembly Resolution 179 (II)); https://treaties.un.org/pages/ ViewDetails.

aspx?src=TREATY&mtdsg_no=III-2&chapter=3&lang=en; and International Organizations Immunities Act, 1945 22 USC § 288d(b); see also Steven Herz, "International organizations in U.S. courts: reconsidering the anachronism of absolute immunity," *31 Suffolk Transnat'l. Law Review 471* (2007-2008). The International Organizations Immunities Act provides that "International organizations, their property and their assets wherever located, and by whomsoever held, shall enjoy the same immunity from suit and every form of judicial process as it enjoyed by foreign governments." In essence the World Bank has been declared the equivalent of a sovereign State and given diplomatic immunity. Yet, this law has been applied selectively. Lawsuits against Cuba are not only allowed but consistently won by plaintiffs.

75 Claire Provost, "Farmers sue World Bank lending arm over alleged violence in Honduras," *The Guardian,* 8 March 2017. Available from www.theguardian.com/global-development/2017/mar/08/farmers-sue-world-bank-lending-arm-ifc-over-alleged-violence-in-honduras; Valentina Stackl, "Honduran Farmers Sue World Bank Group for Human Rights Violations," *EarthRights International,* 8 March 2017. Available from www.earthrights.org/media/honduran-farmers-sue-world-bank-group-human-rights-violations; the absolute immunity of heads of State has already been reduced since the arrest of General Pinochet and the indictment by the International Criminal Court of President Al Bashir. See www.ejiltalk.org/the-bashir-case-has-the-south-african-supreme-court-abolished-immunity-for-all-heads-of-states/; and Asad Kiyani, "Al-Bashir and the ICC: The Problem of Head of State Immunity," *Chinese Journal of International Law,* vol. 12, No. 3 (September 2013). Available from https://academic.oup.com/chinesejil/ article/12/3/467/323940/Al-Bashir-amp-the-ICC-The-Problem-of-Head-of-State.

76 International Monetary Fund Fiscal Affairs Department, *Manual on Fiscal Transparency* (Washington, D.C., 2007).

77 Human Rights Watch, "Human Rights Watch submission re international financial institutions and human rights," 25 April 2017. Available from www.hrw.org/news/2017/04/25/human-rights-watch-submission-re-international-financial-institutions-and-human.

78 Human Rights Watch, "IMF: withhold funds to Angola: require detailed explanation of $32 billion accounting gap," 27 March 2012. Available from www.hrw.org/news/2012/03/27/imf-withhold-funds-angola.

79 See https://spcommreports.ohchr.org/TMResultsBase/DownLoadPublicCommunication File?gId=3320.

80 Ibid.

81 Oxfam International, "No breakthrough on the big issues at spring meetings," 23 April 2017. Available from www.oxfam.org/en/pressroom/reactions/no-breakthrough-big-issues-spring-meetings.

82 International Monetary Fund, "Spillovers in international corporate taxation," policy paper, 9 May 2014. Available from www.imf.org/external/np/pp/eng/2014/050914.pdf.

83 Anne Krueger, First Deputy Managing Director, International Monetary Fund, "A new approach to sovereign debt restructuring," address given at the National Economists' Club Annual Members' Dinner, American Enterprise Institute, Washington, D.C., 26 November 2001. Available from www.imf.org/en/News/Articles/2015/09/28/04/53/sp112601; and "Sovereign debt restructuring and dispute resolution," speech given at the Bretton Woods Committee Annual Meeting, Washington, D.C., 6 June 2002. Available from www.imf.org/en/News/Articles/2015/ 09/28/04/53/sp060602.

84 Elaine Moore, "Anne Krueger: the economist in a hurry," *Financial Times,* 7 August 2015. Available from www.ft.com/content/e3fb48a2-3bae-11e5-8613-07d16aad2152?mhq5j=e3.

85 Juan Pablo Bohoslavsky, "Towards a multilateral legal framework for debt restructuring: six human rights benchmarks States should consider," 26 January 2015. Available from http://unctad.org/meetings/en/Presentation/gds_sd_2015-02-03-05_Bohoslavsky_en.pdf; Juan Pablo Bohoslavsky and Jernej Letnar Cernic, eds., *Making Sovereign Financing and Human Rights Work* (Hart Publishing, 2016); and Business and Human Rights Resource Centre, "Argentina: United Nations experts say the government's debt agreement with private lenders is to the detriment of peoples' human rights," 11 March 2016. Available from https://business-humanrights.org/en/argentina-un-experts-say-the-govts-debt-agreement-with-private-lenders-is-to-the-detriment-of-peoples%E2%80%99-human-rights.

86 International Monetary Fund, "Sovereign debt restructuring—recent developments and implications for the fund's legal and policy framework," 26 April 2013. Available from www.imf.org/external/np/pp/eng/2013/042613.pdf.

87 United Nations Conference on Trade and Development, "United Nations General Assembly adopts basic principles on sovereign debt restructuring processes," 11 September 2015. Available from http://unctad.org/en/pages/newsdetails.aspx?OriginalVersionID=1074.

88 Disciples Center for Public Witness, "Pope Francis calls for global bankruptcy process," 17 August 2015. Available from http://disciplescenter.blogspot.ch/2015/08/pope-francis-calls-for-global.html.

89 Juan Pablo Bohoslavsky, Independent Expert on the effects of foreign debt on human rights, "Vulture funds and human rights," remarks at the fourteenth session of the Human Rights Council Advisory Committee, 25 February 2015. Available from www.ohchr.org/Documents/Issues/Development/IEDebt/VultureFundsAndHumanRights2014.pdf.

90 Jonathan Ostry, Prakash Loungani and Davide Furceri, "Neoliberalism: oversold?," *Finance and Development*, vol. 53, No. 2 (June 2016). Available from www.imf.org/external/pubs/ft/fandd/2016/06/ostry.htm; and Rick Rowden, "The IMF confronts its N-word," Foreign Policy, 6 July 2016. Available from http://foreignpolicy.com/2016/07/06/the-imf-confronts-its-n-word-neoliberalism/.

91 Ibid.

92 Benjamin Dangl, "After empowering the 1 per cent and impoverishing millions, IMF admits neoliberalism a failure," 31 May 2016. Available from https://towardfreedom.com/archives/globalism/after-empowering-the-1-and-impoverishing-millions-imf-admits-neoliberalism-a-failure/.

93 Available from www.imf.org/external/mmedia/view.aspx?vid=5406736503001.

94 Era Dabla-Norris and others, "Causes and consequences of income inequality: a global perspective," staff discussion note 15/13, 15 June 2015. Available from www.imf.org/en/Publications/Staff-Discussion-Notes/Issues/2016/12/31/Causes-and-Consequences-of-Income-Inequality-A-Global-Perspective-42986.

95 Independent Evaluation Office, "The IMF and Social Protection" (IMF, 2017). Available from www.ieo-imf.org/ieo/pages/CompletedEvaluation279.aspx.

96 Ibid.

97 Ayn Rand, *Capitalism: the Unknown Ideal* (New American Library, 1966); and Introduction to Objectivist Epistemology (New American Library, 1979).

98 United Nations Sustainable Development Solutions Network, "World Happiness Report 2016 update ranks happiest countries," 16 March 2016. Available from http://unsdsn.org/news/2016/03/16/world-happiness-report-2016-update-ranks-happiest-countries/; and http://unsdsn.org/news/2017/03/21/media-roundup-on-2017-world-happiness-report/.

99 John Helliwell, Richard Layard and Jeffrey Sachs, eds., *World Happiness Report 2017* (New York, Sustainable Development Solutions Network, 2017), p. 34. "The quality of a country's democratic processes was based on the average of the remaining two World Bank measures: voice and accountability, and political stability and absence of violence. The results showed that for all countries taken together, the quality of delivery mattered more for well-being than did the presence or absence of democracy."

100 United Nations News Centre, "Ban: new economic paradigm needed, including social and environmental progress," 2 April 2012. Available from www.un.org/apps/news/story.asp?NewsID=41685.

101 Ibid.; see also www.un.org/esa/socdev/ageing/documents/noteonhappinessfinalclean.pdf.

102 See www.happinessday.org/resolutions/.

103 Karin Lissakers, "Dateline Wall Street: Faustian finance," *Foreign Policy*, No. 51 (Summer 1983), pp. 160–175.

104 Pepe Escobar, "The G20 From Hell," 11 July 2017. Available from www.counterpunch.org/2017/07/11/the-g20-from-hell/; Kevin Zeese and Margaret Flowers, "Power Dynamics Changing In World Order," 11 July 2017. Available from www.counterpunch.org/2017/07/11/power-dynamics-changing-in-world-order/.

105 See www.globalpolicy.org/social-and-economic-policy/the-three-sisters-and-other-institutions/ internal-critics-of-the-world-bank-and-the-imf/42796-joseph-stiglitz.html.

106 See www.imf.org/external/np/sec/memdir/memdate.htm. More than 90 per cent of the 189 countries that are members of the World Bank and International Monetary Fund have ratified four or more international human rights treaties. Human rights are also protected to varying degrees in most countries' constitutions or legislation. All but 1 have ratified the Convention on the Rights of the Child; 189 have ratified the Convention on the Elimination of All Forms of Discrimination against Women; 178 have ratified the International Convention on the Elimination of All Forms of Racial Discrimination; 169 have ratified the International Covenant on Civil and Political Rights; 165 have ratified the International Covenant on Economic, Social and Cultural Rights.

107 International Monetary Fund, *Articles of Agreement* (Washington, D.C., 2016). Available from www.imf.org/external/pubs/ft/aa/.

108 *World Economic and Social Survey 2017* (United Nations publication, Sales No. E.17.II.C.1). Available from www.un.org/development/desa/dpad/wp-content/uploads/sites/45/publication/WESS_2017-FullReport.pdf.

109 "The G20 and the Inequality Crisis," 7 July 2017. Available from www.project-syndicate.org/print/g20-solutions-to-ending-inequality-by-helle-thorning-schmidt-2017-07.

110 See www.un.org/esa/ffd/ffdforum/wp-content/uploads/sites/3/2017/04/2ndInformal_Statement-by-G77.pdf.

111 Ernesto Crivelli, Ruud De Mooij and Michael Keen, "Base erosion, profit shifting and developing countries," working paper No. 15/118 (International Monetary Fund, 2015).

Chapter 12

MISSION TO VENEZUELA

"The Special Rapporteur calls on all States to review and lift targeted sanctions in accordance with principles of international law, the rule of law, human rights and refugee law, to guarantee the possibility of state officials of Venezuela to represent the state on the basis of the principle of sovereign equality of states, and to guarantee rights of targeted individuals to the presumption of innocence, procedural guarantees, access to justice and other fundamental rights."

PROFESSOR ALENA DOUHAN
Special Rapporteur on the negative impact of unilateral coercive measures on the enjoyment of human rights,
Caracas, 12 February 2021[i]

After I had completed 13 thematic reports to the Human Rights Council and General Assembly, I considered that the exercise of my mandate also required that I conduct at least one country visit, so as to concretely and empirically test the principles of international order that I myself had formulated in theory.

Country visits are conducted only with the consent of the state concerned. The procedure is simple, the rapporteur formulates the object and purpose of a planned visit, sends a note verbale to the Mission of that country and then waits for a positive or negative decision. Some countries like Israel do not invite rapporteurs, and if a rapporteur enters the territory without permission, he/she is detained at the airport and expelled, as happened to Professor Richard Falk, the Special Rapporteur on issues concerning Palestine.[ii] Whereas Falk's visit was fully within its mandate and the Rapporteur is himself Jewish, he was not allowed to carry out any investigations on the ground.

Most States accept visits by rapporteurs on an ad hoc basis. This is a sovereign decision that each State is entitled to take, depending on a variety of factors. Obviously, States welcome advisory services and technical assistance from the United Nations and rapporteurs who will offer such assistance are welcome. Alas, some rapporteurs understand their mandate only as one of "naming and shaming" and specifically go to countries to interview the opposition, document both true and alleged violations of human rights and make a big show at the

---

i https://www.ohchr.org/EN/NewsEvents/Pages/DisplayNews.aspx?NewsID=26747
https://www.ohchr.org/EN/Issues/UCM/Pages/SRCoerciveMeasures.aspx

ii https://ips-dc.org/detaining_the_united_nations/
https://www.democracynow.org/2008/12/17/days_after_calling_israeli_blockade_of

concluding press conference with the attendance of the international media. It is not surprising that some countries that are already targets of a non-conventional information war do not want to facilitate the collection of data that would not be used to help the government solve its problems but would only add to the psychological pressure that the media can generate when they decide to target a country for demonization and "regime change." It is not difficult to understand that if the State perceives a given rapporteur as a priori hostile and not independent, and has reason to anticipate that the rapporteur will only grandstand instead of listening to all stakeholders and formulating constructive recommendations, no invitation will be forthcoming.

When in August 2017 I sent a note verbale to the Venezuelan Mission delineating the thrust of my proposed investigation, I had limited expectations that I would receive a positive response—despite the fact that in my five years as rapporteur I had built a solid reputation for neutral methodology and independence of judgment, and my 13 reports to the Council and General Assembly demonstrated a result-oriented approach, offering pragmatic solutions to concrete problems.

I was pleased to have been the first UN rapporteur to receive an invitation to Venezuela in 21 years, and used this opportunity to open the door for two other rapporteurs. Since, Professor Alena Douhan, the rapporteur on unilateral coercive measures, was invited and conducted a two-week visit in February 2021.[i] I also proposed the opening of a permanent office of the High Commissioner for Human Rights in Caracas—a proposal that materialized in 2019. Other visits by rapporteurs are in preparation.

From 25 November to 4 December 2017, I carried out the first visit to Venezuela by a UN rapporteur since 1996. Admittedly, I was not a "super rapporteur" and my competences were limited by the terms of reference of the mandate.[ii] I could not focus on problems of freedom of expression, the independence of judges, arbitrary detentions or the right to food and health, for which other rapporteurs are competent, but I did receive and transmit petitions on these issues and incorporated some into my own recommendations, which I formulated in a six-page memorandum that I personally gave to the Venezuelan Foreign Minister, Jorge Arreaza. I was pleased that as a direct result of my intercession with the government, eighty detainees were released very shortly after my visit and new cooperation arrangements were crafted between UN agencies and the government.[iii]

In 2016, prior to my visit, Venezuela had been examined under the Human Rights Council's Universal Periodic Review. Venezuela's fourth report to the

---

i https://www.ohchr.org/EN/NewsEvents/Pages/DisplayNews.aspx?NewsID=26747
ii https://www.ohchr.org/en/NewsEvents/Pages/DisplayNews.aspx?NewsID=22457&LangID=E
iii https://www.ohchr.org/en/NewsEvents/Pages/DisplayNews.aspx?NewsID=22569&LangID=E

Human Rights Committee and its third report to the Committee on Economic, Social and Cultural Rights had been examined in 2015, with both Committees issuing recommendations, which I consulted before undertaking the mission. Keenly aware of the methodological imperative to listen to all sides, *audiatur et altera pars*. I also accessed reports by the Inter-American Commission on Human Rights, the UN Human Rights Commissioner, Human Rights Watch, etc.

When in Venezuela I met with stakeholders of all political colours, members of the opposition, of the National Assembly, chamber of commerce (Fedecameras), university professors, churches, non-governmental organizations including Amnesty International, PROVEA, Fundalatin and the Grupo Sures, who helped me to understand the complexities of the para-institutional and constitutional conflicts as well as the current scarcity in certain foods, medicines and personal hygiene products, hoarding, black market, contraband, corruption, sabotage and induced inflation.

It is, of course, insufficient to simply observe the existence of an economic crisis. The challenge is to understand its causes—which became apparent after digesting masses of documentation and statistics. One major problem is the dependence of the Venezuelan economy on the sale of petroleum—a situation prevailing for more than a hundred years. Although the government has endeavoured to diversify, conversion is slow. The dramatic fall in oil prices was followed by a series of unilateral coercive measures including sanctions and financial blockades, exacerbating the situation. For example, when in November 2017 Venezuela needed anti-malaria medicine, Colombia refused to deliver, and Venezuela had to purchase it in India. I learned that to avoid U.S. penalties and complications, many banks closed Venezuelan accounts and other banks refused to effect transfers, routine international payments, even for the purchase of foods and medicines. It is not difficult to understand that economic sanctions kill. Perhaps the principal finding of my mission and post-mission evaluation of documents and statistics was that the cause of the economic crisis and the widespread suffering in Venezuela had to be attributed primarily to the economic war against the Venezuelan economy.

It is also important to recognize that the economic war did not start with the 2015 sanctions, but began with the arrival of Hugo Chávez to power twenty-three years ago. Outside interference with the Chávez government included helping to organize and finance the failed coup of April 2002. This parallels the economic war waged by the U.S. against Salvador Allende of Chile 1970–73, which ended with the Pinochet putsch. As Nixon told Kissinger in 1970, an alternative socioeconomic model would not be tolerated, and the Chilean economy would be made to scream.[i]

---

i https://nsarchive2.gwu.edu/NSAEBB/NSAEBB110/

Whereas the international law principle of non-intervention stipulated in the UN Charter and the clear language of Chapter 4, Article 19 of the OAS Charter specifically prohibits interference in the political or economic affairs of States, killer sanctions have been imposed that aim at asphyxiating Venezuela's economy and imposing "regime change." Before my mission I was overwhelmed by the media campaign aiming at creating the impression that there was a serious "humanitarian crisis" in Venezuela characterized by famine, death and uncontrolled emigration toward neighbouring countries. When I was in Venezuela I saw a different situation.I walked the streets incognito, entered supermarkets and pharmacies. I spoke in my native Spanish with the local population. It became clear that a majority of those with whom I spoke blamed the U.S. and the sanctions for their misery—not the Maduro government.

I came to understand that the media narrative was a collection of evidence-free allegations intended to prepare the ground for a military "humanitarian intervention," as in Libya in 2011.[i] The playbook was as clear as it was old. The intent was to persuade world public opinion of the legitimacy, morality and necessity of a military intervention in order to help the Venezuelan people reclaim democracy and their human rights. However, the situation in Venezuela did not then and does not today reach the threshold of a humanitarian crisis, as was confirmed to me by FAO and CEPAL officials—nothing comparable to the situation in Gaza,[ii] Haiti,[iii] Somalia,[iv] Sudan[v] or Yemen.[vi]

Bearing in mind that the noblest task of the Human Rights Council is to help all peoples live in peace and dignity, the solution to Venezuela's crisis must be through good faith negotiations and mediation, such as that conducted in 2016-18 in the Dominican Republic between the Venezuelan government and the Venezuelan opposition under the guidance of former Spanish Prime Minister José Luis Rodríguez Zapatero. On the day of signature, 7 February 2018, and to general surprise, the Venezuelan opposition refused to sign the long-negotiated

---

i UN Security Council Resolution 1973, https://www.un.org/securitycouncil/s/res/1973-%282011%29

https://www.huffpost.com/entry/clinton-emails-on-libya-e_b_9054182
https://foreignpolicy.com/2016/03/22/libya-and-the-myth-of-humanitarian-intervention/

ii Norman Finkelstein, Gaza, University of California Press, 2018.

iii https://reliefweb.int/report/haiti/haiti-humanitarian-situation-report-april-2017

iv https://www.care.org/emergencies/somalia-humanitarian-crisis

v https://www.unocha.org/story/south-sudan-humanitarian-crisis-catastrophic-proportions

vi https://www.c-span.org/video/?c4670011/murphy-young-yemen-murphy-saudis-deliberately-create-famine-yemen

https://www.ohchr.org/EN/NewsEvents/Pages/DisplayNews.aspx?NewsID=21496
https://www.firstpost.com/world/when-protectors-turn-tormentors-un-finds-war-crimes-breaches-of-humanitarian-law-in-syria-and-yemen-2639034.html

compromise.[i] *As it has been reported, a last-minute phone call to Julio Borges instructed him "no firme" ("don't sign"). He obeyed. In my report presented to the Council during its 39th session, I proposed renewed negotiations and the immediate lifting of sanctions and the financial blockade, which demonstrably have caused so much suffering and death. Many professors, journalists and politicians*[ii] *have echoed my demands.*

Following my visit I continued to follow developments and study documentation, statistics and arguments from all sides. My diagnosis: The crisis is not caused by the ideological "failure of socialism as an economic model" (socialism has not failed in Norway, Sweden, China), but by concrete and palpable causes, the dramatic fall in the price of crude oil, the over-dependence on exports, the failure to diversify the economy, an excess of ideologues and relative scarcity of technocrats in key areas. Most importantly and demonstrably, the crisis is the result of the cumulative impacts of 23 years of internal and external economic war, financial blockades, and sanctions. The mainstream narrative attributes the crisis to incompetence and corruption on the part of Venezuelan officials, but these problems plague most Latin American countries including Brazil, Chile, Colombia, Ecuador, Guatemala, Honduras, Paraguay, Peru, etc., as they also affect efficiency in North America, Europe, Africa and Asia. Besides, many argue that the level of corruption in Venezuela in the 1980s and 1990s was higher and we remember that Chávez won the 1998 elections on a wave of disgust at the corruption of the neoliberal governments. I wanted to investigate this aspect of the mainstream narrative and spent hours with the current Attorney General in Caracas, Tarek William Saab, from whom I received ample documentation on the government's vigorous anti-corruption campaign, investigations and ongoing prosecutions and convictions—not only in cases of corruption, but also in cases of police brutality. Unlike in many other countries in Latin America and the world, there is no institutionalized impunity in Venezuela today.

U.S. efforts to topple Chávez started early, and the CIA cooperated with the Venezuelan oligarchy in the failed coup against Chávez on 11/12 April 2002. The 48-hour President Pedro Carmona had promptly issued a decree doing away with 49 pieces of social legislation, suspending the Supreme Court, the Chávez National Assembly, dismissing governors, etc. Although there is nothing more undemocratic than a coup—Carmona and the U.S. media spoke of "restoring democracy" in Venezuela, "democracy" being understood as the capitalist socioeconomic system.

---

i https://www.lechuguinos.com/zapatero-respondio-julio-borges/
https://www.elciudadano.com/politica/rodriguez-zapatero-niega-que-haya-amenazado-con-carcel-a-julio-borges/08/15/

ii https://www.youtube.com/watch?v=UHqMxs50d7k

It is high time to recognize the simple fact that "human rights" has nothing to do with the U.S. Venezuela policy. As it was in Iraq 2003 and Libya 2011, it is OIL. The U.S. covets the largest oil reserves in the world, as well as the third largest reserves in gold and coltan. If Maduro is toppled, it will be a bonanza for U.S. investors and transnational corporations. It's sad that some countries ostensibly committed to democracy, the rule of law and human rights, are supporting the sanctions and the attempted coup d'état by Juan Guaidó. We observe a Machiavellian, cynical instrumentalization of human rights and humanitarian aid for purely geopolitical reasons. Indeed, there is nothing more vulgar and more undemocratic than yet another right-wing coup in Latin America.

Before reproducing excerpts of my 2018 report, I would like to share with the reader some spontaneous reflections I jotted down shortly after my mission.

1. Realpolitik

As heads of government democratically entrusted with safeguarding the welfare of all Venezuelans, Chávez and Maduro do bear responsibility for the economic crisis—but they are not alone. Surely it was a mistake to continue the risky politics of all previous governments by maintaining the dangerous dependence on the export of petroleum and failing to take timely and effective measures to diversify the economy, ensure food security, achieve a prudent self-sufficiency in the production and supply of generic medicines, etc.

Both Chávez and Maduro naively relied on the benefits of globalization, without sufficiently taking into account their vulnerability in case of an economic war, financial blockade and sanctions such as had already caused chaos and suffering in Cuba, Chile, Nicaragua and Iraq.

Responsible politicians cannot act solipsistically, ignoring Realpolitik. While Chávez and Maduro had the democratic legitimacy to try out a socialist economic model, they should have taken precautionary steps before challenging the U.S.-dominated neoliberal world economy. The international law doctrine of State sovereignty cannot afford to ignore the reality of power politics. In other words, if Chávez wanted to challenge the U.S. model, he should have taken measures to survive the predictable unilateral coercive measures surely to come from Washington. One does not simply provoke the continent's hegemon, expecting somehow to survive unscathed. Chávez and Maduro should have had contingency plans—a plan B, a plan C—to address the consequences of a financial blockade. Back in 1970 President Nixon had clearly told Kissinger that he would not tolerate an alternative economic model in Latin America and that the Chilean economy would be made to scream.

It is not wise to rely on international legal norms and treaties on freedom of commerce, freedom of navigation, etc., since these norms are difficult to enforce, and meaningless when countered by a hegemon that does not hesitate to play hard ball and break international law when it suits him. The U.S. has frequently flouted the International Court of Justice and its judgments on Nicaragua, on the La Grand brothers, on the Avena death penalty cases, etc. And the U.S. has done it and continues to do it in total impunity, and with the acquiescence or connivance of many other States.

Here lies the principal responsibility of Chávez and Maduro—to have ignored Realpolitik as the leaders of Melos naively did during the Peloponnesian war in the fifth century BC, when the Athenian general reminded them of the basic rule of power politics, that the powerful do as they want and the weak suffer as they must.[i]

2. Estoppel

Responsibility for the aggravation of the economic crisis brought about by the fall in the price of oil lies with those inside and outside Venezuela who have conducted an economic war; those who have hoarded foods and medicines, only to release them to the black market at exorbitant prices; those who have speculated on the currency; those who have engaged in smuggling of subsidized food and medicine to Colombia, Brazil, even Aruba; those who have imposed a financial blockade on Venezuela; those who have made it nearly impossible for Venezuela to borrow, issue bonds, etc.; those banks who have closed the Venezuelan government accounts, or who refuse to transfer payments to or from Venezuela; those who impose sanctions and penalize banks and businesses for doing business with Venezuela. Besides the United States, the governments of Canada and of European States bear responsibility for the deaths of Venezuelans from malnutrition or of those who have had no access to anti-malaria medicines, to anti retroviral drugs, insulin, etc. It is a disgrace that some Venezuelan opposition leaders actually demand more sanctions from the United States, in full knowledge that sanctions kill their own people.

Those in the "international community" who shout "humanitarian crisis" and demand humanitarian intervention are estopped from so doing if they, like the U.S., Canada and the European Union, are substantially to blame, because it is they who have criminally aggravated the economic crisis through crippling sanctions and other forms of non-conventional warfare. There is a corruption of logic here, as there is with the cynical offer of "humanitarian aid" by the United States to Venezuela. One cannot be torturer and savior at the same time. One cannot be oppressor today and good Samaritan tomorrow. This is too Machiavellian for words.

---

i Thucydides, *The Peloponnesian War,* Melian Dialogue, 16th year.

Not only do we see a classical estoppel here, but we must draw attention to the tortious and penal implications of sanctions. Both common law and civil law jurisdictions recognize a "duty to rescue" and penalize the "omission of help" or "abandonment of persons." It is not difficult to understand that if sanctions prevent a country from obtaining medicines or medical equipment, people may die as a direct consequence. Creating an artificial scarcity of medicines can be considered under the rubric "reckless endangerment" or failure to assist a person in distress.[i] *Clearly there is responsibility both on the part of the government that imposes sanctions and on those who implement them. Thus, if a businessman engaged in the export of medicines refuses to deliver medicines because of potential penalties, he/she may be guilty of denial of assistance to persons in distress. The only ethical approach to the dilemma is that the businessperson must deliver the medicines and that his/her government must exercise the international legal obligation of diplomatic protection and vindicate not only the right—but the obligation—of the businessperson to provide the medicines. Under no conditions can a sovereign State legally allow the criminal extra-territorial application of foreign legislation in its territory. If responsibility to protect means anything, it must include a responsibility to protect persons put in distress and danger of death by the imposition of unilateral coercive measures. The evidence is before us that there is a direct nexus between economic sanctions and death. This is an inescapable conclusion and a matter that the International Court of Justice should address in an Advisory Opinion.*

3. How best to restore full enjoyment of civil and political rights

Experience shows that when a country is at war—any kind of war—it usually derogates from civil and political rights. Similarly, when a country is enduring non-conventional hybrid warfare and is subjected to economic sanctions, the result is not an expansion of human rights, but exactly the opposite. When sanctions trigger economic and social crises, governments routinely impose extraordinary measures and justify them because of the "national emergency." Accordingly, as in classical war situations, when a country is subject to a siege, it closes ranks in an attempt to regain stability through the temporary restriction of certain civil and political rights.

Article 4 of the International Covenant on Civil and Political Rights does envisage the possibility that governments may impose certain temporary restrictions, e.g. the derogation from Art. 9 (detention), Art. 14 (fair trial proceedings), Art. 19 (freedom of expression), Art. 21 (freedom of peaceful

---

i Allen, Michael. *Textbook on Criminal Law.* Oxford University Press, Oxford, 2005. See also the French penal code which stipulates: *"Selon l'article 223-6 du Code pénal, est considéré comme non-assistance à personne en danger le fait pour quiconque de s'abstenir volontairement de porter a une personne en péril l'assistance...."*

assembly), Art. 25 (periodic elections). In principle, no one welcomes such derogations, but every state's priority is survival, defending its sovereignty and identity. International law recognizes that governments have a certain margin of discretion in determining the level of threat to the survival of the state posed by sanctions, paramilitary activities, currency speculation and sabotage.

Thus, instead of facilitating the improvement of the human rights situation, economic sanctions often result in emergency domestic legislation intended to safeguard vital interests. In such cases sanctions reveal themselves as counter-productive, as a lose-lose proposition. Similarly, the overused practice of "naming and shaming" has revealed itself as ineffective. What has been effective in the past is quiet diplomacy, dialogue, compromise, advisory services and technical assistance.

If the international community wants to help a country improve its human rights performance, it should endeavour to eliminate the threats that make governments retrench instead of opening-up. By now it should be obvious that sabre rattling, sanctions and blockades are not conducive to positive change. Precisely because they aggravate the situation and disrupt the proper functioning of state institutions, they actually weaken the rule of law and lead to retrogression in human rights terms.

In the light of the continuing threats by some politicians against countries subjected to sanctions, it would seem that an old French adage has application:

— la bête est très méchante, lorsqu'on l'attaque, elle se défend.
(*The beast is very nasty—when you attack it, it defends itself.*)

What follows are excerpts from my 2018 report on my visit to Venezuela.[i] —AdeZ

* * *

The present report summarizes the results of the mission of the Independent Expert on the promotion of a democratic and equitable international order to the Bolivarian Republic of Venezuela and Ecuador, two member States of the Bolivarian Alliance for the Peoples of Our America,[1] at the invitation of the respective Governments. The mission focused on alternative social and economic models and their implications for a democratic and equitable international order, with one leg in the Bolivarian Republic of Venezuela from 25 November to 4 December and another in Ecuador from 4 to 9 December 2017. The particularities of each country are sui generis and should not be amalgamated. The parameters of the mission were announced in a statement issued on 27 November 2017.[2]

---

i https://undocs.org/A/HRC/39/47/Add.1

The Human Rights Council, in its resolution 18/6 creating the mandate of the Independent Expert, reaffirmed the determination to establish conditions under which justice and respect for the obligations arising from treaties and other sources of international law can be maintained, to promote social progress and better standards of life in larger freedom. It also reaffirmed the need to continue working urgently for the establishment of an international economic order based on equity, sovereign equality, interdependence, common interest and cooperation among all States, irrespective of their economic and social systems. It instructed the mandate holder to work in cooperation with States in order to foster the adoption of measures at the local, national, regional and international levels aimed at the promotion and protection of a democratic and equitable international order.

The duty of the special procedures mandates is to learn about the situations on the ground, listen to stakeholders on all sides, evaluate documents, ask targeted questions, and formulate constructive recommendations. A result-oriented mission aims at understanding the problems in a political, economic, psychological and historical context, so as to propose measures to better realize all human rights. A comprehensive approach requires, *inter alia*, consideration of the constitutions, laws and practices of States, as well as of reports by intergovernmental organizations and conferences, including the Economic and Social Council (ECOSOC), the World Health Organization (WHO), the International Labour Organization (ILO), the Food and Agriculture Organization (FAO) of the United Nations, the Organization of American States, the Inter-American Commission on Human Rights, the Community of Latin American and Caribbean States (CELAC), the Bolivarian Alliance for the Peoples of Our America, the Latin American Economic System (SELA), the Southern Common Market (MERCOSUR), the Union of South American Nations, the Non-Aligned Movement, Summits of the Americas and People's Summits, reports issued by the Office of the United Nations High Commissioner for Human Rights, national reports submitted for the Universal Periodic Review and State party reports to the treaty bodies. In drafting the present report, the Independent Expert benefited from studying mission reports by the Independent Expert on human rights and international solidarity, Virginia Dandan, the Independent Expert on the effects of foreign debt and other related international financial obligations of States on the full enjoyment of all human rights, particularly economic, social and cultural rights, Juan Pablo Bohoslavsky, and the Special Rapporteur on the negative impact of unilateral coercive measures on the enjoyment of human rights, Idriss Jazairy. He also consulted publications by Human Rights Watch, Amnesty International, the International Commission of Jurists, the Fundación Latinoamericana por los Derechos Humanos y el Desarrollo Social, civil society organizations and universities.

As one of the few special procedure mandate holders to be given access to the Bolivarian Republic of Venezuela and Ecuador, expectations for the mission were high.

While the Independent Expert could not fulfil the hopes of some sectors of civil society and remain within the parameters of his mandate, he listened to their grievances and transmitted their concerns to the competent rapporteurs and working groups. He informed his interlocutors that he was not "the United Nations," a super-rapporteur, a plenipotentiary or a country rapporteur, but an independent expert for international order. He invited interlocutors to give him information and petitions on issues which could be examined in depth by the Special Rapporteurs on the promotion and protection of the right to freedom of opinion and expression, on the rights to freedom of peaceful assembly and of association, on the independence of judges and lawyers, on the right to food, on the right of everyone to the enjoyment of the highest attainable standard of physical and mental health, on adequate housing as a component of the right to an adequate standard of living, and on the right to non-discrimination in this context, on the rights of indigenous peoples, and by the Working Group on Arbitrary Detention. He took the opportunity of informing government authorities of these concerns, which he incorporated into his preliminary recommendations.

The present report gives a fresh look at the realities of the Bolivarian Republic of Venezuela and Ecuador, two countries that have adopted differing socioeconomic models when tackling internal issues of poverty, health care, housing and education. In both countries, the Independent Expert learned of problems associated with corruption, financial constraints, para-institutional failures, and lingering difficulties in ensuring free, prior and informed consent in the extractive field, particularly concerning indigenous communities. In the Bolivarian Republic of Venezuela, he observed the adverse impacts of inflation, price controls,[3] contraband,[4] inefficient distribution, mismanagement, and repression of dissent.

He listened to hundreds of stakeholders, including representatives of United Nations agencies and the Organization of American States (), and received a wealth of information. The visits included meetings with ministers of both countries, ambassadors, diplomats, government officials, church leaders, academics, economists, students, and civil society organizations. In particular cases, he was approached by, and heard the stories of, individual victims. He balanced his meetings between different groups and was proactive in demanding targeted information. After the mission, he requested and received additional information, which he duly reflected, confident that the dialogue begun with each Government will continue through the visits of other rapporteurs.

His methodology followed the principle *audiatur et altera pars* (listen to all sides), and the letter and spirit of the Code of Conduct for Special Procedures Mandate Holders of the Human Rights Council, article 3 (a) of which stipulates that mandate holders shall act in an independent capacity and exercise their functions in accordance with their mandate. Article 6 requires mandate holders to establish the facts, based on objective, reliable information emanating from relevant credible sources that they have duly cross-checked to the best extent possible; take into account in a comprehensive and timely manner in particular information provided by the State concerned on situations relevant to their mandate; evaluate all information in the light of internationally recognized human rights standards relevant to their mandate, and of international conventions to which the State concerned is a party. In assessing the evidence, the Independent Expert was critical both of governmental and civil society sources, conscious of the possibility of distortions and suppression of evidence. He considered whether specific cases were representative and avoided extrapolation. He kept an open mind, ready to change perspective in the light of evidence received from stakeholders on all sides.

After his mission, he continued to follow developments in the Bolivarian Republic of Venezuela, including the refusal of the opposition to sign the negotiated agreement of 7 February 2018, the Declaration of the Summit of the Americas[5] and that of the People's Summit,[6] both held in Lima in April 2018.

Having arrived at his own diagnoses, he proposes how best to enhance the enjoyment of all human rights by the populations of both countries, including through dialogue, increased international cooperation, and reform of treaties, legislation and practices. The mission examined efforts to advance social progress and better standards of living consistent with the provisions of the International Covenant on Economic, Social and Cultural Rights, the International Covenant on Civil and Political Rights and the agendas of the World Social Forums since the first one was held in 2001 in Porto Alegre, Brazil. He paid special attention to the reports presented by the Bolivarian Republic of Venezuela and Ecuador to the Human Rights Committee and the Committee on Economic, Social and Cultural Rights and studied the concluding observations of those bodies. He compared their analyses with the relevant reports issued by the Inter-American Commission on Human Rights between 2013 and 2018[7] and the responses of the Bolivarian Republic of Venezuela and Ecuador thereto.

The present report considers the relevance of General Assembly resolutions on international order, including 2625 (XXV) on friendly relations, 72/4 on the United States embargo against Cuba, and 60/1 on the 2005 World Summit Outcome, which reaffirms that democracy is a universal value based on the freely expressed will of people to determine their own political, economic, social and cultural systems and their full participation in all aspects of their lives; that democracy, development and respect for human rights and fundamental freedoms are interdependent and mutually reinforcing; and that while democracies share common features, there is no single model of democracy. Thus, the models of democracy of the "Revolución Bolivariana"[8] in the Bolivarian Republic of Venezuela and the "Revolución Ciudadana"[9] in Ecuador deserve attention.[10]

The socioeconomic models prevalent in both countries, as well as in the Plurinational State of Bolivia, Cuba and Nicaragua, reveal possibilities of greater regional integration and cooperation with international organizations, particularly the United Nations system, which can assist governments to achieve social progress and strengthen civil liberties. The Independent Expert noted the eradication of illiteracy,[11] free education from primary school to university, and programmes to reduce extreme poverty, provide housing to the homeless and vulnerable, phase out privilege and discrimination, and extend medical care to everyone.

It is appropriate for rapporteurs to highlight beneficial initiatives and recognize lessons learned. In the Bolivarian Republic of Venezuela, the *Gran Misión Vivienda* low-cost housing programme has contributed to saving millions of persons from homelessness. Over two million housing units have been delivered to persons who would otherwise live in shanty towns. In order to address hunger, the Local Supply and Production Committees provide needy Venezuelans with 16kg packages containing sugar, flour, dried milk, oil, etc., as the Independent Expert was able to verify at the Urbanización Nelson Mandela. Another social acquis, *El Sistema*, established by the late José Antonio Abreu, has offered free musical education to over one million youngsters,[12] contributing to a reduction in juvenile delinquency. Gustavo Dudamel,[13] Music and Artistic Director of the Los Angeles Philharmonic, is a product of *El Sistema*.

Achievements and engagement by other human rights mechanisms

In June 2015, the Human Rights Committee examined the fourth periodic report of the Bolivarian Republic of Venezuela. In its concluding observations, it welcomed numerous legislative initiatives, including the adoption of the Indigenous Peoples and Communities Act and the Act on Women's Right to a Life Free from Violence, and the establishment of the Ministry of People's Power for Indigenous Peoples and of the Ministry of People's Power for Women and Gender Equality. The Committee noted with satisfaction that the Constitution provided that human rights treaties were immediately and directly applicable by the courts and other public bodies (see CCPR/C/VEN/CO/4, paras. 3 and 5).

The Committee expressed concern at reports of the alleged commission of human rights violations during protests. While taking into account that some protesters might have resorted to violence, the Committee was concerned at numerous reports of cases of excessive and disproportionate use of force, torture and ill-treatment, arbitrary detention and failure to uphold fundamental legal safeguards. While it took note of the investigations that were under way, only seven civil servants had been convicted at that time (ibid., para. 14).

Also in June 2015, the Committee on Economic, Social and Cultural Rights examined the third periodic report the Bolivarian Republic of Venezuela. In its concluding observations, it noted with satisfaction the progress made in combating poverty and reducing inequality, and in the fight against malnutrition through the expansion of the school meals programme and the food allowance for low-income families (see E/C.12/VEN/CO/3, para. 5). It noted the delegation's commitment that, despite the economic difficulties caused by, among other factors, the fall in oil revenues, the State party would continue to make every effort to prevent the situation from affecting social investment and the progressive realization of economic, social and cultural rights (ibid., para. 6).

The Committee expressed concern at reports that consultations with indigenous peoples were not held regularly and with full guarantees, particularly when granting concessions for the exploration and development of natural resources. It was also concerned by reports that the legally established procedure for appointing and removing judges was not applied and by the large number of judges appointed to posts on a temporary basis, who, without security of tenure, might find that their independence significantly affected (ibid., paras. 9–10). It was further concerned by reports of acts of violence and intimidation against trade union leaders and members (ibid., para. 20).[14]

The Universal Periodic Review of the Bolivarian Republic of Venezuela took place in November 2016. As at June 2017, the Bolivarian Republic of Venezuela had committed to implementing 193 of the 274 recommendations made, and had noted the remaining 81.

A problem in assessing the situation is the widening gulf between the Government's and the opposition's narratives, and the media disinformation, simplification and extrapolation. The Independent Expert consulted data from multiple sources, including presentations by non-governmental organizations (NGOs) to the Human Rights Council.[15]

Undoubtedly, Venezuelans are suffering from an economic crisis that has generated dysfunctions, scarcity in foods and medicines,[16] delays in distribution, and accompanying violations of human rights.[17] Critics in and outside the country see it as a failed State and blame the crisis on socialism,[18] but few look for other contributing factors. By contrast, the Government tends to blame outside causes, notably the drop in oil prices, international smuggling rings, contraband, sanctions, and 19 years of economic warfare, not unlike the non-conventional wars waged against Cuba, Chile and Nicaragua. With political will and international solidarity, solutions can be found, since the Bolivarian Republic of Venezuela is a rich country with the largest oil reserves in the world and major gold, bauxite and coltan deposits,[19] enough to finance the needs of the Venezuelan people, provided that the country is allowed to function free of embargoes and financial blockades.[20]

Observers have identified errors committed by the Chávez and Maduro Governments, noting that there are too many ideologues and too few technocrats in public administration, resulting in government policies that lack coherence and professional management and discourage domestic investment, already crippled by inefficiency and corruption,[21] which extend to government officials, transnational corporations and entrepreneurs.[22] Critics warn about the undue influence of the military on government and on the running of enterprises like Petróleos de Venezuela. The lack of regular, publicly available data on nutrition, epidemiology and inflation are said to complicate efforts to provide humanitarian support.[23]

Meanwhile, the Attorney General, Tarek Saab, has launched a vigorous anti-corruption campaign,[24] investigating the links between Venezuelan enterprises and tax havens, contracting scams, and deals by public officials with Odebrecht.[25] It is estimated that corruption in the oil industry has cost the Government US$ 4.8 billion.[26] The Attorney General's Office informed the Independent Expert of pending investigations for embezzlement and extortion against 79 officials of Petróleos de Venezuela, including 22 senior managers. The Office also pointed to the arrest of two high-level oil executives,[27] accused of money-laundering in Andorra. The Ministry of Justice estimates corruption losses at some US$ 15 billion.[28] Other stakeholders, in contrast, assert that anti-corruption programmes are selective and have not sufficiently targeted State institutions, including the military.[29]

Bearing in mind that the mission had to follow the terms of reference of the mandate, the Independent Expert did not undertake a global inquiry into violations of civil, cultural, economic, political and social rights. Those issues are being dealt with by treaty bodies and deserve investigation by other rapporteurs. The mission necessarily focused on those issues related to the promotion of a democratic and equitable international order, including the need to promote increased regional and international cooperation,[30] survey policies aimed at stopping illicit financial flows and tax havens, ensure freedom of commerce and financial transactions without discrimination, address problems of sovereign debt restructuring,[31] obtain information on policies concerning the distribution of resources and regulation of the private sector,[32] and explore ways of strengthening mutual legal assistance in criminal matters.

Private sector actors have pointed to the State acquisition of private property, price controls[33] and worsened working conditions as reducing private sector confidence, and thus contributing to an economic crisis in the country. Private sector unions question strict controls on currency exchange, which they say cause businesses to hesitate to price and sell goods for fear of violating the law. In addition, as raised in an ongoing complaint to the ILO, businesspeople and some workers' unions have alleged that they are excluded from dialogue that impacts the labour sector and that they have been subject to persecution by the State, contrary to ILO conventions on freedom of association, tripartite consultation and setting minimum wages.[34] In March 2018, in the absence of progress, the ILO Governing Body decided to appoint a Commission of Inquiry.[35]

It has been suggested by entrepreneurs that the Government should exercise more flexibility with monetary policies and provide incentives to the private sector—as has been done in other countries that maintain progressive social models, while easing exchange and loosening price controls—so as to ensure that entrepreneurs are not driven out of business by high replacement costs and a feeling of insecurity, which discourages domestic and international investment.

Obstacles to the enjoyment of human rights: Economic warfare

The Independent Expert asked the Government and the opposition about the impact of measures adopted by several States aimed directly and indirectly at affecting the functioning of the Venezuelan economy. He also looked at the problem of currency speculation, one of the preferred tools to destabilize targeted economies, and the activities of credit rating agencies,[36] which, although they have neither democratic legitimacy nor oversight, have a significant impact on the financial ability of States to issue bonds and obtain financing. The Banco Central de Venezuela informed him that risk rating agencies, primarily Standard & Poor's, Moody's and Fitch, have consistently issued negative ratings based on the country's ability to make external payments, forgetting that the Government has a history of excellent debt response. That has had a significant effect on the country's risk level and has essentially shut down its possibilities of accessing the financial market.

Illicit flows, or the illegal transferring of funds from one jurisdiction to another, has had an adverse impact on the ability of States to meet their financial obligations, as has the use of tax havens. International cooperation is necessary to ensure the repatriation of these funds.[37] It also appears that international criminal groups are responsible for the theft of public resources, food items and medicines, which have found their way into neighbouring countries. The United Nations Office on Drugs and Crime (UNODC) can help States tackle some of these problems. There have been cases of hoarding[38] of food, medicines and personal hygiene items, with the items subsequently released onto the black market.[39] In some cases, the hoarding has been so prolonged that hidden food and medicines have perished.[40] Government officials also shared concerns about the widespread sabotage of public property,[41] arson attacks on public buildings, buses, ambulances, hospitals, maternity wards and other institutions, destruction of electricity and telephone lines, paramilitarism[42] in frontier regions[43] and other violent acts tantamount to terrorism.

Economic sanctions

While arms sales embargoes may be justifiable against some countries, especially to facilitate dialogue and peacemaking, economic sanctions that hurt innocent populations contravene the spirit and letter of the Charter of the United Nations. Over decades, United Nations bodies have condemned unilateral coercive measures,[44] notably in the landmark 2000 study of the Sub-Commission on the Promotion and Protection of Human Rights,[45] documenting the adverse human rights impact of those measures. Multilateral sanctions, even those imposed by the Security Council under Chapter VII of the Charter, can also cause suffering and death. In the 1990s, two United Nations Assistant Secretary-Generals, Denis Halliday and Hans-Christof von Sponeck,[46] quit their Humanitarian Coordinator functions in Iraq to protest against sanctions, which had caused more than a million deaths among Iraqis, particularly children,[47] and which they qualified as a form of genocide.[48]

On 23 March 2018, the Human Rights Council condemned unilateral coercive measures by a vote of 28 in favour, 15 against and 3 abstentions,[49] because economic sanctions demonstrably cause death, aggravate economic crises, disrupt the production and distribution of food and medicine, constitute a push factor generating emigration,[50] and lead to violations of human rights. The refusal of Colombia to deliver anti-malaria medicine that had been ordered to combat an outbreak in November 2017,[51] as well as the absence of condemnation from the international community, entails joint responsibility for the aggravation of the crisis. In that case, the anti-malaria medicine had to be imported from India.

The effects of sanctions imposed by Presidents Obama and Trump[52] and unilateral measures by Canada and the European Union have directly and indirectly aggravated the shortages in medicines such as insulin and anti-retroviral drugs. To the extent that economic sanctions have caused delays in distribution and thus contributed to many deaths, sanctions contravene the human rights obligations of the countries imposing them.

Moreover, sanctions can amount to crimes against humanity[53] under Article 7 of the Rome Statute of the International Criminal Court. An investigation by that Court would be appropriate, but the geopolitical submissiveness of the Court may prevent this.

Modern-day economic sanctions and blockades are comparable with medieval sieges of towns with the intention of forcing them to surrender. Twenty-first century sanctions attempt to bring not just a town, but sovereign countries to their knees. A difference, perhaps, is that twenty-first century sanctions are accompanied by the manipulation of public opinion through "fake news," aggressive public relations and a pseudo-human rights rhetoric so as to give the impression that a human rights "end" justifies the criminal means. There is not only a horizontal juridical world order governed by the Charter of the United Nations and principles of sovereign equality, but also a vertical world order reflecting the hierarchy of a geopolitical system that links dominant States with the rest of the world according to military and economic power. It is the latter geopolitical system that generates geopolitical crimes, hitherto in total impunity. It is reported that the United States is currently training foreign lawyers in how to draft legislation to impose further sanctions on the Bolivarian Republic of Venezuela in an effort to asphyxiate Venezuelan State institutions.[54]

The Banco Central de Venezuela informed the Independent Expert that the sanctions, besides hindering access to external financing and international payments, had affected the normal performance of the national productive apparatus, resulting in a reduction in the supply of local goods and services. For the previous year and a half, the bank had been experiencing difficulties with the correspondent investment of high-level banks; from a total of 33 correspondent accounts, it currently had 14, which operated under a discretional compliance system, with many limitations that resulted in certain operational restrictions, mostly focused on public debt payments. The problems had worsened relating to the operation of correspondent banks, mainly Citibank, Commerzbank and Deutsche Bank, which currently handled only public debt payment. The situation was resulting in obstacles to the realization of public sector payments (i.e. foods and medicines). Demonstrably, unilateral coercive measures and financial blockades have aggravated the economic crisis and caused unemployment and emigration to Colombia, Brazil and Ecuador, among other countries.[55]

Economic asphyxiation policies are comparable to those already practised in Chile, the Democratic People's Republic of Korea, Nicaragua and the Syrian Arab Republic. In January 2018, Middle East correspondent of the *Financial Times* and *The Independent*, Patrick Cockburn, wrote on the sanctions affecting Syria:

> There is usually a pretence that foodstuffs and medical equipment are being allowed through freely and no mention is made of the financial and other regulatory obstacles making it impossible to deliver them. An example of this is the draconian sanctions imposed on Syria by the U.S. and EU which were meant to target President Bashar al-Assad and help remove him from power. They have wholly failed to do this, but a UN internal report leaked in 2016 shows all too convincingly the effect of the embargo in stopping the delivery of aid by international aid agencies.[56] They cannot import the aid despite waivers because banks and commercial companies dare not risk being penalised for having anything to do with Syria. The report quotes a European doctor working in Syria as saying that "the indirect effect of sanctions...makes the import of the medical instruments and other medical supplies immensely difficult, near impossible."[57]

In short: economic sanctions kill.

International mediation process

There is nothing more in keeping with the letter and spirit of the Charter of the United Nations than mediation. For two years, the former Spanish Prime Minister, José Luis Rodríguez Zapatero, with the support of the Vatican,[58] headed a negotiating team in the Dominican Republic which facilitated talks between the Government of the Bolivarian Republic of Venezuela and the opposition. Negotiations advanced to a balanced document entitled "Agreement of Democratic Coexistence" that should have been signed by all sides on 7 February 2018. The Government signed, but, as was reported, a telephone call from Colombia frustrated the two-year negotiating process with the instruction: "Don't sign."[59] Some believe that certain countries do not want to see a peaceful solution of the Venezuelan conflict and prefer to prolong the suffering of the Venezuelan people, expecting that the situation will reach the "humanitarian crisis" threshold and trigger a military intervention.

Bearing in mind that Venezuelan society is polarized, what is most needed is dialogue between the Government and the opposition,[60] and it would be a noble task on the part of the Secretary-General of the United Nations to offer his good offices for such a dialogue. Yet, opposition leaders Antonio Ledezma[61] and Julio Borges,[62] during a trip through Europe to denounce the Government of the Bolivarian Republic of Venezuela, called for further sanctions[63] as well as a military "humanitarian intervention."[64] This attitude generates a palpable malaise in the Government, which remembers the coup of 11–12 April 2002, known as the *Carmonazo*, which caused dozens of deaths, but ultimately failed.[65] Some current opposition members still endorse the coup that installed as President the head of Fedecameras, Pedro Carmona, and the Carmona decree dissolving all elected bodies, including the National Assembly, governorships and municipal authorities, shutting down the government television channel as well as community radio stations.[66] Today, millions of Venezuelans worry that foreign interests may again finance a coup to impose a neoliberal government that would abolish public services and destroy the social acquis. This could engender civil war, since a significant percentage of the population still identifies with the ideals of *Chavismo*.[67] In an interview with *The New York Times*, opposition leader Leopoldo López expressed views endorsing interventionism: "In 1958, there was a military coup that began the transition to democracy.... And in other Latin American countries, there have been coups that called elections. So I don't want to rule anything out, because the electoral window has been closed. We need to go forward on many different levels. One is street demonstrations; a second is coordination with the international community."[68] Those who shout "humanitarian crisis" should inquire whether the economic war and the sanctions are not a major cause. The principle of estoppel prevents those contributing to the crisis from invoking it to demand intervention (*ex injuria non oritur jus*).

Humanitarian crisis and humanitarian intervention

A disquieting media campaign seeks to force observers into a preconceived view that there is a "humanitarian crisis" in the Bolivarian Republic of Venezuela. An independent expert must be wary of hyperbole, bearing in mind that "humanitarian crisis" is a *terminus technicus* that can be misused as a pretext for military intervention.[69]

Instead, international solidarity with the Venezuelan people should facilitate the free flow of food and medicines in order to alleviate the current scarcity. Help should be genuinely humanitarian and not pursue ulterior political purposes. The International Committee of the Red Cross (ICRC), Caritas Internationalis and other organizations could assist in coordinating the importation and distribution of aid; the Bill and Melinda Gates Foundation could help wipe out malaria in the Bolivarian Republic of Venezuela.[70] Thanks to the UNDP, the Independent Expert was able to convene a meeting with all the United Nations agencies and other regional organizations in the Bolivarian Republic of Venezuela with a view to coordinating assistance, an initiative that bore fruit shortly thereafter.[71]

Although the situation in the Bolivarian Republic of Venezuela has not yet reached the humanitarian crisis threshold, there is hunger, malnutrition, anxiety, anguish and emigration.[72] What is crucial is to study the causes of the crisis, including neglected factors of sanctions, sabotage, hoarding, black market activities, induced inflation[73] and contraband[74] in food and medicines.

The "crisis" in the Bolivarian Republic of Venezuela is an economic crisis, which cannot be compared with the humanitarian crises in Gaza,[75] Yemen,[76] Libya,[77] the Syrian Arab Republic,[78] Iraq,[79] Haiti,[80] Mali,[81] the Central African Republic,[82] South Sudan,[83] Somalia,[84] or Myanmar,[85] among others. It is significant that when in 2017 the Bolivarian Republic of Venezuela requested medical aid from the Global Fund to Fight AIDS, Tuberculosis and Malaria, the plea was rejected, because it "is still a high-income country ... and as such is not eligible."[86] During his mission, the Independent Expert discussed the issues of food and medicine scarcity with experts from FAO[87] and obtained pertinent data from the Economic Commission for Latin America and the Caribbean.[88] The December 2017 FAO report and the March 2018 report list food crises in 37 countries. The Bolivarian Republic of Venezuela is not among them.[89]

It is pertinent to recall the situation in the years prior to the election of Hugo Chávez,[90] when the International Monetary Fund (IMF) imposed on Venezuela the "Washington consensus" of restructuring programmes, austerity and privatization (see A/72/1787), which led to mass public demonstrations and a military crackdown, the *Caracazo* of 1989, leaving some 3,000 dead.[91] Corruption was ubiquitous and in 1993, President Carlos Pérez was removed because of embezzlement.[92] The Chávez election in 1998 reflected despair due to the corruption and neo-liberal policies of the 1980s and 1990s, and rejection of the gulf between the super-rich and the abject poor.[93]

International monitoring of elections in the Bolivarian Republic of Venezuela

Participatory democracy in the Bolivarian Republic of Venezuela, called "protagónica," is anchored in the Constitution of 1999 and relies on frequent elections and referendums. During the mission, the Independent Expert exchanged views with the Electoral Commission[94] and learned that in the 19 years since Chávez, 25 elections and referendums had been conducted, 4 of them observed by the Carter Center. The Independent Expert met with the representative of the Carter Center in the Bolivarian Republic of Venezuela, who recalled Carter's positive assessment of the electoral system.[95] They also discussed the constitutional objections raised by the opposition to the referendum held on 30 July 2017, resulting in the creation of a Constitutional Assembly.[96] Over 8 million Venezuelans voted in the referendum, which was witnessed by international observers,[97] including from the Council of Electoral Specialists of Latin America.[98]

Ad hominem attacks

An atmosphere of intimidation accompanied the mission, attempting to pressure the Independent Expert into a predetermined matrix. He received letters from NGOs asking him not to proceed because he was not the "relevant" rapporteur, and almost dictating what should be in the report. Weeks before his arrival, some called the mission a "fake investigation." Social media insults bordered on "hate speech" and "incitement." Mobbing before, during and after the mission bore a resemblance to the experience of two American journalists who visited the country in July 2017.[99] Utilizing platforms such as Facebook and Twitter, critics questioned the Independent Expert's integrity and accused him of bias, demonstrating a culture of intransigence and refusal to accept the duty of an independent expert to be neutral, objective, dispassionate and to apply his expertise free of external pressures. The idea that an independent expert should think independently and weigh evidence does not seem to have occurred to some critics, for whom human rights are weapons of demonization, not only against governments, but also against experts.[100] The Independent Expert explained to critics that he must evaluate independently, not only from governments, but from lobbies, non-governmental organizations and even from other rapporteurs.[101]

CONCLUSIONS

As the first United Nations rapporteur to visit the Bolivarian Republic of Venezuela in 21 years,[102] ...the Independent Expert is conscious of his responsibilities and limitations. Six years into the mandate, he has learned that governments are not always the "bad guys." As demonstrated in 13 thematic reports, other players impact on the enjoyment of human rights, including the World Trade Organization, the World Bank, the International Monetary Fund, transnational corporations and some lobbies like the military-industrial-financial complex. These actors often wield more influence than States. Moreover, the national and international economic orders are distorted by bilateral investment treaties, free-trade agreements, credit rating agencies, vulture funds, boycotts and unilateral coercive measures, which have often resulted in the suffering of billions of individuals. Rapporteurs should focus not only on States and their failures, but also on other actors and the pervasive lack of accountability.

Rapporteurs should conduct country visits with a view to helping rather than condemning. Rapporteurs must strive for objectivity, and rigorously observe the code of conduct, particularly article 6. Whereas some civil society organizations think that the goal is "naming and shaming," this rarely brings results, because the "namer" is not always perceived as independent or possessing moral authority. When the country being named has reservations about the integrity and objectivity of rapporteurs or of the Inter-American Commission on Human Rights, their invitations to the OHCHR will not be forthcoming. The incentive for governments is the expectation that rapporteurs will make constructive proposals.

The solution to the Venezuelan "crisis" lies in good faith negotiations between the Government and the opposition, an end to the economic war being waged against Venezuela, and the lifting of sanctions. In pursuance of the principle of international solidarity (see A/HRC/35/35), United Nations agencies should provide advisory services and technical assistance to the Government. The Special Rapporteur on the promotion of truth, justice, reparation and guarantees of non-recurrence may wish to address the interplay between State crime and international order, both from the positive and the natural law perspective, and formulate recommendations concerning reparations due to populations affected by sanctions and economic war. Rich States should facilitate humanitarian assistance in coordination with neutral organizations such as ICRC, the priority being how to effectively help Venezuelans while respecting State sovereignty.

While the Bolivarian Republic of Venezuela is undergoing a severe economic crisis, the Government is not standing idle; it is seeking international assistance to overcome the challenges, diversifying the economy and seeking debt restructuring. Sanctions only aggravate the situation by hindering the imports necessary to produce generic medicines and seeds to increase agricultural production. Sanctions have also led to emigration.

RECOMMENDATIONS

The Independent Expert recommends that the Government of the Bolivarian Republic of Venezuela:

(a) Continue efforts at dialogue with opposition parties, revive the negotiations hosted in the Dominican Republic by the former prime minister of Spain, José Luis Rodríguez Zapatero, and promote national reconciliation by releasing detainees and granting commutations of sentence;

(b) Invite other special procedures mandate holders to visit the country, besides the Special Rapporteurs on unilateral coercive measures and on the right to development, who have already been invited. The Special Rapporteurs on food, on health, on adequate housing, on the independence of judges and lawyers, the Independent Expert on foreign debt, the Special Rapporteurs on the promotion of truth, justice, reparation and guarantees of non-recurrence, on the promotion and protection of the right to freedom of opinion and expression, and on the rights to freedom of peaceful assembly and of association, the Working Group on Arbitrary Detention and other experts would offer valuable expertise;

(c) Welcome humanitarian aid offered by governments, inter-governmental organizations and the private sector;

(d) Continue constructive cooperation with the United Nations treaty bodies and implement their recommendations;

(e) Continue cooperation with FAO and WHO and ask UNODC for assistance in combating the scourge of food and medicine smuggling by national and international rings;

(f) Strengthen cooperation with ILO, deal expeditiously with contentious cases and implement ILO recommendations, including those related to Case No. 2254, by establishing a social dialogue table and action plan;

(g) Strengthen South-South cooperation, including with the Bolivarian Alliance for the Peoples of Our America, the Union of South American Nations, SELA and CELAC. In particular, strengthen technical and institutional cooperation between SELA and the Organisation for Economic Co-operation and Development for the promotion of sustainable and inclusive economic growth in Latin America, as well as joint actions in the economic, social and trade areas;

(h) Engage proactively with entrepreneurs and a diverse group of non-governmental actors so as to resolve together the prevailing social and political problems.

The Independent Expert further recommends that the General Assembly:

(a) Invoke article 96 of the Charter of the United Nations and refer the following questions to the International Court of Justice: Can unilateral coercive measures be compatible with international law? Can unilateral coercive measures amount to crimes against humanity when a large number of persons perish because of scarcity of food and medicines? What reparations are due to the victims of sanctions? Do sanctions and currency manipulations constitute geopolitical crimes?

(b) Adopt a resolution along the lines of the resolutions on the United States embargo against Cuba, declaring the sanctions against the Bolivarian Republic of Venezuela contrary to international law and human rights law;

(c) Create a consolidated central register of unilateral coercive measures likely to have a human rights impact, to be maintained and updated by the Secretary-General, as proposed by the Special Rapporteur on unilateral coercive measures in his 2015 report to the General Assembly (A/70/345) and his 2017 report to the Human Rights Council (A/HRC/36/44).

The Independent Expert recommends that the Human Rights Council:

(a) Reaffirm the Code of Conduct for Special Procedures Mandate Holders, particularly paragraphs 3 and 6 concerning their independence and the commitment to evaluate all information in good faith, including submissions by governments;

(b) Defend experts against ad hominem attacks, intimidation and threats.

(c) That the Office of the United Nations High Commissioner for Human Rights proactively support special procedure mandate holders in the exercise of their professional judgment and independence; facilitate consultation with and coordination among the rapporteurs, including through their Coordination Committee of Special Procedures, and ensure that apparent contradictions emanating from different points of view do not send wrong signals; and implement the decisions on coordination adopted at the 2016 meeting of rapporteurs so as to strengthen the coherence and credibility of special procedures.

The Independent Expert recommends that the International Criminal Court:

(a) investigate the problem of unilateral coercive measures that cause death from malnutrition, lack of medicines and medical equipment. The examination should not only be quantitative, but should determine whether, objectively treated, economic war, embargoes, financial blockades and sanctions regimes amount to geopolitical crimes and crimes against humanity under Article 7 of the Rome Statute.

(b) That the meeting of States parties to the Rome Statute continue the normative work on the Rome Statute and recognize geopolitical crimes, including unilateral coercive measures and currency manipulations that induce hyperinflation, as within the scope of Article 7 of the Statute. Normative clarity has significant pedagogical value.

(c) That, until the International Court of Justice and the International Criminal Court address the lethal outcomes of economic wars and sanctions regimes, the Permanent Peoples Tribunal, the Russell Tribunal and the Kuala Lumpur War Crimes Commission undertake the task so as to facilitate future judicial pronouncements.

* * *

It is befitting to finish my report on Venezuela with a quotation by the former UN High Commissioner for Human Rights, Navi Pillay. In her thematic report of January 2012, devoted entirely to the adverse human rights impacts of unilateral coercive measures A/HRC/19/33, the High Commissioner wrote

> "Unilateral coercive measures encompass a range of actions, including trade embargoes, financial restrictions, acquisition of property, freezing of assets, visa restrictions, and withholding of vital medical supplies and spare parts for various machineries. the measures in question often extend extraterritorial application of domestic rules, adversely affecting the interests of third States and their nationals." (para. 31)

In her conclusions she recommended:

> "The actions of States in the international arena must be consistent with customary international law principles and the Charter of the United Nations as also interpreted by the International Court of Justice.
>
> "States must refrain from adopting unilateral coercive measures that breach their human rights obligations under treaty or customary international law.
>
> "All States Members of the United Nations should avoid the application of any coercive measures having negative effects on human rights." (paras. 39-41).

POSTSCRIPT

I concluded my mission to Venezuela and Ecuador and returned to Geneva without giving a press conference in Venezuela or Ecuador, precisely because I needed time to digest all my impressions and to study the immense amount of information given to me by the governments, the opposition leaders, civil society—testimonies from victims, reports, analyses and statistics. When in Geneva, I did call a rather informal press conference at the Palais des Nations on 12 December 2017 to communicate very preliminary conclusions, particularly on the issue of the economic crisis in Venezuela and how to help the suffering population. If anything, I had learned that although the crisis had multiple sources, the principal causes of the dangerous aggravation of the human rights situation were the sanctions and financial blockade. I was disappointed that only four journalists showed up, and although the AP did issue a brief news item, it was not picked up by the media.[i] Many months later, in May 2018, the *Tribune de Genève* published a long article,[ii] as did the *Courrier de Genève* in September 2018.[iii]

My six-year mandate as independent expert ended on 30 April 2018. The Club Suisse de la Presse honoured me by hosting a two-hour conference, also attended by my colleague, the late Dr. Idriss Jazairy, then Rapporteur on unilateral coercive measures, and moderated by the President of the Press Club, Guy Mettan.

---

i https://apnews.com/article/24a388879c944144b0756f8fff3b561a
ii https://www.tdg.ch/monde/insoumis-alfred-zayas-jette-dernier-pave/story/25869696
iii https://lecourrier.ch/2018/09/10/les-sanctions-tuent/

It was my successor, Dr. Livingstone Sewanyana, who presented my mission report to the Human Rights Council on 10 September 2018. I was away from Geneva during the entire month of September, but colleague rapporteurs informed me on the session. As it happened, the report was received with deafening silence. Evidently it did not sing the song that the narrative managers expected from me. Thus, the report was filed away and forgotten, like so many others.

It was not until Juan Guaidó auto-proclaimed himself interim president of Venezuela on 23 January 2019 that my report resurfaced. It was thanks to a long interview with the British journalist Michael Selby-Green[i] of *The Independent* that my report received some attention and that other news services started calling me for interviews, including Euronews, Skynews, *Time, Newsweek*,[ii] France 24, Aljazeera, ABC (Sydney), Pax Press Agency, Global Catholic Network, Xinhua, CGTN, RT, Sputnik, Prensa Latina, Telesur, etc. I gave long interviews to the Swiss-German newspapers *Zeit-Fragen and Zeitgeschehen im Fokus*. Yet, I was never approached by CNN, Fox, CNBC, CBC, BBC, *Foreign Affairs*, the *Times, DW, Le Monde, El Pais, Frankfurter Allgemeine Zeitung* or other major "mainstream" outlets. I had sent op-eds to the *New York Times, Washington Post, Guardian,* which were either not acknowledged or not accepted for publication. A noted academic journal did ask me for an article on the Venezuelan crisis, but it was never published, "because of its content." I gave interviews to Amy Goodman of Democracy Now,[iii] Abby Martin of the Empire Files,[iv] Greg Wilpert of The Real News Network,[v] collaborated in the documentary film by Aris Chatzistefanou "Make the Economy Scream,"[vi] and in another documentary for ARTE/ZDF, "Venezuela in Crisis."[vii] My report was picked up by numerous internet platforms including Modern Diplomacy.[viii]

Among the issues that I addressed in my interviews were the negative human rights impacts of the sanctions and my conviction that they constitute crimes against humanity for purposes of article 7 of the Statute of Rome, and that the International Criminal Court should examine the sanctions under this perspective, bearing in mind that tens of thousands of Venezuelans have died prematurely as a direct result of the sanctions and financial blockade, which have effectively

---

i https://www.independent.co.uk/news/world/americas/venezuela-us-sanctions-united-nations-oil-pdvsa-a8748201.html

ii https://www.newsweek.com/venezuela-maduro-military-block-humanitarian-aid-1321214

iii https://www.youtube.com/watch?v=vnH_cV-FWOg&t=81s

iv https://www.youtube.com/watch?v=ii5MlQgGXyk

v https://therealnews.com/de-zayas-un-human-rights-councils-report-on-venezuela-is-unbalanced-1-2

vi https://maketheeconomyscream.com/en/

vii https://www.arte.tv/en/videos/087647-000-A/venezuela-in-crisis/

viii https://moderndiplomacy.eu/2019/02/11/what-the-press-hides-from-you-about-venezuela/

crippled the government and made it extremely difficult to obtain sufficient food and medicines in a timely fashion. Professor Jeffrey Sachs and Marc Weisbrot of the Washington Center for Economic and Policy Research published in April 2019 a study estimating that some 40,000 Venezuelans died as a consequence of the sanctions in 2018 alone.[i] On 13 February 2020 the Venezuelan Foreign Minister Jorge Arreaza filed a complaint with the ICC Chief Prosecutor, Fatou Bensouda, documenting the impacts of the sanctions and justifying the conclusion that they amount to crimes against humanity.

I also elucidated my concerns about the growing credibility gap of both the UN and OAS. I expressed the view that the current Secretary General of the Organization of American States, Luis Almagro, grossly overstepped his mandate by recognizing Juan Guaidó as the interim President of Venezuela, without having a majority vote from OAS members and in spite of the strong protest from CARICOM.[ii] Not only was Almagro's action *ultra vires,* beyond his competence, but it entailed grave violations of the OAS Charter itself, in particular articles 3, 19 and 20.

Closer to home, the behaviour of the former UN High Commissioner for Human Rights Zeid Ra'ad Al Hussein, was unhelpful and not conducive to a peaceful solution of the Venezuelan crisis. He issued two reports on Venezuela, both of them without being asked by either the Human Rights Council or the UN General Assembly to do so—hence, without a solid legal basis. General Assembly Resolution 48/141, which created the HC's mandate, does not authorize the HC to pick and choose arbitrarily what reports to present to the Council. One can easily imagine the kind of manipulation possible when an HC can choose to monitor and condemn violations only in some countries, while keeping silent on others. Worse still, both reports were flawed, because they failed to properly evaluate and incorporate a considerable amount of information made available to the OHCHR by experts and civil society. The reports are methodologically inacceptable, because they breach the fundamental rule of every researcher: *audiatur et altera pars.* Both reports are partisan, relying on information provided primarily by the opposition and systematically suppressing pertinent information and statistics provided by the Venezuelan government and by numerous non-governmental organizations including Fundalatin, Grupo Sures and the Red Nacional de Derechos Humanos. As I learned during my mission to Venezuela, this information had been given to the HC personally in Geneva and provided to his staff in March, June and September 2017, but it was not reflected in the High Commissioner's reports.

---

[i] https://cepr.net/images/stories/reports/venezuela-sanctions-2019-04.pdf
[ii] https://venezuelanalysis.com/analysis/14302

After I had successfully broken the ice by being the first UN rapporteur to be invited for an official visit to Venezuela, I thought that the Office would rejoice, because this would provide an opportunity to establish direct contact with the government and to mediate between government and opposition. I saw myself as the bridge, as the rapporteur who would defuse the polarization by proposing confidence-building measures. I wanted to coordinate my mission with OHCHR, so as to make the maximum impact and pave the way for the visit of other rapporteurs. Yet, when I requested to be personally received by the HC, both before and following my mission, I was not received, not even for a simple briefing, and when I requested substantive support from the Venezuela desk at the OHCHR—assistance that every rapporteur is entitled to receive—it was withheld, manifesting a pattern of bias—and a regrettable lack of professionalism.

My mission report, which does have legal basis, was essentially ignored by the OHCHR and by the mainstream media, although I had written it following consultation with all relevant stakeholders and studying the reports of Amnesty International, Human Rights Watch, OHCHR, IACHR, etc., after conferring personally with members of the Venezuelan opposition, Chamber of commerce, churches, diplomatic corps, professors, NGOs, etc., after listening with respect and objectivity to all sides. At the Human Rights Council there was no discussion on my findings and recommendations, certainly no rebuttal by anyone. Presumably an open debate would have given the report too much attention!

According to the Code of Conduct of Rapporteurs, all well substantiated information must be taken into account and reflected in a report. I did so in my report, and this was recognized by the government in its comments formally submitted to the OHCHR.

The very specific information and statistics submitted by the Venezuelan government further substantiate the findings in my report and illustrate concretely the adverse impact of the sanctions and financial blockade. Paragraph 45 of the government's report lists numerous cases concerning the government's efforts to obtain urgently needed medicines and the preclusive impact of the sanctions. Paragraph 46 illustrates some of the positive outcomes of my mission.

> (xvi) As a result of this on 23 December 2017, 80 people arrested for acts of violence during the protests in the country were released; and on 1 June 2018, 39 more people were released.

> (xvii) On these people, the Judicial Power through the criminal courts of the different judicial districts issued a series of procedural benefits for citizens prosecuted for the alleged commission of crimes sanctioned by law.

(xviii) In this regard, the Venezuelan Government values the willingness and disposition of the Independent Expert, who was pleased to inform the competent authorities of the requests he received from some relatives of the persons deprived of their liberty. His recommendations were accepted. [i]

All in all, it can be concluded that my pragmatic, result-oriented approach during the Venezuela mission was successful in building confidence. For instance, in December 2018, I interceded on behalf of Billy Six, a young investigative German journalist, at the time detained at *El Helicoide* secret service prison under suspicion of espionage. Billy was released on 16 March 2019, and he subsequently visited me in Geneva.[ii] Maybe the good will created by my non-confrontational approach will still bear fruit for the suffering people of Venezuela.

With regard to Venezuela, Dr. Idriss Jazairy, Special Rapporteur on the adverse impact of unilateral coercive measures (2015-19) issued several press releases concerning the artificial economic crisis unleased by the U.S., Canadian and EU sanctions. In a press release dated 31 January 2019, Dr. Jazairy warned that sanctions lead to starvation and medical shortages:

> I am especially concerned to hear reports that these sanctions are aimed at changing the government of Venezuela.... Coercion, whether military or economic, must never be used to seek a change in government in a sovereign state. The use of sanctions by outside powers to overthrow an elected government is in violation of all norms of international law.... Economic sanctions are effectively compounding the grave crisis affecting the Venezuelan economy, adding to the damage caused by hyperinflation and the fall in oil prices. This is a time when compassion should be expressed for the long-suffering people of Venezuela by promoting, not curtailing, access to food and medicine.[iii]

In February 2021 Dr. Jazairy's successor, Professor Alena Douhan, conducted a two-week mission to Venezuela. Her report to the Human Rights Council will be presented at the Council's 48th session in September 2021. In preparation of her report Professor Douhan called an expert meeting in Geneva on 26 April 2021, attended in person and virtually by economists and professors of international law. At this meeting I summarized the conclusions of my 2018 report and

---

[i] http://ap.ohchr.org/documents/dpage_e.aspx?si=A/HRC/39/47/Add.2.

[ii] "UNO-Sonderberichtserstatter mahnt" Deutschland Magazin 83/84, pp. 62-67. Billy is now writing a book about his experiences in Venezuela. I had the opportunity to provide him with numerous ngo documents which he had not seen and turned out pertinent to his investigation.

[iii] https://www.ohchr.org/en/NewsEvents/Pages/DisplayNews.aspx?NewsID=24131&LangID=E

recalled the need to provide immediate assistance to the Venezuelan people, especially during the pandemic. Already during my mission, I had convened all UN agencies in Venezuela to discuss ways in which their expertise could be used to assuage the suffering of the people. Meanwhile greater cooperation has been achieved between these agencies and the Venezuelan authorities, but even the UN is impeded in its work by the adverse impact of the sanctions.

At Professor Douhan's consultation I also emphasized the importance of exploring cause and effect. No one doubts that Venezuela is suffering a major economic crisis, that scarcity of foods and medicines has taken and continues to take a toll among the population. Any objective observer of the situation will realize that the crisis is real—and artificial at the same time, that it was caused partly by the dramatic fall of oil prices but primarily and demonstrably by the non-conventional war waged against Venezuela by the United States since 1999 and by the draconian sanctions regime imposed on the country in an adamant attempt to impose regime change. Without a doubt, it is the cumulative effect of sanctions, financial blockades, cyber attacks, sabotage of utilities and other installations, paramilitary activities at Venezuela's borders and repeated attempts at coups-d'état that has generated the insecurity and *zozobra* that the Venezuelans endure today. The international community has a responsibility to recognize this cause and effect and to assign the blame where it belongs, on those who have taken the population hostage in a geopolitical game.

Our priority must be to end the suffering by taking constructive measures to help the Venezuelan people. This requires an immediate lifting of the sanctions and financial blockade, an end of international support of paramilitaries and other forces engaged in sabotage and contraband. It is time for the international community to recognize that economic sanctions kill, that they are illegal and counter-productive. All UN member States are obliged under the UN Charter to reject all interference in the internal affairs of sovereign states. Finally, it is imperative to reject the propagandistic mainstream narrative as contrary to human rights and human dignity. The Venezuelan people need international solidarity—not "fake news."[i]

In her press release of 12 February 2021 Professor Douhan rightly concluded:

> While recognizing a devastating effect of unilateral sanctions on the broad scope of human rights, especially the right to food, right to health, right to life, right to education and right to development, the Special Rapporteur calls upon the Government of Venezuela and the Office of High Commissioner for Human Rights to implement fully

---

i Jacques Baud, *Gouverner par les Fake News: Conflits internationaux : 30 ans d'Intox utilisées par les pays occidentaux* (Chevilly Larue: Max Milo, 2020), Chapter 12, pp. 355–384.

the cooperation agreement signed between them, to strengthen the OHCHR presence on the grounds to monitor *inter alia* the impact of unilateral sanctions and to organize visits of relevant Special procedures to the country.

The Special Rapporteur calls on the Government of Venezuela, the UNDP, other UN agencies and OHCHR in Venezuela to negotiate an agreement to guarantee the transparent, fair and non-discriminatory distribution of essential goods and humanitarian aid under the control of international institutions regardless of race, gender, nationality, age, religious belief or political views with due account of groups with special needs."[i]

Notes

1 https://albainfo.org/; www.sela.org/media/2087752/di-11-alba-tcp-ing.pdf. The Peoples' Trade Agreement emerged in contrast to the proposed Free Trade Area of the Americas, which was never adopted. See www.ftaa-alca.org/alca_e.asp.

2 www.ohchr.org/en/NewsEvents/Pages/DisplayNews.aspx?NewsID=22457&LangID=E.

3 http://reason.com/archives/2017/09/19/venezuelan-price-controls-lead-to-predic.

4 www.fenavi.org/index.php?option=com_content&view=article&id=2914:el-contrabando-desde-venezuela-tiene-al-menos-35-rutas-de-entrada-por-el-norte-de-santander&catid=293:centro-de-noticias&Itemid=1363;

www.semana.com/nacion/articulo/contrabando-de-medicamentos-negocio-de-alto-costo/400145-3; www.elpais.com.uy/economia-y-mercado/venezuela-hunde-contrabando-florece. html; www.infobae.com/politica/2016/07/04/desbaratan-millonario-contrabando-de-medicamentos-a-venezuela-de-un-empresario-ligado-a-de-vido/.

5 Sixteen States issued the Declaration on Venezuela, calling on the Government to ensure that the elections were conducted in a free, fair and transparent manner.

6 "Condenamos enérgicamente la agresión imperialista, la guerra económica y el acoso político contra la Venezuela Bolivariana. Exigimos respeto a la soberanía de la patria del pueblo venezolano que desde 1999 inició un proceso constituyente popular que ha marcado la senda ... por la unidad latinoamericana ... exigimos el cese de las sanciones ilegítimas y unilaterales contra el pueblo bolivariano, rechazamos la pretensión de la intervención militar en Venezuela bajo el pretexto de ayuda humanitaria."

7 www.oas.org/en/iachr/reports/pdfs/Venezuela2018-en.pdf; www.cancilleria.gob.ec/ecuador-rejects-the-precautionary-measures-of-the-inter-american-commission-on-human-rights-iachr/.

8 www.cepal.org/MDG/noticias/paginas/7/40987/VENEZUELA_es.pdf; www.alainet.org/images/dossier_Venezuela_2013.pdf; https://progresismohumano.wordpress.com/2015/12/07/verdaderas-causas-de-la-perdida-de-la-revolucion-en-venezuela-6d-2015/.

9 www.alianzapais.com.ec/tag/revolucion-ciudadana/;
www.presidencia.gob.ec/wp-content/uploads/downloads/2016/01/REVOLUCION-CIUDADANA.pdf;
www.planificacion.gob.ec/wp-content/uploads/downloads/2017/01/10-RC.pdf.

---

i https://www.ohchr.org/en/NewsEvents/Pages/DisplayNews.aspx?NewsID=26747&LangID=E
https://www.ohchr.org/en/NewsEvents/Pages/DisplayNews.aspx?NewsID=26749&LangID=E
https://www.ohchr.org/EN/Issues/UCM/Pages/Activities.aspx

10 Fernando Casado Gutiérrez, Antonio Salamanca Serrano and Rebeca Sánchez, "La nueva ola de constituciones en Ecuador, Bolivia y Venezuela: una revolución democrática y jurídica en ciernes" *LíneaSur*, vol. 3, No. 11 (January–April 2016).

11 http://portal.unesco.org/es/ev.php-URL_ID=42262&URL_DO=DO_TOPIC&URL_SECTION=201.html; https://knoema.com/atlas/Venezuela-Bolivarian-Republic-of/topics/Education/Literacy/Adult-literacy-rate.

12 www.ve.undp.org/content/venezuela/es/home/presscenter/articles/2018/04/10/pnud-venezuela-celebra-la-incorporaci-n-del-integrante-n-1-mill-n-del-sistema-nacional-de-orquestas-y-coros-juveniles-e-infantiles-de-venezuela-el-sistema-0.html; www.ve.undp.org/content/venezuela/es/home/presscenter/articles/2016/01/25/funcionarios-del-pnud-en-venezuela-visitan-el-cnasplm-n-cleo-de-el-sistema-instituci-n-con-la-que-coopera-hace-m-s-de-12-a-os-ininterrumpidos.html; www.ve.undp.org/content/venezuela/es/home/presscenter/articles/2016/01/06/desarrollo-sostenible-y-empresas-un-imperativo-a-la-acci-n-paloma-dur-n.html. On 2 December, the Independent Expert visited *El Sistema*, interviewing students and teachers. www.flacsoandes.edu.ec/libros/digital/56778.pdf.

13 Tricia Tunstall, *Changing Lives: Gustavo Dudamel, El Sistema, and the Transformative Power of Music* (New York, W.W. Norton, 2012).

14 Many civil society organizations participated in the examination of the report, including the Red Nacional de Derechos Humanos (https://fundalatin.webnode.es/news/discurso-de-asdrubal-gonzalez-coordinador-de-red-nacional-de-derechos-humanos/).

15 http://china.embajada.gob.ve/index.php?option=com_content&view=article&id=2426%3Avenezuela-presenta-ante-la-onu-estudios-que-develan-estrategias-de-la-guerra-economica&catid=3%3Anoticias-de-venezuela-en-el-mundo&Itemid=17&lang=es.

16 "Monitoreo del derecho a la salud en Venezuela: índice de escasez de medicamentos," *Boletin* Nro. 4, Dic. 2017; https://issuu.com/conviteac/docs/boleti n 4_convite; http://efectococuyo.com/principales/el-derecho-a-la-salud-y-a-la-alimentacion-entre-los-mas-vulnerados-por-el-gobierno-en-2016; but compare with http://mppre.gob.ve/2017/11/18/en-espana-la-economista-venezolana-pascualina-curcio-denuncia-a-las-trasnacionales-de-alimentos/.

17 http://unionradio.net/red-nacional-derechos-humanos-resalta-visita-alfred-zayas/.

18 www.jpands.org/vol22no2/huntoon.pdf; www.crisisgroup.org/latin-america-caribbean/andes/venezuela; www.forbes.com/sites/nathanielparishflannery/2018/03/22/venezuelas-economic-crisis-worsens-in-2018/#41f4cb6f1f17.

19 www.laht.com/article.asp?ArticleId=345496&CategoryId=10717.

20 www.legrandsoir.info/la-verite-sur-le-venezuela.html; www.alainet.org/es/articulo/190685; www.globalresearch.ca/us-regime-change-in-venezuela-the-truth-is-easy-if-you-follow-the-money-trail-the-opposition-is-pro-washington-not-pro-democracy/5601933; http://nuso.org/articulo/la-ruina-de-venezuela-no-se-debe-al-socialismo-ni-la-revolucion/.

21 https://transparencia.org.ve/project/informe-anual-corrupcion/; www.transparency.org/whatwedo/publication/global_corruption_barometer_people_and_corruption_l atin_america_and_the_car; www.business-anti-corruption.com/country-profiles/venezuela/; Edgardo Lander, "Venezuela: la experiencia bolivariana en la lucha por trascender al capitalismo," 28 August 2017. Available at www.aporrea.org/ideologia/a251495.html.

22 www.worldbank.org/en/topic/governance/brief/anti-corruption; www.theguardian.com/business/2018/apr/22/city-faces-corruption-crackdown-as-imf-investigates-wealthy-countries.

23 www.derechos.org.ve/informes-anuales.

24 https://venezuelanalysis.com/News/13470; www.occrp.org/en/27-ccwatch/cc-watch-briefs/7636-unsealed-indictment-charges-venezuelan-oil-officials-with-corruption; www.hispantv.com/noticias/venezuela/369245/tramas-corrupcion-pdvsa-perdidas-millonarias; www.hispantv.com/noticias/venezuela/352168/fiscal-saab-acusa-luisa-ortega-desfalco-petrolera; https://venezuelanalysis.com/news/11848; www.telesurtv.net/news/fiscalia-venezuela-detiene-dueno-portal-ilegal-divisas-20180412-0045.

html; https://venezuelanalysis.com/news/13773; www.telesurtv.net/news/aprehenden-dueno-de-portal-divisas-dolar-pro-venezuela-20180416-0040.html.

25 www.efe.com/efe/america/portada/saab-vincula-a-fiscales-venezolanos-con-corrupcion-en-el-caso-odebrecht/20000064-3405927.

26 https://venezuelanalysis.com/News/13577.

27 www.reuters.com/article/us-venezuela-corruption/venezuela-arrests-ex-oil-refining-boss-for-alleged-graft-sources-idUSKBN1GV2V3; https://converus.com/venezuelan-economy-losing-billions-corrupt-importers/; www.wtrf.com/news/us-lawsuit-venezuela-cheated-of-billions-by-rigged-oil-bids/1021936369.

28 www.reuters.com/article/us-venezuela-oil/venezuelas-pdvsa-sues-oil-traders-over-corruption-scheme-lawyer-idUSKCN1GL04U.

29 www.insightcrime.org/news/analysis/evolution-militarization-venezuela-drug-trade-report/; https://d2071andvip0wj.cloudfront.net/065-containing-the-shock-waves-from-venezuela.pdf.

30 www.paho.org/ven/index.php?option=com_content&view=article&id=419:mas-de-450-trabajadores-de-salud-venezolanos-han-sido-entrenados-por-la-ops-para-el-manejo-de-casos-de-malaria&Itemid=0.

31 www.reuters.com/article/us-venezuela-bonds-q-a/implications-of-venezuelas-proposed-foreign-debt-restructuring-idUSKBN1D3250. See the guiding principles on foreign debt and human rights.

32 www.reuters.com/article/us-venezuela-bonds-q-a/implications-of-venezuelas-proposed-foreign-debt-restructuring-idUSKBN1D3250. See the guiding principles on foreign debt and human rights.

33 Lauren Leatherby, "Venezuela's economic and political crisis in charts," *Financial Times*, 25 July 2017.

34 www.ilo.org/gb/GBSessions/GB320/ins/WCMS_237898/lang--en/index.htm.

35 www.ilo.org/global/about-the-ilo/newsroom/news/WCMS_622567/lang--en/index.htm; www.ilo.org/wcmsp5/groups/public/---ed_norm/---relconf/documents/meetingdocument/wcms_619151.pdf; www.ilo.org/wcmsp5/groups/public/---ed_norm/---relconf/documents/meetingdocument/wcms_546649.pdf.

36 https://tradingeconomics.com/venezuela/rating.

37 See Human Rights Council resolution 34/11.

38 https://venezuelanalysis.com/news/11861.

39 www.el-nacional.com/noticias/economia/bachaqueros-venden-medicinas-para-tension-tiroides-antibioticos_218920.

40 www.avn.info.ve/contenido/venezuela-revoluci%C3%B3n-asume-salud-como-derecho-humano-y-social; www.japantimes.co.jp/news/2017/11/26/world/science-health-world/venezuela-government-distributes-medicine-amid-shortages-nearly-drugs/#.Wsu7pi5ubIU; www.youtube.com/watch?v=PcnwUuCsHX8&feature=youtu.be.

41 www.youtube.com/watch?v=v9AcrvknLEU.

42 http://misionverdad.com/la-guerra-en-venezuela/en-10-claves-paramilitarismo-y-violencia-en-venezuela%20; www.derechos.org.ve/paramilitares/funcion-del-paramilitarismo-en-el-contexto-venezolano; http://elvenezolanonews.com/grupos-paramilitares-intentan-dominar-frontera-entre-venezuela-y-colombia/.

43 www.venezuelasolidarity.co.uk/venezuela-closes-colombia-border-amid-paramilitary-violence/.

44 www.ohchr.org/EN/NewsEvents/Pages/DisplayNews.aspx?NewsID=22072&LangID=E. The Movement of Non-Aligned Countries has also repeatedly condemned sanctions. See https://venezuelanalysis.com/analysis/12896.

45 www.ohchr.org/Documents/Events/WCM/MarcBossuyt_

WorkshopUnilateralCoerciveSeminar.pdf;
Sub-Commission on Human Rights resolution 2000/25.

46 Hans-Christof von Sponeck, *A Different Kind of War: The UN Sanctions Regime in Iraq* (Berghahn Books, Oxford, 2006).

47 www.unicef.org/newsline/99pr29.htm.

48 http://news.cornell.edu/stories/1999/09/former-un-official-says-sanctions-against-iraq-amount-genocide. In a 1996 interview, when asked about reports that half a million children had died in Iraq owing to the sanctions, the United States Secretary of State, Madeleine Albright, replied "we think the price is worth it." See https://fair.org/extra/we-think-the-price-is-worth-it/.

49 It is regrettable that resolution 37/21 was not adopted unanimously, bearing in mind that economic sanctions are a toxic medicine worse than the disease.

50 www.telesurtv.net/news/colombianos-venezuela-desplazados-conflicto-interno-20180621-0043.html; www.euronews.com/2018/03/26/colombia-s-venezuelan-migrant-influx; www.washingtonpost.com/news/world/wp/2018/03/02/feature/i-cant-go-back-venezuelans-are-fleeing-their-crisis-torn-country-en-masse/?noredirect=on&utm_term=.b1b0262fd262.

51 www.colombiainforma.info/santos-bloquea-venta-de-medicamentos-a-venezuela/; https://venezuelanalysis.com/news/13782;
http://m.avn.info.ve/contenido/venezuela-denuncia-que-euroclear-mantiene-secuestro-recursos-destinados-medicinas-y-alimen.

52 https://obamawhitehouse.archives.gov/the-press-office/2015/03/09/fact-sheet-venezuela-executive-order;
http://money.cnn.com/2015/03/09/news/economy/united-states-sanctions-venezuela/index.html; https://venezuelanalysis.com/news/12885;
http://uk.businessinsider.com/trump-venezuela-top-priorities-iran-north-korea-2017-12?r=US&IR=T; http://foreignpolicy.com/2018/01/12/why-more-sanctions-wont-help-venezuela/; https://therealnews.com/stories/un-rapporteur-us-sanctions-cause-death-in-venezuela; www.treasury.gov/resource-center/sanctions/Programs/Documents/13692.pdf.

53 https://libya360.wordpress.com/2018/04/11/trumps-crimes-against-venezuela-must-be-brought-before-the-international-criminal-court/.

54 www.mcclatchydc.com/news/politics-government/white-house/article207971169.html.

55 https://foreignpolicy.com/2018/01/12/por-que-mas-sanciones-no-ayudaran-a-venezuela/; https://venezuelanalysis.com/analysis/13332.

56 https://assets.documentcloud.org/documents/3115191/Hum-Impact-of-Syria-Related-Res-Eco-Measures-26.pdf;
www.independent.co.uk/voices/syria-syrian-war-us-eu-sanctions-bashar-al-assad-patrick-cockburn-a7350751.html.

57 www.independent.co.uk/voices/economic-sanctions-north-korea-syria-hospital-supplies-a8168321.html.

58 www.aporrea.org/actualidad/a258744.html;
www.diariolasamericas.com/america-latina/zapatero-denuncia-doble-rasero-venezuela-y-resalta-el-dialogo-crisis-n4149344.

59 On 16 February 2018, the Permanent Mission of the Bolivarian Republic of Venezuela issued a statement to all Permanent Missions to the United Nations Office and other international organizations in Geneva, explaining what had happened.
www.el-nacional.com/noticias/mundo/rodriguez-zapatero-pidio-oposicion-suscribir-acuerdo-dialogo_222314;
www.infobae.com/america/venezuela/2018/02/24/julio-borges-afirmo-que-jose-luis-rodriguez-zapatero-se-quemo-como-mediador-en-el-dialogo-entre-el-regimen-de-nicolas-maduro-y-la-oposicion-venezolana/;
www.elplural.com/politica/2018/02/14/mas-de-200-personalidades-reaccionan-ante-el-virulento-ataque-de-el-pais-contra.

60 https://edition.cnn.com/videos/spanish/2017/12/02/cnnee-brk-sot-julio-borges-republica-dominicana-dialogo-venezuela-oposicion-elecciones-voto.cnn.

61 "« Maduro est acculé, mais cela le rend encore plus dangereux »; Ancien maire de Caracas, l'opposant Antonio Ledezma a fui le Venezuela il y a trois mois. Rencontre à Genève," *Tribune de Genève*, 21 February 2018 (« oui, j'appelle à une intervention humanitaire ... c'est à la communauté internationale de préciser la forme »).

62 www.el-nacional.com/noticias/oposicion/borges-venezuela-convertido-problema-para-region_225386.

63 http://contrapunto.com/noticia/desde-madrid-borges-vecchio-y-ledezma-piden-mas-sanciones-y-aumentar-presion-al-gobierno-194508/.

64 www.lefigaro.fr/international/2018/02/23/01003-20180223ARTFIG00339-antonio-ledezma-il-faut-une-intervention-pour-renverser-maduro.php.

65 http://news.bbc.co.uk/hi/spanish/latin_america/newsid_3718000/3718810.stm; http://elestimulo.com/blog/pedro-carmona-a-15-anos-del-carmonazo-ni-arrepentido-ni-con-miedo/.

66 Miguel Tinker Salas, *Venezuela: What Everyone Needs to Know* (Oxford, Oxford University Press, 2015), pp. 157–58.

67 Ibid., pp. 154 ff. See also Lander, "Venezuela"; https://luisbrittogarcia.blogspot.ch/2018/04/en-una-guerra-si-te-atacan-tienes-que.html.

68 www.nytimes.com/2018/03/01/magazine/can-venezuela-be-saved.html.

69 Stephen Kinzer, *Overthrow: America's century of regime change from Hawaii to Iraq* (New York, Times Books, 2006); Norman Solomon, *War made easy: how presidents and pundits keep spinning us to death* (John Wiley & Sons, Hoboken, New Jersey, 2005); www.un.org/ga/president/63/interactive/protect/noam.pdf; https://consortiumnews.com/2018/02/14/regime-change-fails-is-a-military-coup-or-invasion-of-venezuela-next/.

In its judgment of 27 June 1986 in the Nicaragua v. United States case, the International Court of Justice noted that "while the United States might form its own appraisal of the situation as to respect for human rights in Nicaragua, the use of force could not be the appropriate method to monitor or ensure such respect." The Court held that "the United States of America, by training, arming, equipping, financing and supplying the contra forces or otherwise encouraging, supporting and aiding military and paramilitary activities in and against Nicaragua, has acted, against the Republic of Nicaragua, in breach of its obligation under customary international law not to intervene in the affairs of another State"; www.aporrea.org/ddhh/a260597.html.

70 www.who.int/malaria/news/2018/interview-bill-gates/en/.

71 www.ve.undp.org/content/venezuela/es/home/presscenter/articles/2016/12/08/gobierno-de-la-rep-blica-bolivariana-de-venezuela-y-naciones-unidas-fortalecen-cooperaci-n-en-materia-de-prioridades-nacionales.html;
http://mppre.gob.ve/?p=22182;
http://mppre.gob.ve/2018/06/13/gobierno-revolucionario-establece-acuerdos-con-la-organizacion-panamericana-de-la-salud/.

72 www.unhcr.org/news/briefing/2018/3/5aa793c14/venezuelans-flee-throughout-latin-america-unhcr-issues-new-protection-guidance.html.

73 To solve the hyperinflation problem, the United States economist Steve Hanke proposes dollarization. See www.panorama.com.ve/politicayeconomia/Dolarizar-al-pais-acabaria-con-la-inflacion-Economista-Steve-Hanke-a-PANORAMA-audio-20161219-0002.html. See also www.boeckler.de/pdf/v_2017_11_10_kulesza.pdf; www.alainet.org/es/articulo/188447; www.resumenlatinoamericano.org/2018/04/16/venezuela-sobre-las-dolarizaciones-por-pasqualina-curcio/.

74 https://venezuelanalysis.com/news/11468. According to information received from the Supreme Court, in the period 2015–2017, a total of 10,713 cases of contraband, hoarding and speculation were dealt with by the courts, and in 2017 the Court processed 79 extradition requests, mostly concerning Colombia, Spain and the United States.

75 Norman Finkelstein, *Gaza: an inquest into its martyrdom* (Oakland, California, University of California Press, 2017).

76 www.c-span.org/video/?c4670011/murphy-young-yemen-murphy-saudis-deliberately-create-famine-yemen.

77 https://reliefweb.int/report/libya/unicef-libya-humanitarian-situation-report-july-september-2017.
78 www.icrc.org/en/where-we-work/middle-east/syria.
79 https://reliefweb.int/report/iraq/mosul-humanitarian-crisis-01-june-2017-enarku.
80 https://reliefweb.int/report/haiti/haiti-humanitarian-situation-report-april-2017.
81 https://reliefweb.int/report/mali/unicef-mali-humanitarian-situation-report-april-june-2017.
82 www.unhcr.org/news/press/2018/1/5a659f6ca/global-report-10-under-reported-humanitarian-crises-2017.html.
83 www.unocha.org/story/south-sudan-humanitarian-crisis-catastrophic-proportions.
84 www.care.org/emergencies/somalia-humanitarian-crisis.
85 www.aljazeera.com/news/2018/02/rohingya-allowed-return-myanmar-180213195617187.html.
86 https://plataformalac.org/en/2017/02/global-fund-denies-humanitarian-support-to-hiv-people-of-venezuela/.
87 www.fao.org/3/a-br323e.pdf.
88 https://venezuelanalysis.com/news/12754.
89 www.fao.org/giews/country-analysis/external-assistance/en/.
90 https://revista.drclas.harvard.edu/book/venezuela-1980s-1990s-and-beyond.
91 In 1998, the Inter-American Commission on Human Rights condemned the Caracazo and other actions of the Pérez Government, referring the case to the Inter-American Court of Human Rights, which in 1999 found violations of the American Convention on Human Rights.
92 Naoko Kada, "Impeachment as a punishment for corruption? The cases of Brazil and Venezuela" in *Checking executive power: presidential impeachment in comparative perspective*, Jody C. Baumgartner and Naoko Kada, eds. (Westport, Praeger, 2003); www.nytimes.com/1993/05/21/world/venezuelan-leader-quits-to-face-trial.html.
93 www.imf.org/external/pubs/ft/silent/index.htm; Lander, "Venezuela."
94 www.medelu.org/Ils-confondent-votes-et-arme-de.
95 www.youtube.com/watch?v=rI4z_N2L3nI&feature=youtu.be.
96 www.legrandsoir.info/venezuela-un-vote-contre-la-violence.html.
97 https://venezuelanalysis.com/news/13442.
98 https://theglobalamericans.org/2017/10/council-electoral-specialists-latin-america-ceela/; https://venezuelanalysis.com/news/13783.
99 In the podcast "Unauthorized Disclosure," hosted by Rania Khalek and Kevin Gosztola, journalists Abby Martin and Michael Prysner reported how they were threatened with physical violence and endured a campaign of demonization as "intelligence agents," collecting protester photos for Venezuelan police. They described the violent demonstrations they witnessed as follows: "violent confrontations are happening ... the Guarimbas, which are these huge flaming barricades that are ... going on every single day and night across different areas, usually in middle and upper-class areas.... The opposition does not denounce the violence." Opposition activists "pulled out people from 18-wheelers, stole trucks on the highway, created giant barricades, doused the freeways in gasoline.... When you look at the death toll ... well over half were killed directly or indirectly by opposition violence." https://raniakhalek.com/; www.youtube.com/watch?v=ig6yFP8HjVQ; www.youtube.com/watch?v=YUYWrPiUeWY.
100 Many experts have endured mobbing, including John Dugard, Jean Ziegler, Idriss Jazairy, Richard Falk, Olivier de Schutter, William Schabas and Michael Lynk. Even Virginia Dandan, long-time Chair of the Committee on Economic, Social and Cultural Rights and Independent Expert on human rights and international solidarity, was ridiculed by an NGO because of her press release on her mission to Cuba (A/HRC/38/40/Add.1).
101 www.ohchr.org/EN/NewsEvents/Pages/DisplayNews.aspx?NewsID=20669&LangID=E.
102 The last visit took place in 1996. In its responses of 2005, the Bolivarian Republic of Venezuela elucidated how it had implemented the recommendations (see E/CN.4/2006/6/Add.2, paras. 404–466).

CONCLUSION
REFLECTIONS ON THE WAY FORWARD

"It is in your hands to create a better world for all who live in it."

NELSON MANDELA[i]

In my more than four decades of work in the field of human rights, as a private scholar and researcher, professor of law, United Nations official, president of a human rights non-governmental organization, blogger and UN independent expert, I have come to know the hopes and disappointments of those who genuinely believe in human dignity and who strive for a better and kinder world.

I have met and collaborated with persons working within the UN system whom I would describe as "heroes" of human rights, who have altruistically devoted their lives to improving the lives of others, including John Humphrey, Theo van Boven, Navi Pillay, Elizabeth Evatt, Erica-Irene Daes, Claire Palley, Rosalyn Higgins, Virginia Dandan, Sharon Venne, Isabel Ortiz, Felix Ermacora, Christian Tomuschat, Bertrand Ramcharan, Jakob Th. Möller, Marc Bossuyt, Manfred Nowak, William Schabas, Olivier de Schutter, Nils Melzer, and Bent Sørensen, persons who have demonstrated true professionalism, intellectual honesty, integrity, a sense for ethics, justice and proportions. It is thanks to people like these that considerable progress has been achieved in the promotion and protection of human rights worldwide, that the present international order has devised mechanisms and accommodated a system of monitoring and assistance to victims, advisory services to States and national human rights institutions.

On the other hand, I have also known many diplomats, politicians and journalists who only give lip service to human rights, without believing in them, who instrumentalize human rights for their personal careers or who weaponize human rights for geopolitical purposes. Worse still, I have known colleagues in the academic world, in NGOs, inter-governmental organizations, expert committees, and fact-finding commissions, who are no more than paper-pushers, human rights "operatives," who master the jargon of human rights but are essentially opportunists and could just as well be working in law firms, auditing firms, financial banking, tax consulting, transnational corporations or manufacturing shoes and iphones.

---

i *Notes to the Future: Words of Wisdom* (New York: Simon and Schuster, 2012), p.118, .

When I ended my mandate I was asked whether I could summarize my understanding of the concept "human rights." My answer was succinct:

> Universal human rights constitute a holistic system of interdependent entitlements and freedoms. Yet, "universal" does not mean homologated or insensitive to cultural specificities. The ubiquitous slogan that "all rights are equal" is but a platitude that manifests an absence of a sense for proportions and discernment. Indeed, human dignity, the source of all human rights, necessarily dictates priorities—a hierarchy based on common sense and mutual respect: First and foremost, the right to live in dignity, a commitment to promote and protect the sanctity of life, which encompasses physical integrity, the right to food, water, housing, healthcare, freedom from war, a human right to peace. Secondly, the right to freely develop one's personality i.e. the right to be who we are, the right to our identity, the right to set the priorities of our lives—that essential right of individual and collective self-determination, free from artificial constraints imposed by government or society—and as a corollary the duty to respect the rights of others. Codification of human rights has not been concluded, since continuing standard-setting remains necessary to better protect the practical expression and exercise of our human dignity. All human rights can be subsumed under the two categories above, with the caveat that the letter of the law must not be politicized to subvert the spirit of the law, which must be our credo—the *dignitas humana*.[1]

The "Human Rights Industry"

I do not know whether I can claim to have coined the largely pejorative term, "human rights industry." Certainly, I have employed that neologism for at least two decades to describe the many governmental and non-governmental "players" who have made it their business to instrumentalize the philosophy and ethics of human rights for extraneous purposes, frequently to demonize geopolitical or geoeconomic rivals. I have also warned about the Orwellian corruption of language and the deliberate confusion of terminology practiced by diplomats, politicians, journalists and the media, so that only experts can discover the many scams that are played on society. The concept of "newspeak" can just as well be described as "cognitive dissonance," since we are expected to simultaneously believe in mutually exclusive concepts, to accept the "fragmentation" of international law and the creation of "stand alone" regimes that sabotage the holistic application of the United Nations Charter and the human rights treaties.

It seems that more and more we are surrounded by fake news,[2] fake history, fake law, fake diplomacy and fake democracy. It takes a considerable effort to break out of the stranglehold in which the narrative managers hold most of humanity.

Surely one of the most corrosive developments is the selective application of international law and human rights law, the double-standards, and the intellectual dishonesty of many resolutions of the Security Council, General Assembly and Human Rights Council. It is this linguistic deception and what I call the application of international law "à la carte" that leads to cynicism about the United Nations and to a significant loss in its authority and credibility.

The **weaponization** of human rights has transformed individual and collective entitlement to assistance, protection, respect and solidarity—based on our common human dignity and equality—into a hostile arsenal to target competitors and political adversaries.

In the stockpile of *weaponized human rights,* the technique of "naming and shaming" has become a sort of ubiquitous Kalashnikov. Experience shows, however, that naming and shaming fails to alleviate the suffering of victims and only satisfies the strategic aims of certain governments and non-governmental organizations that instrumentalize human rights for the purpose of destabilizing others, and often enough to facilitate regime change, regardless of how undemocratic that may be and notwithstanding the customary international law principle of non-intervention in the internal affairs of sovereign States. This strategy rests on the false premise that the accuser somehow possesses moral authority and that the accused will then recognize this moral superiority and act accordingly. Theoretically this could function if the accuser did possess moral authority, if the accuser were indeed to practice naming and shaming in a non-selective manner and free of obvious double-standards. Alas, the technique frequently backfires, because the accuser has its own skeletons in the closet. This classic example of intellectual dishonesty usually stiffens the resistance of the accused, who will be even less inclined to take any measures to correct alleged violations.

Another technique of norms-warfare is what is termed "lawfare,"[3] whereby the "law" is in actuality used to subvert the rule of law, and international criminal law is instrumentalized to demonize certain leaders and not others. No self-respecting judge would betray the profession by playing this kind of game—but some do, and instead of safeguarding the ethos of the rule of law these politicized judges corrupt it (remember Roland Freisler's *Volksgerichtshof!*) thus undermining the credibility of the entire system.

The arsenal of weaponized human rights also includes nonconventional wars such as economic wars and sanctions regimes, ostensibly justified on the basis of the alleged human rights violations of the targeted State. The result is that, far from helping the victims, entire populations are held hostage—victims not only of violations by their own governments, but also of collective punishment by the sanctioning State(s). This can entail crimes against humanity, when as a consequence food security is impaired, medicines and medical equipment are rendered scarce or are available only at exorbitant prices. Demonstrably, economic sanctions kill.

Under certain conditions, naming and shaming involves further violations of human rights and the rule of law, contravening Arts. 6, 14, 17, 19 and 26 of the International Covenant on Civil and Political Rights, and could reach the threshold of what is termed "hate speech" (Art. 20). Bottom line: naming and shaming is a thoroughly ineffective instrument of change. States and NGOs would do well to replace this obsolete technique by good faith proposals and constructive recommendations, accompanied by the offer of advisory services and technical assistance so as to concretely help the victims on the ground.

Honest dealing and the pursuit of peaceful relations is a better strategy if humanity is to reap cooperation and progress in human rights terms. What is most needed today is mature diplomacy, result-oriented negotiations, a culture of dialogue and mediation, instead of this petulant culture of grandstanding, intransigence and holier-than-thou pretence that helps no one.

If the international community wants to help a country improve its human rights performance, it should stop the sabre-rattling and eliminate the threats that make governments retrench. By now it should be obvious that demonization, naming and shaming, sanctions and blockades are not conducive to positive change. Precisely because they aggravate the situation and disrupt the proper functioning of state institutions, they actually weaken the rule of law and lead to retrogression in human rights terms.

The bottom line is that "democracy" cannot be exported and imposed by force, that human rights are not the result of a vertical, top-down enforcement but rather require a horizontal recognition of the dignity of every human being, and that the exercise of human rights depends on education, mutual respect and solidarity.

Another victim of instrumentalization and weaponization is the concept of "the rule of law" itself.

The Rule of Law Must Evolve into the Rule of Justice

It is axiomatic that the rule of law functions as a pillar of stability, predictability and the democratic ethos in modern society. Its object and purpose is to serve the human person and progressively achieve human dignity in the larger context of freedom.

Because law reflects power imbalances, we must ensure that the ideal of the rule of law is not instrumentalized simply to enforce the status quo, maintain privilege, and the exploitation of one group over another. The rule of law must be a rule that allows flexibility and welcomes continuous democratic dialogue to devise and implement those reforms required by an evolving society. It must be a rule of conscience, of listening.

Throughout history law has all too frequently been manipulated by political power, becoming a kind of *dictatorship through law,* where people are robbed of their individual and collective rights, while the law itself becomes the main instrument of their disenfranchisement. Experience has taught us that law is not coterminous with justice and that laws can be adopted and enforced to perpetuate abuse and cement injustice. Accordingly, any appeal to the rule of law should be contextualized within a human-rights-based framework.

Already in Sophocles' *Antigone* we saw the clash between the arbitrary law of King Creon and the unwritten law of humanity. Enforcing Creon's unjust law brought misery to all. In Roman times the maxim *dura lex sed lex* (the law is hard, but it is the law) was mellowed by Cicero's wise reminder that *summum jus summa injuria* (extreme law is extreme injustice, *de Officiis* 1, 10, 33), i.e. the blind application of the law may cause great injustice.

The contention that, irrespective of what it stipulates, "the law must be obeyed" has been challenged by human rights heroes for thousands of years. Spartacus fought against the Roman slave laws and paid with his life. Slavery remained constitutional and legal in the Western hemisphere until the mid-nineteenth century; colonialism was deemed constitutional and legal by the colonizers until the decolonization processes of the 1950s, 1960s and 1970s; Germany's racist Nuremberg laws of 1935 were constitutional and legal, as were those of South Africa's apartheid; Stalin's laws, the Holodomor in the Ukraine and the purges of the 1930's were all based on Soviet laws and decrees; segregation in the U.S. was constitutional and legal (see, for instance, the U.S. Supreme Court judgment *Plessy v. Ferguson*) until overturned by the Civil Rights Act of 1964. Civil disobedience by Henry David Thoreau, Zaghioul Pasha, Michael Collins, Dietrich Bonhoeffer, Mahatma Gandhi, Martin Luther King, Nelson Mandela, Ken Saro Wiwa, Mohamed Bouazizi was legitimate and necessary to give example and initiate reforms—but they all suffered the consequences of having opposed the *fetishism of the rule of law.*

Democracy in the twenty-first century requires that the rule of law cease being the rule of power, of might makes right, geopolitics and economics. The rule of law must incorporate human dignity into the equation and enable people power, self-determination and referenda. The rule of law must evolve into the rule of social justice and peace.

Indeed, civilization does not simply require society to have a set of laws and a powerful police force to enforce them. Civilization means ensuring the real welfare of people, creating the conditions necessary for their pursuit of happiness. The true indicators of civilization are not an expanding Gross Domestic Product, ever-growing consumption, and aggressive exploitation of natural resources—but rather respect for human and animal life, sustainable management of the environment, local, regional and international solidarity, social justice and a culture of peace.

Civilization does not entail building ever-higher skyscrapers, producing more gadgets, and accumulating material goods—but affirming individuals' and peoples' identities, uniqueness and history, while celebrating diversity and the common heritage of mankind, demonstrating a sense of proportion and creating beauty for future generations in literature, art and music.

In my 2018 report to the Human Rights Council I proposed a paradigm change that would make it possible to better understand the scope of human rights and to develop strategies for their realization. Indeed, as long as the world is held hostage by the "economy," by the weaponization of human rights, and by their unjustifiable division into those rights supposedly of the first, second and third generations—we will remain handicapped. That is simply a phoney structure, one that prevents us from seeing the true picture.

A New Functional Paradigm on Human Rights

As I explained in my 25 principles of international order, all human rights necessarily derive from human dignity. Codification of human rights is never definitive and never exhaustive, but constitutes an evolutionary *mode d'emploi* for the exercise of civil, cultural, economic, political and social rights.

However, the interpretation and application of human rights is hindered by wrong priorities, inflexible legalisms, and a regrettable tendency to focus only on individual rights while forgetting collective rights. Alas, many rights advocates show little or no interest in the social responsibilities that accompany the exercise of rights, and fail to see the necessary symbiosis of rights and obligations, notwithstanding the letter and spirit of article 29 of the Universal Declaration of Human Rights.

The time has come to change the human rights paradigm away from narrow positivism towards a broader understanding of human rights norms in the context of an emerging customary international law of human rights. Law is neither physics nor mathematics, but a dynamic human institution that day by day addresses the needs and aspirations of society, adjusting here, filling lacunae there. Every human rights lawyer knows that the spirit of the law (Montesquieu) transcends the limitations of the letter of the law, and hence codified norms should always be interpreted in the light of those general principles of law that inform all legal systems, such as good faith, proportionality and *ex injuria non oritur jus*.

The obsolete and artificial division of human rights into those of the falsely called first generation (civil and political), second (economic, social and cultural) and third generation (environment, peace, development) rights—with its obvious predisposition to favour civil and political rights—should be discarded. This generational divide is part of a mental structure that perpetuates a world order that much too often appears to allow injustice.

It should be replaced by a functional paradigm that would consider rights in the light of their function within a coherent system—not of competing rights and aspirations, but of interrelated, mutually reinforcing rights which should be applied in their interdependence and understood in the context of a coordinated strategy to serve the ultimate goal of achieving human dignity in all of its manifestations. Four categories would replace the skewed narrative of three generations of rights:

1. Enabling rights: the rights to food, water, shelter, development and homeland—but also the right to peace, since one cannot enjoy human rights unless there is an environment conducive to the exercise of those rights. Article 28 of the Universal Declaration of Human Rights postulates the right of every human being "to a social and international order in which the rights and freedoms set forth in this Declaration can be fully realized." This entails the basic necessities of life.

2. Inherent or immanent rights: the rights to life, integrity, liberty and security of person, in the light of which other rights must be interpreted and applied. Every such right must necessarily contain within itself the element of equality, the self-evident requirement that it be applied equally and equitably, that there be uniformity and predictability (what the Germans call *Rechtssicherheit*).

There are also inherent limitations to the exercise of rights. The general principle of law prohibiting abuse of rights, *sic utere tuo ut alienum non laedas*—the use of a right without harming others, a principle advocated by Sir Hersch Lauterpacht as an overarching norm prohibiting the egoistic exercise of rights to achieve anti-social results or unjust enrichment. This principle means that every right, including all human rights, must be exercised in the context of other rights and not instrumentalized to destroy other rights or to harm others. There is no right to intransigence in law—as we know from the sad character of Shylock in Shakespeare's *Merchant of Venice*. The letter of the law must never be used to subvert the spirit of the law.

3. Instrumental rights: the rights to due process, access to information, the right to truth, freedom of expression and peaceful assembly, work, education, social security, leisure—rights that we need to achieve our potential, to complete our personalities, to engage in the pursuit of happiness.

4. Outcome rights: the concrete exercise of human dignity, that condition of life that allows each human being to be himself or herself. This ultimate right is the right to our individual identity, to our privacy, the right to be ourselves, to think for ourselves and express our humanity without indoctrination, without intimidation, without pressures of political correctness, without having to sell ourselves, without having to engage in self-censorship.

The absence of this outcome right to identity and self-respect is reflected in much of the strife we see in the world today. It is through the consciousness and exercise of the right to our identity and the respect of the identity of others that we will enjoy the individual and collective right to peace.[4]

The United Nations Human Rights Council should become the international arena where governments compete to show how best to implement human rights, how to strengthen the rule of law, and how to achieve social justice; where they display best practices and give life to this new functional paradigm of human rights. This kind of competition in human rights performance would be a noble goal and challenge for civilization.

The Council should become the pre-eminent forum where governments elucidate what they themselves have done and are doing to deliver on human rights: via good-faith implementation of pledges, adherence to a daily culture of human rights characterized by generous interpretation of human rights treaties and a commitment to the inclusion of all stakeholders.

What the Council must not be is a politicized arena where gladiators use human rights as weapons to defeat their political adversaries and where human rights are undermined through side shows, the "flavour of the month" or the absurd acceptance of "legal black holes." The civilization model to be striven for by the globalized world must not be one of exploitation and consumerism, of positivism, legalisms and loopholes, but one of ethics, direct democracy, respect for the common heritage of mankind, the environment, international solidarity and human dignity.

The Office of the United Nations High Commissioner for Human Rights has undertaken the challenge to revive the legacy of Eleanor Roosevelt,[5] Charles Malik, René Cassin and P.C. Chang. Step by step mechanisms are being established to promote human dignity more effectively, to make human rights juridical and justiciable by expanding the regional human rights courts system and creating an international court of human rights. Humanity looks up at the United Nations as its best chance to build a just world order—for all of us.

* * *

I think it is befitting to end this book with reflections by Pope Francis. —AdeZ

> Once we start to think about the kind of world we are leaving to future generations, we look at things differently; we realize that the world is a gift which we have freely received and must share with others. Since the world has been given to us, we can no longer view reality in a purely utilitarian way, in which efficiency and productivity are entirely geared to our individual benefit. Intergenerational solidarity is not optional, but rather a basic question of justice, since the world we have received also belongs to those who will follow us. (*Laudato Si,* 159)[6]

Notes

1 *Ex Tempore,* Vol. 31, 24 December 2020, p. 123. http://www.extempore.ch/
2 In 2020, the Swiss Colonel Jacques Baud, expert in chemical weapons, anti-terrorism, and mine clearance, and former UN official, published a revealing book, *Gouverner par les Fake News* (Chevilly Larue, France: Max Milo), documenting in 398 pages the corrosive effect of fake news in all current political crises.
3 Professor Nils Melzer, UN Rapporteur on Torture, published in April 2021 a disturbing book, *Der Fall Julian Assange* (Munich, Piper), which reveals in 336 pages the harrowing drama of the unethical "lawfare" waged by the U.S., UK, Sweden and Ecuador against Julian Assange, in contravention of domestic laws and of numerous provisions of the International Covenant on Civil and Political Rights. The revelations are far more serious than those made by Emile Zola in the Dreyfus Affair of 1898.
4 See my 2013 report to the GA A/68/284, paras. 67–68.
5 *Eleanor Lives! A Plan for Humanity,* https://eleanorlives.org
6 "Encyclical Letter *Laudato Si'* of the Holy Father Francis on Care for Our Common Home," Dicastero per la Comunicazione, Libreria Editrice Vaticana, http://www.vatican.va/content/francesco/en/encyclicals/documents/papa-francesco_20150524_enciclica-laudato-si.html.

INDEX

A

Aarhus Convention 261
abuse of rights 31, 49, 208, 240, 241, 244, 257, 261, 267, 268, 270, 273, 286
Advisory Committee 19, 22, 61, 62, 63, 64, 73, 82, 83, 106, 223, 226, 301, 305, 394
advisory opinions of the International Court of Justice 6, 42, 126, 138, 141, 147, 153, 187, 214, 219, 251, 254, 329, 362, 397
advisory services and technical assistance 2, 15, 34, 56, 107, 193, 216, 220, 254, 399, 408, 416, 430, 449
African Charter on Human and Peoples' Rights 208, 243, 285
aggression 2, 10, 22, 44, 51, 52, 58, 59, 63, 70, 75, 76, 79, 124, 126
Agreement on Trade-Related Aspects of Intellectual Property Rights (TRIPS Agreement) 279, 280
Alaska 42, 119, 120
ALBA 4
Alfonso Martínez, Miguel 22
algorithms 55, 173, 174
Al-Khasawneh, Awn Shawkat 22, 139, 142
Allende, Salvador 217, 219, 410
Almagro, Luis 436
Alston, Philip 336, 371
Amnesty International 330, 337, 356, 410, 417, 437
Annan, Kofi 73
Antigone 244, 261, 450
apartheid 193, 219, 450
arbitration 52, 54, 231–234, 237, 238, 240, 241, 248, 251, 254, 256, 263, 264, 267, 269, 271, 272
Archer, Colin 88
Arendt, Hannah 173
Argentina 125, 264, 271, 373, 378, 387–388
Aristophanes 24, 67
Arms Trade Treaty 77, 102
Arreaza, Jorge 409, 436
artificial intelligence 55, 174
Assange, Julian 175, 176, 195, 196, 197, 231
austerity measures 36, 66, 81, 103, 180, 191, 257, 328, 380–389
autonomy 50, 117, 119, 126, 129, 130, 131, 133, 139, 144–150, 160, 167

B

Bachelet, Michelle 195

Bahamas leaks scandal 197, 301
Bangladesh 118, 123, 144
Ban Ki-moon 88, 184
Baud, Jacques 454
Becquelin, Philippe xiv
Bensouda, Fatou 436
Bilderberg Group 5, 177
Bioko Island 42, 118
blockades 53, 194, 211, 221, 222, 410, 412–414, 416, 422, 425, 426, 433, 434, 435, 437, 439, 449
Blum, William 85
Bohoslavsky, Juan Pablo 234, 301, 307, 383, 384, 417
Borges, Julio 412, 427
Bougainville Island 42
Boven, Theo van 12, 13, 34, 85, 446
Boyd, Kirk 13
Brandeis, Louis 31
Bretton Woods 177, 336, 337, 343, 361, 371, 377, 383, 389
Brussels Declaration 108
Bubis 42, 123
business and human rights 3, 25, 47, 231–290, 303, 308, 312, 328, 355, 394

C

Cable, Lieutenant Joe 69
Cáceres, Berta 351
Calvo doctrine 248, 273
Camus, Albert 67
Caracazo 428
Carmona, Pedro 220, 412, 427
Carmonazo 427
Carter Center 429
Carter, Jimmy 46, 429
Cassandra 7, 219
Cassin, René 10, 13, 194, 454
Catalonia 123, 154–169
Cato Institute 264
censorship 4, 8, 9, 28, 29, 31, 173, 174, 178, 179, 182, 183, 186, 188, 192, 351, 453
Central Intelligence Agency (CIA) 412
Centre Europe Troisième Monde (CETIM) 287
CERN (European Organization for Nuclear Research) 247
Chagos Islands 118
Chang, P.C. 10, 13, 454
Charter of the Organization of American States 52, 216, 221, 411, 436

455

Charter of the United Nations *See* United
   Nations Charter
Chatham House 80
Chatzistefanou, Aris 435
Chávez, Hugo 220, 410–414, 422, 428, 429
   National Assembly 220, 412
Chevron 239, 267, 269
Chile 42, 118, 120, 125, 216, 219, 222, 410,
   412, 413, 422, 426
chilling effect 184, 192, 233, 234, 263, 270
China 42, 105, 120, 176, 193, 302, 311, 313,
   314, 320, 321, 348, 412
Chomsky, Noam 85, 284
Chorzow Factory Case 156
Churchill, Winston 78
Cicero, Marcus Tullius 49, 450
Clark, Wesley 203
climate change 5, 79, 93, 109, 111, 112, 242,
   283, 286, 306, 323, 355, 399
cluster bombs 66, 240, 290
coalition of the willing 72, 95
Cockburn, Patrick 222, 426
code of conduct 7, 8, 319, 323, 327, 419, 430,
   432, 437
collateral damage 36, 223, 224
collective rights 6, 450, 451
Commission on Human Rights (UN) 1, 2, 7, 22,
   118, 258, 269, 305, 410, 417, 419, 430
Committee on Economic, Social and Cultural
   Rights 65, 76, 83, 84, 152, 210, 211,
   226, 232, 242, 258, 358, 384, 410, 419,
   421
Committee on the Elimination of Racial
   Discrimination 170
common heritage of mankind 20, 290, 451, 454
competition 3, 18, 46, 184, 185, 194, 208, 302,
   303, 309, 316, 318, 324, 326, 328, 364,
   392, 453
Compliance Advisor Ombudsman 339, 354,
   357, 359, 360, 364, 366
Comunidad de Estados Latinoamericanos y
   Caribeños (CELAC) (Community of
   Latin American and Caribbean States)
   91, 102, 215, 417, 431
conscientious objection 64, 69, 70, 71, 72, 75,
   162, 326, 329, 330
contra bonos mores 231, 234, 241, 243, 244,
   245, 251, 256, 261, 265, 267, 269, 273,
   276, 277, 286
Convention against Torture (CAT) 2, 50, 72, 75
Convention on the Elimination of All Forms of
   Discrimination against Women 21

Convention on the Recognition and
   Enforcement of Foreign Arbitral
   Awards 251, 271, 277, 286
Convention on the Rights of Persons with
   Disabilities 21
Correa, Rafael 201, 321, 334
Corporate Europe Observatory 255
corruption 27, 28, 99, 111, 175, 180, 182, 185,
   195, 197, 208, 243, 255, 262, 271, 275,
   277, 288, 289, 302–304, 306, 308–310,
   312, 315, 318, 322, 325, 328, 330, 337,
   341, 345, 357, 365, 366, 374, 391, 396,
   398, 399, 410, 412, 414, 418, 422, 428
   of language 174, 203, 204, 447
Council of Europe 40, 163, 169, 176, 184, 320
Council on Foreign Relations 5
coup d'état 217, 220, 410, 412, 413, 427
Covid-19 88
credibility gap 436
credit rating agencies 5, 423, 430
Crimea 124
crimes against humanity 3, 39, 52, 53, 65, 70,
   80, 91, 124, 205, 219, 221, 225, 226,
   248, 262, 278, 290, 425, 432, 433, 435,
   436, 449
crimes against peace 76
Cuba 80, 105, 193, 213, 215, 216, 219, 222,
   225, 226, 413, 419, 420, 422, 432
Cuban missile crisis 1
Curcio, Pasqualina 217

D

Damocles, sword of 78, 79, 80, 89
Dandan, Virginia x, 47, 222, 417, 445, 446
Darwinism, social 28, 31
Declaración de Santiago 62
Declaration on the Rights of Indigenous Peoples
   42, 120, 146, 152, 258, 275, 339
decolonization 1, 42, 118, 119, 121, 122, 130,
   138, 143–144, 149, 204, 248, 450
de-escalation committee 81, 97
de facto States 51, 121, 124, 125
demographic manipulation 52, 124
demophobia 5
depleted uranium 66, 80, 290
deregulation 185, 288, 344, 352, 363, 372, 373,
   376, 380, 387, 398
derogation 227, 283, 415, 416
d'Escoto Brockmann, Miguel 65
development, right to 4, 15, 22, 82, 93, 146, 191,
   195, 211, 258, 280, 288, 306, 431, 439
digital technologies 4, 55, 174

direct democracy 32, 33, 41, 94, 168, 181, 329, 454
disarmament for development 88, 93
distress, persons in 415
Doha Development Agenda (DDA) 25, 279, 280, 282, 285
Doing Business project 352
do no harm 343, 376, 396
donors 9, 352
double standards 5, 31
Douhan, Alena 59, 225, 408, 409, 438, 439
Dreyfus, Alfred 175, 454
drones 36, 95, 98
Durban Declaration 51

E

Earth Rights International 337, 353, 390
ecocide 54, 191, 245, 262
economic sanctions 56, 106, 194–195, 210–212, 214, 219, 221–226, 410, 415, 416, 424–426, 438, 439, 449
Ecuador 2, 4, 175, 196, 231, 239, 265, 266, 267, 269, 321, 412, 416, 418, 419, 420, 426, 434
Einstein, Albert 48, 77
Eisenhower, Dwight 96
elections 17, 21, 30, 32, 33, 37, 165, 166, 176, 177, 178, 181, 183, 185, 224, 412, 416, 427, 429
embargo
　against Cuba 213, 215, 226, 419, 432
　　GA resolutions 215, 219, 419
　against Syria 222, 426
　arms 211, 221, 424
enabling legislation 56
enabling rights 15, 186, 452
Energy Charter Treaty 239, 267, 268
enforcement 259, 263, 269, 271, 277, 285, 286, 288, 289, 290
Enforcement 251
environmental impact assessments 233, 242, 249, 250, 275, 284, 285, 287
environmental protection 254, 259, 280, 307, 323, 352, 361, 373
Erasmus of Rotterdam 24
erga omnes 48, 53, 63, 122, 131, 138, 139, 153, 206, 218, 233, 249, 258, 286
estoppel, 20, 49, 149, 241, 261, 414–415, 427
ethnic cleansing 22, 52, 71, 124, 133, 138, 141, 205
European Court of Human Rights 35, 141, 166, 243, 284, 289, 369
European Court of Justice 166, 285

European Parliament 98, 108, 120, 154, 240, 264, 317, 319, 323
European Union 36, 40, 62, 98, 123, 154, 155, 166, 169, 204, 210, 218, 268, 269, 281, 282, 285, 317, 319, 320, 323, 327, 383, 386, 414, 425
"evergreening" of patents 247
ex aequo et bono 245
ex ante/ex post human rights assessment 226, 250, 275, 285, 356, 358, 376
exceptionalism 5, 106, 132
ex injuria non oritur jus 20, 49, 53, 120, 149, 218, 241, 261, 427, 452
expression, freedom of 21, 30, 83, 123, 156, 173, 177, 179, 181, 182, 186, 188, 192, 194, 195, 196, 409, 415, 453
expropriation 235, 237, 245, 246, 265, 266, 288
extraterritorial application of domestic rules 433
extreme poverty 3, 18, 19, 22, 25, 32, 47, 50, 93, 145, 190, 232, 234, 256, 277, 301, 307, 311, 318, 336, 343, 351, 420
ex tunc invalidity 276

F

fake law 174, 203, 448
fake news 173, 182, 196, 203, 221, 425, 439, 448
Falk, Richard 1, 45, 116, 408, 445
family, protection of 191
FAO 212
federalism 50, 119, 129, 130, 132, 139, 147, 149, 167, 186, 187
Ferencz, Benjamin 77
Fernández-Armesto, Felipe 237
fetishism of law 187
financial blockade 53, 221, 222, 410, 412, 413, 414, 422, 425, 433, 434, 435, 437, 439
financial transactions tax 301, 307, 323, 328, 329, 363, 374, 392, 399
Food and Agriculture Organization (FAO) 5, 212, 216, 220, 254, 260, 276, 286, 411, 417, 428, 431
forced population transfers 47, 52, 141, 142
foreign debt 3, 24, 232, 234, 256, 301, 307, 346, 383, 385, 391, 394, 417, 431
Forum on Business and Human Rights 25, 287
Four Freedoms 12, 14, 15, 23, 64, 89, 94
fragmentation of international law 263, 291
Framework Convention on Climate Change 111, 242, 283, 306, 355
Framework Convention on Tobacco Control 234, 239, 260, 268

free, prior and informed consent 52, 145, 146, 152, 269, 339, 345, 355, 418
free-trade agreements 3, 54, 185, 214, 231, 233, 240–245, 248, 249, 250, 251, 252, 253, 254, 278, 284, 286, 288, 289, 430
Freud, Sigmund 48
Frost, Robert 9
Fukushima 239, 267

G

G-7 177
G-20 177, 306, 320, 322, 382
Gandhi, Mahatma 23, 450
Gaza 194, 204, 211, 213, 411, 428
General Agreement on Tariffs and Trade (GATT) 278, 283, 286
General Assembly resolutions 6, 7, 18, 82, 100, 122, 136
31/91 226
36/67 107
39/11 2, 46, 80, 82
48/141 2, 14, 436
53/243 26
55/2 46
60/1 x, 205, 419
60/147 55, 137
61/160 17
63/189 17
65/223 17, 22
65/309 396
66/20 110
67/175 40
68/153 130
68/165 203
68/175 152
69/178 256
69/313 341
69/319 393
70/1 341, 375
71/149 189
71/190 371
72/4 419
1469 119
1654 (XVI) 153
1803 (XVII) 153
2131 (XX) x, 2, 46, 226
2625 (XXV) x, 2, 22, 46, 75, 83, 127, 131, 155, 216, 220, 226, 419
3201 (S-VI) 2, 22
3314 (XXIX) x, 2, 22, 46, 75, 155, 216, 220, 226

general principles of law 20, 49, 121, 218, 237, 241, 247, 261, 262, 286, 452
genocide 39, 46, 50, 52, 65, 70, 123, 145, 204, 205, 208, 221, 424
geopolitical crimes 222, 225, 425, 432, 433
Germany 69, 105, 140, 142, 239, 264, 267, 268, 450
Global Compact 24, 289
Global Food Security Crisis 279
globalization 5, 28, 174, 234, 246, 247, 259, 305, 309, 344, 413
Global Zero campaign 78, 91
Goethe, Wolfgang von 9
good faith 8, 18, 20, 47–49, 63, 84, 94, 101, 102, 129, 132, 146, 161, 167–169, 190, 195, 241, 244, 260, 286, 386, 393, 411, 430, 432, 449, 452
Gorbachev, Mikhail 78, 90
gross domestic product (GDP) 236, 240, 245, 337, 344, 372, 386, 387, 396
gross national happiness (GNH) 105, 396
Guaidó, Juan 413, 435, 436
Guantánamo 211
Guiding Principles on Business and Human Rights 47, 232, 233, 235, 240, 275, 285, 288, 289, 303, 312, 328, 355, 394
Guterres, António 192, 193, 194, 195, 302

H

Halliday, Denis 106, 212, 221, 424
Hawaii 42, 119, 120
health, right to 3, 218, 242, 266, 270, 273, 274, 389, 439
Hessel, Stéphane 24
High Commissioner for Human Rights 2, 7, 12–14, 32, 33, 61, 69, 107, 142, 186, 189, 195, 211, 222, 223, 279, 329, 338, 340, 351, 409, 417, 432, 433, 436, 439, 454
Hiroshima 1, 80
holistic approach 191
homeland, right to 52, 71, 133, 141, 142, 186, 241, 452
Hong Kong 268, 311, 314
—Australia bilateral investment treaty 268
Hong Kong International Arbitration Centre 238
Horace (Quintus Horatius Flaccus) 10, 67
housing and homelessness 420
housing, right to 3, 25, 104, 211, 234, 302, 307, 323, 337, 344, 418, 447
humanitarian crisis 3, 411, 414, 426, 427, 428
humanitarian intervention 3, 53, 98, 204, 209, 411, 414, 427

Human Rights Committee 9, 30, 42, 49, 64, 70, 75, 80, 90, 119, 137, 142, 152, 166, 177, 179, 183, 205, 207, 225, 226, 232, 258, 410, 419, 420
   individual complaints procedure (Optional Protocol) 64, 71, 72, 75, 76, 83, 84
   inter-State complaints procedure (Article 41 ICCPR) 284, 358
Human Rights Council resolutions
   5/2 7
   14/3 19
   17/4 28
   17/16 19
   18/6 2, 15, 22, 72, 77, 92, 108, 182, 189, 232, 417
   19/36 19
   20/15 19
   21/9 72, 92, 232
   24/8 108
   24/14 106
   25/15 88, 92, 232
   26/9 289
   27/9 232
   30/29 278
human rights defenders 3, 28, 55, 180, 182–184, 196, 197, 339, 345, 350, 363, 392
"human rights industry" 9, 194, 447
Human Rights Watch 192, 330, 337, 347, 350, 351, 358–360, 380, 391, 410, 417, 437

I

Igbos of Biafra 118, 123, 144
Ikenson, Daniel J. 264
illicit financial flows 3, 301, 302, 308, 325, 329, 364, 399, 423
IMF *See* International Monetary Fund
immunity from prosecution 341, 353, 365, 390
impact assessments 174, 211, 226, 233, 242, 249, 250, 251, 275, 284, 285, 287, 327, 339, 341, 356, 358, 384
implementation gap 17
implied powers 6, 208
impunity 5, 33, 53, 55, 76, 121, 123, 128, 184, 185, 188, 191, 193, 196, 197, 210, 215, 218, 222, 272, 288, 289, 290, 300, 308, 314, 365, 412, 414, 425
India 23, 143, 221, 226, 268, 320, 347, 348, 350, 353, 359, 360, 410, 424
   WTO dispute settlement 283
Indian Law Resource Centre 344
Indigenous and Tribal Peoples Convention 260

indigenous peoples 3, 22, 25, 34, 42, 46, 47, 52, 117, 119, 120, 130, 131, 141–147, 149, 152, 153, 208, 234, 256, 258, 260, 269, 275, 338, 339, 343, 345, 346, 347, 351, 353, 356, 357, 358, 418, 420, 421
Indignez-vous! 24
information, right to 173–197
Inspection Panel 339, 347, 357–360, 364, 366, 374, 397
intellectual property 1, 235, 247, 322–323, 352
   Agreement on Trade-Related Aspects of Intellectual Property Rights (TRIPS Agreement) 279, 280
   World Intellectual Property Organization (WIPO) 153, 279
Inter-American Commission on Human Rights 269, 410, 417, 419, 430
interference in internal affairs, external 18, 98, 155, 156, 159, 203–205, 209, 210, 215–221, 226, 227, 276, 286, 352, 362, 410, 411, 439
interim measures of protection 47
International Center for Settlement of Investment Disputes (World Bank) 214
International Committee of the Red Cross (ICRC) 427
International Convention on the Elimination of All Forms of Racial Discrimination 21
International Convention on the Protection of the Rights of All Migrant Workers and Members of Their Families 21
International Court of Justice 6, 39, 42, 48, 50, 101, 102, 106, 126, 127, 138, 141, 147, 149, 153, 187, 214, 218, 219, 224, 226, 245, 251, 254, 259, 261, 273, 274, 276, 277, 284, 286, 329, 362, 372, 397, 414, 415, 432, 433, 434
   advisory opinion on Kosovo 51
   advisory opinion on Mauritius 118
   advisory opinion on Nuclear Weapons 49, 80
   judgment on military and paramilitary activities in *Nicaragua v. United States of America* 127, 216, 220, 414
   Statute of, Article 38 49, 218, 241, 261
   Statute of, Article 65 48
International Covenant on Civil and Political Rights 2, 21, 49, 50, 51, 75, 82, 136, 157, 158, 208, 218, 233, 242, 254, 256, 264, 288, 289, 337, 341, 362, 419
   Article 1 119, 122, 152, 156, 166, 241
   Article 2 241, 246
   Article 6 20, 72, 75, 80, 90, 241, 449
   Article 7 75, 166

International Covenant on Civil and Political
  Rights *continued*
  Article 9 64, 166, 241
  Article 10 166
  Article 12 75, 76, 241
  Article 14 140, 166, 233, 259, 269, 274, 276, 449
  Article 17 183, 184, 241, 449
  Article 18 75, 140, 326, 329
  Article 19 75, 140, 166, 178, 183, 195, 196, 241, 242, 263, 327, 449
  Article 20 52, 81, 83, 96, 112, 143, 205, 209
  Article 21 75, 140, 166
  Article 22 75, 140, 166
  Article 24 75
  Article 25 133, 140, 166, 205, 241, 242, 263
  Article 26 166, 241, 449
  Article 27 166, 241
  Article 41 225, 284, 328
  Optional Protocol to 106
International Covenant on Economic, Social and Cultural Rights 2, 21, 50, 64, 66, 75, 76, 82, 122, 157, 158, 208, 211, 218, 233, 242, 252, 254, 256, 288, 289, 300, 328, 337, 341, 362, 384, 419
  Article 1 136, 152, 241
  Article 2 110, 241, 246
  Article 5 110, 241
  Article 6 21, 241
  Article 7 241
  Article 8 21
  Article 9 21, 241
  Article 10 241
  Article 11 21, 241
  Article 12 21, 241
  Article 13 21, 241
International Criminal Court 41, 50, 53, 68, 76, 290, 433
  Rome Statute 3, 52, 54, 68, 76, 141, 221, 226, 261, 290, 425, 433, 435
    Article 5 52
    Article 7 3, 52, 54, 221, 290, 425, 435
    Article 8 52
International Criminal Court Statute
  Article 7 53, 225
international humanitarian law 49, 65, 66, 80, 98, 137, 240
International Labour Organization (ILO) 22, 48, 103, 348, 417
  ILO Convention 169 141, 142, 146, 152, 260
  ILO Conventions 242
International Law Commission 261
international mediation process 426–427

International Monetary Fund (IMF) 3, 25, 41, 103, 189, 303, 306, 322, 324, 325, 329, 336, 337, 338, 340–344, 349, 365, 371–400, 428, 430
international order, principles of 46–56, 74, 408, 451
International Peace Bureau 81, 88, 91, 107
international solidarity 6, 24, 56, 81, 84, 93, 98, 177, 220, 277, 279, 301, 305, 363, 385, 417, 422, 427, 439
international solidarity, right to 3, 47, 54, 74, 213, 247, 256, 375, 430, 451, 454
inter-State complaints procedure 41, 214, 328
intervention, prohibition of 2, 208
investment protection 197, 231, 234–236
investor-state dispute settlement mechanism (ISDS) 3, 54, 208, 231, 233, 240, 255–278, 284, 285, 286, 289, 363
Iran 194, 203, 219, 225, 316
Iraq 36, 56, 73, 95, 175, 197, 203, 211, 212, 221, 413, 424, 428
Israel 125, 219, 318, 408

J

J'accuse 175
James, Deborah 281, 284
Japan 86, 267
Jazairy, Idriss 191–192, 195, 218, 223, 417, 434, 438, 445

K

Kant, Immanuel 10, 23, 73, 74
Kashmir 42, 118, 120, 123, 125, 204
Kaye, David 174
Keller, Ska 264
killer sanctions 222, 226, 410, 411, 414, 426, 439, 449
Kirby, Michael 131
Kissinger, Henry 217, 410, 413
Klein, Naomi 344, 372, 377, 378
Kosovo xi, 51, 121, 124, 127, 142, 358
Kuala Lumpur War Crimes Commission 433
Kurds 123, 125

L

labour rights 1, 347–348
Lamy, Pascal 208
Lancet 227, 390, 404
landmines 240, 290
Lauterpacht, Hersch 453
law schools 309
League of Nations 1, 48
legibus solutus 247

Leningrad, Nazi siege of 221
lethal autonomous weapon systems 81, 89
level playing field 50, 208, 235, 281, 337
liberation movements 123, 204
Lisbon, Treaty of 36, 123, 166
loan conditionalities 338, 344, 361, 362, 363, 371, 373, 384
lobbies 8, 17, 30, 111, 251, 287, 303, 307, 312, 325, 329, 429, 430
Luarca, declaration of 26, 71, 73
Luxembourg 166, 310, 311, 315, 316, 317, 319, 324
LuxLeaks 195, 310, 315, 316, 317, 319, 324
Lysistrata 67

M

Mabo and others v. Queensland 146
Maduro, Nicolás 411, 413, 414, 422
"make the economy scream," 217, 410, 413
Malik, Charles 10, 13, 194, 454
Mandela, Nelson 23, 204, 420, 450
Manning, Chelsea 195
market fundamentalism 28, 236, 252, 274, 309, 344, 372
marriage, concept of 36
Martenson, Jan 14
Mauritius 118
media 4, 5, 8, 28, 29, 33, 37, 55, 68, 81, 89, 96, 97, 107, 123, 163, 173–175, 178–183, 186, 188, 190, 194, 196, 204, 207, 222, 245, 278, 279, 351, 366, 409, 411, 412, 421, 427, 429, 434, 437, 447
Melian Dialogue 414
Melzer, Nils 175, 176, 446, 454
"memory laws" 42, 55, 179, 182, 183
mercenaries 3, 53, 65, 187
Merchant of Venice 244, 453
MERCOSUR 417
Mettan, Guy 434
military expenditures 3, 28, 41, 66, 81, 88–113, 180, 185, 232, 300, 307, 325, 328, 329, 363, 364
military-first economies, conversion of 88, 93, 104, 105, 108, 110
military-industrial complex 28, 35, 66, 80, 89, 93, 97, 99, 109, 111, 240, 325, 430
mining industry 80, 208, 262, 269, 289, 290, 318, 345, 346, 347, 351
Ministry of Truth 173, 174
minorities 35, 46, 121, 130, 131, 139, 140, 143, 144, 156, 174, 191, 223, 234
Mix & Remix xiv
mobbing 9, 31, 68, 195, 429

Molina, Bruna 13
Möller, Jakob Th. v, 14, 44, 45, 60, 85, 86, 100, 115, 171, 172, 370, 446
money-laundering 28, 289, 302, 322, 328, 329, 337, 345, 366, 422
monopolies 208, 247, 281
Montesquieu, Charles-Louis 18, 49, 74, 261, 452
Montevideo Convention 150
moratorium 238, 284, 373, 381, 387, 399
Mossack Fonseca 314
multilateralism 1, 6, 41, 215, 378

N

Nagorno Karabagh 51, 120, 124, 127
Nairobi Ministerial Conference 281
"naming and shaming" 8, 193, 194, 408, 416, 430, 448, 449
national human rights institutions 13, 112, 249, 252, 253, 287, 446
NATO (North Atlantic Treaty Organization) 73, 81, 89, 95, 98, 127, 175, 177, 387
natural law 63, 430
Newman, Frank Cecil 12, 13
Nicaragua 127, 193, 216, 220, 222, 226, 413, 414, 420, 422, 426
Nicaragua v. United States ICJ Judgment 127, 216, 220, 226
Nixon, Richard 217, 410, 413
Non-Aligned Movement 215, 417
non-interference, principle of 18, 203–205, 215, 216, 219, 220, 362
non-intervention, principle of 49, 53, 54, 77, 98, 205, 212, 215, 216, 219, 341, 411, 448
Non-Proliferation Treaty (NPT) 97, 100, 101, 102
non-refoulement, principle of 71, 120
non-retrogression, principle of 54, 220
non-state actors 3, 4, 28, 38, 46, 54, 55, 65, 68, 76, 191, 206, 207, 211, 213, 234, 256, 259, 276, 288, 340
North American Free Trade Agreement (NAFTA) 235, 238, 265, 278
nuclear disarmament 43, 78–81, 83, 91, 100, 101, 102
nuclear energy 239, 268
nuclear weapons 78–80, 84, 90–91, 96, 99–102, 206
  ICJ Advisory Opinion on 49
  Second Conference on the Humanitarian Impact of 100
  Treaty on the Non Proliferation of 97
  UN Convention on the Prohibition of 91

Nuremberg laws 450
Nuremberg Trials 68, 76, 77, 79, 117, 245, 290

O

obligation to assist persons in distress 415
occupation of foreign territory 31, 70, 131,
   140, 191
   peoples living under 43, 120, 122, 130–132,
      136, 142, 144, 149, 153, 155
Oceania 203
ocioeconomic models 420
Ogonis of Biafra 118, 123
oil and gas industries 239, 262, 266, 267, 287,
   290, 347, 378, 410, 412–414, 420, 422,
   438, 439
Okafor, Obiora 301
Okinawa 118
Okonio-Iweala, Ngozi 279
Ombudsman 339, 354, 357, 359, 360, 364–366,
   375, 397
ontology of business 54, 257
ontology of States 54, 231, 257
opinio juris 56, 246, 258
opinion, freedom of 20, 24, 30, 55, 154, 162,
   164, 174, 179, 192, 203, 241, 418, 431
ordre public 50, 54, 234, 241, 246, 261, 262,
   270, 284, 286, 302, 317, 329
Organisation for Economic Co-operation and
   Development (OECD) 303, 305, 306,
   308, 310, 311, 313, 314, 320–322, 324,
   329, 350, 431
Organization of American States (OAS) 52,
   216, 220, 221, 411, 417, 418, 436
Orwell, George 173, 185, 196, 203, 447
outsourcing 233, 348
Owen, Wilfred 24, 67
Oxfam 308, 311, 320, 324, 337, 345, 348, 349,
   356, 373, 392, 395

P

pacta sunt servanda 54, 56, 132, 161, 244, 260
Pakistan 95, 118, 123, 144, 378, 379
Palestine 125, 142, 193, 204, 408
palm-oil industry 353
Panama Papers 309, 310, 313, 314, 330
Pan American Health Organization 216, 220
pandemic 5, 88, 93, 109, 110, 226, 300, 439
paradigm 9, 10, 31, 76, 105, 110, 186, 248, 254,
   283, 304, 355, 361, 396, 451–453
paramilitaries 65, 127, 194, 416, 424, 439
Paris Agreement 283, 307, 355
Paris principles 134
pax optima rerum 47

peace, human right to 61–85
Peloponnesian war 68, 414
People Matter 34
"peoples" definition, Kirby definition 131
Peoples' Tribunals 5, 53
Pérez, Carlos Andrés 428
Permanent Court of Arbitration 267
Permanent Court of International Justice 156,
   181
Permanent Peoples Tribunal 433
petitions 9, 33, 65, 112, 358, 409, 418
Petrov, Stanislas 81, 90
Philip Morris 239, 268, 270
Piketty, Thomas 231, 309, 377, 379, 393
Pillay, Navanethem "Navi" 61, 211, 222, 226,
   433, 446
Pinochet, Augusto 217, 219, 353, 410
Plague, The (book) 67
Pogge, Thomas 300
policy space 235, 236, 240, 246, 248, 254, 280,
   288, 329, 338, 362, 374, 389, 394, 398
"political correctness" 8, 29, 31, 55, 180, 186,
   189, 204, 453
"polluter pays" principle 246
pollution 208, 262, 266, 277, 337, 343, 345, 351
Pope Francis 115, 225, 292, 295, 298, 393, 400,
   406, 454
populism 7, 17, 35, 190, 191
Porto Alegre 5, 419
positivism 5, 18, 41, 49, 148, 187, 244, 253,
   452, 454
poverty 3, 18, 19, 22, 23, 24, 25, 32, 47, 50,
   83, 89, 93, 94, 105, 113, 145, 190, 232,
   234, 256, 277, 280, 281, 301, 307, 311,
   318, 326, 336, 342, 343, 351, 352, 361,
   363, 373, 376, 380, 382, 388, 390, 398,
   400, 418, 420, 421
press releases 4, 154, 188, 189, 190, 280, 301,
   351, 438, 439
privatization 174, 220, 238, 239, 250, 257, 344,
   362, 363, 372, 373, 376, 378, 380, 385,
   387, 389, 398, 428
"privatized justice" 259, 260, 262, 263, 276,
   288
"privatized knowledge" 247, 291
professionalism 342, 437, 446
propaganda 37, 52, 68, 70, 72, 76, 83, 84, 96,
   97, 112, 178, 183, 185, 191, 197, 205,
   329
proportionality 49, 80, 149, 241, 266, 452
"Protect, Respect and Remedy" Framework 232
public-private partnerships 338, 341, 344, 349,
   350, 373

punishment ix, 35, 46, 56, 71, 76, 128, 142, 214, 218, 226, 352, 449

Q

quis custodiet ipsos custodes (Juvenalis) 48, 180, 237

R

Ramcharan, Bertrand 13, 43, 446
Rapa Nui (Easter Island) 118, 125
Rapporteurs 2, 3, 4, 7–10, 13, 22, 24, 55, 71, 104, 117, 118, 122, 139, 147, 174–177, 188–190, 194–195, 212, 214–215, 219, 225, 232, 256, 258, 269, 273–274, 280, 284, 301, 307, 314, 318, 336, 339, 346, 363, 376, 408–409, 417–418, 420, 422, 429–432, 434, 435, 437–440
Realpolitik 413, 414
rebus sic stantibus 241
reckless endangerment 262, 289, 290, 415
recognition of government 124, 125, 127, 160
recognition of statehood 51, 121, 150
Redslob, Robert 141
referendum 36, 37, 41, 50, 51, 122–124, 139, 144, 149, 154, 161, 163–165, 167–169, 187, 263, 278, 284, 287, 329, 429
reform of the United Nations 3, 14, 27, 37–43, 177, 181, 208, 209, 254, 272, 273
  Secretary-General proposal 27
  Security Council 3, 27, 37–41
refugee status 71
regulatory chill 238, 257, 263, 280
rehabilitation 71, 95, 147, 151
religion 5, 64, 69, 70, 71, 179, 225, 440
Remarque, Erich Maria 67
remedy, right to 71, 72, 76, 137, 191, 285
reparation 3, 9, 20, 25, 52, 55, 71, 106, 137, 139, 142, 153, 215, 224–226, 251, 359, 366, 430, 431, 432
reprisals 28, 118, 182, 304, 310, 327, 338, 341, 345, 350, 351, 358, 359, 364, 392
reservation 157, 159
resistance, right to 70, 135
Responsibility of States 261
responsibility to protect (R2P) 53, 65, 98, 128, 207–209
revolving door 255, 316
road map 37, 76, 254, 393
Rodríguez Zapatero, José Luis 411, 426, 431
Rome Statute *See* International Criminal Court, Rome Statute
Roosevelt, Eleanor 10, 12, 13, 194, 454
Roosevelt, Franklin Delano 12, 15, 23, 64, 89, 94

root causes 5, 8, 47, 61, 77, 83, 84, 96, 191, 193, 267, 280
Roth, Kenneth 192–195
Rousseau, Jean-Jacques 24
Roy, Arundhati 24, 43
Ruggie, John 47
rule of law ix, x, 17–19, 21, 28, 33, 35, 48–49, 54–55, 70, 83, 89, 93, 101, 129, 132–133, 146, 148, 150–152, 154, 166, 167, 171, 173–178, 180, 181, 182, 184, 186–187, 192, 195, 196, 206, 211, 219, 233, 237, 247, 253, 262, 269, 272, 276, 396, 408, 413, 416, 448, 449, 450–451, 453
Russell Tribunal 433
Ryukyu 42, 118

S

Saab, Tarek William 412, 422
Sachs, Jeffrey 43, 229, 284, 309, 330, 377, 436
Santiago Declaration 26, 62, 73, 83
sapere aude 10
satyagraha 23
Schlicksup, Daniel 318
Seattle Ministerial Conference 279
secession 50, 117, 119, 121, 126, 130, 138, 144, 148, 150, 152, 155, 167
secrecy 302, 306, 307, 309, 310, 311, 317, 318, 321
secrecy jurisdictions 5, 300, 302, 304, 310, 311, 314, 326, 329
secret treaties 259
Security Council 3, 27, 34, 36, 37, 38, 39, 41, 48, 49, 52, 53, 55, 56, 65, 71, 78, 82, 88, 106, 120, 122, 124, 125, 127, 142, 147, 177, 186, 187, 209, 210, 211, 212, 218, 219, 221, 254, 336, 343, 424, 448
  Article 24 UN Charter 39, 48, 135, 218, 226
  Article 25 UN Charter 48
  Article 39 UN Charter 51
  reform 3, 37, 38, 41
  resolutions 34, 53, 65, 71, 120, 124, 125, 411
Selby-Green, Michael 435
selectivity 5, 14, 31, 36, 48, 49, 53, 65, 83, 121, 127, 169, 183, 191, 195, 207, 319, 349, 373, 381–382, 391, 422, 448
self-censorship 8, 9, 29, 31, 173, 174, 179, 186, 453
self-determination 3, 4, 6, 19, 20, 21, 22, 28, 32, 37, 42, 46, 50, 51, 52, 94, 117–169, 177, 181, 186, 188, 191, 193, 204, 207, 209, 211, 216, 220, 232, 386, 447, 451

Seneca 41
separability, doctrine of 54
Sepúlveda Carmona, Magdalena 301, 307, 318
settlers 117, 125, 139, 140, 141
severability, doctrine of 244, 260, 273
severability, principle of 54, 277
Sewanyana, Livingstone 2, 435
sexual abuse 337, 345, 358
Shakespeare, William
    Shylock (character in *Merchant of Venice*) 244, 294, 453
sic utere tuo ut alienum non laedas 49, 453
si vis pacem, cole justitiam 25, 48
Six, Billy 438
Snowden, Edward 195, 197
social contract 74, 167, 252, 257
social Darwinism 28, 31
socioeconomic models 216, 410, 418, 420
Soering v. the United Kingdom 243
solidarity, international 3, 6, 24, 47, 54, 56, 74, 81, 84, 93, 98, 144, 177, 213, 220, 247, 256, 277, 279, 301, 305, 363, 375, 385, 417, 422, 427, 430, 439, 451, 454
Sophocles' Antigone 244, 261
South Centre 103, 255, 287, 308
South Pacific (musical) 69
sovereignty 2, 6, 17, 18, 19, 22, 27, 28, 32, 36, 51, 52, 54, 104, 129, 131, 134, 143, 147, 150, 160, 161, 181, 210, 213, 218, 219, 226, 240, 248, 253, 256, 263, 276, 277, 318, 323, 353, 362, 386, 413, 416, 430
Spanish Constitution 158, 159, 160, 162
    Article 1 160
    Article 10 (2) 158, 159, 160, 161, 162
    Article 96 (1) 157, 158, 159, 160, 161, 162
    Article 155 165
special procedures, Human Rights Council 3, 7, 16, 24, 41, 191, 196, 214, 232, 258, 273, 305, 338, 391, 397, 417, 419, 431, 432, 440
special purpose entity 324
Sponeck, Hans-Christof von 212, 221, 424
Sri Lanka 42, 118, 120, 122, 123
statehood criteria 150
State of Emergency 57
Statute of Rome *See* International Criminal Court, Rome Statute
Stiglitz, Joseph 234, 235, 236, 259, 284, 336, 344, 372, 377, 393
Stockholm International Peace Research Institute (SIPRI) 81, 92, 95, 107

Sub-Commission on the Promotion and Protection of Human Rights 12, 22, 212, 213, 214, 221, 424
supremacy clause 6, 48, 120, 156, 215, 218, 226, 286, 343
survival clauses 245, 246, 251, 273
sustainable development goals 3, 5, 79, 81, 82, 222, 279–281, 300, 306, 307, 320, 321, 323, 325, 338, 340, 341, 345, 361, 372, 374–376, 381, 397, 398
SwissLeaks 310
Switzerland 63, 239, 311, 315, 316
sword of Damocles 78, 79, 80, 89
Syria 194, 203, 204, 216, 219, 222, 225, 226, 426, 428

T

taboo 9, 31, 207
Tamils 118, 122–125, 204
Tandon, Yash 233
tax competition 3, 302, 303, 318, 324, 328, 364, 392
tax cooperation authority 302, 303, 305, 318, 320, 321, 399
tax evasion, tax havens, and "optimization" 268, 300–330
technology transfer 33, 279
terra nullius doctrine 146
territorial integrity, principle of 119, 123, 126–128, 134, 136, 138, 148, 149, 150, 151, 155, 156, 159, 162
terrorism 36, 96, 123, 184, 204, 225, 424
Tharoor, Sashi 226
Thucydides 414
Tibet 125
Tilburg-Glothro Guiding Principles 344
Tlatelolco, Treaty of 91, 102
tobacco 234, 239, 257, 260, 268, 270, 277
Tobin tax 324
Tomuschat, Christian 44, 295, 446
torture 2, 13, 24, 35, 50, 67, 72, 75, 120, 156, 175, 219, 345, 351, 387, 414, 421, 454
totalitarianism 173, 174, 184
Transatlantic Trade and Investment Partnership (TTIP) 197, 235, 236, 240, 284
"trickle down" effect 227, 287
Trilateral Commission 5, 177
TRIPS Agreement 279, 280
Trojan horse 245, 262
truth commissions 385
truth, right to 3, 55, 71, 173–197, 203, 453
Tunisia 373, 388–389

Index

U

ubi jus, ibi remedium 56
ubi solitudinem faciunt, pacem appellant 68
ultima irratio 150
ultra vires 39, 48, 218, 261, 436
UNESCO Culture of Peace Programme 26, 83, 108, 168
uniform application of law 83, 132
unilateral coercive measures 3, 6, 31, 41, 42, 53, 106–107, 190, 191, 210–215, 218–226, 409, 410, 413, 415, 417, 424, 425, 430–434, 438
unilateralism 5, 76, 106, 132, 212, 213
United Kingdom (UK) 118, 158, 175, 196, 204, 210, 243, 264, 309, 311, 315, 317, 326
United Nations Charter
  Article 1 48, 75, 135, 148, 162
  Article 2 48, 75, 162
  Article 2 (3) 52, 63, 77, 83, 96, 149
  Article 2 (4) 52, 63, 65, 97, 98, 121, 124, 126, 127, 155
  Article 22 40
  Article 24 39, 226
  Article 25 48
  Article 26 78, 88
  Article 33 41, 52
  Article 34 52
  Article 39 51, 127
  Article 40 127
  Article 41 127
  Article 42 127
  Article 51 36, 149
  Article 55 14
  Article 56 14
  Article 57 41, 42
  Article 63 41, 42
  Article 73 41, 153
  Article 96 39, 102, 432
  Article 103 39, 48, 120, 156, 343, 372, 377
  Article 108 27, 38
  Chapter VI 52, 121
  Chapter VII 52, 127, 424
  Chapter XI 42, 119, 120
  Preamble 6, 63, 74, 75
United Nations Children's Emergency Fund (UNICEF) 81, 105, 212, 216, 220, 260, 276, 340
United Nations Commission on International Trade Law (UNCITRAL) 238, 239, 254, 272, 277
United Nations Conference on Disarmament 100
United Nations Conference on Trade and Development (UNCTAD) 25, 235, 255, 286, 305, 320, 324, 341, 377, 394
United Nations Convention against Corruption 262, 275, 289
United Nations Convention against Transnational Organized Crime 289
United Nations Convention on the Prohibition of Nuclear Weapons 80, 91
United Nations Development Programme (UNDP) 94, 153, 216, 220
United Nations Educational, Scientific and Cultural Organization (UNESCO) 25, 26, 69, 94, 108, 130, 133, 153, 167, 168, 216, 220, 340
United Nations High Commissioner for Human Rights, Office of (OHCHR) 2, 7, 12, 13, 14, 32, 33, 61, 69, 107, 142, 186, 189, 195, 211, 222, 223, 279, 329, 338, 340, 351, 409, 417, 432, 436, 439, 454
United Nations High Commissioner for Refugees (UNHCR) 216, 220
United Nations Institute for Disarmament Research (UNIDIR) 26, 103
United Nations Office on Drugs and Crime (UNODC) 329, 424
United Nations tax cooperation body 321
United States 5, 23, 61, 62, 77, 89, 90, 95, 96, 103, 119, 127, 134, 175, 176, 204, 211, 216, 217, 218, 219, 220, 222, 226, 235, 238, 239, 264, 266, 267, 281, 282, 283, 309, 311, 315, 316, 318, 353, 354, 378, 379, 383, 390, 397, 410, 411, 412, 413, 414, 419, 425, 426, 432, 438, 439, 450
Universal Declaration of Human Rights (UDHR) 1, 4, 10, 13, 20, 50, 70, 71, 75, 83, 144, 158, 181, 185, 192, 194, 218, 241, 258, 362, 371, 452
  Article 19 20
  Article 20 20
  Article 21 20
  Article 28 20, 75, 215, 246, 452
  Article 29 20, 185, 194, 452
universal jurisdiction 262, 290, 302
universal periodic review (UPR) 9, 24, 34, 42, 92, 104, 105, 106, 110, 112, 253, 258, 275, 409, 417, 421
Uruguay 239, 268, 270
uti possidetis 121, 143, 144, 149, 209
Utrecht, Treaty of 160

V

Vatican 295, 299, 426, 454
Vattel, Emmerich de x

Venezuela 2-5, 105, 193, 194, 215, 216, 217, 219, 220, 221, 222, 225, 254, 408–440
Verdross, Alfred 243
veto power 37, 38, 39
victim, concept of 8, 9, 13, 15, 20, 31, 34, 39, 71–73, 76, 106, 137, 142, 153, 185, 191, 225–226, 251, 254, 285, 288, 290, 326, 339, 359, 366, 400, 418, 432, 434, 446, 448, 449
Vienna Convention on the Law of Treaties 46, 122, 161, 231, 240, 243, 244, 245, 250, 252, 256, 277, 285
    Article 26 161, 244, 260, 386
    Article 27 161
    Article 31 122, 237, 273
    Article 32 237, 273
    Article 48 243
    Article 49 243
    Article 50 243
    Article 51 243
    Article 52 243
    Article 53 50, 243, 276
    Article 56 243
    Article 60 243
    Article 61 243
    Article 62 243
    Article 64 50
Vienna Declaration and Programme of Action 14, 21, 51, 82, 136, 140, 211, 216, 218, 220, 246
Villán Durán, Carlos 44, 61, 62, 63, 86, 115
Virgin Islands 309, 314, 315
Visible Hand of the Market, The (Curcio) 217
Vitoria, Francisco de 51, 58
vulture funds 5, 301–302, 374, 393–394, 399, 430

W

Wallach, Lori 264
war crimes 5, 52, 65, 70, 79, 124, 141, 175, 197, 205, 208, 433
war on drugs 28, 315
war on terror 28, 184
Washington Center for Economic and Policy Research 436
Washington consensus 283, 380, 428

water and sanitation, right to 3, 25, 191, 232, 234, 252, 323, 338, 349, 398, 399
Weltbürgerrecht 73, 74
Western Sahara 118, 138
whistleblowers 3, 4, 55, 177, 182, 184, 188, 191, 195–197, 303–304, 310, 317–318, 327–328
WHO Framework Convention on Tobacco Control 234, 239, 260, 268
Why War? (book by Albert Einstein and Sigmund Freud) 48
Wikileaks 175, 231, 242, 263
women 21, 32, 33, 83, 178, 180, 211, 213, 420
World Bank 3, 25, 41, 81, 89, 189, 214, 235, 238, 274, 275, 303, 306, 312, 325, 329, 336, 337–366, 371–379, 389, 392, 396–398, 400, 430
    Inspection Panel 339, 347, 357–360, 364, 366, 374, 397
world constitution 1, 6, 20, 48, 63, 121, 206, 226, 247, 260
World Economic Forum 5, 177, 313
World Health Organization (WHO) 5, 153, 216, 220, 234, 239, 241, 242, 246, 249, 254, 260, 268, 276, 279, 340, 355, 365, 417, 431
World Trade Organization (WTO) 3, 25, 41, 231, 254, 270, 273, 275, 277–286, 289, 306, 430
World Wide Web 247
WTO Public Forum 279

Y

Yemen 42, 118, 125, 204, 411, 428
Yugoslavia 121, 126–127, 130, 138, 149, 151, 245
Yukos Universal Ltd. (Isle of Man) 265

Z

Zamora, Luis Roberto (Costa Rican lawyer) 86
Zapatero, José Luis Rodríguez 411, 426, 431
Zeid Ra'ad Al Hussein 436
Ziegler, Jean 106, 301
Zola, Emile 175
zone of peace 91, 102, 212
Zur ewigen Frieden 73

ABOUT THE AUTHOR

Find a biography of Mr. Alfred-Maurice de Zayas, along with links to articles and opinions authored by him between 2012 and 2018, at https://www.ohchr.org/EN/Issues/IntOrder/Pages/AlfredDeZayas.aspx.